The United Nations

International Organization
and World Politics

The United Nations

International Organization and World Politics

Robert E. Riggs
Brigham Young University

Jack C. Plano
Western Michigan University

The Dorsey Press

Chicago, Illinois   60604

© THE DORSEY PRESS, 1988

All rights reserved. No part of this publication may be
reproduced, stored in a retrieval system, or transmitted,
in any form or by any means, electronic, mechanical,
photocopying, recording, or otherwise, without the prior
written permission of the publisher.

This book was set in Times Roman by Weimer Typesetting Co., Inc.
The editors were Leo Wiegman, Mary Lou Murphy, and Jane Lightell.
The production manager was Irene H. Sotiroff.
Malloy Lithographing, Inc., was the printer and binder.

ISBN 0-256-06061-4 (hardback)

ISBN 0-256-05525-4 (paperback)

Library of Congress Catalog Card No. 87–70915

Printed in the United States of America

1 2 3 4 5 6 7 8 9 0   ML   5 4 3 2 1 0 9 8

Preface

The United Nations is now in its fifth decade. It is an established part of the international scene and an important arena for international politics. The national interests of states and frequently the well-being of individuals are affected by what goes on there. Much of international affairs can be understood without reference to the United Nations, but no one's understanding of international politics is complete without knowledge of the United Nations and its processes.

The earliest modern international organizations emerged during the nineteenth century because bilateral diplomacy, and occasional international conferences, proved insufficient to cope with the full range of interstate contacts made possible by developing technology. The problem has since been magnified many times in the wake of a scientific revolution that threatens to outrun human capacity for social inventiveness. The continued growth of international organization—represented in this study by the United Nations and its family of related agencies—is a vast extension of the nineteenth-century effort to come to terms politically with a technologically shrinking, technologically endangered world.

Our treatment of the United Nations in this book is not governed by any single approach to the subject. We draw liberally on history because current organizational arrangements cannot be understood without some knowledge of their ancestry and evolution. We also have concern for institutional forms and structures. Institutions help shape outcomes by setting the limits within which power is exercised and by affecting the way states and other actors communicate with one another. Those matters are addressed specifically in Chapters 2, 3, and 4, but illustrations of institutional impact are found in the chapters dealing with substantive UN activities as well. If there is a special emphasis, it is on UN political processes and the way they affect the distribution of rewards and burdens among states. In surveying "who gets what, when, and how" within the international system, we have repeatedly addressed this question: What difference does the United Nations make?

Although we have tried to be objective in this study, our work has been underpinned by certain normative assumptions. Among them are an acceptance of the necessity of international organization in the contemporary world, a commitment to the democratic processes of decision making through discussion and consensus, and a preference for political pluralism. We have tried to capture the weaknesses and shortcomings of the UN system at the same time that we have noted its strengths and, occasionally, its operational vigor. The United Nations of today is not the same as it was forty years ago, and further change is certain in the decades ahead. Although change is not always progress, we harbor the hope that institutions for international cooperation will one day prove equal to the tasks laid on them. Such an evolution can occur, however, only if national leaders and peoples cultivate what Secretary-General U Thant once called the "common interests based on our habitation of the same planet." Recognition of those common interests provides a focus for our analysis of the United Nations and the role of international organization in the contemporary world.

We acknowledge the help of others in the preparation of this book. Although responsibility for errors rests solely with us, many people share the credit for any merit the book may have. Not least among them are Clarence A. Berdahl, Leland M. Goodrich, and Llewellyn Pfankuchen, who years ago provided intellectual guidance and personal encouragement to us as young scholars embarking on the serious study of international organization. Since then, we have been fortunate in having had good students and good colleagues whose wisdom and spirit of inquiry helped broaden our understanding of this complex and fascinating field. We acknowledge more specific debts as well. Louis Beres, Patrick Callahan, Robert B. Charlick, George A. Codding, Jr., Lawrence Gould, Joseph Lepgold, and Jay Charles Plano read the manuscript in its entirety and offered many helpful suggestions. The book is better because of their thoughtful criticism. Kurt C. Faux, Lorie A. Heimbuck, Robert L. Maxwell, and Theo Sypris rendered skilled, conscientious, indispensable research assistance. In the production of the manuscript, Dorothea Bradford Barr and Mari Miles consistently went beyond the call of duty in meeting deadlines and turning out accurate copy, all with unfailing good humor. To all of these we express gratitude.

Robert E. Riggs
Jack C. Plano

Contents

List of Figures

List of Tables

1

The United Nations in Historical Perspective

International organization can be traced back in history to the time when human beings first began to live in political communities. The ancient Greek city-states attempted through the Achaean League to build a system that would discourage rivalry and conflict and encourage some measure of cooperation. A thread runs through history from these early and rudimentary peace efforts to the contemporary world of the United Nations. Despite monumental and continuing failures to eliminate war, peoples and governments continue to reach beyond existing political boundaries to build on the orderly, brotherly, and cooperative side of human nature rather than give free rein to the suspicious, destructive, dark side. The founding of the United Nations is in this tradition. While falling short of its high ideals and purposes, the UN system nevertheless represents that human outreach toward peace and cooperation. In this chapter we will place the United Nations in historical perspective by looking at the modern state system that gave rise to it, describing the emergence of earlier international institutions, and briefly reviewing events leading to the establishment of the United Nations at the end of World War II. In the chapter that follows, the structure and operation of the United Nations will be discussed.

THE STATE SYSTEM AND INTERNATIONAL ORGANIZATION

Since its legal inception in the Peace of Westphalia in 1648, the modern state system has been characterized by powerful centrifugal forces producing disunity and conflict. Simultaneously, other forces have moved peoples and nations toward closer cooperation.

As the many separate political units created during the European feudal era were fused into larger communities, the national state, on which the contemporary UN system rests, began to emerge as the dominant political unit. The number of small

1

political entities was progressively reduced through conquest and annexation. Contacts among the new states increased as the larger community of Europe began to take shape. In addition, a new awakening occurred in the realm of economic activity. As trade and commerce flourished, mankind's concern with material enrichment became a powerful force affecting political rivalries. Rules were established under which the conflicts that inevitably arise through commercial intercourse could be adjusted. A rudimentary development of international law and consular interchange appeared in response to these needs. As trade competition among the new nations increased, it began to spill over into a race to acquire overseas colonies. This, in turn, produced a need for international rules by which nations could recognize one another's titles to new lands, settle boundary disputes, and undertake joint action against piracy. Nations began to deal more directly with such problems by entering into agreements and treaties with one another. Hence rivalries and antagonisms, while continuing to grow, tended to produce countervailing forces leading to increased cooperation.

Near the end of the eighteenth century, powerful new political forces evolved that have had a profound effect on the nature of the state system. These were the twin concepts of laissez-faire and democratic nationalism, each of which dramatically recognized the new role to be played by the individual in human affairs. At the same time the philosophy of laissez-faire was buttressed by a new technology that provided the means for producing goods with machines. The Industrial Revolution not only radically changed the economic methods of production but also spectacularly increased the interdependence of states.

The forces of science and invention responsible for developing the new machine technology also helped shrink the world through new and better devices for communication and transportation. The steamship, railroads, telegraph, and telephone made closer contacts possible, accelerated trade expansion, and produced a new awareness in the mind of Western man of his common societal relationship in a larger community of nations. Thus, in a progressive and dramatic way, the old patterns of individual and national self-sufficiency began to erode and give way to new and rapidly developing systems of interdependence, which, in turn, produced the rudiments of a new philosophy of internationalism among Western nations. Closer international cooperation and codes of international law began to develop as the respect and freedom accorded the individual within these nations increased. It has not been a historical accident that modern international law and institutions have been created largely at the initiative of those nations enjoying the greatest measure of freedom.

The Process of International Organization

With the appearance of democracy in the Western world, the stage was set for the emergence of modern international organization. Democracy in national government fostered the growth of international organization because both involve, in essence, commitment to a *consensual process*. Just as democracy in a national political setting implies a process of public decision making by consent of the governed, international organization implies a process of international action through the consent of states.

The process of international organization is thoroughly pragmatic—most, if not all, international institutions have been created to achieve specific, practical objectives. The process assumes the multistate system as fact and seeks only to provide an effective means to reconcile the conflicts and contradictions that emerge from this system. As Dag Hammarskjöld, the second Secretary-General of the United Nations, observed,

> The United Nations is not in any respect a superstate, able to act outside the framework of decisions by its member governments. It is an instrument for negotiation among, and to some extent for, governments. It is also an instrument for concerting action by governments in support of the Charter. Thus the United Nations can serve, but not substitute itself for, the efforts of its member governments.[1]

In the absence of supranational government, only voluntary agreement can succeed in mitigating international conflicts, and international organization provides an institutionalized means for eliciting such agreement. It provides the principles, the machinery, and the encouragement, but the catalytic agent needed to bring about tangible results is the will to cooperate. When cooperation is forthcoming, great things can be accomplished by international organs and agencies; when it is lacking, they become mere "debating societies." An international organization like the United Nations is as strong as, and no stronger than, its members want it to be.

Judged by the vast scale of UN activities, it appears that most nations have accepted the premise that collective action can be very useful. There can be no certainty, however, that international organization will continue to be accepted merely because collective action is considered useful. Important gains in the past have, with deadly swiftness, been destroyed by a reversion to open conflict. And it is not only war that can weaken or destroy an international organization; the slow but progressive sapping of its strength through stalemate and deadlock over numerous lesser issues can render it ineffectual and meaningless. As with national governments built on the democratic process, the greater danger is not that of making the wrong decision but of failing to make decisions when they are desperately needed. The record of the United Nations over more than forty years calls for a guarded optimism about the future of the process of trying to solve international problems through collective action.

One crucial test for the process of international organization is the prevention of war or, viewed affirmatively, the maintenance of peace and security. This was the *raison d'être* of the United Nations in 1945; it is of central importance today. It corresponds to the fundamental objective of every national government—putting an end to conflict within its own borders.

Until the twentieth century, war was regarded in the Western state system as a major concern only to the states engaged in it. The entire body of neutrality law was erected on the supposition that other states would remain substantially aloof. With the growth of interdependence in economic and social matters, the concepts of national individuality and isolation slowly began to be supplemented with the idea of community. Modern war in the twentieth century swept away most of the remnants of disinterestedness and aloofness. State after state found itself churned into the maelstrom of World War I, which had begun with a quarrel between Austria-Hungary and Serbia. President Woodrow Wilson recognized the significance of this change when he declared in 1916 that the day of the neutrals was past.[2] Formal acceptance of community responsibility was embodied in the Covenant of the League of Nations, Article 11, which provided that "any war or threat of war, whether immediately affecting any of the Members of the League or not, is hereby declared a matter of concern to the whole League." The UN Charter incorporates this principle in Article 2: "All Members shall give the United Nations every assistance in any action it takes in accordance with the present Charter."

Maintaining peace and security in the world is not the only purpose of international organization, although it is the most crucial. Indeed, the problems with which the United Nations concerns itself include most of those facing states in their foreign relations. These problems range from environmental protection to economic development, from population concerns to outer space. Each year finds the agenda of the General Assembly crowded with problems, new and old, created by the ever-changing international milieu. While many remain unsolved, the members of the United Nations continue to accept the purposes and processes by which solutions are sought through common action.

THE EMERGENCE OF INTERNATIONAL INSTITUTIONS

International institutions dating from the early nineteenth century represent a creative response to the need for a joint approach to common problems in such fields as commerce, communication, and transportation. The first examples of modern international organization were the river commissions in Europe. The Central Rhine Commission, for example, was created in 1804 by an agreement between France and Germany that provided for extensive regulation of river traffic, the maintenance of navigation facilities, and the hearing and adjudication of complaints for alleged violations of the Commission's rules. The European Danube Commission was created in 1856 to regulate international traffic on the Danube River. Both river commissions function today much the same as they did when they were first established.

The development of international organization was carried a step farther with the creation of international public unions in the latter half of the nineteenth century. In many cases the public unions were developed as a result of demands placed on national governments by the members of private international associations. Such demands resulted in the establishment of the International Telegraphic Union in 1865 and the Universal Postal Union in 1874. The success of these two unions paved the way for the creation of numerous international public agencies in such diverse fields as narcotic drugs, agriculture, health, weights and measures, railroads, patents and copyrights, and tariffs. The prolific growth of technical international agencies reflected the new world of science and technology that was compressing space and overcoming political boundaries. States offered collaboration because it was essential to carrying on business and commerce and useful in protecting the lives, health, and other interests of their citizens.

As cooperation among states increased during the nineteenth century, a pattern of organization and procedures developed. Each new international agency established institutional machinery that was unique in some respects, yet possessed certain basic characteristics in common with its contemporaries. The following pattern was typical:

1. Membership was usually limited to sovereign states. Unless regional in scope, such an organization typically held membership open to all states without political conditions.

2. Each organization was created by a multilateral treaty. The treaty served as a constitution that specified the obligations of members, created the institutional structure, and proclaimed the objectives of the organization.

3. A conference or congress was usually established as the basic policy-making organ. The conference included all members of the organization and met infrequently, typically once every five years.

4. Decision making was based on the principle of egalitarianism, with each member having an equal vote and decisions reached by unanimous consent. In time this gave way to majoritarianism, especially in voting on procedural questions.

5. A council or other decision-making organ of an executive nature was often created to implement policies. It usually had a limited membership, and its primary responsibility was to administer the broad policy decisions laid down by the conference.

6. A secretariat was established to carry out the policies of the conference and council and to conduct routine functions of the organization. The secretariat was headed by a secretary-general or director-general, a professional civil servant with an international reputation.

7. Some organizations, such as the river commissions, exercised judicial or quasi-judicial powers. Some created special international courts to decide controversies arising out of their administrative operations.

8. Many organizations were endowed with a legal personality enabling them to own property, to sue and be sued in specified areas, and, in some cases, to enjoy a measure of diplomatic immunity.

9. Financial support was provided by contributions from member governments, using a formula for contributions based on a principle such as "ability to pay," "benefits derived," "equality" or on a combination of such principles.

10. The competence of the organization was usually limited to a functional or specialized problem area, as set forth in its constitution. Organizations of general competence in political, economic, and social areas were not established until the twentieth century.

11. Decision making was carried on in two ways: by drafting international treaties and submitting them to member governments for ratification, and by adopting resolutions recommending action by member governments. A few organizations possessed administrative and minor policy-making powers.

An important by-product of political cooperation on technical matters was the growth of the belief that political cooperation might be equally productive in securing agreement among states in the more weighty matters of war and peace. Such thinking helped prepare the ground for the calling of two conferences at The Hague, Netherlands, in 1899 and 1907, the first general international conferences concerned with building a world system based on law and order. The first Hague Peace Conference was attended by delegates from only twenty-six nations and was largely European in complexion; the second conference, however, moved toward universality, with representatives from forty-four states, including most of the countries of Latin America. The principle of the sovereign equality of states was accepted at the conferences, with the result that the Hague system helped break the monopoly of the great powers of the Concert of Europe in handling matters of war and peace and economic and colonial rivalry. The Hague system also established precedents that contributed to the later development of international parliamentarianism. Headquarters at The Hague provided international machinery to facilitate the pacific settlement of international disputes. The Hague system in effect proclaimed a new era of cooperation and indicated that a global political organization to keep the peace and promote interstate cooperation was now a possibility. The League of Nations and the United Nations were in time to emerge as products of the creative thought produced by the Hague system.

THE LEAGUE EXPERIMENT

Americans were living in an age of innocence when the United States declared war against the Central Powers in 1917. Both sides were then close to exhaustion and had had much of their idealism and fiery nationalism wrung out of them by nearly three years of savage fighting. In the early years of the war, the carnage in Europe produced an American consensus that involvement should be avoided at all costs. But as the war dragged on, that consensus was eroded by a growing belief that the New World somehow had to save the Old World from extinction. If Europeans of all nationalities could live in peace under the American system of democracy, why not apply these same principles to the international community?

Americans entered World War I fired with a holy mission to "make the world safe for democracy." American idealism was summed up in President Woodrow Wilson's peace program, submitted to Congress on January 8, 1918, in which he enunciated Fourteen Points aimed at rekindling Allied idealism and determination and weakening the enemy's resolve by promising a just peace and a new world of security and democracy. In his Fourteenth Point Wilson declared that "a general association of nations must be formed under specific covenants for the purpose of affording mutual guarantees of political independence and territorial integrity to great and small powers alike."

The chief architect of the League, unquestionably, was Woodrow Wilson. Without his support the idea of a League of Nations would probably not have gone beyond the point of intellectual germination. While many Allied statesmen thought more cynically of how the victory won at a terrible cost could be exploited for national gain and future security, Wilson sought to materialize his dreams of a just world based on law and democracy. Because his program appealed to millions of Europeans emerging from the trauma of war, Allied leaders were forced by public opinion to pay at least lip service to his ideas. Wilson's vision of a just peace was focused on the building of a League of Nations, and Allied statesmen accepted his demands that the League be created as an integral part of the peace treaty. The subsequent failure of the United States to ratify the League Covenant, because of political conflict between President Wilson and Senate Republicans, is one of the great ironies of history.

Structure and Functions of the League

The League Covenant provided for the establishment of three permanent or-gans—the Assembly, the Council, and the Secretariat. Two semiautonomous bodies were created outside the Covenant framework—the Permanent Court of International Justice and the International Labor Organization. Their objectives were similar to those of the League, however, and the budgets of both were part of the League budget. The Council and Assembly also elected the judges of the World Court. Of greater importance than structures were the obligations that members assumed toward the organization and toward one another. Each state undertook to "respect and preserve as against external aggression the territorial integrity and existing po-litical independence of all Members of the League." Members agreed to submit all of their disputes to arbitration, adjudication, or Council inquiry and in no case to resort to war until three months after a settlement was offered. If any state resorted to war in violation of the Covenant, members would apply diplomatic and economic sanctions and consider the violation an act of war against the world community. Members further agreed to work together to control national armaments and to co-operate in solving social, economic, colonial, humanitarian, and other common problems.

League Innovations

In its basic design and role, the League was both old and new. It was old in the sense that the system was based firmly on the sovereignty of the member states; no new obligation could be imposed on a member without that member's consent. As with earlier attempts to establish some degree of international order, the powers of the League were limited to recommendations. The Covenant, in keeping with the traditional guidelines of international law, did not seek to outlaw war but only to regulate a state's resort to this ultimate action. A special peacekeeping role was accorded to the great powers, a role that they had always played (along with war-making) in the international political system. The League's decisions were made on the basis of mutual agreements that reflected each state's particular interests, a decision-making system as ancient as the state system itself. Progress in technical, social, economic, and humanitarian fields was, as in the past, founded on common treaty actions and on recommendations for national statutory enactments. All in all, there was much in the new League of Nations system that was merely a continuation of the old traditions, customs, institutions, and decision-making procedures of the pre-League world.

But there was also much that was new, some quietly evolutionary in nature, some dramatically revolutionary in scope. The League, for example, was the first attempt to establish a permanent international organization of a general political nature with machinery functioning on a continuing basis. For the first time a community responsibility to use the collective force of the state system against an international law-breaker was given institutional flesh and bone. Although the League could hardly be compared to a domestic political system with its superior authority, independent police force, and automatic action against lawbreakers, it was, nonetheless, a step toward internationalizing the responsibility of peacekeeping. In the past, action against an aggressor had been a right of states; under the Covenant it became a duty.

The League in Action

The two major functions of the League, as stated in the Preamble to the Covenant, were "to achieve international peace and security" and "to promote international cooperation." These functions were expected to be complementary, since a secure world would encourage state cooperation in many fields and a common attack on the economic, social, and technical problems facing all governments would develop a sense of community that would help deter states from violence. Of the two functions, the security function was regarded as the more pressing.

There was little agreement, however, on how the League should pursue its security objectives. France, for example, regarded enforcing the provisions of the peace treaties and guarding against a resurgence of German military power as the League's primary responsibilities. Britain, in contrast, viewed the League as an agency for fostering the peaceful settlement of disputes and protecting the vital interests of the Empire. Each member, in fact, tended to define the League's peace-preserving role largely in terms of its own national interest, so that when the League was confronted with threats to the peace, it often spoke in a cacophony of voices rather than with a single voice.

In its approach to the problem of war, the Covenant made no general statement that war was illegal. The traditional legal right of states to engage in war was circumscribed in the Covenant by provisions that made it illegal in most situations, enjoined delay in all cases, and prescribed community sanctions against the warmaker.

The Manchurian Case

The League's first test in meeting aggression committed by a great power came in 1931, when Japan, claiming Chinese destruction of its railway properties, attacked Manchuria and occupied the capital city of Mukden. China, charging aggression by Japan, appealed to the League under Article 11 of the Covenant. Attempts by the Council to secure a cease-fire and a Japanese withdrawal were vetoed by Japan, which requested that an on-the-spot inquiry into the facts be made before League action was undertaken.

As fighting spread in Manchuria, the Council appointed a Commission of Inquiry under Lord Lytton's direction to go to Manchuria to dig out the facts. By the time the Commission arrived in the Far East, in April 1932, the Japanese had changed Manchuria into the new independent state of Manchukuo and had begun an attack upon China proper at Shanghai. China, deeply affronted by Council procrastination, asked for transference of the dispute to the Assembly. The Assembly condemned the Japanese aggression and adopted the American-initiated Stimson Doctrine of nonrecognition of new states or governments created illegally by the use of force. A voluminous report from the Lytton Commission condemning Japan's aggressive actions in Manchuria was adopted unanimously by the Assembly but was too late to affect the outcome since the conquest was an accomplished fact. The Assembly's action in fixing blame and condemning aggression, however, led to the withdrawal of Japan from the League of Nations.

The Manchurian case emphasized that situations involving overt aggression could not be successfully handled by using League procedures for peaceful settlement. Japan proved, and the lesson was not lost on potential European aggressors, that the cumbersome machinery and procedures of the League could be used to stifle effective collective action. The League suffered also because great power leadership was lacking on the Council and because the United States, the major power most concerned about Japanese aggressive tendencies, was not a League member. American concern was expressed by sending an observer to Geneva who sat quietly listening to the debates and offered nothing but moral condemnation of Japan's actions. Clearly, this was not enough. The first major test found the League weak and indecisive.

The Ethiopian Case

A second critical test for the League was not long in coming. In the winter of 1934, League-member Italy attacked League-member Ethiopia in violation of their mutual Covenant obligations to respect each other's political and territorial integrity and to adjust their differences peacefully. Italy, following the Japanese example, launched a diplomatic offensive in Geneva, claiming that Ethiopian forces had attacked first. Ethiopia, not recognizing the Italian master plan to build an African empire, sought to negotiate and to use the power of the League facilities for conciliation rather than collective action. Under cover of negotiations, Mussolini mobilized Italian reserves for war, granting minor concessions each time it appeared that the

Council would intervene. Outside the main arena of the League, a diplomatic web of intrigue developed as Britain and France, concerned more with the rising power of Nazi Germany, sought to keep Italy as a buffer to Germany. Permitting Mussolini to seize a piece of African territory seemed to the statesmen in London and Paris a small price to pay for the containment of German power. Incredibly, the United States remained aloof and President Roosevelt refused Emperor Haile Selassie's request that he call on the parties to observe their commitment under the Kellogg-Briand Pact of 1928 not to use war as an instrument of national policy.

By the autumn of 1935 Italy had completed its mobilization, and on October 2, disregarding many League resolutions and Covenant provisions, it launched a full-scale attack on Ethiopia. Ethiopia at once invoked Article 16 of the Covenant, holding that Italy's resort to war before fulfilling Covenant requirements must be considered an act of war against each League member. The Ethiopian delegate at Geneva argued that all members must honor their Covenant obligations by applying immediate economic sanctions against Italy, and he called on the Council to recommend military sanctions as well. Under an interpretation of the Covenant agreed on in 1921, however, neither the Council nor the Assembly was empowered to determine that aggression had been committed; each member state was entitled to decide for itself. The levying of economic and other sanctions was likewise controlled by each state, emphasizing the veto power held by each member under the League system. Of the fifty-four League members polled, fifty indicated that Italy was the aggressor, thus obligating them to apply economic sanctions at once and to undertake military sanctions if these were recommended by the Council.

For the first time in history, economic sanctions were levied against an international lawbreaker, with fifty member states participating. Numerous questions arose immediately concerning what kinds of materials should be embargoed, whether imports from Italy should be banned, what would happen to private long-term contracts, and whether an effort should be made to prevent nonmember states from violating the embargoes. A League consensus soon developed that economic sanctions should include an embargo on arms and essential war materials, a ban on all loans and other kinds of financial help, a restriction against all imports from Italy and its possessions, and mutual support among League members to minimize their economic injury from the embargoes. By November 1935 the economic sanctions were in effect, and within a period of several months the sanctions began to have a telling effect on Italy's economy.[3]

In spite of economic sanctions, the Italian armies swept into Addis Ababa, and on May 5, 1936, Mussolini boasted that victory had been achieved. Eight months after sanctions had been imposed, the Assembly voted to withdraw all sanctions against Italy. Why had the economic sanctions failed? Why were they terminated after Italy had completed its conquest, thus condoning the aggression? Why had the Council not recommended military sanctions? These and similar questions were aired in Assembly debates following the withdrawal of sanctions, and the answers to them, incomplete as they may be, help explain the difficulties of carrying out an effective collective security action against a great power within the context of the international milieu of that day.

Basic to the League's problem was the realpolitik British and French objective of building a coalition to balance the power of Hitler's Germany. In much the same way that the East-West split has weakened the great power concert on the UN Security Council, the struggle in the 1930s to contain Nazi power replaced collective security as the prime concern of British and French statesmen.

Other nations contributed to the weak-sanctions syndrome. The United States condemned Italian aggression but avoided any cooperation with the sanctions decision other than placing both belligerents off-limits for arms shipments under the Neutrality Acts. American trade, especially shipments of oil, increased sizably, with most of the increase going to the Italian African colonies, which were supply bases for the military campaign. Many Latin-American countries, nearly suffocating under gluts of primary commodity surpluses, agreed in principle to sanctions but failed to apply them in practice. Four League members refused to apply any kinds of sanctions, one refused to reduce imports from Italy, and seven never applied the arms embargo. The bait of stimulating national economies stagnated by the world economic depression proved to be a more powerful motivator of national actions than idealistic considerations of collective security.

Yet, ironically, the gains of appeasement were illusory. Italy joined the Axis powers, the United States was eventually drawn into war against the dictators, and potential aggressors in Europe and the Far East were encouraged by the League's vacillation and irresoluteness. As for the League, the imposition of sanctions by an international organization for the first time in history was a signal achievement; but the Ethiopian case illustrated that it takes more to deter aggression than covenants, organizations, institutions, procedures, and decisions. In the final analysis, effective collective security depends on the states that make up international organizations and the policies they pursue. With Hitler's attack on Poland in September 1939 and the beginning of World War II, the League experiment in collective security ended.

An Appraisal: The League's Balance Sheet

A review of the League record might be summarized as a study in utility and futility. Conclusions about the degree of success or failure attained by the League must obviously depend on the standard of measurement employed. If it is measured by what the Covenant framers intended, or what millions of people hoped for, or what the principles of the Covenant actually called for, the League fell far short. If, on the other hand, it is measured by what other international organizations in the past had accomplished, or what skeptics and critics predicted for it, or what the nature of the rivalry-ridden state system would permit, the League probably rated high. Any evaluation faces the danger of falling into the old pro-League–anti-League controversy that characterized the great American debate on the subject and kept it on a largely emotional level for twenty years.

A Capsule History of the League

Obviously, an appraisal of the League must recognize that its effectiveness varied in response to changes in the international environment. The peace, stability, and relative prosperity of its first decade permitted the League to make a promising start in a number of directions. Numerous international disputes were settled peacefully, the complex problem of disarmament was tackled, and the Kellogg-Briand Pact of 1928 attempted to close a gap in the League Covenant by outlawing war as an instrument of national policy. Cooperation in welfare areas was explored, and foundations were laid for extensive programs that flowered during the subsequent decade.

The period from 1930 to 1935 was one of challenge and uncertainty for the League. The economic depression that started with the American stock market crash in 1929 and spread across the world in a chain reaction reduced the League's carefully cultivated channels of cooperation to a shambles. Economic nationalism and ideological rivalries spawned in the depression's wake split the status quo world into hostile camps. Japanese, Italian, and German fascism posed successive political and military challenges with which the organization and its members were unwilling or unable to cope. A new wave of nationalism erased many of the gains of internationalism during the 1920s as League members became increasingly obsessed with their own limited conceptions of national security and with domestic problems. Government after government fought desperately to rescue its people from the brink of economic and financial collapse, social disintegration, and political revolution. As Germany rearmed, disarmament talks collapsed and the world witnessed the start of a new arms race. Economic and monetary conferences failed, and the world depression deepened. The world of the 1930–35 era was not of the League's making, but it was the one in which the League had to operate.

The world stage was now set for the League's inevitable collapse. Nine members withdrew between 1935 and 1939, some for political reasons, others claiming financial problems. A desperate reform movement initiated by the Assembly in 1936 sought for three years to stem the tide and refurbish the League's tarnished image by updating its security provisions and by divesting the Covenant of all references to the peace treaties of World War I. The Axis powers, bent on aggression, were not interested in returning to the League, nor were other former member states, which continued to pursue independent courses. With the failure of the reform movement, the League became inoperative in the security field, except for voting the Soviet Union's expulsion because of its attack on Finland in 1939, and a majority of the members professed neutrality in the crises growing out of German annexations in Central Europe. When general war came to Europe in September 1939, the League became quiescent, a posture it retained through the five years of World War II. A shell of the League organization lived on at the Geneva headquarters through the war period, only to be ignored by the architects of a new world organization, who did not want their creation tainted by association with the League's failure.

An Autopsy

Just as friends of the League in its early years tended to exaggerate its novelty and its potential, critics have in retrospect emphasized its failures and undervalued its contributions. All evaluations, however, eventually return to the central question:

Why did the League fail to keep peace? Since the maintenance of peace and security was the primary objective of the League, it is only natural that the historical verdict on the League has been delivered mainly in that area and in condemnatory terms.

In fixing blame, some observers have sought to explain the League's demise as a failure of its member states to support the principles of the Covenant. Such a rationalization fails to recognize that in the field of international organization members *are* the organization, that the League had no real existence independent of its component parts. No organization made up of sovereign and independent entities can possibly be stronger than the will and support for common action that exists within the group. Thus, to blame the members rather than the League is a circular argument. One could as well make the point that the pre–World War I balance of power functioned well in keeping the peace but eventually failed because the states involved did not play their proper roles within the system.

Procedural difficulties growing out of the League's machinery have also been blamed for its failure. It is quite true that the requirement of unanimity in both Council and Assembly on most substantive questions enabled aggressor nations to veto some countermeasures. Also, because war was not outlawed, the Covenant permitted some members to use the provisions regulating resort to war to block effective collective action. Covenant provisions dealing with disarmament were so loosely worded that no definite responsibility existed for members to reduce their arms. The sanctions system was weakened in the League's early years by a Covenant interpretation permitting each member to decide for itself the question of invoking an economic embargo. Many other technical deficiencies also contributed to the League's failure, but it would be inaccurate to assign organizational weaknesses a major role in the debacle since most of the weaknesses could be, and many were, overcome by interpretation and by the use of alternative pathways.

Probably the most popular explanation for League failure, in the United States at any rate, was American defection. Unquestionably the refusal of the United States to participate in a world organization sponsored by its own president created a psychological and power vacuum that the League never fully overcame. In the security field American policymakers offered only moral condemnation of aggression, while permitting American businessmen to continue extensive trade with the aggressors. The popular myth that American military force combined with that of other League members would have made the League successful against aggressors overlooks the fact that American power during the 1920s and 1930s was only a potentiality awaiting the full mobilization of World War II. Contributions from the small, garrison-bound American army could hardly have influenced the outcome of any major military action during the League period, and Americans were psychologically unprepared for a major effort until Pearl Harbor. American defection, then, weakened the League but was not the central reason for its ultimate collapse.

Some critics of the League have sought to explain its failure as resulting from its close association with the "unjust" peace treaties of World War I. The League, it is argued, was placed in the impossible position of defending the status quo of the victors against the attempts of the vanquished to undo the peace treaties imposed on them. The League itself recognized this argument officially when it appointed a committee in the late 1930s to propose reforms that would free it from this incubus and, hopefully, regain the support of nations—especially Germany—that had been alienated. Yet the League would still have had to operate within a world based on the peace settlements even if it had in no way been associated with them. Moreover, to the League's credit, the status quo was not tenaciously defended and justice often took precedence over the status quo, as in the case of the Saar, whose people, in a League-supervised plebiscite, voted for reunion with Germany.

Finally, some groups of critics have seen in the League's failure an example of the fundamental inability of a collective security system to keep the peace. One such group rejects the League as an impractical and idealistic concept that was foredoomed to failure because it ignored the power realities of the world. Only by fostering a balance of power through military preparedness and alliances can peace be preserved, so runs the argument of these critics, and the League diverted the status quo great powers from such a course, making disaster inevitable. Another group has also criticized the League's utopianism, but its alternative is a world government acting with substantial powers directly on individuals. Since peace can be adequately preserved within nations by a federal government, this group has argued, the world scene likewise demands a world authority with a near monopoly of power. Compelling as arguments favoring world federalism may be in theory, the world of sovereign states was hardly ready then, nor is it now, to undergo such a radical metamorphosis. Moreover, if the will to resist the aggressors had been broadly based and deeply rooted, if conditions approaching a consensus had existed, the cooperation of member states could probably have done the job as expeditiously as a world federal system. Conversely, the absence of consensus under either system would have had equally deleterious results.

In conclusion, no single theory suffices to explain the League's failure. One might even conclude that bad luck had something to do with it. A combination of many factors, often appearing at inopportune times, made success in the security field a difficult and elusive quarry. Unquestionably the economic nationalism engendered by the world depression created an environment uncongenial to international cooperation. And once the world had been irretrievably split between revisionist and status quo powers, the malfunctioning of the League's collective security apparatus became a matter of course.

ORGANIZING THE UNITED NATIONS

Like the First World War, World War II created an international climate of opinion receptive to the ideas of international cooperation. In the early war period, as the Allied powers suffered serious military reverses, the role of international organization was blurred from international consciousness. The League remained immobilized and discarded, playing no role in the global struggle it had sought to prevent. But as the Allies marshaled their power and launched a worldwide offensive, some thinking, official and unofficial, began to take shape concerning the nature of the postwar world. What kind of a world would emerge from the carnage of the most deadly war in history? How would the mistakes made by the previous generation be avoided? Could the peace be won just as the war was being won? How could talent and effort be mobilized on a massive scale to build the new world of peace?

The Road to San Francisco

The UN Charter, which emerged from the San Francisco Conference on International Organization, was a product of extensive wartime planning. The seed of the idea for a new postwar world organization was planted by President Franklin Roosevelt and Prime Minister Winston Churchill in the Atlantic Charter of August 14, 1941. The date is significant because it was four months before the Japanese attack on Pearl Harbor and the entry of the United States into the war. Churchill wanted explicit endorsement of a postwar international political organization included in the joint statement of aspirations. Roosevelt, however, recognized that American public opinion, still basically isolationist, might react unfavorably to such a clear-cut internationalist objective. In final form the Atlantic Charter called for "fullest collaboration between all nations in the economic field" and hinted of the future "establishment of a wider and permanent system of general security." Even in this watered-down form it carried the clear implication that progress toward a world organization having security and economic responsibilities was a joint objective of the two leading democracies. On January 1, 1942, with the United States now in the war, twenty-six nations subscribed to a Declaration by United Nations that reaffirmed the principles of the Atlantic Charter. This declaration established the United Nations military alliance, to which twenty-one other nations subsequently adhered, each agreeing to employ its full resources against the Axis, to cooperate with one another, and not make a separate peace.

The vague references to international organization in these early war documents were made explicit in the Moscow Declaration on General Security signed in October 1943 by the foreign ministers of the Big Four (Hull, Eden, Molotov, and Foo Ping-sheung). The Moscow Declaration pledged continuance of wartime cooperation "for the organization and maintenance of peace and security" and explicitly recognized "the necessity of establishing at the earliest practicable date a general international organization." It was also the first definite commitment by the Soviet Union to support the establishment of a world organization.

The Dumbarton Oaks Conference

With the three major powers diligently working on drafts of a constitution for a general international organization, the American State Department suggested to the Russian and British governments that they meet to work out a single set of proposals. After negotiations the three governments agreed that they would participate in the drafting of a proposed charter and that China should participate, although not directly with the Soviet Union, since the latter desired to preserve its position of neutrality in the Far Eastern war. The four governments met at Dumbarton Oaks, an estate in Washington, D.C., in two separate phases. Conversations were held among the American, Soviet, and British delegations from August 21 to September 28, 1944, and among the American, British, and Chinese delegations from September 29 to October 7, 1944. At the conclusion of the conference, the areas of joint agreement were published as the Dumbarton Oaks Proposals.

A surprisingly large area of agreement emerged from the conference in an atmosphere that was cordial and cooperative. Although the Allies were taking the offensive on all fronts by the summer of 1944, victory was not yet assured and all four governments still felt the close attachment of nations seriously threatened by common enemies. This wartime spirit of unity and common cause that prevailed during the years leading up to the drafting of the UN Charter is sometimes obscured from view by the hindsight of the cold war.

The Dumbarton Oaks Proposals were intended by the four governments to constitute a basis for discussions at the forthcoming general conference on international organization. The following summarizes some of the major areas covered by the Proposals:

Purposes: The primary function of the new organization was to maintain international peace and security. Beyond this, it was to encourage friendly relations among nations and achieve international cooperation.

Nature: The new organization was to be based on the sovereign equality of its members. Thus, in its fundamental character it was to follow in the tradition of early international organizations and the League of Nations.

Membership: All peace-loving states were to be eligible for membership. Universalism was not established as a definite goal, but it could be assumed that in time all states would become "peace-loving" and, hence, eligible for membership. New members would be admitted through action by the Security Council and the General Assembly.

Organs: Five major organs were suggested for the new organization, plus such subsidiary agencies as might be found necessary. A Security Council including all great powers as permanent members and a General Assembly comprising all members would be the two major organs. In addition, there would be a Secretariat, a Court, and an Economic and Social Council.

Competence: The Security Council would have primary responsibility for maintaining peace and security. There was full agreement that all decisions in this crucial area would be reached only with the unanimity of the permanent members.

The Yalta Conference

Several important topics were not settled in the Dumbarton Oaks conversations. No decision was reached on whether a new court should be established to replace the existing Permanent Court of International Justice. The question of how the new world organization would deal with the mandates system and the general problem of colonialism was avoided. More important than the omissions were disagreements that arose in several areas and were to prove too fundamental to settle at any but the highest levels. These disagreements were eventually resolved at the final wartime conference of the Big Three—Roosevelt, Churchill, and Stalin—meeting at Yalta in the Russian Crimea February 4–11, 1945. At Dumbarton Oaks the Soviets had demanded a comprehensive and unlimited veto power in the Security Council; at Yalta Stalin accepted a compromise that the great power veto would not apply to decisions on procedural matters and could not be invoked by a party to a dispute. At Dumbarton Oaks the Soviets had sought the admission of each of the sixteen Soviet republics as original members; at Yalta this demand was reduced to additional seats for two republics, the Ukraine and Byelorussia, and was accepted by Roosevelt and Churchill. The term *peace-loving,* adopted at Dumbarton Oaks as a criterion of fitness for membership, was defined at Yalta to provide original membership for any state that had declared war on the common enemy by March 1, 1945, a definition that was somewhat anomalous but operational. Agreement was reached on the question of territories then governed under mandates from the League of Nations: a trusteeship system would be established, and the territories placed under it would include existing League mandates, colonial holdings from the enemy states, and other areas voluntarily placed under trusteeship. A Trusteeship Council would be established to oversee the trust system. Finally, the Big Three agreed at Yalta that the five great powers would sponsor a UN Conference on International Organization to meet on April 25, 1945. San Francisco was selected as the site of the Conference.

The Yalta Conference helped resolve outstanding issues among the Big Three, but the publication of the Dumbarton Oaks Proposals raised murmurings among the small powers. The views of some of the small states were carefully set forth, somewhat to the annoyance of the U.S. delegation, at the Inter-American Conference on Problems of Peace and War held at Mexico City in February and March 1945. These states called for universality of membership, a more powerful General Assembly, more emphasis on a world court, a special agency to promote intellectual and moral cooperation, adequate representation for Latin America on the Security Council, and the settlement of regional disputes by regional organizations, such as the Inter-American system, acting in harmony with the new organization. Clearly, the small powers were not going to accept passively great power domination in the framing of the new Charter or in the power structure of the organization itself.

To some extent, the Dumbarton Oaks Proposals also collided with the views of informed public opinion in the United States. The wartime propaganda for a new world organization had fostered a wave of idealism bordering on utopianism among segments of the public. The Proposals, conversely, were based on the bedrock of diplomatic realism, as were the compromises reached at Yalta. Consequently, many idealists regarded the Proposals as a step backward from the League of Nations Covenant, pointing out that the principle of national sovereignty was proclaimed more strongly that it had been in 1919, that great power domination was more solidly entrenched, and that references to law and justice were vaguer. Idealists who had been thinking in terms of a world federal union were brought harshly back to reality.

The great powers, however, could not wait for the building of a full public consensus; to prolong the process of constructing the framework of the new organization might run the risk of destroying existing areas of agreement as the war drew to a close. Suggestions for revisions and improvements could be explored at San Francisco. In the words of Franklin D. Roosevelt, addressing the Congress on his return from Yalta, "This time we shall not make the mistake of waiting until the end of the war to set up the machinery of peace."

The UN Conference on International Organization (UNCIO)

The UN Conference on International Organization opened in San Francisco on April 25, 1945, with forty-six nations represented. Four additional delegations representing Argentina, Denmark, Byelorussia, and the Ukraine were subsequently admitted to participate in drafting the Charter. The fifty nations represented plus Poland became the original members of the United Nations. The latter did not participate in the San Francisco Conference because the United States and Britain refused to recognize the Soviet-sponsored Provisional Government, but Poland was permitted to sign the completed Charter as an original member. The controversy over Poland's participation hinted strongly of the coming ideological conflicts within the new organization.

The process of writing the UN Charter resembled that of a democratic constituent body drafting a constitution. The Big Five provided the leadership and initiative in most of the decision making. The U.S. delegation was particularly conspicuous in its role as godfather of the new organization. Although diplomatic practice demands that the foreign minister of the host country be chosen as the presiding officer of an international conference, in the interest of great power unity the Conference chose the foreign ministers of the four sponsoring governments as cochairmen.[4]

The Conference agenda was based on the Dumbarton Oaks Proposals as modified by the Yalta Conference. The Conference rules provided for freedom of discussion, voting equality, and substantive decision making by a two-thirds vote of those present and voting. These ground rules theoretically gave the small states an opportunity to undo the work of the great powers, but in fact no substantial change in the great power position was effected. The threat of empty great power chairs at the UN table was incentive enough for the majority to defer to the few. The middle and small powers did sometimes obtain concessions on matters of secondary importance that, in total, added up to a significant modification of the Proposals. Bloc politics were also used at the Conference, with the twenty Latin-American states and five Arab states particularly active and effective. The Commonwealth states, however, did not join Britain in a voting bloc, preferring to provide leadership to the attempts to modify the great power position.

The completed Charter was signed on June 26, 1945, by the delegates of fifty nations. On the same date the delegates also established a Preparatory Commission consisting of representatives of all member states. The Preparatory Commission met in London during November to make arrangements for the first meetings of the new organization's major organs and for the transfer of certain activities from the League of Nations.

Public Support and Ratification

After signing the UN Charter, the fifty-one signatory states undertook its ratification through their respective constitutional processes. The process of ratification varies from state to state, although it generally involves some measure of approval by the national legislative body. Such approval may be automatic in authoritarian states, and it may even be perfunctory in democratic states, but in some nations, such as the United States, it may be the crucial test for a treaty. Although the great majority of treaties submitted to the U.S. Senate over the years have received its consent, some of the most important ones, such as the Covenant of the League of Nations and the Statute of the first World Court, have been rejected. Many others have been effectively killed by remaining buried in the Senate Foreign Relations Committee.

On July 28, 1945, the Senate of the United States approved the Charter of the United Nations by a vote of 89 to 2. The lopsided vote surprised no one. Never before in American history had a treaty been studied and debated so extensively both before and after its writing. Never had the Senate participated so directly in the major steps of the treaty process or had bipartisanship operated so successfully in removing a major treaty from politics. Never before, or since, had the State Department been so successful in stimulating organized group support for a major policy objective. In a very real sense the American decision to participate in the United Nations was in accord with the democratic principle expounded in the Preamble of the Charter: "We the peoples of the United Nations . . . have resolved to combine our efforts . . . and do hereby establish an international organization to be known as the United Nations."

On August 8, 1945, President Truman ratified the Charter of the United Nations and the Statute of the International Court of Justice, which was annexed to it. The United Nations came into being on October 24, 1945, since established as United Nations Day. At that time the Soviet Union deposited its ratification and the Secretary of State, James F. Byrnes, signed the Protocol of Deposit of Ratifications affirming that a majority of the fifty-one original signers (twenty-nine nations), including all five great powers, had deposited ratifications with the United States. All fifty-one signers of the Charter had ratified it by December 27, 1945. On January 10, 1946, with the opening of the First General Assembly, the United Nations began to function.

NOTES

1. *New York Times Magazine,* September 15, 1957, p. 21.
2. Switzerland and Sweden, despite Wilson's pronouncement, were able to remain neutral during World War I and World War II. Switzerland has also refused to join the United Nations because of a belief that membership would violate its centuries-old policy of neutrality. In a referendum vote in 1986, the Swiss people reaffirmed this policy of not joining the United Nations. Switzerland, however, lends strong support to most UN programs, and many UN agencies and operations are headquartered in Geneva.
3. Within two months following the levying of sanctions in November 1935, Italian exports had declined 43 percent over the same month of the previous year, and imports had dropped 47 percent. In three months imports fell to 56 percent of the previous year and imports of strategic items such as iron ore, tin, and raw rubber had almost ceased. Thus, within a short period of time economic sanctions proved effective in significantly reducing Italy's economic activity.
4. France was invited to become a sponsoring government but declined.

SELECTED READINGS

BRETTON, HENRY L. *International Relations in the Nuclear Age*. Albany: State University of New York Press, 1986.

BURTON, M. E. *The Assembly of the League of Nations*. Chicago: University of Chicago Press, 1943.

CHURCHILL, WINSTON. *The Gathering Storm*. Boston: Houghton Mifflin, 1948.

DAVIS, M.; H. GILCHRIST; G. KIRK; and N. PADELFORD. "The United Nations Charter . . . Its Development at San Francisco." *International Conciliation,* no. 413, September 1945.

EAGLETON, CLYDE. *International Government*. New York: Ronald Press, 1948.

GOODRICH, L. M. "From League of Nations to United Nations." *International Organization,* February 1947, pp. 3–21.

HULL, CORDELL. *The Memoirs of Cordell Hull*. 2 vols. New York: Macmillan, 1948.

KEGLEY, CHARLES W., JR., and EUGENE R. WITTKOPF. *World Politics: Trend and Transformation*. New York: St. Martin's Press, 1985.

LEONARD, L. LARRY. *International Organization*. New York: McGraw-Hill, 1951.

MANGONE, GERARD J. *A Short History of International Organization*. New York: McGraw-Hill, 1954.

POTTER, PITMAN B. *An Introduction to the Study of International Organization*. New York: Appleton-Century-Crofts, 1948.

REINSCH, PAUL S. *Public International Unions*. Boston: Ginn, 1911.

Report to the President on the Results of the San Francisco Conference, by . . . the Secretary of State. Department of State Publication 2349, Conference Series 71. Washington, D.C.: U.S. Government Printing Office, 1945.

REUTER, PAUL. *International Institutions*. New York: Rinehart, 1958.

RUSSELL, RUTH B., and JEANETTE E. MUTHER. *A History of the United Nations Charter: The Role of the United States, 1940–45*. Washington, D.C.: Brookings Institution, 1958.

SMITH, S. S. *The Manchurian Crisis: A Tragedy in International Relations*. New York: Columbia University Press, 1948.

WALTERS, F. P. A. *A History of the League of Nations*. London: Oxford University Press, 1952.

WATKINS, JAMES T., and J. WILLIAM ROBINSON. *General International Organization: A Source Book*. Princeton: D. Van Nostrand, 1956.

2

Legal Framework, Institutional Structures, and Financial Realities

THE CONSTITUTIONAL STRUCTURE

Formally written and ratified as a multilateral treaty, the UN Charter became a de facto constitution with the establishment of the UN organization. Like most constitution makers, the framers had sought to create a working system that would facilitate the development of an administrative substructure, allocate responsibilities, grant and circumscribe powers, demarcate jurisdictions—in short, do the jobs that are typical of a national constitution. Also common to every constitution is the enunciation, usually in hortatory language, of the principles and objectives underlying the organization. The framers fulfilled this responsibility more than adequately.

The real test of any constitution comes in the transition from principle to practice. Meeting this test is an ongoing process. Words constantly take on new meanings as different people interpret them and as changing situations and fresh problems call for solutions not in keeping with older interpretations. This is the process of constitution building; it exists because constitution makers can never fully anticipate the changes that will occur.[1] Although the Charter is a lengthy and verbose document, its framers, whether by intent or accident, wrote much flexibility into it, as the more than forty-year history of the United Nations indicates.

Constitutional Evolution

Constitutional development for an international organization like the United Nations may closely parallel that of a national constitutional system. A comparison can be a useful enterprise if the analogy is not carried too far. Over the years the U.S. Constitution, for example, has developed largely through the process of executive, legislative, and judicial interpretation. Similarly, the Charter of the United Nations has evolved through interpretation by its members and by its major organs, particularly the General Assembly, the Security Council, the Secretariat, and the Court. Custom and usage, where mandates are lacking or ambiguous, have been significant forces in shaping both national constitutional systems and the UN system. In both instances, when the constitutional text has been too confining, ways and means have been found to bypass or ignore the strict letter of the law. Formal amendments have been adopted only infrequently in American constitutional history and for the United Nations as well, since there have been only three formal Charter amendments in over forty years. Two amendments to the Charter were proposed by the Eighteenth General Assembly in 1963, one enlarging the Security Council from eleven to fifteen and changing its voting majority from seven to nine, the other increasing the size of the Economic and Social Council from eighteen to twenty-seven. Both amendments were ratified and took effect in 1965. A third amendment, which took effect in 1973, enlarged the Economic and Social Council to fifty-four members. The Charter amendment process provides that amendments proposed by a two-thirds vote of the General Assembly must be ratified by two thirds of the members, including all permanent members of the Security Council. Each great power thus retains a veto over all *formal* changes to the Charter, but not over changes brought about by interpretation.

The process of constitutional development is not so clearly delineated in the United Nations as in most national systems. As a multilateral treaty, the Charter was a product of extensive international negotiations, with the precise meaning and application of many words and phrases in the Charter masked by the need for agreement at the time of negotiations. Since 1945, difficulties in translations, the vagaries of power politics, conflicts of national interests, the admission of new members, ideological rivalries, and the lack of a final judge have all contributed to the continuing problems of interpretation and development.

Like the U.S. Constitution, the Charter does not establish a definitive constitutional umpire. Who, then, shall decide what the Charter means when questions of jurisdiction, powers, competence, and procedures arise? Should the International Court of Justice as the principal judicial organ appoint itself "guardian of the UN constitutional system" and undertake a role similar to that assumed by the U.S. Supreme Court in the historic case of *Marbury* v. *Madison?* Should that guardian be the General Assembly, in which all members are represented and on which the Charter has bestowed the power to "discuss any questions or any matters within the scope of the present Charter or relating to the powers and functions of any organs provided for in the present Charter"? Should each major organ determine the nature and extent of its own jurisdiction and procedures? Should unanimity prevail, as it did traditionally with multilateral treaties, with constitutional issues resolved through agreement of all signatory governments? Or should each member interpret the Charter for itself?

The question of establishing a constitutional umpire was never resolved at San Francisco, nor was it specifically considered. The result has been that all of the above methods, and many others, have been used to deal with constitutional issues in the UN system. Decisions on constitutional questions have included interpretations made by presiding officers, by majority and extramajority votes in major organs and other bodies, by decisions of the Secretary-General and other Secretariat officials, by advisory opinions of the Court, and by decisions of member governments made outside the UN framework but based on interpretations of Charter provisions. Thus, most interpretations of the Charter leading to development of the UN system have been made *politically* by political organs or individuals rather than *juridically* by the International Court or some other legal body.[2]

Charter Principles

The analogy between national constitutions and the constitutional system of the United Nations can also be extended to the realm of principles. Underlying the American governmental system, for example, are basic principles that provide the philosophical underpinning and moral justification for the constitutional structure. Most of these principles are also found, explicitly or implicitly, in the UN system, supplemented by others that are more germane to an international body. Those that can be observed or implied from the operations of the United Nations include democracy, self-determination, parliamentarianism, majoritarianism, the rule of law and justice, horizontal federalism (regionalism), and the separation of powers. In addition, principles set forth in Article 2 of the UN Charter, which members accept by ratifying the Charter, include (1) the sovereign equality of all members, (2) good faith fulfillment of Charter obligations, (3) peaceful settlement of international disputes, (4) nonuse of force or the threat of force for aggressive purposes, (5) support for UN enforcement action, and (6) nonintervention by the United Nations in matters that are essentially within a state's domestic jurisdiction. Together these principles constitute basic rules of international conduct that all member states are ostensibly committed to observe. These rules are a projection into the international arena of purposes and principles already having national validity. In this sense the Charter takes a first step in the direction of an organized international community independent of the organs set up for international decision making. Even in the most democratic of states, these ideals are never perfectly realized, and certainly a great gulf exists between theory and practice in the United Nations. Nevertheless, they can provide guidelines for action and they are frequently invoked in General Assembly debates. Although these and other principles will be discussed throughout the book as they relate to the operations of the United Nations, two of them—domestic jurisdiction and regionalism—will be examined now in their constitutional context.

Domestic Jurisdiction.   In some states, such as Canada, Mexico, Germany, and the United States, federalism provides by a written constitution for a division of powers between a central government and regional or subdivisional governments. In a somewhat related manner, Article 2 of the Charter recognizes a dual authority when it proclaims that nothing in the Charter should be interpreted to "authorize the United Nations to intervene in matters which are essentially within the domestic jurisdiction of any state." The application of enforcement measures to maintain peace and security under Chapter VII is specifically excluded from the limiting clause. The domestic jurisdiction clause resembles the Tenth Amendment of the U.S. Constitution in that it makes explicit a division of powers and responsibilities between two levels of political organization and provides a limitation on the higher level to safeguard the lower from unwarranted intrusions. In effect, this Charter principle simply states that only *international* problems and issues are proper subjects for UN inquiry and action and that *national* questions remain within the complete jurisdiction of member states. The Charter leaves open to controversy, however, the questions of who shall determine what is national and what is international, and how that determination should be made.

Controversy within the organization has also centered on the nature and intent of the domestic jurisdiction clause, with differences over whether it provides a *legal* limitation or merely proclaims a *political* principle. In practice, the latter has generally been accepted, with decisions made by UN organs in keeping with the political realities of the situation. Problems within the Republic of South Africa, for example, have been debated extensively, and resolutions condemning the apartheid system and maltreatment of Africans have been adopted despite repeated invocation by South Africa of the domestic jurisdiction clause. The United Nations has been singularly ineffectual in trying to force South Africa to take corrective action in its gross violations of human rights even though most UN members have taken the position that South African domestic practices constitute a threat to international peace and security and are therefore subject to UN jurisdiction. Some states—France and Portugal, for example—invoked the domestic jurisdiction clause for many years in refusing to submit reports to the United Nations on conditions in their colonies, holding that their overseas possessions were part of their "metropolitan territory" and therefore matters of purely local concern. Granting independence to these colonies eventually solved that controversial problem.

Over a period of forty years, domestic jurisdiction has become increasingly ineffective as a deterrent to UN consideration of an issue. UN majorities have grown more and more inclined to define UN competence so broadly that virtually nothing is left to domestic jurisdiction. On the other hand, UN resolutions are generally ineffective when addressed to matters believed by affected states to be within their domestic jurisdiction. Whether or not observed by UN majorities, the domestic jurisdiction clause in fact reflects the normal and natural limits of a world organization operating in a world of sovereign states, each zealously guarding its power over what it regards as its internal affairs.

Regionalism.   Interstate cooperation, a halfway house in the American constitutional system between the central government and the state units, has its international counterpart in the form of regionalism. The U.S. Constitution refers to this middle-level organization as "interstate relations"; in its politically activist form it is known as "horizontal federalism," connoting an extensive system of teamwork among the American states to solve common problems through uniform laws, joint actions, and common agencies.

International regionalism is a recognition by participating governments that not all problems are either national or global in scope. Some international problems may be confined to a geographic region; their solutions may require action by only a limited number of states, or psychological, technical, or administrative difficulties may limit the ability of international agencies to function beyond the region. International regionalism exists, therefore, because groups of states have found it to be the most appropriate means of solving some common problems.

The framers of the UN Charter, although theoretically committed to universalism, recognized the political investment in regional organizations and accepted the feasibility of decentralizing some international operations concerned with security, political action, and economic and social welfare. The framers compromised on the issue by providing that regional organizations would serve as adjuncts of the UN system subject to a measure of control and direction by it. All such arrangements and activities must also be consistent with the purposes and principles of the Charter, although no apparent means exist for enforcing this rule. Under these provisions a host of regional political, security, economic, social, and technical organizations have been established over the past forty years in all areas of the globe.

Collective self-defense, expressly authorized by Article 51 of the Charter, has served as a basis for the construction of numerous regional alliances. Whether such arrangements have contributed to peace and a stable balance of power, or have seriously hampered UN efforts by stimulating the arms race and producing fear and insecurity, remains an unresolved issue.

The Charter further provides that regional organizations should contribute to security by making "every effort to achieve pacific settlement of local disputes . . . before referring them to the Security Council" (Article 52). The framers recognized, wisely as it turned out, that the Security Council would be suffocated by an avalanche of disputes and situations if some intermediate agencies for handling them did not exist. Yet the problem of distinguishing between a case that involves only regional considerations and one that concerns international peace and security persists. The handling of the Cuban and Dominican crises by the Organization of American States, for example, produced angry charges from some UN members that these crises threatened world peace and should be handled by the global rather than the regional organization. Unquestionably, under the Charter the Security Council could step in and "take over" the handling of such situations at any time, but since one of the great powers is likely to be involved in the regional group's action, a veto could result. It has also been generally assumed, though not always borne out in practice, that a dispute would be less likely to escalate if it were handled on a regional level.

Another role for regional organizations involves political, economic, and social cooperation. Here, too, collaboration rather than competition has characterized the relationship between the global organization and such groups as the Colombo Plan, the Organization for Economic Cooperation and Development, the Organization of American States, and the European Community. Economic regionalism, in particular, has flowered as states have tried to solve their trade, balance of payments, economic development, and technical assistance problems through arrangements with neighboring or interdependent states.

Regionalism is offered as either an alternative or a complement to universalism. Debates involving the respective advantages of regionalism and universalism have usually focused on the following points.[3]

Arguments for Regionalism

1. Regionalism is more effective than universalism because its capacities are more realistically attuned to its objectives.

2. Regionalism involves fewer states than universalism and offers greater propensities for consensus because of common traditions; similar political, economic, and social systems; and the regional nature of the problems to be solved.

3. Regionalism tends to produce greater support from the peoples of the participating states than universalism because of a closer identification of common interests.

4. Regionalism permits a more appropriate handling of administrative, technical, and functional problems than universalism because the organization's machinery is better matched with the nature and scope of its operations.

5. Regionalism is a necessary precursor to effective global cooperation because it lays the groundwork for a broader consensus.

Arguments for Universalism

1. Universalism is a more appropriate means for preserving peace than regionalism since peace is indivisible; a war anywhere in the world threatens to engulf all.

2. Universalism encourages a more effective pooling of resources to attack economic and social problems; a pooling of African regional resources, for example, would result only in a sharing of African poverty.

3. Universalism encourages a consensus of mankind based on universal principles; regionalism encourages conflict between rival blocs and economic groups.

4. Universalism recognizes that disease, hunger, illiteracy, and poverty are common to all regions of the world; a common attack carried on by a single organization, therefore, will avoid duplication and make the most effective use of available resources.

5. Universalism as embodied in the United Nations already exercises broader powers over a greater variety of subjects than any regional organization; hence, to speak of regionalism as a necessary precursor to universalism ignores contemporary facts.

Although the arguments on both sides have intrinsic merit, such debates tend to be detached from reality because the operational dichotomy between regionalism and universalism is largely a false one. Both types of international organization exist today; both serve useful purposes; and their functions are often—if not always—complementary.

INSTRUMENTS OF POLITICAL DECISION MAKING

UN operations revolve around the functions of six principal organs: the General Assembly, the Security Council, the Economic and Social Council, the Trusteeship Council, the Secretariat, and the International Court of Justice. The organization and processes of each of these major organs will be discussed in this chapter.

In addition to the six principal organs, sixteen specialized agencies and other autonomous organizations within the overall framework of the United Nations operate in various technical, economic, and social fields (see Figure 2–1). Added to the specialized agencies and related bodies are a number of major programs and organizations that have been created by the United Nations to deal with specific problem areas. These include the UN Relief and Works Agency for Palestine Refugees (UNRWA), the UN Conference on Trade and Development (UNCTAD), the UN Children's Fund (UNICEF), the Office of the UN High Commissioner for Refugees (UNHCR), the World Food Program (WFP), the UN Institute for Training and Research (UNITAR), the UN Development Program (UNDP), the UN Environment Program (UNEP), the United Nations University, the UN Special Fund, the World Food Council, the UN Center for Human Settlements (HABITAT), and the UN Fund for Population Activities (UNFPA). Of these programs and organizations, UNRWA reports directly to the General Assembly, whereas the rest report to the General Assembly through the Economic and Social Council. In addition, certain agencies are concerned with security matters and therefore report to the Security Council. Included in this group are UNDOF (UN Disengagement Observer Force), UNFICYP (UN Peacekeeping Force in Cyprus), UNIFIL (UN Interim Force in Lebanon), UNMOGIP (UN Military Observer Group in India and Pakistan), UNTSO (UN Truce Supervision Organization in Palestine), and the Military Staff Committee. Finally, the UN system includes regional commissions, functional commissions, and a variety of committees that report to the Economic and Social Council and, indirectly, to the General Assembly.

The vast array of agencies and programs subject to supervision by the major organs of the United Nations, or at least reporting to them, testifies to the global nature of the UN *system,* as distinct from political decision-making apparatus headquartered in New York. The latter is merely the tip of a huge organizational and bureaucratic iceberg with its operations carried on in one way or another in almost every country in the world. Isolated, indeed, is the country or society that has not been touched by one of the many UN programs. Hundreds of millions of individuals have benefited directly, and all human beings stand to gain from UN activities directed toward such objectives as reducing conflict, controlling pollution, and improving health. Specific actions and programs, problems and issues, that emerge from many of these agencies making up the UN system will be covered in later chapters.

The General Assembly

Central to the sprawling UN organization, resembling somewhat the British prototype Parliament at Westminster in its unifying role, the General Assembly functions as the focus for UN activities. "Global Parliament," "Town Meeting of the World," "Sun of the UN Solar System"—these and other catchphrases are used to sum up, perhaps somewhat inaccurately, the General Assembly's widely diffused activities and diverse roles. Unlike the Security Council, which pays homage to the elitism of great power politics, the Assembly effuses the democratic ethos of *egalitarianism, parliamentarianism,* and *majoritarianism.*

Equality of Members.   The Assembly's *egalitarian* nature should be obvious to even the casual UN visitor: the Assembly is the only one of the six principal UN organs in which all member states are equally represented, with a maximum of ten delegates and one vote for each member (see Table 2–1). Efforts by some of the great powers to push for a change to a weighted voting system have never been taken seriously by the small and middle powers. The traditional equality of all states, large and small, under international law and as participants in international conferences provides the legitimacy for retaining equal voting. The political defensiveness of the new states, some of which formed their Assembly delegations at the same time that they established their first governments, safeguards the principle. This equality permeates the work of the Assembly, including that carried on by its seven main committees, on each of which all members are represented. The seven main committees of the Assembly are the First (Political and Security); Special Political (originally an ad hoc committee, this committee has remained numberless although it is now a permanent committee); Second (Economic and Financial); Third (Social, Humanitarian, and Cultural); Fourth (Trusteeship); Fifth (Administrative and Budgetary); and Sixth (Legal). Consideration of agenda items usually begins in one of the main committees, which meet and carry on business as committees of the whole. Most matters receive their most thorough airing and consideration at this stage, since the press of time permits the Assembly in plenary session to explore extensively only the most politically explosive issues. Increasingly, as in legislative bodies like the American Congress, a committee's report has been accepted in plenary session with only perfunctory debate. This trend has had the effect of creating eight assemblies with a full complement of members in each, a development that has helped keep the business of the Assembly moving forward but has also added to the general confusion of Assembly decision making. The General Assembly also utilizes various procedural committees and subsidiary bodies in carrying out its decision-making functions (see Figure 2–1).

Parliamentary Role.   The parliamentary nature of the Assembly becomes evident in observing its modus operandi. It may be, as an astute British observer has noted, that the Assembly's operations are "a far cry from anything at Westminster."

TABLE 2–1 _____
Membership of Principal UN Organs in 1987

General Assembly—All 159 UN Members

Security Council

Permanent members: China, France, the USSR, the United Kingdom, the United States.

Non-permanent members (two-year term expires 31 December of the year indicated): Argentina (1988), Bulgaria (1987), Congo (1987), Germany, Federal Republic of (1988), Ghana (1987), Italy (1988), Japan (1988), United Arab Emirates (1987), Venezuela (1987), Zambia (1988).

Economic and Social Council

Fifty-four members (three-year term expires 31 December of the year indicated): Australia (1988), Bangladesh (1987), Belgium (1988), Belize (1989), Bolivia (1989), Brazil (1987), Bulgaria (1989), Byelorussian SSR (1988), Canada (1989), China (1989), Colombia (1987), Denmark (1989), Djibouti (1988), Egypt (1988), France (1987), Gabon (1988), German Democratic Republic (1988), Germany, Federal Republic of (1987), Guinea (1987), Haiti (1987), Iceland (1987), India (1987), Iran (1989), Iraq (1988), Italy (1988), Jamaica (1988), Japan (1987), Morocco (1987), Mozambique (1988), Nigeria (1987), Norway (1989), Oman (1989), Pakistan (1988), Panama (1988), Peru (1988), Philippines (1988), Poland (1989), Romania (1987), Rwanda (1989), Senegal (1987), Sierra Leone (1988), Somalia (1989), Spain (1987), Sri Lanka (1989), Sudan (1989), Syrian Arab Republic (1988), Turkey (1987), USSR (1989), United Kingdom (1989), United States (1988), Uruguay (1989), Venezuela (1987), Zaire (1989), Zimbabwe (1987).

Trusteeship Council

Member administering the Trust Territory of the Pacific Islands: United States.

Non-administering members: China, France, the USSR, the United Kingdom. China does not participate in the work of the Trusteeship Council.

International Court of Justice

Fifteen judges, elected individually (nine-year term ends 5 February of the year indicated, listed in official order of precedence): Nagendra Singh of India (1991), President; Guy Ladreit de Lacharrière of France (1991), Vice-President; Manfred Lachs of Poland (1994), José María Ruda of Argentina (1991), Taslim Olawale Elias of Nigeria (1994), Shigeru Oda of Japan (1994), Roberto Ago of Italy (1988), José Sette-Camara of Brazil (1988), Stephen Schwebel of the United States (1988), Sir Robert Y. Jennings of the United Kingdom (1991), Kéba Mbaye of Senegal (1991), Mohammed Bedjaoui of Algeria (1988), Ni Zhengyu of China (1994), Jens Evensen of Norway (1994), Nikolai Tarasov of the USSR (1988).

SOURCE: *UN Chronicle,* January 1987.

FIGURE 2–1
The UN System

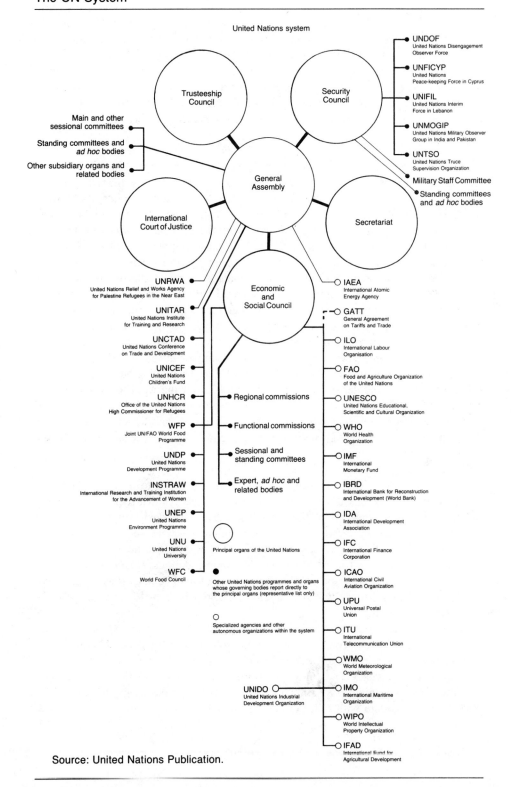

United Nations system

UNDOF
United Nations Disengagement
Observer Force

UNFICYP
United Nations
Peace-keeping Force in Cyprus

UNIFIL
United Nations Interim
Force in Lebanon

UNMOGIP
United Nations Military Observer
Group in India and Pakistan

UNTSO
United Nations Truce
Supervision Organization

Military Staff Committee

Standing committees
and ad hoc bodies

Trusteeship
Council

Security
Council

Main and other
sessional committees

Standing committees and
ad hoc bodies

Other subsidiary organs and
related bodies

General
Assembly

International
Court of Justice

Secretariat

UNRWA
United Nations Relief and Works Agency
for Palestine Refugees in the Near East

Economic
and
Social Council

IAEA
International Atomic
Energy Agency

UNITAR
United Nations Institute
for Training and Research

GATT
General Agreement
on Tariffs and Trade

UNCTAD
United Nations Conference
on Trade and Development

ILO
International Labour
Organisation

UNICEF
United Nations
Children's Fund

FAO
Food and Agriculture Organization
of the United Nations

UNHCR
Office of the United Nations
High Commissioner for Refugees

Regional commissions

UNESCO
United Nations Educational,
Scientific and Cultural Organization

WFP
Joint UN/FAO World Food
Programme

Functional commissions

WHO
World Health
Organization

UNDP
United Nations
Development Programme

Sessional and
standing committees

IMF
International
Monetary Fund

INSTRAW
International Research and Training Institution
for the Advancement of Women

Expert, ad hoc and
related bodies

IBRD
International Bank for Reconstruction
and Development (World Bank)

UNEP
United Nations
Environment Programme

IDA
International Development
Association

UNU
United Nations
University

Principal organs of the United Nations

IFC
International Finance
Corporation

WFC
World Food Council

Other United Nations programmes and organs
whose governing bodies report directly to
the principal organs (representative list only)

ICAO
International Civil
Aviation Organization

UPU
Universal Postal
Union

Specialized agencies and other
autonomous organizations within the system

ITU
International
Telecommunication Union

WMO
World Meteorological
Organization

IMO
International Maritime
Organization

UNIDO
United Nations Industrial
Development Organization

WIPO
World Intellectual
Property Organization

IFAD
International Fund for
Agricultural Development

Source: United Nations Publication.

The British system's "focus" on a legislative program, its emphasis on "responsibility," its "party-whip discipline," and its organized "majority and opposition" are missing or hardly discernible in the Assembly hall. Yet the agenda is adopted, debate proceeds, votes are taken, and decisions are made. Our British observer described the process in this picturesque language: "Like a herd of grazing cattle, that moves as it chews, head down, the Assembly gets through its day [or more often its morning] without any particular drive, yet not without a certain vaguely diffused sense of purpose."[4]

In a search for analogies, the Assembly's parliamentary qualities may be found to resemble the continental European parliaments, with their multiparty coalitions ideological rivalries, and shifting centers of power, more closely than the orderly, compact British model. Or a watchful observer might note some similarities between the Assembly's operations and those of the American Congress. Both are more often than not caught up in clashes of parochial interests and must attempt to harmonize regional, class, creed, and racial conflicts. Both must grapple with procedural rules that often complicate rather than expedite the process of decision making. The American federal system produces an attachment to states' rights in somewhat the same manner that the sovereign states of the world with their attachments to national interests produce a loose, untidy, somewhat anarchic General Assembly. Yet a parliament's main role is concerned with freedom of debate, in which issues can be discussed, decisions made, budgets approved, taxes levied, and administrative operations supervised. The General Assembly resembles all national parliaments in these functions. Although it does not possess a direct lawmaking authority, its competence to discuss and debate extends to *any* problem of the world or of the organization itself that a majority of members regard as proper for Assembly consideration. The only exceptions to this broad power are the domestic jurisdiction clause (Article 2) and the limitation on the Assembly concerning matters under consideration by the Security Council (Article 12).

Majority Rule.   The Assembly's *majoritarian* approach to decision making is an improvement over that of the Assembly of the League, which required unanimity for most actions. Article 18 of the Charter provides that decisions on "important questions" be made by a two-thirds majority of members present and voting. All other questions require only a simple majority. "Important questions" include those mentioned in Article 18 (peace and security recommendations; elections to the three UN councils; admission, suspension, and expulsion of members; trusteeship and budgetary questions and those that the Assembly decides by a majority vote are to be considered "important").

Consensus, not overpowering majority votes, is the objective of Assembly politics. Consensus demands compromise, and compromises in the Assembly are sought through negotiations, pressures, demands, debates, promises, and other techniques of parliamentary diplomacy that, in art and form, closely resemble the "politics" that keeps the wheels turning in a national legislative body. Caucusing groups meet, plan strategy, and negotiate with other groups before decisions are made. The process of forging a majority often resembles that of the continental parliaments where no party has a majority and policy evolves out of coalition governments.* On economic and related issues, however, decision making is dominated by the Group of 77 (G–77), which consists of almost 130 Third World countries that caucus to determine a common approach to issues that arise before the General Assembly.

Formal Organization.   Regular sessions of the General Assembly are held each year, beginning usually on the third Tuesday in September. At the beginning of each session, the Assembly establishes a target date for adjournment, usually mid-December. A three-week period of "general debate" opens each Assembly session, with most delegations taking the opportunity to express their views on the full range of issues on the global agenda. Heads of state or government often participate. Special sessions may be convoked after the Assembly adjourns if requested by the Security Council or if a majority of Assembly members agree. Special sessions of the Assembly have met as follows: Palestine (1947), Palestine (1948), Tunisia (1961), Finance and Budget Problems (1963), Peacekeeping Operations and South-West Africa (1967), Raw Materials and Development (1974), Development and International Economic Cooperation (1975), Financing of UN Interim Force in Lebanon (1978), Namibia (1978), Disarmament (1978), International Economic Cooperation (1980), and Disarmament (1982). It is unusual for the Assembly to confine itself to its regular autumn session, since pressing issues or dispute crises inevitably arise during the year. Emergency special sessions may be convened within twenty-four hours under the Uniting for Peace resolution if a veto in the Security Council blocks action there on a peace and security matter. Adopted in November 1950, this resolution provides the Assembly with authority to recommend, by a two-thirds vote, collective enforcement action against a state that threatens peace and security. By the 1980s, nine emergency special sessions of the Assembly had been called, the most recent dealing with Afghanistan (1980), Palestine (1980, 1982), Namibia (1981), and the Occupied Arab Territories (1982).

The first job facing a new Assembly each year is to elect a President and seventeen Vice Presidents who serve for one year. It has become traditional to select as President a leading international statesman from an important small- or middle-power state, usually from the Third World. The vice presidencies are allocated to the five great powers and to geographic areas of the world to ensure their representative character and a fair apportionment of prestige. In 1963, when the number of Vice Presidents was increased from thirteen to seventeen, a formula was adopted to provide for the election of seven Vice Presidents from Asia and Africa, one from Eastern Europe, three from Latin America, two from Western Europe and "other states" (Canada, Australia, and New Zealand), and one from each of the five permanent members of the Security Council. These figures total eighteen because the region from which the President is elected receives one less than the formula specifies. The President, the Vice Presidents, and the chairmen of the seven standing committees

---

*Decision making in the General Assembly will be discussed in greater detail in Chapter 3.

constitute the General Committee, which functions as a steering committee for each session.

Although his formal powers are limited, the President may accomplish much through his personal influence and political adeptness. Qualities desirable to abet his role as presiding officer of the Assembly include a "refusal to be bored, a memory for faces, a capacity to slough off private and national partialities, a sense of humor coupled with a concern for the dignity of his office, a ready grasp of procedural technicalities, a proper sense of pace, and a quick feeling for the sense of the meeting."[5] Seated beside the President at all Assembly sessions is the Executive Assistant to the Secretary-General, who functions as parliamentarian and adviser to the President in his role of Secretary of the General Assembly. Although the President's formal powers to control or influence the direction of debate and action are weak and tend to resemble those of the President of the U.S. Senate or the Speaker in the House of Commons, the disarray of the Assembly demands a strong yet tactful guidance. The international reputations of the Presidents have helped each of them to weather many verbal storms and to develop the office into a respectable source of Assembly power and influence.

Assembly Functions.   Against a backdrop of politics and diplomacy, the General Assembly carries out its various roles and diverse activities, some assigned by the Charter and others assumed by the Assembly.

One frequently indulged activity is exhortation by means of resolutions aimed at member states, nonmembers, great powers, the Security Council, other major organs, even the General Assembly itself. Sometimes referred to as "manifestos against sin," these resolutions permit the Assembly to carry out what its supporters regard as the role of guardian of Charter principles and the conscience of mankind and what its detractors write off as sheer hypocrisy. Through such resolutions the Assembly has, *inter alia,* called on the permanent members of the Security Council to use the veto with restraint, the great powers to cease their war propaganda, all states to accept the maxim of peaceful coexistence, and disputants to settle their controversies peacefully.

The Assembly's quasi-legislative function, carried on through the adoption of resolutions, declarations, and conventions, goes beyond exhortation in seeking to develop and codify international law. In this role the Assembly most closely approximates the lawmaking activities of a national legislature. Assembly resolutions governing internal matters, such as procedural rules, control of funds and property, and staff regulations, have the force of law. Resolutions directed toward state conduct outside the organization are not binding of themselves, but the rules thus enunciated may have legal force if they are regarded as statements of customary international law or authoritative interpretations of the UN Charter. The Assembly may also engage in lawmaking through the drafting of multilateral treaties. Conventions adopted by the Assembly, such as the Genocide Convention (outlawing acts aimed at the destruction of a national, ethnic, racial, or religious group) or the Law of the Sea

Treaty, become operative as law among the consenting parties after they have been ratified by the required number of states. Just as the Universal Declaration of Human Rights of 1948 typifies Assembly efforts at exhortation, many human rights treaties now in force, prepared under Assembly auspices, illustrate the quasi-legislative function. Where the expectation of common benefits motivates members to act, the Assembly can truly function like a world parliament.

In its investigative role the Assembly complements its quasi-legislative functions. This role can be illustrated by the work of the Assembly's International Law Commission, which since 1948 has conducted studies aimed at the preparation of draft codes to develop and codify international law. As in a national legislature, facts must be accumulated before the Assembly acts. In the settlement of disputes, investigation is an essential prelude to a determination of the issues involved and the working out of a just solution.

Although the Security Council has primary responsibility for international peace and security, the Assembly also has a dispute settlement role. That role becomes especially important when the Security Council is unable to function because of a deadlock or a full agenda. Interposition of an Assembly presence in the Middle East in the form of the UN Emergency Force (UNEF) illustrates this backup role in a very threatening situation. More commonly the Assembly will pursue its peaceful settlement role through discussion and recommendation, tendering good offices, mediation, conciliation, commissions of inquiry, and appointment of individual mediators.

In its peace-preservative role the Assembly fills the void left by Council vetoes. Since 1950 the Uniting for Peace resolution has empowered the Assembly to make appropriate recommendations for collective measures, including "in the case of a breach of the peace or act of aggression the use of armed force when necessary." Assembly actions to maintain or restore international peace and security have been undertaken, for example, in the Middle East, Hungary, Lebanon and Jordan, West Irian, and the Congo. Although the Assembly's role in these cases has not been as forthright as UN critics would have it be, and it has declined in recent years, such action has sometimes helped to moderate, or reduce the threat of, armed conflict.

The Assembly's budgetary function resembles that of a national legislature's traditional "power of the purse." All UN programs and all activities of subsidiary UN bodies come under a measure of surveillance and control since all must be supported financially. Budget decisions have on occasion become the tail that has wagged the dog of substantive actions in the United Nations, as happened during the financial crisis of the 1960s, when lack of funds forced the discontinuance of the UN Congo operation.

Closely related to the Assembly's budgetary function is its supervisory role. It is to the Assembly that the Security Council, the Economic and Social Council, and the Trusteeship Council submit annual and special reports on their respective operations. Although the Security Council is not a subsidiary organ, the Charter empowers the Assembly to make recommendations to it and to call peace-threatening situations to its attention. The Economic and Social Council and the Trusteeship Council, although designated as "principal organs," are actually subsidiary and operate "under the authority of the General Assembly" (Articles 60 and 85). Decisions on economic, social, trusteeship, and related matters are made by the Assembly on recommendations from the two councils. The Secretariat is also primarily concerned with serving the Assembly and in turn is controlled by it. Decisions about the organization, work, personnel, and budget of the Secretariat are regularly made by the Assembly. Annual reports on selected activities and on the work of each organ and agency of the United Nations enable the Assembly to receive, to criticize, and, hence, to supervise the entire UN operation.

The Assembly exercises a twofold elective function. One phase involves the admission of new members into the United Nations; the other relates to the selection of the elective members of other organs. The election to membership takes place following a recommendation by the Security Council, a prerequisite affirmed by the International Court of Justice in an advisory opinion in 1950. Prospective members file an application with the Secretary-General, who transmits it to the Security Council. Some memberships have been delayed in the Security Council, sometimes for years, but once the Council has made its recommendations, Assembly action to admit has been swift. The Assembly's second elective function helps shape the outlook and decision-making capabilities of other major UN organs. Some elections are conducted jointly with the Security Council, as in selecting the judges of the International Court and appointing the Secretary-General. Others occur through Assembly action alone, as in the election of the ten nonpermanent members of the Security Council and all members of the Economic and Social Council. Annual elections to fill vacancies in various organs are preceded by extensive caucusing, which ordinarily, but not always, has prevented sharp wrangling over the more prestigious seats, especially those in the Security Council.

Finally, the Assembly exercises a constituent function in proposing formal amendments to the Charter. To take effect, such proposals must be ratified by two thirds of the member states, including all the permanent members of the Security Council. Amendments to enlarge the Security Council and Economic and Social Council are the only ones that have been added to the Charter.

Proposals to Streamline the Assembly Procedures. Assembly delegations have recognized for years that the Assembly must somehow find the means for streamlining its procedures in order to expedite the work of the organization. The growth in membership has added a degree of urgency as the Assembly often becomes mired in procedural quicksand of its own making. Little agreement, however, has existed on the means of achieving the desired efficiency. Suggestions and recommendations over the years have included the following:

1. Reduce the time wasted during each session. Better scheduling of speakers and the relegation of those not prepared to speak at their appointed time to the bottom of the list have been suggested. Joint statements by a number of delegations with the same viewpoint and written statements instead of oral statements have been encouraged.

2. Expedite the "general debate" with which each Assembly session opens. Often speeches made by heads of government and foreign ministers during general debate are repeated by heads of delegations later in regular debate.

3. Speed up committee work, and organize it better. Committees should start their work early in each session and should coordinate their activities through the steering committee. The creation of more subcommittees would help free the main committees from the detailed work of drafting resolutions.

4. Accelerate the debate and voting process in the Assembly and its main committees.

Many proposals to speed the deliberative process have been considered, such as placing time limits on general debate. Ultimately, the orderliness and dispatch with which a body like the Assembly conducts its procedural work depend on the proficiency of the officers and committee chairmen and on the willingness of heads of delegations to exercise self-restraint in the interest of moving along.

The Security Council

In both the planning and writing of the UN Charter, the primacy of the Security Council was generally accepted. Nothing seemed more certain to the framers than the logic of its role: The primary responsibility of the United Nations is to keep the peace; keeping the peace is mainly a function of the great powers; ergo, the Security Council is the logical focus for this responsibility. For more than forty years, however, the Security Council has failed to measure up to the framers' hopes; no other organ or agency of the UN system has produced a greater discrepancy between promise and performance.

The logic of giving the Security Council powers equal to those of a supreme warmaking organization seemed realistic in 1945, but the hope that the national interests of the great powers would coincide with the world community's interest in peace and security has proved vain. Almost everyone agrees today that the Council has not lived up to expectations. What went wrong? Why has the Council failed to play its intended role? Answers to these questions, of course, may be found in the nature of the cold war and the basic split among the great powers over issues of ideology and territory, as well as in a host of fears and frustrations generated by many years of suspicions, duplicity, threats, cold war, and open warfare. Partly, too, the answer lies in the procedures and decision making of the Security Council itself. It is these that that will be examined here.

Council Procedures.   Unlike the General Assembly with its broad jurisdiction, the Security Council is an organ of specialized responsibility. Its two main functions are to settle disputes peacefully and to meet threats to peace with the concerted action of the organization. Certain other functions were regarded by the framers as having some relationship to security, and so the Council recommends admission of new members, selects the Secretary-General and the judges of the International Court jointly with the Assembly, and supervises strategic trusteeship arrangements.

The unity of the great powers is the core of the peacekeeping plan. The framers reasoned that as long as the great powers remained united in their desire to maintain peace and security, and as long as this desire produced a unity of purpose and fostered a unity of action, no other power or group of powers in the world could stand against them. In some respects the Council is a modern reincarnation of the Concert of Europe system, which functioned sporadically to keep the peace in Europe during most of the nineteenth century. The Council's role was regarded by its architects as both natural and realistic, since World War II had reaffirmed the premise that warmaking, and hence peacekeeping, is largely a great power choice.

The theories underlying the role of the Security Council served as guideposts in dealing with the more mundane problems of organization and procedures for the key security organ. Five countries—China, France, the United Kingdom, the Soviet Union, and the United States—are designated by the Charter as *permanent* members. The ten (originally six) *nonpermanent* or *elected* members are chosen by the General Assembly for staggered two-year terms, five elected each year. On retirement from the Council, elected members are not immediately eligible for reelection. This provision was inserted because under the League the elective seats on the Council were controlled by the middle powers in most elections to the near exclusion of the small powers. Although all members of the United Nations other than the five permanent members are eligible for election, the Charter, as a result of pressures from the middle powers at San Francisco, stipulates that in the selection process due regard be "specially paid, in the first instance to the contribution of members of the United Nations to the maintenance of international peace and security and to the other purposes of the organization, and also to equitable geographical distribution" (Article 23). These two considerations obviously can be contradictory since states with strategic locations, economic resources, or manpower reserves are not evenly distributed about the globe.

During the early years of the United Nations, the Western powers held a majority on the Council. By virtue of a "gentlemen's agreement" in 1946, two elective Council seats were assigned to Latin America and one each to Western Europe, Eastern Europe, the Middle East, and the British Commonwealth, an arrangement that normally assured the West a working majority in making Council decisions.

In the late 1950s, pressed by demands for Asian and African representation, the United States succeeded in shifting the seat allocated for Eastern Europe to Asia. This shift proved to be only a temporary tranquilizer, however, as African, Eastern European, and Asian states clamored for greater representation for their areas. An amendment to the Charter, proposed in 1963 and adopted in 1965 after sufficient ratifications, emerged out of these pressures for greater representation. It provided for enlarging the Council from eleven to fifteen by increasing the elective members from six to ten, and it changed the majority needed for a decision from seven to nine. By Assembly resolution, the ten nonpermanent seats are now allotted as follows: five seats to Asia and Africa, one to Eastern Europe, two to Latin America, and two to Western European and other states. The keen competition in Assembly elections and the demands for "area representation" demonstrate that a seat at the Council table is one of the most coveted honors and crucial power positions available to members of the United Nations. The automatic voting majority that the Western powers relied on for many years is no longer apparent in the decision-making processes of the enlarged Council.

Each Council member, permanent and elective, appoints a representative and an alternate to the Council. Unlike other United Nations organs, the Security Council is in permanent session and meets whenever a need exists. Under its rules of procedure, intervals between meetings should not exceed fourteen days. The President of the Council may convene it at any time on his own initiative, when requested to do so by a member of the Council, or, under circumstances prescribed in the Charter, when requested to do so by the General Assembly or the Secretary-General.

Under the Security Council's rules of procedure, its presidency rotates each month among its members. This provision, while safeguarding the Council from continuing domination or abuse by a presiding officer who is out of sympathy with its objectives, gives the organ a discontinuity and fluidity that are not always in keeping with its high responsibilities. The brief two-year terms of the ten nonpermanent members add to the impromptu quality of the Council. Moreover, debates in the Council also lack spontaneity and continuity because important statements must often be studied thoroughly before they are answered and because comments are often reserved until home governments can be contacted for instructions.

Although debates are carried on in the Security Council under rules of procedure established by the Council, the Charter provides that any UN member may be invited to participate in any discussion if its interests are affected by the question under debate. Also, any state, whether a UN member or not, must be invited to participate in the discussion if it is a party to a dispute being considered by the Council. In neither case does the invited state have a vote.

When debate on a measure has been completed, a vote is taken, with each member of the Council having one vote. Decisions are of two types: *procedural* and *substantive*. The Charter provides that all decisions on procedural questions be made by an affirmative vote of any nine members; thus permanent and elected members have equal voting power on all procedural questions. On all other, or substantive, matters, the Charter specifies that decisions shall be made "by an affirmative vote of nine members including the concurring votes of the permanent members," except that when a member of the Council is a party to a dispute, it must abstain from voting. Although the words of the Charter clearly denote that substantive decisions require a yes vote of all five permanent members, in a practice based on numerous precedents, a permanent member's abstention from voting is not regarded as constituting a veto of the pending measure. To kill a matter of substance that is supported by at least nine members of the Council, a permanent member must cast a negative vote, which constitutes a veto.

The Charter does not specify how the Security Council, in the event of disagreement, decides whether a question is procedural or nonprocedural. At San Francisco the great powers agreed that the issue would be treated as a nonprocedural question and therefore subject to the veto. This meant that a permanent member could gain the right to veto any matter simply by voting against the preliminary motion to declare it procedural. In practice, this so-called double veto has not been attempted often enough to be a serious problem.

Council Functions. The Security Council acts for the entire membership of the United Nations, producing by its decisions an institutionalized political and moral pressure. Any state that threatens the peace and security of the world may be the object of this pressure. As a rule, the Council majority has preferred a modest but sophisticated application of pressure on the disputants rather than a blunt and forceful approach. Whenever possible, the Council has handled situations under Chapter VI of the Charter as simple disputes rather than considering collective action under Chapter VII, even when both sides to the dispute have been engaged in extensive military actions.

Techniques employed by the Council vary from case to case, depending in each situation on the political considerations involved, the degree of unity on the Council, the extent of the danger to peace, and the relationship of the dispute and the disputants to Council members, particularly the permanent members. Typical techniques used by the Council in dealing with peace and security matters include deliberation, investigation, recommendation, conciliation, interposition, appeal, and enforcement. These are discussed at greater length in Chapters 5 and 7. Other functions carried on by the Council are elective, initiatory, and supervisory in nature and were designed by the framers to permit the great powers to maintain some control over organizational matters. These functions are shared with the General Assembly. They include the election of a Secretary-General, the admission of new members, the election of the judges of the International Court of Justice, the deprivation and restoration of members' rights and privileges, and the expulsion of a member. In addition, the Council has the responsibility for supervising strategic trust territories under the trusteeship system, which means some measure of Council oversight concerning the administration of the Pacific Islands Trust Territory by the United States.

Future Role. The Security Council's impact on the organization and the world will continue to depend on its ability to function in peace and security matters. This role, in turn, will be conditioned by the cold war, by the UN budget situation, by the expanding role of the Assembly, and by new alignments and war-threatening situations in the world environment. The role of the Security Council is further examined in Chapters 3, 5, and 7.

The Economic and Social Council

Although afforded the status of principal organ by the Charter, the Economic and Social Council (ECOSOC) functions under the authority of the General Assembly. In many respects its activities resemble those of the main Assembly committees, and it has occasionally been accused of duplicating or competing with the work of the Second (Economic and Financial) and Third (Social) committees of the Assembly.

Originally established with eighteen members, ECOSOC was enlarged to twenty-seven in 1965 and to fifty-four in 1973. Both enlargements were implemented through Charter amendments that were the product of growing demands by the Third World bloc for a greater voice in determining economic and social policy. Members are elected by a two-thirds vote in the Assembly for staggered three-year terms. Although all UN members are equally eligible for election, in practice members representing countries of industrial importance have been consistently elected over the years. This practice contributed to the expansion of the Council in 1965 and again in 1973 to meet the demands of the developing countries for a bigger voice. A president is elected each year from one of the small or middle powers represented on the Council. Sessions are held twice annually, the first in New York in the spring, the second in Geneva in the summer. Decisions are made by a simple majority of those present and voting.

Broadly speaking, ECOSOC carries on worldwide functions aimed at improving the lot of mankind. Charter references to its role, however, are so verbose and repetitive that the organization has been operating for over forty years without a precise mandate. Countless debates have explored a diverse assortment of topics, but successes have been scattered and mostly unnoticed. Many of ECOSOC's operations have been carried on with little public notice, since political controversies have usually monopolized the UN spotlight.

The failure of so many of ECOSOC's debates to materialize into effective action programs has produced a mounting frustration among the developing nations, aggravated by present rivalries and deep-rooted antagonisms of the past. Yet despite grave discrepancies between the hopes of the framers and the accomplishments of the Council, it has carried on a vast amount of useful and potentially useful work. Later chapters on social and economic matters will explore and evaluate these programs. A brief discussion of ECOSOC's functions in pursuit of economic and social goals follows.

Research and Debate.   Far-reaching debates in ECOSOC on a variety of social and economic questions typify its deliberative role. Recent agenda items, for example, have included discussions on housing, human rights, narcotic drug control, water resources, desertification, population problems, trade, UNICEF, industrial development, literacy, refugees, and science and technology.

Two subjects stand out in the Council's deliberations, both in frequency and in intensity. These are economic development and human rights, both emotional subjects for the representatives on the Council from Third World nations. The demands of these representatives for immeasurably greater financial help from the industrial countries, as a rightful legacy of real or imagined exploitations of the past, keep the Western nations on the defensive. Debates on human rights also touch a tender nerve, but participants often fail to see the inherent irony of governmental representatives demanding more rights for individuals in the rest of the world than most are willing to grant their own citizens. The search for agreement in the field of human rights frequently culminates in common condemnations of the easiest target, South Africa.

Probably the most useful function performed by ECOSOC is producing studies that help to overcome the dearth of statistical and other kinds of data on economic and social conditions in the world. Here ECOSOC operates as a research agency and clearinghouse, attempting to coordinate the work of numerous committees, commissions, study groups, and private or nongovernmental organizations. The basic information so gathered is vital to coming to grips with world problems, and no other agency in history has had such a broad research mandate. Most of the studies are carried on by ECOSOC's functional commissions and regional economic commissions. The functional commissions established by ECOSOC are Human Rights, Narcotic Drugs, Population, Prevention of Discrimination and Protection of Minorities (actually a subcommission of the Commission on Human Rights), Statistical, and Status of Women. Regional economic commissions have been set up for Africa, Asia and the Pacific, Western Asia, Europe, and Latin America.

Decision-Making Role.   Based on its deliberations and extensive studies, ECOSOC makes appraisals of its findings and, by Charter directive, may make recommendations "with respect to any such matters to the General Assembly, to the Members of the United Nations, and to the Specialized Agencies concerned" (Article 62). Recommendations usually take the form of a draft resolution, or declaration. The drafts may merely embody a statement of general principles and require only a favorable vote in the General Assembly for implementation, such as the proclamation of the Universal Declaration of Human Rights of 1948. They may also take the form of conventions requiring affirmative action by the Assembly and subsequent ratification by a stipulated number of member states.

Drafting conventions provides a quasi-legislative role for ECOSOC because the Council is often involved in the early phases of consensus building for many UN-sponsored treaties. This resembles the national lawmaking function in that the resulting convention binds consenting states, often limits governments in their relationship to their own citizens, and makes an addition to international law. While ECOSOC cannot make law, it can play an important role in helping members of the United Nations develop law. This is a much more difficult process than the mere proclaiming of principles, and many nations that signed the Universal Declaration of Human Rights in 1948 have failed to ratify the international covenants that would make these rights enforceable.

One such covenant, the Convention on the Political Rights of Women, serves as an example of what can be accomplished in the form of international legislation when states find ground for agreement. Such a consensus, however, was not easily developed. Women's groups from many countries, banding together as an international pressure group, demanded and obtained from ECOSOC a Commission on the Status of Women. They followed this up by pushing the idea of feminine political equality through the Commission, ECOSOC, General Assembly, and national ratification stages. The Convention guarantees women the right to vote and to hold public office equally with men in all adhering states.

Coordination Responsibilities. ECOSOC also exercises a coordination function relating to the sixteen specialized agencies of the United Nations and several autonomous organizations (see Figure 2–1). The Charter charges the Economic and Social Council with bringing the specialized agencies into a relationship with the United Nations through agreements negotiated by ECOSOC and approved by the General Assembly. The specialized agencies range in nature from the highly technical and functionally specific (such as the International Civil Aviation Organization and the International Telecommunication Union) to those that are involved in highly controversial political matters (such as UNESCO and the International Monetary Fund). Each of the specialized agencies began its existence as an intergovernmental organization with its own treaty or constitution. At the initiative of the agency, negotiations are conducted between it and ECOSOC, with the resulting agreement subject to approval by the General Assembly. The agencies that have gone this route and are currently specialized agencies of the United Nations include:

Food and Agriculture Organization (FAO)
International Bank for Reconstruction and Development (IBRD)
International Civil Aviation Organization (ICAO)
International Development Association (IDA)
International Finance Corporation (IFC)
International Fund for Agricultural Development (IFAD)
International Labor Organization (ILO)
International Maritime Organization (IMO)
International Monetary Fund (IMF)
International Telecommunication Union (ITU)
United Nations Educational, Scientific and Cultural Organization (UNESCO)
United Nations Industrial Development Organization (UNIDO)
Universal Postal Union (UPU)
World Health Organization (WHO)
World Intellectual Property Organization (WIPO)
World Meteorological Organization (WMO)

In addition to the above specialized agencies, two other intergovernmental agencies function in a somewhat similar capacity as largely autonomous agencies within the UN system. These are the International Atomic Energy Agency (IAEA) and the General Agreement on Tariffs and Trade (GATT).

Integrating the activities of eighteen diverse intergovernmental agencies that are largely autonomous in their powers, have their own organizational machinery, adopt their own budgets, select their own secretariats, and, in some cases, antedate the UN organization is no simple task. The permissive authorization given to ECOSOC in the Charter has, as a result, not proved adequate to the challenge of securing effective "coordination," although various agreements have been concluded.

The growing assertion of power by the Assembly and its main committees in the 1980s has produced a closer working relationship between them and the specialized agencies than between the agencies and ECOSOC, but this relationship tends to involve general oversight rather than coordination. More effective coordination is carried on by a committee of high officials from the UN Secretariat and the secretariats of the specialized agencies, functioning as an international administrative cabinet. Much of the important work of the UN family is carried on by these eighteen agencies. Most of them will be discussed in their proper context in later chapters.

Future Role. The Economic and Social Council has recognized its inadequate impact on UN policies and has repeatedly examined its methods of operation and role within the organization.[6] This concern, coupled with the more broadly representative nature of the fifty-four-member Council, has in modest ways strengthened ECOSOC's approach to economic and social cooperation. But many problems remain. Not least are the basic conflicts of North versus South, developed versus developing, and industrialized versus preindustrial. Added to these conflicts are the diverse views held by member states on the role of government, the position of the individual, and the types of political, economic, and social systems that should prevail in the world. Finally, the Council itself is a body of very limited powers. It can only study, discuss, and recommend; and even in this it is subordinate to the overriding authority of the General Assembly.

The Trusteeship Council

Although the Charter designates the Trusteeship Council a principal organ of the United Nations, it is, like ECOSOC, subordinate to the General Assembly. Its function, to supervise nonstrategic trust territories for the Assembly and strategic trusts for the Security Council, has involved only recommendation powers.

Membership on the Trusteeship Council is accorded by the Charter to three types of members: (1) states that administer trust territories, (2) permanent members of the Security Council that do not administer trust territories, and (3) enough additional elected members to strike an equilibrium between administering and nonadministering states. No elective member now remains on the Council, and the equilibrium has become impossible to maintain because only one country, the United States, still administers a UN trusteeship. The Trusteeship Council thus consists of the five great powers.

Trusteeship Functions. In carrying out its responsibilities since 1946, the Trusteeship Council has exercised power in performing a variety of functions. Two of these functions have been similar to those of ECOSOC: the Council has deliberated on matters within its jurisdiction through studies and debates, and it has made recommendations for action based on its evaluations. Its recommendations, however, have related to problems of specific trust territories or their administration and, unlike those of ECOSOC, have not usually taken the form of proclamations or treaties.

The Council's supervisory role has involved overseeing the governance of trust territories by administering states. An elaborate questionnaire drawn up by the Council has served as a basic supervisory tool. Questionnaire replies and other reports from administering states have been subjected to rigorous written and oral cross-examinations and evaluations, forcing each trust-holding state to defend its actions or lack of them. Out of these confrontations has emerged the Council's annual report to the Assembly, permitting, this time by the Assembly, another inquiry, another debate, and another evaluation of how well administering states have been living up to their mandated responsibilities. Little wonder that most trust states impatiently pushed their trust territories toward independence and self-government!

Normal supervisory tools have been supplemented by two additional techniques: (1) *petition* to the United Nations from the peoples of trust territories for a redress of their grievances and (2) *on-the-spot investigations* by visiting missions of the Trusteeship Council. Numerous petitions, sometimes several hundred in a single year, have aired real or imagined abuses. Such petitions have been submitted directly to the Council by delegations representing the people of a trust territory or have taken the form of written appeals, with no approval needed from the administering authority in either case. Some petitions have been debated extensively in the General Assembly as well as in the Trusteeship Council.

Each visiting mission was composed of four individuals, two chosen by administering and two by nonadministering states on the Trusteeship Council. The visiting missions checked general social and economic conditions and the extent to which the people were being prepared for self-government, and sought answers to specific questions raised in debates in the Trusteeship Council and the General Assembly. Mission members solicited the views of a cross section of the population, including labor leaders, tribal chiefs, local administrative officials, and private individuals. Reports by the visiting missions indicated the extent to which the administering authority of the trust territory was achieving Charter objectives. These diverse approaches worked successfully, partly because of their intrinsic value and partly because great pressures had developed in the United Nations to grant independence to all subject peoples.

The Trusteeship Council is one of those rare human institutions that are threatened with extinction by their successes. Of the eleven trusteeship agreements concluded by the United Nations, only that of the U.S. strategic trust over the Trust Territory of the Pacific Islands remains. The other trust territories are now independent states, and all but Western Samoa are members of the United Nations. In addition to this record, progress toward the independence of other colonial peoples was encouraged and perhaps speeded up by the example of the Trusteeship Council. The role of the Trusteeship Council as one phase of that revolution of self-determination will be examined in detail in Chapter 8.

The International Court of Justice

Although the International Court of Justice functions largely outside the UN framework as a semi-independent entity headquartered at The Hague in the Netherlands, the Charter recognizes it as one of the six principal organs of the United Nations. The ICJ, or World Court, is the successor to the Permanent Court of International Justice (PCIJ), which functioned as the world's chief judicial organ from 1922 to 1946. The Charter, in Article 92, recognizes this successor status in noting that the annexed Statute for the ICJ "is based upon the Statute of the Permanent Court of International Justice."

Although some of the organization and powers of the ICJ are set forth in the Charter (Articles 92 to 96), most are contained in the ICJ Statute, a multilateral treaty that serves as its basic constitution. All members of the United Nations are automatically parties to the ICJ Statute, but a state that is not a member of the United Nations can join the Court on conditions laid down by the General Assembly following recommendation by the Security Council. Switzerland, for example, has refused to join the United Nations because of its centuries-old position of neutrality, but it has functioned for many years as a regular member of the ICJ. Tiny San Marino and Liechtenstein, neither of which is a member of the United Nations, have nevertheless been accepted as parties to the Statute and serve as full members.

The fifteen judges that make up the International Court of Justice are elected by the Security Council and the General Assembly, voting separately, with five judges elected every three years for nine-year terms. Each judge is eligible for reelection. Article 9 of the Statute of the ICJ provides that judges should be selected on the basis of their individual qualifications and together should represent the main forms of civilization and the principal legal systems of the world. No two judges may be of the same nationality. Although the judges strive for objectivity, their voting behavior on the Court can often be predicted with some degree of accuracy, based on the nature of the cases and the issues involved, their records as national judges, their publications in the field of international law, their ideological persuasions, and other factors that may be calculated to affect their judicial decision making.

The Court's competence to hear and decide cases extends to all controversies submitted to it by contending parties. If there is no judge on the Court of the nationality of one or several of the parties to a case, the party or parties so deprived may under Court rules appoint a judge to participate in that case with full voting rights. While such action is unknown in national courts, the World Court provisions reflect the sovereign independence of the parties in such cases. Some states have accepted the compulsory jurisdiction of the Court in advance under the Optional Clause of the Statute (Article 36), but because of a myriad of reservations and amendments, the general rule is that only those states that are willing to have their controversies adjudicated by the Court will be parties to cases before it. Cases are decided by a majority vote, with a quorum of nine needed for voting. Decisions and awards cannot be appealed. In case of a tie, the President of the Court is entitled to a "casting" (tie-breaking) vote. The court's jurisdiction also extends to the rendering of advisory opinions on legal questions submitted to it by the principal organs of the United Nations and the UN specialized agencies.

To reach a decision, the Court interprets and applies treaties, international custom, the general principles of law, and decision of international tribunals. Decisions of national courts and the teachings of respected international jurists can be used as subsidiary means for determining rules of international law. If the parties agree, the Court can render a decision *ex aequo et bono* (based on the Court's conception of justice and fairness rather than law).

The International Court of Justice represents an ambitious attempt to replace the use of force with the rule of law. The Court has heard a number of disputes and has issued many advisory opinions. Yet it has not played an important role in resolving— or even trying to resolve—many of the major issues that plague mankind today and threaten catastrophic global war. The reasons for this lack of a substantial contribution by the Court in dispute settlement will be explored in depth in Chapter 7.

The Secretariat

The UN Secretariat under Article 7 of the Charter is included as one of the six "principal organs of the United Nations." The Secretariat consists of officials and civil servants who perform administrative, budgetary, secretarial, linguistic, staff, and housekeeping functions for the other principal organs and carry out the programs of the organization. Members of the Secretariat are recruited individually and do not serve as representatives of their governments, as do those who serve as delegates to the General Assembly and the three councils. They are full-time employees of the United Nations who bring diverse skills to the organization. They are supposed to serve the entire membership of the United Nations in a politically neutral manner, although reality sometimes falls short of the ideal.

Role of the Secretary-General.   Heading the Secretariat is a Secretary-General who in Article 97 is designated "the chief administrative officer of the Organization." Appointment of the Secretary-General for a five-year term of office is the culmination of a political process that includes recommendation by the Security Council, with the veto power applicable, and appointment by a two-thirds vote of the General Assembly.

The responsibilities of the Secretary-General and his staff include preparing the agenda for major organs, drawing up the biennial budget of the organization, expending funds, supervising day-to-day operations, taking the initiative in suggesting new programs, offering political leadership when requested to do so by a major organ, serving as a diplomatic agent to iron out difficulties among member delegations, and serving as the ceremonial head of the United Nations in formal affairs. The Secretary-General is the only person in the United Nations who can speak for or represent the entire organization. Each meeting of the General Assembly and the three councils finds the Secretary-General providing essential services and expert advice, the latter only when requested by the body's presiding officer.

One of the regular tasks of the Secretary-General is to oversee the operations of the entire Secretariat. Personnel standards must be maintained by basing them on merit, yet "geographical distribution" must be taken into consideration to give each member state an adequate share of positions. Individuals with diverse backgrounds, ideologies, attitudes, outlooks, and languages must somehow be integrated into a smoothly functioning bureaucracy. Professional standards that reject national partisanship must be encouraged so that members can support both the goals and the operations of the organization.

The Charter emphasizes the "neutrality" of the Secretariat, providing in Article 100 that "in the performance of their duties the Secretary-General and the staff shall not seek or receive instructions from any government or from any other authority external to the Organization." A correlative responsibility is placed on the members of the United Nations, who are required "to respect the exclusively international character of the responsibilities of the Secretary-General and the staff and not to seek to influence them in the discharge of their responsibilities." In the more than forty-year history of the United Nations, apparent lapses in the neutral performance of the Secretary-General have brought criticism from members and efforts to change the top office. These and other challenges to the Secretary-General and to the Secretariat will be reviewed in Chapter 4.

FINANCING THE UNITED NATIONS

The dedication of its members and the effectiveness of a multilateral organization such as the United Nations can often be evaluated by an analysis of its budget. The short history of international organizations reveals that many states have been penurious to an extreme and often grudging in providing financial support. This propensity of members to invest only relatively meager resources in the work of international organizations may reflect the limited character of their commitment, the poverty of their societies, or their disagreement with some of the activities carried on by these organizations. Demands by statesmen for substantial benefits from such organizations are often balanced by inclinations to contribute little more than lip service to their operations.

Assessment Problems

When the United Nations began its work in 1946, the need to find an equitable but adequate financing formula was given high priority. The task of preparing a scale of budgetary assessments was assigned to a special Committee on Contributions under guidelines laid down by the General Assembly. The Committee has since been continued to provide periodic review and recommend necessary revision of the assessment scale. Members of the Committee are supposed to be experienced in financial matters and drawn from states providing a broad geographic representation. In determining assessments, the Committee was originally charged by the General Assembly to utilize the criterion of ability to pay as reflected by each state's total national income, per capita income, economic dislocation caused by the war, and foreign exchange earnings. These factors, with the exception of dislocation caused by war, remain the main criteria for determining assessments today, although "floor" and "ceiling" limitations have been added. The United States pays the largest assessment of the regular budget. Many of the small, poor states of the Third World are assessed the minimum payment of 0.01 percent. Assessments are paid as "contributions," but they are considered binding once the General Assembly has adopted the organization's annual budget. Unlike the technical programs of the League of Nations, whose financing was included within the League's general budget, each of the specialized agencies of the United Nations has its own budget and financial system, with Assembly oversight confined to consultation and recommendations. The UN budget system also differs from that of the League in that budgetary questions are decided in the Assembly by a two-thirds majority rather than by the unanimity rule that often came close to paralyzing League operations.

In 1946 the first scale of assessments reflected the dominant economic position of the United States in a world suffering from the aftermath of war. The American assessment amounted to almost 40 percent, with the remaining 60 percent paid by the other fifty member states. Immediate objections were raised by American leaders who argued that the United States did not have that great a capacity to pay and did not wish to weaken the organization by a heavy dependence on a single source of revenue. American opposition took the form of a demand that a ceiling be established prohibiting contributions of more than one third of the budget by any one state, a position that was gradually accepted over a ten-year period, with the admission of new members and the economic revival of old members easing the transition. The contributions of the United States to the UN system in the past have approached 50 percent despite its regular budget assessment portion of 25 percent, reflecting a sizable American support through voluntary contributions to special UN programs. These heavy American contributions are less impressive if measured strictly in terms of ability to pay, since a number of members contribute a greater percentage of their gross national product (GNP) than does the United States. Moreover, in recent years U.S. voluntary contributions to UN programs have declined to about 25 percent.

The poorer states of the world prefer that budget assessments be based strictly on each state's national income and ability to pay. The use of national per capita income as a factor in the assessment scale has encountered objections from states with high national incomes and small populations. In deference to this protest, the Assembly established a rule that no state should be assessed more per capita than the largest contributor. Canada is the only state that has had its assessment reduced under this rule.

Some members, such as the Soviet Union, have been found to "talk poor" on budget questions, refusing to accept a higher rate of assessment, while in nonbudgetary debates they have proclaimed their great economic advancements and achievements. Much of the debate over budgetary questions involves cold war animus and North-South frictions as well as controversies over money.[7] The Soviet Union's share of the regular budget was 6.34 percent in 1946, but after a vigorous campaign pushed by the United States, its share was increased to 12.95 percent, a figure that includes the separate assessments for the Byelorussian and Ukrainian republics.

Budget Procedures and Politics

Overall UN operations are divided into four major budget categories: (1) the regular budget, (2) the specialized agencies, (3) voluntary programs related mainly to economic development, and (4) peacekeeping operations.

The regular budget pays the day-to-day costs of the organization, including buildings and equipment, conferences, travel, salaries and retirement pay, and other administrative costs arising from the operations of the major UN organs. Each specialized agency has its own budget, which is presented to the General Assembly for formal approval but is in fact arrived at independently. The budget of the voluntary programs includes financial support for economic aid and technical assistance for several major programs, including the UN Development Program (UNDP) and the UN Fund for Population Activities (UNFPA). In addition, other programs, such as the expenses of the Office of the UN High Commissioner for Refugees (UNHCR), operate largely on voluntary contributions but are partly supported by the regular budget. Over the years the peacekeeping budget has been the most controversial of the four budgets because of the political and cold war implications involved in each peacekeeping venture.

The United Nations uses a two-year program budget that requires the administrative staff to plan organizational goals, to establish the programs needed to achieve the goals, and to provide budgetary support for the programs. The budget process is carried on by members of the Secretariat under the direction of the Secretary-General. The Secretary-General proposes; the majority of member states dispose. This means that nations of the Third World, which pay the least, have the most to say about how much should be spent, and for what. The seven richest countries pay 70 percent of the total budget but can be outvoted by the huge Third World majority, which pays only a small portion of the remaining 30 percent (see Figure 2–2). No effective budget ceiling has ever been established; new programs and inflation adjustments for old programs have been approved regularly over the years and added to the total cost of UN operations.

In 1982 several of the major budget contributors rebelled. Protests were placed with Secretary-General Javier Pérez de Cuéllar by the American, British, and Soviet ambassadors, demanding that a ceiling be placed on the 1982–83 budget and that future budgets be further limited. The Soviet Union insisted that there should be no increase whatsoever in future budgets, whereas the United States took the position that there should be no real growth but that some adjustments for inflation might be made. Although the Secretary-General agreed to try to restrain budget growth in the future, he could give no specific pledges, especially because pressures from Third World members to expand various programs were being directed at him in increasing numbers and magnitude. In fact, the budget for 1984–85 was fixed at $1,606 million, an increase of $133 million, or 9 percent, over the previous biennium. The budget

FIGURE 2–2
Relationship of Assessments to Voting Strength in the General Assembly,
September 1986

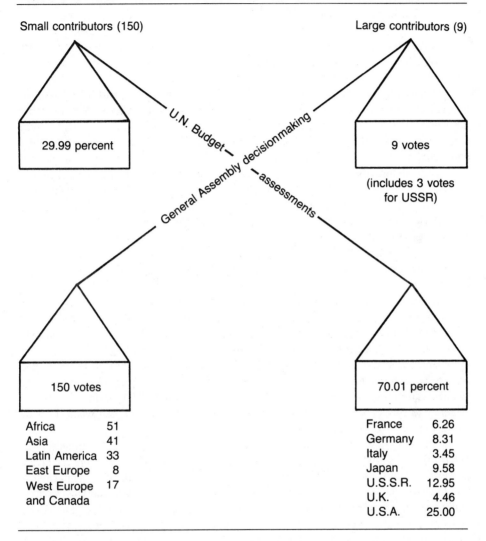

Small contributors (150)

29.99 percent

Large contributors (9)

9 votes

(includes 3 votes
for USSR)

U.N. Budget

General Assembly decisionmaking

assessments

150 votes

Africa	51
Asia	41
Latin America	33
East Europe	8
West Europe and Canada	17

70.01 percent

France	6.26
Germany	8.31
Italy	3.45
Japan	9.58
U.S.S.R.	12.95
U.K.	4.46
U.S.A.	25.00

of $1,660 million for 1986–87 represented only a 3.5 percent rise. In both budget
periods, most of the increase was an adjustment for inflation.

Budgetary positions in the United Nations are a reflection of political realities.
About twenty-five member governments, for example, have withheld portions of their
assessments for political reasons. A number have refused to pay their share for peacekeeping operations because they opposed the use of UN peacekeeping forces in

particular situations, especially those in the Middle East, and because they believe that the veto power should be applicable to the use of all peacekeeping forces. The Soviet Union and France are the major holdouts on peacekeeping funds. In a similar way, the United States since 1982 has refused to make payments for specialized agency and general UN programs involving support of Palestinians, and in 1983 the Reagan Administration notified the Secretary-General that it would no longer pay its share of UN regular budget costs associated with the UN treaty on the Law of the Sea, which it also refused to sign.

Theoretically, continued nonpayment of compulsory assessments could lead to loss of voting rights in the General Assembly. Article 19 of the Charter provides that a member shall lose its vote when its budgetary arrearage equals or exceeds its total assessment for the preceding two years. That sanction lost most of its teeth in 1964 and 1965, however, when the United States tried—and failed—to persuade the Assembly to impose the penalty on the Soviet Union for failure to pay peacekeeping assessments. The Assembly went through the entire 1964 session without taking a formal vote, rather than confront the issue. The United States finally threw in the towel, reserving to itself the right to reject compulsory assessments in the future if compelling reasons should arise.

From the Third World perspective, the major powers—especially the United States—are not interested in providing adequate funding for an organization they no longer control. The almost automatic voting majority of the Third World in the General Assembly has produced a negative budgetary posture on the part of the major contributors. Although Third World spokesmen have probably diagnosed the nature of the problem correctly, solutions to it are not easily found. Each year the positions of the various participants in the UN budget battles become hardened and more intractable. For the Secretary-General, getting a reasonable budget adopted has become a major challenge, with the future of the United Nations hanging in the balance. The problem can perhaps be compared, as noted by an earlier Secretary-General, to that of a prime minister trying to get the budget adopted when most of the members of parliament belong to the opposition.

In the mid-1980s, a financial crisis of major proportions began to emerge. By 1986, the UN's slim cash reserves were exhausted and the failure of many countries to pay their assessments left the organization teetering on the brink of bankruptcy. The most serious threat to UN solvency was a substantial default in the U.S. contribution stemming from funding cuts mandated by Congress. A large part of the default was compelled by the Kassebaum Amendment adopted by the Congress in 1985 which required the United States to reduce its regular budget payments from 25 percent to 20 percent, an action which involved withholding $42 million for 1987. Under the Amendment, this cut would be continued until the United Nations adopted a system of weighted voting on budgetary matters. With the Third World in control of decision making in the General Assembly, such a change is unlikely, although the Assembly agreed in 1986 to give the big contributors greater control of the budget during the early planning stages (see Chapter 12).

With the United States in default, a number of other countries rallied to the support of the United Nations. China, for example, presented the Secretary General with a check for $4.3 million which had been owed for many years as part of the support for peacekeeping forces in the Congo. The Soviets also made a special voluntary contribution to the regular budget, and some key Third World countries, including India and Brazil, found the means to pay their long overdue debts to the organization. By 1987, the United Nations was still functioning, but its financial future was uncertain.

Future Financing Problems

The continuing financial crisis demonstrates that important members are not prepared to accept majority rule when it threatens their vital interests, and decisions cannot be forced upon them against their will. For many years the financing of peacekeeping operations was the root of the UN financing problem, and it is still unresolved. Funding by voluntary contributions is precarious, and funding by budgetary assessment is resisted by countries that disagree with the peacekeeping policies as well as by countries that find the assessments a burden. Even voluntary schemes, such as a permanent peace fund based on voluntary contributions, or arrangements for standby forces earmarked for UN use by states willing to supply them, have been opposed by countries that fear the organization will be used contrary to their national interests.

Today the UN financing problem extends well beyond peacekeeping. Selective withholding of UN assessments has occurred in other areas of UN activity, and the massive U.S. withholding—if not reversed—raises still more serious portents for the future. Should the United States persist, other countries might decide to follow suit.

One answer to the financing problem, at least in theory, is to find sources of income for the United Nations independent of its members. Members have evinced little interest in giving the organization a substantial independent income, but scholarly friends of the United Nations have engaged in speculation concerning potential sources and their technical and political feasibility.[8] Although many such sources would require Charter amendment or basic changes in the UN structure, the principle of revenue production independent of members' contributions is well established. Each year the organization nets several million dollars from its headquarters businesses involving stamp sales, a gift shop, investment income, and guided tours. Although this amounts to only a small percentage of the annual regular budget, other proposals to secure independent sources of revenue would be extensions of this principle, already accepted by all members.

Suggestions for new sources run the gamut from those that would provide minor amounts of supplemental income to those that might in themselves finance most or all UN activities. As might be expected, sources that offer the greatest potential for substantial income are also the least feasible politically. Potential sources for UN income might include the following:

1. Private contributions in the form of individual gifts, inheritances, and foundation grants encouraged through a joint policy of making such contributions deductible from national taxes.
2. Charges levied by UN agencies for services performed; for example, the World Meteorological Organization could charge a service fee for its weather data and the International Telecommunication Union could issue international radio licenses for substantial fees.
3. Tolls charged for various kinds of transportation and communications, facilitated in today's world by UN programs.
4. Fees for international travel imposed through levies on passports and visas or through surcharges on national customs duties.
5. Profits earned through implementation of the 1982 Law of the Sea Treaty by which a UN international investment corporation could exploit the mineral and other forms of wealth in international waters and seabeds.
6. Charters sold to private companies or governmental agencies authorizing them to exploit the resources of seabeds and Antarctica, with royalty rights reserved by the United Nations.
7. Fishing, whaling, and sealing rights in international waters, assigned to countries or private companies upon the payment of "conservation" fees to the United Nations.
8. Rights to the use of outer space, or the operation of outer space programs by the United Nations, aimed at producing revenues through communications satellites, meteorological systems, and the future development of resources on the moon and the planets.
9. Taxes levied on member states, collectible by their governments, and based on ability to pay judged by national income.
10. Taxes levied directly on individuals through the cooperation of member states, based on income and with a mild graduation of rates.
11. Issuance of an international trading currency, backed by national reserves, that could serve the dual function of financing UN programs and providing a supplementary international monetary unit to encourage greater trade.

Several of these proposals are concerned with current international activities related to the new Law of the Sea Treaty and to the issuance of Special Drawing Rights (SDRs) by the International Monetary Fund. The proposals are only a sampling of the possibilities for reducing or eliminating the dependence of the United Nations on national contributions. With a sizable independent source of income, the United Nations could undertake peacekeeping operations and economic and social programs without fear of national reprisals or organizational bankruptcy. Many members, however, may not regard financial independence for the organization as a virtue since it would reduce their control over the organization and its activities.

Aside from regular budget overhead expenses, much of the budgetary activity of the United Nations depends on contributions by member states. In the fields of economic and social development and environmental management, contributions for thirty major programs and special funds are elicited each year through a UN Pledging Conference.[9] The 1985 Pledging Conference, for example, found 110 countries pledging to give $740 million for UN development activities in 1986–87. Some key states, such as Japan and the United States, however, failed to make a pledge at that conference, providing perhaps a harbinger of difficult times ahead for the United Nations.

The budget process of the organization has made it clear that no amount of financial stability will solve the problems of ideological hostility and national particularity. In the final analysis, the problem of financing UN programs is one of developing an international consensus and building a world community. Political accommodation remains a fundamental prerequisite to fiscal solvency.

NOTES

1. For a comprehensive and extremely lucid discussion of constitutional issues, see Inis L. Claude, Jr., *Swords into Plowshares,* 4th ed. (New York: Random House, 1971), chap. 9, "Problems of Constitutional Interpretation and Development."

2. Recognizing that adoption of formal amendments to the Charter to strengthen the organization's role in such areas as peacekeeping remains a dead issue, efforts to achieve the same results through limited political agreements continue. See, for example, Donald J. Puchala, ed., "Review of the UN Charter," in *Issues before the 39th General Assembly* (New York: UNA/USA, 1984), pp. 145–47.

3. Jack C. Plano and Robert E. Riggs, *Forging World Order–The Politics of International Organization* (New York: Macmillan, 1971), pp. 63–64.

4. H. G. Nicholas, *The United Nations as a Political Institution,* 5th ed. (London: Oxford University Press, 1975), p. 104.

5. Ibid., p. 92.

6. "Past suggestions for improvement have addressed such matters as a shift from 'reviewing past activities to examining future programmes'; concentration at each session on a 'limited number of broad issues [defined well in advance] which could form the subject of consideration in depth'; reduction of reports to a 'coherent, assimilable and readily understandable whole'; monthly meetings when necessary . . . [and] reorganization of the committee structure." "Issues before the 20th General Assembly," *International Conciliation,* no. 554 (September 1965), pp. 188–89.

7. For a discussion of the political aspects of UN budget making, see Ruth B. Russell, *The General Assembly: Patterns/Problems/Prospects* (New York: Carnegie Endowment for International Peace, 1970).

8. See, for example, John G. Stoessinger and Associates, *Financing the United Nations System* (Washington, D.C.: Brookings Institution, 1964).

9. For a description of the results of the 1985 UN Pledging Conference, see *UN Chronicle* 18, no. 1 (January 1986), p. 62.

SELECTED READINGS

ALKER, HAYWARD R., JR. "Dimensions of Conflict in the General Assembly." *American Political Science Review* 58 (September 1964), pp. 642–57.

BRETTON, HENRY L. *International Relations in the Nuclear Age.* Albany: State University of New York Press, 1986.

CHASE, EUGENE P. *The United Nations in Action*. New York: McGraw-Hill, 1950.

FELD, WERNER J., and ROBERT S. JORDAN. *International Organizations: A Comparative Approach*. New York: Praeger Publishers, 1983.

GATI, TOBY TRISTER, ed. *The US, the UN, and the Management of Global Change*. New York: New York University Press, 1983.

GOODRICH, LELAND M.; EDVARD HAMBRO; and A. P. SIMONS. *Charter of the United Nations, Commentary and Documents*. 3rd rev. ed. New York: Columbia University Press, 1967.

JACOBSON, HAROLD K. *Networks of Interdependence*. 2nd ed. New York: Alfred A. Knopf, 1984.

KEOHANE, ROBERT OWEN. "Political Influence in the General Assembly." *International Conciliation,* no. 557 (March 1966).

KHAN, MUHAMMAD ZAFRULLA. "The President of the General Assembly of the United Nations." *International Organization*. Spring 1964, pp. 231–40.

LAWSON, RUTH C., ed. *International Regional Organizations*. New York: Praeger Publishers, 1962.

NICHOLAS, H. G. *The United Nations as a Political Institution*. 5th ed. London: Oxford University Press, 1975.

PENTLAND, CHARLES. "Building Global Institutions." In *Issues in Global Politics,* ed. Gavin Boyd and Charles Pentland, pp. 326–66. New York: Free Press, 1981.

PEREZ DE CUELLAR, JAVIER. "The United Nations and World Politics." In *The Global Agenda: Issues and Perspectives,* ed. Charles W. Kegley, Jr., and Eugene R. Wittkopf, pp. 167–75. New York: Random House, 1984.

RIGGS, ROBERT E. *Politics in the United Nations*. Urbana: University of Illinois Press, 1958. Reprinted by Greenwood Press, 1984.

RUSSELL, RUTH B. *A History of the United Nations Charter: The Role of the United States, 1940–1945*. Washington, D.C.: Brookings Institution, 1958.

STOESSINGER, JOHN G., and ASSOCIATES. *Financing the United Nations System*. Washington, D.C.: Brookings Institution, 1964.

TAUBENFELD, RITA F., and HOWARD J. TAUBENFELD. "Independent Revenue for the United Nations." *International Organization,* Spring 1964, pp. 241–67.

3

The UN Political Process

The United Nations provides a setting for states and other actors to practice the art of politics. The principal participants are representatives of governments, secretariat officials, representatives of other international organizations, and spokesmen for non-governmental interests. The UN political process is the sum of their efforts to influence the making and implementing of international decisions. But the United Nations is more than a collection of diplomats and other individuals meeting in an ad hoc multilateral setting. It is an ongoing institution. Who participates—and how effectively—is intimately bound up with the formal and informal UN structures that have developed over the years. This chapter will examine the several types of UN participants, how their interaction is affected by the UN institutional setting, and the consequences that flow from this process.

PARTICIPANTS IN THE UN DECISION PROCESS

Member States

The chief participants in any intergovernmental organization are the official representatives of member states. When decisions are made by voting, these representatives are ordinarily the only ones entitled to vote. They also control most of the resources essential for implementing decisions. What the organization does is thus heavily dependent on who its members are.

But who will its members be? As a general proposition, membership is determined by the objectives of an organization. In this respect the United Nations may be usefully compared with other international organizations. If military security is the goal, membership will be limited to states perceiving a common threat to their security. NATO and the Warsaw Pact illustrate the principle. If cooperation within a given geographic region is the objective, as with the Organization of American States or the Organization of African Unity, membership will be open to states located within the region. Where objectives of international organization have been universal in scope, membership eligibility has tended toward universality. This is notably true of the UN specialized agencies and other limited purpose organizations designed to promote global cooperation in such matters as world health, agriculture, or communications and transit across national boundaries.

The United Nations has a much wider range of functions than any of its specialized agencies, but its purposes and principles—as set forth in the UN Charter—are manifestly broad enough to be shared universally. Its membership provisions, however, reflect World War II animosities and were designed to permit at least temporary exclusion of former enemy states by requiring that members be "peace-loving." Thus the original membership consisted of states that had demonstrated their love of peace by declaring war on the Axis powers prior to March 1, 1945. Membership, under Article 4, paragraph 1, of the Charter was subsequently to be

> open to all other peace-loving states which accept the obligations contained in the present Charter and, in the judgment of the Organization, are able and willing to carry out these obligations.

Such a judgment was not meant to be taken lightly, since favorable action required both an affirmative decision of the Security Council, including the acquiescence of all five permanent members, and a two-thirds majority vote in the General Assembly.

During the first ten years of the United Nations, admission was granted grudgingly—only nine new members were added to the original fifty-one. The reasons had little to do with World War II or love of peace but rather were a product of the emerging cold war. As East-West lines hardened, the U.S.-led majority denied the necessary seven Security Council votes to applicants from the Soviet bloc and the Soviet Union used the veto to block the admission of most other applicants. Understandably, the Soviet Union hoped to use its veto as leverage to secure the admission of its own protégés.

The break in the stalemate came in 1955. With the relaxation of cold war tensions that followed the Korean Armistice and the death of Joseph Stalin, new attitudes toward the membership issue developed. A perceptible loosening in the Western coalition, portents of corresponding fissures in Eastern Europe, and the growing assertiveness of African and Asian countries threw the question of admissions into new perspective. Faced with this changed situation, the United States assented to a package deal involving the admission of sixteen new members, including several Communist applicants. Since then, UN membership has been available virtually for the asking. Table 3–1 shows the present UN member states by years of admission.

The principal exceptions to the new open-door policy were the partitioned states of Germany, Vietnam, and Korea, a persisting legacy of the cold war and the internal politics of the divided countries. Political détente led to the admission of both German states in 1973, and a single Vietnam—unified by force of arms—was admitted in 1977 in the aftermath of the Vietnam War. The problems associated with partition

TABLE 3–1
Growth of UN Membership, 1945–1986

Year	Number	New Member States
1945	51	Argentina, Australia, Belgium, Bolivia, Brazil, Byelorussian SSR, Canada, Chile, China, Colombia, Costa Rica, Cuba, Czechoslovakia, Denmark, Dominican Republic, Ecuador, Egypt, El Salvador, Ethiopia, France, Greece, Guatemala, Haiti, Honduras, India, Iran, Iraq, Lebanon, Liberia, Luxembourg, Mexico, Netherlands, New Zealand, Nicaragua, Norway, Panama, Paraguay, Peru, Philippines, Poland, Saudi Arabia, South Africa, Syria, Turkey, Ukrainian SSR, USSR, United Kingdom, United States, Uruguay, Venezuela, Yugoslavia

Year	Number	New Member States
1946	55	Afghanistan, Iceland, Sweden, Thailand
1947	57	Pakistan, Yemen
1948	58	Burma
1949	59	Israel
1950	60	Indonesia
1955	76	Albania, Austria, Bulgaria, Democratic Kampuchea, Finland, Hungary, Ireland, Italy, Jordan, Lao People's Democratic Republic, Libyan Arab Jamahiriya, Nepal, Portugal, Romania, Spain, Sri Lanka
1956	80	Japan, Morocco, Sudan, Tunisia
1957	82	Ghana, Malaysia
1958	83	Guinea
1960	100	Benin, Burkina Faso, Central African Republic, Chad, Congo, Côte d'Ivoire, Cyprus, Gabon, Madagascar, Mali, Niger, Nigeria, Senegal, Somalia, Togo, United Republic of Cameroon, Zaire
1961	104	Mauritania, Mongolia, Sierra Leone, United Republic of Tanzania
1962	110	Algeria, Burundi, Jamaica, Rwanda, Trinidad and Tobago, Uganda
1963	112	Kenya, Kuwait
1964	115	Malawi, Malta, Zambia
1965	118	Gambia, Maldives, Singapore
1966	122	Barbados, Botswana, Guyana, Lesotho
1967	123	Democratic Yemen
1968	126	Equatorial Guinea, Mauritius, Swaziland
1970	127	Fiji
1971	132	Bahrain, Bhutan, Oman, Qatar, United Arab Emirates
1973	135	Bahamas, Federal Republic of Germany, German Democratic Republic
1974	138	Bangladesh, Grenada, Guinea-Bissau

TABLE 3–1 _____
(Concluded)

Year	Number	New Member States
1975	144	Cape Verde, Comoros, Mozambique, Papua New Guinea, São Tomé and Principe, Suriname
1976	147	Angola, Samoa, Seychelles
1977	149	Djibouti, Vietnam
1978	151	Dominica, Solomon Islands
1979	152	Saint Lucia
1980	154	Saint Vincent and the Grenadines, Zimbabwe
1981	157	Antigua and Barbuda, Belize, Vanuatu
1983	158	Saint Christopher and Nevis
1984	159	Brunei Darussalam

SOURCE: *UN Chronicle* 23, no. 2 (1986), inside front cover.

still keep the two Koreas outside the organization. An exception of a different kind is Switzerland, the former seat of the League of Nations and the present site of UN European headquarters, which has voluntarily remained aloof out of conviction that membership was incompatible with Swiss neutrality. Switzerland and the two Koreas, along with Monaco and the Holy See, presently maintain "Permanent Observers" at the United Nations.

A still different problem was presented by China. An original member of the United Nations, China also became a "partitioned" state in 1949, when the People's Republic seized power on the mainland and the Nationalist government fled to Taiwan. Because neither China would officially admit the reality of partition, the issue was treated as one of representation rather than of membership for both states. Each year from 1950 to 1971, the General Assembly was forced to decide whether China should be represented by delegates from the mainland or from Taiwan. The string of Nationalist voting victories, made possible only by vigorous support from the United States, was finally broken in November 1971, when the General Assembly recognized the People's Republic as the legitimate holder of the China seat. Other UN organs quickly followed the lead of the Assembly, and Nationalist representatives departed the UN scene. Although the Peking government purports to speak for all of China, including Taiwan, that small island remains for practical purposes unrepresented in the United Nations.

The few exceptions aside, new states have valued the status of UN membership and virtually all states have found it a useful forum for the practice of multilateral diplomacy. The United Nations, in turn, has welcomed all comers. For a time some members agonized over the ministate problem—the admission of new states with equal voting rights in the General Assembly but without the population or resources to contribute much to UN programs (or, indeed, exercise much influence in any

TABLE 3–2 _____

UN Membership and Geographic Region, 1945–1986

Date	Western Europe*	Eastern Europe	Asia and Pacific†	Africa‡	Latin America	Others§	Total
1945	9	6	8	4	20	4	51
1950	11	6	15	4	20	4	60
1955	17	10	20	5	20	4	76
1960	17	10	23	26	20	4	100
1986	19	11	41	51	33	4	159

*Includes Turkey.
†Includes Israel.
‡Includes South Africa.
§Includes Australia, Canada, New Zealand, United States.

aspect of international affairs). But the admission of Antigua and Barbuda, the Seychelles, Dominica, and São Tomé and Principe—all with less than 100,000 population—and thirty other states with populations less than one million suggests a precedent too firmly set to be overridden in the foreseeable future.

Current admission policies have brought the membership of the United Nations into consonance with the universality of its objectives, and this in turn has demonstrated another important relationship between membership and objectives. Just as goals determine membership, membership also affects goals. The members, through their participation in the political process, give operational meaning to the goals of the organization. The objectives become whatever the members seek to accomplish. In the case of the United Nations, the effects of unrestricted admission have been profound, as new members have redefined the operational goals of the organization according to their own vision. As shown in Table 3–2, the growth in membership has come primarily from the new states of Africa and Asia. Western, and specifically American, dominance of the United Nations during the first ten years of its existence has given way to the numerical dominance of the Third World. While East-West divisions are still of some importance, the new majority espouses nonalignment and the dominant UN cleavage is now North-South. The United Nations has become a forum for articulating the ideology of the New International Economic Order (NIEO), with its stress on the economic needs of developing states. In dealing with economic issues, the United States and the Soviet Union not infrequently make common cause in opposition to demands on the resources of the industrialized countries. The present UN majority is also militantly anticolonial, to a degree that would have astounded the delegates to the first UN General Assembly. While disputed colonial questions usually find the Soviet bloc aligned with the Third World against a few Western states, the imperialist overtones of Soviet policies in Afghanistan and elsewhere occasionally put the Soviet Union at odds with the anticolonial majority.

The changes wrought by changing membership patterns testify to the central role of member states in the UN political process. All other actors are subordinate because the members collectively have the formal power of decision and provide most of the resources essential to the functioning of the organization.

Private Interest Groups

The twentieth century has seen a very significant meshing of activity by private interest groups ("non-governmental organizations" or "NGOs" in UN parlance) with the processes of intergovernmental organizations ("IGOs"). Although much of the contact is informal in nature, somewhat akin to the lobbying activity of domestic groups in democratic states, a surprising amount of interest group consultation now takes place through constitutionally established forms.

The International Labor Organization has gone the farthest in this direction, allowing participation with full voting rights to representatives of private interests. The ILO permits each member state to send four delegates to its General Conference—two representing the government, one representing employer interests, and one chosen in consultation with national labor organizations. This combination of public and private interest representation dates from the formation of the ILO in 1919 and is still unique; but consultation without right of participation in debate and voting has become common in other intergovernmental bodies.

The UN Economic and Social Council, under Article 71 of the Charter, is authorized to "make suitable arrangements for consultation with non-governmental organizations." It has such arrangements with approximately 750 national and international private organizations, divided into three categories. About thirty are included in Category I, reserved for organizations with broad membership and an interest in most Council activities. Some two hundred others are Category II organizations—those with special competence but concerned with only a few Council activities. The remainder are listed on the "Roster," a third class of organizations not qualified for the first two categories but still able to make a useful contribution. Placement in any of the three categories requires an affirmative decision by ECOSOC.[1] Although consultative status is sought by many organizations, it has contributed less to NGO influence than originally anticipated, at least partly because ECOSOC's role within the UN system has been less important than expected.

The General Assembly has no formal consultative arrangements separate from the ECOSOC system, but representatives of NGOs try to make their presence felt in corridors, lounges, and meeting halls while the Assembly is in session. In 1978, during the tenth special session devoted to disarmament, the Assembly broke precedent by allowing representatives from a number of private organizations to address the assembled delegates.

Observer status has been officially granted to the Palestine Liberation Organization (PLO) and the South West Africa People's Organization (SWAPO), two "liberation movements" recognized by many UN members. The two organizations are not altogether similar, since SWAPO is a response to South Africa's colonial domination of neighboring Namibia, whereas the PLO's professed goal is destruction of the independent state of Israel. Nevertheless, as potential governments of the territories they seek to liberate, SWAPO and the PLO have characteristics both of governments and of nongovernmental organizations. Their representatives actively participate in drafting Assembly resolutions relating to Namibia and the Middle East, respectively, and have been permitted to speak in Assembly bodies. The Security Council, likewise, has admitted the PLO and SWAPO to its discussions.

Most other intergovernmental organizations have formal or informal arrangements for consultation with private groups. The volume of contacts frequently depends on the perceived capacity of the organization to affect group interests. The European Community, for example, is lobbied heavily because it has extensive power to regulate, reward, and punish the conduct of private groups and individuals. On a lesser scale, UNESCO is also an important focus of private group activity. Private groups and individuals are involved directly in many of its programs for educational, scientific, and cultural interchange; and UNESCO can reward some of them with fellowships and scholarships, contracts for writing and publication, and subsidies to support private international societies fostering such interchange. UNESCO maintains additional private contracts through the national UNESCO commissions that have been formed in many member countries.

A notable increase in private group activity has been stimulated by the recent practice of holding special world conferences under UN auspices. As early as 1963, and again in 1970, the FAO sponsored World Food Congresses designed primarily for NGOs as a means of publicizing and enlisting support for FAO objectives. Since the 1972 Stockholm Conference on the Environment, the more common pattern has been to hold intergovernmental conferences on special subjects with informal participation and sometimes "parallel" conference activities by NGO representatives. Participation includes the usual forms of lobbying at meetings and, often, working with secretariat officials or national governments in preparation for the conference program.[2] Increasingly it has included appeals to the media and their mass public audiences. NGOs lobby media representatives at international conferences, hoping to influence the reporting of what is done. Many NGO representatives themselves hold press accreditation from local newspapers or broadcasting stations and send out their own news reports. Such NGO activity has also carried over to General Assembly special sessions on economic development and on disarmament.

Generalizations about the role of private interest groups are difficult. There is wide variation from one intergovernmental organization to another, and it is all too easy to equate activity with influence. Speeches delivered or papers submitted to ECOSOC or some other UN body are easily ignored, and most have little impact beyond the satisfaction felt by the NGO representative in expressing his point of view. UN officials tend to view NGOs as vehicles for building public support for IGO programs rather than as coparticipants in UN decision making.[3] Still, some influence is exerted. Where NGO cooperation is essential or helpful in carrying out IGO programs—refugee relief or cultural exchange programs, for example—influence on details of administration may be considerable. Private group influence may be especially significant in a setting such as the European Community, where Community organs have a capacity to affect private interests in a direct and substantial way. Many of the affected groups have resources to conduct extensive lobbying with Community agencies or member governments and will not hesitate to use those resources if important interests are at stake.

More typical at UN-sponsored meetings is the private group with humanitarian rather than economic motivations and with limited lobbying resources. This is not a recipe for great influence. However, a good idea or a piece of high-quality research may sometimes have an impact. If secretariat officials recognize the need for NGO involvement in preparation for a particular UN conference, NGO influence can be substantial in developing position papers and documentation. If the private group has a strong national base, it may lobby with a national government on some issue before the United Nations. Once a resolution has been adopted, NGOs may serve as gadflies to the international body politic by monitoring compliance by governments and subsequent follow-up by secretariat officials. Some private groups have been very active in finding facts on human rights violations and making them public. If the impact of such activity on any given UN decision is small, the total impact of NGO participation in international organization surely is not insignificant.[4]

The International Official as Political Participant

The political functions of international secretariats are discussed in a subsequent chapter, but a description of participants in the political process would be incomplete without a brief reference to the international civil servant. In any political system the line between the making and execution of decisions—between policy and administration—is hard to draw. The policy decisions of legislative bodies take on color and character from the subsequent administrative decisions that give them effect. Furthermore, administrative officials can be direct participants in the process by which organizational decisions are made.

The executive head of an international secretariat is often in a position to have an effect on policy. In organizations with large budgets for operational programs, he is likely to be the most influential individual participant. He may initiate proposals as well as joining actively in formal and informal discussion of matters to be decided by members of the organization. Influence will of course vary with the type of organization, the nature of the issue, and the individual attributes of the incumbent. All UN Secretaries-General have felt a responsibility to bring the weight of their office to bear on issues confronting the United Nations, some with more success than others.

Secretariat influence on the political process is not restricted to the activities of the chief administrative officer. Others farther down the hierarchy participate as well. Experience and expertise may qualify secretariat officials for the role of counselor or informal adviser to delegates whose respect and friendship they have earned, or sometimes for an intermediary's role when compromise is required. Formal reports or opinions prepared by secretariats provide part of the informational base for some decisions. Decisions relating to the operation of agency programs often depend on information from the officials who administer the programs. Nor can one overlook the substantial policy implications of budget preparation, a task regularly performed by secretariats, albeit with careful supervision by representatives of member states.

International Organizations as Participants

The participation of international organizations in the decisions of other international organizations, including organizations outside the UN system, is now a pervasive feature of international relations. Representatives of the European Community speak for the Community in international tariff negotiations, and the secretariat of the General Agreement on Tariffs and Trade (GATT) maintains contact with Community authorities in Brussels. Members of the European Community frequently address economic matters in UN forums through a common spokesman. In the UN Development Program the participating intergovernmental organizations jockey vigorously to influence the allocation of available funds. At a different level of policymaking, coordination of technical assistance sponsored by different international organizations is facilitated by interagency committees of secretariat officials. Representatives of UN specialized agencies regularly participate in the work of ECOSOC, and regional organizations frequently collaborate with UN bodies in dealing with common problems. The General Assembly has adopted resolutions granting formal consultative status to a number of regional organizations, including the Commonwealth of Nations, the Council for Mutual Economic Assistance, the European Community, the Islamic Conference, the League of Arab States, the Organization of African Unity, and the Organization of American States. Such arrangements illustrate an often ignored political fact—that international organizations are more than mere channels for national diplomatic activity. An international organization with permanent institutions is itself a political entity capable of participating in the political processes of the international system.

UN DECISION MAKING

National interest and power may ultimately determine who gets what in the international arena, but perceptions of interest and use of power are modified by the institutions through which power is exercised. The most significant questions that can be asked about international organization relate to the ways in which participation modifies national perceptions of interest and affects the exercise of national power. Definitive answers have not been found—and perhaps never will be—but the questions should be asked. The following sections present information that may be helpful in framing tentative answers.

National Organization for UN Participation

Membership in the United Nations requires countries to adopt positions on a multitude of issues ranging in diversity from war in the Middle East to stabilization of world prices for copper and cotton to refugee relief in Africa. Many countries feel compelled to formulate policy on specific issues that never would have concerned them except for their participation in the United Nations. There is, of course, a wide variation in the thoroughness of preparation for UN discussions. States with substantial resources and broad foreign policy interests are likely to prepare detailed instructions for their UN representatives. Delegates from tiny states with limited interests and meager resources may have little guidance beyond the country's general foreign policy orientation, level of development, and bloc affiliations and the known predilections of its leaders.

The United States illustrates a very extensive adaptation to UN participation. Within the State Department a Bureau of International Organization Affairs (IO) is concerned exclusively with coordinating U.S. policy in the United Nations and other multilateral agencies. The IO Bureau does not do it alone, however. Every major unit of the State Department is involved in preparation for UN meetings because the agendas run virtually the full range of American foreign policy interests. Indeed, every major department of government has interests in the activities of one or more international agencies, and officials from every department participate in international conferences.

If an issue is to come before the United Nations, the IO Bureau has responsibility for clarifying the possible policy alternatives and preparing position papers to guide American representatives in the UN. This, again, is not a self-contained operation. It is usually accomplished through a small working group—a temporary interoffice committee including representation from geographic and other interested bureaus— to do the groundwork and make the initial policy recommendations. Position preparation may also require coordination with other executive departments through an interdepartmental coordination committee. This is a far cry from the behavior of a microstate, which may send no instructions at all to its UN representatives, but it shows the extent to which a major state must adapt its governmental machinery to the needs of UN participation.

Such complex arrangements for intragovernmental consultation and coordination are essential if U.S. policies in the United Nations are to mesh with other aspects of foreign and domestic policy. Still, a broad base for policy formulation is no guarantee of effective participation. That depends on the quality of the representation, the energy devoted to influencing UN decisions, and a clear sense of what is to be accomplished.[5]

Missions and Delegations.   Nearly all UN members maintain permanent missions to the United Nations in New York. Most also have permanent representation at the UN European Office in Geneva. The mission chief, or Permanent Representative, usually holds the diplomatic rank of ambassador. Mission size varies with the interests and resources of the state. The smaller missions may have only one or two persons of diplomatic rank plus a couple of clerical employees, while the United States maintains a permanent staff of about 125 and the Soviet mission (including personnel assigned to the ostensibly separate missions for the Ukraine and Byelorussia) has been more than twice that size.[6]

The permanent mission represents a country's interests in the United Nations much as an embassy represents that country's interests in a foreign capital. The functions of the permanent mission differ in many respects from those of the traditional diplomatic mission, however, because the UN is a multilateral organization rather than a government. Members of the permanent mission perform the traditional diplomatic functions of representation, negotiation, information gathering, and reporting. But at the UN this is done multilaterally with more than 160 states, including nonmembers with Permanent Observers, rather than bilaterally with one. In any national capital bilateral and multilateral contacts occur among diplomats from various national embassies, but such contacts are incidental to the primary mission of representation to the host government and not the fundamental object. The UN diplomat deals constantly with many national viewpoints and policies and often operates through procedures more congenial to national parliaments than to chanceries and foreign offices. He also deals with a broader spectrum of issues, frequently of a technical nature. This, as Finger observes, "promotes a greater degree of autonomy for the mission, as few governments can keep track of so many details and the government is more dependent on the mission for relevant information."[7]

Permanent representation at the United Nations is essential for the fifteen members of the Security Council, which, under Article 28 of the Charter, must "be so organized as to be able to function continuously." Most other countries also find it useful for a variety of reasons. The Assembly is in session for at least three months of every year. Fifty-four states are members of ECOSOC, which meets twice each year for a few weeks, one session in New York and another at the Geneva UN headquarters. Numerous other UN committees, commissions, and subsidiary bodies hold meetings in New York as well. (See Figure 3–1 for a typical month's meetings calendar.) For states that have no current meeting in session, there is continuing need to prepare for forthcoming meetings, engage in preliminary negotiations, maintain working relations with the UN Secretariat, monitor the operation of UN activities, and stay in contact with other UN missions.

Diplomatic discussions in New York are by no means limited to matters on a UN agenda. The existence of so many diplomatic missions in one location makes the United Nations the world's busiest center for bilateral diplomacy. Most UN members are small states that cannot afford to maintain embassies in very many other countries. If they are geographically distant from one another, the volume of contacts among their governments and citizens does not justify the expense. Yet they may have some common interests, and the United Nations provides a setting where they can exchange views and carry on diplomatic contact, whether or not the matter is a subject of UN discussion.[8] Even for countries that exchange ambassadors, the United Nations is a useful additional channel of bilateral communication. UN contacts may be particularly helpful for hostile states, such as Israel and its Arab neighbors, for which the normal channels of communication are not functioning.

A "delegation" in UN parlance consists of personnel accredited to represent a country at a particular UN meeting or series of meetings. For the General Assembly, each state is entitled by the Charter to five representatives and five alternates, with

FIGURE 3–1 _____
UN Meetings Calendar, March 1985

_____

New York

March 1	Pledging Conference for the International Year of Peace
March 4–15	Group of Governmental Experts to Carry Out a Comprehensive Study on the Naval Forces and Naval Arms Race, Naval Forces and Naval Arms Systems, third session
March 4–22	Committee on the Elimination of Racial Discrimination
March 4–29	Special Committee on the Charter of the United Nations and on the Strengthening of the Role of the Organization
March 11–22	Intergovernmental Working Group of Experts on International Standards of Accounting and Reporting
March 11–22	Committee on Non-Governmental Organizations
March 18–19	Committee on Information (organizational session)
March 18–22	Human Rights Committee—Working Group on Communications
March 18–April 4	Committee on the Peaceful Uses of Outer Space—Legal Subcommittee
March 21	Special Committee against Apartheid—Special Meeting in Observance of the International Day for the Elimination of Racial Discrimination
March 25–29	Consultative Committee on the Voluntary Fund for the UN Decade for Women
March 25–April 4	Ad Hoc Committee on the Indian Ocean
March 25–April 4	Group of Governmental Experts on International Cooperation to Avert New Flows of Refugees
March 25–April 12	Human Rights Committee
March 25–April 12	Ad Hoc Intergovernmental Committee of the Whole to Review the Implementation of the Charter of Economic Rights and Duties of States
March–July (3–5 meetings a week)	Special Committee on the Situation with regard to the Implementation of the Declaration on the Granting of Independence to Colonial Countries and Peoples

Geneva

March 18–29	UNCTAD—Trade and Development Board

Vienna

March 4–13	Commission on the Status of Women Acting as the Preparatory body for the World Conference to Review and Appraise the Achievements of the UN Decade for Women, third session

FIGURE 3–1 _____
(Concluded)

| March 25–April 3 | Advisory Committee for the International Youth Year, fourth session |

Other Locations

March 4–6	Port Moresby	Asian and Pacific Regional Seminar to Commemorate the Twenty-fifth Anniversary of the Adoption of the Declaration on the Granting of Independence to Colonial Countries and Peoples
March 6–8	Kingston	Preparatory Commission for the International Sea-Bed Authority and for the International Tribunal for the Law of the Sea—Group of 77
March 11–29	London (IMO Hqs.)	International Civil Service Commission, twenty-first session
March 11–April 4	Kingston	Preparatory Commission for the International Sea-Bed Authority and for the International Tribunal for the Law of the Sea, third session
March 19–29	Bangkok	Economic and Social Commission for Asia and the Pacific, forty-first session
March 25–28	Baghdad	Western Asia Regional Expert Group Preparatory Meeting for the UN Conference for the Promotion of International Cooperation in the Peaceful Uses of Nuclear Energy
March (1 week)	To be determined	UN Council for Namibia—Regional Seminar on Namibia in Africa
March (1 week)	To be determined	UN Joint Staff Pension Board—Standing Committee

SOURCE: _UN Chronicle_ 22, no. 1 (1985), p. 60.

no constitutional limitation on the clerical or advisory staff, which usually consists of permanent mission personnel as well as officials from foreign offices, diplomatic posts, or other agencies of government. It is customary for the Permanent Representative to be one of the delegates, but he is often outranked on the delegation by his foreign minister—and occasionally his head of state or head of government—who may attend part of a session. Some states send a full delegation of professional diplomats, while others include persons from other ministries of government. Many, including the United States, send one or more members of the national legislature and prominent persons from private life.

The UN delegate is akin to both legislator and diplomat. This duality is recognized by use of the term *parliamentary diplomacy* to designate what goes on at meetings of the United Nations and other international organizations. Procedures for agenda setting, debate, and decisions by vote are not unlike those in a national legislature. So also are the informal activities of discussion, persuasion, and compromise in drafting resolutions embodying areas of common interest sufficient to command a voting majority.

But the delegate is still a diplomat. He comes as a representative of his government to negotiate agreements rather than as a representative of his constituency to enact laws. Except for procedural and organizational matters, General Assembly resolutions are not legally binding on states. As a governmental agent, the delegate must act not only in the interest of his country but also in conformity with his government's instructions. There are, of course, vast differences in the quality of instructions from one delegation to another. As one careful observer has noted, some delegations

> are given lengthy and detailed instructions which severely limit their freedom of manoeuvre. Some governments instruct their delegation in terms of the position of other governments, i.e., "Vote more or less like . . ." or "if . . . votes 'no' you can abstain." Some governments provide no instructions at all, leaving matters to the discretion of the delegation.[9]

Even the most meticulous instructions do not rule out all freedom of action. Like any diplomat, the UN delegate can influence the content of his instructions by the information and advice he sends to his foreign office. The degree of influence depends on his political standing at home, as well as on the force of his arguments. If a government has a strong interest in the United Nations as an institution, it may be more willing to listen to members of the delegation or the permanent mission. On the other hand, if a particular issue touches important interests of a country, the UN representative's margin for maneuver and his ability to influence policy may both be reduced.

The UN setting virtually demands some leeway for the delegate because no government can fully anticipate every twist and turn of UN parliamentary diplomacy. All delegations have a large measure of discretion as to tactics, and at least some discretion to make minor adjustments of substance. If changed instructions are desired, the delegation's judgment will be given weight because of its position on the UN firing line. The bottom line, nevertheless, is the government's control over its diplomats. Notwithstanding the freedom of action and policy influence entailed by the parliamentary setting, delegations to international meetings have a responsiveness to their governments that is unmatched by any ordinary relationship of a national legislator to his constituency or, in democratic societies at least, to his political party.

The Institutional Setting of UN Decision Making

National interest and national power supply the dynamics of the political process in international organization, but the outcome is also affected by the institutional setting. One obvious institutional constraint is the subject matter competence of the organization. Limited purpose organizations such as the UN specialized agencies are confined by their charters to a specific subject area, such as the promotion of world health, development funding, or regulation of maritime transport. Regional organizations, by reason of membership as well as constitutional prescription, focus on matters of particular concern to states of the region. The United Nations, by its nature as a general international organization, is much less restrictive in scope. Its legal purview extends to virtually everything under the sun except matters of "domestic jurisdiction." Practically, its reach extends in the General Assembly to any subject that UN members wish to have considered there, since the issue of jurisdiction has always boiled down to who has the votes to put an item on or keep it off the agenda.

Two other institutional features must be considered in greater detail because they so profoundly affect the perception of national interests and the exercise of national power within the United Nations. One is the body of rules and practices governing voting and formal decision making in the organization. The other consists of the formal and informal communication structures that characterize the UN political process. Each will be examined in the pages that follow.

Voting in the International Arena.   If decision-making procedures within an international organization accurately mirror the actual distribution of national power, the effect of procedure on the exercise of power is minimal. But such a congruence seldom obtains. This is because power is not easily measured, power patterns change over time, less powerful states are generally unwilling to accept rules that clearly reflect their impotence, and larger states have learned to live with rules that emphasize sovereign equality above national power. In practice, the three most common decision rules of modern international organizations are decision by vote, one vote per member state, and majority rule. When these three rules are combined in an organization of wide membership, an imbalance between internal and external power relationships is unavoidable.

Voting has become so common on the international scene that one can easily forget its recent origins. Modern international organizations date only from the nineteenth century, and voting as a means of international decision making is a product of that development. The international conferences of an earlier period were primarily negotiating bodies without "action" responsibilities. Their function was to negotiate agreements to be embodied in treaty form for ratification by the respective national governments. Voting implies a process of deciding—and the final right of decision belonged to governments individually, not to representatives of states gathered at an international meeting. The principles of national sovereignty and sovereign equality demanded nothing less than complete dispersal of decision-making authority among national units.

With the development of international organizations having permanent secretariats, organizational budgets, and special subject matter competences, a new dimension was added to interstate relations. The organizations themselves became entities with legal personalities distinct from those of their member states. Budgeted funds, though raised primarily through national contributions, were disbursed by the organization, and secretariats did the bidding of the collectivity—not of the individual members. A growing number of decisions of international organizations became operative immediately, without referral to the treaty ratification process. Voting, a time-honored practice in domestic politics, was readily transferred to the new setting.

The shift of real, if limited, decision-making power to international organizations placed unavoidable strain on national sovereignty and equality. In a strictly juridical context states may be equal in their legal rights and duties with respect to the world community. In any other context, including that of international organizations, state equality is pure fiction. States have neither equality of interest in the substance of organizational decisions nor equal capacity to implement them. Sovereign equality suggests that each state should have an equal voice in the decisions of the organization. But this can only result in divorce of power to decide from responsibility for implementing the decision.

The principle of sovereignty gives rise to the further implication that no state can be bound without its consent. Carried to a logical conclusion, this could mean that decisions should be taken only by a unanimous vote.[10] But such a requirement strikes at the capacity of the organization to produce meaningful decisions at all. If unanimity must prevail on every matter, decisions may never be made for lack of the requisite agreement. Or, if agreement is reached, it may represent a common denominator so diluted that nothing of substance has been agreed on. Some decisions, of course, cannot be carried out very effectively without the concurrence of the states most directly connected. Economic aid programs will falter without the support of the wealthier contributors. Resolutions calling for cessation of Soviet intervention in Afghanistan, Libyan support of international terrorism, or even Israeli withdrawal from the West Bank will not achieve their aims without acceptance by the Soviet Union, Libya, and Israel, respectively. But many decisions, certainly those involving joint action among states disposed to cooperate, can be made and acted on without the concurrence of other states having little practical interest in or responsibility for the matter.

International organizations presently display varying kinds of compromise between principle and practicality. Equality of voting rights is the general rule, although its impact has been blunted in several ways and it has been rejected by a few organizations in favor of a distribution of voting rights more accurately reflecting differences in national interests and the distribution of power. This is true of some organizations whose primary function is the handling of money—the International Bank, the International Monetary Fund, the International Finance Corporation, and the International Development Association—where voting power is governed by amount of contribution. Commodity councils, such as the Wheat and Sugar councils, allot votes according to the volume of imports and exports of the commodity. Still another form of unequal or weighted voting is found in the Central Commission for the Navigation of the Rhine, where voting rights, for certain purposes, are roughly proportional to river frontage. These illustrations suggest that weighted voting is most feasible where the weighting principle can be tied to a single measurable criterion directly related to the primary function of the organization.

When weighted voting is not acceptable, organizations often recognize differences among states by the creation of special executive or deliberative bodies of limited membership on which representation can be granted according to some rough approximation of interest and power. Thus the five largest states in the wartime UN coalition were made permanent members of the Security Council, ten of the twenty-eight governmental seats on the ILO Governing Body are allotted to states of "chief industrial importance," states of "chief importance in air transport" are given preference in the election of the ICAO Council, and eligibility for selection to the Council of the International Maritime Organization is determined by a state's interest in shipping and maritime trade. As further recognition of their special status, the five permanent members of the Security Council are always represented on the UN Trusteeship Council, ECOSOC, and most other UN bodies on which they desire membership. A national of each permanent member is usually chosen to sit on the fifteen-member International Court of Justice.

If sovereign equality has been somewhat eroded by schemes of weighted voting and unequal representation on limited-membership bodies, the rule of unanimity has suffered a more far-reaching eclipse. Unanimity still governs some organizations of limited membership, including the NATO Council, the Arab League Council, COMECON, and the Council of the Organization for Economic Cooperation and Development (OECD), but most international organizations now conduct business by concurrence of a simple or a qualified majority. Even in the UN Security Council, which retains the principle of unanimity for permanent members, decisions require only nine of fifteen votes.

Majority voting, with its inherent derogation from sovereign prerogatives, is the price paid for some degree of organizational efficiency. The spread of majority voting in international organizations does not necessarily mean the triumph of "majority rule" in international affairs, however. To pass a resolution by majority vote is one thing; to take action that is practically effective and legally binding on all members is quite another. A careful examination of the law and practice of international organizations reveals that majorities have much more authority to recommend than to command and that their authority to command is largely limited to matters eliciting a high degree of consensus or not seriously impinging on the vital interests of states. The Universal Postal Union, for example, can alter certain postal regulations by a two-thirds majority vote. This is possible because of the substantial consensus on UPU objectives. Most international organizations can adopt binding rules governing the operations of their secretariats, the filling of electoral offices, the expenditure of budgeted funds, and other housekeeping activities. Although such "lawmaking" power is important, it does not ordinarily affect the vital interests of states.[11]

Except for power over internal operations, one looks almost in vain for authority to make binding decisions in any of the policy-making organs of the United Nations. The General Assembly, the Economic and Social Council, and the near-defunct Trusteeship Council are clearly limited to nonbinding recommendations. Under Chapter VII of the Charter, members are obligated to assist with military, economic, and diplomatic sanctions imposed by the Security Council in dealing with a "threat to the peace, breach of the peace, or act of aggression." However, the Security Council's authority to make binding decisions for the use of military force was nullified by its failure to reach accord, as contemplated by Article 43, on the composition of forces to be available on call for UN use. And rarely has a majority been available to order compulsory nonmilitary sanctions.[12] For most purposes the Security Council, like the General Assembly, has been limited to exhortation rather than command.[13]

Voting in the General Assembly.   General Assembly decision procedures combine the elements of sovereign equality and majority voting with persistent reluctance to let majorities legislate. Each member state is allotted one vote, regardless of size or capacity to contribute to the purposes of the organization. Decisions on "important questions" require a two-thirds majority of members present and voting. Certain types of "important questions" are specified in the Charter.[14] Other matters are decided by a simple majority vote, including the decision to designate other questions or categories of questions as "important" enough to require a two-thirds majority. In calculating the existence of a required majority, the General Assembly has adopted the practice of including both formal abstentions and absences among those not present and voting. With a large number of abstentions, even an important measure can be adopted by considerably fewer than a majority of the total membership.[15] Just a few categories of decisions require a majority based on total membership. These include an absolute majority for election to the International Court of Justice, under Article 10 of the ICJ Statute, and a two-thirds majority for the proposal of Charter amendments as provided in Article 109 of the UN Charter.

In the decades since the framing of the UN Charter, dissatisfaction with Assembly voting rules has frequently been voiced. Equality of voting rights has been the most persistent source of concern. The expansion of the United Nations to include many small states created since 1945 has multiplied the voting disparity of small states over large. Third World states now have the voting strength to obtain a two-thirds majority on any issue of importance to them. Mathematically, a two-thirds vote could even be mustered by states collectively representing less than 15 percent of the world's population. This extreme case does not occur, however, because the prevailing majority of anticolonial, developing states includes such populous countries as China, India, and Indonesia.

Even in the days of U.S. ascendance, the Assembly was prone to adopt resolutions that were totally unacceptable to states in the minority whose cooperation was essential to achieving the purposes of the resolutions. Today, with voting dominance of mostly small and poor developing countries, the gap between the power to decide and the power to implement decisions has further increased. The readiness of small states to use their collective voting power to influence UN outcomes is understandable. It is a form of political leverage, one of the few that many of them have. It can sometimes be used to win meaningful compromises from industrialized states. It can in any event be used to win parliamentary victories. But major power disenchantment with equality of voting rights is also understandable. And the effectiveness of the organization is diminished when groups of states, through frustration with the slow pace of negotiations or enthusiasm for a parliamentary cause, resort to an empty display of voting power that cuts short the hard search for genuine agreement. Various forms of weighted voting have been suggested as a remedy to this problem, but no one has yet devised a plan acceptable to a majority of states, not to mention the two-thirds majority required for Charter amendment. Small states, certainly, are unlikely to voluntarily relinquish the advantage they enjoy under the present system. The remedy, if any, must lie in national self-restraint.

Even though formal amendment of UN voting arrangements has not been possible, the members have come to recognize the need for alternatives to deciding by majority vote. The result has been extensive use of a "consensus" approach to decision making. Instead of taking a vote on a proposed resolution, a procedural decision, or some other matter, the presiding officer simply announces his understanding that the measure commands general support and is hence to be considered adopted by consensus. This expedites the decision procedure when there is genuine consensus on an agreed text. It is also useful when general agreement has been reached on action to be taken, but drafting a specific text might prove difficult. Approving the chairman's more or less vague summation averts possibly extensive wrangling over details. Sometimes the consensus procedure is used when substantial disagreement exists, but the meeting is willing to adopt a particular text without a vote. This permits a decision without forcing a defeated minority to make their opposition or abstention part of the permanent public record, although some members may still choose to express their objections or reservations to the adopted text. In recent sessions of the Assembly, decisions by consensus have outnumbered decisions by majority vote.[16]

Voting in the Security Council.   At the 1945 San Francisco Conference the great powers insisted that their special responsibility for maintaining international peace and security should be recognized in the voting procedures of the Security Council. Thus China, France, the United Kingdom, the United States, and the Soviet Union were made permanent members of the Security Council and each was given a veto over "nonprocedural" matters. The issue involved far more than mere concern for great power status. Without the concurrence of all the major powers, the United

Nations could conceivably find itself in the position of starting enforcement action that it could not finish for lack of cooperation from an essential collaborator. Worse yet, a decision to use force in the name of the United Nations over the objection of a state controlling large military forces could be the means of turning localized conflict into world war. The veto was intended to avoid such situations and, above all, to preclude initiation of enforcement action directly against one of the major powers. In the words of one of the architects of the Charter, "This would be the equivalent of a world war, and a decision to embark upon such a war would necessarily have to be made by each of the other nations for itself and not by any international organization."[17]

In practice, the United Nations has not had the important military enforcement role envisioned by the framers, but the veto has still served a useful purpose in preventing the organization from overreaching itself by intruding too forcefully on the interests of the great powers. All of the permanent members continue to value its protection. From 1946 to 1969, the Soviet Union cast 105 vetos and the United States none. Since 1970 the roles have been reversed, with the United States vetoing many more proposals than the Soviet Union. Britain, France, and China have also found occasion to use this right. (See Table 3–3.)

Vetoes have been a source of irritation to states on the opposite side of the issue but have not seriously hampered the United Nations in performing its security functions. Fifty-one of the Soviet vetoes, all before 1960, were used to deny approval of UN membership applications that had been pressed to a vote over Soviet objection. All of the applicants except Vietnam and South Korea were admitted in 1955, however, and Vietnam was admitted in 1977. Other vetoes have been almost frivolous or inconsequential in their practical effects. In 1949 the Council was unable to tender official congratulations to the Netherlands and Indonesia upon successful conclusion of their negotiations for Indonesian independence. In 1963 the Security Council was not permitted to utter official condemnation of the murder of two Israelis in an incident along the Syrian border. Still other vetoes have been circumvented through action by the General Assembly. This was notably true of the Korean War, the 1956 Suez crisis, and the 1960 UN Congo operation. It has also been true of numerous resolutions of condemnation or censure first vetoed in the Security Council and subsequently adopted, with perhaps some change in wording, by the General Assembly. Assembly resolutions disapproving Soviet intervention in Hungary and Afghanistan, U.S. intervention in Nicaragua and Grenada, and many Israeli actions in the Middle East are examples of the practice.

Some vetoes, of course, have achieved their purpose of preventing UN action opposed by one or more of the permanent members. British and U.S. vetoes have thus far fended off mandatory UN sanctions against South Africa, except for an arms embargo. China's veto in 1981 denied a third term as Secretary-General to Kurt Waldheim, and the U.S. veto barred the election of Tanzanian Salim A. Salim. The 1961 Soviet veto of a resolution calling for a cease-fire and withdrawal of Indian forces from Goa was never contradicted by the Assembly, and Soviet vetoes of cease-fire resolutions in December 1971 left India uninhibited in its military action against

TABLE 3–3

Vetoes in the Security Council, 1946–1985

Time Period	China	France	United Kingdom	United States	Soviet Union
			Number of Vetoes		
1945–50	0	2	0	0	47
1951–55	1	0	0	0	30
1956–60	0	2	2	0	15
1961–65	0	0	1	0	11
1966–70	0	0	2	1	2
1971–75	2	2	8	11	5
1976–80	0	5	4	10	5
1981–85	16*	4	7	28†	2
1986	0	1	2	8	0
Total	19	16	26	58	117

*All 16 vetoes by China were cast in closed session to block the reelection of Kurt Waldheim as Secretary-General in 1981. The vetoes are not recorded in the official records but appear in press accounts.

†Five of the 28 U.S. vetoes were cast in closed session to block the election of Tanzanian candidate Salim Ahmed Salim as Secretary-General in 1981.

SOURCES: Sydney D. Bailey, *Voting in the Security Council* (Bloomington: Indiana University Press, 1969); *Report of the Security Council to the General Assembly,* 1968–1984, UN Documents A/23/2 through A/39/2; UN Security Council, Provisional Verbatim Records (S/PV), 1985–86.

Pakistan, which secured the independence of East Pakistan (now Bangladesh). Likewise, a British veto of a call for cessation of hostilities in the Falklands permitted the fighting to be resolved on British terms before the Assembly, meeting later in the fall of 1982, could intervene.

Thus the veto has given protection to the interests of the permanent members but has seldom prevented UN action in a situation where effective UN action was possible. When action has been feasible and desired by member states, the General Assembly has usually found a way to act. If a UN resolution will not alter any state's behavior for the better, a veto of that resolution can scarcely be considered a disservice to the organization or to the cause of peace. The veto simply prevents the Security Council from undermining its own authority by issuing orders that cannot be carried out.

Viewed in another perspective, the veto may be crucial to UN viability as a world organization. During the years of Western dominance in the General Assembly, the Soviet Union might have left the United Nations altogether if it had been forced to accept the will of the Western coalition in the Security Council as well. Through hard diplomatic times the Soviet Union stayed, perhaps in part because the veto provided an institutional power base that could not be shaken by numerical majorities. The Soviet Union is no longer politically isolated in either the Assembly or the Security Council. But the United States, now often confronted with hostile Third World majorities, has reason to be grateful for its veto in the Security Council. The scenario thus has changed, but the significance of the veto remains. It continues to provide an institutional foundation on which the permanent members can maintain "a tolerable political position within the United Nations."[18]

The veto has also had the salutary effect of promoting the search for consensus. Some of the same forces that encourage consensus in the Assembly are at work in the Security Council, but the veto provides an additional incentive. If the Council is to act at all, it must have the concurrence—or at least the abstention—of each permanent member. The need for great power consensus was the fundamental assumption underlying the UN security system, and the veto was the institutional embodiment of that assumption. The passing decades have demonstrated both the correctness of the assumption and the utility of the veto as an incentive to reach consensus.

The United Nations as a Communications Network.   Voting procedures set important constraints on decision making. The flow of information among the participants that precedes the voting is even more important in determining the kinds of decisions that will be reached.

The United Nations generates a constant stream of information that must be evaluated by foreign offices. The United Nations also stimulates a heavy flow of information directly between governments. The approach of a General Assembly session, for example, is always the signal for increased intergovernmental consultations both through regular diplomatic channels and in New York. Members with a special interest in an issue use presession discussion to obtain the widest measure of support for their positions. On issues in which they have no special interest, they consult to obtain the information necessary to appraise their own policies intelligently in the light of positions held by others.

Whatever the scope of presession consultations, the beginning of an Assembly session brings a new phase in the communication process. The character of the United Nations as a generator of information affecting national policy merges with its character as a system that receives and circulates information relevant to its own decision processes. National governments now become sources of information flowing into the UN system.

The UN provides both formal and informal channels for continuing the dialogue. Formal debate in committee and plenary session has symbolic importance but usually does little to facilitate agreement on disputed questions. A public address may dramatize or occasionally clarify positions, but a committee of 159 members is too large for useful document drafting or for the working out of detailed compromise. Furthermore, reconciliation of differences requires give-and-take in a more private setting. This can occur among smaller groups of states in vacant rooms of the UN building or perhaps in delegation offices. Social gatherings also have their part in the communication process. Although casual meetings in a UN bar or lounge, luncheon engagements, cocktail parties, or formal receptions are unlikely settings for resolution drafting, they can provide occasion for significant exchanges of views and information.

Caucusing Groups.   The private, ad hoc interchange between delegates drawn temporarily together by their common interest in an issue is a persistent and inevitable part of the UN process. But other forms of interchange occur on a more routinized basis. The least formal may include the regular luncheon engagements of two friendly delegates sharing a range of common interests. At a higher level of activity and significance are organized caucusing groups having more or less regular meeting times, established routines for the conduct of discussion, and secretarial assistance drawn from one or more of the delegation staffs.

Caucusing groups have formed at the United Nations for the obvious purpose of achieving common objectives through concerted action. Consultation within regional groups received its initial impetus from electoral contests in the General Assembly. By seeking agreement beforehand, groups of members might hope to obtain an "equitable share" of Assembly officers and elective positions on the Security Council, ECOSOC, and other UN bodies with rotating membership. This ultimately led to agreed arrangements for allotting such positions among geographic regions and permitting regional groups to nominate candidates to fill the allotted positions. For electoral purposes nearly every UN member is assigned to one of five regional groups—the African group, the Asian group, the Latin-American group, the socialist states (the Soviet Union and its allies in Eastern Europe), and the "Western European and other states" group[19] (see Figure 3–2). Albania, Israel, and South Africa meet with no regional group. The United States is not a member of any group but consults with Western Europe on electoral matters.

The formal geographic groups exist primarily for elections and exchange of relevant information, but other groups are concerned with policy matters. Such groups reflect common interests, and often organizational ties, developed outside the United Nations. Thus members of the League of Arab States, the Organization of African Unity, the Organization of American States, the Association of South East Asian Nations, the European Community, the Organization for Economic Cooperation and Development, the Nordic Group, the Islamic Conference, and the Non-Aligned Nations meet periodically, or as their interests dictate, to exchange views and canvass the prospects for common action. Occasionally an issue may call for consultation among members of the North Atlantic Treaty Organization, the Warsaw Pact, or the Commonwealth. Not infrequently a group appoints a common spokesman to represent its views in debate on a particular issue. No group has matched the voting unity of the East European states over the years, but coordination of policy initiatives and UN voting has been a frequent product of group consultation, with considerable effect on voting outcomes. The overlapping membership of various groups is shown in Figure 3–3.

FIGURE 3–2

UN Membership: Regional Groups

Much of the work of the United Nations is done after consultations within five regional groups. These groups have not been created by the General Assembly, but have evolved over the years for many practical reasons. Four countries—Albania, Israel, South Africa, and the United States—are not members of any regional grouping. For election purposes the United States is considered under "Western European and Other States."

African States

Algeria, Angola, Benin, Botswana, Burkina Faso, Burundi, Cameroon, Cape Verde, Central African Republic, Chad, Comoros, Congo, Djibouti, Egypt, Equatorial Guinea, Ethiopia, Gabon, Gambia, Ghana, Guinea, Guinea-Bissau, Ivory Coast, Kenya, Lesotho, Liberia, Libyan Arab Jamahiriya, Madagascar, Malawi, Mali, Mauritania, Mauritius, Morocco, Mozambique, Niger, Nigeria, Rwanda, São Tomé and Principe, Senegal, Seychelles, Sierra Leone, Somalia, Sudan, Swaziland, Togo, Tunisia, Uganda, United Republic of Tanzania, Zaire, Zambia, Zimbabwe.

Asian States

Afghanistan, Bahrain, Bangladesh, Bhutan, Brunei Darussalam, Burma, China, Cyprus, Democratic Kampuchea, Democratic Yemen, Fiji, India, Indonesia, Iraq, Islamic Republic of Iran, Japan, Jordan, Kuwait, Lao People's Democratic Republic, Lebanon, Malaysia, Maldives, Mongolia, Nepal, Oman, Pakistan, Papua New Guinea, Philippines, Qatar, Samoa, Saudi Arabia, Singapore, Solomon Islands, Sri Lanka, Syrian Arab Republic, Thailand, Turkey,* United Arab Emirates, Vanuatu, Vietnam, Yemen.

Eastern European States

Bulgaria, Byelorussian SSR, Czechoslovakia, German Democratic Republic, Hungary, Poland, Romania, Ukrainian SSR, USSR, Yugoslavia.

Latin-American States

Antigua and Barbuda, Argentina, Bahamas, Barbados, Belize, Bolivia, Brazil, Chile, Colombia, Costa Rica, Cuba, Dominica, Dominican Republic, Ecuador, El Salvador, Grenada, Guatemala, Guyana, Haiti, Honduras, Jamaica, Mexico, Nicaragua, Panama, Paraguay, Peru, Saint Christopher and Nevis, Saint Lucia, Saint Vincent and the Grenadines, Suriname, Trinidad and Tobago, Uruguay, Venezuela.

Western European and Other States

Australia, Austria, Belgium, Canada, Denmark, Finland, Federal Republic of Germany, France, Greece, Iceland, Ireland, Italy, Luxembourg, Malta, Netherlands, New Zealand, Norway, Portugal, Spain, Sweden, Turkey,* United Kingdom.

*Turkey, which for election purposes is in the Western European Group, is also a member of the Asian Group.

SOURCE: *UN Chronicle* 22, no. 10–11 (November–December 1985), inside back cover.

FIGURE 3–3
Regional and Other UN Groups: Overlapping Membership

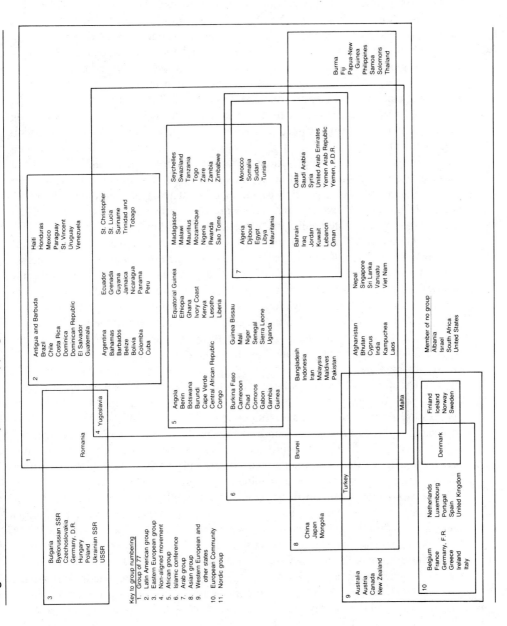

During the past two decades two interrelated groups have achieved preeminence as forces in UN politics. One is the Group of 77 (G–77), representing the interests of the developing countries, which are the vast majority of UN members.[20] The other is the Non-Aligned Movement (NAM).[21] The Group of 77 took shape at the first meeting of the UN Conference on Trade and Development (UNCTAD) at Geneva in 1964, when the seventy-seven Third World[22] participants developed a unified approach to global economic and trade problems. Their well-organized caucusing system worked so effectively that it was retained and extended to include not only UNCTAD meetings but also the General Assembly and the entire UN system. The membership has since expanded from the initial 77 to include 127 in 1986 (among them four non-UN members—the two Koreas, Tonga, and the Palestine Liberation Organization), but the "Group of 77" label has been retained. The Group has been the driving force in the United Nations for promoting developing country interests in trade, aid, investment, technical cooperation, and related matters. Developed countries have come to expect position papers or other statements from the Group of 77 at most UN meetings, and draft resolutions are frequently submitted on behalf of the whole Group by the state holding the current chairmanship.

The Group of 77 has maintained a high degree of cohesiveness on issues of economic development. Unity is greatest in formulating broad statements of principle or general concepts reflecting the interests of developing countries vis-à-vis the industrialized states. On specific issues, differences in levels of development and particular economic interests have often made negotiation of a common position difficult. At the UN Law of the Sea Conference, for example, members of the Group were frequently divided on the basis of their differing maritime interests, their location as landlocked or coastal states, or their position as importers or exporters of certain minerals.

The Group of 77 has the voting strength to override all opposition in the United Nations, and frequently it does. Since meaningful action often depends on voluntary cooperation from industrialized states, however, the Group has shown a gradually increasing tendency to negotiate consensus decisions. In the negotiation process the numbers and unity of the Group provide political leverage but are far from determinative. Sometimes the negotiations break down and end in a display of raw voting power. At other times a degree of genuine consensus can be reached.

The Non-Aligned Movement is organized separately from the Group of 77, although the two share economic goals and reinforce each other on matters of common interest. A recent U.S. Permanent Representative to the UN has called the NAM "the most important bloc of all" because of its size and effectiveness.[23] The NAM has a somewhat smaller membership than the Group of 77, 100 states in 1986 (including non–UN member North Korea), plus the PLO and the South West Africa People's Organization. Some of the more moderate G-77 states, such as Brazil, Mexico, and Venezuela, have chosen not to become full members of the NAM. The Non-Aligned Movement dates from a 1961 summit conference in Belgrade, convoked by Marshal Tito for the purpose of exploring a common foreign policy independent of the superpowers. Since then, summit meetings have been held approximately every three years (except 1967), with annual meetings of foreign ministers during the fall meeting of the UN General Assembly and meetings of specialized lower-level representatives as necessary. The NAM has no headquarters or permanent secretariat.

Although summit meetings of the NAM are held apart from the United Nations, the desire to influence decisions of UN agencies is now the most important reason for its existence. The NAM takes positions on a broader range of issues than the Group of 77. In addition to economic development, the NAM has been highly active on issues pertaining to the Middle East and southern Africa, as well as other political questions. Its anticolonial, anti-Western bias has frequently put the Movement at odds with the United States. This was particularly true during the chairmanship of Cuba, 1979–83. In its summit pronouncements and UN voting, the NAM is far less likely to make common cause with the United States than with the Soviet Union, which assiduously courts the NAM through a posture of general support and encouragement. The Movement, of course, has its internal divisions. Group discipline generally precludes outright opposition to Group decisions in UN voting on core issues, such as the Middle East and South Africa, but there is some flexibility on less politically sensitive issues.

Opinions differ on whether the caucus group system has a salutary effect on UN politics. On the negative side, the group system introduces elements of rigidity into the political process. When a group has agreed on its position, the need for constant reference back to the group may make negotiation of compromise solutions more difficult. An individual member of the group also loses flexibility when pressures to conform to the group position prevent the public expression of any misgivings that the member may have. The dilemma may be excruciating when an individual spokesman for a group passes off his own extremist views as the group position or when the group position in fact represents the views of its more extremist elements. The caucus system has the further disadvantage of fostering power relationships within the United Nations that are at variance with the actual distribution of national power. Large groups of small states can dominate voting, but they may have little power to carry out the mandates they have issued. From the standpoint of the United States and other Western, industrialized states, there is one further patent disadvantage to the system: the prevailing majority frequently espouses an anti-Western point of view. Many small states are much more anti-Western in their Assembly votes than in their bilateral foreign policies, in large part because of group influence.

The system nevertheless has a positive side. For the smaller or less developed countries, which constitute the majority of UN members, groups play a very useful role in promoting shared interests—most notably in dealing with issues of economics and anticolonialism. For new and smaller members, the groups perform an important socializing function, helping new governments and delegates to find their roles in the UN community. For nearly all members, the groups provide additional channels of communication and a forum for harmonization of views. Caucusing is an important means of building consensus at the group level, in some instances eliminating the need for an extensive series of bilateral negotiations. If the formulation of group positions adds rigidity to UN decision making, that rigidity is mitigated by the gradual trend toward consensus decisions in UN meetings generally. As a further benefit, the caucus system saves time in meetings by permitting speaking assignments to be filled by one or a few delegates from a group in place of the many who might otherwise speak.

UN Decisions: Who Wins?

Action by the General Assembly or the Security Council, as in most other intergovernmental bodies, is symbolized by the adoption of a resolution. The winners, in a parliamentary sense, are those who vote for a resolution that succeeds or against a resolution that fails. When the political process works at its best, an adopted resolution is the expression of a common interest among states having the will and the ability to do whatever its implementation requires. At other times the "win" is purely parliamentary.

Pressure and Influence.   Most resolutions are the product of extensive negotiation and compromise. The frequent adoption of resolutions by consensus indicates that this process can be successful in finding the requisite area of common interest (or at least in watering down the resolution so that no one is seriously offended). Often, however, opinion in the Assembly is strongly divided, so that adoption of a resolution is a victory for some and a defeat for others. In such a situation the delegations most directly interested will lobby vigorously to achieve victory or avoid defeat. Every delegation with a stake in the outcome of course tries to persuade others that its cause is just. But if winning is important, a determined delegation will resort to methods extending beyond arguments for the merits of its position.

In the usual case such methods involve the exploitation of some important relationship between the parties concerned—ties of friendship, military security, cultural homogeneity, or economic dependence. Regional and group solidarity have become especially important in UN meetings, particularly for the small or less developed countries whose parliamentary strength lies in unity. On many issues group pressures are determinative. As between individual governments, pressure may consist not so much in what is said as in how it is said. When reluctant delegates are repeatedly buttonholed in New York and their governments subjected to insistent appeals at home, the pressure is noticed. In this context an appeal for "good relations" carries an unmistakable hint that relations may be strained by failure to cast an appropriate vote. For a large country merely to communicate a strong opinion to a smaller dependent country may constitute pressure. If no more is said, the smaller country is left to weigh the uncertain consequences of taking a position displeasing to its more powerful patron. Such interchanges constitute a kind of diplomatic pressure and are a common occurrence in connection with UN meetings.

The crasser forms of threat or promise are also used, but they are too costly to invoke often. Threats arouse resentment, and bribes do not build mutual esteem and respect over the long run. Most Assembly decisions are not important enough to justify the threat to alter levels of foreign aid or to take other forms of retaliatory

TABLE 3–4
Regional Group Voting Agreement with the United States:
Fortieth General Assembly, 1985 (201 recorded votes)

Group	Percent Agreement	Group	Percent Agreement
Western Europe and others	59.6	Africa	15.1
(NATO members only)	67.9	Eastern Europe	12.4
The Americas	23.7	Arab states	12.2
Asia and the Pacific	17.0	No affiliation (Israel)	91.5
		All UN members	22.5

SOURCE: U.S. Department of State, *Report to Congress on Voting Practices in the United Nations,* submitted pursuant to Public Law 99–190 and Public Law 98–164, June 6, 1986, pp. I-7, II-3–II-14.

action.[24] Only on very important issues do the stakes of UN action appear to justify strong bilateral pressures. Undoubtedly the occasions when such pressures would bring a favorable vote are even fewer. Another form of pressure, exerted primarily as a deterrent to action, is the threat of noncooperation with proposed UN programs. This kind of bargaining power is still important for a country like the United States, whose cooperation may be essential to the effective functioning of particular economic programs.

The discussion of pressure tactics might convey the picture of a superpower whipping its "friends" into line by effective use of threats and promises. Within the Soviet bloc this may be true: the Socialist states still have great voting solidarity with one another. But unfortunately for the superpower image, the Soviet Union has never had enough reliable friends to constitute anything close to a UN majority and the days of a dependable U.S.-led majority have faded into history. As Table 3–4 indicates, except for Western Europe, no regional group of states votes with the United States on contested votes even half of the time. In point of fact, neither the Soviet Union nor the United States has consistently voted with the majority as often as most members. A tabulation of majority agreement scores for seventy-nine resolutions adopted by roll-call votes during the 1954, 1959, and 1962 sessions of the Assembly shows that the United States voted in the minority more often than did 93 of the 110 member states and that only 4 members had a poorer win-loss record than the Soviet Union.[25] More recently the position of the United States has grown even worse, as judged by percentage agreement with the majority. For the 1954, 1959, and 1962 sessions the United States voted with the majority 71 percent of the time, as compared with 58 percent for the Soviet Union. During the 1971–75 regular sessions of the Assembly the agreement score for the United States dropped below 40 percent, while the Soviet figure rose to 65 percent.[26] In the 1980s U.S. agreement

TABLE 3–5 _____

U.S. and Soviet Union Percentage
Agreement with the Majority, UN General
Assembly Roll-Call Votes, Regular Plenary
Sessions, 1946–1985

	Percent Agreement with Majority	
Years	United States	Soviet Union
1946–50	74.0	34.1
1951–55	60.1	52.4
1956–60	72.5	47.2
1961–65	54.5	54.7
1966–70	43.9	59.4
1971–75	38.9	65.1
1976–80	32.6	67.4
1981–85	14.3	79.3

SOURCE: Roll call voting data obtained from
Inter-University Consortium for Political Research,
Ann Arbor, Michigan.

with the majority on recorded roll-call votes has fallen below 15 percent. The U.S.
decline and the corresponding rise in Soviet agreement with the Assembly majority
are shown in Table 3–5 and Figure 3–4. The improved Soviet position is not the
result of Soviet leadership initiatives or of pressures effectively exerted on smaller
states. It reflects mainly the growing dominance of the anticolonial majority, with
which the Soviet Union has been able to make common cause.[27]

Clearly, the superpowers have a monopoly neither of pressure tactics nor of influence within the United Nations. Some of the most effective participants in the UN
political process come from the Non-Aligned Movement and the Group of 77, which
now consistently determine the outcome of Assembly voting. Intragroup pressures
stemming from trade, aid, and security relationships, or from political, ideological,
and cultural affinities, or from appeals to regional or group solidarity, are an important component of that effectiveness.

Size is a factor in a state's influence. It is easier for a large country to devote the
resources necessary to maintain active, well-informed representation at the United
Nations. But even small countries may play a significant role in the decision process
if their representatives are persuasive, facile at compromise, and adept at fostering
helpful contacts. Officeholding can also enhance the influence of a state through
added prestige, access to information, control over procedure, or the right to participate in the deliberations of select bodies. Election to the Security Council is a sure
ticket to increased influence in UN affairs for the next two years.

The Structure of Winning Coalitions.   The makeup of winning coalitions differs in detail with the nature of the issue, but UN membership patterns now guar-

FIGURE 3–4 _____

Graph of U.S. and Soviet Union Percentage Agreement with the Majority, UN General Assembly Roll-Call Votes, Regular Plenary Sessions, 1946–1985

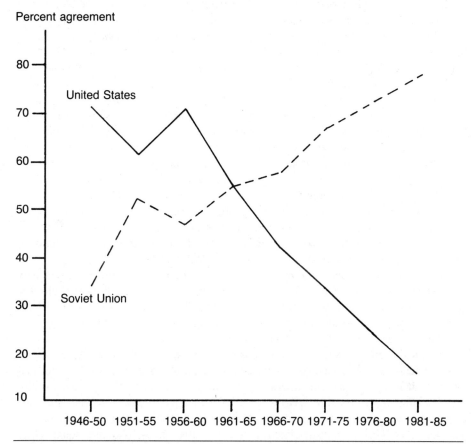

Percent agreement

SOURCE: Roll call voting data obtained from Inter-University Consortium for Political Research, Ann Arbor, Michigan.

antee that any majority must depend heavily on votes from African, Asian, and Latin-American countries. Western industrialized countries win when their views coincide with those of the developing, non-Western majority. The same is true of the Soviet bloc. The rest of the time they lose. On many issues the industrialized states and the superpowers have important leverage in the negotiation process because their cooperation is essential to carrying out proposed resolutions. But the UN issue is resolved at the Third World's threshold of tolerance, not that of the big powers. If compromise is unacceptable, the Third World automatic majority rings up the votes even though nothing much will be changed in the world outside.

On East-West issues the UN majority purport to be nonaligned, although UN speeches and votes indicate more suspicion of the United States than of the Soviet Union. The majority would also like to legislate a massive redistribution of the world's wealth in favor of the poorer countries. They clearly have not bought the Soviet argument that the world is divided between the "progressive" and "imperialist" blocs rather than between the rich and poor countries. In dealing with Israel, South Africa, and the remaining scraps of dismantled colonial empires, Assembly majorities routinely run roughshod over the small minority that may choose to dissent or abstain. On a number of issues, the United States and Israel have stood alone on the losing side of the vote, with some American allies abstaining.

On many questions negotiations are pursued to consensus because of the need for big power cooperation and, perhaps, because some of the questions do not threaten important interests. But the Third World has been willing to use its clout on even the most sensitive political questions when an important principle is at stake. Thus the Assembly did not hesitate to run its majority steamroller over Soviet, U.S., or British objections in condemning military intervention in Afghanistan and Grenada and in urging Britain to negotiate with Argentina on the sovereignty of the Falklands. Resolutions on economic and humanitarian questions also are often negotiated to consensus, but again the sticking point is the Third World's threshold of tolerance. When that point is reached, the voting machine does the rest.

Perhaps the best clue to the current UN political situation is the extreme rarity of close votes. The African, Asian, and developing countries simply overwhelm the opposition when agreement cannot be negotiated. The division of 53 to 30 with 45 abstaining that occurred during the Fortieth Assembly on a vote expressing concern about alleged human rights violations in Iran was a close decision by UN standards. More typical examples from the same session were the vote of 128–8–18 calling for a comprehensive nuclear test ban treaty and a resolution condemning Israeli occupation of the Golan Heights, which was opposed only by Israel, with ten states abstaining. Winning coalitions thus have a remarkable quality of sameness. Nothing can pass that does not minimally satisfy the Non-Aligned Movement or the Group of 77. The fact that Western industrialized states, Socialist states, and individual Third World states slide in and out of the majority is almost incidental to the outcome. With small, poor, developing states winning far more often than large, rich, developed states, the UN General Assembly has become a place where, to parody Thucydides' maxim, "the weak do what they can and the strong suffer what they must."

But that is not quite the whole story. Another view of Assembly voting alignments is presented in Table 3–6. In recent years the United States has prepared an annual report on General Assembly voting practices for the purpose of identifying how frequently other UN members vote with the United States. One feature of the report is identification of the ten "key votes" taken during the preceding session of the Assembly that most significantly affected U.S. interests.[28] Table 3–6 shows the voting alignments, by regional groups, for the ten key issues of the 1985 session of the General Assembly. Although the United States voted with the majority on less than 15 percent of all contested issues in the Fortieth Assembly, the U.S. position prevailed on seven of these ten key votes. This outcome indicates that the United States can still win frequently when it is willing to lobby intensively for a position that is not diametrically opposed to interests of great importance to Third World states.

The growth in the voting power of the Third World states does not necessarily make the General Assembly either a useless or a dangerous place for the others.[29] The Assembly's resolutions have only the force of recommendations. A parliamentary victory may induce temporary euphoria in the winners, and even have some weight as an expression of world opinion, but no dissenting state is bound to comply. Also not to be overlooked is the UN function of harmonizing differences and promoting action in the common interest. The numerous resolutions adopted without objection suggest that differences are frequently harmonized; and widely approved UN programs in such disparate areas as peacekeeping, economic development, and refugee relief indicate that the agreement extends beyond rhetoric. The Assembly undoubtedly could accomplish more if its members behaved better, but it has utility for all of them. At the very least it is a good place for listening and learning.[30]

THE CONSEQUENCES OF UN ACTION

The UN political process normally focuses on the adoption of a resolution. But what are the consequences of this action? Will the resolution be enforced, ignored, acted on in any way? There is no single answer to these questions because UN resolutions are not all alike and much depends on the circumstances. Partial answers will be supplied as particular UN activities are examined in subsequent chapters. Here we will present a more general framework for identifying and explaining the differing consequences of differing UN actions. In developing this analysis, an examination of conditions that give weight to the decisions of national governments will be helpful. These include the sanction of physical force, the authority of law, customary obedience, and the economic and human resources available to carry out programs.

Physical force is important, primarily as a deterrent to law violation. Without it society would be at the mercy of the deviant lawbreaker, vulnerable to a general breakdown in order and respect for law. Physical coercion works best when its use is the exception rather than the rule. A government that must habitually resort to violence to obtain compliance with its rules is unstable at best. In a well-ordered state people obey the law because it is the law. The law is respected because it is legitimate; that is, the people accept the government's right to make it. The legitimacy of the law is also reinforced by customs of compliance. While the state's coercive power may lurk in the background, the daily homespun of obedience is woven from threads of habit, legitimacy, underlying consensus on the goals of the state, and rational recognition that general obedience to law is in the general interest. The viability of a state and its government rests heavily on the capacity to command widespread compliance without the necessity of physical coercion.

The protective and regulatory functions of government require general obedience to law. Governments also perform service functions, and these are dependent not so much on the obedience of the citizenry as on the availability of material resources

TABLE 3–6
Regional Alignments on Ten Key Votes Affecting Important U.S. Interests, Fortieth General Assembly, 1985

Issue	Yes–No–Abstain/Absent*	Regional Group	Yes–No–Abstain/Absent	Vote of United States and Israel	Vote of Soviet Union
1. Kampuchea intervention	114–21–23	Africa,	34–4–12	Yes	No
		Asia and Pacific	29–6–7		
		Americas	30–2–2		
		Eastern Europe	1–9–1		
		Western Europe	18–0–1		
2. Afghanistan intervention	122–19–17	Africa	37–4–9	Yes	No
		Asia and Pacific	31–6–5		
		Americas	32–1–1		
		Eastern Europe	2–8–1		
		Western Europe	18–0–1		
3. Human rights in Afghanistan	80–22–56	Africa	19–4–27	Yes	No
		Asia and Pacific	18–7–17		
		Americas	23–2–9		
		Eastern Europe	1–9–1		
		Western Europe	17–0–2		
4. Human rights in Iran	53–30–75	Africa	8–10–32	Yes	Absent
		Asia and Pacific	6–14–22		
		Americas	20–2–12		
		Eastern Europe	0–3–8		
		Western Europe	17–1–1		
5. Israeli credentials	80–41–37	Africa	17–12–21	Yes	No
		Asia and Pacific	13–21–8		
		Americas	29–2–3		
		Eastern Europe	2–6–3		
		Western Europe	17–0–2		
6. Chemical weapons	112–16–30	Africa	39–1–10	Yes	No
		Asia and Pacific	24–6–12		
		Americas	27–1–6		
		Eastern Europe	1–8–2		
		Western Europe	19–0–0		

#	Issue	Vote	Region	Regional vote		
7.	Criticize United States, Namibia	54–63–41	Africa	23–11–16	No	Yes
			Asia and Pacific	18–13–11		
			Americas	3–18–13		
			Eastern Europe	10–0–1		
			Western Europe	0–19–0		
8.	Criticize United States, Middle East	64–33–61	Africa	22–1–27	No	Yes
			Asia and Pacific	28–4–10		
			Americas	3–10–21		
			Eastern Europe	10–0–1		
			Western Europe	1–16–2		
9.	Criticize U.S. embargo of Nicaragua	91–6–61	Africa	29–2–19	No	Yes
			Asia and Pacific	23–0–19		
			Americas	18–2–14		
			Eastern Europe	11–0–0		
			Western Europe	10–0–9		
10.	UN budget	127–10–21	Africa	48–0–2	No	Yes
			Asia and Pacific	38–0–4		
			Americas	30–0–4		
			Eastern Europe	1–8–2		
			Western Europe	10–0–9		

Synopsis of 10 key issues:

1. Call for the withdrawal of Vietnamese forces from Kampuchea.
2. Call for the withdrawal of Soviet forces from Afghanistan.
3. Resolution expressing concern over human rights violations in Afghanistan.
4. Resolution expressing concern over human rights violations in Iran.
5. Motion to accept Israeli credentials.
6. Resolution calling for strict observance of prohibitions on chemical and biological weapons.
7. Proposal to retain a passage critical of U.S. policy in a resolution on Namibia.
8. Proposal to retain a passage critical of U.S. policy in a resolution on the Middle East.
9. Resolution criticizing the U.S. trade embargo against Nicaragua.
10. Resolution on the 1986–87 biennium UN budget.

*The number of states shown as voting yes or no or as abstaining or absent totals 158. South Africa did not participate in the voting and is not included in the tally of those abstaining or absent. Voting figures given in the text do not include absences with abstentions and thus total something less than 158 in each instance.

SOURCE: United States Department of State, Report to Congress on Voting Practices in the United Nations during 1985 (1986).

and of administrative apparatus for application of the resources to the task at hand. All governments have the power to raise money by various forms of compulsory levy, and all have some type of administrative machinery. Given a satisfactory level of obedience to law, the effectiveness of government action is closely correlated with the availability of taxable resources and the efficiency of public administration. The states of Western Europe and North America, for example, have effective governments not only because of general obedience to law but also because their resources are adequate and their administrative machinery is relatively efficient. In contrast, some of the smaller poorer countries lack resources, administrative capacity, and even an adequate level of obedience to law.

To what extent can the United Nations draw on the sources that give force to decisions of national governments? On its face the UN Charter appears to confer on the United Nations a legal monopoly of physical coercion in international affairs, with the exception of the right to self-defense. The self-defense loophole is vast, however, and in practical terms the United Nations neither has a monopoly of such force nor makes any grandiose claim to it. At best, the United Nations can serve as a catalytic agent for mobilizing international force for UN objectives when enough members are willing to cooperate.

Most UN decisions also lack the force of law. The organization has much authority to recommend, but little to command. Recommendations might be effective if they were supported by a strong tradition of customary obedience, but the United Nations has not yet developed such a tradition. Some UN specialized agencies do much better. The regulations of the Universal Postal Union, for example, are observed with a regularity that would do credit to national administrations. All the elements of customary obedience are there—habit, legitimacy, broad consensus on goals, and recognition of a common interest in international postal operations. As one moves away from purely technical activities to the more political subjects debated by the General Assembly and other UN organs, the degree of customary obedience declines markedly. States have not yet developed habits of indiscriminate compliance with General Assembly recommendations. As a result, compliance is left to rest on a coincidence of national interests in particular UN policies and programs. The action of a UN majority may sometimes create political pressure in favor of compliance, but that is no substitute for the kinds of forces that induce voluntary compliance with national laws.

International organization also stands in a different position from that of national governments in its ability to command financial and other resources. Although standards for budgetary assessments are customarily adhered to, international organizations are ultimately dependent on the resources that individual states are willing to supply, not on what majorities are moved to demand. This should not suggest that the sums raised by contribution are inconsequential. For the 1986–87 biennium a regular UN budget of $1.66 billion was approved, with an additional assessment of $175 million for Middle East peacekeeping, and voluntary contributions for special UN programs (technical assistance, refugee relief, population activities, etc.) exceed a billion dollars annually.[31] Nevertheless, the United Nations must depend on the willingness of members to provide funds. The sale of UN publications and postage stamps does not yet constitute an important source of independent income, and substantial revenues from resources of the common seabed area are yet in the distant future.

The remaining condition of effective action, administrative capability, will be discussed in more detail in the following chapter. Here we may observe that the UN Secretariat has performed reasonably well the administrative tasks imposed on it, while decisions dependent on member state compliance have frequently been dead letters.

Given UN capabilities as we have assessed them, the consequences of UN action may be briefly summarized. Where UN resolutions have initiated programs to be administered by the Secretariat, and members are willing to contribute the necessary resources, the consequences of UN action have been significant. The United Nations has solid accomplishment in areas ranging from research studies to development assistance to peacekeeping operations. On the other hand, where resolutions have depended on compliance by member states, the record is very checkered. In many instances members comply because they are in sympathy with the resolution. Occasionally states are moved to compliance, or a show of compliance, by a desire not to appear out of step with a large UN majority. In numerous other instances UN recommendations are flatly ignored by governments that perceive no self-interested basis—however broadly or narrowly construed—for compliance. No UN majority could persuade the Soviet Union to withdraw its troops from Afghanistan or induce the United States to pull out of Grenada before either was ready. No amount of repeated UN urging has yet moved Israel to give up control of Jerusalem or the West Bank. In the absence of rules having the force of law, compelling habits of obedience, and physical sanctions to support the rules, the United Nations must rely on a convergence of national interests to secure compliance.

Identifying limitations on UN action does not mean that UN decisions are inconsequential. Resources exceeding $4.5 billion were available for disposition by the United Nations and its related agencies in 1985. This sum is small in comparison with the $900 billion 1985 budget of the United States, but it is a good deal larger than the annual governmental expenditures of many small states.[32] As we have noted, states also render varying amounts of compliance with UN recommendations on a voluntary basis.

There is still another way in which UN resolutions affect international politics, without the expenditure of financial resources and even without the voluntary cooperation of states to which a resolution may be directed. More than two decades ago Inis L. Claude, Jr., observed that the United Nations "has come to be regarded, and used, as a dispenser of politically significant approval and disapproval of the claims, policies, and actions of states."[33] He called this phenomenon "collective legitimization" and argued that statesmen took it seriously. "A state may hesitate to pursue a policy that has engendered the formal disapproval of the Assembly," he suggested, "not because it is prepared to give the will of that organ priority over its national interest, but because it believes that the adverse judgment of the Assembly makes the pursuit of that policy disadvantageous to the national interest."[34] More recently former UN Ambassador Jeane J. Kirkpatrick, a persistent critic of UN decision making, made a similar point in explaining why UN decisions have significance for the conduct of foreign affairs:

> U.N. votes define "world opinion" on major issues. Since there are no other arenas in which all the countries of the world express their opinions on policy, the decisions of the U.N. bodies are widely taken as the most valid expression of "world opinion."[35]

UN resolutions, by the very fact of their adoption, become intangible resources for their supporters and liabilities for their opponents. UN decisions may not confer the legitimacy of law, but they do confer the legitimacy of majority approval in a body representing virtually every sovereign state. The legitimizing force of a resolution varies according to the size and composition of the voting majority and the forcefulness and clarity of the language used. Specificity cuts sharper than ambiguity. A unanimous Security Council resolution is weightier than one on which several permanent members abstain. Overwhelming approval in the Assembly is more convincing than a two-vote margin. A series of resolutions reaffirming a position will have more impact than an isolated case. Repeated UN reaffirmations of support for decolonization, aid to developing countries, and human rights have helped to make such concepts almost articles of faith (if not of unfailing practice) in the global system. Even states that deny the validity of particular UN pronouncements are sometimes reluctant to violate them, or appear to violate them, in tacit recognition of the significance of collective legitimization.

The United Nations is not the center of the international system. Its resources are limited; its words are not law; its mandates can seldom be enforced against an unwilling state. But its decisions do make a difference. Funds are raised and expended; economic and social programs are launched; peacekeeping missions are maintained. Much voluntary cooperation is encouraged. And no state can totally disregard UN processes without paying some penalty, or losing some benefit, in its relations with other states.

NOTES

1. Political considerations sometimes enter into the selection process, which requires a recommendation by the ECOSOC Committee on Nongovernmental Organizations. In the Committee's 1985 session, 48 of 105 applicants received a favorable recommendation. The Committee deferred until its 1987 meeting the requests of a number of human rights organizations with headquarters in the West. *New York Times,* March 31, 1985, sec. 1, p. 7.

2. These have included UN world conferences on Population (1974), Food (1974), International Women's Year (1975), Human Settlements (1976), World Employment (1976), Water (1977), Desertification (1977), Racial Discrimination (1978), Technical Cooperation among Developing Countries (1978), Agrarian Reform and Rural Development (1979), Science and Technology for Development (1979), UN Decade for Women (1980), Energy (1981), Outer Space (1982), Palestine (1983), Racial Discrimination (1983), Population (1984), Fisheries (1984), Status of Women (1985), and Peaceful Uses of Nuclear Energy (1986).

3. See Chiang Pei-heng, *Non-Governmental Organizations at the United Nations: Identity, Role, and Function* (New York: Praeger Publishers, 1981), especially pp. 230–34.

4. Some observers believe that NGOs have had an especially important influence on UN deliberations in the field of human rights. See David P. Forsythe, "The United Nations and Human Rights, 1945–1985," *Political Science Quarterly* 100, no. 2 (Summer 1985), pp. 261–62, and sources cited there.

5. See John Gerard Ruggie, "The United States and the United Nations: Toward a New Realism," *International Organization* 39, no. 2 (Spring 1985), pp. 354–56.

6. In 1986 President Ronald Reagan ordered the Soviet Union to reduce its mission staff from 275 (the number in March 1986) to 170 by April 1, 1988. The President expressed concern about "inappropriate activities" by Soviet mission personnel. *New York Times,* March 8, 1986, sec. 1, p. 1.

7. Seymour Maxwell Finger, *Your Man at the UN* (New York: New York University Press, 1980), p. 20.

8. As Berridge points out, the United Nations is not the small states' only alternative to exchanging ambassadors. Other possibilities are unilateral representation (receiving but not sending an ambassador), multiple accreditation (accrediting an ambassador in one country to others in the area), third-country representation (communicating with a second country through the embassy of a third), and joint representation (two governments accrediting a single envoy). Berridge concludes that permanent UN representation is "useful but—in normal circumstances—not indispensable to the bilateral diplomacy of small states." It cannot adequately replace direct representation in countries most important to small states, but "it helps them in their dealings with states which lie outside this inner core, especially in the forming of propaganda alliances; it provides for dramatic symbolic assertion of the state; and it can double as representation to one of the world's two great powers, the United States." G. W. Berridge, "'Old Diplomacy' in New York," in *Diplomacy at the UN,* ed. Berridge and A. Jennings (New York: St. Martin's Press, 1985), p. 180.

9. Johan Kaufmann, *United Nations Decision Making* (Alphen aan den Rijn: Sijthoff & Noordhoff, 1980), p. 110.

10. The problem is practical rather than legal. If a state joins the organization, it consents to the decision rules of the organization. Thus it is not bound without its consent. In practice, however, states are very reluctant to assume particular obligations to which they object even if they have given general assent to the voting procedures.

11. See Robert E. Riggs, "The United Nations and the Development of International Law," *Brigham Young University Law Review,"* 1985, no. 3, pp. 411–52.

12. Economic sanctions were imposed on the Ian Smith regime in Rhodesia in 1966 and again in 1968. An embargo on arms shipments to South Africa was ordered in 1977. See discussion of UN sanctions in Chapter 5.

13. For a good argument that the Security Council's authority to make legally binding decisions is not limited to enforcement action under Chapter VII of the Charter, see Rosalyn Higgins, "The Advisory Opinion on Namibia: Which UN Resolutions are Binding under Article 25 of the Charter," *International and Comparative Law Quarterly,* 21, part 2 (April 1972), pp. 270–86. In practice, most Security Council resolutions not based on Chapter VII have been treated by the Security Council and by UN members as hortatory rather than obligatory.

14. As enumerated in Article 18, such questions include

    recommendations with respect to the maintenance of international peace and security, the election of the nonpermanent members of the Security Council, the election of members of the Economic and Social Council, the election of members of the Trusteeship Council . . . , the admission of new Members to the United Nations, the suspension of the rights and privileges of membership, the expulsion of Members, questions relating to the operation of the trusteeship system, and budgetary questions.

15. Decisions in the Economic and Social Council, the Trusteeship Council, and subordinate UN committees and commissions are made by a simple majority of the members present and voting,

but their decisions are all subject to review by the General Assembly, with its two-thirds requirement for important questions.

16. Of 353 resolutions and decisions adopted by the 1985 General Assembly, 201 were decided without a vote or by consensus. In the 1984 Assembly, 187 issues were resolved by consensus and 153 by vote. See U.S. Department of State, *Report to Congress on Voting Practices in the United Nations,* submitted pursuant to Public Law 99–190 and Public Law 98–164, June 6, 1986, p. I-3; and U.S. Department of State, *Report to Congress on Voting Practices in the United Nations,* submitted pursuant to Public Law 98–151 and Public Law 98–164, May 20, 1985, p. 3.

17. Leo Pasvolsky, "The United Nations in Action," in *Edmund J. James Lectures on Government* (Urbana: University of Illinois Press, 1951), pp. 80–81.

18. Robert E. Riggs, "The United States and Diffusion of Power in the Security Council," *International Studies Quarterly* 22, no. 4 (December 1978), p. 542.

19. The "others" are Canada, New Zealand, and Australia.

20. See Robert Mortimore, *The Third World Coalition in International Politics* (Boulder, Colo.: Westview Press, 1984).

21. See Richard L. Jackson, *The Non-Aligned, the UN, and the Superpowers* (New York: Praeger Publishers, 1983).

22. The term *Third World* does not carry the connotation of an institution or an organized lobby, such as the Group of 77, the NAM, or another UN caucusing group. It is a looser concept, coined in France during the early 1950s, having reference to less developed states generally. Since most such states are in the southern hemisphere, they are sometimes collectively designated as the "South" in a North/South or developed/underdeveloped classification of the world.

23. Jeane J. Kirkpatrick, *The Reagan Phenomenon—and Other Speeches on Foreign Policy* (Washington, D.C.: American Enterprise Institute for Public Policy Research, 1983), p. 83.

24. Foreign aid is usually too blunt an instrument to apply effectively to UN votes. As Finger observed in 1983, "Adjusting the aid spigot to accord with U.N. votes can be difficult, given all the other factors that must be considered. For example, the Soviet Union votes with the United States nearly as often as Jordan does, and Zimbabwe, the recipient of the largest U.S. aid program in Sub-Saharan Africa, votes with the United States less often than Libya." Seymour Maxwell Finger, "The Reagan-Kirkpatrick Policies and the United Nations," *Foreign Affairs* 62, no. 2 (Winter 1983–84), p. 442.

25. Catherine Senf Manno, "Majority Decisions and Minority Responses in the UN General Assembly," *Journal of Conflict Resolution,* March 1966, p. 8.

26. Riggs, "United States and Diffusion of Power," p. 525.

27. This state of affairs led UN Ambassador Jeane J. Kirkpatrick to observe, with perhaps some degree of overstatement, that the United States had no influence at all in the Assembly. In a speech at Georgetown University, June 14, 1983, she said of her UN experience: "It soon became clear to me that I was watching what political scientists call power processes—the processes that Harold Lasswell characterized as who gets what, when, and how. I observed that some countries exercise a very large share of control, other countries have some influence, and some have none at all. I regret to tell you that the United States is—or long has been—in the last category." Kirkpatrick, "The United Nations as a Political System: A Practicing Political Scientist's Insights into U.N. Politics," *World Affairs* 146, no. 4 (Spring 1984), pp. 358–59.

28. E.g., U.S. Department of State, *Report to Congress on Voting Practices in the United Nations,* submitted pursuant to Public Law 99–190 and Public Law 98–164, June 6, 1986.

29. At least two book titles have referred to the United Nations as "a dangerous place"—Abraham Yeselson and Anthony Gaglione, *A Dangerous Place: The United Nations as a Weapon in World Politics* (New York: Grossman Publishers, 1974); and Daniel Patrick Moynihan, *A Dangerous Place* (New York: Berkley Books, 1980). Donald J. Puchala is perhaps closer to the mark: "Those who have called the United Nations 'a dangerous place' are correct only in that it is a microcosm of the cleavages, contentions, insecurities, and volatilities of a very dangerous world." Puchala, "American Interests and the United Nations," *Political Science Quarterly* 97, no. 4 (Winter 1982–83), pp. 571–88.

30. A former U.S. diplomat with lengthy UN experience has emphasized the importance of the quiet diplomatic interchanges:

    "Speeches and resolutions are not all that happen at the United Nations, even though they consume the bulk of its time and are most visible to the public. Most speeches and General Assembly resolutions are soon forgotten. Important actions can be taken only by governments, and influence on them can usually be effected by informal conversations and a persuasive ear rather than public rhetoric and votes. Indeed, in my own 15 years at the United Nations, I found these informal conversations more important and productive than public rhetoric." (Finger, *Your Man at the UN,* pp. 438–39).

31. Contributions to all agencies within the UN system amounted to about $4.5 billion in 1985. The major lending agencies within the system—the World Bank group, the International Monetary Fund, and the International Fund for Agricultural Development—have income from previous lending operations which relieves dependence on national contributions.

32. For example, total governmental expenditures for Belize during 1984 were $97 million; for Cyprus, $515 million; for Dominica, $27 million; and for Fiji, $299 million. *The Europa Yearbook, 1986,* vol. 1 (London: Europa Publications, 1986), pp. 487, 823, 887, 980. Dollar equivalents are calculated from exchange rate figures.

33. Claude, *The Changing United Nations* (New York: Random House, 1967), p. 73.

34. Ibid., p. 93.

35. "Testimony of U.S. Permanent Representative to the United Nations Jeane J. Kirkpatrick before the Senate Foreign Operations Subcommittee of the Senate Appropriations Committee, March 25, 1985," reproduced in U.S. Department of State, *Report to Congress on Voting Practices in the United Nations,* submitted pursuant to Public Law 98–151 and Public Law 98–164, May 20, 1985, p. 3.

    Kirkpatrick further observes: "U.N. votes focus world attention on some problems and away from others and, in the process, greatly influence the definition of what constitutes a problem. Thus, repeated actions of the General Assembly and the Security Council define Israeli presence in Lebanon as a pressing international problem, while inaction defines Syria's larger military presence as not a problem requiring world attention." Ibid.

SELECTED READINGS

ALKER, HAYWARD R., and BRUCE M. RUSSETT. *World Politics in the General Assembly.* New Haven: Yale University Press, 1965.

AMERI, HOUSHANG. *Politics and Process in the Specialized Agencies of the United Nations.* Aldershot, Eng.: Gower Publishing, 1982.

ARANGIO-RUIZ, GAETANO. *The United Nations Declaration on Friendly Relations and the System of the Sources of International Law.* Alphen aan den Rijn: Sijthoff & Noordhoff, 1979.

BAEHR, PETER R. *The Role of a Delegation in the General Assembly.* Occasional paper no. 9. New York: Carnegie Endowment for International Peace, 1970.

BAILEY, SIDNEY D. *Voting in the Security Council.* Bloomington: Indiana University Press, 1969.

BEICHMAN, ARNOLD. *The "Other" State Department: The United States Mission to the United Nations—Its Role in the Making of Foreign Policy.* New York: Basic Books, 1968.

CHIANG PEI-HENG. *Non-Governmental Organizations at the United Nations.* New York: Praeger Publishers, 1981.

Cox, Robert W.; Harold K. Jacobson; and others. *The Anatomy of Influence: Decision Making in International Organization*. New Haven: Yale University Press, 1973.

Finger, Seymour M. *American Ambassadors at the U.N.* 2nd ed. New York: Holmes & Meier Publishers, 1986.

Franck, Thomas M. *Nation against Nation: What Happened to the U.N. Dream and What the U.S. Can Do about It*. New York: Oxford University Press, 1985.

Hovet, Thomas, Jr. *Bloc Politics in the United Nations*. Cambridge, Mass.: Harvard University Press, 1960.

Jackson, Richard L. *The Non-Aligned the UN and the Superpowers*. New York: Praeger Publishers, 1983.

Kaufmann, Johan. *United Nations Decision Making*. Alphen aan den Rijn: Sijthoff & Noordhoff, 1980.

Kirkpatrick, Jeane J. *The Reagan Phenomenon—and Other Speeches on Foreign Policy*. Washington, D.C.: American Enterprise Institute, 1983.

Koo, Wellington, Jr. *Voting Procedures in International Political Organizations*. New York: Columbia University Press, 1947.

McWhinney, Edward. *United Nations Law Making*. New York: Holmes & Meier Publishers, 1984.

Mortimore, Robert. *The Third World Coalition in International Politics*. Boulder, Colo.: Westview Press, 1984.

Moynihan, Patrick. *A Dangerous Place*. New York: Berkley Books, 1980.

Peterson, M. J. *The General Assembly in World Politics*. Winchester, Mass.: Allen & Unwin, 1986.

Riches, Cromwell A. *Majority Rule in International Organization*. Baltimore: Johns Hopkins University Press, 1940.

Riggs, Robert E. *Politics in the United Nations: A Study of United States Influence in the General Assembly*. Urbana: University of Illinois Press, 1958. Reprinted Greenwood Press, 1984.

Rubinstein, Alvin Z., and George Ginsburgs, eds. *Soviet and American Policies in the United Nations*. New York: New York University Press, 1971.

Sauvant, Karl P. *The Group of 77: Evolution, Structure, Organization*. Dobbs Ferry, N.Y.: Oceana Publications, 1981.

Stoessinger, John G. *The United Nations and the Superpowers*. 4th ed. New York: Random House, 1977.

Yemin, Edward. *Legislative Powers in the United Nations and Specialized Agencies*. Leyden: A. W. Sijthoff, 1969.

Yeselson, Abraham, and Anthony Gaglione. *A Dangerous Place: The United Nations as a Weapon in World Politics*. New York: Grossman Publishers, 1974.

4

Politics and the UN Secretariat

Modern international organization was born with the creation of the permanent international secretariat. Without a staff to administer its affairs between meetings, an international organization is little more than a series of conferences. With a permanent secretariat, the organization is no longer just an arena where states and other actors play out their roles but is itself an actor on the international scene. A permanent staff creates the capacity to gather and disseminate information, monitor state compliance with rules and recommendations of the organization, and provide services to member states and their people.[1] Within its sphere of operation, the organization becomes a continuing influence on states in their relations with one another and often in their domestic policies.

Secretariat employees perform many tasks that have little direct effect on the substance of UN decisions or the relations of states. Internal housekeeping activities, such as personnel management, financial administration, property maintenance, and supply procurement, are important institutionally but usually politically neutral. So also are conference servicing activities. Hundreds of language specialists are employed to interpret speeches at UN meetings, often simultaneously, into each of six official languages—English, French, Russian, Spanish, Chinese, and Arabic—and to prepare documentation in the same six languages.[2] The United Nations conducts its own postal service, including the issuance of postage stamps, and maintains a large-scale publishing operation to supply the world with reports, records of meetings, and other UN publications. These services are useful, in some degree essential, but for the most part they do not give rise to political controversy among states.

But secretariats also do much that is politically significant. At meetings of the United Nations and other international agencies, the staff is concerned not only with translation and documentation but also with the substantive problems being discussed. Whether the subject is human rights, social welfare, disarmament, environmental protection, or the pacific settlement of disputes, staff members are assigned duties of information gathering, research, and reporting. Staff reports are often the basis for discussion and decision in meetings of UN bodies. Specialists in economic development, international law, or specific political problem areas must be prepared to advise the Secretary-General and, on occasion, national delegates. Countries lacking qualified experts available for service with national UN delegations sometimes rely heavily on the expertise of secretariat officials. In organizations whose principal business is supplying technical assistance and other services to member states, the budget proposal prepared by the secretariat dominates the organization's agenda.

Even internal matters such as staff recruitment can become intensely political as member states intervene to secure secretariat positions, especially high-level positions, for their nationals. Budgeting in any international agency is also an intensely political process. Staff members and governmental representatives consult extensively in negotiating a budget that will satisfy their special interests and yet win the necessary majority of votes. Budget battles are ultimately resolved by governments, but secretariats are intimately involved in the political give-and-take.

Before considering the political role of the UN Secretariat in detail, this chapter will briefly examine the origin of the international civil service and some of the special problems that it raises for those who serve in it. The discussion will then turn to the UN Secretariat, with emphasis on political problems associated with personnel recruitment and the difficulties of preserving staff independence from national influences. A final section will elaborate the principal theme of the chapter—the role of secretariats in organizational decision making and their impact on international politics. The discussion will center on the United Nations and its Secretary-General, but a broader perspective will be added by occasional comparison with other international organizations.

THE INTERNATIONAL CIVIL SERVICE

Origin

The international civil service dates only from the establishment of the League of Nations and the International Labor Organization at the close of World War I. Before that time the permanent bureaus or secretariats of such technical organizations as the Universal Postal Union were not international in composition. The personnel were typically citizens of the headquarters host state, and often they were national officials on leave from their normal assignments to serve the international organization.

The League Covenant made no express provision for internationalization of the staff. It simply stated, "The Secretariat shall comprise a Secretary-General and such secretaries and staff as may be required." To Sir Eric Drummond, first Secretary-General of the League, goes the credit for insisting on a truly international secretariat. The decision to establish a multinational civil service recruited individually rather than as contingents of national representatives has been called, in an authoritative history of the League, "one of the most important events in the history of international politics."[3]

Codifying the experience of the League and the ILO, the UN Charter expressly provided for a secretariat that was to be appointed by a Secretary-General as its administrative head, recruited individually on the basis of merit, and responsible in official conduct only to the organization. These provisions embodied the ideals of the international civil service—*efficiency*, *loyalty* to the organization, *independence* from national pressures, and *impartiality* toward all member states. Wide geographic distribution of appointments was recognized as an important subsidiary principle. Other intergovernmental organizations have looked to these standards and have applied them to an ever-growing international public service. At their peak the staff of the League and ILO together numbered scarcely more than a thousand. In the present UN system, including the specialized agencies and related intergovernmental organizations, the number of secretariat employees has grown to more than 50,000.

Problems of Diversity and Political Support

An international secretariat faces the problems that bureaucracies face everywhere—problems of internal decision making, communication, lines of authority and responsibility, and recruitment and retention of competent personnel. But compared with national civil services, an international secretariat has special problems stemming from its political environment.

One obvious challenge is to integrate within a single administrative machine the diverse attitudes, tongues, backgrounds, and abilities of personnel recruited from the four corners of the earth.[4] The central problem here is the absence of a shared political culture. A national civil service operates within a relatively homogeneous value framework. There is broad consensus on the functions of government, the means by which political decisions are reached, and the limits of legitimate governmental authority. With no shared global political culture, the secretariat lacks both the guidelines that would make its own choice of actions easier and the legitimacy that would make its functions acceptable to its clientele. In any governmental system the conduct of administration requires some bargaining and negotiation with the clientele to be served or regulated. In international administration the lack of shared political values greatly widens the range of issues that must be negotiated. Even when norms for specific activities are developed through practice, such as standards for technical assistance programs, the process is complicated by the need to adapt standards to differing national contexts.

The international secretariat also lacks sustaining links with sources of political support that national civil services enjoy. At the apex of the national administrative structure is a president or prime minister who is himself a very influential figure. In the United States the President draws power from his constitutional prerogatives, his control of the executive branch, his electoral mandate, and his relationship with his political party and other influential groups within the society. The administrative departments work under his direction and draw political support from that relationship. Parliamentary systems have the further advantage of a chief executive who speaks for a dominant political party or coalition within the national legislature. In addition, administrative agencies often receive support from groups within the community that benefit from agency services.

In contrast, the links that join an international secretariat to sources of power within the international system are more fragile and tenuous. The typical secretary-general or director-general has very limited political prerogatives, no significant ties with a public constituency, no broad electoral mandate, and scarcely anything resembling leadership of a dominant political party or legislative coalition. The executive head can cultivate the support of governments within his organization. But governments change, as do their UN representatives, and governments are motivated very little by a sense of loyalty, obligation, or feelings of support for a UN Secretary-General.

Sometimes international bureaucracies can develop important ties of mutual interest with their counterparts in national ministries of government. Periodic personal contacts at international meetings and regular communication between staff of national and international agencies concerned with similar problems can lead to mutually supportive behavior. Thus officials in national ministries of health may feel a vested interest in the work of the World Health Organization, or national finance ministries may provide support for the work of the International Monetary Fund. Such relationships are more likely to be developed in technical, relatively noncontroversial fields and in economic and social activities rather than matters affecting national security.

Some international secretariats, such as UNESCO, the International Labor Organization, the International Civil Aviation Organization, the World Bank, and even the United Nations, have mutually beneficial relationships with private groups; but in range and intensity of support, they cannot be compared to the agency-clientele relationships that sustain national bureaucracies.

THE UN SECRETARIAT

The UN Secretariat is by far the largest of any global international agency, with more than 25,000 authorized positions in 1986, exclusive of the specialized agencies (see Table 4–1). It also suffers from most of the weaknesses that have overtaken the international civil service.

Recruiting the UN Official

The UN Secretariat, like a national bureaucracy, faces the constant problem of recruiting competent employees to fill available positions. For "general service" or "manual worker" positions, the problems of recruitment are much the same as those faced by other employers. Such jobs are commonly filled by local recruitment without regard to geographic distribution and mostly with nationals of the host country.

TABLE 4-1
Staff of the UN Secretariat and other UN Organs, June 30, 1986

Organization	Regular Budget				Extrabudgetary Sources				Grand Total
	Professional and Above	Technical Assistance Project Personnel	General Service and Others	Total	Professional and Above	Technical Assistance Project Personnel	General Service and Others	Total	
UN Secretariat	3,553	145	6,984	10,682	322	989	2,228	3,539	14,221
UN Development Program	—	—	—	—	603	689	4,040	5,332	5,332
UN High Commission for Refugees	113	3	166	282	336	149	1,022	1,507	1,789
UNICEF	—	—	—	—	950	344	2,351	3,645	3,645
UN Institute for Training and Research	—	—	—	—	15	5	21	41	41
UNRWA*	14	—	2	16	69	—	8	77	93
International Trade Center	59	—	76	135	18	79	54	151	286
International Civil Service Commission	3	—	25	48	—	—	—	—	48
International Court of Justice	5	—	26	41	—	—	1	1	41
United Nations University	—	—	—	—	45	5	79	129	129
Total	3,777	148	7,279	11,204	2,358	2,260	9,803	14,421	25,625

*The UN Relief and Works Agency for Palestine Refugees (UNRWA) also has 16,669 area personnel.

SOURCE: Adapted from table C, Composition of the Secretariat, Report of the Secretary-General, UN Document A/41/627, September 20, 1986, p. 8.

About two thirds of the employees at UN headquarters in New York and Geneva fall into these categories.

For higher-level employees, the search for talent is limited to persons with the necessary language skills and the willingness to live in an alien environment. There is also the very serious problem of reconciling competence with the demands of wide geographic distribution. This applies to positions at the professional level and higher, except for language specialists. In 1986 they numbered about 2,750, less than 11 percent of the UN Secretariat, but clearly the most important as to pay, perquisites, prestige, and responsibility.

According to Article 101 of the UN Charter, the "paramount consideration" in recruitment and conditions of service should be "the necessity of securing the highest standards of efficiency, competence, and integrity." Article 101 further provides that "due regard shall be paid to the importance of recruiting the staff on as wide a geographical basis as possible," but the Charter makes this clearly secondary to the merit principle. In practice, the Secretary-General has tried to place efficiency first, with substantial support from the United States and countries of Western Europe, which have always been heavily represented in the UN Secretariat. Areas less well represented, especially Eastern Europe and newer states of Asia and Africa, have fought for the principle of equitable geographic distribution as though it were the paramount consideration. They contend that efficiency in the broader sense is not possible unless all national viewpoints are adequately represented in the Secretariat.

Initially the principal basis for geographic distribution was budgetary contribution. In 1962 the General Assembly adopted a formula that took into account membership (one to five per member state regardless of other factors) and population, in addition to budgetary contribution. Desirable ranges for each country and region, derived from the formula, were to serve as a guide to the Secretary-General in the recruitment of staff. Since then, greater weight has been given to the membership factor, which now places the minimum desirable range at two to fourteen. The majority of UN members, being small and poor, fall within this range.[5] The distribution of such posts in 1986, by geographic region, is presented in Table 4–2. Most governments have come to regard the ranges as entitlements rather than guidelines, and some have generated great political pressure on the Secretary-General to conform. Even for regions within or very close to their desirable ranges, merely maintaining the balance is a drag on recruitment by merit, and individual countries continue to press the Secretary-General for the maximum number of posts. The Assembly has kept up the pressure by setting targets for the appointment of candidates from underrepresented countries.[6] Ironically, the most grossly overrepresented countries are themselves from developing areas. This is possible because no hiring disadvantage is imposed on overrepresented states from underrepresented regions.[7]

In recent years the developing countries have gone even farther, demanding not only overall geographic equity but also equitable representation (i.e., more positions for their nationals) in the senior and policy-formulating posts.[8] There is ample precedent for politicizing recruitment among top-echelon UN administrators. The initial

TABLE 4–2 _____
UN Staff in Posts Subject to Geographic Distribution, Classified by
Region, June 30, 1986

Region	Desirable Range*	Number of Staff	Percent of All Posts	Region Budget Assessment (percent)
Africa	346–469	442	16.1	1.66
Asia and the Pacific	468–634	460	16.8	14.67
Eastern Europe	303–410	273	10.0	15.53
Western Europe	589–797	619	22.6	32.87
Latin America	198–268	224	8.2	4.11
Middle East	149–202	131	4.8	2.94
North America and Caribbean	496–671	561	20.5	28.22
Other (stateless, nonmembers)	—	30	1.1	—
Total	—	2,740	100.0	100.00

*In 1986 the desirable ranges were recalculated on an assumption of 3,000 posts subject to geographical distribution rather than the figure of 3,350 posts previously established by General Assembly Resolution 35/210 of December 17, 1980. This was done because the UN Industrial Development Organization (UNIDO) became a specialized agency and its staff—including 347 occupied posts which had been subject to geographical distribution—was formally separated from the UN Secretariat on January 1, 1986.

SOURCE: Adapted from tables in *Composition of the Secretariat, Report of the Secretary-General,* UN Document A/41/627 September 20, 1986.

distribution of top-level posts was determined by informal agreement among the permanent members of the Security Council to have a national of each of them appointed as an Assistant Secretary-General. The Soviet Union was specifically awarded the top post in political and Security Council affairs and has held it ever since, except for a few years in the mid-1950s. France, Britain, the United States, and China have also staked their respective claims to a position at the highest administrative level.

Intimately related to geographic distribution is the problem of the fixed-term appointment. Short-term appointments are appropriate for positions at the highest levels where some rotation is desirable, for needed specialists who are not willing to make a career of UN service, and for posts that are temporary because of the nature of the work (for example, technical assistance projects). Nevertheless, a career service is the heart of the international civil service ideal. With the large-scale admission of new members after 1955, the career ideal came into conflict with the principle of equitable geographic distribution. Many new members did not have a large pool of qualified candidates whom they could afford to lose permanently; but they wanted to be "represented," and they were willing to send persons who would

TABLE 4–3 _____

Fixed-Term Appointments and Appointments of Women in Posts
Subject to Geographic Distribution, Classified by Region,
June 30, 1986

Region	Fixed-Term Staff		Female Staff		Total Staff from Region
	Number	Percent	Number	Percent	
Africa	171	38.7	48	10.9	442
Asia and the Pacific	135	29.3	134	29.1	460
Eastern Europe	269	98.5	15	5.5	273
Western Europe	187	30.2	177	28.6	619
Latin America	69	30.8	63	28.1	224
Middle East	44	37.0	21	16.0	131
North America and Caribbean	107	19.1	209	37.3	561
Other (stateless, nonmembers)	8	26.7	9	30.0	30
Total	990	36.1	676	24.7	2,740

SOURCE: Adapted from tables in *Composition of the Secretariat, Report of the Secretary-General,* UN Document A/41/627 September 20, 1986.

return after a short period, often better qualified because of the UN experience. Thus fixed-term appointments of one to five years became a tool for achieving desired geographic distribution of UN jobs. The result has been an increase in the percentage of fixed-term appointments from about 10 percent in 1955 to about 25 percent in 1965 to more than 35 percent in 1986. (See Table 4–3.)*

The developing countries do not bear the sole responsibility for this trend. East European states, with the exception of Yugoslavia, have always insisted on fixed-term appointments for their nationals. They reject the civil service ideal of placing loyalty to international organization above loyalty to country, and they are unwilling to run the risk that national ties will become attenuated through long residence abroad. They also oppose a career service on principle, insisting that an international civil servant is less effective if he has lost touch with life in his own country.[9]

Even though governments may press for equitable geographic distribution of UN positions and urge an increase in fixed-term appointments, the Secretary-General has ultimate responsibility for individual appointments. Under the UN Charter hiring is supposed to be between him (or his subordinates) and the individual applicant. In fact, governments frequently sponsor the candidacy of particular nationals not only

_____

*To its credit, the Assembly has also given priority in recent years to the recruitment of women. See resolutions cited in note 6. The 1986 percentage of women in positions subject to geographic distribution, classified by region, is shown in Table 4–3.

for higher-level posts but for posts at lower professional levels as well. The Secretary-General is entitled to resist their importunings, but this is often difficult. Sometimes geographic considerations and government pressures override all else, and government-sponsored candidates are hired with little effort to canvass the field of available applicants. Announcements of vacancies are commonly sent to governments, universities, professional societies, and other agencies where persons with needed qualifications may be contacted. But if a department already has a particular person in mind for the job, the distribution of announcements may be limited to UN permanent missions and a few international organizations. Numerous appointments, apparently, are made with no circulation of a vacancy announcement at all.[10]

The recruitment of able personnel is also affected by conditions of service, which appear to have deteriorated in recent years. Staff salaries thus far have been maintained above national levels,[11] but large-contributor efforts to hold the line on budgetary increases have reduced career advancement prospects through periodic hiring freezes and staff reductions in some areas. A much greater problem is the politicization of personnel decisions. Promotion prospects for the career civil servant are necessarily limited when many higher-level positions are filled from the outside, frequently by fixed-term appointments. When an increasing proportion of the staff is on fixed-term appointment, the service becomes that much less career oriented. Perhaps most debilitating is the introduction of geographic considerations into the promotion process, with occasional overt interventions by governments on behalf of particular candidates. When extraneous factors such as national origin and political influence determine promotion, the whole concept of a career service based on merit is undermined.[12]

Loyalty, Independence, Impartiality

The international civil service ideal requires that national loyalties be transcended by a primary professional loyalty to the international organization and the cause of international cooperation. The question is often raised whether international officials can and do make this transition in fact. The Swiss scholar William Rappard, speaking as a delegate to the League Assembly in 1930, was not too hopeful. He observed that "truly international officials are possible but very difficult to find. You have to transform into devoted servants of the international community men who are naturally attached to their native soil, and this is almost a miracle." A much less equivocal conclusion was later voiced by a distinguished group of League officials, reflecting on twenty years' experience with the world organization: "Experience shows," they said, "that a spirit of international loyalty among public servants can be maintained in practice." UN experience bears out both observations. Many UN officials have put international interests above the interest of any single state or group of states. But some have not, and the UN record clearly demonstrates that observance of the international ideal declines when it is undermined by the conduct of member states.

The elements of international loyalty, set forth in the Staff Regulations, are integrity, impartiality, and independence. From the viewpoint of the individual, *integrity* is the key. A person of integrity will not be false to either his own standards or his responsibility to others, including his oath to put the interests of the organization first.

Impartiality requires the UN official to act neutrally toward all states, except as the interests and objectives of the United Nations dictate. Since appearances are important, impartiality embodies an element of prudence in not publicly taking sides on controversial matters. More fundamentally, impartiality is an expression of integrity in acting as the office demands. Dag Hammarskjöld made the point forcefully in defending his own actions during the Congo crisis:

> I am not neutral as regards the Charter. . . . I am not neutral as regards facts. . . . But what I do claim is that even a man who is in that sense not neutral can very well undertake and carry through neutral actions, because that is an act of integrity.[13]

The ideal of impartiality probably goes no farther than integrity requires, and does not presume that an international official must or will free himself from all cultural bias or previously developed political values and attitudes. Certainly Hammarskjöld never assumed that he should abandon his deepest values, drawn from the Western cultural heritage.

Independence in a secretariat official is the ability to act without regard to political pressure from any national government or any group of countries. The Charter (Article 100) states that the Secretary-General and his staff "shall not seek or receive instructions from any government or from any other authority external to the Organization." Members, on their part, undertake "to respect the exclusively international character of the responsibilities of the Secretary-General and the staff and not to seek to influence them in the discharge of their responsibilities." Independence is thus a two-way street. It requires determination by the official to be independent and a willingness of governments, particularly his own government, to let him be independent.

Unfortunately, the independence ideal has not always been realized. During the League days the governments of Nazi Germany and Fascist Italy attempted, with some success, to control their nationals on the Secretariat. No one doubts that the Soviet Union does the same today, since the East European states make no pretense that international loyalty ought to come first. Nor has the problem been limited to the Soviet bloc. From 1953 to 1986 the United States subjected its nationals to a loyalty check before their appointment to the Secretariat. The practice was discontinued following a federal court decision that the loyalty program violated the First Amendment rights of American citizens. A number of other governments screen their nationals informally, which is less obvious but equally incompatible with Secretariat independence.

Other practices may be even more inimical to Secretariat independence. Some governments make supplementary payments to their nationals on the Secretariat, in clear violation of the Staff Regulations, which prohibit acceptance of "any honour, decoration, favour, gift or remuneration from any Government excepting for war services." The dangers of creating dependence on the government making the payment are obvious. Independence is similarly threatened when an initial appointment or a subsequent promotion results from government intervention on behalf of the candidate.

The increased number of fixed-term appointments also has implications for staff independence, since persons with a career stake in the United Nations may have more incentive to serve the organization single-mindedly. Many fixed-term employees do in fact measure up to the international civil service ideal, and the threat to independence is probably more acute with seconded employees, that is, national civil servants on temporary duty with the UN who anticipate returning to government service when the UN appointment expires. Even in such cases, personal integrity and government respect for the Secretariat's role may preserve the official's independence of action, but the risk of partiality and special influence is undoubtedly magnified by secondment.

THE SECRETARIAT IN THE POLITICAL PROCESS

Every aspect of international administration is affected by its political milieu, and the Secretariat is far more a creature of its environment than a controller. Nevertheless, secretariats do affect political outcomes through initiative and leadership in the administration of programs, participation in the decisions of policy-making organs, and the practice of quiet diplomacy. The following pages will examine each of these avenues of influence.

Policy through Administration

Administration is the process of carrying into action the commands of policy-making bodies. Legislative commands vary in their specificity, however, and at a minimum leave room for administrative discretion in the application of rules to particular cases. In this sense administration is simply policy-making at a relatively high level of specificity. Sometimes commands are stated so broadly that important decisions of substance must be made by administrators, and the administrators literally become the organization's policymakers. In UN political affairs this kind of implicit delegation reached its height during the administration of Dag Hammarskjöld. His actions in the 1956 Suez war and the 1960 Congo crisis substantially affected the course of events there.[14] Since Hammarskjöld, neither the Security Council nor the General Assembly has been willing to allow that much Secretariat discretion in political and security affairs, but UN policy bodies continue to impose quite broad mandates on the Secretary-General in the field of economic and social policy.

Administration also becomes entwined with large policy decisions in less direct ways. Research studies and reports prepared by Secretariat officials add to the information base for government policy. A League historian estimates that the monumental *Nutrition Report* issued in 1937 by a special committee of the League Assembly had far-reaching effects on the attitudes of governmental officials and private groups in many countries by calling attention to the abysmally low levels of nutrition in most parts of the world. Nearly every international organization can point to reports drafted by expert secretariat personnel that were the basis for subsequent action by policy-making bodies.

Successful performance of assigned duties by secretariat personnel can lead to requests for more of the same. The first UN peacekeeping force in Palestine had to be built almost from the ground up when the Suez crisis arose; but that precedent made a peacekeeping force the logical UN response in the Congo, Cyprus, and elsewhere, including current UN operations in the Middle East. On the other hand, ineffective administrative performance may lead to modification or abandonment of programs.

Secretariat Participation in Decision Making

International officials also participate directly in the decision-making processes of their governing bodies. Among existing international organizations, probably no secretariat enjoys greater influence than the staff of the World Bank, which not only frames the program for discussion by its Executive Directors and Governing Board but generally secures their approval for what the Bank President and his staff recommend. Governments are of course closely consulted in the preparation of the recommendations. The UNESCO Secretariat also fixes the agenda and prepares a program of action for its governing body. Although the UNESCO General Conference is sometimes disposed to alter the program, the Director-General is undoubtedly the most important decision-maker in the organization. The European Common Market represents yet a different relationship. By constitutional fiat, policy-making authority is divided between the Council of Ministers, which speaks for governments, and the Commission, which heads the administrative establishment. Some types of decisions are made by the Commission alone, some by the Council alone, and others of considerable importance by the concurrent action of both.

These organizations are to be contrasted with the UN General Assembly, where most agenda items are proposed by member states, or mandated by previous resolutions, and simply compiled by the Secretariat in a preliminary agenda. Although the Secretary-General may suggest additional items, he does not submit a legislative program, as is done in some other international agencies. However, most items represent continuing business from a previous session and are usually accompanied by a Secretariat report that helps shape consideration of the issue. Where the issue involves programs administered by the Secretariat, the views of the Secretariat have considerable weight, especially since the positions of member states are likely to have been solicited in formulating the Secretariat positions.

The Secretary-General is also responsible for preparation of the biennial UN budget. His estimates are, for the most part, based on the amounts required to carry out programs already authorized by the policy-making bodies, but the choice of figures nevertheless involves discretion. The Secretary-General is normally required to defend his budget vigorously and usually loses something to the budget cutters. In recent years the large contributors have put great pressure on the Secretary-General to produce a "no-growth budget," even though many smaller members would like to see continuing expansion of UN programs of special benefit to them.

Whether or not the secretariat of an international agency has a large role in initiating program proposals, other avenues of participation in the policy process are open. Executive heads are usually authorized to take part in formal discussion and debate of agenda items. All UN policy-making organs have provision for hearing the Secretary-General. Other UN officials conduct their own lobbying operations with varying degrees of directness. Individual civil servants are often consulted by national officials because of their expertise in a subject, and the Secretary-General will certainly be consulted if members are seriously considering the proposal of new functions or responsibilities for the Secretariat. On some questions the Secretary-General may be drawn into informal negotiating processes because he represents a relatively neutral and impartial viewpoint on an issue or because he can serve as a useful channel of communication. At a tactical and procedural level, secretariat officials are storehouses of information on such policy-relevant matters as the conduct of meetings, the drafting of resolutions, and tactics of effective advocacy.

The Practice of Diplomacy

International officials also influence organizational policy and the larger international system by means of "quiet diplomacy." Here we refer to the secretariat role in promoting agreement among states through quiet discussion and reconciliation of differences, as contrasted with public discussion and voting.

Opportunities for quiet diplomacy are presented in a wide variety of situations. Continuing diplomatic activity is required to carry out the programs of an organization and to obtain compliance with its resolutions. No peacekeeping mission can be launched without extensive negotiations with countries supplying the troop contingents and necessary matériel, as well as with the host country and any other country directly involved with the underlying threat to peace. No mission is maintained without continuing negotiation to resolve problems and differences as they arise. The same is true of other operating programs of international organization. Every technical assistance project is the product of extensive and detailed interchange among governments and the responsible international agency. Programs for refugee relief often require negotiation among representatives of one or more international organizations, the host country, the countries supporting the refugee program, and private organizations that cooperate in the relief activities. When UN resolutions call for government action rather than establishing operating programs, secretariat officials may perform a diplomatic function in seeking compliance from member states. The object of the negotiation is as varied as the subject matter of the resolutions—from urging financial support of UN development programs to encouraging South Africa to cease racial discrimination.

Another form of diplomatic activity is the resolution of controversy between states. The role of mediator, conciliator, and consensus-builder often appears in the quiet negotiations that occur behind the scenes of conference diplomacy. While government representatives often fill that role, not a few compromises later embodied in a resolution have been forged with the help of a timely suggestion or the mediatory services of a secretariat official. The expertise, impartiality, and continuity of secretariats become especially important in negotiating issues that persist over a long period of time within the UN framework, such as arms control or economic development.

The UN Secretary-General and his staff may also mediate particular disputes between countries. Frequently this involvement comes through a mandate from the Assembly or the Security Council. The diplomatic services of the Secretary-General, acting personally or through his representatives, have been enlisted by the Assembly or Council in such recent problem areas as the Iran-Iraq war, Afghanistan, Kampuchea, Namibia, the Falkland Islands, Lebanon, the Middle East, Grenada, and continuing Greek-Turkish conflict in Cyprus.[15] Sometimes Secretaries-General have not waited for the Council or Assembly to act but have attempted a mediating role on their own initiative. Dag Hammarskjöld, for example, initiated a successful mediation effort in a 1958 dispute between Cambodia and Thailand. U Thant attempted, with less success, to be a mediating influence in the Vietnam War, as did Kurt Waldheim in the Soviet invasion of Afghanistan and the Iranian hostage crisis. Pérez de Cuéllar has attempted independent initiatives in Africa, Central America, the Middle East, and elsewhere, without, however, achieving spectacular successes.

The Secretary-General and Political Leadership

Political leadership and initiative cut across all avenues of secretariat influence—administration, policy-making, and diplomacy. In the United Nations the focus of political leadership within the Secretariat must necessarily rest on the Secretary-General as the "chief administrative officer" of the organization. In contrast to all subordinate UN civil servants, the Charter makes his appointment subject to a uniquely political process. Under Article 97, he is "appointed by the General Assembly upon the recommendation of the Security Council." Since the Security Council recommendation is a nonprocedural matter, the recommendation is subject to all the hazards of great power politics. In practice, whenever the Security Council has been able to agree on a candidate, the General Assembly has hastened to add its formal approval.

Agreement in the Security Council has not always come easily. In 1950, when Trygve Lie's first five-year term was about to expire, the Soviet Union vetoed Lester Pearson of Canada and Paul-Henri Spaak of Belgium, and the United States then threatened to veto any candidate other than Lie. In this impasse the Secretariat was prevented from going leaderless only by the constitutionally questionable expedient of extending Lie's term an additional three years by General Assembly resolution. Since then, the appointment of a Secretary-General has sometimes gone to several

ballots in the Security Council, but disagreement has never forced such an extracon-
stitutional extension of tenure. In 1981 the Council was deadlocked for more than
six weeks. Through sixteen ballots China vetoed Kurt Waldheim's bid for an unprecedented third five-year term, while the United States blocked his Tanzanian chal-
lenger, Salim A. Salim. When these two candidacies were finally withdrawn, Javier
Pérez de Cuéllar was nominated on the first ballot from a list of nine Third World
hopefuls.

Given the political considerations that surround the appointment, it is not surprising that all successful candidates have come either from small, neutral European
countries or from the Third World: Norway (Trygve Lie), Sweden (Dag Hammarskjöld), Burma (U Thant), Austria (Kurt Waldheim), and Peru (Javier Pérez de
Cuéllar). (See Table 4-4.) The election of Pérez de Cuéllar in 1981 undoubtedly
reflects the personal reputation for fairness and ability that he acquired as Peruvian
Permanent Representative to the United Nations and as Undersecretary-General to
Kurt Waldheim. It also suggests that Peru and other Latin-American countries have
come to be identified in the United Nations more as Third World states than as U.S.
allies in a cold war context.

The Charter appointment process assures that the new incumbent will have the
support—or at least the acquiescence—of all permanent members and of a UN majority. This is a political asset, but leadership demands that he continue to seek
support wherever he can—primarily among governments but also with private interest groups and the general public. Since governments are the principal clients of the
Secretariat and the direct beneficiaries of most of its service, earning their goodwill
begins with trying to serve them well. It also requires careful counting of costs
before taking action or assuming a public stance that will antagonize influential
members. Lie's outspoken endorsement of UN action in Korea totally alienated the
Soviet support he had formerly enjoyed. Hammarskjöld's handling of the Congo
crisis also enraged the Soviet Union, but his cultivation of Afro-Asian support paid
off handsomely in that crisis. U Thant's efforts at mediation in the Vietnam conflict
brought a significant cooling in his relations with the United States, and his withdrawal of the UN Emergency Force from Egypt in May 1967 under Egyptian pressure brought severe criticism from many sides—especially after it proved a prelude
to the June 5 Israeli attack. Waldheim made no implacable enemies during two terms
in office, but his bid for an unprecedented third term was blocked by China's veto.
The Chinese position reflected a strong preference for a Third World candidate rather
than antagonism to him personally.[16]

Secretariat links with private groups can also be a modest source of support.
Private groups supply helpful information, and some have field operations that can
be harnessed to UN objectives in such areas as refugee and disaster relief or development assistance. Private groups may also lobby national governments and mobilize
public opinion in favor of the United Nations. In most instances the effect of private
groups on government behavior toward the organization is marginal, but the Secretariat must cultivate support wherever it can. Thus the Office of Public Information
maintains liaison with numerous national and international groups having an interest

TABLE 4–4

UN Secretaries-General, 1946–1986

Secretary- General	Nationality	Term of Office	Previous Experience
Trygve Lie	Norway	1946–53	Norway Foreign Minister at time of appointment; head, Norway delegation to San Francisco Conference (1945); former Minister of Justice, Commerce; politician and trade union negotiator
Dag Hammarskjöld	Sweden	1953–61	Minister of State (Finance) of Sweden at time of appointment; former chairman, Bank of Sweden; high-level civil servant, academic (political economy)
U Thant	Burma	1961–71	Permanent Representative of Burma to United Nations at time of appointment; former government press director, free-lance journalist, high school teacher
Kurt Waldheim	Austria	1972–81	Permanent Representative of Austria to United Nations at time of appointment; former foreign minister, ambassador to Canada, foreign service officer; unsuccessful candidate for President of Austria (1971)
Javier Pérez de Cuéllar	Peru	1982–*	Representative of UN Secretary-General in Afghanistan at time of appointment; former UN Undersecretary-General; Representative of UN Secretary-General in Cyprus; Permanent Representative of Peru to United Nations; ambassador to Switzerland, Poland, Venezuela; foreign service officer, professor of international law and relations

*Elected to a second five-year term in 1986.

in its work. UN staff also try to inform and accommodate the numerous nongovernmental organizations that hold consultative status with the Economic and Social Council. As for the general public, busy information clerks and smartly uniformed tour guides minister to the throngs of people who visit the UN headquarters each year to see the sights and observe UN public meetings. The United Nations reaches out to the much vaster world audience through a constant stream of news releases from New York, Geneva, and UN information centers around the world. Publications range from documentary reports of proceedings and Secretariat research to slick brochures lauding the accomplishments of the United Nations and its related agencies.

The object of building a power base is to influence the affairs of the organization and the larger political community. All incumbents have considered themselves spokesmen for the world community and have not hesitated to take positions in support of UN purposes and principles. Lie, as he later recalled in his memoirs, "was determined that the Secretary-General should be a force for peace."[17] Hammarskjöld also insisted on the right to take a stand on international issues whenever it could "be firmly based on the Charter and its principles."[18] Thant, Waldheim, and Pérez de Cuéllar have continued to defend the Secretary-General's right to speak out, whether the issue be Vietnam, Iran, Afghanistan, the Falklands, human rights, economic development, or the staffing of the Secretariat. Such statements have seldom had much impact on the course of events, but the right to speak remains intact.

The Secretary-General's opinion carries more weight if the Secretariat has special expertise or interest in the issue, other than his role as global community spokesman. Matters of administrative structure and budget fall into this category. So also do programs administered by the Secretariat, where the Secretary-General and his agents are closer to the facts of the issue than the representatives of most governments, and his arguments weigh accordingly. The same is true where the Secretary-General is engaged in mediatorial activities, either in person or through an appointed mediator.

In taking political initiatives, the Secretary-General has certain formal powers of office to draw on. He enjoys the privilege of speaking to UN deliberative bodies or placing items on their agendas. Under Article 99 of the Charter, he is specially authorized "to bring to the attention of the Security Council any matter which in his opinion may threaten the maintenance of international peace and security." While this right has rarely been exercised—almost always some member state will raise an issue if it is appropriate for Security Council consideration—Article 99 clearly stamps the office as one of political as well as administrative functions. A seemingly innocuous clause in Article 98, authorizing the Secretary-General to "perform such other functions as are entrusted to him" by the other major organs, has also been interpreted as an important grant of power. For Dag Hammarskjöld it was a mandate to do whatever he found necessary to implement directives from the General Assembly and the Security Council relating to the Middle East, the Congo, and other problem areas.

Hammarskjöld went even farther in finding broad political responsibilities inherent in the office of Secretary-General. When deadlock in the Security Council prevented enlargement of the UN Observer Group in Lebanon in the summer of 1958, he enlarged it on his own initiative, explaining to the Security Council that under the Charter he "should be expected to act without any guidance from the Assembly or the Security Council should this appear to him necessary towards helping to fill any vacuum that may appear in the systems which the Charter and traditional diplomacy provide for the safeguarding of peace and security."[19] U Thant continued the practice of taking independent political initiatives. The UN temporary executive authority in West New Guinea (1962), the observer mission in Yemen (1963), and the UN plebiscite in North Borneo and Sarawak (1963) were initiated by Thant on his own responsibility, although each action was subsequently approved by the General Assembly or the Security Council. At the height of the 1962 Cuban missile crisis, Thant's appeal for a voluntary suspension of Soviet arms shipments to Cuba and of American quarantine measures provided a formula that helped avert a direct confrontation at sea. After 1964 he made various attempts, all unsuccessful, to assume a mediating role in the Vietnam conflict. Waldheim actively sought a solution to the Afghanistan crisis, without success, while Pérez de Cuéllar has quietly but determinedly attempted to mediate the crises arising in Lebanon, the Falklands, the Iran-Iraq War, Grenada, and elsewhere.

The freewheeling, vigorous assertion of political prerogative characteristic of the late Hammarskjöld years has since given way to a quieter, more restrained approach to political leadership. This is in part a result of lessons learned from that experience. If Hammarskjöld opened new vistas of executive action, his clash with the Soviet Union—like that of Lie—plainly marked its limits. The Security Council has also held tighter rein on the Secretary-General in political matters, and more great power agreement on the scope of appropriate UN action in political crises has left fewer occasions for either the General Assembly or the Secretary-General to exercise broad discretion. Undoubtedly there is still room for the strong statement of principle by a Secretary-General calling member states to a sense of their responsibilities to the global community. But the evolution of the office suggests that effective political leadership, in the present United Nations, lies less in flamboyant public activities than in the arena of quiet diplomacy.[20]

The Basis of Secretariat Influence

International secretariats and their executive heads have extensive involvement in the political processes of international organizations. But involvement and effectiveness vary from one organization to another,[21] and even within a single organization, over a period of time. What accounts for these differences? Although an adequate answer to that question would require a book in itself, some of the reasons will be briefly summarized here.

1. Legal Powers. The charter of an organization gives the executive head certain rights, powers, and duties that help define the office. Others may be conferred by action of the organization's governing bodies. The UN Charter gives more authority to the Secretary-General than did the League Covenant. The constitutional grant of authority to the Commission of the European Community, as contained in relevant treaties, is still greater. Legal rights are a source of positive influence.

2. An Administrative Organization.   A secretariat is a working organization, often embracing hundreds or, in the case of the United Nations, thousands of employees. It can perform or withhold service. Its programs affect the welfare of numerous people. The ability to control such an organization is a source of power to the Secretary-General, or whoever is in charge.

In some, perhaps most, secretariats the executive head is never fully in charge. This may be because he lacks the personal skills to administer effectively. In part it results from the inherent unwieldiness of large bureaucracies. In some instances geographic distance from headquarters, or the support of governmental clients, or the strong personality of an able subordinate, may reduce the Secretary-General's control over particular units of the staff. A higher-level official who owes his appointment primarily to the political influence of his government may feel some independence from the executive head. Within the United Nations the General Assembly has been prone to create special programs, such as the UN Development Program, the UN Children's Fund (UNICEF), the UN High Commissioner for Refugees, and the UN Relief and Works Agency for Palestine Refugees, for which the Secretary-General has little or no administrative responsibility. In addition, the Assembly frequently creates committees, consisting of national representatives, to carry out some of its mandates. The work of the staff assigned to these committees is subject to the control of the committee rather than the Secretary-General. With such bodies as the Council for Namibia, the Committee on the Exercise of the Inalienable Rights of the Palestinian People, or the Special Committee to Investigate Israeli Practices Affecting the Human Rights of the Population of the Occupied Territories, a Secretary-General who wishes to mediate in these areas might find a portion of his staff working at cross-purposes to him in supporting a much harder committee line. When an executive head lacks full control, his administrative power base is thereby diminished.

3. Information.   Many states rely on the secretariat to provide reliable information and advice on a wide variety of subjects. This "information power" may result from the technical expertise of secretariat personnel, continuity of service and depth of experience, or access to sources of information not directly available to governments. Sometimes the balance of influence as between government representatives and international civil servants hinges on relative expertise, particularly if the organization performs primarily technical functions. If government representatives possess the technical expertise, they will certainly dominate the policy process. If secretariat officials are more technically qualified, their prospect of influencing policy will be greater.

4. Neutrality.   However difficult the achievement of absolute neutrality in international affairs, one source of secretariat strength is the secretariat's position as spokesman for the whole community. A reputation for neutrality, impartiality, and integrity increases trust and thereby the prospect for successful mediation of disputed questions.

5. Personal Qualities of the Incumbent.   Each executive head brings his own talents and interests to the office. He may be a good administrator or a good politician, or both, or neither. He may be interested in administration or in politics. He may be more adept, or less adept, at building coalitions of support among governments and private groups and at inspiring his staff to a sense of unity and purpose.

Albert Thomas, first Director-General of the ILO, was a promoter of causes, heavily involved in broad questions of organizational policy. This presumably reflected his background as "a politician, a trade unionist, a social campaigner and reformer."[22] On the other hand, Sir Eric Drummond brought to the League the self-effacing anonymity of the British civil servant who, while leaving center stage to others, exerted his influence through management, counsel, and negotiation behind the scenes. Trygve Lie, like Thomas, delegated administration to deputies and emphasized the political function of the UN Secretary-General both as a public figure and as a quiet negotiator. Dag Hammarskjöld appeared in many ways to combine the best aspects of both the Lie and Drummond types—concern for administrative detail, mastery of quiet diplomacy, and zealous advocacy of secretariat initiative. Although Hammarskjöld's successors have struggled to preserve the political functions of the office, theirs of necessity has been a less assertive approach.

6. The Organizational Task.   The nature of the organizational task has important consequences for secretariat influence on policy. Highly technical tasks usually generate less controversy than broad political questions and hence provide safer subjects for secretariat initiative. An organization that administers programs is likely to have greater staff influence on policy than one that makes rules for state behavior or tries to settle international disputes. Within the United Nations one should expect more secretariat influence on the form of technical assistance programs than on the outcome of resolutions dealing with South African apartheid. If task performance generates its own financial resources, as with the lending operations of the World Bank, the reduced dependence on member states for funds is almost certain to give the staff a greater policy role.

7. The Political Environment.   The political environment of an organization may be the most important variable affecting secretariat influence and, indeed, every other aspect of international organization. One kind of environmental impact consists of unplanned events that may frustrate organizational goals or, contrarily, offer new opportunity for initiative and constructive accomplishment. Another is the persistent influence of government attitudes, preferences, and control of resources that set limits on any attempted secretariat initiative. The environment, far more than the skills of the executive head, determines the support that may be available from governments and nongovernmental groups. Attitudes can of course change, and sometimes the process of participation precipitates change. But environment, even a changing environment, controls the organization, and not vice versa.

NOTES

1. Information, rule-making, and service functions of UN agencies in economic, social, and technical fields are discussed in Chapters 9, 10, and 11. These functions comprise an awesome range of activities—lending money, giving advice on farming, eradicating malaria, fighting illiteracy, improving national meteorological services, regulating labor standards, promoting human rights, and providing refugee relief, to name only a few. UN activities relating to international peace and security are examined in Chapters 5 through 8.

2. The designation of "official" and "working" languages has been a political issue. Initially the UN had five "official" languages but only two "working" languages—English and French—into which all documents were routinely translated. Arabic was subsequently added to the official languages, and all of the official languages have been made working languages, at some increase in convenience to members and a vast increase in the costs of producing documentation.

3. F. P. Walters, *A History of the League of Nations* (New York: Oxford University Press, 1952), p. 76.

4. Some problems of the international civil service here represented as unique may in fact be pertinent to governmental administration in some less developed countries where diversity of language, a heterogeneous political culture, and the absence of a well-developed administrative tradition also exist to a substantial degree. See Fred W. Riggs, "International Relations as a Prismatic Society," *World Politics* 14 (October 1961), pp. 144–81.

5. See *Composition of the Secretariat, Report of the Secretary-General,* UN Document A/41/627, September 20, 1986.

6. See, e.g., UN General Assembly Resolutions 35/210 (1980), 37/235 (1982), 38/231 (1983), 39/245 (1984), and 40/258 (1985).

7. As of June 30, 1986, twenty-nine states were overrepresented. All were from Asia, Africa, or South and Central America and the Caribbean. Of thirty-six underrepresented (or unrepresented) states, twenty-six were from the same areas (one was Japan), five were from Eastern Europe (Albania, Czechoslovakia, German Democratic Republic, Romania, Yugoslavia), and five were from Western Europe (Federal Republic of Germany, Greece, Italy, Luxembourg, and Norway). *Composition of the Secretariat, Report of the Secretary-General,* UN Document A/41/627, September 20, 1986.

8. See, e.g., UN General Assembly Resolutions 39/245 (1984) and 40/258 (1985).

9. Not all short-term appointments are inconsistent with a career system. A two to five-year contract may provide a probationary period before a career appointment is granted. Some fixed-term appointments are followed by career appointments, and others become de facto career vehicles by virtue of periodic renewal.

10. See Theodor Meron, *The United Nations Secretariat* (Lexington, Mass.: D. C. Heath, 1977), p. 57.

11. As of June 30, 1986, UN pay rates, for matching grades at the professional level, averaged 120.9 percent of the pay rates for the U.S. federal civil service. See *Report of the International Civil Service Commission,* UN Document A/41/30 (1986), p. 78.

12. In 1978 Secretary-General Waldheim issued a plea for relief from "mounting pressure from all sides to secure jobs" and appealed for states "to exercise great restraint" in the matter. "No civil service," he said, "can hope long to survive if it fails to compensate adequately, through reasonable career prospects, those of its staff who have served it for long periods, conscientiously and with dedication." UN Document A/33/1 (1978), p. 10.

13. Quoted in Sydney D. Bailey, *The Secretariat of the United Nations,* rev. ed. (New York: Praeger Publishers, 1964), p. 28.

14. See Chapter 5.

15. See, e.g., UN General Assembly Resolutions 40/7 (1985) (Kampuchea), 40/12 (1985) (Afghanistan), and 40/21 (1985) (Falkland [Malvinas] Islands); and UN Security Council Resolutions 566 (1985) (Namibia), 575 (1985) (Lebanon), and 580 (1985) (South Africa).

16. For useful profiles of Thant and Waldheim, see Alan James, "U Thant and His Critics," *Year Book of World Affairs, 1972* (London: Stevens & Sons, 1972), pp. 43–64; and James, "Kurt Waldheim: Diplomats' Diplomat," *Year Book of World Affairs, 1983* (London: Stevens & Sons, 1983), pp. 81–96. For their own views of the UN experience, see Thant, *View from the United Nations* (Garden City, N.Y.: Doubleday, 1978); and Waldheim, *In the Eye of the Storm: A Memoir* (Bethesda, Md.: Adler & Adler, 1986).

17. Trygve Lie, *In the Cause of Peace* (New York: Macmillan, 1954), p. 42.

18. Address in Copenhagen, May 2, 1959, reprinted in *United Nations Review* 5 (June 1959), p. 25.

19. Official Records of the Security Council, 13th year, 837th meeting, July 22, 1958, p. 4.

20. A strong argument for a "private" rather than a "public" role for the Secretary-General is made in James Barros, "The Importance of Secretaries-General of the United Nations," in *Dag Hammarskjöld Revisited: The UN Secretary-General as a Force in World Politics,* ed. Robert S. Jordan (Durham, N.C.: Carolina Academic Press, 1983), pp. 25–37.

21. See, e.g., Robert I. McLaren, *Civil Servants and Public Policy: A Comparative Study of International Secretariats* (Waterloo, Ont.: Wilfrid Laurier University Press, 1980).

22. Georges Langrod, *The International Civil Service* (Leyden: A. W. Sijthoff, 1963), p. 311.

SELECTED READINGS

BAILEY, SIDNEY D. *The Secretariat of the United Nations.* Rev. ed. New York: Praeger Publishers, 1964.

BARROS, JAMES. *Office without Power: Secretary-General Sir Eric Drummond, 1919–1933.* New York: Oxford University Press, 1979.

FINGER, SEYMOUR M., and JOHN MUGNO. *The Politics of Staffing the United Nations Secretariat.* New York: Ralph Bunche Institute on the United Nations, 1974.

GORDENKER, LEON. *The UN Secretary-General and the Maintenance of Peace.* New York: Columbia University Press, 1967.

GRAHAM, NORMAN A., and ROBERT S. JORDAN, eds. *The International Civil Service: Changing Role and Concepts.* New York: Pergamon Press, 1980.

JORDAN, ROBERT S., ed. *Dag Hammarskjöld Revisited: The UN Secretary-General as a Force in World Politics.* Durham, N.C.: Carolina Academic Press, 1983.

LANGROD, GEORGES. *The International Civil Service.* Leyden: A. W. Sijthoff, 1963.

LIE, TRYGVE. *In the Cause of Peace: Seven Years with the UN.* New York: Macmillan, 1954.

LOVEDAY, ALEXANDER. *Reflections on International Administration.* Oxford: Clarendon Press, 1956.

McLAREN, ROBERT I. *Civil Servants and Public Policy: A Comparative Study of International Secretariats.* Waterloo, Ont.: Wilfrid Laurier University Press, 1980.

MERON, THEODOR. *The United Nations Secretariat: The Rules and the Practice.* Lexington, Mass.: D. C. Heath, 1977.

PECHOTA, VRATISLAV. *The Quiet Approach: A Study of the Good Offices Exercised by the United Nations Secretary-General in the Cause of Peace*. New York: UNITAR, 1972.

RANSHOFEN-WERTHEIMER, EGON F. *The International Secretariat: A Great Experiment in International Administration*. New York: Carnegie Endowment for International Peace, 1945.

REYMOND, HENRI, and SIDNEY MAILICK. *International Personnel Policies and Practices*. New York: Praeger Publishers, 1985.

ROVINE, ARTHUR W. *The First Fifty Years: The Secretary-General in World Politics, 1920–1970*. Leyden: A. W. Sijthoff, 1970.

ROYAL INSTITUTE OF INTERNATIONAL AFFAIRS. *The International Secretariat of the Future*. London: Oxford University Press, 1944.

SCHWEBEL, STEPHEN M. *The Secretary-General of the United Nations: His Political Powers and Practice*. Cambridge, Mass.: Harvard University Press, 1952.

THANT, U. *View from the UN*. Garden City, N.Y.: Doubleday, 1978.

URQUHART, BRIAN. *Hammarskjöld*. New York: Alfred A. Knopf, 1972.

WEISS, THOMAS G. *International Bureaucracy: An Analysis of the Operation of Functional and Global International Secretariats*. Lexington, Mass.: D. C. Heath, 1975.

ZACHER, MARK W. *Dag Hammarskjöld's United Nations*. New York: Columbia University Press, 1970.

5

Security through Collective Action

Safeguarding international peace and security was the primary reason for the establishment of the United Nations in 1945. The aspiration "to save succeeding generations from the scourge of war" is enshrined in the opening lines of the UN Charter. Maintaining peace and security appears first in the Charter's statement of purposes and principles. UN functions are not narrowly limited to promoting military security, but even the nonmilitary functions are justified in the Charter by their potential contribution to peace.[1]

The great frequency of armed conflict since 1945 testifies that the UN security system has not worked as intended. Security is still the central concern of all states, but the United Nations is less central to the security of its members than the Charter might indicate. States rely primarily on their own might and that of their allies to deter aggression against themselves and, should peace fail, to vindicate their interests by force of arms. Lack of centrality does not mean irrelevance, however, and the United Nations has in many situations affected the way states pursue their security interests. The UN role in dispute settlement, arms control, and establishment of the economic and social foundations for peace is discussed in succeeding chapters. This chapter will examine efforts through the United Nations to prevent and limit war and to organize coercive sanctions against states that violate Charter norms.

The UN war-prevention role has often been called "collective security," although in practice the United Nations has been largely an adjunct to the operation of local and global balances of power. Before examining UN activities in detail, this chapter will present a brief historical and theoretical analysis of the balance of power and collective security concepts. A second section will discuss the largely unsuccessful efforts of the United Nations to achieve the collective security ideal. A third section recounts the evolution of UN "peacekeeping" as a means of war limitation that depends, not primarily on coercion, but on the willingness of the affected states to accept a pacifying UN presence.

122

BALANCE OF POWER AND COLLECTIVE SECURITY BEFORE THE UNITED NATIONS

Alliances and the Balance of Power

Historically, the most common security arrangement among independent political entities has been the military alliance. The Book of Genesis gives accounts of alliances and wars among rival groups of kings in the days of Abraham. Thucydides' *History of the Peloponnesian War* is the story of alliances and counteralliances among contending groups of Greek city-states. The modern state system has followed the same pattern from its inception, and even today arrangements for military cooperation among two or more states—secret or open, simple or highly organized—maintain undiminished popularity.

Balance of power is the term usually applied to a system in which states rely on international alliances to promote their individual security interests.[2] The concept of "balance" refers to a distribution of power among states such that no state is strong enough to mount a military challenge to the status quo. As traditionally conceived, the balance-of-power system functions without central coordination and without much regard to any common ideals, except the obvious concern to prevent undue concentration of power in others. Security decisions are made by states, acting individually or in concert with allies. Combinations to deter prospective warmakers are formed by the actions of governments whose individual national interests are threatened by a common danger. Such combinations are generally limited in objective, temporary in duration, and shifting in composition. The balance system is supposed to be called into play when a state or a group of states seeks to alter an existing power relationship. The action of the "revisionist" states produces a reaction from the "status quo" powers, which band together to preserve their interests. The outcome, depending on the circumstances, might be deterrence through strength, accommodation through bargaining, or war through failure of the system.

The outbreak of World War I convinced all doubters that the balance-of-power system had weaknesses as a peacekeeping mechanism. A system in which coalescence of states depended on the coincidence of particular national interests, rather than recognition of general interest in keeping the peace, did not always deter aggressors. Apparently, also, statesmen were not as rational in calculating the odds as the proper working of the system would presume, and even rational judgments were subject to serious miscalculation. The size of the stakes sometimes outweighed the risks—as in Napoleon's dream of European hegemony; or, contrarily, the very narrowness of the immediate issue could blind the powers to the intensity of the possible repercussions and lead governments to unwittingly topple the first domino—as at the outbreak of World War I. In the years preceding 1914, moreover, the system had developed a rigidity of alignments that robbed it of the fluidity that theory—and apparently practice—required for the effective operation of the balance-of-power mechanism.

The Advent of Collective Security

The task of finding a workable substitute for the balance of power was undertaken by the Versailles peacemakers in 1919, under the prodding of President Woodrow Wilson. The available precedents for bringing two or more states within a common security system were not promising. The principal historical precedents were conquest, political federation, and, at a lower level of integration, the military alliance. Conquest was a wholly unacceptable model, and voluntary extinction of separate sovereignties through political federation was not feasible, given deep-seated nationalisms and global diversity in economic development, social organization, and political values. The military alliance made few inroads on national sovereignty, but as a security system it was discredited by the onset of World War I.

Another nineteenth-century precedent was the Concert of Europe, a loose-knit system of great power consultation spawned by the Napoleonic Wars and continued sporadically to the eve of World War I. The Concert was more a state of mind than an organized security system, and it was only indifferently effective. When the Serbian crisis arose in the summer of 1914, the Concert technique of great power consultation was not even called into play. In addition to the Concert, there was the legacy of the 1899 and 1907 Hague Conferences and the considerable experience of organized international cooperation in economic and social fields. Although suggestive of organizational forms and procedures, the international conference and the public administrative union were not security systems. The hard fact was that nothing in history constituted a working precedent for an effective system of security within a community of sovereign states.

The peacemakers at Versailles thus were forced to innovate. They took the ideal of a universal security system, hitherto the domain of political dreamers, and fused it with nineteenth-century international organization, using in the process much of their own ingenuity to forge the essential compromises between ideals and realities. The result was the world's first major attempt at "collective security" through the League of Nations.

The Nature of Collective Security

The League died in the ruins of World War II, but the notion of collective security has lived on. What it means, however, varies with the context. The term *collective security* has been applied indiscriminately to almost any arrangement among two or more countries that involves the possibility of joint military action. After World War II it was used to describe military alliances such as NATO in order to give them more respectability. In this context it became almost a synonym for a "good" or a "defensive" alliance, as contrasted with a "bad" (someone else's) alliance, which might be used for "aggressive" purposes. More recently the term *collective defense*, rather than collective security, has been applied to multilateral alliances aimed primarily at threats to security created by countries outside the coalition.

In its more specialized and correct meaning, collective security is an arrangement among states by which all are committed to aid any country threatened with armed attack by any other country. The object is to deter aggression by confronting a potential aggressor with the power of an overwhelming coalition and, should war nevertheless occur, to bring the aggressor quickly to heel. A collective security system is distinguished from an alliance by its inward orientation. While an alliance is geared to threats from foes of the alliance, collective security focuses on threats arising within the system. Among the states involved, there are no predetermined alignments. All of them, presumably, are friends until one of them chooses to become an aggressor. That state then becomes the enemy of all the others until the threat of aggression has been removed.

As originally conceived, collective security was intended to be worldwide in scope. In theory, however, a collective security system might include any smaller number of states as long as preponderant power could be marshaled against any one of them. Some regional organizations presently have collective security aspects. The Inter-American Treaty of Reciprocal Assistance (the Rio Pact) makes explicit provision for resisting possible aggression by one Latin-American state against another. NATO, the Organization of African Unity, and the Arab League have also tried to deal with armed conflict among their own members. Such organizations fall short of the collective security ideal in many respects; and to the extent that they are concerned with external threats, they must be regarded as alliances or collective defense arrangements.

The essential elements of an effective collective security system are *consensus, commitment,* and *organization.* At the minimum level of *consensus,* states must agree that peace is indivisible and that threats to peace anywhere are the concern of all. But more is required. There must be a *commitment* to act in accordance with the collective security principle. The commitment has both a positive and a self-denying aspect. States are bound affirmatively to combine their force to meet any threat to the security of the world community. They are also committed to refrain from unilateral use of force to achieve purely national objectives. Ideally, the commitments should be so binding and so widely embraced that any attempts "to change the *status quo* by violence are unlawful and doomed to frustration through opposition in overwhelming force."[3] Without this commitment consensus remains a meaningless abstraction. But commitment, too, may fail in time of crisis if there is no *organization* to make it effective. Every such commitment is necessarily a generalized commitment until a specific crisis arises. If each state is then free to decide how and when its commitment will be honored, enforcement may be highly selective. An effective collective security system requires a central decision-making organ that is empowered to say how and when collective force is to be used, with adequate military forces available on call to carry out that decision.

For practical purposes collective security has a fourth prerequisite. Power should be widely enough dispersed that no state can hope to challenge all the others. The effectiveness of the system depends on its capacity to deter most potential violators and to defeat an actual aggressor in short order. If one state is substantially stronger than the rest, it may be willing to act militarily in defiance of the system. Even though the collectivity may ultimately put down the aggression, the system fails if protracted or devastating war occurs.

The League Security System

The League of Nations did not satisfy any of the conditions for effective collective security, except perhaps the last. During the interwar period no country was strong enough to defy all the others if the others were united. But League members, and the United States as the major nonmember, were not sufficiently convinced that every war anywhere was a threat to them. And certainly they lacked commitment to use their combined force against any and every case of aggression, regardless of who the aggressor might be.

The League Covenant did not even require such a commitment. Far from it. In disputes coming before the League, the Covenant expressly permitted aggressive war against a state that refused to comply with recommendations unanimously endorsed by the Council and against any party to a dispute on which the Council was divided. These so-called gaps in the Covenant were widely deplored, but even more enfeebling was the absence of obligation to act when unauthorized aggression occurred. Article 10 of the League Covenant declares unequivocally that "the Members of the League undertake to respect and preserve as against external aggression the territorial integrity and existing political independence of all Members of the League." Yet Manchuria, Ethiopia, and ultimately a host of other members fell victim to violence without a shot being fired in their defense in the name of the League and without any state being obligated by the Covenant to fire such a shot.

Article 11 seemed to embody both the necessary consensus and commitment in its grand assertion that "any war or threat of war, whether immediately affecting any of the Members of the League or not, is hereby declared a matter of concern to the whole League, and the League shall take any action that may be wise and effectual to safeguard the peace of nations." But when the obligations were spelled out in greater detail, League decisions to take military action had only the force of recommendations (Article 16). Even the supposedly automatic "severance of all trade or financial relations" was vitiated by League resolutions adopted in 1921 emphasizing the right of each state to determine for itself how and when to apply economic sanctions. The League was also hampered by its rule requiring a unanimous vote for most decisions. Whenever the League was moved to action against threats to the peace during the troubled 1930s, it was almost always too little and too late. In short, the League system did not work well because the disposition of members to view their own security as separable from that of others was reinforced by weak legal commitments and ineffective decision-making procedures.

THE UNITED NATIONS AND COLLECTIVE SECURITY

The Charter Framework

The framers of the UN Charter were not willing to abandon the collective security concept of peace enforced by the community of nations. Although they recognized the need for some compromise with the ideal, they hoped that improved institutions and a new will to cooperate would succeed where the League had failed.

Taking a cue from the 1928 Pact of Paris, the UN Charter commits all members to "refrain in their international relations from the threat or use of force against the territorial integrity or political independence of any state, or in any other manner inconsistent with the Purposes of the United Nations" (Article 2, section 4). The only exceptions to the use of force are (1) self-defense, individual or collective (Article 51); (2) action against "enemy" states of World War II (Article 107); (3) joint action by the Big Five on behalf of the organization, pending the availability of troops under Article 43 (Article 106); and (4) any other use of force authorized by the Security Council. The Charter does not ban internal armed revolt and civil wars which, strictly speaking, are not concerned with the use of force in "international relations."[4]

Equally important was the attempt to put sharper teeth into the Charter. Instead of economic sanctions that were automatic in theory but discretionary in practice, the Security Council was given the right to impose nonmilitary sanctions, with all members obligated "to accept and carry out the decisions of the Security Council." In place of the League Council's right to recommend military sanctions, the Security Council was to have earmarked troops supplied by prior agreement with members and awaiting only the Council's call to action. Abandoning the unanimity requirement, the Security Council was empowered to take military action by vote of seven of eleven (now nine of fifteen) members, including the concurring votes of the five permanent members.

The retention of a great power veto was, admittedly, a conscious compromise with the principle of collective security, but one dictated by common sense. Critics had constantly pointed out that collective security treated all wars as incipient world wars, with the practical danger of turning localized wars into global war if powerful forces were ranged on both sides. The veto was intended to prevent such an eventuality. With the great powers all committed to collective enforcement through the organization, the prospect of quickly squelching an outburst of violence would be very good indeed.

On paper the UN Charter seemed a reasonable approach to collective security, subject to the limitation of the veto. The Charter registered broad consensus that peace is indivisible and that any threat to international peace and security is the concern of all. Members were legally committed to accept and carry out Security Council decisions, and the Council could make binding decisions (not just recommendations) to impose both military and nonmilitary sanctions. Here then was consensus, commitment, and central decision-making machinery merged in a coherent collective security system.

The Demise of Collective Military Sanctions

The Charter system never worked as intended. The root problem was lack of genuine consensus and commitment to match the paper responsibilities. Even while the United Nations was being planned, leaders of the Big Three had little faith in the collective security concept or the efficacy of particular institutional arrangements. Roosevelt, Churchill, and Stalin all regarded a new balance-of-power system as inevitable. Churchill and Stalin hoped to stabilize it by recognizing spheres of influence in areas of special interest to them—particularly the Balkans. Roosevelt looked more to a "Four Policemen" concept (including a rehabilitated China) modeled after the old Concert of Europe as a means of providing order in the system. Great power cooperation, not collective security, was the answer. Roosevelt ultimately yielded to the pressure of domestic groups calling for the establishment of the United Nations, but the germ of his Four Policemen idea was preserved in the provision for permanent members of the UN Security Council.[5]

Events subsequently confirmed President Roosevelt's judgment about collective security, if not his optimism about the prospects for East-West cooperation. Wartime collaboration quickly degenerated into cold war, revealing discordant national security interests that could not be harnessed to the collective security requirement of all for one and one for all. Soviet-American rivalry brought deadlock to the Security Council, where a Western majority was held in check by the Soviet veto. But the veto was only a symptom. Fundamental divergence of interest was the underlying problem.

One of the early institutional casualties was the UN security force envisioned by Charter Article 43. The capacity of the Security Council to take military action on its own initiative was dependent on the subsequent negotiation of special agreements with member states to make standby military forces and facilities available to the Council at its call. Each such agreement required ratification by the states concerned according to their respective constitutional processes. The ratification requirement meant that member states, in accepting the Charter, had made only a moral commitment to support UN military sanctions, while postponing to a later day any limitation on the right to control their own military forces. In fact, no Article 43 agreement ever reached the ratification stage, because the major powers could not agree on the size and character of their respective national contributions or on where the units should be based. The Security Council and its Military Staff Committee (Articles 46, 47) were never able to resolve their differences.[6]

Without agreement on guidelines for UN military forces, no special agreements under Article 43 could be negotiated. The broad Charter commitment to collective security was never translated into a specific commitment to supply troops and matériel. Despite the intent of the Charter, members retained the right to decide for themselves, according to the circumstances of each case, how their military forces should be used. If collective military action were to be taken at all, it would be on a voluntary basis.

While the Security Council was struggling with Article 43, the General Assembly embarked on the project of defining aggression. Nearly thirty years later, in 1974, the Assembly approved a compromise definition embodying a fair degree of international consensus but containing enough ambiguities to leave the identification of aggression in many situations still an ad hoc political act.[7]

Korea and Collective Action

Korea provided the test of voluntary collective security under UN auspices. In a number of respects, the conditions for voluntary UN enforcement action were highly favorable. When fighting broke out in June 1950, a UN observation group already in South Korea was able to provide immediate confirmation that an armed attack by North Korean troops had in fact occurred. The absence of the Soviet delegate, in protest against the continued seating of Nationalist China, eliminated the prospect of a veto and allowed a quick Security Council endorsement of the U.S. request for military aid to South Korea. In Japan and Okinawa the United States had troops that could be quickly moved to the scene of the fighting. Thus the "UN" action was commenced, relying almost totally on American initiative and resources.

When the return of the Soviet delegate in August snuffed out the Security Council's capacity to act, the issue was removed from the Security Council to the General Assembly. At first, the Assembly was able to act on crucial issues with some dispatch. As the months wore on, however, Chinese intervention, military stalemate, and rising concern about touching off a third world war brought division and dissension to the United Nations. Nearly all members breathed a sigh of relief when the Korean Armistice was arranged, in July 1953.

UN action helped preserve the independence of the Republic of Korea, but it brought no renewed enthusiasm for collective security, on a voluntary basis or otherwise. At first seen as the rebirth of collective military action, the Korean War proved to be its requiem.[8] The reasons are now fairly clear, and they speak to characteristics of the world and of the United Nations that persist to the present time.

One reason is the ambiguous form in which armed conflict has occurred since Korea. Civil wars, revolutions, guerrilla warfare, clandestine infiltration, and subversion, with foreign intervention in the guise of assistance to contending domestic factions, are the common forms of violence that have ruptured the peace of the world. This new dimension of conflict brings into question the appropriateness of a collective military response, which may strike at symptoms without reaching any of the underlying problems. Internal war increases the already difficult task of singling out an aggressor. Should the United Nations support the rebels, or should it weigh in on the side of the status quo? Should enforcement action be taken against the foreign sponsor or abettor? The probability that the Korean experience may have encouraged the subsequent use of more covert forms of aggression in place of overt military invasion does little to enhance the usefulness of collective military sanctions in meeting the kinds of threats that do exist.

The Korean War also highlighted basic defects of the United Nations as an instrument for launching collective military sanctions. Its decision-making apparatus was shown to be unsuited to decisive action in times of crisis. Only the absence of the Soviet delegate made the initial Security Council action possible, and no permanent member has since repeated that mistake. Indeed, the Soviet Union insisted that Security Council resolutions adopted in its absence were void, although other members argued that an absence was the equivalent of an abstention, which, by precedent, was not a veto. Whatever the legal merits, the Security Council was immobilized by the Soviet return. When responsibility for decisions was then shifted to the General Assembly, that body proved too large, too unwieldy, and too divided in counsel to direct a military operation effectively.

Korea further revealed the disadvantages of dependence on voluntary commitment of forces in time of crisis. Just twenty-two of the sixty member states offered military forces, and only sixteen of the offers were of usable size and quality. The United States contributed over half of the ground forces, 85 percent of the naval forces, and nearly 95 percent of the air force contingents, with South Korea providing most of the remaining personnel. Less than 10 percent came from the other contributors. This means that the Korean War was largely an American operation. It was directed by a Unified Command, a euphemism generally understood to mean U.S. command. This fact was emphasized when President Harry Truman removed Supreme UN Commander Douglas MacArthur from the post because of political differences over how the war should be conducted. The Unified Command reported to the United Nations, but only what the United States saw fit to report. The United Nations undoubtedly provided a valuable political cover for U.S. operations in Korea, but a collective response so heavily dependent on a single great power, and so closely tied to its national interests, is a questionable kind of collective security.

If UN institutions and member response fell short of the collective security ideal, in one respect the Korean action exceeded the carefully delimited bounds of the Charter. The United Nations wielded arms against the interests of a permanent member of the Security Council, with all the explosive potential for a third world war that the veto had been designed to prevent. Korea did not lead to a direct military confrontation of the giants and to world war, but at times the thread by which the Damoclean sword hung suspended seemed perilously slender. The enduring lesson of the Korean venture was not that it repelled aggression but that it was too risky to try again.

Korea also demonstrated the absence of a fundamental precondition for effective collective security: consensus on the kind of world that is to be made secure. Enforcement of peace in a national political system is possible because of general agreement on political goals and the existence of machinery for the peaceful settlement of most disputes as they arise. Collective security, by attempting to outlaw violent change, assumes that existing methods of peaceful change and dispute settlement are adequate to resolve international differences and satisfy legitimate national aspirations. The unreality of this assumption is well illustrated by the Korean War, where the only settlement possible was an agreement to exchange prisoners and to stop fighting along a line roughly corresponding to the status quo ante. A divided Korea was perpetuated, and the underlying problems that precipitated the crisis remained unresolved. Within the United Nations itself opinion was so divided that the members could scarcely agree on the roster of participants in a proposed political conference on Korea. Without greater agreement on the kind of world that was to be made secure, the nations were not ready for collective security.

One enduring institutional legacy of the Korean conflict is the Uniting for Peace resolution, adopted by the Assembly in early November 1950, when total UN victory seemed imminent.[9] The resolution was a U.S. proposal intended to make the United Nations more efficient in dealing with future threats to the peace. The UN system had worked reasonably well in repelling North Korean aggression (or so it appeared at the time), but only because of fortuitous circumstances (the Soviet boycott, nearby U.S. forces) that might not occur again. Next time the Assembly should be prepared to act quickly from the outset, whatever the circumstances.

The resolution formally affirmed the responsibility of the General Assembly for dealing with international violence when the Security Council was unable to act, including the right to recommend collective military action. It established a procedure for calling the General Assembly into "emergency special session" by a vote of any seven (now nine) members of the Security Council or on request of a majority of UN members. In addition, it created a "Peace Observation Commission" to send observers to tension-laden areas on request, authorized a "Collective Measures Committee" to study and report on methods of strengthening international peace and security, and urged members to earmark national military units for use by the United Nations. The last three provisions of the resolution have fallen into disuse, but the emergency special session procedure has survived. It was invoked in the Suez and Hungarian crises of 1956, the Lebanon crisis of 1958, the 1960 Congo crisis, and the 1967 Suez War. After a period of disuse, it was revived again to deal with Afghanistan (1980), Palestine (1980, resumed 1982), Namibia (1981), and the Occupied Arab Territories (1982). Removed from the context of collective military sanctions, the special emergency session has become an accepted feature of UN practice. The Uniting for Peace system was originally sponsored by the United States largely as a means for containing Soviet and Chinese power and blunting their aggressive moves. With the Third World now exercising voting control over the General Assembly, the system is being used to serve its interests.

Nonmilitary Sanctions

Like the League Covenant, the UN Charter provides for nonmilitary sanctions against states that threaten peace. Article 41 authorizes the Security Council to enforce its decisions through "complete or partial interruption of economic relations and of rail, sea, air, postal, telegraphic, radio, and other means of communication, and the severance of diplomatic relations." Moral condemnation is also available as a sanction for noncompliance.

None of these sanctions has been very successful in accomplishing UN objectives. Moral condemnation, although frequently invoked, has seldom been very effective in getting states to comply with UN directives.[10] States may sometimes act with an eye to avoiding UN condemnation, but UN scolding after the fact is more likely to harden positions than evoke repentance. Israel and South Africa have been the constant object of UN railing, with little discernible effect on their policies. China was totally undeterred by the "aggressor" label attached to its Korean intervention, and UN censure did nothing to hamper Soviet suppression of the 1956 Hungarian revolt or, more recently, Soviet repression in Afghanistan. Nor has the United States responded penitently to UN disapproval of its support for Israel or such ventures as the 1983 occupation of Grenada.

Diplomatic and economic sanctions have scarcely been more effective.[11] A 1946 Assembly recommendation for withdrawal of ambassadors and ministers from Spain did not achieve its object of undermining the Franco regime and was withdrawn in 1950. An Assembly-sponsored embargo on arms bound for Albania and Bulgaria in 1949, aimed at cutting aid to Communist rebels in Greece, was wholly ineffectual, and an Assembly ban on shipment of strategic goods to China in 1951 had no dampening effect on China's resistance to the United Nations in Korea. A nonmandatory Security Council embargo on arms shipments to Israel and the Arab states was quite widely observed from 1948 to 1955 but thereafter was disregarded.

Modest success might be claimed for UN efforts to topple Ian Smith's white minority regime in Rhodesia through use of nonmilitary sanctions. The initial Security Council response to Rhodesia's 1965 unilateral declaration of independence from Britain was to apply a limited range of voluntary economic and diplomatic measures. This was followed in 1966 with the first ever UN *mandatory* sanctions under Chapter VII of the Charter. Although limited at first to an embargo of arms, oil, and motor vehicles and a boycott of Rhodesian exports, the sanctions were expanded in subsequent years to include a ban on most economic intercourse with Rhodesia. The sanctions contributed to Rhodesia's economic deterioration, despite nonobservance by a number of states. They were lifted in 1980 when power was transferred to the black majority and Rhodesia was renamed Zimbabwe. This outcome was attributable primarily to the pressures of internal civil war, combined with persistent British efforts to promote a settlement, but the UN sanctions linked with general delegitimization of the Rhodesian regime by the world community undoubtedly had some effect.

South Africa has been the most frequent target of UN nonmilitary sanctions, aimed at altering its racial policies and securing the independence of Namibia. Since 1962 the General Assembly has repeatedly called for severance of economic and diplomatic relations as well as an embargo on arms and war materials. The arms embargo was endorsed as a voluntary measure by the Security Council in 1963 and eventually made mandatory under Chapter VII in 1977. The UN sanctions were not well observed and did not substantially affect the economic and military strength of South Africa or its racial and colonial policies. South Africa occasionally made modest concessions to satisfy its Western friends but has been quite contemptuous of the UN majority.

South African relations with the world entered a new phase in 1985 and 1986, when the white government's stern reaction to internal dissent induced a number of countries to take a hard look at their own policies toward South Africa. The Security Council, with the United States and the United Kingdom abstaining, at last moved to recommend economic sanctions. Further economic sanctions were voluntarily imposed by a number of countries, including some of South Africa's Western trading partners. Private multinational firms also moved toward disinvestment in South Africa. The ultimate impact of these external and internal pressures on South African racial policies remains to be seen, although a weakening of the economy was evident. While neither the internal dissent nor the economic measures taken by foreign governments have been the direct result of UN sanctions, both have undoubtedly been encouraged by four decades of UN dealings with South Africa.

The Regional Alternative

The UN Charter places primary responsibility for international peace and security on the Security Council, with regional organizations playing a secondary role. The principal proponents of regionalism at the San Francisco Conference were delegates from the American states who wished to preserve the developing Inter-American security system, and the relevant provisions, Articles 51–54, are a compromise. These provisions focus on three central issues—peaceful settlement, self-defense, and enforcement action (the use of diplomatic, economic, or military sanctions). Regional associations are expressly encouraged to take the initiative in settling local disputes (Article 52). Article 51 recognizes an "inherent right of individual or collective self-defense" against armed attack; but all action taken in self-defense must be immediately reported to the Security Council and that body retains authority to take any concurrent action it finds necessary. The Security Council's predominance with respect to enforcement action is even more forcefully established. With the exception of measures against the enemy states of World War II, the Charter states categorically that "no enforcement action shall be taken under regional arrangements or by regional agencies without the authorization of the Security Council" (Article 53).

In practice, the roles have been reversed. Because of bitter East-West rivalries the Security Council never acquired its military capability, and members utilized Article 51 to expand collective self-defense arrangements out of all proportion to the puny enforcement arm of the general system and, in some instances, to justify outright aggression. The United States led the stampede to regional security and autonomy. From the Pact of Rio de Janeiro (1947) to NATO (1949) to ANZUS (1951) to SEATO (1954) to CENTO (1955) and numerous bilateral military pacts, the United States became the hub of the most complex and extensive system of alliances the world has ever known. Other states followed suit in a more modest way with such arrangements as the Arab League, the Warsaw Pact, and the Organization of African Unity, as well as a host of bilateral alliances. Part of this system has since disintegrated. The Southeast Asian component of the U.S.-sponsored system (SEATO) was formally abandoned in 1977, and CENTO, the Middle East segment, in 1979. New Zealand's participation in ANZUS was effectively suspended in 1986 because of that state's refusal to let U.S. nuclear-powered or nuclear-armed ships into its ports. The Rio Pact has experienced severe strains because of revolutionary regimes in Cuba and Nicaragua, U.S. support of Britain in the Falklands War, and other sources of disunity. So also, to some extent, have NATO, the Warsaw Pact, the Arab League, and the OAU. But the alliance system is still in place, and it presents a striking contrast to the security system envisioned at San Francisco.[12]

THE PEACEKEEPING ALTERNATIVE

Collective security never became a reality, but the United Nations has found other ways to remain relevant, if not central, to the control of international violence. The most significant and innovative is UN "peacekeeping." In a UN context the term *peacekeeping* was first used to describe the work of the UN Emergency Force (UNEF), created by the General Assembly during the 1956 Suez War to take temporary control of the Suez Canal area and facilitate the withdrawal of Anglo-French and Israeli forces from Egyptian territory. It has since become the generic term for a UN-sponsored nonfighting military "presence" that may occur in a variety of forms.[13]

Peacekeeping contrasts sharply with the collective military sanctions contemplated by Article 41. Instead of acting to deter or defeat an aggressor, the UN peacekeeping mission is deployed against no identified enemy. Its purpose is to help maintain peace when tension is high but no party is determined to pursue armed conquest. It may perform this function by observing border violations, policing a cease-fire or truce line, serving as a buffer between hostile forces, and even helping to maintain domestic order during a transition period. A peacekeeping force is deployed only with the consent of the sovereign of the territory where it operates, and usually with the consent or acquiescence of all the governments concerned. While UN forces or military observers are normally armed, weapons are to be used only in self-defense and not to enforce the UN will on any of the contending parties. Except for the Congo operation, 1960–64, UN peacekeeping operations have never been large enough to enforce order against serious military opposition.

Secretary-General Dag Hammarskjöld conceived UNEF as part of a UN strategy to prevent local disputes or power vacuums from becoming extensions or inciting escalations of the cold war. This concept, fathered and nurtured by the Secretary-General, became known as "preventive diplomacy." Hammarskjöld later articulated the theory of preventive diplomacy in a report to the General Assembly:

Preventive action in such cases must, in the first place, aim at filling the vacuum so that it will not provoke action from any of the major parties, the initiative from which might be taken for preventive purposes but might in turn lead to a counter action from the other sides. The ways in which a vacuum can be filled by the United Nations so as to forestall such initiatives differ from case to case, but they have this in common: Temporarily, and pending the filling of the vacuum by normal means, the United Nations enters the picture on the basis of its non-commitment to any power bloc, so as to provide to the extent possible a guarantee in relation to all parties against initiatives from others.[14]

Most UN peacekeeping missions have embodied a large element of preventive diplomacy.

In some respects the peacekeeping force is more akin to the machinery of peaceful settlement than to enforcement action under the Charter. It serves to separate combatants that are willing to be separated, to bring order and stability to an area by reason of its presence, and to perform nonfighting police functions. Ideally, the return of peace and stability will permit a negotiated settlement of political differences. And yet the function of the force is not to settle disputes but to curb disorder, prevent the spread of violence, and inhibit outside intervention. It thus defies ready classification in one of the traditional categories of sanctions or pacific settlement. The Charter neatly separates its prescriptions for pacific settlement of disputes (Chapter VI) from enforcement action (Chapter VII), but in the real world the peacekeeping function involves a variety of specific means that cannot readily be compartmentalized. The principal UN peacekeeping missions—their size, function, and duration—are shown in Table 5–1.

Early UN Experiments

Early UN experiments with a nonfighting military presence occurred in Greece, Indonesia, Kashmir, and Palestine. Although the term *peacekeeping* was not used at the time, these UN ventures have since been recognized as examples of the small UN peacekeeping mission. From 1947 to 1949, a UN Special Committee on the Balkans (UNSCOB) kept a small team of observers (up to twenty) along the northern frontiers of Greece to monitor border violations by Soviet-bloc states in support of leftist Greek rebels. Another temporary field mission was conducted in Indonesia from 1947 to 1951. UN military observers associated with the UN Commission for Indonesia (UNCI) and its predecessor Good Offices Committee aided Security Council peacemaking efforts in the Indonesian war for independence from the Netherlands and observed the subsequent repatriation of Dutch forces. Two observer missions dating from the pre-UNEF period proved to be more than temporary. The UN Truce Supervision Organization (UNTSO), established in 1948 to police a truce between Israel and its Arab neighbors, grew to nearly 700 in number before armistice agreements were concluded in 1949. The size of UNTSO has since fluctuated with events, but lack of permanent peace in the area has made its continuance necessary. UNTSO currently maintains about 300 observer personnel to monitor situations in Lebanon, the Golan Heights, and the Sinai. The UN Military Observer Group in India and Pakistan (UNMOGIP) has experienced a similar longevity. Set in operation during

TABLE 5–1

Principal UN Peacekeeping Missions, 1947–1986

Mission	Date	Peak Force Size	Force Size (December 1986)	Function
UNSCOB	1947–49	20	—	Monitor violations of Greek border
UNCI	1947–51	63	—	Observe Indonesian cease-fire and Dutch troop withdrawal
UNTSO	1948–present	700	298	Report on Arab-Israeli cease-fire and armistice violations
UNMOGIP	1949–present	102	38	Observe Kashmir cease-fire
UNEF	1956–67	6,000	—	Observe, supervise troop withdrawal and provide buffer between Israeli and Egyptian forces
UNOGIL	1958	600	—	Check on clandestine aid from Syria to Lebanon rebels
ONUC	1960–64	20,000	—	Maintain order in the Congo, expel foreign forces, prevent secession and outside intervention
UNSF	1962–63	1,600	—	Maintain order during transfer of authority in New Guinea from Netherlands to Indonesia
UNYOM	1963–64	189	—	Supervise military disengagement in Yemen
UNFICYP	1964–present	6,500	2,350	Prevent internal conflict in Cyprus, avert outside intervention
UNIPOM	1965–66	89	—	Observe India-Pakistan border
UNEF II	1973–79	4,000	—	Supervise cease-fire and troop disengagement, control buffer zone between Egypt and Israel
UNDOF	1974–present	1,330	1,330	Patrol Syria-Israel border
UNIFIL	1978–present	6,000	5,800	Supervise Israeli troop withdrawal, maintain order, help restore authority of Lebanese government

SOURCE: Henry Wiseman, ed., *Peacekeeping: Appraisals and Proposals* (New York: Pergamon Press, 1983); David W. Wainhouse, *International Peace Observation: A History and Forecast* (Baltimore: Johns Hopkins University Press, 1966).

December 1986 figures from *United Nations Peacekeeping: The Facts,* UN Department of Public Information, DPI/905–40005, January 1987.

January 1949 to help curb fighting in Kashmir, it has never quite outlived its usefulness in watching over the cease-fire and restraining conflict along the India-Pakistan
border. Its peak number was 102, but it now functions with fewer than 50 observers.

UN Emergency Force I (UNEF)

UNEF, like the earlier observer missions, was a nonfighting UN military presence designed to help bring international violence under control. The violence in this
case was precipitated by an October 1956 Israeli invasion of Egypt, launched in
coordination with Anglo-French seizure of the Suez Canal, which Egypt had nationalized the previous July. Security Council action was prevented by the British and
French veto, but the General Assembly called for a cease-fire and authorized Secretary-General Hammarskjöld to prepare a plan for an international emergency force.
Because of the large hostile armies and the extent of the area to be patrolled, UNEF
went far beyond any previous UN peacekeeping operation in size and function.
UNTSO at its largest had numbered seven hundred; UNEF fielded six thousand
troops from ten countries. Earlier missions had been concerned largely with observation and reporting. UNEF was intended not only to observe, report, and supervise
troop withdrawal but also to serve as a buffer between the contending forces and to
keep order in the areas under its control.[15]

UNEF fulfilled this assignment well for nearly eleven years. As a face-saving
device to secure troop withdrawal, it proved its value almost immediately. Although
American pressures provided the principal incentive for Britain, France, and Israel
to withdraw, the three countries could pretend that the UN operation was in some
sense theirs and that further military action by national forces was unnecessary. The
last Israeli soldiers left in March 1957. UNEF performed its important buffer role
until June 1967, when the remaining 3,400 troops were withdrawn, on Egyptian
demand. UNEF's withdrawal proved a prelude to the outbreak of the 1967 Middle
East war.

The Congo Force (ONUC)

When the Congo crisis erupted in July 1960, the United Nations turned without
hesitation to the UNEF model even though conditions in the Congo (now Zaire)
were quite different from conditions in the Middle East. The Congo had achieved
independence from Belgium on June 30 with obviously inadequate preparation for
statehood. Widespread rioting, tribal disorders, and mutiny in the Congolese army
broke out almost immediately, and Belgium intervened militarily on July 8 to protect
the lives and property of its nationals. Three days later the mineral-rich province of
Katanga seceded to form an independent state with economic ties to Belgium. Faced
with breakdown of internal order, outside intervention, and secession, the government of the Congo appealed to Secretary-General Hammarskjöld for UN military
assistance. The Security Council authorized Hammarskjöld to prepare a plan for
military and technical aid and thereafter approved his proposal for a UN Operation

in the Congo (ONUC, using the French acronym). The ONUC peacekeeping force eventually reached a strength of twenty thousand troops from twenty-nine countries, cost more than $400 million in its four-year existence, and, with its massive civilian aid component, helped restore a measure of internal stability to the Congo.

From the UNEF experience a number of principles had emerged to govern the organization and functioning of a large peacekeeping force. Among the more important were the following: (1) A peace force should be established only by authorization of the General Assembly or the Security Council. (2) While responsible to the organ that established it, the force should be administratively integrated with the UN Secretariat under the political control of the Secretary-General. (3) Troops from the great powers should not participate in the force. (4) The force should remain politically neutral as between the various contending parties. (5) The force should be limited to nonfighting functions—those that could be performed with the consent or acquiescence of all the governments concerned—but weapons might be used in self-defense. (6) Troop-supplying states should pay the costs that would be incurred if the military units remained in national service; all other costs should be borne by UN members in accordance with the normal UN scale of contributions.

Although most of these principles have continuing validity as peacekeeping guidelines, several of them were bent or broken in the course of the Congo operation. The U.S.-Soviet consensus that permitted initial authorization of ONUC quickly evaporated, and responsibility shifted from the establishing organ to the General Assembly. Political neutrality also suffered. A fair degree of neutrality with respect to outside powers was maintained (the Soviet Union thought otherwise), but internal factions were not treated evenhandedly. Early actions of the force tended to favor an anti-Soviet faction over a leftist faction striving for control of the central government. Later on, ONUC supported the central government in its struggle to prevent the secession of Katanga. Support for the government also meant abandonment of ONUC's nonfighting role, since the Katanga secessionists and their foreign mercenaries could be suppressed only by the use of force. Throughout the Congo operation the principle of financing by assessment of all UN members was maintained, but the Soviet Union, France, and some other countries refused to pay. The skyrocketing deficit brought financial and political crisis to the United Nations (see discussion in Chapter 2) and ultimately forced the premature withdrawal of ONUC before internal stability had been fully achieved.

Whatever its shortcomings under extremely trying circumstances, ONUC had notable accomplishments to its credit. The Belgian troops, mercenaries, and foreign military advisers were gone; the secession of Katanga and other areas of the Congo had been forestalled; and a modicum of law and order had been maintained.[16] The civilian side of the operation had kept essential public services in operation—transport and communication, health, education, public administration—while providing needed technical training for Congolese personnel and supplying emergency relief throughout the country. The threat of intervention by foreign governments was substantially reduced, and the Congo was insulated from the worst effects of cold war rivalry.

UN Forces in West New Guinea and Cyprus

The UN Security Force (UNSF) in West New Guinea (West Irian) and the UN Peacekeeping Force in Cyprus (UNFICYP) were both initiated while the Congo operation was still in progress. They followed the UNEF/ONUC organizational pattern in most respects, with some differences in the force composition. Of some 1,600 UNSF personnel, more than 1,500 were Pakistani troops and the others were U.S. and Canadian air force personnel assigned to an air contingent for supply and liaison activities. The Cyprus force was much larger, about 6,500 in the initial stages. It was more widely international in composition, but the largest contribution came from one of the large powers—the United Kingdom—for reasons of direct interest and immediate availability. Both UNSF and UNFICYP departed from precedent in their mode of financing, in recognition of the growing impasse over the financing of peacekeeping forces by mandatory assessment on the regular UN budgetary scale. The Netherlands and Indonesia—the two parties directly involved in the West Irian dispute—agreed to share all UN expenses equally. UNFICYP has been financed by the countries supplying troops, the government of Cyprus, and voluntary contributions, largely from the states of the Atlantic Community.

UNSF, unlike the other peacekeeping forces, came into being as the result of prior political settlement between the disputants. After years of dogged resistance to Indonesian claims, the Dutch government finally agreed to give up West Irian and to use the United Nations as a convenient mechanism for the transfer. An August 1962 agreement committed the Netherlands to turn over the administration of the territory to a UN Temporary Executive Authority (UNTEA) on October 1. UNTEA, in turn, was to transfer governmental authority to Indonesia after May 1, 1963, subject to the right of the native Papuans to determine their own political fate by a plebiscite before the end of 1969. The Security Force was created to maintain the authority of UNTEA and supplement existing Papuan police in preserving law and order.

When the force was withdrawn at the termination of UN administration, it had the distinction of being the only peacekeeping force to leave the scene of action with its mission fully accomplished. The only sour note was sounded in 1969, when Indonesia substituted an "act of free choice" by eight consultative assemblies in West Irian for a genuine popular plebiscite on the territory's political future. The predictable result of this engineered act of self-determination was perpetuation of Indonesian rule.

The UN Force in Cyprus was created to cope with conflict between Greek and Turkish communities in Cyprus and the threat of military intervention by Greece and Turkey.[17] A British dependency since 1878, Cyprus was granted independence in 1960 under a constitution drafted as a compromise minimally acceptable to the United Kingdom, Greece, Turkey, and the local Cypriot leaders. Under the constitution, majority rule—which would have meant rule by leaders of the Greek Cypriots constituting 80 percent of the island's 600,000 population—was modified by placing a legislative veto in the hands of the Turkish minority. In the absence of good faith, goodwill, and rational behavior, all of which were in short supply, the constitution was scarcely workable. And without consent of the Turkish minority and of the British, Greek, and Turkish governments, it could not lawfully be amended.

Not surprisingly, the machinery of government stalled, the Greek Cypriot majority set about to amend the constitution unilaterally, and domestic violence ensued. Bloodshed and the formation of rival terrorist groups on Cyprus brought Greece and Turkey to sword's point once more, with Britain in the middle as mediator, peacemaker, and policeman. Unable to quell the violence, Britain turned to the Security Council, which established UNFICYP in March 1964.

The UN force has been on duty in Cyprus ever since, though its initial strength of 6,500 has been scaled down to a present force of under 2,500. The initial function of UNFICYP was to create a buffer between Greek and Turkish communities in Cyprus but not to interfere with freedom of movement throughout the island. Subsequently its functions included resolving conflicts between the two groups, adjudicating local disputes, and, with the assistance of a special UN civilian police force, helping to maintain local order. A new crisis erupted in 1974, when a military coup in Cyprus and the prospect of closer military ties between Greece and Cyprus prompted Turkey to invade the island. UNFICYP became involved in the fighting and suffered a number of casualties before a cease-fire could be arranged. The result was a de facto territorial division strongly favoring the Turkish community, followed by a resumption of UNFICYP functions along a now distinct dividing line.

UNFICYP has competently performed its mandate to curb violence and contribute to the maintenance of law and order. The original Security Council resolution authorized the Secretary-General to appoint a mediator to assist the parties with a political settlement, but such efforts have been fruitless. No better result has been accomplished by a personal representative of the Secretary-General, serving at the request of the governments of the United Kingdom, Greece, Turkey, and Cyprus since January 1964. UNFICYP, through repeated Security Council extensions of its mandate, performs a useful and perhaps indispensable function in maintaining order. But the political issues remain impervious to solution.

Small Observer Missions after UNEF

The invention of the large peacekeeping force did not make small observer missions obsolete. Besides perpetuating UNTSO and UNMOGIP, the UN deployed new observer teams during the 1958 Lebanese crisis and in Yemen and India-Pakistan during the mid-1960s. A token UN observer presence was also sent to the Dominican Republic in 1965 to report on U.S. military intervention there.

The largest of the three small observer missions was the UN Observation Group in Lebanon (UNOGIL), a mission of six hundred men that was established in June 1958 at Lebanese request to check on clandestine aid from Syria to rebel groups in Lebanon. UNOGIL reported only minor border infiltration, but in July the border problem was completely overshadowed by a violent pro-Soviet coup in Iraq that raised fears of a similar upheaval in Lebanon. UNOGIL appeared wholly inadequate to cope with this new threat, and fourteen thousand American troops were rushed to

Lebanon at the request of the Lebanese President. In retrospect, the American intervention was a patent overreaction. The external threat to Lebanon had been exaggerated, and domestic strife declined markedly after the July 31 election of a new president. UNOGIL's presence, however, continued to serve a useful purpose by providing a diplomatic rationale for the early withdrawal of U.S. troops. The UNOGIL mission was terminated in December, having played a significant role in relieving a potentially serious crisis.

The UN Yemen Observation Mission (UNYOM) had a more difficult mandate to fulfill. It was established in July 1963 to observe a military disengagement agreement between parties to Yemen's civil war, which posed a serious international threat because of intervention by Egypt and Saudi Arabia on opposite sides. UNYOM's small team, never more than 189 observers, exerted a modest restraining influence on hostilities in the area, but repeated violations of the disengagement agreement led to its withdrawal in September 1964.

Political conditions permitted a happier conclusion to the work of the UN India-Pakistan Observation Mission (UNIPOM), which supplemented UNMOGIP in observing a cease-fire between India and Pakistan from October 1965 to February 1966. The Tashkent Agreement of January 1966 led to mutual troop withdrawal and to the disbandment of UNIPOM with its work successfully completed. Of the three observer missions, UNIPOM and UNOGIL were financed by regular budget assessments. The expenses of UNYOM, however, were jointly shared by Saudi Arabia and Egypt.

The Mission of the Representative of the Secretary-General in the Dominican Republic (DOMREP) consisted of a three-man team sent at the request of the Security Council to report on the situation, but its role was very limited because of opposition from the United States and other parties. DOMREP served mainly to confirm the proposition that UN peacekeeping is unlikely to be viable within the regional sphere of a superpower.

Recent Experience with Peacekeeping

From 1965 to 1973, no new peacekeeping missions were established, although UNTSO, UNMOGIP, and UNFICYP continued to function under repeated extensions of their mandates. In 1973 an attack on Israel by Egypt and Syria made UN peacekeeping again seem a necessary collective response to crisis. The Security Council authorized a UN Emergency Force (UNEF II) of four thousand men to supervise a cease-fire and troop disengagement on the Egyptian front and subsequently to control a UN buffer zone between the combatants. On the Syrian front military action persisted until May 1974, when a disengagement agreement was signed at Geneva by Syria and Israel, with provision for a UN peacekeeping force. Pursuant to the agreement, the Security Council established a UN Disengagement Observer Force (UNDOF) of approximately 1,300 to supervise disengagement and patrol the border area. UNEF II and UNDOF were financed by a specially scaled budgetary assessment designed to reduce the proportionate share of the developing countries.

Both UNEF II and UNDOF performed their assignments successfully and kept hostile incidents to a minimum. Warming relations between Egypt and Israel culminated in the 1978 Camp David accords and the March 1979 treaty of peace, the first political settlement between Israel and any Arab country, which included agreed withdrawal of Israeli forces from the Sinai, to be completed by April 1982. Both parties requested that UNEF II be reconstituted to serve within the framework of the peace agreement, but Soviet and Arab opposition to the treaty made continued UN involvement impossible. UNEF II was terminated in 1979 through nonrenewal of its mandate, leaving a few UNTSO observers as the only UN presence in the Sinai. The gap was filled temporarily by expanding the duties of the U.S. Sinai Field Mission (staffed by civilians, most under private contract), which had been established in 1976 to monitor two strategic passes within the UNEF II buffer zone by means of highly sophisticated electronic surveillance equipment. In 1982 a Multinational Force and Observers (MFO) was created outside the United Nations to monitor the final stages of Israeli troop withdrawal and serve as a continuing border watch. Its 2,500-man force has included troops from the United States and ten other countries, with 60 percent of the cost defrayed by the United States.

UNDOF was not a precursor of a Syria-Israel settlement, but it continues to keep peace by patrolling a forty-seven-mile-long corridor separating opposing forces in the Golan Heights area. That tenuous peace has survived a 1981 exchange of threats over Syrian missiles in the nearby Bekaa Valley, Israeli annexation of the Golan Heights, and Israeli invasions of Lebanon in 1978 and 1982.

A third peacekeeping force, the UN Interim Force in Lebanon (UNIFIL), was a Security Council response to the 1978 Israeli invasion of Lebanon. UNIFIL was given the broad mandate of "confirming the withdrawal of Israeli forces, restoring international peace and security, and assisting the Government of Lebanon in ensuring the return of its effective authority in the area."[18] This mission proved impossible for its six thousand troops to carry out. Although Israel eventually withdrew under heavy international pressure, UNIFIL lacked the resources to maintain order among the numerous armed Christian and Muslim groups or to restore government control over southern Lebanon. Israel complained that UNIFIL was unable to prevent continued PLO raids across the border, while Israel itself continued to make retaliatory strikes against PLO forces both within and beyond the UNIFIL area. UNIFIL troops frequently came under fire, suffered many casualties, and—though a "defensive" force—sometimes had to initiate preventive military action against one or another of the domestic military groups.[19] UNIFIL also encountered financial difficulties. Its budget exceeded $100 million annually during its first four years of operation, and voluntary contributions had to be sought because a number of states refused to pay their assessments.

UNIFIL was brushed aside by Israeli forces in the June 1982 invasion of Lebanon, but it subsequently resumed its efforts to provide a buffer and reduce violence in the area. At the conclusion of the 1982 hostilities, a non-UN Multinational Force (MNF) consisting of British, French, Italian, and U.S. contingents was established to monitor withdrawal of PLO forces from Beirut and help maintain domestic order.

The MNF was unable to remain neutral in the ensuing civil war. American and, to a limited extent, French troops found themselves fighting not only in self-defense but in support of the Lebanese army against Druze, Shiite, and Palestinian militias. Their position proved untenable, as illustrated by the October 1983 truck bombings that killed 299 American and French troops. The MNF withdrew in early 1984, unable to provide for even its own security.

The UN Peace Force: Retrospect and Prospect

In retrospect, the peacekeeping force marks a return to the Charter assumption that the military arm of the organization should not be used to coerce a great power. Even more, it is a tacit admission that the United Nations is ill suited to organizing military sanctions against any country, large or small. The framers of the Charter foresaw the dangers of making the organization a potential catalyst of general war between the giants, and they devised the Security Council veto to preclude such a UN role. What they could scarcely foresee was the extent to which the pervasiveness of East-West rivalry would give to nearly every armed conflict, or threat of conflict, the potentiality of great power involvement on opposite sides. In practical terms, the use of any kind of military sanctions under UN auspices now appears either too dangerous or politically unfeasible, or both.

The United Nations is still capable of a constructive role in matters of global security, however, when the large powers see a common interest in the termination of hostilities and the maintenance of order. Over the past four decades violence has been curbed through UN intervention in such diverse places as Indonesia, the Middle East, Kashmir, Cyprus, and the Sinai Peninsula without resort to international military sanctions. This suggests that UN sanctions forces, while politically unacceptable in any event, are practically unnecessary when Soviet and American interests converge. In such a setting the peace force becomes a highly useful instrument for performing local police functions while a settlement is being effectuated or, in the more usual case, for encouraging restraint and separating combatants in a volatile situation where the parties have accepted peace without settlement.

The peacekeeping force has been politically feasible when the major powers have acquiesced in its role and the consent of all parties immediately concerned could be obtained. The financial feasibility of such forces remains a critical problem. Considering the apparent contribution of UNEF I and ONUC to peace and stability, their combined cost was relatively small—some $15 million to $20 million a year for the former and approximately $100 million a year for the latter. Nevertheless, the unwillingness of some members to pay the costs of peacekeeping brought the United Nations to the verge of bankruptcy. The financial impact of the Congo crisis was temporarily cushioned by the issuance of UN bonds, but ONUC had to be disbanded and withdrawn from the Congo in 1964 because of the financial drain on the organization, not because its usefulness had ended.

The financial problem, while serious in its own right, was symptomatic of a more fundamental political problem—disagreement over the establishment and control of peacekeeping operations. Both France and the Soviet Union maintain that sole control of UN forces should rest with the Security Council, where each of the five permanent members holds the veto. They object to the deployment of UN forces without their consent, and to the principle that a state can be required to pay for any UN security function that a majority of the Assembly decides to make chargeable to the organization as a whole.

The assessment issue was sidestepped in the creation of the UN Cyprus force (1964) by making it dependent on voluntary contributions, and nine years passed before another UN peacekeeping force was created. The three UN forces since established—UNEF II (1973), UNDOF (1974), and UNIFIL (1978)—have all been authorized and controlled by the Security Council and financed by an Assembly-approved mandatory assessment formula that minimizes the contributions of developing countries. Although the Soviet Union initially voted for UNEF II and UNDOF, and abstained on the UNIFIL authorization, it now pays assessments only for UNDOF. Along with some twenty East European and Arab states, it refuses to support UNIFIL on the theory that Israel as the "aggressor" in Lebanon should pay the costs of peacekeeping. Soviet contributions to UNEF II ceased after 1976 because the Israeli-Egyptian disengagement agreement was negotiated under American rather than UN auspices.

Although the UN peacekeeping presence has proved its worth in the field, and five such missions are currently in operation (UNMOGIP, UNTSO, UNFICYP, UNDOF, and UNIFIL), the future of UN peacekeeping is problematic. A Special Committee on Peacekeeping Operations, established during the financial crisis of 1964–65, has labored for more than twenty years without resolving the thorny issues of finance and control. Apart from the merits of particular operations, the United States has favored an active supervising role for the Secretary-General, while the Soviet Union would confer sole power on the Security Council. In practice, since 1973 peacekeepers have followed guidelines prepared by the Secretary-General and approved by the Council. The expertise of the Secretariat and a small cadre of peacekeepers in the field is an international asset of great potential value in future operations. Several middle powers have been willing to supply needed troops and have also accumulated valuable experience in the process. The most frequent contributors of military contingents have been Canada, Sweden, Finland, Denmark, Ireland, Norway, the Netherlands, Italy, Austria, New Zealand, and India. The Scandinavian states have earmarked troops and facilities to be available on a few weeks' notice. As sympathetic observers have noted, however, none of this will "lower the level of international violence unless the UN's member countries rededicate themselves to using the world organization."[20]

No new UN peacekeeping force has been put into the field since the establishment of UNIFIL in 1978, although three major peacekeeping efforts have been launched outside the United Nations. Their experience is instructive. The Multinational Force (MNF) in Beirut, Lebanon, 1982–84, as noted above, lost its neutrality, became involved in the local fighting, and withdrew with little accomplished. The

Multinational Force and Observers (MFO) in the Sinai Peninsula has been more successful, largely because it was modeled closely on the UN pattern and provided a buffer for two countries that genuinely desired peace. A peacekeeping force sponsored by the Organization of African Unity was deployed in December 1981 in Chad to help maintain peace among rival factions. Some six months later it withdrew in disarray—underfinanced, poorly managed, and unwilling to continue fighting to maintain its position between the rival groups.

A peacekeeping operation can be effectively conducted outside UN auspices if the parties are willing to have peace and if financial support and acceptably neutral troops are available. The success of the MFO in Sinai illustrates that. Experience with the MNF and the OAU force in Chad, however, suggests that maintaining a neutral, nonfighting stance may be more difficult for peacekeeping forces not subject to the discipline of UN rules and the UN commitment to neutrality. The OAU force in Chad also suffered from lack of financial resources and management expertise. In both Beirut and Chad a UN force would probably have served better than the alternatives that were used, if a UN force could have been created. Some local conflicts, of course, are beyond the ability of a peacekeeping force to contain, regardless of whether the sponsor is the United Nations, another international agency, or even a superpower.

The main problem of the UN force is political feasibility. Sometimes the permanent members of the Security Council are divided, so no action is possible. Sometimes a UN force is not feasible because the states directly concerned oppose UN involvement or are unwilling to stop fighting or because states in a geographic region prefer to handle the matter themselves. But when political conditions permit recourse to the United Nations, its neutrality, organizational capability, and peacekeeping experience make it a valuable international asset.[21]

GLOBAL SECURITY AND THE UNITED NATIONS

In the fall of 1961, the United States submitted to the General Assembly a plan for "General and Complete Disarmament." An integral part of the plan was a proposal to build a "United Nations peace force" strong enough, ultimately, to "deter or suppress any threat or use of force in violation of the purposes and principles of the United Nations." In the final stage of disarmament, the force would be so strong that "no state would have the military power to challenge" it.[22] The proposal was breathtaking, to say the least, if it could be taken seriously. It went much farther along the road to collective security than anything the conferees of Versailles and San Francisco had dreamed of. The proposal created a noticeable ripple on the UN diplomatic pond, but the reaction was in no way commensurate with the drastic alteration of the conditions of international life that it contemplated. Most observers regarded it as lip service to collective security that would bring no more practical results than predecessor proposals. The episode illustrates the paradox of global security today.

People cherish the ultimate ideal of an orderly, peaceful world made secure by force wielded in the common interest; but their actions negate the very notion of a common interest.

Stanley Hoffmann aptly characterized the UN security effort when, at the time of the Suez crisis, he compared it to the mythological Sisyphus, forever commanded to roll a stone uphill and never permitted to reach the top.[23] But perhaps the plight of world organization is not so eternally void of hope as that of Sisyphus. No one can feel very confident about getting to the top, but occasionally the stone is rolled upward to a new plateau that marks a gain over previous efforts to promote world peace and security. The establishment of the League of Nations was such an advance, for all the League's inability to stave off aggression and a catastrophic world war. If international security arrangements changed very little from the days of Abraham to the assassination of the Austrian Archduke at Sarajevo, the creation of the League of Nations interjected a new and lasting element into the international system. The League symbolized widespread acceptance of the principle of common interest in the maintenance of peace and security, and it was an institutional embodiment of the principle. Even World War II could not wipe out this concept; the United Nations reflected the same sense of common interest.

This development, of course, is no more than a step toward world order. If twentieth-century international organization marks a plateau in the ascent toward world peace and security, it is still very far from the top. Both the League and the United Nations have had to exist in a world where national armaments, alliances, and some form of the balance of power are the chief reliance of states in their quest for security. The polarization of military power and the availability of nuclear weapons have worked far greater modifications in the balance-of-power system than has the advent of international organization. Indeed, the central feature of the system—collective security—has heretofore proved unworkable, and substantial doubts of even its desirability remain unallayed. Honest critics have yet to be satisfied that doctrinaire versions of collective security hold no danger of turning localized wars into general wars and of creating a collective force that, if it were strong enough to do its job, would itself constitute a threat to world peace and security.

Nevertheless, if doctrinaire collective security has little relevance for present problems, the same pessimistic appraisal is not applicable to the whole gamut of UN security techniques. The present global balance of power has a need for services that the United Nations can provide as a means of communication, mediation, and judicious intervention in time of crisis. Giving a reverse twist to collective security, which calls for universal involvement in every international conflict, the United Nations can serve to insulate the conflicts of other states from the worst effects of large power rivalry.[24] This was the UN function that Dag Hammarskjöld called "preventive diplomacy." By contributing to local stability, a UN presence might promote the stability of the global system. It cannot help, of course, unless it is used. But if this UN capacity is not permitted to atrophy through disuse, it can help the world inch upward in the troubled ascent toward peace.

NOTES

1. The rationale for international economic and social cooperation, for example, as set forth in Article 55 of the UN Charter, is "the creation of conditions of stability and well-being which are necessary for peaceful and friendly relations among nations." Peace and security also figure prominently in Charter prescriptions for dependent territories and peoples. See Articles 73(c) and 76(a).

2. The term *balance of power* has not been given a consistent meaning in the literature of international relations. A *system* is only one of its meanings, and not all definitions of the system are the same. As Claude points out, the term may also refer to a *situation* (the existing distribution of power, whether an equilibrium or a balance in some state's favor) or a *policy* (promoting an equilibrium, confronting power with countervailing power, combining against a potential aggressor, or simply striving for increased power). A classic critique of the concept is found in Inis L. Claude, Jr., *Power and International Relations* (New York: Random House, 1962), especially chaps. 2, 3.

3. Andrew Martin, *Collective Security* (Paris: UNESCO, 1952), p. 7.

4. See John F. Murphy, *The United Nations and the Control of International Violence: A Legal and Political Analysis* (Totowa, N.J.: Allanheld, Osmun, 1982), p. 135.

5. See Gordon A. Craig and Alexander L. George, *Force and Statecraft: Diplomatic Problems of Our Time* (New York: Oxford University Press, 1983), pp. 106–12.

6. A detailed analysis of these differences is found in Leland M. Goodrich and Anne P. Simons, *The United Nations and the Maintenance of International Peace and Security* (Washington: Brookings Institution, 1955), pp. 398–405.

7. General Assembly Resolution 3314 (XXIX), December 14, 1974. The preamble to the definition observes that "the question whether an act of aggression has been committed must be considered in the light of all the circumstances of each particular case." Article 1 of the definition proscribes "the use of force against the sovereignty, territorial integrity or political independence" of another state and labels it "aggression." Article 2 makes "the first use of armed force by a State in contravention of the Charter" prima facie evidence of aggression, subject to Security Council determination that the act in question did not constitute aggression. Article 3 lists several other acts that may be labeled aggression, subject again to the Security Council's decision to the contrary. Article 7 specifically excludes from the definition of aggression acts by and in support of peoples struggling to achieve "self-determination, freedom and independence" from "colonial and racist regimes or other forms of alien domination."

8. A very thorough and authoritative study of the UN role in Korea, published in 1956, concluded that "the successful repulse of the aggression gave renewed vitality to the United Nations collective security system." Leland M. Goodrich, *Korea: A Study of U.S. Policy in the United Nations* (New York: Council on Foreign Relations, 1956), p. 211. This was the general feeling of informed persons at the time, but the "renewed vitality" proved to be only a temporary phenomenon.

9. General Assembly Resolution 377/(V), November 3, 1950.

10. As Orbach observes, many such resolutions are adopted as a substitute for action because UN members recognize that nothing more concrete can be done. See William W. Orbach, *To Keep the Peace: The United Nations Condemnatory Resolution* (Lexington: University Press of Kentucky, 1977), pp. 9–10.

11. For a careful, detailed study of economic sanctions, see Margaret P. Doxey, *Economic Sanctions and International Enforcement*, 2nd ed. (New York: Oxford University Press, 1980).

12. A useful commentary on regional approaches to military cooperation in the Atlantic area, Africa, the Pacific, Latin America, and the Middle East is Gavin Boyd, ed., *Regionalism and Global Security* (Lexington, Mass: D. C. Heath, 1984).

13. A recent review of UN peacekeeping is Henry Wiseman, ed., *Peacekeeping: Appraisals and Proposals* (New York: Pergamon Press, 1983).

14. *Introduction to the Annual Report of the Secretary-General on the Work of the Organization*, June 16, 1959, to June 15, 1960, General Assembly, Official Records, 15th sess., supp. no. 1A, p. 4.

15. A good account of UNEF in its early years is Gabriella E. Rosner, *The United Nations Emergency Force* (New York: Columbia University Press, 1963).

16. Ernest W. Lefever's *Uncertain Mandate: Politics of the U.N. Congo Operation* (Baltimore: Johns Hopkins University Press, 1967) emphasizes "the inherent and inescapable limitations of the United Nations as an instrument for states that want to contain conflict or facilitate peaceful change" (p. 221). Nevertheless, this study acknowledges, "given the limitations of the UNF and the magnitude of the problem, its modest accomplishments are noteworthy" (p. 213). See also Georges Abi-Saab, *The United Nations Operation in the Congo, 1960–1964* (New York: Oxford University Press, 1978).

17. The standard work on the origin and early years of UNFICYP is James A. Stegenga, *The United Nations Force in Cyprus* (Columbus: Ohio State University Press, 1968).

18. Security Council Resolution 425, March 19, 1978.

19. UNIFIL forces suffered 103 deaths during the period from March 1978 to January 1985—42 from mines and gunfire, 48 as the result of accidents, and 13 from natural causes. *UN Chronicle* 22, no. 1 (1985), p. 29.

20. Ann Florini and Nina Tannenwald, *On the Front Lines: The United Nations' Role in Preventing and Containing Conflict* (New York: United Nations Association of the United States, 1984), p. 54.

21. For an analysis of the advantages of UN over non-UN peacekeeping, see Indar Jit Rikhye, *The Theory and Practice of Peacekeeping* (London: C. Hurst, 1984), p. 239.

22. *Department of State Bulletin* 45 (October 16, 1961), pp. 653–54.

23. Hoffmann, "Sisyphus and the Avalanche: The United Nations, Egypt and Hungary," *International Organization,* 11, no. 3 (Summer 1957), pp. 446–69.

24. Geoffrey L. Goodwin, a leading British student of international affairs, emphasizes this aspect of peacekeeping: "The record in the peace-keeping field has been mixed but not unimpressive and it can be claimed that in several instances, Suez (1956), Lebanon (1958), the Congo (1960), in the Sinai (1973) and intermittently in Cyprus, UN peace-keeping forces have helped to contain conflicts which could have further exacerbated great power tensions." Goodwin, "Power Politics and the United Nations," in *Diplomacy at the UN*, ed. G. R. Berridge and A. Jennings (New York: St. Martin's Press, 1985), p. 5.

SELECTED READINGS

ABI-SAAB, GEORGES. *The United Nations Operation in the Congo, 1960–1964*. New York: Oxford University Press, 1978.

BOYD, GAVIN. *Regionalism and Global Security*. Lexington, Mass.: D. C. Heath, 1984.

BOYD, JAMES M. *United Nations Peace Keeping Operations: A Military and Political Appraisal*. New York: Praeger Publishers, 1971.

CLAUDE, INIS L., JR. *Power and International Relations*. New York: Random House, 1962.

DOXEY, MARGARET P. *Economic Sanctions and International Enforcement*. 2nd ed. New York: Oxford University Press, 1980.

FABIAN, LARRY L. *Soldiers without Enemies: Preparing the United Nations for Peacekeeping*. Washington, D.C.: Brookings Institution, 1971.

FINKELSTEIN, MARINA S., and LAWRENCE S. FINKELSTEIN, eds. *Collective Security*. San Francisco: Chandler Publishing, 1966.

FLORINI, ANN, and NINA TANNENWALD. *On the Front Lines: The United Nations' Role in Preventing and Containing Conflict.* New York: United Nations Association of the United States, 1984.

GOODRICH, LELAND M. *Korea: A Study of U.S. Policy in the United Nations.* New York: Council on Foreign Relations, 1956.

GOODRICH, LELAND M., and ANNE P. SIMONS. *The United Nations and the Maintenance of International Peace and Security.* Washington, D.C.: Brookings Institution, 1955.

HIGGINS, ROSALYN. *United Nations Peacekeeping.* 4 vols. London, Oxford: Oxford University Press, 1969–1981.

JAMES, ALAN. *The Politics of Peacekeeping.* New York: Praeger Publishers, 1969.

LEFEVER, ERNEST W. *Uncertain Mandate: Politics of the U.N. Congo Operation.* Baltimore: Johns Hopkins University Press, 1967.

MURPHY, JOHN F. *The United Nations and the Control of International Violence: A Legal and Political Analysis.* Totowa, N.J.: Allanheld, Osmun, 1982.

ORBACH, WILLIAM W. *To Keep the Peace: The United Nations Condemnatory Resolution.* Lexington: University Press of Kentucky, 1977.

RIKHYE, INDAR JIT. *The Peacekeeping Handbook.* New York: Pergamon Press, 1984.

————. *The Theory and Practice of Peacekeeping.* London: C. Hurst, 1984.

ROSNER, GABRIELLA E. *The United Nations Emergency Force.* New York: Columbia University Press, 1963.

ROYAL INSTITUTE OF INTERNATIONAL AFFAIRS. *International Sanctions.* London: Oxford University Press, 1938.

STEGENGA, JAMES A. *The United Nations Force in Cyprus.* Columbus: Ohio State University Press, 1968.

WAINHOUSE, DAVID W. *International Peace Observation: A History and Forecast.* Baltimore: Johns Hopkins University Press, 1966.

————. *International Peacekeeping at the Crossroads: National Support—Experience and Prospects.* Baltimore: Johns Hopkins University Press, 1973.

WISEMAN, HENRY, ed. *Peacekeeping: Appraisals and Proposals.* New York: Pergamon Press, 1983.

6

Disarmament and Arms Control

A variety of approaches to peace are utilized within and outside the UN system, but each has its drawbacks. Regional and global alliance systems, for example, offer pathways to peace, but both may ultimately lead to a major war. Deterrence based on a "balance of terror" poses the threat of the annihilation of entire populations, or perhaps of all life on planet earth, if a major escalation to the use of nuclear weapons occurs or if a human, electronic, or mechanical error results in a massive nuclear exchange. Economic, social, and human rights programs may ultimately eliminate the causes of war, but such a happy state of affairs cannot be foreseen at this time.

Disarmament, on the other hand, offers an approach to security that eliminates the need for balancing power with power or for energizing the world community into action against a lawbreaker; peace is simply a consequence of a world without weapons. Although the Charter does not mention disarmament in its basic purposes and principles, disarmament and arms control negotiations fostered by the United Nations have been carried on since it came into being. Hundreds of proposals and thousands of meetings later, no substantial evidence of successful disarmament exists and insecurity is rife. This chapter will explore this ill-fated campaign by examining the history of negotiations, analyzing the modest successes in the field of arms control (as distinct from disarmament), evaluating the reasons for failure, and positing some potential strategies to break the disarmament deadlock. Such a broad-based analysis of the theory and practice of arms control is necessary to place UN actions in their global context and to help explain why the United Nations has brought forth so little fruit in this area.

DISARMAMENT IN HISTORICAL PERSPECTIVE

Historically, disarmament negotiations have had limited objectives, such as an arms reduction, a "freeze" in the level of armaments, the limiting of weapons to an agreed ratio, the prohibition of specified types of arms, or a local demilitarization. It was

150

not until 1960 that "general and complete disarmament" as a goal for the entire state system was proclaimed by a unanimous vote of the UN General Assembly. Schemes envisioning universal peace through general disarmament written by Immanuel Kant, Jean-Jacques Rousseau, William Penn, and other visionaries had postulated the ideal of a completely disarmed world prior to the nineteenth century, but these utopian schemes had had little impact except in intellectual circles. Arms control, as contrasted with general disarmament, may include various forms of agreements and understandings that have an impact on the arms race. These might include arrangements to avoid misunderstandings that could lead to war, the substitution of one type of weapon for another through mutual agreement, or "confidence-building measures" aimed at reducing the tensions of the arms race. Arms control thus focuses on mutual restraint and stability sought through agreement.

Although Russian, British, French, and Italian statesmen made practical proposals for arms reduction during the nineteenth century, the only successful agreement reached during that period was the Rush-Bagot Treaty of 1817, by which the United States and Britain agreed to demilitarize the Great Lakes in perpetuity. The agreement remains to this day the most successful disarmament understanding ever negotiated.

The first international conference with disarmament as its major objective was called by Czar Nicholas of Russia at The Hague in 1899. Although no agreement was reached on the limitation of armaments and war budgets, the First Hague Conference did adopt declarations proscribing the use of certain weapons so that war could be made more humane. Few of the countries represented were cooler toward disarmament negotiations than the United States. The chief American delegate, Captain (later Admiral) Alfred Mahan, received instructions that arms limitation "could not profitably be discussed" because of the inferior position of American arms to those of leading European powers. Instead of agreeing to a naval limitation, he openly stated that the United States planned to increase the size of its Pacific fleet to strengthen its role in the competition for Asian markets. On the question of banning dumdum bullets and asphyxiating gas as barbaric weapons, Captain Mahan joined with the British delegate to vote against outlawing the former and cast the lone negative vote on the latter.[1]

Two innocuous resolutions calling on the twenty-six states represented at the Conference to consider the limitation of their war budgets "for the increase of the material and moral welfare of mankind" were adopted unanimously. At the Second Hague Conference, in 1907, the delegates accepted the fact that the arms race had made disarmament impracticable and so pursued other avenues to avoid war. A brief discussion, another meaningless resolution, and the subject was laid to rest. Ironically, some delegates expressed the opinion that the question of disarmament should be reopened at another conference in 1915, a year in which most of the world was to be at war. In spite of the failure of the two Hague Conferences to achieve agreement on disarmament or arms control, they did establish the precedent—still followed in the United Nations—that coping with the arms race is a responsibility of the world community.

Disarmament Efforts during the League Years

The Covenant of the League of Nations followed the prescription advocated by Woodrow Wilson in one of his Fourteen Points. It provided that armaments, as a recognized cause of war, should be "reduced to the lowest point consistent with national safety" but retained in sufficient quantities to provide for "the enforcement by common action of international obligations." This close relationship between disarmament and collective security as two phases of a basic approach to peace and security was augmented by three approaches to arms limitation that were employed within the framework of the postwar peace settlements. First, through League efforts and treaty provisions, the Rhineland, Danzig, the Aaland Islands, and certain other territories were completely demilitarized. Second, the Versailles Treaty imposed extensive limitations on Germany's military forces and provided for inspection and control by Allied authorities. Third, the League encouraged and sponsored disarmament studies and conferences aimed at implementing Covenant provisions.

The first postwar effort to limit arms, however, took place outside the League framework. In 1921 the Washington Naval Conference—called by the United States and attended by representatives of Britain, France, Italy, and Japan—set the pace for arms limitation negotiations. A treaty signed the following year limited the size of warships, restricted the construction of battleships and aircraft carriers for ten years, limited new construction thereafter by a ratio agreement (United States, 5; Britain, 5; Japan, 3; France, 1.67; and Italy, 1.67), and imposed limitations on naval bases in the Pacific. Subsequently some of the parties violated the spirit and others the letter of the treaty. Britain and the United States engaged in a "cruiser race," Japan devised ingenious variations of the prohibited vessels to nullify the intent of the treaty, and France refused to implement any limitation in the absence of a general European security arrangement. The record of violations and subterfuge that followed the Washington Naval Arms Limitation Treaty and the countermeasures undertaken in response to evasions call attention to the difficulty of implementing a disarmament agreement without international inspection and enforcement machinery.

The League was even less successful in its efforts to promote a general reduction in armaments. Several commissions appointed by the League Council to study and recommend disarmament plans failed to find a formula acceptable to the great powers. Each major state had a different approach to the subject, and its own conception of how security could be safeguarded; the only area of mutuality was a common suspicion of one another's intentions.

Encouragement for the League's efforts during the 1920s came with the signing of the Locarno Treaty of 1925, which sought to normalize relations between France and Germany by a collective guarantee against aggression in the frontier areas between the two nations. The spirit of Locarno fostered a hope that general disarmament would soon prove feasible, and a Preparatory Commission established in 1925 was assigned the task of providing the groundwork for a major international disarmament conference. After five years of sporadic effort, the Commission prepared a Draft Convention in 1930 that reflected mostly the inability of its members to reach accord on limiting their armed forces. The main provisions of the Draft Convention called for the reduction of military budgets, some reductions in naval armaments, and the establishment of a Permanent Disarmament Commission. The deepening economic depression, however, served notice that, although states could not agree on disarmament, the coming struggle to preserve fiscal solvency might force them to curtail arms production.

The long-heralded World Disarmament Conference was finally convened at Geneva in 1932, with sixty-one states represented. Each of the major nations in turn offered its scheme to a skeptical group of delegates. The French plan envisaged a comprehensive security system that included qualified disarmament, an international control system, compulsory arbitration, and an international police force under League jurisdiction to guarantee security. Britain offered a plan that would outlaw the use of "offensive" weapons through a reinforced League security system, provide for disarmament by stages over a five-year period, and outlaw weapons of mass destruction. Germany demanded equality with France in any disarmament program. The United States proposed a uniform reduction in forces so that each nation would retain the same arms ratio with all other nations that it had before the agreement. The American plan was regarded by some Conference delegates as an oversimplified scheme that would encourage aggression and penalize defensive armies.

The flicker of hope that an acceptable formula might be discovered through conference debate was extinguished when Adolf Hitler was appointed Chancellor in 1933 and withdrew Germany from the Conference and the League. The Conference, immobilized almost from the start by the basic conflict between German demands for arms equality and the French insistence on arms superiority over Germany, finally adjourned in 1934 in complete failure. The Conference, however, was not a total loss. Agreement on broad principles, though never formalized, indicated a general revulsion against the use of chemical and bacteriological weapons, a consensus that arms should be reduced and military budgets curtailed, and a general acceptance of the idea that an international authority should be established to supervise any disarmament agreement that could be reached. Debates at the Conference and in the League Assembly over a period of twenty years helped prepare the world for the next round in the disarmament cycle under the United Nations.

The United Nations and Disarmament

The effort to secure disarmament during the UN era differs from that of the League period in several respects. For one, the pressures to reach agreement have been more persistent and have grown out of a sense of grave urgency. The dropping of an atom bomb on Hiroshima several months after the writing of the Charter alerted the world to the potentiality for a calamity far greater than the destructiveness of World War II. The period after 1946 of cold war with full-scale rearmament, the framing of the North Atlantic and Warsaw pacts, intermittent crises, and the development of intercontinental missiles with thermonuclear warheads—all occurring within a setting of frenetic ideological hostility—forged a link in many minds between disarmament and sheer survival. New Third World nations, whose people had ignored the arms race and the threat of war in quiet colonial subservience during the 1930s, now joined the rising chorus of those awakened to the danger of global war. The United Nations provided them with a ready forum to air their demands for great power retrenchment in the arms race.

The Charter framers did not assign disarmament a prominent role in pursuing the primary goal of peace and security. Their failure to stress disarmament can perhaps be ascribed mainly to their ignorance about the nuclear device that American scientists were secretly preparing to test at the very time the Charter was being written. Added to this, the frustrations of the League period and the emphasis on the use of an international army to maintain peace and security through community force influenced the framers against setting forth extravagant disarmament goals that would be unrealizable.

Unlike the League Covenant, which had called for an outright *reduction* in arms, the Charter merely proclaims the objective of arms *regulation*. Regulation implies the need for a strategically balanced ceiling on armaments so that the collective security machinery of the United Nations can function in a world not obsessed with fear of an imminent and massive attack. The close relationship between the two objectives—arms regulation and collective security—led the framers to assign responsibility for both functions to the Security Council aided by the Military Staff Committee (Articles 26 and 46, respectively). Giving the same bodies the responsibility of formulating plans for arms regulation *and* the use of military forces offered no contradiction for the framers, who considered progress in both areas essential to the maintenance of peace and security. Moreover, arms regulation was to *follow*, not precede, the full implementation of a global security system. The innovation of the atom bomb, however, invalidated the otherwise logical plan of the framers by destroying the potential for strategically balancing the forces of the great powers. The result was the emergence of two nuclear superpowers with tremendously destructive arsenals.

ARMS NEGOTIATIONS IN THE UN ERA

Early Failures

Initial efforts in the disarmament field were undertaken by the UN Atomic Energy Commission, established in January 1946 by the first General Assembly resolution. In recognition of the fact that atomic energy possessed great potentialities for peaceful purposes as well as grave dangers for all of mankind, the Assembly rather than the Security Council was chosen by the great powers to create and empower the Commission. The Assembly resolution called on the Commission to develop "with the utmost dispatch" a plan to provide for (1) the exchange of scientific knowledge for peaceful purposes, (2) the control of atomic energy to limit its use to peaceful purposes, (3) the elimination of atomic and other weapons of mass destruction, and (4) the establishment of an inspection and enforcement system to safeguard against evasions.[2]

At the first meeting of the Atomic Energy Commission, the United States, with a monopoly of atomic weapons, offered a plan that would eventually provide for a sharing of its atomic secrets under an international control system. The proposal, based on recommendations made in the Acheson-Lilienthal Report, was presented by elder statesman Bernard Baruch. In its fundamentals the Baruch Plan provided for a transition to peaceful atomic control by stages, with each stage dependent on the successful implementation of the preceding stage before further progress would be attempted. It called for the creation of an International Atomic Development Authority that would operate an elaborate inspection and control system under Security Council direction unhampered by the veto power. All atomic weapons would be destroyed once the control system became operational, and the manufacture of new atom bombs would be outlawed. The Authority would then exercise exclusive ownership of atomic raw materials, control all atomic activities, encourage their beneficial use by all nations, hold a monopoly on research and development in the field of atomic explosives, and license national atomic research for peaceful purposes. In sum, the plan would establish a world federal government restricted to the field of atomic energy, in which its powers would be virtually supreme. Although many of the specifics have changed, the broad framework of this position has remained substantially unchanged as an American debating posture in the many years of negotiations that have followed the presentation of the Baruch Plan.

The Soviet Union emphatically rejected the American proposal in favor of the immediate outlawing of all atomic weapons followed by the establishment of a minimum system of control. In the Soviet view, each state should accept responsibility for the peaceful development of atomic power and for the policing of the prohibition against atomic weapons within its borders, subject to periodic oversight by an international authority. Enforcement action would be undertaken by the Security Council against violators, but only with the agreement of all permanent members. Thus the first confrontation between the United States and the Soviet Union produced basic disagreements over the timing (which comes first, complete disarmament or an inspection and control system?), peaceful development (by national or international authority?), inspection (what powers should the international authority possess, and how frequently should it conduct inspections?), and control (should the veto power apply to action against violators?). The gulf between the major parties over the details of controlling armaments has been altered little since that initial encounter.

The Soviets, placed on the defensive by the Baruch Plan and outnumbered on the Atomic Energy Commission, took the offensive in the latter part of the General Assembly's first session in 1946 with a proposal for general and complete disarmament, including conventional and nuclear weapons. The proposal apparently was an effort to overcome the propaganda advantage gained by the United States in offering to relinquish its atomic monopoly and to contribute its know-how to the peaceful development of atomic power for mankind. Moreover, the special treatment accorded atomic disarmament overlooked the fact that the atom bomb figured prominently in the assessments of the major power rivals as a weapon that could decisively affect the power ratio in conventional arms. The Soviet Union obviously preferred to discuss the broad, innocuous subject of general disarmament while carrying on a crash program to develop an atom bomb to offset the American advantage. In 1949 the Soviets tested their first atom bomb, and thereafter the arms race was converted into a nuclear race between superpowers.

The Search for Effective Discussion Forums

The initial failure to reach agreement via the Baruch Plan has been repeated in many different forums. A multitude of discussion and negotiating committees and commissions, some within the UN framework and others outside it, have been created to seek agreement on disarmament and arms control measures. Disarmament forums have varied in size, composition, and subjects for negotiation. The first, the Atomic Energy Commission, consisted of the permanent members of the Security Council (Britain, China, France, the Soviet Union, and the United States) plus Canada. When the AEC failed to achieve agreement, a five-power subcommittee consisting of the same nations minus China met in closed session from 1954 to 1957. Since 1957 most arms control negotiations have been conducted, not in UN organs, but in ad hoc bodies that have only a tenuous connection with the United Nations. Participants have often utilized UN facilities and staffs and, at the request of the General Assembly, have altered the size and composition of the negotiating forums and submitted reports to that body. In 1965 the idea of a World Disarmament Conference was endorsed by the General Assembly, but thirty years of efforts by nonnuclear states have failed to secure the agreement of the nuclear weapons states to the use of that forum.

In 1958 a special Three-Power Conference consisting of Britain, the Soviet Union, and the United States was established at the initiative of the parties and with Assembly support to reach agreement on the ending of nuclear tests. The next year, in response to Soviet demands for parity, the now familiar East-West pattern of representation was initiated with the establishment of the Ten-Nation Committee on Disarmament. Bulgaria, Czechoslovakia, Poland, Romania, and the USSR represented the Eastern bloc on this Committee, and Britain, Canada, France, Italy, and the United States represented the Western bloc. In 1961 the Ten-Nation body, under pressure from the Third World for its failure to achieve disarmament results, was enlarged into an Eighteen-Nation Disarmament Committee (ENDC). The ENDC was empowered by the General Assembly to "undertake negotiations with a view to reaching . . . agreement on general and complete disarmament under effective international control." The new body continued the East-West parity arrangements and added eight nonaligned countries. When success proved elusive, the ENDC was converted in 1969 into the Conference of the Committee on Disarmament (CCD), with an expanded Third World representation that brought its membership to twenty-six. In 1979 the General Assembly expanded the CCD into a new forty-member Conference on Disarmament (CD) in the hope that additional members could apply greater pressures on the nuclear powers to reach agreement.

Although most of the actual negotiations on general disarmament have taken place in ad hoc bodies created with the agreement of the major powers, since 1952 the General Assembly has provided for a UN Disarmament Commission to discuss major issues. At first, the Disarmament Commission consisted of the eleven members of the Security Council plus Canada. In response to the Soviet Union's pressures for a broader forum for expounding its views on disarmament issues, the Assembly expanded the Disarmament Commission to twenty-five in 1957 and in 1958 increased it to include all members of the United Nations. This new "negotiating forum" was not expected to produce tangible results, but many nations supported the idea as a means of marshaling world pressures to force concessions from the great powers. Meeting sporadically, this huge body, true to its critics' forecasts, failed to resolve any arms control issues, but its sessions did prove useful in breaking the Soviet boycott of negotiations in other bodies and in exploring approaches not ordinarily considered by the great powers, such as including the People's Republic of China in disarmament talks and calling for a World Disarmament Conference. Later the General Assembly determined that its First (Political and Security) Committee, composed of all members of the United Nations, should thereafter function as the UN Disarmament Commission, particularly in making recommendations to the General Assembly and through it to the various negotiating bodies.[3]

Special Sessions of the General Assembly

In addition to these efforts, the General Assembly twice called special sessions on disarmament (SSOD I, 1978; and SSOD II, 1982). Each special session took the form of a five-week conference that placed the United Nations in the center of arms control discussions. In 1982, for example, nineteen heads of state and fifty foreign ministers joined in discussions of the dangers of the arms race and made suggestions concerning how it might be brought under control. At that time, in what was perhaps the largest disarmament rally in history, an estimated 750,000 people demonstrated their support for disarmament. Despite the evidence that almost everyone supported the idea of disarmament, no concrete actions to reduce the arms race emerged from either session. Nevertheless, the first Special Session on Disarmament established what is currently known as the UN Department for Disarmament Affairs. This UN body seeks to generate support for disarmament by fostering studies, training diplomats, organizing conferences, and distributing its annual *United Nations Disarmament Yearbook*.

Both special sessions were noteworthy for the amount of public interest generated, the high quality of debate carried on by the participants, and the universal concern manifested in the search for peace on planet earth. All the major problems growing out of the arms race were extensively discussed, and many general and specific solutions were proposed. The UN Disarmament Commission, inactive for several years, was reinvigorated by the actions of SSOD I. Future special sessions of the General Assembly focusing on disarmament can be anticipated, but none is currently scheduled. Perhaps most important, SSOD II produced a World Disarmament Campaign that recruited as disarmament activists thousands of community leaders, professionals, academics, and others from most regions of the world.

SALT and START Bilateral Negotiations

From the beginning of UN arms control efforts, there has been a general recognition that large, cumbersome disarmament forums can address the issues and explore approaches but that progress toward agreement depends on the pace and substance of superpower talks. In 1969 at Helsinki, the United States and the Soviet Union recognized this fact of life by initiating Strategic Arms Limitation Talks (SALT). The objective was to reach agreement on the control of strategic nuclear warheads, delivery systems, and related offensive and defensive weapons systems through continuing bilateral negotiations. By undertaking the SALT negotiations, the two nuclear giants redeemed a pledge that they had made to other UN members at the July 1, 1968, signing of a UN-sponsored treaty on the Non-Proliferation of Nuclear Weapons (NPT).

Face-to-face superpower negotiation proved to be a moderate success. Several limited-time-span agreements, whose main emphasis was placed on limiting defensive systems, were concluded in the form of SALT I, and a major treaty to limit offensive weapons emerged from the second-phase SALT II discussions. The SALT II treaty, unlike the SALT I agreements, needed the consent of the U.S. Senate, which was not forthcoming.

Bilateral negotiations have also periodically taken the form of summit conferences between Soviet and American leaders. One of these was a two-day meeting between President Ronald Reagan and General Secretary Mikhail Gorbachev in October 1986 in Reykjavik, Iceland. Great progress was initially made in the negotiation process. Tentative agreement was apparently reached on such broad and significant topics as the ultimate elimination of strategic missiles and warheads, the substantial reduction of medium-range missiles in both Europe and Asia, and the application of on-site inspection in both the United States and the Soviet Union. Yet all of these and other potential gains were wiped out when the two leaders disagreed completely over the continuation of the American Strategic Defense Initiative, often referred to as "Star Wars." For a fleeting moment the world was treated to the prospect of a substantially disarmed world reached through bilateral superpower negotiations, but this was not to be.

Despite the uncertainties involved in efforts to reach a bilateral agreement, observers have generally praised the idea of a superpower forum for negotiations.[4] The results achieved in SALT and START negotiations will be examined in the next section.

Multilateral Negotiations

The superpower arms control dialogue was supplemented by multilateral talks on mutual and balanced force reductions (MBFR), which began in Vienna in 1973. The participants have included twelve NATO and seven Warsaw Pact members. The purpose of these negotiations is to reduce the likelihood of conflict in Central Europe and to engender greater East-West stability. From NATO's perspective, this has meant that the main objective has been to achieve parity between Eastern and Western conventional forces in Central Europe. Currently, the Warsaw Pact countries have a force of approximately 6 million, of which about 4 million face NATO forces in Europe. In contrast, NATO forces total about 4.5 million, with about 2.6 million in Europe. Both sides, however, agree that the biggest need is for an understanding that reduces the possibilities of conflict. Although the Soviet Union suspended the superpower START (Strategic Arms Reduction Talks) and INF (Intermediate-Range Nuclear Forces in Europe) negotiations following the deployment of American missiles in Western Europe in 1984, it later agreed to continue all of these talks.

Another multilateral approach to peace in Europe began in Helsinki in 1975 with a Conference on Security and Cooperation in Europe (CSCE) aimed at producing a general rapprochement between the East and West. A treaty known as the Helsinki Accord or the Helsinki Final Act was signed by thirty-five participants that included the NATO countries, the Warsaw Pact nations, and thirteen neutral and nonaligned European states. Although neither a disarmament nor an arms control measure, the treaty nevertheless made a contribution to general security by achieving some reduction in the tension and hostility that had pervaded East-West relations in the European arena. The success of this Conference led to the inclusion in the Final Act of provision for periodic review conferences to continue the multilateral process of building security in Europe.

The use of forums of varied size and composition in the search for disarmament and arms control provides some lessons for the future. Large forums, for example, have proved ineffectual in furthering agreement, although they have been useful in building public pressures to encourage the superpowers to commence or recommence talks. Over the years the forum that has devoted the most time and effort to discussions of arms control and disarmament topics has been the General Assembly.[5] Much of the "general debate" at the start of each regular session has focused on arms control, and topics ranging from confidence-building measures to ultimate "general and complete disarmament" have often been placed on the Assembly's agenda. In addition, two special sessions devoted exclusively to disarmament topics gave the Assembly and its members an opportunity to broadcast their individual and collective views to the world.

Progress in arms control, however, has been largely a product of small negotiating bodies, although typically the decisions of such bodies have been transmitted to a larger UN body to gain broader support. The two superpowers and the five permanent members of the Security Council have clearly provided the most useful forums for negotiation. Once the Third World nations have been included, both major nuclear powers have been tempted to undertake propaganda campaigns. The search for agreement then becomes a search for a ploy that will discredit one's opponent in the eyes of the world and build one's own reputation as a lover of peace.

Although most observers of disarmament and arms control efforts have been highly critical over the years, others have marveled over the fact that some agreements have emerged from the negotiating process. It is to these limited successes that we now turn our attention.

DISARMAMENT AND ARMS CONTROL—A FORTY-YEAR BALANCE SHEET

The pursuit of security in a dangerous nuclear world over a period of four decades has produced no results that can assure the global community that Armageddon can be avoided. Yet substantive progress in a variety of negotiating areas has been made in a number of arms control and related fields. These fields include (1) achieving demilitarization and denuclearization of specific geographic areas, (2) halting nuclear proliferation, (3) banning nuclear weapons tests, (4) avoiding a nuclear weapons race in outer space, (5) limiting or reducing nuclear warheads and delivery systems, (6) developing confidence-building and communication measures to avoid accidental war, (7) banning chemical and biological weapons, and (8) reducing tension by economic and political policies. Each of these fields will be examined in this section.

Demilitarization and Denuclearization

If global disarmament is beyond reach in the contemporary world, limited disarmament within specific geographic areas may still be possible. Proceeding on that assumption, both sides in the arms race have demonstrated a willingness to consider regional demilitarization and denuclearization proposals. In addition, the Third World has demonstrated a continuing concern about the impact of a great power war on the peoples of Africa, Asia, and Latin America.

The first arms control agreement to emerge after World War II provided for the complete demilitarization of the Antarctic continent. The Antarctic Treaty of 1959, signed by twelve governments with interest in the region (including the United States and the Soviet Union), contains these provisions:

1. The use of the region for military activities of any kind is forbidden.
2. Each signatory has the right to inspect the installations of the others to ensure that no treaty violation has occurred.
3. Territorial claims on the continent remain unrecognized, and no new claims may be made.
4. No nuclear explosions or dumping of radioactive wastes is permitted.
5. Disputes under the terms of the treaty will be settled peacefully.
6. The signatories will cooperate in scientific investigations in the region.

The Antarctic Treaty provides a model for the potential demilitarization of other regions in the world. No known violations have occurred, and the right of national inspection has been fully acknowledged. Although no joint arrangements exist for governing the area, Antarctica is at least partially "internationalized" by the voluntary system.

Guided by the example of the Antarctic Treaty, in 1964 an American and a Soviet scientist proposed a similar plan for the demilitarization of the Arctic.[6] The two advanced their scheme as a potential first step in a zonal disarmament that could incorporate additional zones after each successful demilitarization. The Antarctic, however, has proved to be a unique example for demilitarization purposes. Unlike the Arctic, with its proximity to a major military confrontation, the Antarctic is far removed from the power centers of the world.

Although the idea of setting up a demilitarized zone or region to separate two potentially hostile armies is not a new one, the approach at first attracted only minor attention in the field of disarmament diplomacy. In 1957, however, the Communist side indicated an interest through a proposal made by Adam Rapacki, Foreign Minister of Poland. The Rapacki Plan called for the denuclearization of Central Europe (Czechoslovakia, Poland, East and West Germany) followed by a "disengagement" of Soviet and Western forces through a staged withdrawal from the region. The interest aroused by the Rapacki Plan produced much explorative debate in various UN forums, and a virtual avalanche of disengagement proposals were placed before the General Assembly by the East and the West.[7]

The object of disengagement is to reduce tension and avoid incidents between two major armies within a specific geographic area in order to avoid a major clash. The proximate confrontation of Western and Soviet forces in the heart of Europe has made the demilitarization of Germany the crucial issue in most disengagement schemes. All of the proposals foundered, however, because neither West Germany nor other NATO members were willing to consider the question of German neutralization. Western advocates of disengagement argued that it would release several Warsaw Pact members from Soviet control, facilitate settlement of the historic "German problem," and constitute a valuable experiment in controlled disarmament. Moreover, it would be likely to reduce East-West tensions and make further disarmament measures feasible. Western statesmen and military leaders objected mainly on the ground that it would place NATO in a militarily weak position by the withdrawal of West Germany and the severe reduction of NATO's system of defense in depth. Denuclearization of the region, moreover, would be disadvantageous to the West because of Soviet superiority in conventional weapons.

Numerous proposals aimed at reducing the threat of nuclear war through denuclearization of various regions of the world have since been presented in the General Assembly or developed by regional groups. The prototype nuclear-weapons-free zone was concluded in the Treaty of Tlatelolco in 1967. This Treaty for the Prohibition of Nuclear Weapons in Latin America has been signed by twenty-five Latin countries and ratified by twenty-two of them. Two protocols, in which the major powers agree not to bring nuclear weapons into the region, supplement the Treaty. All of the major nuclear powers—the United States, the Soviet Union, Britain, France, and China—have accepted this limitation, but the three Latin-American countries most likely to build or deploy nuclear weapons—Argentina, Brazil, and Chile—have not ratified the treaty.

Other regions have tried to establish nuclear-weapons-free zones. A resolution adopted by the General Assembly in 1961, for example, requested all countries to "consider and respect the continent of Africa as a denuclearized zone." The Organization of African Unity (OAU) followed up by adopting a Declaration on the Denuclearization of Africa, which led the General Assembly to call for an African nuclear-weapons-free zone. Similar calls for action over the years have not produced a treaty that follows the Latin-American precedent. In fact, some African leaders have decided that it is too late to proscribe nuclear weapons in Africa and have called on Africans to follow the nuclear path. The long-standing efforts to create nuclear-weapons-free zones in the Middle East and in South Asia have also been stymied, the former largely because of Arab-Israeli hostility, the latter by India's fear of China and Pakistan.

Each annual session of the General Assembly finds much lip service paid to the idea of freeing geographic areas from the threat posed by nuclear weapons. Yet Third World countries find it as difficult as the major powers to reach agreement to limit such weapons. The general feeling of these countries is that none can escape the fury of nuclear war and that superpower agreement is the essential element needed to save the world from annihilation. They are also fearful that a great military and diplomatic advantage would be gained by their current or potential enemies in the Third World that do not sign such treaties or are willing to violate them. An observer can only conclude that the denuclearization of geographic regions is at best only a supplementary approach to security.

Demilitarization and disengagement proposals have aroused interest and debate, but they have failed to evoke the support of the major powers directly involved. The main obstacle has been the difficulty of defining a zone or region for neutralization that would not strategically disadvantage either side. Years of debate indicate that such proposals are unlikely to prove acceptable unless they are part of a broader political or general disarmament agreement or, as in the Antarctica Treaty of 1959, unless they apply to regions of little strategic importance.

Nuclear Proliferation—The Growing Brotherhood of the Bomb

Closely related to the efforts to denuclearize geographic regions has been the problem of dealing with nuclear proliferation. That problem began in 1949, when the Soviet explosion of an atomic device ended the American postwar monopoly of atomic weapons. Three years later Britain exploded a fission bomb, followed by France in 1960 and China in 1964. Each member of the "nuclear club" also exploded test fusion warheads thousands of times more powerful than the Hiroshima fission bomb. India became the first Third World country to join the brotherhood of the bomb in 1974, when it successfully tested a "peaceful nuclear explosive." At least ten nations having the scientific and technological capability to join the club are perhaps debating whether or not to expend the effort and the money necessary for membership. As many as ten additional nations may soon have that capability. Moreover, the spread of nuclear power for peaceful uses involves a risk that fissionable materials may be diverted for military purposes, and more than fifty countries now have nuclear reactors. The countries most likely to join the nuclear club within five to ten years include Argentina, Brazil, Israel, North Korea, Pakistan, South Africa,

South Korea, and Taiwan. A number of European countries and Canada, Australia, New Zealand, and Japan have the capability to develop nuclear weapons but have refrained from doing so. Several nations, such as Pakistan, Israel, and South Africa may have already secretly developed a nuclear weapons capability.

What happens if the number of nuclear states expands to fifteen or to twenty-five? Would the threat of a major war be greater, or would nuclear proliferation reduce the danger of conflict? Does a state like India need a nuclear weapons capability for its defense against a nuclear-armed neighbor, or will guarantees from a friendly great power suffice? Could an international control system help prevent additional states from "going nuclear"? What can be done about the criticism of Third World leaders who charge that the major nuclear powers seek only to restrict "horizontal proliferation" involving the spread of nuclear weapons to additional countries while they foster "vertical proliferation" by adding thousands of new warheads to their nuclear arsenals? Much controversy exists among experts and statesmen on the answers to these and related questions.

The debate over proliferation has tended to polarize. One group regards nuclear diffusion as an obvious danger that will increase the possibility of nuclear war, probably more than proportionally to the addition of each new state. The other group views the dissemination of nuclear weapons as inevitable and wants major consideration given to the problem of how to manage a multinuclear world.

The process of expanding the nuclear club tends to be self-propelling. Each new entry strengthens the political and strategic motivations of another or several other states to follow its example. If, for example, Israel explodes an atomic test bomb, several Arab states would unquestionably embark on a crash program to catch up. Since India has an atomic weapons capability, why not Pakistan? It is difficult to foresee where the drive to achieve nuclear capability will end.

As the nuclear club expands, nuclear weapons may be increasingly viewed as an acceptable means for waging war, and the probability that they will be used by design or accident mounts with each additional finger on the trigger. States caught up in the nuclear race will also find it far more difficult to meet other priorities, such as financing economic development. The result may be a growing internal instability and revolution-proneness in Third World states that could encourage rash or even irrational actions by their leaders. Worst of all, a "catalytic war" could be touched off by a small power that surreptitiously uses an atom bomb to destroy a major Russian or American city.

Efforts to Halt Nuclear Proliferation

The problems of a nuclear-diffused world may have to be faced in the future, but contemporary efforts are directed at trying to avoid them through international agreement. After seven years of debate, discussion, and intensive negotiation in the Eighteen-Nation Disarmament Committee and in the Political and Security Committee, a Treaty on the Non-Proliferation of Nuclear Weapons was approved by the

General Assembly in 1968.[8] The main provisions of the eleven-article treaty are found in the first two articles, which assign obligations to nuclear and nonnuclear states as follows:

Article I

Each nuclear-weapon State Party to this Treaty undertakes not to transfer to any recipient whatsoever nuclear weapons or other nuclear explosive devices or control over such weapons or explosive devices directly, or indirectly; and not in any way to assist, encourage, or induce any non-nuclear-weapon State to manufacture or otherwise acquire nuclear weapons or other nuclear explosive devices, or control over such weapons or explosive devices.

Article II

Each non-nuclear-weapon State Party to this Treaty undertakes not to receive the transfer from any transferer whatsoever of nuclear weapons or other nuclear explosive devices or of control over such weapons or explosive devices directly, or indirectly; not to manufacture or otherwise acquire nuclear weapons or other nuclear explosive devices; and not to seek or receive any assistance in the manufacture of nuclear weapons or other nuclear devices.

The treaty also obligates each nonnuclear state to enter into an agreement with the International Atomic Energy Agency to provide safeguards, through verification by the Agency, to prevent any diversion of nuclear energy from peaceful uses to nuclear weapons. Other provisions of the treaty call for cooperation in the development of nuclear energy for peaceful purposes and for the nondiscriminatory transfer of nuclear explosive devices to nonnuclear states for peaceful purposes. Each of the parties to the treaty also agrees "to pursue negotiations in good faith on effective measures relating to cessation of the nuclear arms race."

The major obstacle to the treaty in the Assembly debates had been the fear prevalent among nonnuclear states that renouncing their right to acquire nuclear weapons might leave them open to nuclear blackmail. To meet this problem, three of the nuclear powers—Britain, the Soviet Union, and the United States—in Article 6 of the Non-Proliferation Treaty agreed to guarantee the security of nonnuclear states against such actions or threats. This guarantee was underwritten by the Security Council when it adopted a resolution affirming the decision of three of the four nuclear powers on the Council to provide "immediate assistance, in accordance with the Charter, to any nonnuclear-weapon State that is a victim of an act or an object of a threat of aggression in which nuclear weapons are used."

With Assembly approval of the treaty, the problem remained of getting all states to become parties to it. States that have refused to sign the treaty include two nuclear powers, France and China, and a number of nonnuclear countries that might aspire to develop a nuclear capability.[9] Until all existing and potential nuclear powers renounce proliferation, the danger of expanding the nuclear club remains. Currently, 121 non-nuclear-weapons states have ratified the Non-Proliferation Treaty, whereas over thirty, including Argentina, Brazil, India, Israel, and South Africa, have refused to do so.

Limiting Nuclear Testing

After years of unsuccessful negotiations on limiting nuclear weapons testing, a consensus suddenly evolved in 1963. Conditions had ripened so that the three parties that negotiated the Partial Test-Ban Treaty—Britain, the United States, and the Soviet Union—regarded it as fully complementary to their respective national interests. Both the United States and the Soviet Union had exploded bombs of immense power and had perfected sophisticated devices for use as both strategic and tactical nuclear weapons. The bombs had reached such a magnitude of power that testing more powerful ones had become dangerous and nonsensical. Levels of radioactive fallout from Soviet and American tests in the early 1960s had reached proportions that might pose a health threat to the present generation and future generations. Moreover, the rising clamor of world opinion demanding a cessation to all testing had become increasingly difficult to ignore.

The Moscow Partial Test-Ban Treaty of 1963 capped years of frustration, propaganda exchanges, and fruitless negotiations. Each state adhering to the treaty agrees

to prohibit, to prevent, and not to carry out any nuclear test explosion, or any other nuclear explosion, at any place under its jurisdiction or control . . . in the atmosphere; beyond its limits, including outer space; or underwater, including territorial waters or high seas.

Because of the seismological problem of detecting underground nuclear tests and distinguishing them from natural earth tremors, subsurface tests were not prohibited by the 1963 agreement. The Soviet Union and the United States have each carried out numerous underground tests since the treaty took effect.

Although there was a clear implication that the "partial" nature of the test ban would be made complete as soon as technology had advanced to the point of ensuring the detection of all nuclear tests, negotiations have lagged behind scientific advances. Moreover, the treaty is a partial one in another equally significant respect: although 120 nations have subscribed to the treaty, two nuclear powers—France and China—have refused to sign it, and both of these powers have conducted atmospheric tests since 1963.

In the 1970s the Disarmament Commission of the United Nations continued to push for agreement on a Comprehensive Test Ban (CTB) treaty. Advocates perceive a clear relationship between testing and the development of new weapons systems. Stopping all nuclear testing would, they believe, slow down the arms race and decrease the likelihood of using nuclear weapons. Negotiations for a Comprehensive Test Ban treaty, however, ended in 1980, and the Reagan Administration refused to continue the talks, concluding that the problems of inspection and verification were insurmountable. Although the Partial Test-Ban Treaty was a major achievement, a meaningful brake on the arms race would require a cessation of *all* nuclear tests, including underground tests. In 1985, the Soviets proclaimed a moratorium on all nuclear tests and called for agreement on a Comprehensive Test Ban Treaty, a campaign probably motivated by Soviet efforts to stop the Reagan administration's Strategic Defense Initiative. By early 1987, however, the Soviet leaders announced that the failure of the United States to agree to end all testing meant that Soviet testing would be resumed. Shortly thereafter, the Soviets ended their moratorium and conducted several underground tests.

The Partial Test-Ban Treaty represents an acknowledgment by the three major nuclear states that the dangers of an uncontrolled arms race may outweigh the fear that the other side may not honor the agreement. It represents a substantial compromise in the American position against entering into any disarmament or arms control agreement without the safeguards of inspection, verification, and control. The treaty, however, has not seriously restricted either side's military efforts in the arms race even though both sides have complied with its provisions for more than twenty years. It has, however, greatly reduced the level of radioactive fallout around the globe.

Peaceful Uses of Outer Space

The launching of the first earth satellite in 1957 by the Soviet Union added to the complex of disarmament issues the problem of preventing military exploitation of outer space. The General Assembly took an initial action the following year, when it established a special Committee on the Peaceful Uses of Outer Space to draft a set of principles governing national conduct in the new environment. After early failures and a long deadlock over legal issues, the United States and the Soviet Union reached agreement within the Committee. The General Assembly thereupon unanimously adopted the Committee's draft in the form of a Declaration of Legal Principles Governing the Activities of States in the Exploration and Use of Outer Space.

Major principles to guide states in using and exploring space were enunciated in the Declaration. Outer space and celestial bodies were "internationalized"; international law was made applicable to them; states were made internationally responsible for their activities in outer space; and the responsibility of rendering emergency assistance to astronauts and their vehicles and of returning them safely to their country of origin was proclaimed. The Declaration also endorsed the exchange of scientific information on space programs and the establishment of a world "weather watch" under the sponsorship of the World Meteorological Organization.

From 1958 to 1963, the General Assembly adopted six other resolutions relating to outer space. These resolutions affirmed several additional guidelines for space activity:

1. The exploration and use of space should be "only for the betterment of mankind."
2. All states, regardless of their scientific or economic development, should benefit from space activities.
3. The United Nations should serve as a center for coordinating space activities and for the exchange of information regarding such activities.
4. International cooperation in space activities will foster closer relations between nations and peoples.

Space cooperation between the United States and the Soviet Union got off to a good start with bilateral agreements in 1962 and 1964. These provided for a coordinated weather satellite program and for joint satellite communications tests. Subsequent activities by both countries pointed to the potential military use of space and dramatized the need for agreement on a space treaty. In December 1966 a consensus was finally achieved and a draft treaty was approved by the General Assembly without a dissenting vote. The following year, a decade after the launching of the first Soviet sputnik, the Outer Space Treaty came into force, with the United States and Soviet Union included among the eighty-four signatory nations.

The main provisions of the treaty (1) prohibit placing nuclear or other weapons of mass destruction in orbit or on the moon and other bodies in outer space, (2) ban military bases on the moon and the planets, (3) reject all claims of national sovereignty in outer space, (4) require that explorations and uses of outer space benefit all countries, and (5) provide for international cooperation in exploring space, in rendering assistance to astronauts and space vehicles, and in exchanging scientific information. The treaty culminated ten years of negotiations aimed at avoiding a military space race and achieving the internationalization of space.

The Outer Space Treaty has not succeeded in its basic objective of avoiding a military space race. Both the United States and the Soviet Union have sought to develop antisatellite weapons that could destroy each other's orbiting communication and reconnaissance systems. This is a new and dangerous phase of the superpower arms race. Each of the two superpowers would like to deny the other the ability to conduct military operations from satellite command posts in outer space. Each would like to be able to destroy nuclear-armed satellites if the other should decide to orbit them in violation of the Outer Space Treaty. Efforts by the General Assembly to pressure the superpowers to negotiate an end to the new space race have found neither the United States nor the Soviet Union particularly receptive. In 1983 President Ronald Reagan proposed a new Strategic Defense Initiative (popularly known as "Star Wars") that helped fuel the growing space race by calling for the development of new laser and other weapons into an ultimate outer space defense system.[10] Strategic experts disagreed over the costs, feasibility, and utility of developing such a system, but the President's speech itself helped throw disarmament negotiations into disarray.

Control of Nuclear Warheads and Delivery Systems

SALT negotiations involving bilateral discussions between the United States and the Soviet Union began, as already noted, in 1969 in Helsinki. Some measure of success in the talks emerged following President Richard M. Nixon's trip to Moscow in 1972. The first Soviet-American agreement, known as SALT I, limited each country to the development of two antiballistic missile (ABM) defense systems, and a second agreement sought to limit the number of missile-delivery systems with nuclear warheads for a five-year period. Efforts to limit the number of multiple warheads on each missile (i.e., MIRVing—attaching multiple independently targeted reentry vehicles) failed, leading to a MIRVing race. SALT II guidelines worked out at the Nixon-Brezhnev summit meeting in Washington in 1973 were aimed at (1) achieving permanent ceilings on offensive strategic forces, (2) controlling the size and number of warheads, and (3) ultimately carrying out a mutual reduction of strategic forces. In the 1974 Nixon-Brezhnev summit meeting in Moscow, two nuclear weapons treaties were signed that limited ABM systems to one for each country and limited the magnitude of underground nuclear tests. SALT II negotiations continued, and in late 1974, at the Ford-Brezhnev summit in Vladivostok, agreement was reached to place a limit of 2,400 on the the total number of delivery systems with nuclear warheads that each side could possess and a limit of 1,320 missiles on the number that each side could MIRV. Major agreements were linked together into a comprehensive SALT II treaty, but President Jimmy Carter was unable to secure the Senate's consent to ratification and President Ronald Reagan rejected the treaty on the ground that the United States had negotiated it from a position of weakness. Failure to ratify the SALT II treaty led to a greater acceleration in the arms race during the 1980s even though both the United States and the Soviet Union informally agreed to respect the provisions of the treaty. This agreement led to numerous charges and countercharges of violations of the treaty's provisions, adding to the suspicious and mean-spirited relationship between the two superpowers.

In 1981 supplementary Intermediate-Range Nuclear Forces (INF) bilateral negotiations were undertaken at Geneva by the United States and the Soviet Union. The objective was to reach an agreement that would reduce or eliminate the threat of Soviet missiles against Western Europe and to avoid the deployment of American intermediate-range missiles aimed at the Soviet Union and Eastern Europe. The Soviet Union claimed that a balance already existed and that any agreement should start with a recognition of this fact. The United States held that the Soviet Union had a great missile advantage in the European region and that unless it agreed to reduce the number of missiles and warheads aimed at Western Europe, the United States would deploy Pershing II and cruise missiles in Europe to counterbalance the Soviet threat. This positional difference arose mainly from the fact that the Soviet Union counted British and French missiles and warheads, whereas the United States regarded them as "national deterrents" and refused to include them in the bargaining. An American proposal for a zero-zero option that would involve the elimination of all the intermediate-range missiles of both parties failed because the British and French forces were not involved in the calculations. The Soviet Union rejected other American initiatives that included bombers as well as missiles and provided for equal levels of longer-range INF missiles globally.

In 1982 a new phase in the Soviet-American arms control dialogue began in Geneva with the renaming of SALT as the Strategic Arms Reduction Talks (START). The emphasis was now on actually reducing the size of each nation's intercontinental missile arsenal. The United States proposed that each of the superpowers reduce its arsenal to 850 long-range missiles, and the Soviet Union countered with a proposal that each be governed by a ceiling of 1,800 missiles and bombers.

As negotiations proceeded, very little compromise was evident as each side began to develop new missile and bomber delivery systems. In 1983, when the INF negotiations failed and American Pershing II and cruise missiles were deployed in Western Europe, the Soviet Union withdrew from the START and INF negotiations. It then retaliated by deploying missiles in several East European countries and by stationing missile-carrying submarines off the coast of the United States. With each side apparently convinced that the other was hopelessly intransigent and that its security could be assured only through a massive arms buildup, superpower bilateral arms control efforts appeared to have reached their nadir in 1986. However, a 1987 initiative by Soviet leader Mikhail Gorbachev offering some hope of success was aimed at reaching agreement to withdraw all Soviet and American missiles from Eastern and Western Europe.

Avoiding Accidental War

For the foreseeable future, all of the nuclear powers appear to have accepted the dictum that to engage in nuclear war is to commit national suicide. The logic of MAD (Mutual Assured Destruction) has convinced most observers that the balance of terror and the deterrence it evokes make a nuclear attack an irrational action. Yet nuclear war may come about by a means other than a planned attack—by misinterpretation of the other side's actions, by electronic or mechanical error, or by human derangement. The Soviet Union has been particularly concerned about the human element, recognizing that in the American system of government one individual, the President, has the power as commander in chief to order a nuclear attack—a unique power, since in all the other nuclear weapons states there is collective decision making in the nuclear field. But whatever the causes of a nuclear attack, the consequences could be deadly for all concerned. For this reason, the nuclear superpowers have sought to reach agreement on methods for avoiding accidental war.

The 1962 Cuban missile crisis dramatized the need in the nuclear age for some means of direct and rapid communication between the leaders of the Soviet Union and the United States. To reduce the possibilities of a great power clash through miscalculation, accident, or failure of communication, the United States in its bilateral negotiations with the Soviets proposed in 1963 that each side give advance notice of major military movements, that ground observation posts be established at key transportation centers, that aerial observation be permitted by both sides, and that a teletype communications link be established between Washington and Moscow. The Soviet representative initially dismissed all of these proposals as potential sources of espionage but later announced that his government would accept the teletype cable as a step that "might have certain positive benefits." The two governments signed an agreement, and a "hot line" in the form of a teletype system stretching from the Kremlin in Moscow to the White House in Washington was installed. Subsequently hot lines were established between Paris and Moscow and between London and Moscow.

Although some observers hailed this communications link as a major step forward in reducing the threat of accidental war, others expressed amazement that no such precautionary arrangement had existed between the two governments during years of major crises. At the height of the Cuban missile crisis, for example, President Kennedy had had to fall back on commercial facilities to communicate with the Kremlin. The main danger of war through misunderstanding occurs during a crisis, when each side's preparations *against* a surprise attack may appear to the other to be a preparation *for* an attack. Between crises, other situations may develop that the hot line may help to explain or moderate. For example, radar distorted by meteors or other natural phenomena could lead one side to believe that an attack is under way or a major city may be destroyed through human or mechanical error. If a large American or Russian city were suddenly atomized, would the leaders of the country in which this happened undertake an immediate full-scale retaliatory attack, or would they first communicate with the leaders of the other country? The former action could lead to the complete destruction of both countries, with hundreds of millions of casualties; the latter action might prevent an all-out nuclear exchange but would not resolve the problem of "compensation" for the destroyed city.

With the deployment of nuclear missiles in Eastern and Western Europe, the time from firing to impact has been reduced for Russian, French, and British target cities to from eight to ten minutes. No past experience in warfare can give satisfactory answers to the new dangers of the atomic age. The communications link is merely an improvisation to reduce the threat of irrational responses; only complete nuclear disarmament with adequate safeguards can eliminate the threat of nuclear war.

In recognition of the dangers of accidental war, thirty-five NATO and Warsaw Pact nations met at Stockholm in 1984 in a Conference on Confidence and Security Building Measures and Disarmament in Europe (CDE). The NATO group developed a package for consideration that would (1) reduce the risk of surprise attack, (2) develop predictability regarding the military activities of NATO and Warsaw Pact countries, (3) reduce the risk of war by accident or miscalculation by greater openness about military activities, and (4) improve communication during crises.

Despite the dire need for such controls, the acceleration in the arms race and the deteriorating relations between the United States and the Soviet Union have further decreased the already slim chances for a breakthrough on arms control measures of this kind. Moreover, the Soviet Union has remained skeptical, holding that more openness about military activities is actually a means by which the West, especially the United States, seeks to obtain intelligence information about the Eastern bloc. But at least both sides have been willing to recognize the great dangers of accidental war and to discuss measures that might reduce its possibility.

Banning Chemical and Biological Weapons

Ever since chemical weapons were used with devastating results in World War I, the world community has sought to ban them. This objective was achieved in the Geneva Protocol of 1925, which incorporated a legal ban on the *use* of chemical and biological or bacteriological weapons. Most nations, including the United States and the Soviet Union, became signatories to that agreement. Both nations, however, have built up substantial stockpiles of chemical agents since the Geneva Convention prohibits their first use but not their production or stockpiling. In addition, the United States has ended its development and production of "offensive" biological weapons but continues to develop counteractive defensive agents.

Beginning in 1969, the issue of chemical and bacteriological weapons has been regularly included in each annual agenda of the UN General Assembly, with the two types of weapons considered separately since 1971. As a result of UN efforts, a Convention on the Prohibition of the Development, Production, and Stockpiling of Bacteriological (Biological) and Toxin Weapons and on Their Destruction was signed in 1972 and entered into force in 1975. Banned by the treaty are pathogenic agents, such as bacteria and viruses, and toxins from microbes, plants, and animals. Since 1972 the General Assembly has tried to write a treaty that would also ban the development, production, and stockpiling of chemical weapons, as well as their use, and that would require the supervised destruction of existing stockpiles and production facilities. In addition, the General Assembly in 1982 authorized the Secretary-General to investigate alleged violations of the Geneva Protocol or applicable customary law. In 1986, following a 17-year self-imposed moratorium, the United States resumed production of chemical weapons in the hope that this would spur the Soviet Union to accept a ban on such weapons.

Although both the United States and the Soviet Union have indicated an interest in achieving such a ban, the Reagan Administration took the position that the United States must first expand its chemical arsenal in order to bargain with the Soviet Union on a plane of equality. One of the main problems standing in the way of agreement—on-site inspections by an international body—has been a persistent sine qua non of American negotiators in all disarmament fields. In 1984 the Soviet delegate to the Geneva sessions of the Committee on Disarmament announced that the Soviet Union was prepared to agree to a treaty incorporating the establishment of a permanent international committee to supervise and verify the destruction of chemical stockpiles. Although the Soviet Union has not agreed to the principle of "automatic inspections" carried out on-site and irregularly, a major treaty banning chemical weapons may be within reach.[11] Other issues that remain to be resolved, however, include (1) a definition of chemical weapons, (2) the means and timetables for destruction of existing stocks and production facilities, (3) provisions for ensuring compliance and providing opportunity for challenge, and (4) a foolproof system of verification.

Meanwhile, charges and countercharges concerning the alleged use of chemical and biological weapons have shocked the world community. The Soviet Union and China, for example, charged the United States with using chemical weapons in Vietnam, and the United States has more recently claimed that the Soviet Union used chemical and toxin weapons in Afghanistan, Laos, and Kampuchea. Although the United States and the Soviet Union have the world's largest stockpiles of chemical weapons, the technology for developing these weapons is finding its way to the Third

World. This problem became more evident in 1984, when the Security Council is-sued a declaration condemning the use of chemical weapons in the Iran-Iraq War. The Council declined to name the country that had violated the Geneva Convention, but evidence supplied by newsmen and Iranian gas casualties flown to European hospitals made it clear that Iraq was the culprit.

Unless some arms control measures can be adopted and the political climate between the superpowers moderated, the world may be engulfed in a major new chemical/bacteriological arms race of massive proportions. As in other areas, the United Nations cannot impose an agreement on the superpowers, but it can continue to provide pressure, negotiation facilities, and encouragement.

Tension Reduction through Political Agreement

Many agreements and policies have contributed toward a lessening of tension among the nuclear powers. The expansion in East-West trade and the opening of China to Western trade in recent years have clearly contributed to better relations, although other irritants have frequently tended to negate the gains achieved from closer economic ties.

Perhaps the main accomplishment in the area of tension reduction was the Con-ference on Security and Cooperation in Europe (CSCE) in 1975 and the Helsinki Accord or Final Act that it produced. Divided into four sections or "baskets," the Helsinki Final Act included provisions for (1) security in Europe, including the de-velopment of confidence-building measures (Basket I); (2) cooperation in economics, science and technology, and the environment (Basket II); (3) cooperation in promot-ing human rights, cultural exchanges, education, and the free flow of people, ideas, and information throughout Europe (Basket III); and (4) the holding of review conferences "to continue the multilateral process initiated by the Conference" (Basket IV). The Helsinki Accord included no provisions for disarmament or arms control, but it was a major effort to reduce hostility between the East and West by getting all the nations of Europe plus the United States to accept the post–World War II status quo in Europe. Programs of cooperation and understanding, it was believed, would engender a relaxed atmosphere that would encourage good relations and perhaps promote demilitarization in Europe. Although the Final Act was a dip-lomatic agreement and not a binding lawmaking treaty, the signatories were expected to honor the spirit as well as the letter of the agreement, and the periodic review conferences were aimed at goading them into meeting that expectation. Two review conferences were called, the first in Belgrade (1977–78) and the second in Madrid (1980–83). Both conferences, and especially the second, were weakened by a rising tide of distrust and fear growing out of deteriorating political relations and an accel-erated arms race.

OBSTACLES TO DISARMAMENT

The UN objective in seeking disarmament through agreement—in contrast to the more pragmatic objectives of arms control—is to build a peaceful world by ridding it of weapons of war. This solution is so simple, so obvious, so preferable to its alternative that an impartial observer from another planet might think that only a dedicated warmonger or a potential aggressor could resist its logic. Yet the historical record of efforts to achieve disarmament through agreement reveals appallingly few and mostly short-lived examples. Why have the United Nations and its members failed to achieve this almost universally acclaimed objective? There are many reasons—some technical, others related to the nature of the state system, and still others rooted in human nature. What follows is an analysis of some of the major problems that help explain the disarmament impasse.

Security Questions

The difficulty of securing disarmament can perhaps be understood best if it is related to the question of why nations arm in the first place. If an arms race causes war, what causes the arms race? Obviously, the building of weapons of war is related to the objectives of states, especially national survival. Nations arm for security, to protect their existence, but they also arm to pursue political and economic objectives. For centuries arms have offered the opportunity and provided the means for states to carry out national policies. So long as leaders regard military capacity as essential to the fulfillment of their state's vital interests, the abandonment of that capability through international agreement is unlikely. The pursuit of security through the arms race is based on the ancient Roman maxim *Si vis pacem, para bellum* (If you seek peace, prepare for war). In today's nuclear world, however, efforts to increase one's security by building more and more deadly weapons tend only to produce greater insecurity. Therein lies the paradox of the contemporary arms race and of UN efforts to end it. Both the United States and the Soviet Union are feverishly developing new weapons systems in their search for security, but they are both producing only greater amounts of insecurity, while security through disarmament remains only a theoretical abstraction.

Sovereignty and Nationalism

The search for explanations of the failure to achieve disarmament leads to the heart of the disarmament dilemma. Controversies over means and details are only symptomatic of the basic contradiction between international needs and national prerogatives that has stymied most disarmament efforts. Two forces that emerged early in the history of the modern state system—state sovereignty and nationalism—constitute the major legal and emotional barriers to the idea of reaching agreement with "foreign" elements. A disarmament agreement, by its very nature, would limit the sovereign power of a state to exercise full control over the area most vital to its security. The ardent nationalist resents the access, free movement, and "snooping" within his state that must accompany a disarmament enforcement system.

An effective disarmament arrangement in the contemporary world must be based on some form of effective international control. For example, in formulating the

Acheson-Lilienthal proposals that became the basis for the Baruch Plan, Dean Acheson insisted that inspection would be inadequate if the production of fissionable materials remained under national control and that enforcement would be insufficient unless a veto-free international body could punish a violator. The question of the feasibility of disarmament essentially boils down to this question: Is the world ready for a measure of world government? Although such a curtailment of national prerogatives may be a logical necessity for sheer survival, there is as yet no consensual support for it in any country. The sovereign state system may be obsolete when it is objectively evaluated within the context of intercontinental missiles and thermonuclear weapons systems, but in the minds of human beings nationalism and sovereignty still offer the best approach to security. A successful disarmament system, then, requires a basic change of attitude among the populations of the great powers. The question most central to the arms race today is whether attitudes will change rapidly enough to avert a war, planned or accidental, that brings final catastrophic dissolution to the state system.

"Vested Interests"

Disarmament in today's world must take account of the armaments that nations already possess. How does a nation communicate pacific intent to a rival when it has the military capability to destroy the rival instantly? How can the arms race be reversed in a world in which enormous amounts are spent each year for military purposes, millions of people serve in the armed forces, and other millions are engaged in military production? There may well be too many vested interests in the world of armaments and the military services to challenge the status quo successfully.

The economic consequences of disarmament are viewed ambivalently in some states. Total disarmament would permit states to devote the huge savings to economic betterment. Many observers, however, fear that it would result in a loss of jobs and profits or a dislocation of the national economy. Communists argue that capitalism depends on the artificial stimulus provided by arms production and war. Although little evidence exists to substantiate that charge, many Americans have reacted adversely to the closing of defense plants and the cancellation of procurement contracts in economy moves. The military-industrial complex functions as a powerful force in both the Soviet Union and the United States against any disarmament proposal that threatens a loss of status or income. A successful disarmament plan, therefore, would have to take economic consequences into full account.

Threats of Deception

The technological revolution that has dramatically changed the mode of warfare has also increased the difficulty of disarmament. Arms reduction in a world of conventional weapons might mean that one side could achieve an initial advantage through deception. Though this advantage is not likely to be decisive, a violation in these circumstances could give the attacking state a significant edge. With the advent of thermonuclear, chemical, and biological weapons, however, treachery in a disarmament agreement could be decisive. Moreover, the ability to deceive has increased; it is far easier to hide a few intercontinental rockets and their thermonuclear warheads than to conceal several divisions of troops or a fleet of battleships. Fear of deception has led the United States to insist that an effective system of on-site inspection be operational *before* any disarmament measures are implemented.

Deception may also relate to intentions and the fear of a surprise attack. Both the Soviet Union and the United States—general publics and decision makers alike—are still obviously affected in disarmament matters by the national shocks experienced as a result of the invasion of the Soviet Union by the armies of Adolph Hitler in June 1941, and the Japanese attack on Pearl Harbor in December 1941.

Ideological Rivalry

A world of conflicting values offers a poor milieu for reaching agreement on disarmament. When one side in an ideological struggle becomes convinced that the other is bent on conquest or destruction, any proposal for a reduction in arms is regarded as a devious inducement for a nation to weaken itself, providing the enemy with an opportunity to attack. Any disarmament agreement must depend on some minimal amount of good faith and a belief that the other side will live up to its terms. But a deep gulf between ideological enemies makes trust a rare commodity.

In more than forty years of disarmament negotiations between the Soviet Union and the United States, ideological hostility has often led to a "deaf man's dialogue." Both sides favor the reduction of arms and propose various schemes to accomplish it, but each side is wary of the proposals of the other side because it fears a trap. Each believes its plan is logical and responsible and that if the other side were sincerely interested in disarmament, it would cease its diversionary tactics and accept the plan. The will to survive, however, may in time force a moderation in the two ideological camps and build enough understanding to permit a start toward mutual arms reduction.

Full Participation Needed

A meaningful disarmament agreement requires the participation of all the great powers. If one or several states with sizable military strength were not included, the delicate balance of power provided by a carefully worked-out schedule of arms reductions would be in constant danger of being upset. It is difficult to get all the major powers to support disarmament, because one or several may prefer an independent policy or may regard the existing power distribution in the world as favorable to their national interests. France between World War I and World War II, for example, was interested in maintaining arms superiority over Germany, not in a general disarmament. Both China and France have refused for many years to participate in disarmament negotiations. It is doubtful that the United States and the Soviet Union would ever agree to reduce their nuclear weapons in a meaningful way or subject them to substantial control without the participation of all nuclear powers. The non-proliferation treaty that limits the right of some states to secure nuclear weapons but not those refusing to sign it is also a dubious approach. Full participation in each case is a sine qua non for achieving some measure of agreement.

The Propaganda Barrier

The appeal of disarmament to millions of human beings has made it a prime subject of psychological warfare. Diplomats confident that the other side will reject their proposals are free to advance radical schemes designed to make their country appear avant-garde in its search for peace. The simpler the proposal and its approach to the problem, the more likely it is to receive the approbation of an observing world.

The majority of states, neutralist in their orientation toward the cold war struggle, regard their foreign policy mission to be chiefly one of achieving great power rapprochement and disarmament. This desire has resulted in obvious efforts by both sides to appeal in their proposals to the great mass of nonaligned states rather than to the negotiators sitting across the table. Sweeping Soviet proposals for general and complete disarmament, with control machinery to be established *later,* have been matched by American plans providing for a maximum of elaborate international inspection and enforcement but de-emphasizing the problems of overseas bases and German rearmament, which are central to Soviet security considerations.

Pressures for great power agreement on disarmament emanate regularly from the majority of the states in the General Assembly, challenging both sides to find new platitudes they can endorse while tabling concrete proposals "for further study." Each side must try to preserve its image—that of a peace-loving, humanitarian, but horrendously powerful nation that would gladly lay down its arms and contribute the savings to economic development but for the intransigence and uncompromising hostility of the other side. It is noteworthy that one of the most significant agreements in the arms control field during the past forty years—the Partial Nuclear Test-Ban Treaty of 1963—was reached through closed negotiations among American, British, and Soviet diplomats and that the SALT I and SALT II agreements were the products of bilateral superpower negotiations.

The Speed of Change

An increasingly significant factor working against consensus to end the arms race is the realization that much scientific research and development for peaceful purposes can be related to weaponry; hence no disarmament agreement can really stop progress in military technology. The development of a decisive new weapon that could upset the agreed balance of arms is a potential danger that both sides would have to assume in any arms control or disarmament agreement. No inspection or control system could offer full protection against such an eventuality. In an age of intensive exploration of the atom and of new ventures with particle beams and lasers in outer space, any disarmament agreement could be rendered obsolete within a short period of time unless it provided for periodic updating. It may be that the day has already passed when disarmament through agreement was rationally practicable.

Over the years disarmament negotiators have faced a basic dilemma: As scientific knowledge grows and technology changes with revolutionary speed, disarmament agreements become increasingly dependent on trust; but trust is vitiated by the fear of new, secret weapons spawned by advancing technology. Science and technology, the very forces that have made it necessary to end the arms race in order to save the human race from destruction, are the forces that appear to make agreement to disarm too dangerous for national security interests. These forces must somehow be released from their subservience to the gods of war and converted into allies of disarmament and peace. This is the great challenge to the world community today.

Timing Problems

There is a pervasive tendency for both sides in an arms race to procrastinate in the belief that the future will offer a more propitious time for entering into a disarmament agreement. That right moment never seems to occur. Instead, new weapons, military confrontations and other crises, and the burgeoning of military capabilities on both sides increase the need for disarmament but decrease its likelihood.

The Western-Soviet arms race since 1945 is a case in point. When the military rivalry commenced, both sides had just finished fighting a major war and were faced with major problems of recovery from it. One side had suffered the destruction of its cities and calamitously high civilian and military casualties. The other side had a monopoly of nuclear weapons that it offered to sacrifice in return for a world security system. In restrospect, those first few years following World War II appear to have been an ideal time for disarmament; yet negotiations fostered by the United Nations failed dismally. Since then, the cold war has developed, alliance systems and overseas bases have been established, new weapons of mass destruction have been perfected, both sides have become peripherally or directly involved in local wars, and there has been a proliferation of nuclear weapons. The grounds for insecurity and fear are no longer hypothetical or based on a future potentiality; mass extermination is now a proximate danger. Yet each side continues to manufacture "overkill" capacity in a vain effort to achieve a preferred position in disarmament negotiations.

The conventional wisdom on military and defense matters dies slowly. Both sides, it appears, still follow the old maxim that national security is a function of spending money, manufacturing weapons, and fielding armies. In the preatomic age, such efforts may have increased a nation's security when they outstripped those of an opponent; today, with both sides already in possession of military capabilities far in excess of those needed to destroy each other, the dangers of war from overheating the arms race or as a result of human aberration or mechanical error may in fact *decrease* a nation's security. Conditions may once again be ripe for disarmament, but neither of the major opponents shows any signs of recognizing this. The psychology of the arms race produces a relentless "falling behind, catching up, going ahead" channel of thought that repeats itself endlessly. A disarmament agreement may finally be obtained when both sides simultaneously break the arms race psychosis and decide that the opportune time has arrived.

"Ratio" Problems

During negotiations the future power relationship among the parties becomes a matter of grave concern. Each nation seeks a minimum goal of maintaining parity and a maximum advantage of arms superiority from a prospective agreement. Because power and security are never absolute but always relative, each proposal must be carefully weighed to determine its potential impact on all the parties. The result is an unending series of calculations by military tacticians who prefer to err on the conservative side, in keeping with their general distaste for disarmament as a security objective. The problem of balancing different categories of forces (strategic versus tactical, air versus naval, nuclear versus conventional) provides an additional complication.

Although general and complete disarmament or a system of enforcement by a global police force might overcome the fear of disadvantage, the difficulty of phasing out arms through stages remains. At each stage, no party can be left relatively weaker than at an earlier point and each strives to compare more favorably with its power rivals. Since it is impossible to achieve complete parity, each state must be led to believe that it will be advantaged by successive stages of disarmament. The difficulty in successfully pulling off this sleight-of-hand maneuver is evidenced by the forty-year disagreement between the United States and the Soviet Union over the numbers and types of forces to be disarmed at each stage and the ratio of forces that would remain. Despite the difficulty of determining ratios, the problem remains central to disarmament and must be faced.

Inspection and Enforcement

From the earliest postwar discussions of the Baruch Plan in 1946, most of the hundreds of disarmament discussions have concerned "inspection and control." American proposals have consistently offered to exchange a dependence on armaments for an international system that could safeguard security through enforcement. The Soviet Union has accepted the general proposition that inspection and control are necessary, but the details of implementing those vague terms have resulted in little more than an exchange of recriminations.

An effective inspection system to verify disarmament accords must resolve such issues as (1) the extent of access to each country's territory; (2) the frequency of on-the-spot surveillance; (3) the timing—whether inspection arrangements are to go into effect before or after the disarmament measures that they will verify; (4) the nature of aerial and ground reconnaissance to guard against the possibility of a surprise attack; (5) the means of detecting weapons in outer space; (6) the determination of what constitutes a weapon or a potential weapon; (7) the selection of the areas to be included in a progressive territorial demilitarization; and (8) the composition, powers, and number of inspection teams.

The technical questions concerning the detection of violations lead to a second and equally difficult set of issues that involve the political and military consequences of a violation once it has been detected. To what extent, for example, will world opinion contribute to enforcement and sanctions? What role should the injured state or states play if they detect an evasion? What kind of international authority should be set up, and what should be the nature of its sanctions? Should the injured state be entitled to undertake "restorative measures" following a detected violation to restore the military balance that would have existed without a disarmament agreement? What role should the United Nations and regional organizations undertake in the enforcement of sanctions? No disarmament agreement is possible in the contemporary world until a consensus can provide answers to such questions.

STRATEGIES AND TACTICS TO BREAK THE DEADLOCK

When Columbus undertook his epic voyage, scientists had thought for years that the earth was round; yet the fear among mariners that the earth might after all prove to be flat had postponed the discovery of the New World. Similarly, nations which recognize that a major war would be too catastrophic to contemplate are yet fearful to venture onto the uncharted seas of general disarmament. Is there a strategy that the United Nations could offer that might prove useful in breaking the deadlock by overcoming the uncertainties about the viability and effects of a disarmament agreement? What additional partial disarmament measures might contribute to building a better base for general disarmament? A small sampling from the profusion of approaches offered by statesmen and scholars to overcome the dilemma or afford a partial remedy will be examined here.

The Direct Approach

The problem of developing a useful approach to disarmament starts with the question of whether the major effort should be placed on reducing arms or on developing security. Those who advocate a "direct" approach regard the arms race itself as the main source of fear and insecurity. The solution they offer is simple: "The way to disarm is to disarm." These words have reverberated through the chambers of the League and the United Nations on many occasions. As arms are reduced, so holds the theory, the familiar cycle that produces the upward spiral in the arms race (increased arms produce greater fear and insecurity, which, in turn, produce greater expenditures on arms, and so on) will be reversed. Reduced international tensions will follow in the wake of disarmament, encouraging agreement in other areas of controversy. The Soviet Union as well as India and most other Third World nations have been vocal proponents of the direct approach during the UN era; the United States and Britain, which supported the direct approach during the League period, have changed since 1946 to the indirect approach.

The Indirect Approach

Those who advocate an indirect approach regard armaments as a reflection of the deep insecurities of the state system. Disarmament, therefore, should be recognized for what it is—a fundamentally *political* problem that involves the totality of relations among the nations caught up in the arms race. Disarmament becomes the secondary, not the immediate, objective. Major political conflicts must first be ameliorated, an effective collective security system must be established, and carefully planned inspection, verification, and sanctions arrangements must be made operational. Disarmament cannot be feasible, therefore, until there is a convergence of national policies on these issues. For the United States, this might mean that preconditions for disarmament would include resolution of the Afghanistan issue, creation of an operational UN police force without a Security Council veto, and establishment of an inspection and control system meeting American standards for safeguarding against violations.

Little wonder, then, that when the Soviet Union offered package proposals for full and complete disarmament, the West with its indirect orientation to disarmament did not take the offers seriously. On the other hand, American preoccupation with political details may have convinced the Soviets that Western avowals of willingness to disarm were merely perfidious cold war strategies. Whatever the interpretations by each side of the other side's motives, years of deadlock provide substantial evidence that general disarmament is not plausible unless the two opposing approaches can be reconciled or unless one side proves willing to change its tactics.

Unilateral Disarmament

Some disarmament advocates offer the radically novel strategy of one-sided initiative to secure an arms reduction breakthrough. Once such an action has started the disarming process, reciprocation would theoretically give it the motive power necessary to accelerate its momentum. Underlying unilateral disarmament theories is an assumption that the reduction of arms is really a matter of common interest but that inertia, tension, mistrust, fear, and habit make it appear to be beyond realization.

Several religious groups advocate a complete unilateral disarmament. If the other side uses the opportunity to impose its control, a Gandhian passive resistance would be employed against the conqueror. While no one can be certain that utopian schemes of this nature would fail, they are impracticable because neither side in the arms race would be likely to place its national security or way of life in the hands of its opponent.

Disarmament theoreticians have worked out unilateral schemes that depend on reciprocal initiatives and responses rather than an abject surrender of retaliatory power. Unilateral initiatives are not posited as a substitute for bilateral negotiations but only as a "psychological primer" to reverse the trend of the arms race by demonstrating good intentions. If the other side fails in due time to reciprocate or tries to take advantage of the unilateral reductions or withdrawals, such plans call for a return to a hard-line policy.

Although a partial unilateral disarmament would be unlikely to threaten the security of a state that has the power to destroy its opponent many times over, it lacks mass appeal because it violates the injunction not to encourage a potential aggressor through signs of weakness. Would the Soviet Union accept an opportunity to reverse the arms race by reciprocating American initiatives, and vice versa, or would each side pass off such initiatives as "Trojan horse" tactics? The nature and history of the contemporary arms race present some evidence that unilateral initiatives by either side might produce useful responses. Neither participant has strained its capabilities to the utmost in developing its arsenal, preferring some semblance of balance to an all-out drive for a massive superiority. Moreover, periods of lessened tension during the cold war have reduced the rate of growth in arms on both sides. None of these reductions, however, has had a lasting impact. New crises have had a tendency to boost the rate of arms production in both the United States and the Soviet Union to more than counterbalance previous cuts. Although unilateral disarmament schemes may be rational enough in their inherent logic, they must function in a highly irrational arms race environment. Their value could be proved or disproved only by submitting them to adequate testing, a testing that neither side shows any inclination to initiate.

A Nuclear Freeze

Polls have shown that many people in the world support the idea of a freeze on nuclear weapons. In the United States, for example, two thirds of those quizzed stated their support for this approach.[12]

Proponents of this approach hold that if the arms buildup could be effectively halted by a nuclear freeze agreement, the next step of negotiating an actual reduction in nuclear weapons could begin. Hopefully, the anticipated change in atmosphere from hostility to détente resulting from a nuclear freeze could then produce a disarmament agreement.

Opponents of a freeze agreement argue that this is a dangerous step because it is impossible to fully verify the halt in the development and building of nuclear weapons. Only through on-site inspection could an effective verification be carried on, and even then opponents fear treachery. The Russians have traditionally rejected on-site inspection, although the 1986 Reykjavik summit meeting indicated a softening of this position. Supporters of the freeze approach point out that only those aspects of production, testing, and deployment that can be verified effectively will be included in the agreement. In the mid-1980s the Reagan Administration proposed that the testing, production, and deployment of missiles should be omitted from a freeze agreement so long as the total number deployed did not exceed an agreed ceiling, and that new types of missiles should be completely excluded from the agreement. This approach left very little to freeze.

Despite popular pressures in the United States and Western Europe, a nuclear weapons freeze appears unlikely. Somewhat similarly to unilateral disarmament, the freeze agreement might function as a "psychological primer" to demonstrate good intentions on both sides of the disarmament table. The nuclear freeze proposals indicate that more than public support for an arms control or disarmament initiative is essential. The elite groups that control the arms race and disarmament policies in both camps must agree with public views if the proposal is to materialize.

Total Disarmament

Arms control schemes and tangible progress achieved through partial disarmament measures are unquestionably useful elements in the battles waged to bring the arms race under a semblance of control. Such measures as a comprehensive test ban treaty, universal adherence to an antiproliferation agreement, and regional demilitarizations would be significant steps in their own right as well as reducing tension and encouraging additional steps. Only *total* disarmament, however, holds any real promise of wholly removing the nuclear threat to human survival.

That contemporary weapons of mass destruction offer the dismal prospect of human extinction can no longer be doubted. At the Hiroshima kill ratio of approximately four deaths per ton of explosive power, the billions of tons of TNT equivalent in the combined nuclear arsenals of the United States and the Soviet Union have the capability to destroy the entire population of the earth many times over. When the deadly effects of radioactive fallout and of chemical and biological weapons of mass destruction are added to this estimate, only the most imperturbable optimist can talk about a meaningful aftermath to a major war.

Yet, as the survey of disarmament diplomacy since 1946 indicates, the propensity to move toward agreement on general disarmament does not increase proportionally to the growing dangers. The constant reiteration of old positions by both sides has enabled each to gain a fluent understanding of what the other will not accept, but little effort has gone into a search for consensus on other than basic principles. Both, apparently, believe that armaments are necessary to the achievement of their objectives, or at least that the status quo is less risky than the unknown risks of a disarmed world.

CONCLUSION

The problem of controlling armaments is fundamentally a problem of abolishing war and providing for security through world law and order. This means that any general disarmament agreement must operate within some broader framework for maintaining global security. The two major nuclear powers have shown no proclivity to return to the UN framers' concept of collective security to keep the peace in a disarmed world; but states are unlikely to give up their arms without some alternative guarantee of national security.

Nor is disarmament a problem that can be isolated from the development of an international legal, political, economic, and social system. Armaments will become obsolete only when the bonds of world community, which depend on progressive evolution in each of these fields, become strong enough to moderate the conflicts and tensions that make armaments seem necessary. The transformation of international relations from that of a system exuding power, tension, fear, and conflict to one of cooperation, understanding, and common action may be an impossible undertaking. If so, general disarmament may prove to be an ever-elusive quarry and long-term survival on planet earth may become increasingly problematic.

NOTES

1. A lively account of the personalities and issues involved in the two Hague Peace Conferences can be found in Barbara W. Tuchman, *The Proud Tower* (New York: Macmillan, 1962), pp. 229–88.

2. *Department of State Bulletin* 13 (1945), p. 782. The Soviet Union backed the Commission's objectives and called for an early agreement on all points.

3. For a summary of the work of the 158-member Disarmament Commission in 1984, see "Disarmament Commission: The Search for Consensus," *UN Chronicle* 21, no. 5 (1984), pp. 40–45.

4. For an analysis of current American and Soviet positions in arms control policy, see, for example, "Nuclear Arms: Positions of the 'Superpowers,'" *UN Chronicle* 21, no. 2 (1984), pp. 12–15.

5. See, for example, the documented discussions of arms control and disarmament efforts expended over the first forty years of the United Nations as set forth in annual editions of *Issues before the _____ General Assembly,* published by the United Nations Association of the United States of America. A recent review, *Issues before the 40th General Assembly of the United Nations, 1985–1986,* ed. Frederic Eckhard (New York: UNA/USA, 1985), summarized areas of negotiation undertaken in 1985–86.

6. See Alexander Rich and Aleksandr P. Vinogradov, "Arctic Disarmament," *Bulletin of the Atomic Scientists,* November 1964, pp. 22–23. Their plan was the first specific disarmament proposal jointly authored by scientists of the United States and the Soviet Union.

7. For a review of these early proposals, see Eugene Hinterhoff, *Disengagement* (London: Stevens & Sons, 1959). In a two-year period sixty plans were offered by Western scholars and statesmen and about twenty proposals came from the Warsaw Pact countries.

8. United Nations Document A/RES/2373 (XXII), June 12, 1968. The Assembly vote recorded ninety-five in favor of the draft treaty, four against (Albania, Cuba, Tanzania, and Zambia), with twenty-one abstentions and several nations absent. Although France abstained from the vote and has refused to sign the treaty, its representatives have indicated that it accepts the intent of the treaty and will refrain from any action that might proliferate nuclear weapons. China has more recently given such assurances.

9. See "Nuclear Proliferation" in *Issues before the 39th General Assembly of the United Nations,* ed. Donald J. Puchala (New York: UNA/USA, 1984), pp. 62–65.

10. "Star Wars and Arms Talks: Debating the Link," *Interdependent* 2, no. 3 (May-June 1985), pp. 1–6. For a British view, see Robert Chesshyre, "The Star Wars Stampede," *World Press Review,* August 1985, p. 40.

11. "New Proposals Offered on Chemical Weapons Ban," *UN Chronicle* 21, no. 5 (1984), pp. 36–40.

12. See Herbert Scoville, Jr., "A Freeze Is Verifiable," *New York Times,* October 25, 1984, p. 29. Also see Denise Harrington, "The 'Freeze' Analyzed," excerpted from the *Toronto Star* and reprinted in *World Press Review,* November 1984, p. 38.

SELECTED READINGS

BARKER, CHARLES A., ed. *Problems of World Disarmament*. Boston: Houghton Mifflin, 1963.

BURNS, E. L. M. "Can the Spread of Nuclear Weapons Be Stopped?" *International Organization*, 19, no. 4 (Autumn 1965), pp. 851–69.

BURTON, JOHN W. *Peace Theory*. New York: Alfred A. Knopf, 1962.

CRAIG, PAUL P., and JOHN A. JUNGERMAN. *Nuclear Arms Race—Technology and Society*. New York: McGraw-Hill, 1986.

ECKHARD, FREDERIC. In *Issues before the 40th General Assembly of the United Nations, 1985–1986*, pp. 50–63. New York: UNA/USA, 1985.

FALK, RICHARD A., and SAUL H. MENDLOVITZ, eds. *The Strategy of World Order*. Vols. 1–4. New York: World Law Fund, 1966.

HARRIS, JOHN B., and ERIC MARKUSEN, eds. *Nuclear Weapons and the Threat of Nuclear War*. New York: Harcourt Brace Jovanovich, 1986.

JACOBSON, HAROLD KARAN, and ERIC STEIN. *Diplomats, Scientists, and Politicians: The United States and the Nuclear Test Ban Negotiations*. Ann Arbor: University of Michigan Press, 1966.

KEGLEY, CHARLES W., JR., and EUGENE R. WITTKOPF, eds. *The Nuclear Reader—Strategy, Weapons, War*. New York: St. Martin's Press, 1985.

LEVINE, HERBERT M., and DAVID CARLTON. *The Nuclear Arms Race Debated*. New York: McGraw-Hill, 1986.

MATTHEWS, ROBERT O., et al., eds. *International Conflict and Conflict Management*. Scarborough, Ont.: Prentice-Hall of Canada, 1984.

MYRDAL, ALVA. *The Game of Disarmament*. New York: Pantheon Books, 1982.

SCIENTIFIC AMERICAN. *Progress in Arms Control?* San Francisco: W. H. Freeman, 1979.

SMOKE, RICHARD. *National Security and the Nuclear Dilemma*. Reading, Mass.: Addison-Wesley Publishing, 1984.

STOESSINGER, JOHN G. *Crusaders and Pragmatists*. 2nd ed. New York: W. W. Norton, 1985.

WASKOW, ARTHUR I. *Keeping the World Disarmed*. Santa Barbara, Calif.: Center for the Study of Democratic Institutions, 1965.

WOOLSEY, R. JAMES, ed. *Nuclear Arms—Ethics, Strategy, Politics*. San Francisco: ICS Press, 1983.

7

The Settlement of International Disputes

Collective security, even when supplemented by a "system for the regulation of armaments" (Charter Article 26), was never seen as the answer to all global problems of peace and security. Whatever the deterrent effect of UN enforcement machinery, many underlying sources of international tension and conflict would still exist. Countries would continue to have disputes with one another, with the ever-present possibility that some of them might get out of hand and lead to violence. The UN Charter acknowledges this problem by encouraging states to use existing methods of peaceful settlement and by providing additional options through the United Nations.

Before examining the UN role in the pacific settlement of disputes, this chapter will briefly describe the traditional settlement procedures that have become an accepted part of international law and practice and through which most disputes are settled. We will then look at UN practice to see what it has added to the procedures and machinery already available. This includes an appraisal of the International Court of Justice, which technically is a principal organ of the United Nations but renders decisions independent of the other organs. A subsequent section examines a sampling of disputes before the General Assembly and Security Council to illustrate how the system operates in practice, including its capabilities and limitations. A concluding section renders judgment on the UN performance in dispute settlement.

PROCEDURES FOR SETTLING INTERNATIONAL DISPUTES

The international norm of peaceful settlement is set forth in Article 2, paragraph 1, of the UN Charter, which states, "All Members shall settle their international disputes by peaceful means in such a manner that international peace and security, and justice, are not endangered." On its face the injunction to settle appears obligatory. The rule is best understood, however, if Article 2 is read with emphasis on the word *peaceful* rather than the word *settle,* because the United Nations has no authority to require states to settle a dispute or to accept any particular form of settlement. A dispute could go unresolved indefinitely without constituting a Charter violation. The obligation, rather, is to *try* peaceful settlement and, in any event, not to seek resolution of a controversy by use of violence.

Most of the common procedures for settlement of international disputes are cataloged in Article 33, paragraph 1, of the Charter:

> The parties to any dispute, the continuance of which is likely to endanger the maintenance of international peace and security, shall, first of all, seek a solution by negotiation, enquiry, mediation, conciliation, arbitration, judicial settlement, resort to regional agencies or arrangements, or other peaceful means of their choice.

All of these techniques of dispute resolution were embodied in international law and practice well before the advent of the United Nations. The Charter merely recognizes their existence and encourages their use. The procedure of "good offices," to be discussed below, is another time-honored approach to dispute settlement. Unlike the procedures listed in Article 33, which parties to a dispute are urged to use, good offices depends entirely on the initiative of third parties.

Except for negotiation, each of the procedures requires the assistance of third parties, that is, representatives of states or organizations not directly involved in the dispute. Most are also *political* rather than *judicial* modes of settlement, in the sense that parties are left free to accept or reject proposed settlements, as their interests dictate and their capacities permit. Third-party assistance is concerned primarily with finding some common ground where agreement can be reached. Arbitration and judicial settlement, however, are in the judicial mode because (1) the basis of decision is supposed to be international law rather than national interest and power and (2) the decisions are legally binding on the parties that accept these settlement procedures in a particular case.

Negotiation among parties to a dispute is as old as the state system and is the most common method of settlement. It involves direct discussion by diplomatic representatives of the states concerned, for the purpose of reaching agreement on matters at issue. Successful negotiation normally requires a good faith effort to achieve compromise solutions that serve the national interests of all parties.

Good offices (not mentioned in Article 33) is the name given to friendly assistance rendered by a third party for the purpose of bringing disputants together so that they may seek to reach a settlement. Good offices may be tendered by a state, a group of states, or even an individual of international standing such as the UN Secretary-General. The third-party representative meets with each disputant separately but may, with consent, convey messages between them. Technically, good offices are limited to facilitating negotiation by the states directly concerned and do not include discussion of substantive issues. Good offices are particularly useful where the disputing parties have broken off diplomatic relations or where negotiations have been interrupted and neither side takes the initiative to resume them, out of pride or out of fear that such action would be an indication of weakness.

Mediation occurs when the third party actively participates in the discussion of substantive issues and offers proposals for settlement. If the disputants are not speaking, the mediator may also tender good offices as a prelude to mediation. A mediator may meet with the parties either separately or jointly and is expected to maintain an attitude of impartiality throughout. He can expect little success unless he enjoys the confidence of all parties. His proposals are suggestions only, with no binding force on any party. Disputants are of course free to reject an offer to mediate.

Enquiry, or *inquiry*, may be used when the disputing parties are unable or unwilling to agree on points of fact relating to a controversy but are willing to let an impartial commission investigate and report on the facts. The parties need not accept the findings of the inquiry, but they usually do. The inquiry is limited to findings of fact and does not include proposed terms of settlement. Many international disputes hinge on disputed questions of fact, and inquiry may be a means of lowering tensions as well as reducing the area of disagreement.

Conciliation is a procedure for settling a dispute by referring it to a commission, or occasionally a single conciliator, charged to examine the facts and recommend a solution that the parties are free to accept or reject. Conciliation is more formal and less flexible than mediation. Whereas mediation is a continuing process of assisting negotiations among parties to a dispute, conciliation involves formal submission of the dispute to a conciliation body in anticipation of a final report containing the conciliator's findings and recommendations for settlement. The boundaries between the two tend to blur in practice because the conciliator usually confers informally with the parties, hoping to find an area of agreement. Moreover, in UN parlance, the terminology of mediation, conciliation, and good offices is frequently used without careful reference to the legal distinctions among them. Thus a UN conciliator may in reality be a mediator who also finds it necessary to render good offices and never has occasion to publish a formal recommendation for settlement.

Arbitration is a procedure by which disputants agree to submit a controversy to judges of their own choosing, who render a legally binding decision based on principles of international law. Commonly each side names one or two arbitrators, and those two or four designate one additional arbitrator to complete the panel. The essential characteristics of arbitration are (1) free choice of judges (arbitrators), (2) respect for international law, and (3) obligation to comply with the award. The parties frequently stipulate in the arbitral agreement *(compromis)* the particular rules of law or equity, or even special rules, that are to be applied. The parties are relieved of their obligation to accept or carry out the award only if the arbitrators disregard instructions laid down in the *compromis*. Arbitration is at least as old as the Greek city-states, and within the modern state system it enjoyed a substantial renaissance during the nineteenth and early twentieth centuries. Since 1945 arbitration has been used extensively in resolving trade and investment disputes but less frequently to resolve political disputes between states. One notable recent example is the U.S.-Iran agreement to arbitrate claims arising in the aftermath of the hostage crisis. Many treaties include a provision that controversies arising over the interpretation or application of the treaty shall be resolved by arbitration.

Judicial settlement or *adjudication,* like arbitration, produces legally binding awards or judgments based on rules of international law. Unlike arbitration, however, the judges are not chosen by the parties for their particular case but are members of a preconstituted international tribunal. Settlement of disputes by international courts is based on voluntary acceptance by the parties, either through advance agreement to accept the jurisdiction of the court in special types of cases or through agreement at the time the dispute is submitted. The same is generally true of arbitration. The International Court of Justice (ICJ) and its predecessor from League of Nations days, the Permanent Court of International Justice, provide the principal examples of judicial settlement at the global level. The League Court was not widely used, and the ICJ docket has been even less crowded. Decisions have generally been carried out, but no effective means have been available to enforce Court decisions against a few recalcitrants that have ignored their obligation to comply. Noncompliance is most common in cases involving controversies over the Court's jurisdiction. At the regional level the Court of Justice of the European Community has been an extensively used and highly successful organ of judicial settlement.

UN PRACTICE

The Charter provides broad authorization for UN involvement in any dispute serious enough to threaten international peace and security. Although the Security Council is given preeminence, the General Assembly is also authorized to consider peace and security questions. The Assembly may not, however, make any recommendation as long as the Security Council is exercising jurisdiction over a question. A dispute may be submitted to the Council or the Assembly by one of the parties, by any member of the United Nations, or by the Secretary-General. Neither body can *impose* a final settlement on any party to a dispute, but the Charter places no limits on UN organs in *recommending* procedures or terms of settlement.

UN organs utilize most of the traditional techniques of dispute settlement, and submission of a dispute to the Security Council or the Assembly has something in common with the procedure of conciliation. The United Nations becomes a third party that examines the facts of the dispute and renders a decision that the parties are free to accept or reject. But the UN political setting and procedures make the process considerably different from traditional forms of conciliation. Recourse to conciliation generally assumes that both sides are willing to submit the issue to an impartial commission in hope of finding an acceptable compromise. Most disputes before the United Nations, however, come not as agreed submissions but as complaints brought by one party against another or by a third state without necessarily obtaining the consent of either party to the dispute.

The United Nations, moreover, can seldom be regarded as impartial toward the disputes brought before it. Its members are highly partisan on most issues and often bitterly divided. Complaints are frequently brought there, not for the purpose of seeking an agreed compromise, but to legitimize the position of one side or the other.

The parties themselves participate in the discussion and may be more interested in scoring debating points before the bar of world opinion than in honestly seeking common ground for agreement. Such exchanges may widen the gulf between them, harden their positions, and inflame rather than repair relations.[1] The public nature of UN debate facilitates the appeal to world opinion but is a far cry from the privacy and quiet deliberation of traditional conciliation.

The UN process then becomes sui generis, a new approach to dispute settlement having strengths as well as weaknesses. The public debate pattern is only part of the picture, and even that is not wholly negative. Public debate makes UN members aware of the conflicting positions and sometimes helps clarify facts. Although speeches and supporting documentation submitted by the parties are mostly self-serving versions of the case, they can be informative as well. Public debate also provides governments with a way to "blow off steam," particularly in situations where an objectionable act has been committed, no redress is in sight, and retaliation is not feasible. When the Soviet Union invades Afghanistan or shoots down a civilian airliner, denunciation in the United Nations is a way to express outrage, uphold principle, and score a few propaganda points at little cost or risk. The same is true of Soviet responses to U.S. military adventures in the Caribbean and Central America.[2] UN consideration serves the further purpose of legitimizing the involvement of other states that may sometimes be able to exert a moderating influence on the disputants. In the days before the UN anticolonial majority became automatic, the United States frequently used its influence in the United Nations to steer parties to colonial disputes away from extreme positions.

The Security Council

The Security Council has firmly established its preeminence among UN organs in the field of peace and security. During the early postwar years the United States was the prime mover in an effort to enhance the security role of the General Assembly as a means of overcoming the Soviet veto in the Security Council. The effort was so successful that during the early 1950s the Council sometimes went months without discussing a substantive question. The shift of activity away from the Council was only temporary, however. The growing numbers and solidarity of Third World countries undermined American dominance in the Assembly and made the Security Council a relatively more attractive forum for the United States. It became clear that American as well as Soviet interests might require the protection of the great power veto. These developments paved the way for the reemergence of the Security Council as the central security organ of the United Nations. This resurgence was hastened by the Council's inherent advantages over the Assembly stemming from its smaller size, its capacity to function continuously, and the primacy assigned to it by the UN Charter.

Despite the high visibility of public debate, quiet consultation and negotiation are the most effective elements of the Security Council process when the parties are willing to listen. The point is well made in the recollections of a former President of the Security Council:

> The most striking feature of the Council's working procedures was the careful and prudent preparation by way of extensive informal consultations. . . . members were in contact almost daily. The methods of consultation ranged from daily informal, bilateral contacts . . . to full, informal consultations in the President's office in the presence of permanent representatives, assisted by their own staffs, and senior Secretariat officials, normally including the Secretary-General himself.
>
> Formal meetings were called for two reasons: (a) to give the parties an opportunity to present their case formally and officially; (b) to record any agreement or decision reached during the consultations. No substantial negotiations took place during the formal meetings. They were, rather, the end-product of a long process.[3]

The Security Council is not obligated to discuss every complaint that a state chooses to submit to it, and potentially inflammatory debate may sometimes be avoided by prior consultation and informal decision not to place an item before the Council. Such was the case with a Mexican request in the fall of 1975 for the Council to suspend Spain's UN membership privileges, following a number of executions by the Franco regime that were widely believed to be in violation of fundamental human rights. Preliminary consultation revealed that a majority of Council members were unwilling to discuss the issue, and Mexico was advised informally by the Council President that the Third Committee of the General Assembly (which deals with social and humanitarian questions) might be a more appropriate forum in which to raise the matter. Mexico took the advice and used the Third Committee as a forum for deploring Spain's conduct. Occasionally the Council has discussed a proposal to inscribe an item on its agenda but failed to obtain the necessary votes to do so. A decision by the Council to discuss a peace and security matter is considered a "procedural question" and thus not subject to the veto.

When the Security Council decides to consider a dispute or a threatening situation, numerous techniques are available for dealing with it. Whatever is said in the debating chamber, members of the Council will usually approach the parties quietly to explore the possibilities for agreed settlement. Sometimes debate will be adjourned, at least temporarily, while exploratory discussions are conducted. Quick agreement on a solution to the underlying substantive dispute is uncommon, but an understanding is frequently reached as to the appropriate limits of Security Council action. The understanding may be that the Council will adjourn without adopting a formal resolution, or will simply urge the parties to seek a solution by negotiation or other peaceful means. This was done, for example, with Chad's complaint of Libyan intervention in March 1983. The persisting civil war had proved totally immune to OAU peacemaking efforts, and there was little prospect of Security Council agreement on a strong resolution. Such action is not necessarily to be taken as abdication by the Council, since tendering of good offices and informal mediation by a Council member or the Secretary-General may follow. In most situations the decision to terminate debate, or to avoid substantive recommendations, is an act of prudence. Further debate would probably generate more heat than light, and recommendations, if any could be agreed on, might be disregarded.[4]

Sometimes more is called for by the situation or demanded by members of the Council. The Secretary-General can be authorized to appoint a mediator, or to consult with the parties and mediate himself as circumstances permit. The Council may occasionally create a special commission of inquiry or conciliation body to deal with the problem. Alternatively, the dispute may be referred to an appropriate regional organization, such as the Organization of American States or the Organization of African Unity. If hostilities seem imminent, the Council or its President may urge the parties to refrain from taking any action that might aggravate the dispute. Should fighting break out, the Council will in all likelihood issue an order for a cease-fire. If one party has occupied the territory of another, the cease-fire order may be accompanied by an order for troop withdrawal. In a number of situations, most notably in the Middle East, the Security Council has authorized peacekeeping forces and observer missions to help police a cease-fire and prevent violence that might further aggravate the dispute.

When the Security Council speaks, the disputants do not always listen. In his 1982 report on the work of the United Nations, Secretary-General Pérez de Cuéllar lamented that the Council's resolutions "are increasingly defied or ignored by those that feel themselves strong enough to do so."[5] There is substance to this lament. Israel and South Africa, the most frequent targets of Security Council censure, have repeatedly disregarded Council resolutions in pursuit of their national interests. Other countries have done the same. Argentina, for example, in the spring of 1982 ignored a Security Council demand for a cease-fire in the Falklands; and Iraq and Iran have persistently flouted Council requests to terminate hostilities.

Nevertheless, disregard of Security Council recommendations is not undertaken lightly. This is true even of states that sometimes disregard them. According to a former Director-General of Israel's Foreign Ministry, Israeli actions in times of crisis have been heavily influenced by anticipation of what the Security Council might do. In his words,

> Throughout the thirty years of conflict the estimated timing of intervention by the Security Council in the fighting had engaged the closest attention of the military planners of both sides. Strategists and field commanders planned and conducted their campaigns virtually with an eye on the ticking of the United Nations clock. They accelerated the advance or slowed down the retreat of their forces in synchronization with the movements of the clock's hands. The ringing of the Security Council bell was never absent from their mind because they knew that military means would not finally decide the outcome of the conflict.[6]

Israel's concern was no doubt justified by the history of active Security Council intervention in the Middle East, as well as Israel's dependence on American support, which might be alienated if Israel ignored Council actions taken with the approval of the United States. Argentina, Iran, and Iraq, on the other hand, could anticipate that Council intervention in their wars would go no farther than harsh words. But even words can sometimes have an impact. To disregard them risks disapproval of the international community, which no state wantonly invites.

The General Assembly

The General Assembly has also been extensively involved in disputes among UN members, but since it is a very large public forum, its debates and decisions are better adapted to legitimizing the position of one side or another than to promoting a negotiated settlement. During the first ten years of the United Nations, the Assembly overshadowed the Security Council as a forum for airing disputes and threats to the peace. This enhancement of the Assembly's security role occurred mainly as an American-led response to Soviet vetoes in the Security Council. Even then, the most obvious function of the Assembly was legitimizing U.S. and Western positions rather than promoting agreed settlement of the issues.

Although the Assembly has since relinquished its primacy to the Security Council, security questions still make up a substantial part of its agenda. Issues relating to the Middle East and southern Africa tend to predominate from year to year, but conflicts in Kampuchea, Grenada, Central America, the Falkland Islands, Afghanistan, and elsewhere find their way to the Assembly as well as to the Security Council. Now, however, the Assembly tends to legitimize Third World positions rather than Western positions on the issues.

The legitimization approach to dispute settlement, whether indulged in by the Security Council or the Assembly, is sometimes more than a propaganda exercise or a shouting match. If consensus is high and the interest is not vital, the offending party may look for ways to bring its conduct more into line with the views of the majority. Numerous disputes arising out of the decolonization process have been considered by the Assembly, and progress toward self-government and independence was undoubtedly hastened by diplomatic pressures mobilized in the Assembly. Such pressures would of course have been ineffectual if the colonial powers had continued to perceive a vital interest in maintaining their colonial relationships.

Occasionally the Assembly has been able to play a third-party role extending beyond legitimization. It authorized peacekeeping operations that helped defuse the 1956 Suez crisis, for example, and it facilitated West Irian's transition from Dutch to Indonesian rule in 1962–63. It took over control of the UN Congo force in 1960 when the Security Council became deadlocked. It fielded a border watch team in Greece from 1947 to 1951 and in Korea prior to the outbreak of the Korean War. Since the West Irian mission, however, the authorization of field missions for security purposes has become the exclusive province of the Security Council.

The Assembly can enlist the services of its President or one of its officers in promoting quiet negotiations among disputing parties. It can formally appoint a UN mediator to assist the parties in reaching agreement, as it did in the early stages of the Arab-Israeli conflict, although mediation is now more likely to be undertaken by the Secretary-General or the Security Council. Like the Security Council, the Assembly has authorized and supported the Secretary-General's peacemaking efforts in the Falklands War, Afghanistan, the Iran-Iraq War, southern Africa, Cyprus, Palestine, Lebanon, and other conflict situations. The convening of the General Assembly each year also provides occasion for high-level diplomatic representatives of most countries to gather in New York and, if they choose, to meet privately for the exchange of views and the resolution of differences.

The Secretary-General

The Secretary-General—at the direction of the Council or the Assembly, on his own initiative, or at the request of a party—is a very important UN dispute settlement resource. His operations as a third-party intermediary, acting personally or through a special representative or mediator, are generally carried on without the disadvantages of vast publicity and public debate. His purposes are also more exclusively focused on settlement, in contrast to the substantive biases that frequently motivate governmental representatives to UN bodies. Where there is genuine room for agreement, the Secretary-General can perform an effective third-party function. The political role of the Secretary-General is discussed at greater length in Chapter 4.

The United Nations and Regional Dispute Settlement

The United Nations was not expected to handle every international dispute that might endanger international peace and security. Article 33 of the Charter urges disputants first to "seek a solution" through "peaceful means of their own choice," including "resort to regional agencies or arrangements." During the past four decades regional organizations have become an important supplement to UN procedures for pacific settlement. A recent study found that four regional agencies—the Organization of American States, the Organization of African Unity, the Arab League, and the Council of Europe—had dealt with a total of 84 disputes from 1945 to 1981, compared with 146 for the United Nations during the same period. Twenty of the disputes were considered by both the United Nations and a regional organization.[7]

There are no clear guidelines for determining whether a dispute should be handled by a regional organization or by the United Nations. Before 1955 the typical regional dispute tended to be of low intensity, between small and middle powers, with minimal armed conflict. Since then, regional organizations have entertained a range of disputes not much different from those handled by the United Nations, and referral to one or the other hinges on the political circumstances of each case. A dominant state within a region might prefer to have intraregional disputes settled locally, where it has greater control, but one of the parties often sees a political advantage in appealing to the United Nations. Until the mid-1960s the United States had considerable success in keeping hemispheric disputes within the Organization of American States. With declining U.S. leadership in both the Organization of American States and the United Nations, inter-American controversies now frequently appear on UN agendas. The Arab League has always had trouble keeping its quarrels at home because its members are often so divided on issues as to make regional dispute resolution impossible. The Organization of African Unity, embracing the vast expanse of the African continent and its associated islands, also finds consensus difficult to achieve.

The techniques of dispute settlement used by regional organizations do not differ significantly from those used by the United Nations. Good offices, inquiry, informal mediation, conciliation, formal debate, adoption of resolutions, cease-fire pleas—the whole gamut of approaches is available. Regional organizations have even resorted to various forms of "peacekeeping" by a military presence. The Organization of American States authorized a peacekeeping force in the 1965 Dominican crisis, although the OAS action was largely a post hoc ratification of U.S. military intervention. The Arab League established a peacekeeping force in Kuwait, mostly Egyptian and Saudi Arabian troops, to ward off the threat of Iraqi attack in 1961. In 1976, the Arab League legitimized Syrian intervention in Lebanon's civil strife by creating an Arab League force dominated by Syrians. More recently the Organization of African Unity fielded an abortive peacekeeping force in Chad for two months in early 1980 and for a six-month period in 1981 and 1982. The force was withdrawn with no appreciable effect on the shifting tides of revolution and outside intervention in Chad.

In dealing with international disputes, the OAS commonly follows the UN pattern of debate and decision by formal vote. Within the OAU and the Arab League, heads of state or their representatives generally seek decision by consensus rather than by voting.

Judicial Dispute Settlement

As noted in Chapter 2, the International Court of Justice is named in the UN Charter as one of the six principal organs of the United Nations, its budget is included within the regular UN budget, and its fifteen members are selected by action of the Security Council and the General Assembly. All UN members are ipso facto parties to the ICJ Statute. The Court nevertheless carries on its judicial functions independently of the other UN organs and is supposed to reach its decisions on the basis of international law rather than international politics. Although its decisions apply only to the parties and do not constitute precedents binding on others, its opinions—like those of the League Court before it—have been recognized as important statements of existing international law.

In twenty-five years the League Court rendered decisions in thirty-two cases and gave twenty-seven advisory opinions at the request of League organs. This was not a heavy caseload, and the ICJ has been no busier. From 1946 through July 1986, the Court entertained just fifty-three cases and in addition wrote seventeen advisory opinions. Its use has been declining. Thirty-four cases were filed from 1947 to 1960, but only nineteen since that time (through July 1986). Of the advisory opinions, ten were rendered through 1960 and just seven since then.[8] The record is still less impressive when the nature of the Court's action on the fifty-three contentious cases is taken into account. Just twenty-three of the fifty-three went to judgment on the merits, with three cases pending. The others were dismissed for lack of jurisdiction, lack of applicant standing to raise the legal issues involved, mootness, request of the parties, and other procedural grounds.

There are a number of reasons why the World Court has been used so sparingly. The most obvious reason is its limited jurisdiction. Only states—not individuals or organizations—can be parties to a dispute before the Court. A private claimant cannot be represented there unless he can persuade his own government to plead his cause. Requests for advisory opinions may be submitted only by the General Assembly, by the Security Council, or by other UN organs or specialized agencies previously authorized by the Assembly to make such requests on legal questions pertaining to their activities. Thus the number of entities entitled to invoke the jurisdiction of the Court is strictly limited.

A still more stringent limitation on use of the Court is the requirement that all parties consent to the Court's jurisdiction. The complaining state (the "applicant") signifies consent by its act of submitting the dispute to the Court, and the respondent state may of course consent at that time by special agreement or by filing a response accepting jurisdiction. But agreed submissions to the Court after a dispute has arisen are not numerous. Few defendants in a civil suit would appear in national courts if they were not required to do so, and very few plaintiffs would file lawsuits if the courts could not compel the defendant to respond. Lacking any general compulsory jurisdiction, the World Court is in precisely that position: few applications are filed, because the country complained against can usually ignore the Court if it wishes.

The docket would be even shorter if the Statute did not provide for methods of consent conferring a limited degree of compulsory jurisdiction on the court. This is done by permitting states to give consent *before* a dispute has occurred, through treaty or other agreement accepting the Court's jurisdiction for a specified class of cases that might arise in the future. For example, an optional protocol to the 1961 Vienna Convention on Diplomatic Relations provides that disputes arising out of the interpretation or application of the Convention fall within the compulsory jurisdiction of the Court. Any party to the protocol may invoke the jurisdiction of the Court against any other party in that class of cases. This optional protocol allowed the Court in 1979 to entertain the U.S. claim that Iran had violated the Vienna Convention by holding U.S. diplomatic personnel hostage in the Tehran embassy. Iran denied the Court's jurisdiction at the time of the U.S. application, but the Court nevertheless took jurisdiction because of Iran's prior consent in ratifying the protocol. The United States also claimed jurisdiction for the Court under a bilateral treaty between the United States and Iran that had a dispute settlement clause conferring jurisdiction on the Court. Other bilateral or multilateral treaties similarly confer jurisdiction on the Court, although they have seldom been invoked.[9]

The ICJ Statute provides a further avenue for states to grant compulsory jurisdiction to the Court by depositing a declaration to that effect with the Secretary-General of the United Nations. Because no state is required to do so, this provision (Article 36, Section 2) is commonly known as the "optional clause." It applies only between states that have made the optional declaration, but for them it extends the Court's jurisdiction to a very broad range of cases. In the words of the Statute, it includes

all legal disputes concerning

   a. the interpretation of a treaty;
   b. any question of international law;
   c. the existence of any fact, which, if established, would constitute a breach of an international obligation;
   d. the nature or extent of the reparation to be made for the breach of an international obligation.

As of July 1986, the requisite declaration was in force for 46 of the 162 parties to the Statute.[10]

In accepting the optional obligation, many states have given with one hand and taken away with the other by attaching reservations that substantially limit the scope of the jurisdiction accepted. The most common reservation is to exclude disputes within the domestic jurisdiction of the state concerned. An extreme form of this reservation is illustrated by the U.S. declaration of acceptance in 1946, which excepted "disputes with regard to matters which are essentially within the domestic jurisdiction of the United States *as determined by the United States of America.*" The italicized phrase, added on the floor of the U.S. Senate as the so-called Connally amendment, greatly weakened the acceptance by allowing the United States rather than the Court to determine the existence of domestic jurisdiction. Because of the reciprocity principle recognized by the Court, other states could invoke the same exception against the United States if the United States brought an action against one of them. At least five other countries have adopted similar "self-judging" reservations. For the United States, the reservation became moot on April 7, 1986, when the United States officially withdrew its declaration of acceptance following a six-month notice of termination. Its withdrawal was prompted by the Court's decision to entertain Nicaragua's complaint of U.S. intervention.

Another reason for the Court's scanty caseload is the expensive, time-consuming, and highly public nature of the Court proceeding. Settling a dispute by quiet negotiations between the parties is much to be preferred. If the World Court is involved, the parties can expect at least a two-year wait between submission of the case and final judgment, and often longer. Legal action entails the time and expense of preparing memorials (legal briefs), exhibits, countermemorials, replies, and supporting documents, as well as conducting a formal hearing with witnesses, expert testimony, and oral argument. The parties may then wait many months for the Court to render its decision. If preliminary decisions on jurisdictional questions or provisional orders are necessary, this argumentation process may occur more than once. The costs of legal counsel can run high, especially when—as is commonly done—private counsel is hired to assist with an ICJ proceeding. Common sense suggests settling in some quicker, cheaper way if at all possible. If the dispute is not already a matter of serious public concern, submission to the Court may have the further disadvantage of publicizing conflict between otherwise friendly states.

Third World states and Communist-bloc countries have had additional reasons for avoiding the Court. International law evolved to accommodate the needs of a state system that was dominated by Europe and oriented to the status quo. Many new states believe that the international legal system inherited from European practice does not adequately reflect their needs and perspectives. The distinction may be less one of geography than one of vested interests. Law tends to protect established rights and thus to work against demands for change by states in a less favored position. European dominance has also been reflected in the composition of the Court itself. Although the balance is now changing, half of the elected judges of the Court since 1945 have been drawn from Europe, the United States and the English-speaking Commonwealth. It is not surprising, then, that only twenty African and Asian states, and no Communist-bloc states, have accepted the optional clause and that the United States and Western European countries have been parties to more than three fourths of the contentious cases before the Court. This pattern may also be changing, however. Of ten contentious cases filed from 1976 through July 1986, seven were initiated by Third World countries.

While all of these reasons help explain the reluctance of states to bring disputes before the World Court, a still greater deterrent is loss of control over the decision process. If important interests are at stake, the risks of an unfavorable decision by members of the Court are too great. Prolongation of the dispute may be preferable to a settlement on unsatisfactory terms. In nonlegal approaches to dispute settlement, the parties remain the final judges of settlement terms, and matters of primary national interest are not compromised. In legal settlements, a majority of the judges make the decision, which is binding on the parties. In extreme circumstances a state might reject the award of the Court, but, given the legal obligation to comply with the decision, this can be done only at considerable diplomatic cost by any state that wishes to be known as law-abiding.

The unpredictability of judicial decisions is one aspect of the problem. Not all international law is uncertain, but the disputes most likely to be brought before an international court are those in which the relevant law or facts are uncertain. The numerous dissenting opinions reflect a wide divergence of opinion on the Court in many cases. Moreover, uncertainty in the law increases the probability that a judge, consciously or unconsciously, may be influenced by political considerations. As one legal scholar has observed, "This casts doubt on his impartiality; and states may be forgiven for thinking that political decisions should be taken by states and not by courts."[11] Faced with such unpredictable and uncontrollable factors, states are understandably reluctant to accept a broad commitment to appear before the Court.

But unpredictability is only half the problem. If uncertainty discourages advance acceptance of the Court's jurisdiction, certainty as to the applicable law may also discourage submission by the side with the weaker legal position. In either situation, loss of control over the outcome of the dispute, and consequent risk of injury to important interests, discourages submission to the Court. Under these circumstances the limited use of both the ICJ and its League predecessor is wholly understandable.

With such formidable deterrents to the use of the Court, one may reasonably ask why it is used at all. A close look at the cases submitted since 1945 reveals that the motivations are almost always intensely practical, having to do with specific questions of national interest rather than generalized allegiance to the ideal of a world governed by law. Recourse to the Court is often merely an incident in a larger process of bargaining and political conflict. A strong legal position can give the application some deterrent or harassment value against an antagonistic state, even if the Court ultimately fails to establish jurisdiction. This probably helps explain U.S. resort to the Court in three aerial incidents of the 1950s in which the Soviet Union twice and Bulgaria once were charged with illegally shooting down foreign aircraft. Undoubtedly it was also a factor in Nicaragua's 1984 decision to seek ICJ action on its complaint against the United States for mining Nicaraguan harbors and aiding Nicaraguan rebels, although the Court subsequently found jurisdiction in that case and, indeed, ruled in favor of Nicaragua.

Among friendly states, recourse to the Court may be a means of isolating a dispute to prevent it from tainting otherwise cordial relations.[12] Australia and New Zealand had this consideration in mind when they asked the Court in 1973 to declare that French atmospheric nuclear testing in the South Pacific was illegal. That objective was largely achieved, even though France never admitted the competence of the Court to hear the case. In Australia, in particular, the Court action helped appease the more aggressive elements of domestic opinion without seriously alienating France. France continued its testing during 1973 but announced a voluntary cessation the following year.

The outcome of the nuclear testing cases suggests another reason for initiating litigation—to encourage a negotiated settlement. Resort to the Court by Australia and New Zealand came only after ten years of unsuccessful bilateral negotiation and UN debates on the subject. A similar motivation has accompanied numerous other applications to the Court. The United Kingdom and West Germany, for example, brought suit against Iceland in 1972 primarily to communicate the seriousness of their determination to resolve their long-standing dispute over Iceland's unilateral extension of its fishing boundaries. The Court rendered a judgment favoring the applicants' position, but a more important effect of the litigation was to encourage subsequent negotiation among the parties. In 1973 Pakistan found the Court helpful in breaking a stalemate with India in negotiations over the release of Pakistani prisoners of war taken during the hostilities in East Pakistan (now Bangladesh) in 1971. The application was filed in May, negotiations were resumed in July, the case was withdrawn from the Court in December, and a final agreement for release of the prisoners was signed in April 1974.

A variety of other reasons may enter into the calculations of an applicant state in deciding for judicial settlement. If settlement of a dispute among friendly states is slow in coming, the bargaining process may reach a point where finding a settlement is more important to both sides than striking a particular kind of bargain. In the

North Sea continental shelf cases (1967–69) pitting Denmark and the Netherlands against West Germany, the controversy was submitted by agreement of all the parties because just such a plateau had been reached. The Court decision broke the deadlock over the division of the oil-rich shelf, although final resolution of all the disputed issues required still further negotiation and a compromise settlement. One additional motive for the agreed submission, at least on the part of Denmark, was to "save face" with domestic public opinion. If territorial concessions were the price of settlement, a Court judgment would make them more politically acceptable. Occasionally, also, parties to a dispute may see the opportunity for judicial clarification or development of the law as worth the risk of an unwanted substantive result. This was true to some extent of both the fisheries dispute and the North Sea continental shelf case.

Despite its underutilization, the Court has been a helpful addition to the tools of pacific settlement. Judicial settlement was never intended to replace negotiation among the parties as the primary means of resolving international disputes, and it has not done so. Nevertheless, it has settled a number of cases brought before it and it symbolizes the ideal of dispute resolution by law rather than force. Its widely cited decisions have contributed to the development of international law. Compliance with its judgments has been high in cases that have proceeded to judgment with the consent of all the parties, although not when the Court has accepted jurisdiction over the objection of the responding party. Several recent decisions have not been honored with compliance, including the court's judgment against the United States in the Nicaragua case, but in each instance the noncomplying party denied the Court's jurisdiction throughout the proceeding. The record is mixed; but if some accomplishment is better than none at all, the balance sheet is positive. Establishment of the International Court of Justice has not brought a world rule of law, but it has been a small step in that direction.

The legal approach to international dispute settlement will become more effective only as weaknesses in the international legal system are remedied. The main flaws may be briefly summarized:

1. The law is often uncertain, and in some areas it reflects earlier power relationships that have become anachronistic in a world no longer centered on Europe.

2. The system has no effective contemporary lawmaking body.

3. While international courts and arbitral tribunals are prepared to interpret and apply international law, there is no general system of compulsory jurisdiction to ensure legal settlement of disputes that evade a negotiated solution.

4. The system lacks effective procedures to bring offenders to justice and to ensure compliance with judgments.

5. The Court, and most areas of international law, have no direct application to individuals and provide no criminal sanctions for individual law violators.

These weaknesses are fundamental and are not to be remedied merely by calling for stronger institutions. Stronger legal institutions could not survive without a firm foundation in widely shared values. Until the requisite links of community have been forged at the international level, judicial settlement and international law will continue to defer to politics in the settlement of international disputes.

CASE STUDIES IN UN CONFLICT RESOLUTION

Disputes before the United Nations have had a variety of causes, but most frequently they have involved East-West controversies, conflicts produced by the decolonization process, territorial and boundary questions, or disputes arising from intervention by one or more states in the internal quarrels of another. The following pages present a number of case studies that have been selected to illustrate the range and difficulty of the disputes placed on UN agendas.

South Africa and the United Nations

Questions arising from South Africa's racial policies have been before the United Nations since its inception and have preoccupied UN discussions more than any other political issue. Some twenty subsidiary UN offices, committees, or funds are now concerned solely or mainly with southern African issues. At one recent General Assembly session, South Africa was verbally attacked in 62 of 111 plenary meetings and criticized in one fifth of all the resolutions adopted.[13]

Not all of the questions relating to South Africa can legitimately be labeled international "disputes," since much UN discussion has been directed toward South Africa's treatment of its own nationals—a subject not readily characterized as a dispute between South Africa and any particular foreign state. Because South Africa's racial policies invoke the wrath of its neighbors, however, and have often led to mutually hostile actions, those policies would clearly appear to create a "situation," as anticipated by Article 34 of the Charter, that falls within UN jurisdiction because it could "lead to international friction or give rise to a dispute."

South African discrimination against minorities first came before the General Assembly in 1946. The complaint was brought by India, alleging South African violation of the Capetown Agreements of 1927 and 1932, which guaranteed equality of treatment for each other's resident nationals. The Indian complaint was never resolved, and it was a perennial subject of Assembly discussions and resolutions until it was merged in the 1950s with a broader attack on South African racial discrimination, focusing on the policy of apartheid, or separation of whites from the nonwhite majority. The debate on that issue has persisted to the present time, with the practical result of politically isolating South Africa from nearly all the other members of the United Nations. South Africa has persistently refused to heed Assembly resolutions demanding that it abandon its apartheid policies, and the Assembly has responded with increasingly bitter denunciation. In 1976 the Assembly began to explicitly advocate "armed struggle" in South Africa as a means of eradicating the evil. The Assembly has repeatedly urged UN members to cut all political and economic ties with South Africa and called on the Security Council to impose mandatory sanctions.

Action on apartheid by the Security Council has been somewhat more restrained because of the moderating influence of the American and British vetoes. The Council first addressed the issue in 1960, criticizing South African behavior in the Sharpesville incident, in which police killed sixty-seven people during an antiapartheid demonstration. Three years later the Council called for a voluntary embargo on the sale of arms to South Africa, and in 1977 it made the embargo mandatory. The 1977 resolution also banned nuclear cooperation with South Africa. Third World and East European states have called for much stronger measures, including a total severance of economic relations with South Africa, but thus far the Western members of the Council have refused to cut all ties. They argue that total isolation of South Africa would give up the leverage that present economic contact provides and injure black South Africans as well as white. In 1985, with Britain and the United States abstaining, the Security Council recommended nonmandatory economic sanctions against South Africa. Many private multinational businesses moved toward voluntary disinvestment in South Africa, and public pressures in Western states began to force serious consideration of tough economic sanctions.

UN encounters with South African racial discrimination represent a failure of the dispute settlement process, if elimination of apartheid is the criterion of success. South Africa has modified some of its stricter segregation measures in response to external pressures, and in 1982 it conceded limited political participation to its Indian and colored (mixed race) minority populations. But Pretoria's solution to the racial problem has been focused mainly on a program to denationalize all blacks (70 percent of the country's population) and make them citizens of "independent" homelands or "bantustans" supposedly separate from South Africa. Thirteen percent of South Africa's territory has been set aside for the bantustans, in which all of its blacks are to be politically accommodated. Even if creation of the bantustans represented genuine self-determination, which it does not, millions of urban blacks will still remain in South Africa, where they enjoy neither the rights of South African nationals nor the rights generally accorded to aliens. The government at Pretoria has hinted at granting limited political rights to these urban blacks, but by 1986 nothing concrete had materialized.

The full force of the criminal law, including the death penalty, has been used against internal opponents of apartheid. Members of the antiapartheid African National Congress (ANC) have been the most frequent targets. Externally, South African forces have periodically raided neighboring countries harboring ANC guerrillas and South Africa has unabashedly given aid to insurgents seeking the overthrow of leftist governments in Angola and Mozambique. South Africa constitutes a perpetual affront to UN ideals and majority interests that four decades of UN involvement have failed to alleviate.

Namibia

Closely related to apartheid has been the issue of South African rule in Namibia. Large (half the size of Europe), arid, and small in population (about 1.5 million),

Namibia borders South Africa to the northwest. A German colony prior to World War I, the territory (known as South West Africa until the late 1960s) was invaded and occupied by South Africa in 1915 and governed by South Africa as a League of Nations mandate after 1920. At the end of World War II, South Africa refused to accept UN supervision under the trusteeship system, as other holders of League mandates had done, but instead took steps to integrate the territory with South Africa and impose its apartheid system there.

The General Assembly responded to these developments with alarm, criticism, attempted negotiation, and legal action against South Africa. A 1950 advisory opinion of the International Court of Justice ruled that the South West African mandate should be subject to UN supervision, but this opinion was totally ignored by South Africa. Subsequently the Assembly encouraged Ethiopia and Liberia, as former League members, to file an ICJ action against South Africa to obtain a binding legal decision on the former mandate. This effort failed when the Court in 1966 determined that Ethiopia and Liberia had insufficient legal interest to pursue the claim. According to the Court, the right to sue in such a cause belonged to the League, as distinct from its individual members, which left no legal remedy since the League had ceased to exist.

The General Assembly then acted unilaterally to terminate the mandate and declare Pretoria's continued occupation of Namibia illegal. This position was subsequently endorsed by the Security Council and by advisory opinions of the International Court of Justice. In 1967 the Assembly created an eleven-member Council for South West Africa, subsequently renamed the UN Council for Namibia, to take over administration of the territory from South Africa. The Council for Namibia was never permitted to perform that function, but it became a center for constant UN agitation against South African occupation of Namibia. Many UN members blamed the failure of UN efforts on the United States and its Western allies because their vetoes in the Security Council prevented tougher sanctions against South Africa.

In addition to external UN pressures, South Africa has faced growing opposition within Namibia. The principal opposition organization, the South West Africa People's Organization (SWAPO), was formed in 1960 and began guerrilla warfare in 1966. The United Nations now recognizes it as the true representative of the Namibian people, and most observers regard it as having majority popular support.

Hostility between South Africa and the UN majority has disabled the United Nations from serving as an effective third party or a forum for negotiations. The Secretary-General has been designated as a UN representative to negotiate with Pretoria, but his office has little credibility there either. Since 1977 the five Western members of the Security Council, called the "contact group," have succeeded in promoting dialogue between South Africa and SWAPO without as yet bringing a final settlement. In 1978 the contact group negotiated a plan for Namibian independence that was accepted by both South Africa and SWAPO and subsequently embodied in Security Council Resolution 435 (1978). The UN Secretariat prepared an elaborate plan for a UN Transition Assistance Group (UNTAG) including a 7,500-

man peacekeeping force to supervise elections and oversee the transition to independence. South Africa persistently balked at the details for implementation, however, and beginning in 1981 the issue was further complicated by the efforts of the United States and South Africa to link a Namibian settlement to agreement for withdrawal of the 20,000–25,000 Cuban troops stationed in neighboring Angola. This linkage is not totally without factual underpinning, since Angola has provided a haven for SWAPO guerrillas, but most UN members have regarded the linkage as a ploy to postpone settlement. Until this and other issues of implementation are resolved, UNTAG must remain waiting in the wings.

Arab-Israeli Conflict

The Arab-Israeli conflict, like South African racial policies, has been a perennial concern of the United Nations almost from the beginning of the organization. It was first placed before the United Nations in 1947 and has been there ever since. For centuries a land of Arabs, Palestine in the twentieth century became a haven for Zionist Jews returning to their ancient homeland. Conflicting Arab and Zionist attitudes toward continued Jewish immigration and, indeed, the whole political future of the area, reached a crisis in a rising tide of violence after World War II. Britain, as administrator of Palestine under a League of Nations mandate, declared its mandate unworkable and turned to the General Assembly for a solution.

The General Assembly at first recommended partition of the mandate into separate Arab and Jewish states, each politically independent but forming an economic union. When Arab opposition thwarted peaceful implementation of the partition plan, the United Kingdom terminated the mandate on May 15, 1948, and the Jewish groups by force of arms secured their own independence over a territory extending well beyond the boundaries specified in the UN partition plan. Through the offices of a UN mediator appointed by the General Assembly and a Truce Commission authorized by the Security Council, a cease-fire, truce, and four armistice agreements were worked out.

Since that time no annual session of the Assembly has been free from the Arab-Israeli problem in its many aspects. Among the specific issues have been refugee relief and resettlement, Arab property rights in Israel, human rights violations, Israeli withdrawal from conquered territories, the status of Jerusalem, the creation of an independent Palestinian state, and a host of security questions ranging from specific acts of terrorism to military border clashes and full-scale war.

The Security Council has also been heavily involved in the Arab-Israeli conflict. Scarcely a year has passed without one or more Palestine security questions appearing on its agenda. Major hostilities have broken out at least once every decade since the 1948–49 war for Israeli independence. In 1956 (the Suez War) Egyptian nationalization of the Suez Canal provided the occasion for an invasion of Egypt by Israel, Britain, and France. In 1967 (the Six-Day War) Israel launched a preemptive military strike against Egypt in a bold attempt to remove once and for all the threat to the security of its borders. In 1973 (the Yom Kippur War) Egypt and Syria struck the first blow in hope of regaining lost territory and, perhaps, inflicting a mortal blow on Israel. In 1978 and again in 1982, Israeli forces initiated major hostilities in Lebanon in response to Palestinian raids into Israel over the Lebanese border.

The 1948 war resulted in an independent Israel, but none of the subsequent wars brought lasting security. Israel and Egypt were finally able to bring some stability to their common borders through the Camp David accords of 1978 and the peace treaty of 1979. The other Arab states of the region remain legally at war with Israel, although their activities are restricted by military armistices. Hostility and great insecurity continue to characterize Israel's relationship with these Arab states and with Palestinian Arabs. The dangers of the situation and the difficulties facing the United Nations are exacerbated by superpower rivalry, with the United States strongly supporting Israel and the Soviet Union giving aid to the Arabs. No other area of the world has so persistently involved the United Nations in threats to peace and security, and no ultimate solution is yet in sight.

Over the years the role of the General Assembly has changed from that of a relatively evenhanded third party to that of a shrill partisan of the Arab cause. In early attempts at mediation, a Palestine Conciliation Commission, established by the General Assembly in 1948 and composed of France, Turkey, and the United States, was able to secure the release of blocked Arab accounts in Israeli banks and to prepare lists of real and personal properties left behind in Israel by Arab refugees. Attempts at settling more fundamental differences were fruitless, but at least both sides were engaged in dialogue. When vetoes by Britain and France blocked Security Council action in the 1956 Suez War, the Assembly was able to respond with an innovative peacekeeping force as a means of facilitating a cease-fire and troop withdrawal, and subsequently of providing a buffer between contending forces.

In recent years the Third World–dominated Assembly has substituted condemnation of Israel for any genuine attempt at settlement. Israel has given the Assembly ample grounds for reproach, including its complete absorption of Jerusalem within the Israeli state, its determined colonization of the West Bank territory occupied during the 1967 war,[14] and its frequent resort to violence (often in response to Arab terrorist acts) in dealing with its neighbors. Still, the Assembly has given up all pretense of neutrality in dealing with Israel and as a result has lost the capacity to be a positive influence on Israel's policy.

The Security Council has been no haven for Israeli interests either, but in the Council the U.S. veto has prevented some of the anti-Zionist excesses that have characterized Assembly action. Thus the Council has been able to play a more constructive role in times of extreme crisis, particularly in bringing major hostilities to an end and authorizing peacekeeping forces to supervise the tenuous peace. The peacekeeping function, discussed in Chapter 5, is not to be minimized as a UN contribution to order in the Middle East. One other contribution of special importance, applicable to both the General Assembly and the Security Council, is the opportunity for informal contacts between Israeli and Arab representatives at the United Nations. This makes some degree of dialogue possible despite the absence of formal diplomatic relations.

In addition, Security Council resolutions have established certain principles to which all the participants repeatedly refer in Middle East negotiations. Security Council Resolution 242, adopted unanimously on November 22, 1967, in the aftermath of the Six-Day War, is by far the most important. Its two cardinal principles, often reaffirmed, are (1) Israeli withdrawal "from territories occupied in the recent conflict" and (2) "respect for and acknowledgement of the sovereignty, territorial integrity, and political independence of every State in the area and their right to live in peace within secure and recognized boundaries."

Agreement in the 1967 Security Council has not been followed by agreement among the parties to the conflict. The Palestine Liberation Organization has opposed Resolution 242 because it makes no reference to Palestinian self-determination, and Arab states (except Egypt) have balked at recognizing Israel's right to existence. Israel, moreover, has interpreted the withdrawal provision as though it reads "some but not all" occupied territories. Thus Israel eventually withdrew from Sinai and most occupied Syrian territory but has steadfastly refused to give up the West Bank and the Golan Heights. If any settlement is ever reached, however, it will probably embody the principles of Resolution 242.

Viewed in perspective, the United Nations has operated in the Middle East as a fire brigade that helps limit damage and keep the flames from spreading. It has assisted in the resolution of subsidiary issues but has been unable to promote permanent settlement of the underlying conflict. In the one instance where political differences were successfully resolved, the Egypt-Israel accord, the United States rather than the United Nations played the role of third-party mediator.

India-Pakistan

Territorial and other disputes between India and Pakistan have been a periodic feature of the UN landscape. The India-Pakistan issue first came before the Security Council in January 1948 at the complaint of India. When the two countries gained independence in August 1947, more than 500 princely states of the subcontinent were given the choice of joining one or the other. For most, the choice was easily made on the basis of geographic proximity and predominance of Moslem or Hindu populations. But Kashmir (also called Jammu and Kashmir) with its Hindu Maharaja, predominantly Moslem populace, and geographic contiguity with both India and Pakistan, faced a difficult choice. Invading tribesmen from Pakistan, allegedly supported by the Pakistani government, forced the Maharaja's hand, and he sent out a plea for help with the announcement that he had decided to join India. Indian troops moved to protect the new accession, Pakistani forces formally entered the fray, and Kashmir became the scene of large-scale armed combat.

The Security Council appointed a UN Commission on India and Pakistan (UNCIP) to investigate and mediate the dispute. After months of negotiation, UNCIP was able to secure a truce and cease-fire, effective January 1, 1949, and acceptance in principle of a plebiscite to resolve the accession question. A UN Military Observer Group was established to supervise the cease-fire. The proposed plebiscite was never held, primarily because India occupied the larger part of Kashmir and regarded this fait accompli as preferable to a free vote in which the Moslem majority would in all likelihood opt for union with Pakistan.

In August 1965 renewed fighting shattered the truce; but prompt Security Council action, mediation by the Secretary-General, and close coordination of diplomatic efforts by the Soviet Union and the United States brought a cease-fire in September. A UN observer group helped make the cease-fire effective. In 1971 serious conflict again broke out, although the major hostilities were in East Pakistan, where Indian armies intervened in support of Bengali separatists fighting for independence from Pakistan. The Soviet Union vetoed a Security Council call for a cease-fire, and a similar resolution adopted by the Assembly was ignored by India until the creation of an independent Bangladesh was assured.

In perspective, the United Nations has been quite effective in terminating hostilities between India and Pakistan when the superpowers were in agreement. But the political stalemate over Kashmir has persisted to the present day. The efforts of UNCIP (discontinued in 1950) and two special mediators (1950 and 1951) and mediation efforts at various times by the President of the Security Council and the UN Secretary-General have been virtually fruitless. The intensity of the national interests involved and the irreconcilability of legal and moral positions have left little room for compromise.

UN-Assisted Negotiated Settlements

As the problems of Kashmir, Palestine and South Africa demonstrate, the United Nations offers no talisman for the solution of complex and deep-seated problems that divide nations. It is a place to talk, to bring collective pressures to bear, and sometimes to help bring international violence under control. Sometimes, too, it has made significant contributions to the settlement of particular disputes. Following the 1956 Suez War, for example, Secretary-General Dag Hammarskjöld was assigned to arrange for and supervise clearance of the Suez Canal, which Egypt had blocked with the hulks of sunken ships. The underlying political differences between Israel and Egypt were not resolved, but clearing the canal was a significant accomplishment in its own right.

The American Airmen. The release of American air force personnel imprisoned by China in violation of Korean Armistice arrangements is another instance of successful UN negotiation of a particular dispute. The issue arose in November 1954, when the Peking government unexpectedly announced that eleven crewmen of a B–10 bomber shot down near Korea in January 1953 had been tried by a military tribunal and sentenced to long prison terms for espionage. Four American jet pilots were already known to be similarly detained. The United States immediately appealed to the General Assembly, which in this case proved surprisingly effective. At the request of the Assembly, Dag Hammarskjöld departed for Peking in early January, and shortly after his visit Peking announced that relatives of the airmen would be permitted to visit China. Four months later, in a letter to the Secretary-General sent through the Swedish ambassador in Peking, the Chinese government informed Hammarskjöld that the four jet pilots would be deported. In August the eleven crewmen were freed. Whatever the motivation of the Chinese, the United Nations played an important mediating role in obtaining release of the fliers.

Thailand-Cambodia, Equatorial Guinea, Bahrain, Greenpeace.   An important mediating contribution by the UN Secretary-General has also been recognized in a number of other cases. In 1958–59 and again in 1962–64, a representative of the Secretary-General was instrumental in resolving border disputes and hostile incidents between Thailand and Cambodia. The representatives were sent at the request of both parties, which undoubtedly helps explain the success of the missions. The second UN mission remained on the scene for two years, with expenses jointly shared by the two governments. The Secretary-General's personal representative was also successful in assisting the peaceful withdrawal of Spanish troops from Equatorial Guinea (a former Spanish colony) in the spring of 1969. Again, the assistance was requested and received with cooperation by the parties.

A potentially much more explosive situation was defused by a representative of the Secretary-General in the 1970 controversy over the status of Bahrain, a small, oil-producing British protectorate off the coast of Saudi Arabia in the Persian Gulf. Iran's claims to sovereignty over Bahrain were disputed by Britain, and the good offices of the Secretary-General were enlisted to help resolve the controversy. All of the parties subsequently accepted a report by his personal representative, reinforced by UN consultation in Bahrain, that the islands should become independent. The report was unanimously endorsed by the Security Council, and Bahrain became a member of the United Nations the following year.

More recently Secretary-General Pérez de Cuéllar successfully mediated a dispute between France and New Zealand arising from the clandestine bombing of the Greenpeace ship *Rainbow Warrior* by French agents while the ship was in Auckland harbor. Greenpeace had planned to use the ship to protest French underground nuclear tests on a South Pacific atoll. One life was lost as a result of the incident, and two French agents were convicted of manslaughter by a New Zealand court. The agreed settlement, announced in July 1986, called for $7 million compensation to New Zealand, an apology by France, and the lifting of a French embargo on the import of food from New Zealand. New Zealand, in return, released the two agents on condition of their transfer to a French military garrison in the South Pacific for a period of three years.

The Cuban Missile Crisis.   The United Nations also had a modest role in the resolution of the 1962 Cuban missile crisis arising from the discovery of Soviet missiles and jet bombers in Cuba in the fall of 1962. Agreement on dismantling the missile sites and removing the missiles and bombers from Cuba was reached primarily through great power negotiation, but the UN contribution is not to be discounted.

Most obvious at the time was U.S. use of the Security Council as a forum to display evidence that missiles were indeed being installed in Cuba. Aerial photographs laid before the world made Soviet denials no longer credible. The United Nations also had a part in the less public negotiation processes. Both superpowers used their UN ambassadors to channel informal suggestions and semiofficial messages that supplemented more direct communication. At various times during the crisis, Secretary-General U Thant served personally as an intermediary. After the acute stage of the crisis had passed, the United Nations was the site of extensive negotiations on means of verifying the weapons withdrawal. At this stage U Thant was the principal point of contact between Castro and the superpower representatives in New York.

Another important UN contribution to settlement was a face-saving formula that gave Soviet Premier Nikita Khrushchev an excuse to call for the return of Soviet freighters bearing additional missiles to Cuba, and ultimately to agree to withdrawal of all missiles and equipment. At a crucial moment in the Khrushchev-Kennedy dialogue, Secretary-General U Thant offered a proposal for a voluntary suspension of Soviet arms shipments to Cuba in return for a voluntary suspension of the American naval quarantine. This suggestion was quickly accepted by Khrushchev as an excuse for Soviet freighters already under way with a missile cargo and a submarine escort to steer clear of the quarantine fleet, even though Kennedy's reply to Thant made suspension of the quarantine contingent on removal of offensive weapons already in Cuba. At this point the UN role may have been crucial. Kennedy could scarcely have made such a proposal, and if he had, Khrushchev could not easily have accepted it. But Thant, as impartial spokesman for a community of states, was able to elicit a degree of restraint that neither of the parties could as easily have exercised under pressure from the other.

Decolonization.   The United Nations has been involved in numerous disputes arising from the decolonization process, and in several instances it has made a significant contribution to their settlement. During the course of the Indonesian struggle for independence from the Netherlands, 1945–49, a Security Council Good Offices Committee (later reconstituted as the UN Commission for Indonesia) arranged cease-fires in the field, maintained a small truce observation team, and assisted with negotiations. At UN headquarters, debates and resolutions kept continual pressure on the Dutch to grant Indonesian independence. When the United States finally took sides in the controversy, the United Nations helped legitimize American diplomatic and economic pressures on the Dutch. The final agreement on independence, in December 1949, owed much to UN involvement. As discussed in Chapter 5, the subsequent controversy over Western New Guinea (West Irian), which the Netherlands refused to relinquish to Indonesian rule in 1949, was also resolved with UN assistance when the Dutch were finally ready to deal. The terms of the transfer of West Irian to Indonesia were arranged by a UN mediator and executed with the help of the UN Temporary Executive Authority and the UN Security Force.

The United Nations also peacefully resolved the fate of the former Italian colonies of Libya, Eritrea, and Italian Somaliland. France, the Soviet Union, the United Kingdom, and the United States had agreed in the World War II treaty of peace with Italy to let the UN General Assembly decide the future status of the colonies if the powers were unable to agree among themselves by September 1948. Disagreement prevailed, and the decision fell to the Assembly. The question occupied several sessions of the Assembly, but ultimately Libya was granted independence (proclaimed in December 1951), Somaliland was placed under Italian trusteeship until independence was achieved in 1960, and Eritrea was associated in a federal arrangement with Ethiopia.

Unsuccessful Settlement Efforts

UN successes in dispute settlement have sometimes come after the outbreak of violence between the parties, and some of the partial successes in curbing violence have left the controversy still unresolved. Other conflicts, including some very serious ones, have been totally impervious to UN settlement attempts. Two recent cases illustrate the problem.

The Iran-Iraq War.   All international machinery of pacific settlement has thus far been irrelevant to the war between Iran and Iraq. Iraq struck in September 1980 in the aftermath of the Iranian revolution, hoping for a quick victory that would nullify Iran's support of Shiite revolution in Iraq, gain control of the Shatt al Arab waterway, and establish Iraqi dominance in the Persian Gulf area. Iraq miscalculated. Although the tides of battle periodically shifted, the overall result was stalemate. After years of fighting, Iraq has become readier than Iran to end a war entailing hundreds of thousands of casualties, material losses running to billions of dollars, severe economic damage to both countries from drastically reduced oil production and shipment, and war-caused oil leaks that threaten to pollute large sections of the Gulf coast.

Security Council cease-fire appeals were regularly rejected by Iran, and sometimes by Iraq. Several mediation missions by a representative of the Secretary-General, acting under Security Council authorization, proved fruitless. A fact-finding mission dispatched by the Secretary-General in May 1983 was praised by Iran for its objectivity but brought the war no closer to an end. The General Assembly also called for an end to the fighting, but Iran refused to support any resolution that did not brand Iraq as an aggressor. In June 1984, in response to an appeal by the Secretary-General, the two combatants agreed to stop deliberate attacks on civilian population centers. The agreement has been generally, if imperfectly, observed. Conciliation efforts by the Islamic Conference, the Gulf Cooperation Council (formed for this purpose by Saudi Arabia and five small Arab states bordering the Persian Gulf), and the Non-Aligned Movement have been totally without avail.

When both parties are willing to stop fighting, the United Nations may help supply the modalities; but without that political will there is little that the United Nations can do.

The Falklands War.   Located 300 miles off the Argentine coast, the 4,700 square miles of the Falkland Islands (called the Malvinas by Argentina and other Latin-American states) have been a British dependency since 1833. The 1,800 inhabitants are largely of British descent, and in response to a 1982 questionnaire they showed a clear preference for continued association with the United Kingdom. Argentina's claim to the Falklands is through succession from Spain, dating from the Argentine declaration of independence in 1816. Argentina has periodically disputed British rule there and has done so insistently since 1965, when the UN General Assembly first considered the question and urged a peaceful solution.

On April 2, 1982, Argentina invaded the islands in an attempt to make good its claim by force of arms. The modest sheep raising and wool industry of this cold and barren land offered little economic incentive for military conquest, although suspected oil deposits beneath Falkland waters might yet prove a reality. More likely the military regime in Argentina launched its attack to divert attention from serious domestic problems and, perhaps, out of frustration with the long diplomatic impasse. Both the British Isles and the British navy were a long way from the South Atlantic, and a fait accompli in the name of anticolonialism might deter a major effort by the United Kingdom to regain control.

Even more than Iraq in 1980, the Argentinians seriously miscalculated. In the United Nations support for anticolonialism was undercut by concern about the use of naked force to resolve territorial disputes. One day after the invasion the Security Council adopted a British-sponsored resolution demanding an immediate halt to the fighting and total withdrawal of Argentine forces. Argentina ignored the Council's demand, but it could not ignore the massive British expeditionary force that reestablished British control of the islands and forced the surrender of the main Argentine garrison on June 14. In early June Argentina suddenly became the partisan of a cease-fire resolution, but its adoption by the Security Council was vetoed by the United States and the United Kingdom.

During the course of the conflict, U.S. Secretary of State Alexander M. Haig, Jr., and subsequently UN Secretary-General Javier Pérez de Cuéllar, mounted major efforts at mediation, but neither was successful. Once the fighting stopped, the diplomatic action shifted to the UN Committee of 24 (Decolonization Committee) and to the General Assembly when it convened in the fall. A resolution calling for resumed negotiations was adopted by an overwhelming majority, which left the matter much as it had been before the war. The United Kingdom voted against the resolution because it suggested that "sovereignty" over the Falklands was negotiable and failed to emphasize the importance of self-determination by the Falklanders. The Assembly has since reiterated its position, but no meaningful negotiations have occurred.

Other Controversies Resistant to UN Settlement.   The Falklands War and the Iran-Iraq War illustrate a principle that underlies all UN attempts to promote peaceful settlement of disputes. Where there is no common ground, no common desire for settlement, the United Nations can do little. The Vietnam War proved totally resistant to UN attempts at mediation. The same has been true of Soviet intervention in Afghanistan, U.S. intervention in Grenada, Nicaragua's differences with its neighbors and with the United States, and a long list of other disputes since 1945 in which one or more parties have been hostile to UN involvement or unwilling to settle on mutually acceptable terms. The United Nations can sometimes be a useful third party, but it cannot produce agreement where no basis for agreement exists.

CONCLUSIONS ON DISPUTE SETTLEMENT

Most states settle most of their disputes with one another most of the time without resort to force and without need for assistance from third parties. The vast bulk of day-to-day transactions between nationals of different countries and their governments are mutually beneficial, and all parties have an interest in peacefully resolving differences that may arise. Most differences between governments are settled by diplomatic negotiation without recourse to courts, the United Nations, or complicated procedures and pose no threat to international peace and security. The United States alone concludes perhaps two hundred treaties and executive agreements with foreign governments every year, each of which settles some disputed question. One legal authority estimates that "each major state settles annually scores or even hundreds" of disputed matters with other states through letters and memoranda, without resorting to the formality of a treaty.[15] If one could identify and count all of the disputes between governments that have been peacefully resolved, the statistical evidence in support of peaceful settlement as an international norm would be overwhelming.

By contrast, the UN record of peaceful settlement is statistically not strong. Although people may reasonably differ in their judgment of UN impact on particular disputes, knowledgeable observers agree that the United Nations has contributed to the settlement of well under half of the disputes brought before it.[16] Table 7–1 presents findings of Ernst Haas in a study of disputes considered by the United Nations from 1945 to 1981. During that time, by his methods of calculation, 123 disputes were referred to the United Nations for settlement.[17] Of this number, the United Nations helped settle just twenty-eight, and most of the successes occurred before 1970. In nine of the disputes, the organization's contribution to settlement was judged substantial; in the other nineteen, it was significant but nevertheless modest in relation to other influences working toward settlement. An additional thirty-five disputes, for a total of sixty-three, were in some degree ameliorated because of UN efforts at conflict management. *Conflict management,* as Haas defines the term, includes not only settling disputes but also abating the conflict (reducing its intensity), isolating the conflict (inhibiting third parties from intervening diplomatically or militarily in support of the disputants), and stopping armed hostilities. UN success in

TABLE 7–1
UN Success in Conflict Management, 1945–1981

Time Period	Number of Disputes Referred to United Nations	Disputes Settled with UN Help		Disputes Ameliorated with UN Help*	
		Number	Percent	Number	Percent
1945–50	20	3	15	13	65
1951–55	12	4	33	4	33
1956–60	16	7	44	12	75
1961–65	25	7	28	10	40
1966–70	14	5	36	9	64
1971–75	12	0	0	5	42
1976–81	24	2	8	10	42
Total	123	28	23	63	51

*Includes disputes in which the United Nations helped abate the intensity of the conflict, stop hostilities, and inhibit expansion of the conflict to other states, as well as disputes actually settled.

SOURCE: Ernst B. Haas, "Regime Decay: Conflict Management and International Organizations, 1945–1981" *International Organization* 37, no. 2 (Spring 1983), pp. 189–256, especially the data in tables I, M, and N.

conflict management was characterized as "great" in thirty-one cases and "limited" in the other thirty-two.[18] If the concept of pacific settlement is expanded to embrace Haas's definition of conflict management, the UN success level through 1981 rises to just 51 percent, including cases in which the organization made only a limited contribution. No similar study has covered the period after 1981, but no informed person has suggested that the UN record of peaceful settlement has improved since then.

This record is not necessarily cause for despair. The United Nations would undoubtedly do better if it had the legal right and the practical capability to enforce settlements. In this respect the United Nations mirrors the shortcomings of the larger international system, which lacks sufficient sense of community to support central coercive institutions. States in their bilateral settlement procedures also operate within the constraints of the existing system, but that is an unfair comparison because the United Nations never deals with routine disputes susceptible of ready compromise. Bilateral negotiation has already failed in most disputes brought to the United Nations, and parties have often resorted to the threat or use of force. In many UN disputes, one or more of the parties is willing to settle only for the complete capitulation of the other side. Not all UN disputes are this intractable, but as a class the disputes that reach the United Nations are those that are the most difficult to resolve.[19] Viewed in this light, the spotty UN settlement record is understandable. Given the nature of the disputes that come to the United Nations, one may reasonably conclude that a contribution to the settlement of any of them is a net gain.

The trend of the past two decades nevertheless gives cause for concern. The United Nations' ability to settle disputes has been in decline, with no corresponding increase in the dispute resolution capacity of regional organizations. Moreover, the apparent cause of the decline offers little hope of an early or easy reversal. That cause, expressed in broadest terms, is the decline of a consensus within the United Nations having links with effective centers of power outside the organization.

For a number of years, U.S. leadership was able to engineer the needed consensus on many issues, and that consensus was supported by American influence. The organization was seldom effective in resolving conflicts between opposing cold war coalitions, but promoting settlement between an aligned and a nonaligned state was often possible. The organization was quite effective in dealing with decolonization disputes, perhaps the typical case of aligned versus nonaligned. In the past two decades U.S. leadership has been replaced by Third World dominance. The new majority readily musters a united front on issues of Western colonialism, on Israel and South Africa, and usually on opposition to superpower military interventions. But the few remaining vestiges of vanished colonial empires are a small and declining portion of the UN agenda, and when a superpower opposes the consensus, the prevailing majority lacks the power to carry out its mandates. This in turn often leads to name-calling and denunciation in place of a genuine search for settlement. Other serious quarrels and threats to peace occur within the Third World, and here the requisite consensus is often lacking. Thus, while Israel, South Africa, and the remaining colonial enclaves evoke strong UN disapproval, the new majority has been much less decisive in dealing with disputes between nonaligned states, such as those arising from the 1975 Indonesian conquest of East Timor, Vietnamese military occupation of Kampuchea, China's 1979 incursion into Vietnam, the Iraqi attack on Iran, and Indian aid to secessionist Bangladesh.

The Charter framers at San Francisco never contemplated that the United Nations would abolish differences of interest among states. They did believe that international disputes should be kept within peaceful bounds and that the United Nations could help with this task. In this they were not wrong or mistaken. Peaceful settlement of international disputes is still a worthy goal, and the United Nations has been a helpful adjunct to other settlement techniques. No war of global extent, no conflict severe enough to threaten the system of independent states has emerged since the United Nations was established. To this conflict containment, the United Nations has made a contribution. A decline in its effectiveness is to be lamented, especially since the persistence of unresolved disputes and the occurrence of numerous local wars leave the world far short of the peaceful settlement ideal. One may regard such conflict at the periphery as a reasonable price to pay for stability at the center if that is in fact the trade-off. But if the framers were right in believing that no war is necessary, it represents a persisting challenge to extend the reach of UN peaceful settlement procedures.

NOTES

1. Former UN Ambassador Jeane J. Kirkpatrick has emphasized the adverse UN impact on international conflicts, asserting that the United Nations makes "conflict resolution *more difficult* [emphasis in original] than it would otherwise be, at least in a good many cases." Address before the Foreign Policy Association, New York City, January 26, 1986, reproduced in Kirkpatrick, *The Reagan Phenomenon—and Other Speeches on Foreign Policy* (Washington, D.C.: American Enterprise Institute for Public Policy Research, 1983), p. 95. The reasons she gives are use of the forum for name-calling and invective rather than negotiation, extension of the conflict from a few states to all that participate and vote, and polarization that results from the necessity for countries to take sides.

2. Critics have challenged the "safety valve theory"—that the world is made safer because injured or outraged nations can release pent-up indignation there—as inoperable in the present United Nations, and especially the General Assembly. Writes one critic:

   It cannot be said that this beneficial outcome has never occurred. It must also be said that in today's General Assembly, such occurrences are very rare. All evidence points to the safety-valve theory being turned on its head. The venting of steam is for the most part hypocritical, stage-managed and conflict-oriented. Far from cooling passions, the techniques of name-calling and lying are intended to mobilize the Assembly on the side of the speaker, to discredit and isolate adversaries, and to cultivate climates of opinion inhospitable to [r]ational argument. (Maurice Tugwell, "The United Nations as the World's Safety Valve," in *A World without a U.N.: What Would Happen if the United Nations Shut Down,* ed. Burton Yale Pines [Washington, D.C.: Heritage Foundation, 1984], p. 163)

3. Olof Rydbeck, "Conflict in the Western Sahara," in *Paths to Peace: The UN Security Council and Its Presidency,* ed. Davidson Nichol (New York: Pergamon Press, 1981), p. 270.

4. A number of scholars concerned with the Council's future capability have studied how Security Council procedures might be improved. A good source is Davidson Nicol, *The United Nations Security Council: Towards Greater Effectiveness* (New York: UNITAR, 1982). Suggestions have focused on the mediating role of the President of the Council, increased private consultations, Council initiatives to instigate change in areas that present a danger to peace—before a crisis arises, and establishment of a precrisis monitoring committee, among other possibilities.

5. "Report on the Work of the Organization," *UN Chronicle* 19, no. 9 (October 1982), p. 2.

6. Gideon Rafael, *Destination Peace: Three Decades of Israeli Foreign Policy* (New York: Stein & Day, 1981), p. 235. This subject is elaborated in Istvan S. Pogany, *The Security Council and the Arab-Israeli Conflict* (Aldershot, Eng.: Gower Publishing, 1984).

7. Ernst B. Haas, "Regime Decay: Conflict Management and International Organizations, 1945–1981," *International Organization* 37 (Spring 1983), p. 195, n. 7.

8. At the end of July 1986, an additional advisory opinion was pending. The figures are compiled from *International Court of Justice Yearbook, 1983–84,* vol. 38 (The Hague, 1984); and *Report of the International Court of Justice,* UN Document A/41/4 (1986).

9. According to a 1985 UN estimate, "about 160 bilateral and trilateral treaties involving at least 64 States contain clauses relating to the jurisdiction of the Court in contentious proceedings." Some eighty-seven multilateral treaties authorize the Court to decide disputes about the application or interpretation of the treaties. *UN Chronicle* 22, no. 1 (January 1985), p. 8.

10. *Report of the International Court of Justice,* UN Document A/41/4 (1986), lists the forty-six states adhering to the optional clause on July 31, 1986. The United States withdrew its acceptance effective April 7, 1986, as noted in the text below.

11. Michael Akehurst, *A Modern Introduction to International Law,* 4th ed. (London: Allen & Unwin, 1982), pp. 211–12.

12. Reasons for using the Court are examined in Dana D. Fischer, "Decisions to Use the International Court of Justice," *International Studies Quarterly* 26 (June 1982), pp. 251–77.

13. Donald J. Puchala, ed., *Issues before the 38th General Assembly of the United Nations, 1983–1984* (New York: UNA/USA, 1983), p. 31.

14. Under the original General Assembly decision (1947) to partition Palestine into an Arab state and a Jewish state, a large land area west of the Jordan River was allotted to the Arab state. During the 1948 war much of this territory was occupied by Jordan, an occupation that endured until Jordanian forces were driven beyond the Jordan River during the 1967 war.

15. Gerhard von Glahn, *Law among Nations*, 5th ed. (New York: Macmillan, 1986), p. 523.

16. See, e.g., Robert Lyle Butterworth, *Moderation from Management: International Organizations and Peace* (Pittsburgh: University of Pittsburgh Center for International Studies, 1978); Haas (1983), "Regime Decay"; and Mark W. Zacher, *International Conflicts and Collective Security, 1946–77* (New York: Praeger Publishers, 1979).

17. Haas identified a total of 146 cases referred to the United Nations during that period. However, he excluded from his analysis twenty-three cases in which no "management" was possible (i.e., there was nothing for the United Nations to do short of taking enforcement action) or which were brought to the forum for propaganda reasons with no expectation of UN action. Among the excluded cases were Israeli abduction of Eichmann from Argentina, Israeli bombing of the Baghdad nuclear reactor, and various airplane incidents pitting the United States against the Soviet Union. See Haas, "Regime Decay," p. 195, n. 7.

18. Ibid., tables M and N, pp. 254–55.

19. See William D. Coplin and J. Martin Rochester, "The Permanent Court of International Justice, the International Court of Justice, the League of Nations, and the United Nations: A Comparative Empirical Survey," *American Political Science Review* 66, no. 2 (June 1972), pp. 520–50, which compares the disputes coming before the United Nations and the International Court of Justice with those brought to the League of Nations and the Permanent Court of International Justice, and shows that armed conflict was involved in a greater percentage of the former than of the latter. Moreover, of 123 disputes referred to the United Nations from 1945 to 1981, Haas classified 52 as "serious disputes involving military operations and fighting." Haas, "Regime Decay," table 2, p. 197.

SELECTED READINGS

BAILEY, SYDNEY D. *How Wars End: The United Nations and the Termination of Armed Conflicts, 1946–1964.* 2 vols. New York: Oxford University Press, 1982.

BOYD, ANDREW. *Fifteen Men on a Powder Keg: A History of the United Nations Security Council.* New York: Stein & Day, 1971.

BUTTERWORTH, ROBERT LYLE. *Moderation from Management: International Organizations and Peace.* Pittsburgh: University of Pittsburgh Center for International Studies, 1978.

COLL, ALBERTO R., and ANTHONY C. AREND, eds. *The Falklands War: Lessons for Strategy, Diplomacy, and International Law.* Winchester, Mass.: Allen & Unwin, 1985.

FISHER, ROGER. *International Mediation: A Working Guide.* New York: International Peace Academy, 1978.

FORSYTHE, DAVID P. *United Nations Peacemaking: The United Nations Conciliation Commission for Palestine.* Baltimore: Johns Hopkins University Press, 1972.

GROSS, LEO, ed. *The Future of the International Court of Justice.* 2 vols. Dobbs Ferry, N.Y.: Oceana Publications, 1976.

LALL, ARTHUR S. *Multilateral Negotiation and Mediation.* New York: Pergamon Press, 1985.

MERRILLS, J. G. *International Dispute Settlement.* London: Sweet & Maxwell, 1984.

NICOL, DAVIDSON. *The United Nations Security Council: Towards Greater Effectiveness.* New York: UNITAR, 1982.

————, ed. *Paths to Peace: The UN Security Council and its Presidency.* New York: Pergamon Press, 1981.

PECHOTA, VRATISLAV. *The Quiet Approach: A Study of the Good Offices Exercised by the United Nations Secretary-General in the Cause of Peace.* Peaceful Settlement Series no. 6. New York: UNITAR, 1972.

RAMAN, K. VENKATA. *Dispute Settlement through the United Nations.* Dobbs Ferry, N.Y.: Oceana Publications, 1977.

RAMCHARAN, B. G. *Humanitarian Good Offices in International Law.* Hingham, Mass.: Kluwer Academic Publishers, 1983.

ROSENNE, SHABTAI. *The World Court: What It Is, How It Works.* Dobbs Ferry, N.Y.: Oceana Publications, 1974.

TAYLOR, ALASTAIR. *Indonesian Independence and the United Nations.* London: Stevens & Sons, 1960.

VON GLAHN, GERHARD. *Law among Nations.* 5th ed. New York: Macmillan, 1986.

YOUNG, ORAN R. *The Intermediaries: Third Parties in International Crisis.* Princeton: Princeton University Press, 1967.

8

The Revolution of Self-Determination

During the past half century the international system has been transformed by the disintegration of colonial empires and the rise of independent Third World states. Nearly two thirds of the present UN members were colonial dependencies before World War II. In this vast revolution of self-determination, the United Nations has played an integral part. While the League of Nations was content to exercise minimal supervision over the administration of a few ex-enemy territories, the United Nations became an advocate of self-government for colonial peoples everywhere. Decolonization would have come in any event, but the United Nations helped reinforce the anticolonial mood and hasten the transition process. This chapter will examine the evolution of international concern for dependent peoples from the League mandate system to the UN trusteeship system and UN involvement with the broader process of decolonization.

MANDATES UNDER THE LEAGUE

At the end of World War I, the European imperial system was still alive and well. Despite an earlier wave of anticolonial revolution in North and South America, and more gradual emancipation in Canada, Australia, New Zealand, and South Africa, European powers still held fast to vast territories in distant lands inhabited by native peoples rather than settlers of European stock. The empires of the European Allies emerged from the war intact, and the victors fully expected to extend their rule to German and Turkish possessions by right of conquest. Some of the Allies had already concluded among themselves secret wartime agreements to this effect.

Disposition of the defeated enemies' colonies proved not to be that simple. Direct annexation was not acceptable because it conflicted with often repeated claims that the war was being fought for the rights and freedoms of peoples and for the defense of democracy. In the waning months of the war, the British Labour Party and the

French Socialist Party had publicly urged that German colonies be placed under the trusteeship of the proposed League of Nations. More important was the position of President Woodrow Wilson at the Versailles Peace Conference. Determined that the war he had fought for principle should not now appear as an imperialist venture, he steadfastly opposed the annexation that the other leading Allies preferred. Another theoretical option, restoration of the conquered territories to their former masters, was not viewed with enthusiasm by any of the Allies. There was also general agreement that most of these territories were not ready for self-government.

Such a situation called for inventiveness, and the resulting compromise among the peacemakers, based on a proposal by Jan Smuts of South Africa, had a touch of political genius. The territories were parceled out among the victors, but control was to be exercised subject to League of Nations supervision. Article 22 of the Covenant declared to the world that the "well-being and development" of the peoples in the conquered territories was "a sacred trust of civilization" accepted by certain "advanced nations" serving "as Mandatories on behalf of the League." This doctrine had something in common with the still more patronizing notion of the "white man's burden," but the recognition of an international trust for conquered territory undoubtedly represented a step forward from the days of the old imperialism. For the first time in the history of the state system, the relationship between imperial powers and their subject peoples was subjected to international supervision.[1]

The impact of compromise is also evident in the classification of the conquered territories into three groups, subsequently known as A, B, and C mandates, on the basis of their political development, geographic location, economic conditions, and "other similar circumstances." The relative political sophistication of the Arabs, and British wartime commitments to them, made the Turkish dominions candidates for the Class A mandate. According to Article 22, their status as independent nations could be "provisionally recognized subject to the rendering of administrative advice and assistance by a Mandatory until such time as they are able to stand alone." The tutelage stage lasted longer than the local peoples desired, but Iraq gained independence in 1932 and the other mandated areas of the Middle East achieved full statehood in the wake of World War II without undergoing a period of UN trusteeship. (See Table 8–1.)

At the other extreme were the Class C mandates—South West Africa and the German Pacific islands, which were to be "administered under the laws of the mandatory as integral portions of its territory." Sparse population, small size, and "remoteness from the centres of civilization" were mentioned in the Covenant as reasons for this classification. Unmentioned was the political constraint: Class C status was the maximum degree of internationalization that annexationists in Australia, New Zealand, and South Africa (the mandatory states) would gracefully accept. Class C mandates were thus linked directly with the government of the mandatory power, and their peoples were not regarded as subjects for self-government in the foreseeable future. The remaining German territories in Africa were placed in Class B. They were not to be administratively annexed but were

TABLE 8–1
Territories Placed under League Mandate and UN Trusteeship

Territory	Class of Mandate	Administering Authority (League of Nations)	Administering Authority (United Nations)	Present Status
Iraq	A	United Kingdom	—	Independent (1932)
Palestine	A	United Kingdom	—	Independent, Jordan (1946), Israel (1948)
Syria and Lebanon	A	France	—	Independent, Syria (1946), Lebanon (1946)
Cameroons	B	France	France	Independent, Cameroon (1960)
Cameroons	B	United Kingdom	United Kingdom	Part merged with Nigeria, part with Cameroon (1961)
Ruanda Urundi	B	Belgium	Belgium	Independent, Rwanda, (1962), Burundi (1962)
Tanganyika	B	United Kingdom	United Kingdom	Independent (1961); merged with Zanzibar as United Republic of Tanzania (1964)
Togoland	B	United Kingdom	United Kingdom	Merged with Gold Coast as Ghana (1957)
Togoland	B	France	France	Independent, Togo (1960)
Nauru	C	Australia, New Zealand, United Kingdom	Australia, New Zealand, United Kingdom	Independent (1968)
New Guinea	C	Australia	Australia	Independent, Papua New Guinea (1975)
North Pacific islands	C	Japan	United States	Strategic trusteeship
South West Africa	C	South Africa	—	Mandate terminated (1966); independence as Namibia pending
Western Samoa	C	New Zealand	New Zealand	Independent (1962)
Somaliland	—	—	Italy	Independent, merged with British Somaliland as Somalia (1960)

nevertheless to be governed as colonies without explicit provision for ultimate independence or self-government.

The means of enforcing Covenant obligations were minimal. Article 22 provided for a "permanent Commission . . . to receive and examine the annual reports of the Mandatories and to advise the Council on all matters relating to the observance of the mandates." This Permanent Mandates Commission consisted of nine (subsequently ten) persons appointed by the League Council as private experts rather than governmental representatives. A majority were drawn from nonmandatory states, but nearly all came from countries with colonial possessions, which enabled them to understand the problems faced by the mandatory countries. They were, for the most part, able people who took their international responsibilities seriously.

Being only advisory, the Commission had no power to affect the policies of the mandatory states other than through persuasion and publicity. Its principal means of supervision consisted of reviewing annual reports submitted by the mandatories and making recommendations to the Council. The Commission developed comprehensive questionnaires to facilitate uniform and complete reporting, and a representative of each mandatory participated in all Commission discussions of its mandate. Written petitions were also entertained, but petitions from indigenous inhabitants had to be routed through the mandatory and all other petitions were sent to the mandatory for comments. The majority of petitions came from the Class A mandates.

The Permanent Mandates Commission made its recommendations to the Council rather than directly to the mandatory. Although the Council usually agreed with the Commission, it was a political body not prone to giving needless offense to the mandatories and, in any event, it had no more legal authority than the Commission to coerce a mandatory that failed to honor its "sacred trust." The Assembly, without any special authorization in the Covenant, also developed the practice of making recommendations each year on some aspect of mandate administration. Like the Commission and the Council, it too was limited to exhortation and the sanction of publicity.

Given the political milieu from which the mandate system emerged, its record of accomplishment was bound to be spotty. Its greatest achievement probably lay in establishing the principle of international accountability for dependent territories. It is doubtful that prevailing attitudes toward the treatment of colonial peoples would have been altered so rapidly in the past half century without the conditioning effect of the League mandate system. Administration of the conquered territories was also improved in some details as a result of suggestions from the Commission. The mandatories, for example, generally refrained from mass naturalization of mandate peoples and did not enlist them for general military service—two practices specifically disapproved by the Commission. The mandate system fell short of idealistic hopes and expectations, but there is wide agreement that the League's methods of friendly persuasion helped fix the welfare of indigenous peoples as the standard of administration.

THE IMPACT OF WORLD WAR II

The League mandate system was a symbol of change in world attitudes toward colonialism, but it left European imperialism untouched in most parts of the world. The great catalyst for change was World War II, which destroyed the political balance that had made imperialism viable. The war severely weakened the colonial powers and for a time brought total or partial severance of contacts with their overseas possessions. The war also stimulated the growth of existing native nationalist movements.[2] The quick collapse of Belgium, the Netherlands, and France, and Britain's hurried retreat to a beleaguered island, destroyed at a stroke Europe's long-standing image of invincibility in the eyes of colonial peoples. The immense loss of respect for Europe was most apparent in Southeast Asia, where the ease of Japanese conquest revealed the weakness of the former white masters and exploded the myth of racial superiority. The Japanese victory was clear proof that the West no longer enjoyed the monopoly of technological and military potential that had been the basis of its dominance.

Japanese occupation physically eliminated European administrative and economic personnel and systematically destroyed existing colonial institutions. Japan did not encourage nationalist aspirations for autonomy, but the necessity of entrusting high administrative responsibilities to local elites, which previously had been systematically confined to lower-grade positions, provided training for independence. At the close of the war, native nationalists in Indonesia and Vietnam took advantage of the sudden collapse of Japan to seize control of abandoned ammunition stocks and proclaim independence. Independence did not come to Indonesia until 1949, and to Vietnam until much later, in both cases only after protracted struggle with the former colonial powers. But the nationalist movements ultimately could not be denied.

The war also speeded decolonization in areas not occupied by the Japanese.[3] India used its leverage as an important partner in the war effort to obtain political concessions from Britain and was invited to participate in the San Francisco Conference as a founding member of the United Nations. Formal independence came in 1947, along with the creation of Pakistan. Independence for Burma and Ceylon followed shortly. In the Middle East wartime pressures and Arab nationalism brought an early termination of British and French mandates. Syria, Lebanon, and Jordan[4] became independent in 1946, and Israel—with some help from the United Nations—emerged in 1948. In French North Africa the war also gave new impetus to nationalist movements, although independence did not arrive until 1956 for Morocco and Tunisia and, after years of internal rebellion, until 1962 for Algeria. The war also accelerated the growth of nationalism in sub-Saharan Africa. In addition to the weakening of European control during the war, wartime demand for raw materials and agricultural products brought more people to the cities, where tribal links were weaker and nationalist currents stronger. The first black African country to achieve independence after the war was Ghana, in 1957. Guinea followed in 1958, and sixteen more African countries were admitted to the United Nations in 1960. The movement was worldwide and irreversible.

UN TRUSTEESHIP

Trusteeship at San Francisco

At the UN San Francisco Conference, meeting in April 1945, the new currents were being felt but were not fully appreciated. Although no state seriously objected to continuing the League mandates in some form, proposals to extend the principle of trusteeship to the whole colonial system met with vehement opposition from Britain, France, Belgium, the Netherlands, and South Africa. The United States, so enthusiastic for self-determination at Versailles, wavered in support of international supervision, in part because of a growing security interest in the Japanese-mandated Pacific islands.

Other forces, however, compensated for the foot-dragging of the colonial powers and the waning of Wilsonian zeal in the United States. At San Francisco the anticolonial viewpoint had new and vigorous spokesmen from Egypt, Syria, Iraq, India, and other former dependencies that loudly trumpeted the cause of fellow nationalists still under colonial domination. The Soviet Union, unrepresented at Versailles, was another forceful anticolonialist voice. The trusteeship cause was also aided by a growing belief that the just treatment of colonial peoples and their evolution toward self-government were connected with the maintenance of international peace and security. In the League Covenant the "well-being and development" of colonial peoples provided the rationale for League action. In the UN Charter, by contrast, the first objective of the trusteeship system is "to further international peace and security."

The states supporting wider involvement of international organization were able to achieve a modest increase in its power and responsibilities. A strengthened trusteeship system replaced the mandate system, and a declaration on non-self-governing territories committed members to submit economic and social information on all of their colonies. A greater departure from the League Covenant was the announced goal of ultimate "self-government or independence" for trust territories and "self-government" for all other dependencies. Although the consequences of these changes may not have been fully anticipated in 1945, they constituted the opening wedge for what subsequently became a broadside attack in the United Nations on the old colonialism in all its manifestations.

The Nature of the Trusteeship System

Despite the shift in goals, the new machinery of trusteeship made full allowance for the interests of the administering powers. The Trusteeship Council, as successor to the Permanent Mandates Commission, was composed of governmental representatives instead of private experts, with equal representation for administering and nonadministering states (UN Charter, Article 86). Each trust territory was to be brought within the system by an agreement drawn up by the administering member and approved by the General Assembly. Although the Assembly could reject a proposed agreement, the alternative was no trusteeship at all. Once the trusteeship was agreed on, both the Assembly and the Trusteeship Council were limited to information gathering, discussion, and recommendation, with no legal powers of coercion.

The Trusteeship Council was given means of inquiry into the conduct of trust administration superior to those of the League system. The practice of the annual report, based on a comprehensive questionnaire, was borrowed from the Permanent Mandates Commission. To this was added the right to receive petitions directly, without relying on the administering power as intermediary, and the right to send visiting missions to gain firsthand knowledge of conditions in trust territories. The administering powers thus matched their effective control of the trust territories against the organization's capacity to publicize, criticize, and mobilize the weight of diplomatic opinion.

The United States obtained an additional safeguard against UN interference with its administration of the Pacific Islands trusteeship. If an administering authority, in the trusteeship agreement, chose to designate all or part of a trust territory as a "strategic area," all matters relating to the area became the province of the Security Council, where the veto could forestall any adverse recommendation. The Trust Territory of the Pacific Islands under American supervision was so designated.

The Functioning of Trusteeship

The Class A mandates were not candidates for trusteeship, because they were scheduled for early independence, but all of the Class B and C mandates except South West Africa were placed under trusteeship through agreements approved in 1946 and 1947. The Charter also made trusteeship an option for territories "detached from enemy states as a result of the Second World War," as well as any other colonies a state might choose to place within the system. No state accepted the latter invitation, although Italian Somaliland, which had been taken from Italy during the war, was given a period of trusteeship under Italian administration. The legal evolution of the territories placed under mandate and trusteeship is shown in Table 8–1.

Of eleven trust territories, ten have achieved the promised independence or have been united, on the basis of a UN-approved plebiscite, with an adjoining independent country. Only the Trust Territory of the Pacific Islands (Micronesia), with 150,000 inhabitants scattered over 2,141 islands and atolls, remains within the system. After years of negotiations, its four separate political entities—the Northern Mariana Islands, the Federated States of Micronesia, the Marshall Islands, and Palau—reached agreement with the United States on the terms for achieving self-government.[5] In 1975 the Northern Marianas voted to become a U.S. commonwealth when trusteeship was ended. In 1983 UN-observed plebiscites in each of the other three jurisdictions approved compacts of "free association" providing local autonomy in domestic affairs while leaving foreign relations and defense responsibilities with the United

States. The Palau plebiscite was ruled invalid by the Palau court because the voters had rejected a second ballot measure providing for the stationing of nuclear weapons on the island, and the two measures were held nonseverable. A revised compact of association was ultimately approved by Palau voters in February 1986.[6] Termination of the trusteeship may thus be anticipated in the near future if the Soviet Union can be persuaded not to veto the U.S. proposal when it comes before the Security Council. When the Pacific Islands trusteeship ends, the Trusteeship Council will cease to function unless new duties are found for it.

The Charter goal of independence or self-government for trust territories has for most practical purposes been reached—an achievement for which the United Nations may claim considerable credit. Criticism in the Trusteeship Council and the General Assembly spurred the administering authorities to put the best possible face on their conduct of territorial affairs. This in turn affected administration of the territories, as policies were formulated with an awareness that the United Nations was watching. Occasionally specific governmental practices were modified in response to Council recommendations.

Petitions and visiting missions permitted detailed scrutiny of trust administration and thereby increased the pressure on administering authorities to justify their policies. At the height of its activity, the Trusteeship Council received several hundred written petitions annually and considered as many as 250 in a session, besides granting an occasional hearing to an oral petitioner. Aside from the informational function, the petitioning procedure made administering authorities more alert to the legitimate grievances of the local populace and sometimes resulted in direct relief to the complainant. In one instance two inhabitants of the Pacific Islands accomplished through oral petition what three years of direct negotiation with the United States had failed to achieve—a settlement of their claim against the government for property taken without just compensation.

Visiting missions, conducted every three years, also proved a valuable source of information as well as an outlet for native views and grievances. Reports of the visiting missions appeared to receive serious attention from the administering authorities and in some instances foreshadowed policy changes. Australia, for example, took steps to give the New Guinea territorial legislature an elective majority in response to the recommendations of a 1962 visiting mission. In several territories the United Nations sent plebiscite teams and election observers during the final stages of preparation for self-government, which increased the international acceptability of the regimes thereby established.

Considered as a whole, trusteeship helped raise standards of administration in the trust territories and hastened the coming of independence. Suggestions and criticisms from the Trusteeship Council and the Assembly strengthened progressive elements within the administering authorities and kept them mindful of their obligations to the peoples of the territories. Trusteeship encouraged more articulate native demands for national independence and may have fostered some increased readiness for self-government. Given the growth of nationalism, the changes in power relationships wrought by two world wars, and the increasing economic liabilities of the colonial system, independence would have come to most of these areas without the intervention of the United Nations. Nevertheless, the system provided a more orderly and peaceful process of change. In none of the trust territories was the transition to independence marked by serious violence.

Trusteeship must be seen in perspective as but one aspect of a much wider movement for decolonization. Several African and Asian dependencies of France and Britain became independent before the first trust territories achieved that status in 1960. While ten trust territories were gaining independence from 1960 to 1975, several times that number of former colonies were undergoing the same transformation outside the trusteeship system. Trusteeship contributed to a climate of world opinion congenial to decolonization, but the system itself was swept along in the broader current.

The trusteeship system never achieved the scope that its more enthusiastic supporters at San Francisco had envisioned. Except for Somaliland, it did not expand territorially beyond the League mandates, and South West Africa never came within its purview. The UN Charter option of placing other dependent territories under trusteeship appears never to have been seriously considered by any colonial power. In meeting the larger problem of colonialism, the United Nations has consistently turned to other means.

THE UNITED NATIONS AND TOTAL DECOLONIZATION

Unlike the League Covenant, the UN Charter went beyond prescribing conditions for mandated territories and extended its concern to dependent peoples everywhere. In the Declaration regarding Non-Self-Governing Territories, contained in Chapter XI of the Charter, the colonial powers acknowledged a "sacred trust" to promote the well-being and self-government of all their dependencies. They were not willing to make independence a goal for their colonies or to accept international supervision, but they agreed to submit data "of a technical nature relating to economic, social, and educational conditions in the territories" for "information purposes." There was general accord at San Francisco that the Declaration embodied only moral commitments, dependent on the good faith of the colonial powers for their fulfillment and involving no UN right to intervene in what was regarded by the colonial powers as a matter of domestic jurisdiction.

Today the picture is drastically altered. Independence has become not merely a goal but an accomplished fact for the vast majority of the colonial peoples of 1945. Within the United Nations the original Charter assumption "that each colonial power should at its own discretion and in an unhurried way lead its dependent peoples to well-being and self-government" soon gave way to the proposition that colonialism is "an intolerable and illegitimate abuse to be done away with as speedily as possible by the international community."[7] This revolutionary change in ideology was accompanied by an organizational assault on the whole structure of colonialism that erased any essential distinction between trust territories and other non-self-governing areas. The change mirrored new global realities, but it amounted to a Charter amendment without the niceties of ratification.

The Committee on Information

The first step toward establishing UN responsibility for all dependent territories occurred in 1946 with the establishment of a Committee on Information from Non-Self-Governing Territories. Its purpose was to examine the information transmitted by the administering authorities and make recommendations to the Assembly. In composition it was modeled on the Trusteeship Council, having an equal number of administering and nonadministering members. It had no provision for permanent representation of the Big Five, however, and the Soviet Union and China generally did not hold membership on it. Like the Trusteeship Council, the Committee prepared a questionnaire to guide members in reporting.

With the built-in moderation arising from its composition, the Committee on Information was not an aggressive instrument of anticolonialism. Its original terms of reference debarred it from examining "political" information, although such information was voluntarily submitted by some countries. Even on economic and social matters, the Committee could make recommendations of general application but could not single out individual territories. It was not given the right to accept petitions or send out visiting missions.

Because of the Committee's limited powers, the anticolonial initiative remained largely with the General Assembly and its Fourth Committee, which soon requested governments to include political information in their annual reports. Later the Assembly began to demand that administering authorities submit sufficient information on constitutional changes in the territories to enable it to determine whether self-government had in fact been attained. The Assembly's right to make such a determination was a much more sensitive issue than its demand for information, and the colonial powers vehemently rejected the idea.

The admission of Spain and Portugal to UN membership in 1955 raised the related question of who decided when and whether new members must begin to transmit information. The question was far from academic since Spain and Portugal, both of which had overseas dominions, assured the United Nations that they had no "non-self-governing territories." In 1960 the Assembly resolved the question by informing both states of their obligation to transmit information. Spain capitulated to the pressure, but Portugal refused to comply.

Self-Determination and Political Crisis

While the Assembly was attempting to turn all non-self-governing territories into quasi trusteeships, the United Nations was also faced with a series of political crises arising from the breakup of colonial empires. During the early years the alignment of colonial and anticolonial forces was not sharply drawn and the issues were sometimes perceived as having a complexity inconsistent with the taking of doctrinaire positions. The question of Palestine came before the United Nations in 1947 at the initiative of a harassed mandatory power that was no longer willing to bear the impossible burden of reconciling Arab and Jewish claims to the Holy Land. The issue was not whether self-determination should be granted but how and by whom it should be exercised. In the Indonesian struggle for independence from the Netherlands, mediated in part by the Security Council from 1947 to 1949, the continuation of colonial rule was more clearly at issue, but the threat to international peace and security was the Security Council's foremost concern. Assembly debates on the former Italian colonies of Libya, Eritrea, and Somaliland, from 1949 to 1951, were also relatively free from the kind of anticolonial diatribe that subsequently came to characterize UN debates on colonial questions.

Assembly debates on Morocco and Tunisia brought the anticolonial position more sharply into focus during the early 1950s, but a two-thirds majority was never available for anything stronger than a call for "free political institutions" and continued negotiations among the parties. Both states were granted independence from France in 1956.

The emergence of anticolonial dominance in the United Nations is illustrated by its handling of the Algerian question. The General Assembly considered Algeria each session from 1955 through 1961. In 1955 no action at all was taken; in 1956 the Assembly expressed the hope that a peaceful, democratic, and just solution in conformity with the Charter would be found. In 1957 the Assembly went so far as to urge negotiations, but in 1958 and 1959 no recommendation was able to command a two-thirds majority. This stalemate reflected the unwillingness of the anticolonial bloc to support a weak statement and its inability to obtain a strong one. In 1960, with the admission to UN membership of seventeen former colonies, the inhibitions of the earlier period vanished. The right of the Algerian people to "self-determination" was vigorously asserted, despite France's bitter objection to discussing the matter at all. A year later the Assembly demanded nothing less than full "self-determination and independence." These resolutions may have had no greater influence on the French decision to grant Algerian independence in 1962 than on the granting of independence to Morocco and Tunisia in 1956. But the temper of the Assembly was plainly different.

Anticolonialism Triumphant

By 1960 the anticolonial revolution was rapidly approaching its zenith. Four decades of mandate and trusteeship had established the principle of international accountability for the administration of a select group of territories, with independence as the ultimate goal. Fifteen years of gradually expanding activity under the Charter Declaration Regarding Non-Self-Governing Territories had gone far to establish the principle of international accountability for the well-being and self-government of all colonial peoples. Repeated recourse to the United Nations in crisis situations had established at least a prima facie connection between colonialism and the periodic outbreak of violence. Within the world community the day of colonialism was rapidly passing. Thirty-five territories that had achieved full independence since 1945 were now members of the United Nations. Most other dependencies of any substantial size were moving toward independence with the consent and cooperation of their colonial overseers.

An Anticolonial Manifesto.   Amid these signs of a revolution well on its way to completion, the General Assembly in 1960 took a step of unusual symbolic importance. In previous years the anticolonial forces had been forced to compromise in their attack on the old colonial order. With domination of the Assembly now assured, they turned the organization into an instrument for the complete legitimization of their cause. In a historic Declaration on the Granting of Independence to Colonial Countries and Peoples, the General Assembly proclaimed that the subjection of any people to alien domination was a denial of fundamental human rights, contrary to the UN Charter, and an impediment to world peace and that all subject peoples had a right to immediate and complete independence.[8] No country cast a vote against this anticolonial manifesto, although eight colonial powers (Australia, Belgium, France, Portugal, Spain, South Africa, the United Kingdom, and the United States) and the Dominican Republic abstained. It was an ideological triumph. The old order had not merely been challenged and defeated in the field—its adherents were no longer willing to be counted in its defense.[9]

As long as colonial rule prevailed in any territory, the Declaration provided a rationale for efforts to undermine or overthrow it. The anticolonial principle was carried to its logical conclusion when India, on invading Portuguese Goa in December 1961, assured the Security Council that the invasion was an "embodiment of the principles" in the Declaration and a "new dictum of international law." Some Western states were unconvinced that an Assembly resolution, which was legally binding on no country, could create international law that overrode express Charter prohibitions on the use of force. But the basic issue, as the Indian representative admitted, was moral, not legal. Portugal's centuries-old occupation of Goa constituted permanent aggression, and India was justified in "getting rid of the last vestiges of colonialism . . . Charter or no Charter, Council or no Council."[10] Like the American Declaration of Independence, the Declaration of 1960 was an appeal to a higher law to which all lesser claims were subordinate.

The Special Committee.   Within the United Nations the Declaration presaged a more vigorous assault on the last bastions of colonialism. In 1961 the Assembly expanded the role of the Committee on Information by authorizing it to discuss political information and to make recommendations specifically directed at the problems of territories located in the same area or region. The Fourth Committee also broke new ground by granting, for the first time, a hearing to petitioners from two non-self-governing territories.

Of considerably more importance for the future was the creation of a Special Committee on the Situation with regard to the Implementation of the Declaration on the Granting of Independence to Colonial Countries and Peoples. Known as the Committee of Seventeen (increased to twenty-four in 1962, twenty-five in 1979), it was assigned to study the Declaration and make appropriate recommendations for its implementation. Parity of representation was discarded as the Assembly packed the Special Committee with an anticolonial majority. For its terms of reference, the Committee was given a blank check—a mandate to do whatever it was able to do in implementing the 1960 Declaration. Under this broad grant of authority, the Committee assumed powers to hear petitions, send missions to the field, and make recommendations directed at specific territories—powers that the Trusteeship Council had exercised but that had been denied to the Committee on Information. By 1963 the Committee of Twenty-four had so plainly overshadowed the Committee on Information in its systematic harassment of the colonial powers that the latter was formally abolished.

The Demise of the Old Colonialism.   The United Nations was able to launch its massive assault on colonialism because colonialism was already in full retreat. The Committee of Twenty-four was engaged mainly in a mopping-up operation. In its 1963 report to the Assembly, the Committee listed sixty-four colonies, mandates, and trust territories that had not yet achieved self-government. Only ten of these could claim as many as a million inhabitants, and the total population of all sixty-four was less than fifty million. Forty of the sixty-four were British, consisting, as one writer put it, mostly of "little islands scattered about the face of the globe, representing the days when Britain was an indefatigable collector of scraps of empire."[11]

Rhodesia (Zimbabwe), Namibia, and the Portuguese African colonies of Angola, Mozambique, and Guinea were significant exceptions to the "scraps of empire" characterization. Rhodesia's white minority government unilaterally declared independence from Britain in 1965 and endured fifteen years of international ostracism, UN economic sanctions, and internal strife before finally accepting majority rule in 1980 and receiving admission to the United Nations as the state of Zimbabwe. Portugal's hard-line policy collapsed in 1974 under the weight of colonial wars that had absorbed nearly half of the Portuguese national budget. The Caetano dictatorship fell victim to an internal coup, and Portugal's African policy fell with it. Portuguese Guinea (now Guinea-Bissau) became independent in 1974, and Mozambique and Angola followed in 1975, despite serious internal divisions in Angola that have continued to the present. Namibia, the former South West Africa mandate, remains the last major holdout. This problem is discussed at greater length in Chapter 7 as a persistent challenge to UN dispute resolution capabilities.

By 1985 the Special Committee's list had been reduced to eighteen dependencies, most of them small islands with minuscule populations (see Table 8–2). In a more controversial category are Gibraltar, Western Sahara, East Timor (an island territory of 5,700 square miles), and Namibia. Britain has been engaged in continuing negotiations with Spain on the future of Gibraltar. Western Sahara was relinquished by Spain in 1975, and the present controversy pits Moroccan claims to

TABLE 8–2 _____

Territories to which the Declaration on the Granting of Independence to
Colonial Countries and Peoples Continues to Apply (as of October 1985)

	Territory	Administering Authority	Area (sq. km.)	Population (est.)
Africa	Namibia*	United Nations	824,292	1,465,000
	Western Sahara†	Spain	266,000	147,000
Asia	East Timor‡	Portugal	14,925	616,000
Atlantic and the Caribbean	Anguilla	United Kingdom	96	78,000
	Bermuda	United Kingdom	53	55,000
	British Virgin Islands	United Kingdom	153	13,000
	Cayman Islands	United Kingdom	250	19,000
	Falkland Islands (Islas Malvinas)	United Kingdom	12,173	2,000
	Montserrat	United Kingdom	103	13,000
	St. Helena	United Kingdom	412	5,000
	Turks and Caicos Islands	United Kingdom	430	8,000
	U.S. Virgin Islands	United States	343	101,000
Europe	Gibraltar	United Kingdom	6	29,000
Pacific and Indian Oceans	American Samoa	United States	197	34,000
	Guam	United States	540	111,000
	Pitcairn	United Kingdom	5	55
	Tokelau	New Zealand	12	2,000
	Trust Territory of the Pacific Islands	United States	1,854	145,000

*In 1966 the General Assembly terminated South Africa's mandate over South West Africa and placed the territory under the direct responsibility of the United Nations. In 1968 the Assembly declared that the territory would henceforth be known as "Namibia," in accordance with the desires of its people. Until independence the legal administering authority for Namibia is the UN Council for Namibia.

†By resolution 39/40 of December 5, 1984, the General Assembly reaffirmed that the question of Western Sahara was a question of decolonization that remained to be completed by the people of Western Sahara. The Assembly requested the parties concerned to undertake negotiations to create the necessary conditions for a peaceful and fair referendum for the self-determination of the people of Western Sahara.

‡On April 6, 1979, and in following years, Portugal informed the Secretary-General that conditions still prevailing in East Timor had prevented it from assuming its responsibilities for the administration of the territory.

SOURCE: *Un Chronicle* 23, no. 1 (January 1986), p. 79.

sovereignty against those of an indigenous nationalist movement called the Polisario Front. A similar situation exists in East Timor, which was annexed by Indonesia in 1976 following intervention in a civil war that broke out during the transfer of authority from Portugal to local entities. Recent developments suggest that both Morocco and Indonesia will eventually make good their respective claims and these items will disappear from the UN agenda. Puerto Rico has also been before the Special Committee with great regularity. Although technically not on the list of non-self-governing territories, Puerto Rico is discussed nearly every year at the special request of Cuba. Of territories still on the list, Namibia is by far the most urgent concern and will undoubtedly remain so until the South African hold is broken.

THE UN ROLE: AN APPRAISAL

Decolonization, after more than four hundred years of colonial rule, is one of the great revolutions of our century. It was brought on by forces that were neither generated nor controlled by international organizations. But the League of Nations and the United Nations have contributed to the speed and direction of the movement and, in some instances at least, have helped promote a more peaceful transition to independence and self-government.[12] The League gave respectability to the principle of international accountability in a limited area of colonialism and moderated some of the worst abuses of the system. Since 1945 the United Nations has done much more. It provided a forum where anticolonial spokesmen could articulate their position; it greatly expanded the principle of international accountability; and it developed more effective instruments for international supervision of colonial administration. Above all, it gave an element of legitimacy to independence movements everywhere in the world. By holding aloft the standard of self-determination, it served as a reminder to the majority of Western colonial countries that such demands were basically consonant with enduring values in their own political tradition. When violence occurred, the United Nations sometimes intervened to curb hostilities, as in Indonesia, Kashmir, and Palestine. In the end, the United Nations hastened acceptance of the new order by legitimizing its tenets. A leading French authority on colonization has called the United Nations "the main anti-colonial driving force of the post-war period."[13]

The UN record on colonial problems has not been without blemishes. In some instances the United Nations at least inadvertently encouraged resort to violence by native nationalists who felt that creating a threat to peace and security was the best way to gain the attention of the organization. The 1960 Declaration has frequently been used to justify violence, including India's attack on Goa in 1961, Argentina's abortive attempt in 1982 to seize the Falkland Islands by force, and the resort to arms by various African liberation groups.

A good case can also be made that the United Nations has pushed many territories to premature independence and has encouraged independence for ministates when association with a larger entity would have produced an economically and politically more viable state. Statehood and full membership in the United Nations has been attained by many new nations that are woefully lacking in trained personnel to administer governmental and economic institutions. In most of the new states, independence has not been followed by hoped-for gains in economic welfare. This has led many Third World peoples to complain that the old colonial system has merely been replaced by neocolonialism in the form of economic exploitation by the developed countries.

The benefits of decolonization were unquestionably oversold, although the United Nations can be held only partly responsible for that. Independence was in principle a good thing, and it brought immediate benefits to those who were able to seize the levers of political and economic power in the new states. But removal of the foreign master did not everywhere bring greater respect for democractic values and individual rights. Indigenous leaders often adopted governmental techniques as repressive and demeaning as those formerly attributed to colonialism. Racial and tribal minorities have sometimes fared ill at the hands of the new rulers, as is attested by the slaughter of the Tutsi in Burundi and Rwanda and of the Ibo in the Nigerian civil war. The mass exodus of refugees from Laos, Kampuchea, and Vietnam since the 1970s further illustrates the internal stresses plaguing new states, although in those countries the internal stresses were augmented by ideological conflict and outside military intervention. Nor has decolonization done much to bring peace and security to former colonial domains. The preindependence era was marked by armed conflict in many dependent areas, but the era of independence has also witnessed internal wars and rebellions, outside interventions, and outright military aggression in these same lands.

The United Nations did not create all the ills of decolonization any more than it produced all the benefits, but a fair appraisal requires recognition that decolonization has its down side as well as its positive aspects. In retrospect, the most important UN contribution may have been to encourage acceptance of the new order before relations between colonial masters and subject peoples became impossibly embittered. With that battle largely won, the United Nations has shifted its energies to problems of political and economic nation building among the newer and less developed sovereignties. The challenge of the postcolonial era is to maintain dialogue among new nations and old through which fruitful and mutually beneficial cooperation in this task can be achieved.

NOTES

1. A standard treatment of the League mandate system during its first decade is Quincy Wright, *Mandates under the League of Nations* (Chicago: University of Chicago Press, 1930).

2. See "The Immediate Consequences of the War (1939–1945)," in Henri Grimal, *Decolonization: The British, French, Dutch, and Belgian Empires, 1919–1963,* trans. Stephan De Vos (Boulder, Colo.: Westview Press, 1978), pp. 113–37.

3. The Philippines, which also were overrun by Japan, became independent on July 4, 1946. This occurred in spite of the war rather than because of it. The independence date had been officially set in 1934 with the passage of the Tydings-McDuffie Act.

4. Jordan became administratively separate from Palestine in 1923, when Britain recognized King Abdullah as ruler of Transjordan. Abdullah accepted British guidance and subsidies, and the mandate remained in force until formal Jordanian independence in 1946. See Richard Allen, *Imperialism and Nationalism in the Fertile Crescent: Sources and Prospects of the Arab-Israeli Conflict* (New York: Oxford University Press, 1974), pp. 273–75, 353.

5. A good discussion of the basic issues is Roger S. Clark, "Self-Determination and Free Association—Should the United Nations Terminate the Pacific Islands Trusteeship?" *Harvard International Law Journal* 21, no. 1 (Winter 1980), pp. 1–86.

6. *New York Times,* February 23, 1986, sec. 1, p. 5

7. Rupert Emerson, "Colonialism, Political Development, and the UN," *International Organization* 19, no. 3 (Summer 1965), p. 486.

8. General Assembly Resolution 1514 (XV), December 14, 1960. The Declaration provides that (1) alien domination is contrary to the UN Charter; (2) all peoples have a right to self-determination; (3) inadequacy of political, economic, social, or educational preparedness is no excuse for delaying independence; (4) all repressive measures against dependent peoples should cease, so that they can freely exercise their right to complete independence; (5) all powers of government should be immediately transferred to the remaining dependent peoples; and (6) disruption of the national unity or territorial integrity of a country is contrary to the UN Charter. The application of the "right to self-determination" is discussed in S. K. N. Blay, "Self-Determination *Versus* Territorial Integrity in Decolonization," *New York University Journal of International Law and Policy* 18 (Winter 1986), pp. 441–72.

9. Edward T. Rowe, "The Emerging Anti-Colonial Consensus in the United Nations," *Journal of Conflict Resolution* 8 (September 1964), pp. 209–30, traces the growth of anticolonial sentiment as expressed in roll-call votes on colonial questions during the first sixteen sessions of the Assembly, 1946–61. Taking two sessions as a unit, Rowe's data show a steady rise in the percentage of anticolonial votes and a persistent decline in colonial votes from biennium to biennium. The trend is explained in part by the admission of new members and in part by a growing anticolonial consensus among the older ones.

10. UN Document S/PV.988, December 18, 1961, pp. 9, 15.

11. Emerson, "Colonialism, Political Development, and the UN," p. 498.

12. A legal scholar has written,

> The relatively peaceful transformation of the vast European empires in Africa, Asia and the Caribbean into dozens of independent states has been one of the major successes of the international community since the ending of World War II. The legal and institutional framework for this task is the United Nations Charter and the norms evolved by the major organs of the United Nations—the General Assembly and the Security Council. (R. H. F. Austin, "Namibia and Zimbabwe: Decolonisation, and the Rule of International Law," *Current Legal Problems* 35 [1982], pp. 203–27)

13. Grimal, *Decolonization,* p. 138.

SELECTED READINGS

CARTER, GWENDOLYN M., and PATRICK O'MEARA, eds. *African Independence: The First Twenty-five Years.* Bloomington: Indiana University Press, 1985.

DORE, ISAAK I. *The International Mandate System and Namibia.* Boulder, Colo.: Westview Press, 1985.

EMERSON, RUPERT. *From Empire to Nation.* Cambridge, Mass.: Harvard University Press, 1960.

GRIMAL, HENRI. *Decolonization: The British, French, Dutch, and Belgian Empires, 1919–1963.* Trans. Stephan De Vos. Boulder, Colo.: Westview Press, 1978.

HALL, H. DUNCAN. *Mandates, Dependencies, and Trusteeship.* Washington, D.C.: Carnegie Endowment for International Peace, 1948.

JACOBSON, HAROLD KARAN. "The United Nations and Colonialism: A Tentative Appraisal," *International Organization,* 16, no. 1 Winter 1962, pp. 37–56.

JESSUP, PHILIP C. *The Birth of Nations.* New York: Columbia University Press, 1974.

JOHNSON, HAROLD S. *Self-Determination within the Community of Nations*. Leyden: A. W. Sijthoff, 1967.

KAY, DAVID A. *The New Nations in the United Nations, 1960–1967*. New York: Columbia University Press, 1970.

MURRAY, JAMES N., JR. *The United Nations Trusteeship System*. Urbana: University of Illinois Press, 1957.

POMERANCE, MICHLA. *Self-Determination in Law and Practice: The New Doctrine in the United Nations*. The Hague: Martinus Nijhoff Publishers, 1982.

SLONIM, SOLOMON. *South West Africa and the United Nations: An International Mandate in Dispute*. Baltimore: Johns Hopkins University Press, 1973.

WAINHOUSE, DAVID W. *Remnants of Empire: The United Nations and the End of Colonialism*. New York: Harper & Row, 1967.

WRIGHT, QUINCY. *Mandates under the League of Nations*. Chicago: University of Chicago Press, 1930.

9

Social and Technical Cooperation

International violence commands world attention when it breaks out, but economic and social programs command most of the resources of international organizations in their day-to-day operations. Agencies within the UN system carry on a great many such programs, as do several hundred other global and regional intergovernmental organizations. Although these activities are supported primarily because of their contribution to economic and social well-being, they are also frequently justified by their asserted contribution to peace.[1] Organizations for international economic and social cooperation are commonly called functional organizations, and people who advocate this approach to global peace are known as functionalists.

This chapter and the two following chapters will evaluate the activities of the United Nations and related organizations in a number of functional fields. This chapter will focus on human rights, international communication, health, the law of the sea, education and information, international relief programs, and aid to refugees. International organization for trade and economic development will be examined in Chapters 10 and 11. Because the growth of functional cooperation has been accompanied by the development of a unique body of ideas to justify and explain it, which has had some influence on the course of events, we will preface the discussion of particular activities with a brief review of functionalist theory.[2]

FUNCTIONAL COOPERATION IN THEORY AND PRACTICE

Functionalist Thought

Students of international organizations have used a variety of theories and approaches borrowed from studies of other social institutions. Functionalism does not fit this pattern. While not without its intellectual debts, functionalism is almost unique as a body of prescriptions, explanatory concepts, and predictions developed

235

with specific application to international organization.[3] As empirical explanation and prediction, its weaknesses are now widely recognized, but its prescriptive aspects have continuing vitality.

Functionalist thought achieved currency in the early twentieth century as writers began to generalize about the multitude of international organizations for economic and social cooperation that had emerged during the preceding half century.[4] The functionalist persuasion was subsequently given impetus by two world wars and by frustration with the inability of the League's collective security machinery to keep the peace. To those who embraced functionalist ideas, the prospect of organizing "peace by pieces" in specific functional areas appeared more hopeful than military approaches, which had failed repeatedly, and more realizable than visionary schemes for peace through global or regional political federations.

As elaborated by its various spokesmen, functionalism is first of all a prescription for more international cooperation in dealing with economic and social problems. Since most people recognize the desirability of cooperative activity, this aspect of functionalism finds few critics. Functionalists also assert that cooperation in "non-political" matters will promote world peace. This too has a ring of self-evident truth. To the extent that needs are met and problems resolved by cooperation, there will be that much less to fight about. Deprivation and inequality generate frustrations that can find an outlet in international conflict. By providing the means for solving such problems on a global basis, functional activities help eliminate the sources of tensions that lead to war.

The asserted link with peace extends well beyond this commonsense assumption, however, to embrace a theory of individual and social learning. Its key element is the belief that the workshop setting of functional activities provides a school for learning cooperative behavior. As individuals and governments work together for their mutual benefit, they develop habits and attitudes conducive to further cooperation. One successful venture leads to another, and the result is an ever-widening circle of shared interests. The genius of this approach is its avoidance of major challenges to state sovereignty and strongly entrenched national interests. Particular functions—health, mail service, telecommunications, and the like—become the subject of international cooperation only as the shared interests are recognized. The process is gradual and pragmatic, searching out areas of mutuality and "binding together those interests which are common, where they are common, and to the extent to which they are common."[5] As the edifice of world community is constructed piece by piece, the roots of political conflict wither and the whole area of international relations is infused with learned habits of cooperation.

Functionalists have also argued that performing needed functions at the international level will be more efficient because it permits a global attack on worldwide problems, unlimited by the constricting effect of national boundaries. Moreover, the relatively low controversiality of technical activities will permit politicians to delegate decision making to experts and professionals, whose main concern will be technical efficiency in performing their work. As a side effect, by providing useful services to people around the world, functional organizations will begin to replace national governments as the focus of human loyalties.

Not all of these assumptions appear to be confirmed by practice. Perhaps most important, international discussion of economic and social problems does not necessarily generate good will and cooperation. Some international issues are undoubtedly more controversial than others, but economic and social issues are not always low in controversy. Dispute rages over South African apartheid and Third World attempts to establish a New International Economic Order, despite their social or economic character. The history of recent adventures in functional cooperation is replete with instances of political wrangling. The process of authoritative value allocation has proved to be inherently political, whether the values are economic, social, or "political" in their content. The technical nature of an activity does not banish the need for value choices or the primacy of self-interest. Nor does the involvement of bureaucrats, however expert or professional, eliminate the push and shove of contending interests, including the interest in building bureaucratic empires. Replacing politicians with bureaucrats may simply be a means of reducing popular control.

Other functionalist assumptions may also be questioned. The functionalist explanation of war, at best, overlooks multiple causative factors. Although social inequality and economic deprivation are contributing causes of some wars, they are not an adequate explanation standing alone. Experience also raises doubt that cooperative habits learned in one functional context will necessarily be transferred to another, or that a widening sphere of functional cooperation will finally lead to elimination of violent conflict in the so-called political sphere. Functional cooperation has increased, but conflict and the threat of it do not appear to have undergone a corresponding decrease. Time may yet vindicate the functionalist thesis, but recent history offers no assurance that it will. Often-sounded complaints about "politicization" of economic and social agencies suggest that political controversy is more likely to hinder functional cooperation than to be mellowed by it.

Nor has the proliferation of functional activities thus far been accompanied by noticeable transference of loyalties from states to international institutions. The European Community, with its relatively high level of economic integration, has had little discernible impact on national loyalties. As for global agencies, it is almost ludicrous to suggest that the World Bank, the International Monetary Fund, UNESCO, or the World Intellectual Property Organization have become the significant focus of human loyalties (except perhaps for their paid secretariats). With so many international agencies now emphasizing assistance to less developed countries, functional organizations have become engaged in promoting the viability of states rather than diverting loyalties from them.

Functionalism nevertheless retains relevance for the real world of international organizations. Despite its obvious weaknesses, the theory offers useful insights. Learning from past experience is undoubtedly a growth accelerator, and successful functionalist ventures have provided models for new applications. If national loyalties remain firm, functional cooperation nevertheless wins support where it is perceived as genuinely serving individual and national interests.

Of more immediate importance, the functionalist prescription is closely attuned to the facts of international life. With time and space compressed by technology, states are constantly faced with new opportunities to promote welfare by joint action and new challenges to avoid problems created by the closeness. Interdependence is an inescapable fact. In such a world, the functional approach makes sense as a practical endeavor, whatever its theories of institutional development or its contribution to peace.[6]

The Organization of Functional Cooperation

The nineteenth-century system of international economic and social cooperation unfolded without plan or means of central coordination. The inevitable result was a patchwork of international institutions tending toward common structural forms, but each juridically and politically separate. Such unplanned growth is a common affliction of national societies. A nation, however, has a central government that can undertake reorganization when its administrative structure grows too cumbersome. The international system has no central authority capable of rationalizing the random growth of its institutions. As a consequence, the pattern of decentralization has continued largely unabated to the present day.

The impact of the League of Nations on nineteenth-century organizational patterns was to multiply institutions and activities without providing effective overall coordination. The League Covenant (Article 24) extended its sheltering arms to existing "international bureaus established by general treaties" if the parties to the treaties consented, and it also provided that any international bureaus or commissions thereafter established were to be "placed under the direction of the League." Only a half dozen or so of the existing agencies chose to accept League direction.

Despite the problems of coordination, League functional programs were widely recognized as being vigorous, constructive, and worth preserving, and this opinion was reflected in the copious UN Charter prescriptions for economic and social cooperation. The impact of League experience was also evident in the establishment of the Economic and Social Council as a special coordinating organ. The principle of decentralization was accepted, however, in the overall system of world economic and social collaboration. The UN Charter abandoned the League Covenant's vain hope that all international bureaus and commissions would be placed under the direction of the general organization. Instead, the various "specialized agencies" were authorized to maintain cooperative relationships with the Economic and Social Council and to accept such coordination as might flow from consultation and recommendation.

In practice, decentralized control has characterized many of the UN functional activities established within the United Nations itself. Agencies such as UNICEF, the UN Environmental Program, the UN Relief and Works Agency for Palestine Refugees (UNRWA), and the UN Development Program, though subject to the general supervision of the Assembly, have separate governing boards or advisory bodies and depend heavily on voluntary contributions to support their programs. Their staffs also respond to mandates of their respective governing bodies and the needs of the governments and other agencies that make up the constituencies they serve. Perhaps the very extent and variety of the economic and social programs administered on a global scale preclude truly effective central coordination. Repeated unsuccessful efforts at coordination launched in the Economic and Social Council certainly suggest such a conclusion.[7]

What Functional Organizations Do

The things done by functional organizations can be classified in a number of ways. The substantive function of an organization—human rights, health, telecommunications, and so on—is a common, even unavoidable, method of classification. Organizational functions can also be usefully classified by reference to the nature of the policy product: Is their primary concern *rules and standards* for state conduct, or is it *operating programs* that provide services to states and their peoples? Some functional organizations are oriented more toward one activity or the other, although most engage in both to some extent. In addition, all such organizations serve an *informational and promotional* function.[8]

Rule making takes a variety of forms. In the broadest sense it includes recommendations and standards that depend on voluntary acceptance as well as international treaties having the force of law and authoritative rule-making by the few agencies empowered to bind their members by majority action. Organizations that make rules also attempt to secure some degree of compliance. Most of the implementation takes the form of publicity and moral pressures, or else technical assistance to states whose noncompliance springs from lack of technical capacity rather than lack of will. Functional organizations generally have little power to enforce compliance through coercive sanctions, although noncompliance may in some instances be grounds for expulsion or loss of organizational benefits (such as future eligibility for loans and grants).

Programs to provide services, such as refugee relief or development aid, are dependent on funds and other resources available to the organization. The influence of secretariats on operating programs is usually substantial because they have responsibility both to prepare proposals and to administer the approved programs. Secretariats are typically in league with recipient states, since both have an interest in expanded programs, while donor states set the ultimate limits by their willingness—or unwillingness—to contribute the resources.

Informational and promotional activities involve the gathering, analysis, and dissemination of information, as well as the airing or propagation of points of view. All organizations have staff that perform these functions. Organizations also provide forums for state representatives and other participants to exchange views and information. Some of this communication is intended simply to inform; much is intended to persuade and promote programs, causes, or points of view.

The discussion that follows will make reference to these functions in examining a number of important social and technical activities within the UN system.

HUMAN RIGHTS RULE-MAKING

The rights of persons have traditionally been matters of domestic jurisdiction and concern. International protection of individuals has not been completely absent from the law and practice of the modern state system, but until World War II such protection was limited to special groups—primarily diplomatic representatives, consular personnel, and aliens—whose status involved the interests of a foreign sovereign. From time to time, states have also undertaken treaty obligations with respect to their own nationals, as evidenced by the various European treaties from the sixteenth century onward guaranteeing freedom of worship to religious minorities. As another example, in 1890 the Brussels Conference produced a treaty providing effective measures to end the slave trade.

In this century the peace architects at Versailles required new states and defeated countries of Eastern Europe to assume treaty guarantees of the linguistic, educational, and other rights of ethnic minority groups incorporated within their territories. Neither the earlier religious guarantees nor the minorities treaties were very effective in securing the rights of persons, and their strictly limited nature underscored the general freedom of a state to deal as it wished with those living within its jurisdiction. The League Covenant went a bit farther in concept, if not in effectiveness, in making the "well-being and development" of subject peoples in mandated territories (Article 22) a matter of international concern and in committing members to "secure just treatment of the native inhabitants" of all their dependent territories (Article 23).

Against this background the UN Charter emphasis on the promotion of human rights, induced in large part by reaction to Nazi atrocities, constitutes a sharp break with tradition. No less than seven references to human rights are found in the Charter—the Preamble, Article 1 (purposes and principles), Article 13 (responsibilities of the Assembly), Article 55 (objectives of economic and social cooperation), Article 62 (functions and powers of ECOSOC), Article 68 (a commission to promote human rights), and Article 76 (objective of the trusteeship system). The new approach did not take the form of specific legal obligations, but it did assert an international interest in the rights of individuals.

Since 1945 proponents of international action have waged a continuing battle with the conservative forces of national sovereignty, although few countries have been consistent in their support of either camp. Positions on humanitarian principles have often been tinged with political expediency. The Soviet Union has consistently displayed a double standard in favor of Socialist states, while the United States has sometimes attempted to shield the questionable conduct of authoritarian states in the Western camp. Many Third World countries have persistently condemned the human rights violations of Israel and South Africa while overlooking transgressions in other parts of the world. Surveying the record in his 1983 annual report, Secretary-General Pérez de Cuéllar probably struck an accurate balance when he saw progress in

the international protection of human rights alongside continuing "gross violations
. . . in many parts of the world."[9]

The UN record in dealing with human rights must be assessed in relation to the
capacity of international organization to affect the conduct of states in this sensitive
area. States, not international agencies, are the primary guarantors of individual
rights. Unlike states, the United Nations has no courts to hear the complaints of
individuals. Even the International Court of Justice permits only states to be parties
to contentious cases brought before it. If a violation is found, the United Nations has
no means of providing redress other than negotiation, censure, or, in extreme cases,
the levying of sanctions. The Charter authorizes economic and military sanctions
only in case of threats to peace and security, and, as discussed in Chapter 5, the
consensus required to use them has seldom existed. Resort to war as a means of
vindicating individual rights would in any event be a questionable expedient.

The difficulty is compounded by disagreement among states on the nature of the
rights to be protected and on the priorities among them. Western industrialized democracies have emphasized political and civil rights, such as freedom of speech,
religion, and press and freedom from arbitrary arrest and imprisonment. Socialist
and Third World states give priority to economic, social, and cultural guarantees—
the right to decent food, shelter, clothing, humane working conditions, and education.[10] Many economic and social rights depend for their realization, not on political
will, but on adequate resources and efficient economic organization. Others, for example equal rights for women, may challenge deeply ingrained social custom. Different societies have different values, and the right to food may seem far more
important to hungry people than the right to an uncensored press. For these reasons,
states guard their sovereign authority to define individual rights and decide what
protection shall be given.

The UN role under these circumstances is limited mainly to formulating standards, encouraging conformity to them, and occasionally condemning egregious
lapses—at least with respect to civil and political rights. Supplying information and
providing forums for exchange of views is one way of encouraging conformity, and
technical assistance may be appropriate for a new state that desires to achieve a
higher standard but lacks experience and the necessary institutional infrastructure.
Economic "rights" may also be promoted by technical assistance and financial aid
channeled through international organizations. Aside from economic aid and some
services rendered directly to persons in need, the United Nations has only an indirect
role in promoting human rights. Even the treaty guarantees formulated through the
UN system and by other international organizations have a limited function. As one
perceptive commentator has noted, they "are designed not to provide human rights
or to enforce human rights provisions but to nudge states into permitting their
vindication."[11]

Setting Voluntary Norms

Voluntary norms are commonly set by an international forum through the declaration of generally applicable rules of behavior. Declaring the rule produces no legal

obligation; it simply expresses a goal, an aspiration, a guide to conduct, and perhaps a moral imperative. The most celebrated such statement in the field of human rights is the Universal Declaration of Human Rights, approved by the General Assembly on December 10, 1948, by a vote of 48 to 0, with 8 abstentions (6 East European members, Saudi Arabia, and South Africa). Its thirty articles encompass a broad range of civil, political, economic, social, and cultural rights and reflect the differing aspirations and values that had to be reconciled in order to secure wide agreement for its adoption. The political and civil rights of the old liberalism are joined with the economic and social ideals of the new, while all are hedged with the right of the sovereign state to limit individual rights and freedoms as necessary to meet "the just requirements of morality, public order and the general welfare in a democratic society." Although the practical application of some of the enumerated economic and social rights might require more governmental control than is consistent with some of the political rights, and others depend on the availability of adequate economic resources, the Declaration as a whole is an admirable and appealing distillation of universal human values. It is reproduced in Appendix D.

Other human rights declarations since approved by the Assembly include the Declaration of the Rights of the Child (1959), the Declaration on the Granting of Independence to Colonial Countries and Peoples (1960), the Declaration on the Elimination of All Forms of Racial Discrimination (1963), the Declaration on the Promotion among Youth of the Ideals of Peace, Mutual Respect and Understanding between Peoples (1965), a Declaration on Territorial Asylum (1967), the Declaration on the Elimination of Discrimination against Women (1967), a Declaration on Social Progress and Development (1969), a Declaration on the Rights of Disabled Persons (1975), a Declaration on the Protection of All Persons from Being Subjected to Torture and Other Cruel, Inhuman or Degrading Treatment or Punishment (1975), a Declaration on the Elimination of All Forms of Intolerance and of Discrimination Based on Religion or Belief (1981), a Declaration on the Right of All Peoples to Peace (1984), and a Declaration on the Human Rights of Individuals Who Are Not Nationals of the Country in Which They Live (1985).

In addition to declarations, which are formalized statements of general principles, the UN General Assembly each year adopts a number of resolutions dealing with some aspect of human rights, broadly defined. Many deal with economic and social conditions, but some are addressed to particular violations of civil and political rights. South Africa and Israel have been the most frequent targets in recent decades, although Afghanistan, Chile, El Salvador, Guatemala, Kampuchea, and other countries have also been urged to observe higher standards.

Such declarations and resolutions have unquestionably influenced the way governments talk about human rights. They are frequently cited by governments as a standard of behavior, most often when criticizing other governments, and lip service is paid both in and out of the United Nations. They have probably brought increased observance of human rights as well, although the impact is difficult to measure. In the short run, most countries do not remedy their conduct in response to UN criticism, and UN action sometimes heightens intransigence. Chile, for example, reacted to UN criticism during the 1970s by holding a national plebiscite to endorse the Pinochet regime, which had been accused of gross human rights violations. In the long run, the picture may be different. Even South Africa has responded to international criticism by making cosmetic changes in its implementation of apartheid.

Other responses to UN declarations suggest that the long-run effects could eventually be substantial. Many of the principles of these declarations have passed into the law of individual countries through embodiment in constitutions, statutes, and judicial decisions. The Universal Declaration, in particular, has been cited in numerous decisions of domestic courts, has served as a model and inspiration for domestic legislation, and is mentioned or partially incorporated into some fifty extant national constitutions. A U.S. federal court recently cited the Universal Declaration as evidence that torture committed by an official of a foreign government against one of his own nationals was a violation of international law.[12] References to human rights declarations in statutes, constitutions, and judicial decisions may in some countries be mere window dressing. In the United States and many other countries, they often are not. Frequent citation does not prove that human rights are being better observed than before, but incorporation of UN declarations into legal instruments and judicial decisions does mean that they are acquiring legal status that may enable them to influence respect for human rights.

Lawmaking Treaties

The United Nations has not been content to let the Universal Declaration filter into national legal systems through the slow and uncertain process of exhortation, example, and action by individual states. When the Declaration was adopted in 1948, it was regarded as preliminary to the drafting of a multilateral treaty that would translate its precepts into binding legal obligations.[13] Since that time the organization has drafted multilateral treaties on a variety of special topics as well as preparing two omnibus covenants—the International Covenant on Civil and Political Rights and the International Covenant on Economic, Social, and Cultural Rights—roughly paralleling the Universal Declaration.

The process of preparing such treaties is lengthy. Typically, it involves initial consideration in the ECOSOC Commission on Human Rights, reconsideration by the ECOSOC parent body, a third detailed examination in the Third (Social, Humanitarian, and Cultural) Committee of the General Assembly, and final approval by the Assembly in plenary meeting. Alternatively, the United Nations has sponsored special conferences to draft lawmaking treaties, including some in the field of human rights. Treaties take effect when a specified number of states individually sign and ratify the documents in accordance with their respective constitutional requirements.

A number of shorter, special purpose treaties passed through the UN pipeline more quickly than the two general covenants, including conventions on slavery, refugees and stateless persons, genocide (defined as "acts committed with intent to destroy, in whole or part, a national, ethnical, racial, or religious group, as such"), the political rights of women, the nationality of married women, the rights of children, and racial discrimination. A UN convention on Elimination of All Forms of Discrimination against Women took effect in 1981, and a convention proscribing torture was opened for signature by the General Assembly in December 1984. Table 9–1 gives a list of the principal UN human rights treaties and their current ratification status.

The two general covenants were not approved by the Assembly until December 1966, eighteen years after the adoption of the Universal Declaration, and both remained inoperative until 1976, when the requisite thirty-five ratifications were finally obtained. Originally the provisions of the two covenants were proposed as a single document, but the United States and some other Western countries viewed as inappropriate and impractical the effort to convert economic and social goals into legally enforceable obligations. The traditional freedoms of speech, press, worship, assembly, security of person and property, political participation, and procedural due process are prohibitions against unreasonable and arbitrary governmental action. Guarantees of an adequate standard of living, education, social security, full employment, medical care, holidays with pay, and a right to leisure, on the other hand, are invitations to a vast expansion of governmental functions with no guarantee that the goals will in fact be attained. It was argued that some states willing to accept treaty obligations for the promotion of political rights would refuse to ratify a treaty including economic and social rights. The answer, over the objections of some, was to write two covenants instead of one.

The United States, spurred by the enthusiasm and dedication of its best-known human rights delegate, Eleanor Roosevelt, played a leading part in drafting the Universal Declaration. Domestic controversy, fueled by fears that UN treaties might override U.S. laws in the field of civil rights, precluded a similar role for the United States in the covenant-drafting process. Shortly after Eisenhower took office in 1953, John Foster Dulles, his Secretary of State, assured the U.S. Senate that the United States would not sign or seek ratification of the UN human rights covenants. This was done to head off impending Senate approval of a proposed constitutional amendment, sponsored by Senator John Bricker of Ohio, designed to limit the impact of treaties on domestic law and to restrict the power of the President to enter into executive agreements with foreign countries. The Dulles assurance had its desired domestic effect but at the price of diminished U.S. influence and leadership in the international protection of human rights. Of the principal UN human rights treaties, the United States has to date ratified only a Supplementary Convention on Slavery and a related protocol, the Convention on the Political Rights of Women, the Genocide Convention, and a protocol relating to the Status of Refugees. The U.S. policy of hostility or indifference to UN human rights treaties was reversed in 1977 by President Jimmy Carter, and several treaties were submitted to the Senate for its approval, including the Genocide Convention. The new policy survived the Carter Administration, with President Ronald Reagan also urging ratification of the Genocide Convention, and the Senate finally complied in February 1986.

TABLE 9–1 _____
UN Human Rights Conventions

Convention (grouped by subject)	Year Opened for Ratification	Year Entered into Force	Number of Ratifications, Accessions, Acceptances (April 1986)
General Human Rights			
International Covenant on Civil and Political Rights	1966	1976	78
Optional Protocol to the International Covenant on Civil and Political Rights	1966	1976	31
International Covenant on Economic, Social and Cultural Rights	1966	1976	80
Racial Discrimination			
International Convention on the Elimination of All Forms of Racial Discrimination	1965	1969	122
International Convention on the Suppression and Punishment of the Crime of Apartheid	1973	1976	70
International Convention against Apartheid in Sports	1985	—	—
Rights of Women			
Convention on the Political Rights of Women	1952	1954	88
Convention on the Nationality of Married Women	1957	1958	55
Convention on Consent to Marriage, Minimum Age for Marriage and Registration of Marriages	1962	1964	39
Convention on the Elimination of All Forms of Discrimination against Women	1979	1981	72
Slavery and Related Matters			
Slavery Convention of 1926, as amended in 1953	1953	1955	77
Protocol Amending the 1926 Slavery Convention	1953	1955	50
Supplementary Convention on the Abolition of Slavery, the Slave Trade, and Institutions and Practices Similar to Slavery	1956	1957	101
Convention for the Suppression of the Traffic in Persons and the Exploitation of the Prostitution of Others	1949	1951	49
Refugees and Stateless Persons			
Convention Relating to the Status of Refugees	1951	1954	95
Protocol Relating to the Status of Refugees	1966	1967	96
Convention Relating to the Status of Stateless Persons	1954	1960	30
Convention on the Reduction of Statelessness	1961	1975	11
Other			
Convention on the Prevention and Punishment of the Crime of Genocide	1948	1951	92
Convention on the International Right of Correction	1952	1962	11
Convention on the Non-Applicability of Statutory Limitations to War Crimes and Crimes against Humanity	1968	1970	24
Convention against Torture and Other Cruel, Inhuman or Degrading Treatment or Punishment	1984	—	—

SOURCES: "Human Rights International Instruments: Signatures, Ratifications, Accessions, etc., 1 September 1983," UN Document ST/HR/4/Rev. 5; Richard B. Lillich, ed., _International Human Rights Instruments_ (Buffalo, N.Y.: William S. Hein, 1985); and _Department of State Bulletin_ 84–86, nos. 2087–2110 (June 1984–June 1986).

Implementing Human Rights

Any discussion of human rights implementation must take account of the global power structure within which the United Nations operates. International organizations provide important linkages within the system, but the principal centers of power are sovereign states. Whether individual rights are violated or vindicated in the territory of a given state depends mainly on decisions made within that state. A state may legitimately complain if its own nationals are mistreated by foreign governments, and sometimes succeed in obtaining redress. But under traditional international law, states have been largely free to treat their own citizens as they will— and this is the source of the most persistent and egregious human rights violations. The new law of human rights, arising from both treaty and custom, offers people more protection against their own governments, but the tradition of national autonomy remains strong. Pressures by one state on another for better observance of human rights generally stop short of coercive action. (The economic coercion currently directed at South Africa is a notable exception.) The reluctance of states to do more reflects the realities of an international system made up of sovereign entities. If states are thus inhibited, the United Nations is still less able to *enforce* individual rights against the wishes of a recalcitrant state.

Useful things can still be done through international action, however. One helpful, and generally inoffensive, way is to supply information and technical assistance. The United Nations has for years conducted a small program of seminars, fellowships, and advisory services for countries requesting special help. The world organization also circulates information about human rights through UN meetings and through studies, reports, and other publications. UN discussions of human rights are all too frequently dominated by political polemics, but on some subjects they serve a useful informational function. It is quite probable, for example, that the ECOSOC Commission on the Status of Women has contributed to the extension of political rights to women through its efforts to gather information and exchange views and experience. In other areas of concern, discussion has been enlightened by special UN studies on such topics as forced labor, slavery, torture, and discrimination in education, employment, and political rights. In addition, national reports on human rights observance are periodically discussed in the ECOSOC Commission on Human Rights.

In dealing with alleged violations of human rights, the United Nations has relied on investigation, discussion, publicity, and censure. These have occurred in a variety of forums, including the General Assembly and its Third Committee, the Economic and Social Council, the Commission on Human Rights, and the Subcommission on Prevention of Discrimination and Protection of Minorities. In a few instances, where marginal national interests have been involved and UN action has been conciliatory, states have reacted favorably to such pressure. Most attempts by the organization to remedy specific violations of human rights have not been efficacious, at least in the short run. Viewed as a deterrent, UN censure seldom outweighs the domestic motivations that lead to rights violations.

Nevertheless, UN organs have persisted in exerting the moral pressure of discussion and recommendation and have strengthened their procedures for doing so.[14] For years the Commission on Human Rights was debarred from taking any action on complaints that particular states were denying human rights. This limitation was modified in 1967, when the Commission was authorized to examine information and make studies of situations revealing gross violations of human rights. The procedure was regularized in 1970 with the adoption of ECOSOC Resolution 1503, permitting the Commission to investigate "particular situations which appear to reveal a consistent pattern of gross and reliably attested violations." This "1503 procedure" restricted the Commission to matters referred by its Sub-Commission on Prevention of Discrimination and Protection of Minorities, which in turn could act only on a recommendation from a working group of five of its members. Even so, it was a step toward more effective UN scrutiny. All such matters remained private until 1978, when the Commission began to divulge the names of countries that it had discussed in confidential sessions. Since 1980 the Commission has publicly disclosed reports of its investigations or discussions in a number of cases, including complaints against Equatorial Guinea, Bolivia, Democratic Kampuchea, El Salvador, Guatemala, pre-Sandinista Nicaragua, the Soviet Union (in Afghanistan), Poland, and Iran.

Another proposal for strengthening UN action in the field of human rights, under discussion since the 1970s, is the creation of a UN High Commissioner for Human Rights. The Sub-Commission, which is composed of elected experts, has reported favorably on the proposal; but the Human Rights Commission, which is composed of governmental representatives, has been reluctant to forward it to the General Assembly. As conceived by the Sub-Commission, the High Commissioner would keep track of developments throughout the world and have authority to contact any government to protect or restore respect for human rights. The Soviet bloc and many Third World states have strongly resisted the proposal, fearing unwanted intervention in their internal affairs by the High Commissioner.

Nongovernmental organizations have been especially active in support of improved UN human rights procedures. While many individuals and groups have communicated with the United Nations from time to time, some of the more active groups—which have their own operations independent of the United Nations—include Amnesty International, the International Commission of Jurists, the International League for Human Rights, the International Federation for Human Rights, and the World Council of Churches. Amnesty International, established in London in 1961, has become widely known for its efforts to publicize and secure the release of political prisoners and to eradicate torture. It is respected as a source of information as well as for its persistence in mobilizing public opinion and encouraging government action to vindicate fundamental human rights.[15]

Some of the human rights treaties have their own provisions for implementation, but most use the same procedures of complaint, investigation, discussion, and censure used by UN bodies outside the treaty framework. Under the International Covenant on Civil and Political Rights, for example, an eighteen-member Human Rights Committee of specialists elected by the parties is empowered to receive reports from states on measures adopted to implement the covenant. The Committee studies the reports and transmits its comments to the parties and the Economic and Social Council. In addition, states may authorize the Committee to receive and consider communications from other parties alleging nonfulfillment of treaty obligations. No state may bring such a complaint unless it has made an appropriate declaration subjecting itself to the procedure. The Committee's powers are limited to discussion and reporting, supplemented by a conciliation procedure with consent of the parties. By accepting an optional protocol to the treaty, a state may empower the Committee to consider communications from private persons within its jurisdiction who claim to be victims of a treaty violation by that state. Any views expressed by the Committee have only the force of recommendation.

Regional Institutions

Perspective on UN efforts to promote human rights throughout the world may be gleaned from a brief look at regional approaches to human rights in the Americas and Western Europe. The Organization of American States was seven months ahead of the United Nations in adopting its own American Declaration of the Rights and Duties of Man, in May 1948. An Inter-American Commission on Human Rights was established in 1959, and in 1965 it was given authority to hear and investigate complaints from individuals and to make recommendations for settlement. The Commission is now the primary implementation mechanism of the American Convention on Human Rights, signed by most American states in 1969 and in force from 1977. Under the Convention a party may by declaration subject itself to complaints from another state. The Convention also creates an Inter-American Court of Human Rights to interpret and apply the covenant in disputes between states voluntarily accepting its jurisdiction. Although the Court has had little activity, the Commission receives numerous complaints. Through quiet persuasion and occasional publicity, it has been a positive influence on the laws and practices of a number of states.

Undoubtedly the most effective arrangement for the international protection of human rights is the European Convention on Human Rights, drafted under the auspices of the Council of Europe and in force since 1953. The Council's twenty-one members have accepted the Convention and thereby agreed to submit certain types of human rights controversies to the binding determination of an international body. Fourteen of the twenty-one have approved an optional provision granting individuals and private associations the right to complain. The emphasis is on quiet negotiation to find a "friendly solution" among the parties involved. For states that have ratified an optional protocol conferring jurisdiction on the European Court of Human Rights, the final decision is left to the Court.

The successful operation of the Convention rests on a number of circumstances. First, the Convention has been limited to traditional civil and political rights already widely guaranteed in Western European countries. Second, the legal systems of the parties have sufficient homogeneity to produce similarity in interpretation and application of the treaty guarantees. Third, the emphasis throughout is on quiet negotiation of settlement, utilizing a judicial or quasi-judicial body as the final arbiter and at no stage providing a public forum for political harassment of one state by another. Fourth, states have seldom utilized the machinery in their dealings with one another, with the great majority of complaints issuing from individuals. Fifth, petitions by individuals are carefully screened to rule out frivolous or insubstantial complaints. These special conditions that contribute to the success of the European experiment do not encourage great hope that it can readily be duplicated elsewhere, especially among a group of states as numerous and as heterogeneous as the United Nations.

Improvement of Labor Standards

Closely related to UN action in the field of human rights are the efforts of the International Labor Organization to upgrade labor standards around the world. The ILO has been a force for higher labor standards since its creation in 1919, when Allied statesmen, responding to labor pressures and honoring their wartime commitments to trade union groups, drafted the constitution of the ILO as Part XIII of the Versailles Treaty. The organization has ever since been marked by a vigorous secretariat, known as the International Labor Office, and a unique form of tripartite representation for employer, worker, and government interests in its policy-making bodies. Each member state sends two government delegates, one employers' delegate, and one workers' delegate to the annual meeting of the International Labor Conference, and the same tripartite distribution is found in its fifty-six-member Governing Body.

Like the United Nations in its human rights programs, the ILO functions by setting standards, giving advice, facilitating the exchange of information, and mobilizing world opinion in support of higher standards. Standards are set through legally binding conventions, subject to state ratification, and through recommendations voicing goals and aspirations that are beyond the reach of some states and hence not proper subjects for lawmaking treaties. The conventions and recommendations taken together are referred to as the International Labor Code. From 6 conventions and 6 recommendations adopted by the first International Labor Conference in 1919, the number had grown to more than 160 conventions and 170 recommendations by 1985. The Code extends to nearly every aspect of working conditions—hours, wages, the right to organize and bargain collectively, employment discrimination, workers' compensation, employment security, vocational guidance and training, and occupational safety and health, among others. A number of the conventions and recommendations deal with special abuses, such as slavery and forced labor, or with special categories of workers—women, children, miners, seamen, dockworkers, and sharecroppers. States vary widely in their ratification of conventions. France has ratified more than a hundred, the United States only seven.

The ILO has unusually well-developed techniques for encouraging compliance with the Code. This is done by a searching annual review of member states' reports, a judicious use of the ILO's powers of investigation, and a procedure for hearing complaints in specific cases. The ILO has seldom been hesitant in pointing out instances of noncompliance and making specific recommendations for remedial action.

In addition to rule-making and implementation, the ILO carries on extensive informational activities through publications, conferences, seminars and fellowships, and technical experts. Its *Yearbook of Labor Statistics* and its quarterly *Official Bulletin* have long been important sources of data on international labor conditions. A monthly *International Labor Review* and numerous special publications provide information on current problems and conditions.

Programs of technical assistance are used to help countries conform to the International Labor Code as well as to promote economic development as a means of providing the social and economic base for improved labor standards. Assistance is provided in areas of ILO interest and expertise, such as vocational training, social security services, occupational health and safety, and labor statistics. Some ILO technical assistance is funded from its own budget, but a larger share draws on resources of the UN Development Program.

The International Labor Organization operates in the same world environment as the United Nations, and it has suffered the effects of political battles between East and West and between North and South. In 1977 the United States withdrew from the organization, after having held continuous membership since 1934. American dissatisfaction sprang from a number of causes. The United States saw the tripartite principle threatened by delegations from the Soviet bloc and some other states whose employer and labor representatives were, for practical purposes, government representatives under a different label. The United States also objected to what it saw as selective concern for human rights, especially as reflected in actions of the International Labor Conference that pilloried friends of the United States and ignored violations in some other countries. Excessive politicization was also alleged, particularly in using the forum to penalize Israel for actions that had little to do with labor standards and in granting observer status to the Palestine Liberation Organization (PLO) in 1975. As early as 1970 the AFL–CIO, with its strong anticommunist tradition, had been seriously alienated by the appointment of a Soviet national as an ILO Assistant Director-General.

Loss of the U.S. financial contribution, amounting to 25 percent of the regular budget, caused severe temporary curtailment of ILO programs. The United States returned in 1980, after some signs that the ILO would behave more circumspectly. An Arab proposal to condemn Israel was defeated, labor rights violations in Eastern Europe were given more attention, and procedures were adopted to bolster employer and worker autonomy within the organization. Perhaps more important, the United States concluded that working from within was a more effective method of influencing labor standards and ILO programs than remaining outside the organization.

RULES IN OTHER FUNCTIONAL SETTINGS

Human rights and labor standards are matters of domestic concern that have traditionally been regulated by individual states. By contrast, many areas of functional cooperation involve interstate contacts that fall beyond the jurisdiction of any single state and must be regulated by international action if they are to be regulated at all.

In recognition of this fact, states have submitted a number of their functional relationships to the regulative processes of international organization. This is the kind of behavior that Leonard Woolf in 1916 termed "international government."[16] Its growth does not necessarily justify the functionalist premise that economic and social cooperation leads to peace, but it does demonstrate that states will subject themselves and their citizens to a degree of international regulation in limited functional areas when self-interest requires it. Some of the more significant ventures in the regulation of international contacts will be briefly examined here.

Postal Service

Among the best-observed international regulations are those of the Universal Postal Union, an organization dating from 1874.[17] Under its auspices letters can be delivered anywhere in the world by the most expeditious route at a modest uniform cost and in accordance with generally uniform procedures. The technical nature of UPU functions is conducive to consensus, and consensus on broad objectives provides the foundation for majority rule within the organization when the goal of complete unanimity cannot be attained. Revisions of the UPU Constitution, initiated at meetings of the Congress of the Postal Union, held every five years, become effective upon ratification by two thirds of member countries. Changes in the rules and regulations governing letter post are effected by a simple majority of the membership, without need for ratification. Between congresses, proposals for amendments to the postal rules are circulated by the Bureau (secretariat) and take effect when enough affirmative replies are received. Compliance with the rules is obligatory from the time of their entry into force, with loss of membership privileges as the sanction. Formal approval of changes is not necessary as long as a state in fact observes the regulations. Compliance is generally forthcoming because the benefits of participation outweigh the burdens of compliance.

Telecommunications

The work of the International Telecommunication Union is in many respects analogous to that of the UPU, especially its efforts to create a homogeneous global communication system by joint regulation of telegraph, telephone, and radio-telegraph services.[18] The two organizations' methods of legislating and of enforcing compliance are also broadly similar. The ITU Conference meets at intervals of five to eight years to make general policy and initiate amendments to the ITU Convention. Decisions are reached through unanimous agreement if possible but by simple and qualified majorities when necessary. A state is permitted to ratify amendments with reservations and still remain in good standing, but the penalty for nonratification is loss of its vote in ITU organs after a two-year grace period. As a practical matter, from the date of their entry into force, amendments are treated as provisionally applicable even to nonratifying states. In a number of technical matters, including the important function of radio frequency regulation, the ITU assigns tasks to specialist, "nonpolitical" experts instead of to negotiating conferences composed of governmental representatives. This approach differs from that of the UPU and is possible because of the highly technical nature of the tasks.

Compliance with ITU rules, a product of necessity and convenience, has been very high except in the special problem area of radio broadcasting. There the ITU has sometimes been faced with defiance by countries refusing to be limited to the use of frequencies allotted by the ITU's International Frequency Registration Board. If a recalcitrant member broadcasts on a frequency not assigned to it, the ITU may punish the offender by freeing other states to use its assigned frequencies. Interference with authorized radio signals, otherwise known as radio jamming, is another special problem. The practice is clearly in violation of ITU regulations, but it is so entwined with the vital interests of states that ITU sanctions are unable to curb it. When faced with a complaint of radio jamming, the ITU has generally resigned itself to the fact that retaliation through release of frequencies would only add to the confusion and further impair radio transmission.

Civil Aviation

In the field of air transportation, international efforts to promote safety, regularity of transport, uniformity, and nondiscrimination are centered in the International Civil Aviation Organization.[19] The rule-making function is exercised principally by the organization's thirty-three-member Council, rather than its triennial Assembly. Standards approved by a two-thirds vote of the Council become effective at a date prescribed by the Council unless a majority of states indicate their disapproval during the intervening period. The organization distinguishes between binding *standards,* which are necessary to the safety or regularity of international air navigation, and nonbinding *recommended practices,* which represent desirable goals.

A state that cannot conform to a new standard may notify the Council within the time period fixed for raising objections and be released from its legal obligation. If the standard relates to the airworthiness of aircraft or the competence of personnel, however, other states are free to close their airspace to the aircraft of the noncomplying state. The ICAO Convention commits all members to the principle of nondiscrimination against the aircraft of any country; but noncompliance with standards revives the discretionary rights of one state against another that would prevail under the rules of customary international law. Compliance with ICAO rules is widespread, and most instances of noncompliance appear to be rooted in lack of economic and technical resources rather than willful disregard of the norms.

ICAO regulation is primarily technical, relating to such matters as air traffic control, communication and navigational aids, safety standards for aircraft, and rules of the air. The organization has not been given the authority to regulate the commercial aspects of civil aviation, including access to the passenger and cargo markets of individual countries. A right jealously guarded by states, the granting of commercial privileges still occurs through bilateral agreement between states.

Health

Health problems have long been a subject of international regulation. The international health councils established during the nineteenth century in seaport cities of North Africa, the Middle East, and Southeast Europe—sometimes by the imposition of the more powerful European states—represented an early form of international action to improve sanitary conditions and prevent the spread of epidemics along the channels of commerce. Later the councils were supplemented by multilateral conventions that established rules for quarantine and other precautionary measures to be taken in ports and prohibited vessels from leaving port without a clean bill of health. Exchange of information through conferences was put on a more systematic basis in 1907 with the establishment of the International Office of Public Health in Paris, and League health machinery subsequently forged ahead with direct efforts to fight disease and improve world levels of health.

Today the World Health Organization as a specialized agency of the United Nations has combined and expanded international cooperation in all of these fields.[20] With respect to its regulatory functions, the WHO Assembly has effective rule-making power in several limited but important areas, including (1) sanitary and quarantine regulations applicable to ground, sea, and air travel; (2) standardization of medical nomenclature; (3) standards for diagnostic procedures; (4) standards on the safety, purity, and potency of biological and pharmaceutical substances passing in international commerce; and (5) advertising and labeling of such products. When approved by the WHO Assembly, health regulations come into force for all members after a specified period of notice, except for states that specifically object or enter reservations. This preserves a right of individual consent but leaves the possibility that the legal obligation to comply may be accepted through inadvertent failure to give notice of objection. Communicable diseases that pose a threat of international epidemics are of special concern for WHO.

The WHO Assembly has the right to formulate conventions and make recommendations on virtually any health-related matter. Although these rules do not take effect until they have been ratified or otherwise implemented by national action, noncomplying members must face the sanction of adverse publicity. The WHO constitution requires all states to accept or reject conventions within eighteen months of their adoption by the Assembly, and to notify the Director-General of the action taken. After the pattern of the ILO, each state must also submit an annual report on the implementation of WHO recommendations and of the conventions it has ratified. Research, collection and dissemination of information, and expert advice are also used extensively to upgrade health standards around the world.

Although the preceding discussion has emphasized WHO's rule-making functions, WHO also has extensive programs of health services and technical assistance to developing countries. Successful campaigns against disease have been particularly notable. A concentrated effort to combat malaria, beginning in the mid-1950s, led to its eradication from most of Asia, much of the Americas, and all of Europe.

Permanent eradication in Africa was not possible until basic health services were improved. The WHO's success in fighting smallpox was even more spectacular. A campaign in the late 1960s and early 1970s reduced the incidence of smallpox to a rare occurrence in most parts of the world. An Expanded Program on Immunization (EPI), launched in 1974, seeks to provide immunization for all children by 1990 against diphtheria, measles, pertussis (whooping cough), poliomyelitis, tetanus, and tuberculosis. These are a major cause of death and disability in the developing countries. The worldwide fight against disease is also aided by WHO's Epidemiological Intelligence Network, which receives reports from member governments immediately upon the outbreak of any case of smallpox, cholera, plague, or yellow fever and transmits the information to health authorities throughout the world by means of daily broadcasts.

A Global Strategy in support of a "Health for All by the Year 2000" campaign, adopted by the WHO Assembly in 1981, has the goal of promoting a world level of health that will permit all persons to lead socially and economically productive lives. Specific objectives include safe water within fifteen minutes' walking distance of every home, immunization against the six EPI diseases, local health care within an hour's travel, and trained personnel to attend childbirth and to care for pregnant mothers and for children up to at least a year old. These ambitious goals are not likely to be reached by A.D. 2000 since neither WHO nor the poorer countries have the resources to do the job.[21] Nevertheless, the goals are admirable and some progress is being made.

In addition to its general health functions, WHO cooperates with the United Nations and related agencies for the control of narcotics and for the limitation of their use to legitimate medical and scientific needs. Systematic efforts at international control date from the Hague Convention of 1912. International cooperation in this area was expanded by the League and further systematized under UN auspices. Under the present Single Convention on Narcotic Drugs, adopted in 1961 to replace a number of earlier treaties, an International Narcotics Control Board sets acceptable limits for the manufacture and import of controlled drugs and monitors treaty compliance. The effectiveness of regulation depends largely on the ability and willingness of states to enforce treaty provisions, but international agencies help states remain sensitive to their obligations. An ECOSOC Commission on Narcotic Drugs is an important forum for discussion of international narcotics problems, and the United Nations maintains research laboratories in several countries. The WHO role is to advise other international agencies on drugs likely to produce addiction, and to sponsor research and technical assistance relating to the prevention and treatment of drug addiction.

The Law of the Sea

The oceans constitute 70 percent of the earth's surface. In the past most of this area has been open to all states. Current developments in the law of the sea would increase national control over large parts of this area through rules expanding the breadth of the territorial sea, creating an "exclusive economic zone" out to two hundred miles from a country's coastline and extending national control of sea-bed resources still farther in many cases. Simultaneously, the new rules would establish an international government for the seabed beyond national jurisdiction, a regime that states have been unwilling to accept anywhere else on earth. This is more than just a rule-making exercise to help regulate matters of technical, social, and economic interest. It is a massive experiment in peaceful political and territo-rial change.

In centuries past the oceans were used for two main purposes—navigation and fishing. Although specific disputes over fisheries and navigation rights sometimes arose, the oceans were treated for the most part as a global commons not subject to the control of any single state. With the increased use of the oceans made possible by new technology, the twentieth century has seen rising demands from states to extend national control over larger and larger ocean areas and the seabed beneath. While oil and fisheries have provided the primary motivation, the extension of na-tional jurisdiction to areas that were formerly part of the high seas necessarily has an impact on navigation rights as well. In addition, intensive use creates problems of depleted fishing resources and increased maritime pollution.

These and other ocean problems have been attacked in a number of international forums. The International Maritime Organization (formerly known as IMCO, Inter-governmental Maritime Consultative Organization), founded in 1948 as a UN spe-cialized agency, has produced important treaties dealing with maritime safety and pollution. The UN Environmental Program (UNEP) encourages global and regional agreements to preserve the ocean environment. A UNESCO-sponsored Intergovern-mental Oceanographic Commission promotes and coordinates scientific research, monitoring of the oceans, and international exchange of oceanographic data. The Food and Agriculture Organization conducts research and provides technical assist-ance on fish as a food resource. The International Labor Organization makes rec-ommendations and sponsors conventions dealing with maritime labor conditions. The International Whaling Commission, through international agreement, jawbon-ing, and economic pressures exerted by sympathetic states, tries to preserve existing stocks of whales from extinction.

While the attack on maritime-related problems has been highly splintered, by far the most ambitious effort to establish rules for the use of the oceans has occurred in UN-sponsored treaty-drafting conferences. As early as 1930 an international confer-ence at the Hague tried to codify the law of the sea in treaty form but failed to reach agreement. In 1958 a UN Conference on the Law of the Sea (UNCLOS I) was more successful. It produced four multilateral treaties—the Convention on the Territorial Sea and the Contiguous Zone, the Convention on the High Seas, the Convention on the Continental Shelf, and the Convention on Fishing and Conservation of the Living Resources of the High Seas—each of which entered into force among the ratifying states during the 1960s. Although the treaties codified much of the existing law of the sea, important issues remained unresolved, including the breadth of the territo-rial sea and the extent of coastal state jurisdiction over fishing rights.

The conventions on the territorial sea and the contiguous zone, the high seas, and fisheries addressed problems that had been at the heart of ocean law for centuries. They codified long-standing rules of customary international law, adapted to modern circumstances. Jurisdiction over the continental shelf, on the other hand, was a new issue because technology had only recently made possible the exploitation of oil resources of the ocean floor. The United States started the rush toward national jurisdiction with President Harry Truman's September 1945 proclamation claiming control over the natural resources of the seabed and subsoil of the U.S. continental shelf. Many states followed suit, and the 1958 convention embodied these claims in treaty law. The Convention was extremely generous to coastal states, recognizing jurisdiction as far out as developing technology might permit exploitation of seabed resources.

A second UN conference (UNCLOS II), held in 1960, was unable to agree on disputed issues, and in subsequent years national jurisdiction over the oceans continued to expand. Several states, most of them in Latin America, went so far as to claim a territorial sea of two hundred miles, which, if established, would include control over navigation as well as ocean and seabed resources. Others claimed an economic zone of varying distances that would not impinge on navigation rights. Faced with such diverse and extensive claims to national jurisdiction, the United Nations set in motion preparations leading to a third UN Conference on the Law of the Sea (UNCLOS III). The initial impetus for this renewed UN effort is traceable to a remarkable speech before the 1967 General Assembly by Ambassador Arvid Pardo of Malta. The need for greater uniformity was obvious. The need to reconcile coastal state jurisdictional claims with flag state claims to "freedom of the seas" and every state's interest in what was left of the "global commons" was also apparent. The genius of Pardo's appeal was to join these concerns with the special needs of developing countries for additional sources of financial aid. To achieve these purposes, he proposed to set fixed limits to national jurisdiction and to declare the resources of the seabed and ocean floor beyond those limits "the common heritage of mankind." This common heritage would be managed by a seabed authority empowered to exploit its resources on behalf of mankind, with particular emphasis on the needs of developing countries.

Preparations for the conference lasted six years, and drafting the Convention took another nine years, from the first brief session held in December 1973 to the closing session in 1982. The new treaty embraced, modified, and amplified the four treaties drafted in 1958 at UNCLOS I and added important new provisions on an exclusive economic zone (EEZ), the rights of landlocked states, a regime for the common area beyond national jurisdiction, preservation of the marine environment, marine scientific research, and machinery for the settlement of disputes arising under the treaty.[22]

A number of notable changes from previous law are written into the treaty. The breadth of the territorial sea, previously claimed at three, four, six, twelve, and up to two hundred miles by different states, and unspecified in the 1958 convention, is fixed at twelve miles, with an additional twelve miles of contiguous zone for enforcing regulations against smuggling. The 1958 convention set the contiguous zone at twelve miles from the coastline. The convention also provides an exclusive economic zone extending two hundred miles from the coastline, in which coastal states have control over the economic resources of the sea and the subsoil beneath but not jurisdiction over navigation. A limit is also put on the breadth of the continental shelf. Although various methods of calculation are given, coastal states are guaranteed jurisdiction over the seabed to a distance of 200 nautical miles, with a maximum in some cases of 350 miles. Any minerals extracted from the continental shelf beyond two hundred miles are subject to a royalty, paid to an international Authority, primarily for the benefit of developing states. The dispute settlement provisions are also noteworthy. Disputes arising under the law of the sea that are not settled by agreement must be submitted to binding arbitral or judicial procedures. An International Tribunal for the Law of the Sea is created as one such alternative.

The most controversial provisions turned out to be those setting aside the ocean floor beyond national jurisdiction (called the "Area") as the common heritage of mankind and creating an International Sea-Bed Authority to administer it. Under the terms of the treaty, governments and private firms may obtain licenses to conduct mining operations in the Area, subject to fees, royalties, and production regulations. However, as a condition to receiving the permit, each national firm must submit two proposed mining tracts to the Authority, which will then select one to be developed by its own operating agency, known as the "Enterprise." National licensees are also required to share technology with the Enterprise. The Authority is to be an autonomous international organization with its own Assembly, Council, and Secretariat. The deliberative organs are constituted to guarantee majority (i.e., Third World) dominance, although a measure of minority protection is provided through requirements for extraordinary majorities on some issues. After a trial period of twenty years from the commencement of commercial production, treaty provisions relating to the system of exploration and production may be amended by a two-thirds majority of the states that are parties to the convention.

Although the United States had earlier indicated that it would accept the seabed provisions of the treaty as part of the overall law of the sea package, the Reagan Administration expressed reservations about the Sea-Bed Authority and subsequently refused to sign the convention. The regulation of seabed mining by private corporations was regarded as too burdensome, and the United States feared that the amendment provisions after twenty years might be used to exclude private enterprise entirely. The United States was also concerned about being perpetually outvoted on critical issues. As a substitute measure, the United States has sought negotiated agreements with other industrialized states likely to have a deep sea mining capability. The uncertain status of the treaty, which does not take effect until sixty states have ratified,[23] and the confusing prospect of two or more differing legal regimes for exploitation of the seabed, is likely to delay any substantial investments of capital. There is the additional possibility that the United States, under a new administration, might decide to ratify the treaty.

Apart from the legal cloud cast on seabed mining, other issues are raised by the refusal of the United States and several other Western countries to ratify. In particular, the United States will certainly wish to claim the benefit of the treaty provisions it approves, including those pertaining to the exclusive economic zone and the right of transit through international straits that have fallen within national jurisdiction as a result of the broadened territorial sea. American claims could be supported by the argument that such provisions have passed into the realm of customary international law and are binding even without treaty ratification. The Law of the Sea Conference has been a major venture in international rule-making and peaceful change, but its ultimate effects remain to be seen. Setting aside the Area as an international territory and creating the Authority to govern and exploit it could be important steps toward international government, at least for that limited area. The failure of critical states to ratify UNCLOS III, however, may substantially reduce the Authority's role.

INFORMATION AND PROMOTION

Every international organization gathers and disseminates information. This is an inevitable by-product of meetings, but it is also done systematically. Many organizations sponsor research in their technical areas and hold conferences for the exchange of information among scholars and experts, including representatives of governments and private groups. Many collect and publish statistical data supplied by research or by their members. All publish various reports of their activities.

"Years," "Decades," and "World Conferences"

All international agencies also engage in promotional activities. Secretariats carry on various "public information" programs designed not only to inform but also to put organizational functions in a favorable light. Speeches made in deliberative bodies, and actions taken by them, have the same objects. While efforts at international consciousness-raising and promotion of worthy causes have become commonplace in international organizations, three techniques repeatedly used by the United Nations merit special emphasis. They are the "year," the "decade," and the "world conference."

Nearly every year is now set aside for some designated promotion. Thus 1983 was designated by the General Assembly as World Communications Year, 1985 as International Youth Year, 1986 as the International Year of Peace, and 1987 as the International Year of Shelter for the Homeless. The "decade" usually involves a more ambitious undertaking, with proposals for programs to achieve the purposes of the decade and periodic reports on progress. The first such decade was the UN Development Decade, 1961–70. The 1970s were subsequently declared the Second Development Decade, and the 1980s the Third. The 1970s and the 1980s were also designated Disarmament Decades. A Decade to Combat Racism and Racial Discrimination was launched in 1973, and a Second Decade to Combat Racism in 1983. A UN Decade for Women was inaugurated in 1976.

The world conference approach has already been noted in Chapter 3, in connection with the involvement of private groups with international organizations. Here we would emphasize that UN-sponsored world conferences since the early 1970s, on such subjects as the environment, population, women, housing, energy resources, refugees, and development, have to a large extent been intended to raise the level of international attention and concern and must be regarded in that light. They always receive press attention, and the participants can normally be expected to transmit some information and concern to the private groups and governmental agencies that they represent.

Education, Science, and Culture

Among international organizations the UN Educational, Scientific and Cultural Organization (UNESCO) has a special responsibility for the dissemination of information. Its activities are very wide-ranging, which has been a source of both weakness and strength. The strength comes from the capacity to appeal to and gain support from many governmental and private constituencies with an interest in one or more of UNESCO's activities. The weakness lies in the dispersion of effort and the limited impact that result from spreading limited resources over a wide area.

A large share of UNESCO's resources has been devoted to technical assistance in education, particularly in programs for the elimination of illiteracy and for training in basic vocational skills essential to economic development. In addition, UNESCO provides technical assistance for the promotion of the natural sciences and, to a lesser extent, the social sciences, the humanities, the development and preservation of national cultural heritages, and mass communication. All of these programs are directed toward the needs of the developing countries, and most are undertaken with financial assistance from the UN Development Program.

UNESCO has also produced a number of treaties in areas of concern to it, including an International Convention concerning the Protection of the World Cultural and National Heritage, the Universal Copyright Convention, the Convention on the Free Flow of Educational, Scientific and Cultural Materials, and the Convention against Discrimination in Education.

The strictly informational activities of UNESCO cover a staggering variety of topics. Titles in the catalog of UNESCO and UNESCO-sponsored publications number in the thousands. Periodical publications range in scope from the *UNESCO Courier* (topical themes and events of popular interest) and the *UNESCO Chronicle* (a running review of the Organization's activities) to the *International Social Science Journal, Diogenes* (humanities), *Impact of Science on Society,* and *Museum*. These titles are illustrative, not exhaustive. Other publications include bibliographies, reports, histories (including the multivolume *History of Africa* and *History of the Scientific and Cultural Development of Mankind*), translations of literary masterpieces, and special studies on all manner of subjects within UNESCO's fields of interest, as well as valuable statistical documentation in education, the social sciences, library services, mass communication, and other fields.

Another important informational activity, often fostered by means of conferences, is the promotion of interchange among scientists, scholars, and artists. To further this interchange, UNESCO has encouraged the formation of international professional societies and has often supported them through financial subventions. Scholarships and fellowships, educational exchange, elimination of barriers to the free flow of information, and improvement of mass communication systems are other elements of the UNESCO approach to dissemination of information. If UNESCO falls short in its efforts to spread education, science, and culture, it is not from lack of variety in its methods.

With such broad objectives, UNESCO's reach has necessarily exceeded its grasp. Falling short of goals need not bring a negative assessment; the task may simply be larger than the available resources. UNESCO has undoubtedly promoted the production and exchange of information in its various fields of activity, and its technical assistance programs have added something to national resources for education and development. Critics, nevertheless, have faulted the diffusion of its efforts and have suggested that its impact might be greater if its focus were sharper.

In response to these criticisms, UNESCO has tried to set priorities, but the pressures for diffusion of its efforts have been irresistible. First of all, its mandate is very broad—education, science, and culture can be construed to embrace almost anything—and the UNESCO Constitution posits the additional goal of contributing to a more peaceful world. Second, UNESCO constituencies—governmental and private—provide constant pressure for the continuation or addition of programs that benefit them. For two decades or more, the Director-General of UNESCO has predominated in setting the direction for UNESCO's programs, and he is responsive to the groups that give him support. These include scientists, scholars, and other private beneficiaries of UNESCO programs and, more important, the prevailing Third World majority in the UNESCO General Conference and Executive Board, whose interests lie in expanding programs. A third reason for diffusion is UNESCO's bureaucracy, with its vested interest in proliferation and expansion. A reversal of the trend would cost some officials their jobs, while other officials might lose perquisites and influence in the constituent communities they serve.

The governments of developed countries that pay most of the bills, including both the United States and the Soviet Union, have repeatedly protested the growth of UNESCO budgets. This has been a much greater source of dissatisfaction than the abstract question of how many programs are too many. UNESCO's cause was not helped by a 1984 report of the General Accounting Office, the investigative arm of the U.S. Congress, presenting detailed allegations of mismanagement in UNESCO's personnel program and financial activities. The report laid responsibility squarely at the door of the Director-General, Amador-Mahtar M'bow of Senegal.[24] Other problems have also seriously eroded support for UNESCO. From the mid-1970s onward, the United States persistently objected to the "politicization" of UNESCO—particularly as expressed in Arab-sponsored resolutions criticizing Israel for its archaeological activity in Jerusalem and its educational policies in the West Bank, and the attempted exclusion of Israel from participation in UNESCO. Still more serious has been the Third World demand for a New International Information Order. The avowed purpose is to redress the imbalance and distortion in the flow of world information alleged to result from control of world news and information channels by the developed states. Redressing the balance is advocated as essential to successful development, but the United States and some other Western governments fear that this would legitimize government control over the news and lead to restrictions on the freedom of journalists and the media.

In December 1984 American frustration with UNESCO finally prompted the long-threatened U.S. withdrawal, and the United Kingdom and Singapore followed in December 1985. Since the United States paid 25 percent of the regular budget and Britain nearly 5 percent, this brought program cuts that no amount of haranguing in the past had been able to achieve. There is of course a possibility that these countries will find a way to reenter UNESCO.

Other Information Activities

Other international organizations also render informational services on which governments, business, the professions, and others throughout the world have come to rely. The Statistical Office of the United Nations, for example, publishes a number of annual basic reference works, including the *Statistical Yearbook,* the *Demographic Yearbook,* the *Yearbook of International Trade Statistics, World Energy Supplies,* and the *Yearbook of National Accounts Statistics.* The *UN Chronicle,* published quarterly (monthly before 1986) by the UN Department of Public Information, contains a review of major UN activities during the preceding quarter. The United Nations also issues periodicals on special subjects, such as the *International Review of Criminal Policy* and the *International Social Service Review.* These and other regular UN publications are supplemented by numerous special reports. The specialized agencies likewise produce a flood of facts in their own special fields of competence and interest. When publications are considered together with the many conferences, seminars, and other meetings whose primary function is the spreading of knowledge, the informational services of the United Nations assume a wide scope indeed.

Units within the United Nations especially concerned with informational activities include the UN Office of Public Information (OPI), the UN Institute for Training and Research (UNITAR), and the United Nations University. The OPI, with its Information Centers in many countries (sixty-seven in 1985), supplies UN publications to the world and carries on a variety of public relations activities designed to present the organization in its most favorable light. UNITAR, established by the General Assembly in 1963, trains individuals for work in economic and social development and conducts training seminars for national government personnel concerned with the work of the United Nations. Its most visible activity is the publication of special studies undertaken by UNITAR staff, often in collaboration with visiting scholars. Since 1975 the United Nations University, with headquarters in Tokyo, has attempted to stimulate research on world problems and has provided fellowships for postgraduate training in collaboration with national research institutes and universities. It is now moving to establish its own research training centers. Both UNITAR and the United Nations University serve as links between the United Nations and the international academic community.

INTERNATIONALLY ADMINISTERED PROGRAMS

Technical assistance is widely used by international organizations to promote economic, social, and technical goals. Reference has already been made to the technical assistance programs of WHO and UNESCO in areas of their special interest, as well as to UN and ILO assistance in promoting human rights. While some organizations, such as WHO, UNESCO, the ILO, and the Food and Agriculture Organization, have large programs of technical assistance, nearly every UN specialized agency offers technical assistance of some sort, financed variously from its regular budget, the UN Development Program, voluntary contributions, and other sources. Chapter 11 will discuss aid to developing countries in detail. Here we will briefly examine programs of international organizations for the aid of refugees and other persons in need of emergency relief.

Emergency Relief

Since World War II international organization has been continuously involved in programs for the relief of people in distress. If League of Nations efforts to protect refugees during the interwar years are included, the period of continuous involvement begins even earlier. Although the long-term problems of economic development absorb the greater part of UN resources, the organization and its related agencies have compiled a substantial record of accomplishment in meeting the short-term needs of selected groups of people in distress.

UNRRA.   A direct forerunner of UN programs was the UN Relief and Rehabilitation Administration, an agency of the wartime United Nations that operated from November 1943 until its disbandment in June 1947. During this period UNRRA expended nearly $4 billion, and at the peak of its activity it employed 27,800 persons. The initiative, the basic planning, and 70 percent of the funds came from the United States, but the implementation involved the concerted action of many governments. Food, clothing, and medicine supplied by UNRRA filled a critical need of millions in Europe and Asia. In China alone, direct food relief was provided to an estimated ten million people. The process of rehabilitation also extended to the revival of agricultural and industrial production and to the support of public health programs, public education, and other social services. In addition, UNRRA assumed the responsibility of caring for millions of refugees and displaced persons.

UNRRA was terminated somewhat precipitately because the U.S. Congress decided to stop funding the organization. Congressional support had been undermined by persistent charges, not altogether unjustified, of UNRRA inefficiency and "political intrigue" and by a suspicion that the Soviet Union was using UNRRA aid to consolidate its hold on Eastern Europe. Whatever the justification for dumping UNRRA, its demise created an alarming gap in the world's machinery for economic and social defense, and provision was made for the assumption of UNRRA functions by other organizations wherever possible. On the initiative of the UN General Assembly, an International Refugee Organization (IRO) was established to deal with the continuing refugee problem; a UN International Children's Emergency Fund (UNICEF), supported by private donations and voluntary government contributions, was created to administer relief programs for children in the war-devastated areas;

and the United Nations itself assumed responsibility for the advisory social welfare services. Portions of the health program were picked up by the World Health Organization.

Korean Relief and Reconstruction.   War in Korea provided the setting for another UN relief operation of substantial proportions. Under a Security Council authorization the UN Unified Command administered a $450 million program of civilian and refugee relief. The U.S. government contributed more than $400 million of the total sum, and American private agencies provided about half of the remainder. A longer-range program of reconstruction was authorized in December 1950 by a General Assembly resolution that established the UN Korean Reconstruction Agency (UNKRA). By the time UNKRA operations were phased out in 1960, to be replaced by massive amounts of direct American aid, approximately $150 million had been expended for the rehabilitation of the Korean economy and public services. The United States limited itself to 65 percent of the total UNKRA budget.[25] Unlike some countries that have absorbed large amounts of UN and U.S. aid, South Korea experienced remarkable postwar economic growth and industrialization, a genuine developing country success story.

UNICEF.   The UN Children's Fund was established in 1946 as a temporary organization to administer residual funds left over from UNRRA. Over the years, the approach that was so satisfactory in assisting the children of war-devastated areas has proved adaptable to the problems of developing countries as well. The General Assembly responded by placing the organization on a permanent basis in 1953. The words *International* and *Emergency* were deleted from the title when it was given permanent status, but the acronym UNICEF was retained in preference to a less pronounceable UNCF. The budget of UNICEF is raised mainly through voluntary government contributions, although a substantial portion comes through private donations and the sale of greeting cards. The fund has its own thirty-nation executive board, elected by ECOSOC, and its executive director and staff are a unit of the UN Secretariat.

The initial program emphasis on emergency supplies of food, clothing, and medicines has shifted toward emphasis on longer-range programs for the benefit of children. UNICEF is still a source of drugs, insecticides, vaccines, and field equipment for disease control campaigns, as well as food and medical supplies in emergency situations. But it is no longer simply a supply program. UNICEF's grants-in-aid, usually matched by two or three times as much in local funds, are now available to governments for help in planning projects and training national personnel. As a condition of a grant, a government must agree to conduct the program as part of its permanent services if the need persists. UNICEF does not operate projects of its own, although it supervises the national programs it sponsors. UNICEF-aided projects are often conducted with the advice and cooperation of such other UN agencies as WHO, FAO, UNESCO, and the ILO. Joint endeavors have included mass disease control, family education in better nutrition practices, teacher training and the local production of teaching materials, and the establishment of child welfare services. UNICEF, aided by the International Red Cross, has coordinated most of the Western humanitarian assistance to Kampuchea in the wake of its domestic upheavals and the 1978 Vietnamese invasion. In 1965 UNICEF received the Nobel Peace Prize for its work on behalf of children.

Disaster Relief. Earthquakes, floods, famine, and other natural disasters have commonly evoked emergency aid from international sources, both public and private. Such aid has necessarily been provided on an ad hoc basis because the precipitating event is always unplanned. As early as 1965 the United Nations provided a small fund for use by the Secretary-General in meeting emergency needs arising from natural disasters. An Office of the Disaster Relief Coordinator (UNDRO) was established in 1971 following a particularly disastrous earthquake in Peru and a tidal wave in Bangladesh the preceding year. UNDRO administers a fund for emergency relief, maintained on a continuing basis through voluntary contributions. It also provides planning assistance to prevent and minimize damage in countries subject to recurring natural disasters. It is not used to administer larger-scale relief operations, however. When famine reached crisis proportions in Ethiopia and other parts of Africa during the 1980s, the Secretary-General created a special Office of Emergency Operations in Africa (OEOA) to mobilize international aid, while UNDRO served a primarily reporting function.

Refugees

The problem of the refugee is not unique to the twentieth century, but sustained intergovernmental cooperation in dealing with it is a hallmark of our era. Governments have tried to regard refugees as a series of temporary problems, each capable of a discrete solution, but from a world perspective the existence of refugees in substantial numbers has become a continuing fact of life.

Refugees and the League. In 1921 the League of Nations established the office of High Commissioner for Refugees as a temporary agency to deal with the influx of nearly two million refugees from the Russian civil war into countries of Eastern and Central Europe. The hard shell of the problem had scarcely been dented when new streams of Greek, Armenian, and Assyrian refugees began to pour out of Turkey, beginning in 1922. The League High Commissioner was still attempting to cope with these problems when the Nazi persecutions of the 1930s produced a new flow of refugees from the Saar, Austria, and Czechoslovakia. The League agency was intended to be temporary, but the problem was continuous and recurrent.

The homeless multitudes of the interwar period needed legal and political protection as well as relief and assistance with resettlement. The League High Commissioner and his small staff, however, never had the resources needed to render direct assistance on any significant scale. On a meager budget they could do little more than serve as an advocate with governments, work for uniform standards of legal protection, give advice to national governments, and attempt to coordinate the efforts of public and private agencies engaged in refugee relief. In the legal field one notable contribution was the Nansen passport, named after Fridtjof Nansen, the first League High Commissioner. This was a certificate issued to refugees by a national government on the recommendation of the High Commissioner; it served as the equivalent of a regular passport and greatly facilitated refugee travel throughout Europe.

Refugees and World War II. World War II produced new millions of homeless persons in Europe, and the responsibility for massive relief and repatriation was undertaken by military authorities and UNRRA. Of some eight million refugees and displaced persons in Allied-occupied zones at the time of the German surrender, five to six million were repatriated within a year through the prodigious efforts of military authorities, and numerous others were assimilated or resettled. UNRRA repatriated an additional 750,000 refugees during its lifetime. A special problem was created by the increasingly large group of persons who refused to be repatriated, particularly those who feared to return to countries dominated by newly ascendant Communist regimes.

The International Refugee Organization. The IRO began operations in July 1947 as a UN specialized agency. During its term of existence, which expired in February 1952, the IRO spent nearly $400 million in assisting more than 1,600,000 refugees who came under its mandate in Africa, the Americas, Asia, and Europe. Approximately 73,000 were repatriated, and more than a million were resettled abroad through the active advocacy and assistance of the IRO. At the termination of the IRO, most of the refugees remaining from its original mandate were of the "hard core" groups—the sick, the aged, and the infirm—for whom resettlement was especially difficult. A number of states urged that the IRO be continued beyond 1952, but the United States, which underwrote more than half of the IRO budget, insisted on the early termination date, claiming that the problem was small enough to be handled by the countries of asylum and by voluntary organizations.[26]

The UN High Commissioner. In anticipation of the IRO's demise, the General Assembly created the Office of UN High Commissioner for Refugees (UNHCR) to serve as a continuing focus for UN refugee activities. Commencing operations in 1951, the High Commissioner was given the assignment of providing international protection for refugees and assisting governments and voluntary organizations to find permanent solutions through resettlement and assimilation. His present mandate excludes refugees receiving aid from other UN programs (such as the Palestine refugees) and refugees who have the rights of nationals in the country of asylum (for example, refugees from India to Pakistan, and vice versa, or East Germans seeking asylum in West Germany). Otherwise the mandate extends to nearly all persons outside their country of origin whose "well-founded fear of persecution for reasons of race, religion, nationality, or political opinion" prevents them from seeking the protection of the home country.

The High Commissioner's primary responsibility of providing international protection is carried out by promoting the adoption and supervising the application of international conventions and by encouraging governments to take other measures for the benefit of refugees. Of special importance is the 1951 Convention Relating to the Status of Refugees and its 1966 protocol, which codify minimum rights in such matters as freedom of religion, access to courts, the right to work, education, social security, and travel documents. The High Commissioner also provides material assistance to refugees from funds made available by voluntary contributions. In relation to needs, his funds have been very modest, although they have increased substantially in recent years. In 1965 UNHCR expenditures amounted to $3.6 million. In 1985 the figure approached $500 million.[27]

In the 1980s Africa has been the locale of major UN refugee relief efforts.[28] An estimated three million refugees were located in Ethiopia, Somalia, the Sudan, Burundi, Rwanda, Uganda, Tanzania, Zaire, Angola, Zambia, and other African countries.[29] Their needs were highlighted by two International Conferences for Assistance to Refugees in Africa, held in 1981 (ICARA I) and 1984 (ICARA II). In a broader perspective, the refugees were simply one highly visible aspect of the emergency brought on by years of extended drought and other natural disasters, political turmoil, and economic mismanagement that had made Africa, by the mid-1980s, the object of world concern and concerted relief efforts. ICARA II specifically recognized that the solution to refugee relief was closely tied to the development and revitalization of African economies.

Substantial refugee problems continue to plague other parts of the world. In 1986 thousands of refugees from Kampuchea remained unrepatriated, more than three million Afghans had taken refuge in Pakistan and Iran, and the number of Central American refugees continued to mount. The UN High Commissioner was also concerned with smaller groups of refugees in other parts of the world. With problems on so grand a scale, the High Commissioner can make only a marginal contribution to the material needs of refugees. His primary role remains that of coordinator, initiator, and catalyst in programs supported largely by individual governments, voluntary agencies, and other international organizations.[30] His effectiveness in carrying out these tasks has been twice recognized by the award of the Nobel Peace Prize, in 1954 and again in 1981.

Palestine Refugees.   Since 1949 a UN Relief and Works Agency for Palestine Refugees in the Near East (UNRWA) has cared for refugee victims of Arab-Israeli conflict.[31] Over the years it has absorbed far more money than any other UN refugee program and yet has brought no final solution. UNRRA, the IRO, and the High Commissioner have had the satisfaction of seeing old refugee groups diminish through repatriation, resettlement, and assimilation, even though new needs have arisen from new refugee groups. But UNRWA, which started with approximately 900,000 Arabs who fled their homes in 1948, had more than two million persons on its rolls in 1986, located in Jordan, Syria, Lebanon, and the Gaza Strip. The increase was largely a result of population growth, although 300,000 new refugees were added at the time of the 1967 war. Thirty-five percent of the Palestine refugees continue to live in camps in the occupied territories and the Arab host countries.

In its early years UNRWA concentrated on providing food, shelter, and clothing to homeless refugees. As larger numbers became self-supporting, its emphasis shifted to longer-term programs. Until a major policy change in 1982, UNRWA was supplying basic rations to nearly half of the refugees, as well as attempting to provide health services, education, and vocational training. In 1982 distribution of food to most refugees was discontinued in order to concentrate available scarce resources on education and health services. Of a projected 1986 budget of $191 million, some 75 percent was allotted to education, 18 percent to health care, and 8 percent to relief.[32] With seventeen thousand Palestinian employees, ten thousand of them teachers, UNRWA is the largest single operating program within the UN system. In recent years contributions have usually fallen short of projected requirements. UNRWA operations have also been hampered by periodic wars in the region, which have disrupted refugee operations and produced new refugees. Lack of organized political authority in parts of Lebanon has made UNRWA's task in that area especially difficult in recent years.

The root of the continuing problem is political rather than economic. Arab governments insist that a Palestinian state be established in territories occupied by Israel after the 1967 war, with compensation or repatriation—at the refugee's option—for pre-1967 refugees. These demands have been reaffirmed in many General Assembly resolutions. Israel, on the other hand, thus far refuses to give up the occupied West Bank and regards mass repatriation as absolutely inconsistent with its national security. Resettling the majority of the refugees in Arab lands, with Israel obligated to accept some and to compensate the rest for property losses, would perhaps be a sensible long-range solution. But the relationship of Arab states with Israel has not been characterized by much goodwill or good sense. As more and more refugees leave the camps and become self-supporting, and as new generations are born, a de facto resettlement is in fact occurring. Without a political settlement and the full integration of refugees into the life of the national communities in which they reside, however, they remain a continuing threat to the stability of the region as well as an object of humanitarian concern. Meanwhile, UNRWA carries on a thankless task, criticized for not doing more while financial contributors grow restive in support of a relief operation that has no end in sight.

CONCLUSION

The contribution of expanding functional cooperation to international peace and security is highly speculative, but its contribution to economic and social well-being is subject to more concrete evaluation. Where interstate transactions have been of a sufficiently technical and noncontroversial character, as in communication and transportation, the UN system has provided widely accepted standards for national conduct. In the field of human rights, where the issue is less one of international cooperation than one of the conduct of the state within its own borders, standards have been set but not well observed. Even here a little progress in securing compliance has been made, and the record of the ILO in upgrading labor standards has been quite respectable. In the special area of the law of the sea, UN forums have contributed to a remarkable alteration of rules governing the use of the oceans and seabeds. International agencies have also promoted the exchange of useful information, and the services they render can stand on their own merits. While most human needs are being met by individual and group action organized within a national setting, UN operations have in many local situations provided a significant margin of difference for the war victim, the refugee, the socially underprivileged, and the economically deprived.

The tradition of decentralization bequeathed to the UN system has continued unabated, along with a steady proliferation of new agencies. This situation has given rise to criticisms of overlapping, duplication of effort, and nonrational overall allocation of resources. There is no world budget for economic and social affairs. The United Nations and each specialized agency sets its own budget and program within limits that its membership will collectively permit. The Economic and Social Council was supposed to have a central coordinating function, but in practice it has been limited to discussion and liaison. Theoretically, governments could bring coordination to the system since the same governments for the most part hold membership in all the agencies of the UN system. But national governments are pluralistic institutions as well, and governmental policy toward a particular international function tends to be set by the government department with an interest in that function, whether health, education, oceans, or international trade. Governmental representatives to different international agencies often speak with different voices. If governments do not always coordinate their own policies effectively, there is little hope that they will provide effective coordination of the programs of many international agencies.

Some mitigating circumstances exist. Although no organization has the capacity to impose coordination, a degree of coordination has been introduced by cooperation across agency lines. An Administrative Committee on Coordination provides a forum in which representatives of the UN and specialized agency secretariats at the highest level can attempt to achieve a substantive meshing of their programs as well as greater uniformity in administrative matters. An International Civil Service Advisory Board, which serves the entire UN system, has helped establish uniformity in position classification, salaries and allowances, and pensions. Organizations engaged in related activities regularly interact at one another's meetings. Intersecretariat liaison, by means of committees and other devices, is a standard operating procedure.

In defense of the system, one might even argue that the present pluralistic state of international society defies consensus on any rational criteria for overall allocation as between regional and universal levels and among individual programs on the same level. Greater centralization of resource allocation could result in different but not necessarily more rational matching of resources to needs.

The most formidable barriers to improved functional cooperation are in fact political, not organizational. Despite the lack of central coordination, and persistent complaints about entrenched international bureaucracies, existing organizational forms have proved serviceable enough to hold all the international cooperation that states have been willing to pour into them. East-West and North-South divisions, as well as other political conflicts, have impinged on most of the functional activities, often turning their forums into ideological battlegrounds and shaping their programs to meet sometimes unrelated political criteria. In the long run, functional cooperation may provide cement for the foundations of world peace; but in the short run, functional growth depends on an expansion of the area of political agreement.

NOTES

1. Article 55, which introduces the Charter provisions dealing with international economic and social cooperation, speaks of "the creation of conditions of stability and well-being which are necessary for peaceful and friendly relations among nations."

2. Useful commentaries on functionalist theory include James Patrick Sewell, *Functionalism and World Politics* (Princeton: Princeton University Press, 1960); Ernst B. Haas, *Beyond the Nation-State* (Stanford: Stanford University Press, 1964); A. J. R. Groom and Paul Taylor, eds., *Functionalism: Theory and Practice in International Relations* (London: University of London Press, 1975); and Robert E. Riggs and I. Jostein Mykletun, *Beyond Functionalism* (Minneapolis: University of Minnesota Press, 1979). An excellent brief analysis is "The Functional Approach to Peace," in Inis L. Claude, Jr., *Swords into Plowshares*, 4th ed. (New York: Random House, 1971), pp. 378–407.

3. The theory of international functionalism is distinct from and should not be confused with the concepts of *functionalism* or *structural functionalism* utilized in some theories of social systems and comparative politics. See, e.g., Talcott Parsons, *The Social System* (New York: Free Press, 1951); and Gabriel A. Almond and James S. Coleman, eds., *The Politics of the Developing Areas* (Princeton: Princeton University Press, 1960). For a recent brief survey of the latter theory and its applications in sociology, see Jonathan H. Turner and Alexandra Maryanski, *Functionalism* (Menlo Park, Calif.: Benjamin/Cummings Publishing, 1979).

4. E.g., Simeon E. Baldwin, "The International Congresses and Conferences of the Last Century as Forces Working toward the Solidarity of the World," *American Journal of International Law* 1 (July 1907), pp. 565–78; Paul S. Reinsch, *Public International Unions: Their Work and Organization: A Study in International Administrative Law* (Boston: Ginn, 1911); J. A. Salter, *Allied Shipping Control: An Experiment in International Administration* (Oxford: Clarendon Press, 1921); and Leonard S. Woolf, *International Government: Two Reports* (New York: Brentano, 1916). International functionalism is now most often identified with the Englishman David Mitrany, especially his small book *A Working Peace System: An Argument for the Functional Development of International Organization*, 1st ed. (London: Royal Institute of International Affairs, 1943). Mitrany published on this theme both before and after 1943.

5. Mitrany, *A Working Peace System* (Chicago: Quadrangle Books, 1966), p. 69. The Quadrangle Books edition is the most accessible version of Mitrany's classic.

6. Although functionalism is a flawed predictive theory and rests on several questionable premises, it has influenced a good deal of research in international political economy and regimes, topics of much current theoretical interest. See, for example, Robert O. Keohane and Joseph S. Nye, *Power and Interdependence* (Boston: Little, Brown, 1977); and Stephen D. Krasner, *Structural Conflict: The Third World against Global Liberalism* (Berkeley: University of California Press, 1985). Theories of international integration are also indebted to functionalism. See, for example, Lèon N. Lindberg and Stuart A. Scheingold, *Regional Integration: Theory and Research* (Cambridge, Mass.: Harvard University Press, 1970).

7. For a discussion of this issue, see Evan Luard, *International Agencies: The Emerging Framework of Interdependence* (London: Macmillan, 1977), pp. 264–87. Luard's chapter on "The Coordination of International Government" is prefaced with this comment: "This teeming family of international agencies, each seeking to organize world services in its own specialized field, has brought

with it a new problem, much discussed but never solved: the need for securing effective coordination among them." Ibid., p. 264.

8. For a more detailed classification of organization functions and decisions, see Robert W. Cox and Harold K. Jacobson, "The Framework for Inquiry," in Cox and Jacobson, *The Anatomy of Influence: Decision Making in International Organization* (New Haven: Yale University Press, 1973), pp. 8–11; and Harold K. Jacobson, *Networks of Interdependence* 2nd ed. (New York: Alfred A. Knopf, 1984), pp. 81–83.

9. *Report of the Secretary-General*, UN Document A/38/1 (1983), p. 3.

10. Students of the subject have been divided about how impartial or balanced UN forums have been in their treatment of the two basic categories of rights—civil and political, on the one hand, and economic, on the other. Some Western critics have complained that civil and political rights have been overshadowed by UN emphasis on economic and social concerns. The respective positions are outlined in Jack Donnelly, "Recent Trends in UN Human Rights Activity: Description and Polemic," *International Organization* 35, no. 4 (Autumn 1981), pp. 633–55; and Philip Alston, "The Alleged Demise of Political Human Rights at the UN: A Reply to Donnelly," *International Organization* 47, no. 3 (Summer 1983), pp. 537–46.

11. John Gerard Ruggie, "Human Rights and the Future International Community," *Daedalus* 112, no. 4 (Fall 1983), p. 106.

12. *Filartiga* v. *Pena-Irala*, 630 F. 2d 876 (2d Cir. 1980); and see *Rodriguez-Fernandez* v. *Wilkinson*, 505 F. Supp. 787 (D. Kan. 1980), which referred to the Universal Declaration in holding arbitrary prolonged detention of an alien to be proscribed by international law.

13. The development of an international law of human rights, through the United Nations as well as through other instrumentalities, is detailed in Theodore Meron, *Human Rights in International Law*, 2 vols. (Oxford: Clarendon Press, 1984).

14. For a balanced but generally optimistic appraisal of UN efforts to promote human rights, see David P. Forsythe, "The United Nations and Human Rights, 1945–1985," *Political Science Quarterly* 100, no. 2 (Summer 1985), pp. 249–69.

15. Forsythe, "United Nations and Human Rights," regards NGO activity as "one of the main reasons why the United Nations record on human rights" has become more balanced in the 1980s. See also Virginia Leary, "A New Role for Nongovernmental Organizations in Human Rights," in *U.N. Law/Fundamental Rights*, ed. Antonio Cassese (Alphen aan den Rijn: Sijthoff & Noordhoff, 1979), pp. 197–210; and Nigel S. Rodley, "The Development of United Nations Activities in the Field of Human Rights and the Role of Non-Governmental Organization," in *The US, the UN, and the Management of Global Change*, ed. Toby Grister Gati (New York: New York University Press, 1983), pp. 263–82.

16. L. S. Woolf, *International Government* (London: Allen & Unwin, 1916).

17. The most extensive treatment of the Universal Postal Union is George A. Codding, Jr., *The Universal Postal Union* (New York: New York University Press, 1964).

18. Two useful studies of the ITU are George A. Codding, Jr., and Anthony M. Rutkowski, *The International Telecommunications Union in a Changing World* (Dedham, Mass.: Artech House, 1982); and David M. Leive, *International Telecommunications and International Law: The Regulation of the Radiospectrum* (Dobbs Ferry, N.Y.: Oceana Publications, 1970).

19. A good discussion of ICAO rule-making is Thomas Buergenthal, *Law-Making in the International Civil Aviation Organization* (Syracuse: Syracuse University Press, 1969). For a more politically oriented study, see Young W. Kihl, *Conflict Issues and International Civil Aviation Decisions: Three Case Studies* (Denver: University of Denver Press, 1971).

20. An often-cited work on the WHO is Robert Berkov, *The World Health Organization: A Study in Decentralized International Administration* (Geneva: Librairie E. Droz, 1957). More recent treatments are Peter Corrigan, *The World Health Organization* (Hove, Eng.: Wayland Publishers, 1979); and David Leive, *International Regulatory Regimes*, vol. 1 (Lexington, Mass.: D. C. Heath, 1976), pp. 1–152.

21. The WHO regular budget for 1986–87 was $554 million, with additional sums for special projects from the UN Development Program, the UN Fund for Population Assistance, and voluntary con-

tributions. *The Europa Yearbook, 1986: A World Survey*, vol. 1 (London: Europa Publications, 1986), p. 87.

22. The best source on the new law of the sea is the Convention itself. It is available in various official and nonofficial formats. One readily available commercial edition is *The Law of the Sea: United Nations Convention on the Law of the Sea, with Index and Final Act of the Third United Nations Conference on the Law of the Sea* (New York: St. Martin's Press, 1984). Useful commentaries on the subject, emphasizing the U.S. perspective, are Bernard Oxman, David Caron, and Charles Buderi, eds., *Law of the Sea: U.S. Policy Dilemma* (San Francisco: ICS Press, 1983); and Ann L. Hollick, *U.S. Foreign Policy and the Law of the Sea* (Princeton: Princeton University Press, 1981).

23. By early 1987, 32 ratifications had been deposited with the UN Secretary-General.

24. See *Interdependent* 10, no. 4 (July–August 1984), p. 4.

25. The United Nations also helped mobilize and coordinate a massive relief operation in Bangladesh, 1971–73, to alleviate some of the human hardship accompanying Bangladesh's violent accession to independence. Aid from bilateral, multilateral, and private sources, coordinated by the UN Relief Operation in Dacca (UNROD), exceeded $1.3 billion. See Thomas W. Oliver, *The United Nations in Bangladesh* (Princeton: Princeton University Press, 1978).

26. The standard work on the IRO is Louise W. Holborn, *The International Refugee Organization* (London: Oxford University Press, 1956).

27. The *Report of the United Nations High Commissioner for Refugees*, UN Document A/40/12 (1985), p. 22, listed expenditures of $458.6 million in 1984. Increased demands were anticipated for 1985.

28. See Ved P. Nanda, "The African Refugee Dilemma: A Challenge for International Law and Policy," *Africa Today* 32, nos. 1–2 (1985), pp. 61–75.

29. *UN Chronicle* 21 (October–November 1984), p. 10. The *World Refugee Survey, 1984* (New York: U.S. Committee for Refugees, 1984), put the figure at 2.6 million. According to the *Survey*, the estimated number of refugees worldwide in need of assistance was 9,091,000. Most of them were in Africa, South Asia (Afghan refugees), and the Middle East (Palestinian refugees).

30. The first two decades of the UNHCR are recounted in Louise W. Holborn, *Refugees—A Problem of Our Time: The Work of the United Nations High Commissioner for Refugees, 1951–1972*, 2 vols. (Metuchen, N.J.: Scarecrow Press, 1975). A recent short survey is Shelley Pilterman, "International Responses to Refugee Situations," in *Refugees and World Politics*, ed. Elizabeth G. Ferris (New York: Praeger Publishers, 1985), pp. 43–81. The international legal status of refugees is treated in Guy S. Goodwin-Gill, *The Refugee in International Law* (Oxford: Clarendon Press, 1983).

31. UNRWA became operative in early 1950, supplanting the UN Relief for Palestine Refugees (UNRPR), which had been established by the General Assembly in November 1948. See Milton Viorst, *UNRWA and Peace in the Middle East* (Washington, D.C.: The Middle East Institute, 1984).

32. *UN Chronicle* 23, no. 1 (January 1986), p. 56. The figures add to 101 percent, apparently due to rounding within each category. A slightly different breakdown of proposed 1986 expenditures is found in *Report of the Commissioner-General of UNRWA*, UN Document A/40/13/Add 1 (1985), p. 3, which includes separate categories for administrative expenses and capital construction.

SELECTED READINGS

BERKOV, ROBERT. *The World Health Organization: A Study in Decentralized International Administration*. Geneva: Librairie E. Droz, 1957.

BOOTH, KEN. *Law, Force, and Diplomacy at Sea*. London: Allen & Unwin, 1985.

BUEHRIG, EDWARD H. *The UN and the Palestinian Refugees: A Study in Non-Territorial Administration*. Bloomington: Indiana University Press, 1971.

BUERGENTHAL, THOMAS. *Law-Making in the International Civil Aviation Organization*. Syracuse: Syracuse University Press, 1969.

CODDING, GEORGE A., JR. *The Universal Postal Union*. New York: New York University Press, 1964.

CODDING, GEORGE A., JR., and ANTHONY M. RUTKOWSKI. *The International Telecommunications Union in a Changing World*. Dedham, Mass.: Artech House, 1982.

CORRIGAN, PETER. *The World Health Organization*. Hove, Eng.: Wayland Publishers, 1979.

COX, ROBERT W., and HAROLD K. JACOBSON. *The Anatomy of Influence: Decision Making in International Organization*. New Haven: Yale University Press, 1973.

CUÉLLAR, JAVIER PÉREZ DE. *United Nations Action in the Field of Human Rights*. New York: Unipub, 1985.

DONNELLY, JACK. *The Concept of Human Rights*. New York: St. Martin's Press, 1985.

FERRIS, ELIZABETH G., ed. *Refugees and World Politics*. New York: Praeger Publishers, 1985.

FORSYTHE, DAVID P. *Human Rights and World Politics*. Lincoln: University of Nebraska Press, 1983.

GALENSON, WALTER. *The International Labor Organization: An American View*. Madison: University of Wisconsin Press, 1981.

GOODWIN-GILL, GUY S. *The Refugee in International Law*. Oxford: Clarendon Press, 1983.

HAAS, ERNST B. *Beyond the Nation-State: Functionalism and International Organization*. Stanford: Stanford University Press, 1964.

HENKIN, LOUIS, ed. *The International Bill of Rights: The Covenant on Civil and Political Rights*. New York: Columbia University Press, 1981.

HILL, MARTIN. *The United Nations System: Coordinating Its Economic and Social Work*. Cambridge: Cambridge University Press, 1978.

HOLBORN, LOUISE W. *The International Refugee Organization*. London: Oxford University Press, 1956.

————. *Refugees—A Problem of Our Time: The Work of the United Nations High Commissioner for Refugees, 1951–1972*. 2 vols. Metuchen, N.J.: Scarecrow Press, 1975.

HOLLICK, ANN L. *U.S. Foreign Policy and the Law of the Sea*. Princeton: Princeton University Press, 1981.

JACOBSON, HAROLD K. *Networks of Interdependence*. 2nd ed. New York: Alfred A. Knopf, 1984.

JOYCE, JAMES AVERY. *World Labour Rights and Their Protection*. London: Croom Helm, 1980.

LEIVE, DAVID M. *International Regulatory Regimes*. 2 vols. Lexington, Mass.: D. C. Heath, 1976.

————. *International Telecommunications and International Law: The Regulation of the Radiospectrum*. Dobbs Ferry, N.Y.: Oceana Publications, 1970.

LUARD, EVAN. *International Agencies: The Emerging Framework of Interdependence*. London: Macmillan, 1977.

MERON, THEODORE, ed. *Human Rights in International Law*. 2 vols. Oxford: Clarendon Press, 1984.

MORSE, DAVID A. *The Origin and Evolution of the ILO and Its Role in the World Community*. Ithaca, N.Y.: Cornell University Press, 1969.

MOWER, A. GLENN, JR. *International Cooperation for Social Justice*. Westport, Conn.: Greenwood Press, 1985.

————. *The United States, the United Nations, and Human Rights*. Westport, Conn.: Greenwood Press, 1979.

OXMAN, BERNARD; DAVID CARON; and CHARLES BUDERI, eds. *Law of the Sea: U.S. Policy Dilemma*. San Francisco: ICS Press, 1983.

ROBERTSON, ARTHUR H. *Human Rights in the World: An Introduction to the International Protection of Human Rights*. New York: St. Martin's Press, 1982.

SEBENIUS, JAMES K. *Negotiating the Law of the Sea*. Cambridge, Mass.: Harvard University Press, 1984.

SEWELL, JAMES P. *UNESCO and World Politics*. Princeton: Princeton University Press, 1975.

VAN DYKE, VERNON. *Human Rights, the United States, and the World Community*. London: Oxford University Press, 1970.

10

Managing International Trade and Finance

In the UN world of international economic activity, the French aphorism *Plus ça change, plus c'est la même chose* (The more things change, the more they remain the same) seems applicable and appropriate. Although a great many new approaches and action programs have been created by the United Nations over many years, the problems besetting member countries remain. Many such problems, in fact, are in much the same form, although in varying intensities, as they were when UN institutions and programs were created to cope with them. Two thirds of the world's peoples, for example, continue to live in grinding poverty in the countries of Africa, Asia, Oceania, and Latin America. Millions suffer from malnutrition or are on the verge of starvation. Populations continue to soar despite some moderation in birthrates, and urban centers groan under the influx of millions of unwanted migrants who are no longer able to survive in the countryside. Inflation, in some societies reaching as high as 400 to 500 percent in a single year, is endemic in the world. Trade has increased tremendously, but serious balance of trade and balance of payments problems remain for most countries. Debt, which has grown steadily during the UN era, has reached astronomical levels for some nations, creating major problems for lenders and debtors alike. Protectionism, that ill-starred economic approach of the Great Depression period, continues to plague trade relationships, and the search for monetary and exchange rate stability goes on.

The continued existence of these problems, some in increasingly virulent form despite the extensive range of UN actions to cope with them, emphasizes their difficult nature and the limits of resolving economic issues through international cooperation. One can only guess what the state of the world would be without the UN system or some similar international framework devoted to harmonizing economic relationships. Without some such institutional cooperation in the state system, a dog-eat-dog kind of economic nationalism might prevail.

Before attempting to evaluate the UN role in the field of economics, however, the reader must first be willing to examine the background and nature of the major economic problems of the global system. Such information makes possible a more meaningful evaluation of the policies, programs, and institutions by which the UN system (including its entire "family" of specialized agencies and other semiautonomous bodies) attempts to come to grips with these perplexing problems. In this chapter we are concerned with the efforts of the United Nations and its related agencies to build an international milieu receptive to the fulfillment of the economic potential of all states. The next chapter will focus on the special problems of economic development and modernization in Third World states and on the role of the UN system in meeting these challenges.

EARLY ECONOMIC MODELS

From the sixteenth century to the latter part of the eighteenth century, a state-dominated system of mercantilism pervaded the economic scene in the Western world. Both domestic and foreign economic activity were regulated and directed by government in support of state power. Each state sought to enhance its power and security by amassing treasures of precious metals useful to buy off opponents and to hire mercenary troops for military campaigns. The major objective of trade was to achieve a favorable balance that would enable states to enlarge their national treasuries through an international payments system that settled accounts by transfers of gold and silver.

In the latter part of the mercantilist era, a rising class of merchants and entrepreneurs began to use its political and economic influence to demand greater measures of economic freedom. The American Revolution, although justified by the new political doctrines of freedom and democracy, was fundamentally a reaction against the mother country's narrowly restrictive trade and tax policies. These policies were aimed at keeping the colonies functioning within the mercantilist framework as suppliers of cheap raw materials and as a market restricted to high-priced British manufactures. It was not an accident of history that Adam Smith published his *Wealth of Nations* in the same year that the American colonists declared their independence. The new liberalism, grounded in the philosophy of laissez-faire, broke down internal restrictions in European states and, following the Napoleonic Wars, fostered the development of an international trading system embracing the concept of free trade. International market forces replaced the dictates of government officials in shaping national specialization and the direction of trade. Under the new system trade flourished and Europe became an industrial and commercial center for the entire world.

The rebirth of economic nationalism in the twentieth century signaled that the long period of relatively free trade was coming to an end. World War I accelerated this movement, and the economic dislocation and rivalry fostered by four years of hostilities carried over to undermine the efforts of political and economic leaders to return to the relatively stable period of the nineteenth century. Attempts to regain stability centered on restoring the unity formerly provided by the gold standard and the British pound sterling. Neither effort was wholly successful; Britain failed during the 1920s to regain the economic strength it had wasted during the war, and the gold standard, functioning out of the London money market, reflected this weakness. Some semblance of free trade was regained by the latter part of the decade, however, and monetary stability appeared within reach by 1928.

The American stock market crash in 1929 and the deepening world depression of the early 1930s dealt a deathblow to hopes of restoring the stability of the prewar era. They ushered in a period of economic nationalism whose intensity was even greater than that of the heyday of mercantilism. The traumatic shock to domestic and international economic institutions produced by the Great Depression was probably matched only by the mass psychological depression that came in its wake. The world of the 1930s was poised on the brink of revolution—economic, social, and political. Millions were unemployed, the economic plant of most countries stagnated, and politicians and statesmen alike groped blindly for solutions to mounting problems. The natural reaction of most leaders was to protect the national economy from foreign competition and to open up bigger foreign markets so as to absorb the growing surpluses resulting from insufficient domestic demand. That these policies of economic nationalism were contradictory made little difference; popular demand for policies of short-range advantage or retaliation could not be resisted.

The multilateral trading system of the nineteenth century, with its relatively low tariffs, virtually disappeared during the 1930s. Although some semblance of a world market economy continued to function, it was rigidly circumscribed by the neo-mercantilist practices of governments. High tariffs became endemic in all countries, and quota restrictions permitting only small amounts of foreign goods to enter the domestic market buttressed the high tariffs in most countries. The use by some countries of currency depreciation to achieve trade advantage was followed by equal or greater depreciation in scores of other countries. Subsidies for domestic producers, state licensing of importers, barter agreements, preferential trade arrangements, quotas, and exchange control were freely used in desperate efforts to stimulate or protect economic activity. Such devices often provided only a brief stimulus, and they were bitterly resented by trading partners as "beggar thy neighbor" policies aimed at improving a nation's economic position at the expense of other nations. Retaliation became the guiding principle for state economic policy, growing ever stronger by feeding on itself. Feeble attempts to arrest the cycle of economic nationalism through League of Nations–sponsored world monetary and trade conferences and the U.S.-sponsored reciprocal trade agreement tariff reduction system produced much verbal support but little action for a return of the trading system from its unilateral and bilateral nature to its former multilateral basis. The division of labor and free trade postulated by Adam Smith as the basis for national productivity disappeared except as ideals for a future world economy.

REBUILDING THE WORLD ECONOMY

World War II arrested the trend toward the unilateral and bilateral determination of economic policies. Under American leadership the Allies implemented a system of economic cooperation to facilitate the war effort and laid plans for rebuilding a working multilateral trading system when peace was restored. Unlike the laissez-faire economy of the nineteenth century, the new liberalized world economy was to be constructed by building regional and global institutions to facilitate agreement on trade, monetary, and investment matters. The new approach offered a compromise between the requirements of a free-trading system and the growing role of government to provide economic stability.

One individual—John Maynard Keynes, an English economist—assumed a natural leadership in the planning process. Keynes's ideas, expounded in numerous articles and books, placed major emphasis on utilizing the fiscal and monetary policies of government to guide and direct a free enterprise economy. The Great Depression, according to Keynes, had lasted a decade because *government* had failed to provide the policies and programs that could have ended it much sooner. His prescriptions for the continued health of national economies were avidly followed by economic planners and governments, so much so that his theories and approaches led to the coining of the term *Keynesianism* to describe them. Lord Keynes (he was made a member of the British nobility in recognition of his contributions to the field of economics) also functioned as the major planner of the post-World War II global economy. It was his firm belief that governmental institutions must play a major role in guiding and directing international as well as domestic economic activity. In the absence of world government, cooperative institutions must be constructed so that common policies could be developed that would lend strength and flexibility to the global economy.

Keynes proposed that the central international economic institutions should in effect constitute a three-legged stool created to support the postwar world economy. The first leg was to be the International Monetary Fund (IMF), with responsibility for maintaining currency exchange stability and for helping member nations deal with short-term disequilibriums in their balances of payments. The second leg was to be the International Bank for Reconstruction and Development, with responsibility for aiding in the reconstruction of war-devastated areas and in the modernization of the underdeveloped countries. The third leg, recognized by Keynes and others as politically the most difficult to secure agreement on, was to be an International Trade Organization (ITO) that would reduce or eliminate tariffs and other barriers to trade and would develop a set of rules to govern trade behavior. The three institutions were expected to function within the general framework of the UN system.

But more was needed than optimism and Keynesian plans for a bright new world of plenty. At war's end, the problems created during the era of economic nationalism remained major hurdles to the reestablishment of a multilateral trading system. Added to them were the problems that had grown out of the devastation and dislocation caused by the war itself. Ideological dangers, too, lurked amid the chaos and despair of Europe; the masses were fearful of a short-lived capitalist recovery that would soon return them to the prewar days of unemployment and general depression, and the middle class believed that the danger of communism from within or outside the state was very real. To meet these problems, planners identified six areas needing immediate attention by the new United Nations: (1) the economic recovery of Europe and other areas suffering economic deprivation from the war must be assigned the highest priority; (2) global trade must be returned to a rational basis freed of most of the restrictive encumbrances instituted since 1930; (3) international monetary stability must be achieved through the harmonization of exchange rates and the expansion of international liquidity; (4) regional economic cooperation should be fostered so that critical areas of the world could develop a viable economic unity; (5) international investment must be encouraged so that capital would be available to support the reconstruction of war-devastated areas; and (6) massive transfers of resources and technology from rich to poor societies should be made to provide for the economic development of underdeveloped peoples. The first five of these areas will be discussed in this chapter, and the sixth will be covered in the next.

Reconstruction of Western Europe

In the spring of 1945, at the end of World War II, the economic plant of Europe was moribund. Heavy shelling and bombing had destroyed industrial and transport facilities, power supplies were low, food was scarce, raw materials were almost nonexistent, and whole populations were dispersed and homeless. The immediate task, the feeding and housing of millions, was directed by the temporary UN Relief and Rehabilitation Administration (UNRRA), which expended almost $4 billion, much of it in direct aid to needy and homeless refugees. Slowly and painfully, displaced persons were sorted out and returned to their homelands, trains started running again, and rebuilding campaigns got under way. But the major problem remained: Where would Europe obtain the huge amounts of capital needed to restore its economic vitality?

The European Recovery Program

The answer came in a commencement address delivered by Secretary of State George C. Marshall at Harvard University in June 1947, a speech that kindled the spark of hope for millions. Marshall called for a massive injection of American aid into both Western and Eastern Europe, but before the assistance would be granted, Europe had to reach agreement on the amount of aid required and on what each participating state could contribute to the common effort. The Soviet Union rejected the offer to include Eastern Europe in the program and attacked the program as a policy of political interference and economic imperialism. Invited countries that refused to participate included Albania, Bulgaria, Czechoslovakia, Finland, Hungary, Poland, Romania, the Soviet Union, and Yugoslavia. American policymakers then began to push the concept of an integrated Western Europe. They believed that integration would not only restore economic viability to the region but would also build political stability and military defense capability on the new economic base. At a major conference called in the summer of 1947 in response to American initiatives, sixteen West European countries worked out a plan for joint recovery, formed a Committee of European Economic Cooperation (CEEC) to determine individual capital needs, and agreed to cooperate in the reduction of barriers to trade and the free movement of labor. From this impetus emerged a European integration movement that was to attain unprecedented objectives of economic and political unity in an area that for centuries had exuded mutual suspicion and hostility through carefully nurtured nationalisms.

The following year the cooperating sixteen nations established the Organization for European Economic Cooperation (OEEC) as a means for jointly implementing the Marshall Plan and building a sound European economy. The initial members of the OEEC were Austria, Belgium, Britain, Denmark, France, Greece, Iceland, Ireland, Italy, Luxembourg, the Netherlands, Norway, Portugal, Sweden, Switzerland, and Turkey. West Germany participated unofficially and became a member when it was granted independence by the occupying countries. To facilitate the expansion of intra-European trade, the OEEC established the European Payments Union (EPU) in 1950 to provide for a common system of payments among its members. The arrangement worked so well that by the late 1950s full convertibility of OEEC currencies was achieved. This signaled that Western Europe had achieved full recovery from the war. The success of the new institutional approach in lifting Europe from despair to prosperity augured well for its global potential.

THE ATTACK ON TRADE RESTRICTIONS

Early success in promoting Western European cooperation raised hopes that the postwar period might be an appropriate time to launch a major offensive against tariffs and other barriers to trade on a global scale. Tariffs have a depressing effect on world living standards because they violate basic economic principles. An international division of labor with its resulting specialization—the key to higher standards of living in all states—is negated by the artificial restrictions of tariffs, which encourage the development of noncompetitive industries and distort the direction of trade.

Psychological factors have often been more decisive than economic considerations in state decisions to increase barriers to trade. It was the need to change popular attitudes about "protectionism" that presented the most difficult obstacle to proponents of freer trade in the postwar era. The architects of an orderly and relatively free trading system recalled how irresistible public pressures in the United States following the stock market crash in 1929 had forced the enactment by Congress of the Smoot-Hawley Tariff of 1930, with its viciously high protective rates. They remembered, too, how that American action "exported" the depression to other countries in the trading system by touching off worldwide retaliation that resulted in a cycle of deepening restrictionism powered by fear, rising nationalism, and deteriorating domestic conditions. To prevent a recurrence of the 1930 tragedy, two needs became obvious: (1) to establish a world trading organization that would provide an orderly, systematic means by which states could carry on their trading activities and devise common policies; and (2) to use that organization to move the trading world toward freer commercial conditions.

ITO—An American Cul-de-Sac

The United States took the initiative in promoting the first objective by preparing and circulating a preliminary blueprint for a world trade organization. The organization was to be one of the three institutions—along with the World Bank and the International Monetary Fund—that would provide support for the world economy. After preliminary conferences in London and Geneva, a final draft Charter for the International Trade Organization was worked out at the UN Conference on Trade and Employment at Havana in 1948. The Havana Charter represented the most extensive attack ever attempted on barriers to trade. Like the Bank and the Fund, the ITO was to function as a specialized agency within the overall framework of the United Nations. After the Charter was drafted, a struggle over ratification took place in the United States, where battle lines were drawn between the advocates of protectionism and the advocates of liberal trade. An American trade expert who had participated in the writing of the Havana Charter warned:

> The ITO is recognized everywhere as an American project. Our country brought the rest of the world along on it, step by step, over a period of five years. If we were now to abandon it, as we abandoned the League of Nations a generation ago, there is small chance that the world could seriously consider another such program proposed by the United States for years to come.[1]

This warning and others went unheeded. The State Department, after having converted most world leaders to the ITO project, failed to get its message across to the Senate. The old fear that in a free world market American producers might not be able to compete effectively with low-wage producers abroad was exploited by lobbyists and pressure groups in a massive trek to Washington. Other groups attacked the ITO as a Communist plot (despite the fact that Communist states had refused to participate in the ITO Conference) and as an organization that would weaken American sovereignty. These arguments carried the day in Congress. Other nations, cognizant that an ITO without the United States would be like an arch without a keystone, refused to ratify the Charter. The first major effort to establish an institutional basis for trade cooperation within the UN system thus fell victim to the American effort to provide leadership in the postwar world without accepting the responsibilities essential to effective leadership.

GATT—An Innovation Succeeds

While early negotiations for the anticipated ITO were going on, many nations urged an immediate attack on trade barriers through an ad hoc conference that would function as a temporary arrangement until the ITO came into operation. Meeting in Geneva in 1947, twenty-three nations worked out a vast number of bilateral tariff concessions that were written into a final act called the General Agreement on Tariffs and Trade (GATT).

The GATT Conference was an adaptation of the reciprocal trade agreement system inaugurated by Secretary of State Cordell Hull in 1934 and subsequently implemented by most of the world's trading nations. That system provided for bilateral negotiations on a selective product-by-product basis, with all tariff reductions based on the principle of reciprocity. Agreements reached through bilateral bargaining sessions were embodied in trade agreements incorporating the most-favored-nation clause, thus making lower tariff rates applicable to all nations participating in the program as well as the two nations that signed the agreement. This application of the nondiscriminatory, most-favored-nation approach made it an outward-looking program aimed at building a liberal trading system. Although numerous trade agreements had been concluded before 1947, tariffs remained generally high and a speeded-up approach was clearly needed to overcome the hiatus of the war period. The GATT Conference was the means selected for accelerating the program by providing for multilateral participation in a series of simultaneous bilateral bargaining sessions.[2]

The failure of the ITO gave impetus to the GATT approach and led to the establishment of permanent international machinery. Unlike the ITO, GATT is based on executive agreements rather than a treaty, which means that American participation in GATT has not involved the Senate in the ratification process. GATT's role progressively expanded after 1947, and it now serves four major purposes:

1. It is a forum for negotiations on tariff reduction and the progressive elimination of other barriers to trade.
2. It functions as a vehicle for developing and articulating new trade policy.
3. It provides a set of rules that govern the conduct of trade policy.
4. It offers a means for interpreting rules and procedures for the adjustment of trade disputes.

GATT operates under the guidance of its informal steering body, the Consultative Group of Eighteen (CG-18), with a membership of nine developed and nine developing countries. Parity between developed and developing states reflects efforts by the industrialized nations to escape from early Third World charges that GATT functioned largely as a Western organization. CG-18 is charged with maintaining a smooth flow of international trade and is responsible for facilitating balance of payment adjustments by fostering coordination between GATT and the International Monetary Fund. GATT has never been given the full status of a specialized agency; but it functions in much the same manner and reports to the General Assembly through the Economic and Social Council. Although known for many years as "the rich man's club," GATT's current membership of full contracting parties and parties associated with the organization on a limited basis includes two thirds of the world's countries. Its members carry on more than 80 percent of world trade.

The hub of the GATT wheel is the rule against discrimination for imports and exports. Except for established systems of preference, tariffs, quantitative restrictions, and other barriers to trade must be administered without favor under GATT rules. New systems aimed at establishing complete preference—a customs union, a common market, or a free trade area—are permitted only if their basic purpose is "to facilitate trade between the constituent territories and not to raise barriers to the trade of other . . . parties." Such exceptions as the European Community have clearly weakened this principle of nondiscrimination. Seven rounds of negotiations to reduce barriers to trade have been carried on by GATT. Two of these were major campaigns to reduce tariffs: the so-called Kennedy Round of negotiations (1964–67), aimed at keeping the European Community open to world trade, and the Tokyo Round (1973–79), which focused special attention on encouraging trade between the developing and developed countries. Efforts continue to institute a third major round of trade negotiations during the 1980s.[3]

Originally concerned only with tariffs, GATT's rules today are also directed toward limiting the use of quantitative restrictions in imports and other nontariff barriers (NTBs). Import quotas are more rigid barriers to trade than tariffs; a tariff is a tax that increases the price for the consumer, whereas a quota permits only a fixed number of imports, regardless of consumer demand. Exceptions to the general rule against import quotas include (1) states that are suffering from a serious deficit in their balance of payments, (2) developing countries that are using quotas to foster economic advancement, and (3) states that restrict the domestic production and marketing of agricultural and fishery products. Because these exceptions include almost all GATT members (including the United States for the first and third exceptions), emphasis is placed on a requirement for consultation with GATT or the International Monetary Fund prior to the imposition of quotas by any state. Other NTBs included in GATT's oversight function are state licensing, special taxes, and exchange control. Individual countries, such as the United States and Japan, clash frequently in GATT sessions over the use of NTBs as protectionist replacements for lowered tariffs. GATT has not been as successful in eliminating nontariff barriers as it has been in reducing tariff rates.

Probably the most useful function performed by GATT is that of helping to resolve disputes over alleged infractions of its trading rules. The lesson of the 1930s, burned indelibly into the pages of economic history, is that the greatest danger to a liberal trading system is retaliation that touches off a spiral of increasing protectionism. With the past as a guide, every complaint brought to GATT over a violation of rules is treated as a grave matter. Disputing parties are first urged to settle their disagreement bilaterally; failing this, the aggrieved party may take the matter to a special GATT panel, which, in consultation with the parties, hears the issues and makes a recommendation. Only if the offending state fails to abide by the panel decision may the complaining state retaliate by withdrawing a concession. The resolution of numerous disputes and the absence of major trade wars testify to the effectiveness of GATT's settlement procedures.

However, these settlement procedures—especially those dealing with nontariff barriers to trade—are sorely strained when world economic conditions take a turn for the worse. A serious economic dislocation in the West can be disastrous for Third World countries. As an old economic aphorism puts it, when the industrialized countries sneeze, the countries supplying raw materials catch pneumonia. These conditions test the ability of GATT to remain the strong bastion of freer trade planned by its architects. In a recent GATT session, for example, GATT Chairman B. L. Das (India) commented on the challenges facing the organization.

> Prices of commodities on which developing countries are highly dependent for their foreign exchange earnings reached their lowest levels . . . since the Great Depression, [and] country after country has registered historically low or negative growth rates, trade growth has also stagnated, . . . the inflation rate has been disturbingly high, balance of payments problems have mounted and unemployment rates have risen to levels unprecedented for decades.[4]

Despite many difficulties in reducing trade barriers, GATT's growing membership and broadened scope of interests have helped it to remain a vigorous and useful tool for achieving freer trade. Tariffs have been cut significantly over its forty-year period of operations, and many other once malignant barriers to trade have been excised from state policies. A degree of orderliness in tariff rate-setting and an acceptance of trading rules unprecedented for such a sizable portion of the world community supplement its success in reducing trade discrimination and unfair business practices. GATT's objective has never been to eliminate all barriers but only to encourage *freer* trade and the acceptance of rules to systematize trade practices and harmonize trade policies. Progress toward these limited objectives has been steady and sturdy since 1947. The ITO ideal, rejected at the front door, has been permitted to sneak in through the back door, so that today the broad institutional framework anticipated by ITO's sponsors has come close to full realization. By 1987, however, actions by the U.S. Congress to combat alleged "unfair" competition for many manufacturing industries and to reduce unemployment threatened to unleash a new world trade war contrary to the objectives of GATT and its trade rules. American concern—and for some, wrath—was aimed mainly at major industrial competitors, such as Japan and Germany, but Third World countries with their inexpensive low-wage raw materials and manufactured products were also threatened with new trade barriers. The long history of Third World efforts to open First World markets to their products through preferential treatment appeared to be moving in the wrong direction once again. It is to that history that we now turn our attention.

UNCTAD—A New Global Approach

The UN Conference on Trade and Development (UNCTAD), owes its existence at least partially to GATT's pre-UNCTAD policies of relative exclusivity. The idea of a new world trade organization started with a developing nations' resolution, adopted by the General Assembly in 1961, calling on the Secretary-General to make preliminary plans for an international trade and development conference. Debated extensively in the Economic and Social Council, the proposal grew out of the developing nations' exasperation over the failure of the developed nations to lower their restrictions on commodity trade. With the slogan "export or die," the Assembly majority pressed ahead with the trade conference despite the objection of seventeen developed nations that it duplicated GATT's work.

In one of the largest international meetings ever held up to that time, the UN Conference on Trade and Development met in Geneva for three months in the spring of 1964. The fact that over two thirds of the 120 delegations represented developing states was reflected in the agenda topics:

1. Expansion of international trade and its significance for economic development.
2. International commodity problems.
3. Trade in manufactures and semimanufactures.
4. Improvement of the invisible trade of developing countries.
5. Implications of regional economic groupings.
6. Financing for an expansion of international trade.
7. Institutional arrangements, methods, and machinery to implement measures relating to the expansion of international trade.

In addition, the Conference's Preparatory Committee dusted off an old idea and proposed that the Conference "set up a completely new specialized agency, a United Nations International Trade Organization, on the basis of universal membership." To many members, GATT was an instrument of cold war policy and unfitted to meet the needs of the developing states; hence a new forum and a new set of rules for removing trade barriers were needed. The Conference's objectives were brought into still sharper focus by a scholarly background paper prepared by Raul Prebisch, Secretary-General of UNCTAD.

The objectives of the developing states at UNCTAD can be summarized as an effort to pressure the developed states into accepting a liberal trade policy as the best means of securing the capital needed to promote economic development. The industrialized states prefer programs of technical assistance and loans as the means for fostering development. Many of these states object to increased imports from developing states because of the impact that such imports have on their domestic economies and because of the low wages paid in the developing world. This viewpoint overlooks the basic comparative cost rationale for international trade. Imports and exports exist simply because countries have advantages in producing particular articles of commerce. If costs were equalized in all states, international trade would become almost an irrelevancy. If each state refused to trade with nations in which labor was cheaper or general costs were lower, very little trade would take place. Moreover, the higher productivity of labor in the advanced states tends to equalize their costs with those of the low-wage countries. The developing states took the position at UNCTAD that since the developed states have professed a willingness to help them develop, why not give this help in the form of liberalized trade opportunities?

The developing countries recognized that political muscle was needed to secure economic concessions. Consequently, they functioned within a voting bloc at the Conference that came to be known as the Group of 77, or G-77,[5] a caucus corresponding to the number of independent Third World countries in 1964. The figure increased to about 130 by the 1980s, but the designation G-77 remained. Regional caucuses and informal contact groups supplemented the major caucus at the Conference. Their political unity made concessions from the advanced nations almost inevitable.

The Final Act of the Conference represented three months of committee sessions, speeches, negotiations, and what some of the disillusioned delegates from Asia and Africa referred to as the "deaf man's dialogue" between the developing states and the developed states. Yet the Final Act also represented a signal victory for the developing states even though no immediate major liberalization of trade resulted from it.

First, the Final Act contained a set of principles setting forth the economic and social development of developing countries as the first concern of international economic relations. Realization of these principles was to be secured by Third World countries through (1) an increase in their export earnings, (2) a stabilization of primary commodity prices, (3) the attainment of a new specialization based on an international division of labor, and (4) the extension of the most-favored-nation principle to developing states without reciprocity. These principles represented a voting victory for the bloc of developing states, but the problem remained: Could the developed states be persuaded to apply these principles in future negotiations?

Second, the Final Act recommended that UNCTAD be established as a permanent organ of the General Assembly, that it be convened at least once every three years, and that its purpose be "to promote international trade, especially with a view to accelerating economic development." In 1964 the Nineteenth General Assembly accorded UNCTAD permanent status to function as a center for harmonizing the trade and development policies of countries and regional groupings, as a coordinator between the Assembly and ECOSOC, and as an initiator of multilateral trade policies.[6] Although neither the Final Act nor the Assembly resolution made mention of it, UNCTAD's main purpose has been to serve as a forum in which developing states can exert pressures on the developed states to relax their restrictionist policies.

Third, the Final Act urged the Assembly to establish a Trade and Development Board to develop policy between UNCTAD sessions. The Board now meets annually and is open to participation by all UNCTAD members. As in the Conference, the developing states hold a voting majority on the Board, although the "principal trading states" are also represented on it so that pressures can be applied continuously on them.

Fourth, the Final Act called for the establishment of a permanent secretariat "within the United Nations Secretariat." The first Secretary-General of UNCTAD, international development expert Raul Prebisch, was appointed by Secretary-General U Thant and confirmed by the General Assembly. After lengthy debate over whether the headquarters of the UNCTAD Secretariat should be located in Geneva or in New York, the Trade and Development Board unanimously selected the European Office of the United Nations at Geneva. Those who preferred New York regarded the coordination of the UNCTAD Secretariat with the UN Secretariat as of the highest priority, but other members argued that the Geneva location would give UNCTAD a proximity to the headquarters of other trade and economic organizations that would prove more useful.

UNCTAD clearly represented a *political* victory for the developing states. Neither the Western states nor the Communist bloc ventured to bring their revised proposals for the Final Act to a vote, sensing that defeat was certain. Whether UNCTAD represented an *economic* triumph is still not clear more than two decades later. From its inception the advanced countries that carry on most of the world's trade accepted the establishment of a new organization reluctantly.

Since the initial 1964 Geneva meeting, subsequently known as UNCTAD I, major international conferences have been held every three or four years. These have included UNCTAD II in New Delhi (1968), UNCTAD III in Santiago (1972), UNCTAD IV in Nairobi (1976), UNCTAD V in Manila (1979), and UNCTAD VI in Belgrade (1983). UNCTAD VII was scheduled for 1987.

UNCTAD VI was a typical UNCTAD Conference. With three thousand delegates from 160 nations attending, the majority of Third World members once again brought tremendous pressure to bear on the industrialized states to open up their markets to the products of the developing states and to increase the prices they paid for these products. No negotiations were conducted; the Conference functioned mainly as a forum for discussion and debate. The main effort of the Third World members was to adopt resolutions that could be followed up with concrete actions. The Conference was motivated by the drastic impact of the high oil prices and the world recession of that period on Third World economies. The theme expounded by the majority of delegates throughout the month-long Conference was a call for an "immediate emergency action program" that included demands for (1) more financial aid for development projects, (2) more credit from the International Monetary Fund and the World Bank, and (3) a new issue of Special Drawing Rights (SDRs) by the Fund that would increase each developing nation's monetary reserves. Unwilling to antagonize the Third World majority by outright rejection of demands, the industrialized nations promised to consider them in other international bodies, including the Fund and the Bank. In both of these institutions, voting power was heavily weighted in favor of the Western nations. Knowing that the transfer of such demands to the Bank and the Fund would only serve to kill or cripple them, the Pakistani delegate may have reflected the views of many other Third World delegates when he described the Conference atmosphere which had failed to produce an immediate action program as "hateful and humiliating."

Another proposal developed by the Group of 77 and presented at the Belgrade Conference was the Commodity Stockpile Fund. The object of the Commodity Stockpile Fund was to stabilize prices worldwide for up to eighteen raw materials. This was to be accomplished by the purchase and stockpiling of commodities during times of abundance so as to sustain prices and encourage production. The financing of the stockpiles would come from a "common fund." Then, when the stockpiled commodities were in scarce supply, they would be sold and the fund would be replenished. The idea is similar to that underlying the American "ever-normal granary" system, which has tried to help American farmers since the 1930s by having the government buy up surpluses during "fat" years and replenishing the funds expended by selling stockpiled crops during "lean" years. Successive fat years have almost overwhelmed that system. Support for UNCTAD's Commodity Stockpile Fund has come from the European Community and a number of Third World countries, but opposition to this proposal has been strong, especially from the United States and from those Third World countries that operate controlled marketing systems. Among the strongest supporters of the proposal have been countries that produce the commodities that are in greatest abundance, such as sugar, coffee, cocoa, and natural rubber. Regardless of what happens to the plan, the Third World search for a means of supporting commodity prices and limiting supply will go on.

The Group of 77, encouraged by its voting successes at UNCTAD conferences, has functioned as a Third World caucus at other UN meetings. This has brought many voting victories since 1964, but it has not changed the basic economic posture of First World trading nations toward the Third World. Over the years the Group of 77 has carried on two major campaigns at UNCTAD conferences. The first was aimed at persuading the industrialized states to adopt a Generalized System of Preferences (GSP) that would improve opportunities for Third World states to sell their products in Western markets.[7] The second sought a drastic reorganization of the world economy through the creation of a New International Economic Order (NIEO). These campaigns, and their impact on development programs, will be discussed in the next chapter. Suffice it now to conclude that UNCTAD has been a political success in producing unity and voting strength for the developing state bloc but that it has done little to alter the basic economic realities in a world market system that favors the rich nations, often at the expense of the poor.

PROMOTING REGIONAL INTEGRATION

While plans to establish a global trading system through the ITO, GATT, and UNCTAD were unfolding, regional integration movements to facilitate trade and economic progress were also under way. These resulted in a spate of new regional organizations, first in Western Europe, then in Latin America and elsewhere. The former are composed of advanced countries seeking means to foster economic growth and broaden the base of their prosperity; the latter are composed of developing countries that are trying through the fusion of their trade policies to gain a taste of the kind of prosperity that was accepted as a starting point for the European model. Although contemporary regional organizations represent different levels of cooperation and integration, they have the common objective, supported by various UN programs, of promoting economic well-being through regional unity.

Many regions of the world are represented in integration arrangements. The most economically and politically advanced of these arrangements, as already noted, is the European Community, which originated in 1952 with the Coal and Steel Community. Its twelve members (Belgium, Britain, Denmark, France, West Germany, Greece, Ireland, Italy, Luxembourg, the Netherlands, Portugal, and Spain) have established a common market, a common external tariff, free flow of capital, and free migration of workers and have developed many common economic policies and programs. It has a common political structure—consisting of a Council of Ministers, a Commission, a European Parliament, and a Court of Justice—which makes economic decisions for the Community.

The Communist world's attempt to promote economic development through regional unity has taken the form of the Council for Mutual Economic Assistance (CMEA or COMECON). Its members include the Soviet Union and six East European states (Bulgaria, Czechoslovakia, East Germany, Hungary, Poland, and Romania) plus Angola, Cuba, Mongolia, and Vietnam. Established in 1949, its main objective is to foster an integration of Communist economies based on national specialization. COMECON operates through a Council and an Executive Committee supplemented by various committees and commissions.

Several integration efforts have been undertaken in Latin America. One of these, the Latin American Integration Association (LAIA), seeks to reduce tariffs among its members with concessions based on each country's level of development: (1) less developed (Bolivia, Ecuador, and Paraguay), (2) medium developed (Chile, Colombia, Peru, Uruguay, and Venezuela), and (3) more developed (Argentina, Brazil, and Mexico). These countries represent three fourths of the population of Latin America. LAIA emerged in 1980 as a successor to the Latin American Free Trade Association (LAFTA), which had failed in its mission to establish a regional free trade area. Another group, the Andean Common Market, was established mainly to improve its members' bargaining power within the larger framework of LAFTA and later LAIA. Unlike most non-Communist integration schemes, the Andean Common Market promotes the ideas of "central planning" and "directed economies," and it has encouraged the imposition of controls over foreign investments and multinational corporations. By 1980 essentially all tariffs had been eliminated among its members and a common external tariff had been established. The Caribbean Community and Common Market (CARICOM) is still another effort to promote economic development through economic/political integration. Established as a customs union in 1973, CARICOM has made slow but steady progress toward political and economic unity, using the European Community as a model. Its members include most of the independent states and the nonsovereign entities of the Caribbean region, divided in terms of their responsibilities into more developed countries (MDCs) and less developed countries (LDCs), with special benefits and protections accorded to the latter.

A different approach to economic well-being is used by the Organization of Petroleum Exporting Countries (OPEC), which consists of thirteen oil-exporting countries that have established an intergovernmental cartel to seek agreement on regulating production and pricing in the world oil market. The membership of OPEC comprises seven Middle East Arab states (Algeria, Iraq, Kuwait, Libya, Qatar, Saudi Arabia, and the United Arab Emirates), two African states (Gabon and Nigeria), two Asian states (Indonesia and Iran), and two Latin-American states (Ecuador and Venezuela). Although the political and economic unity of its members helped produce high levels of income for them during the 1970s, a massive oil glut in the 1980s created frictions among them and drove world oil prices and OPEC incomes down substantially.

Why Regional Integration?

The simultaneous development of UN organizations fostering the growth of a world trading system and of regional groupings raises the question whether these developments are complementary or contradictory. Does a regional common market, for example, contribute to global multilateralism, or is it a new form of bloc nationalism that hampers world trade? Does the integration of national economies within regions promote or impede the goal of an orderly world economy? Does it foster political unity or rivalry? In sum, are the benefits of regional economic integration local or global, and what, if any, are its disadvantages?

Governments representing hundreds of millions of people in Western Europe, Eastern Europe, Asia, Africa, the Caribbean region, and Latin America have applied theories of economic integration in their efforts to solve common economic problems through various levels of regional organization. Although each of these experiments in integration has indigenous characteristics, they are all aimed at promoting *national* welfare through *regional* cooperation. The common denominator among the diverse approaches used in the integration movements is the creation of a free trade area. Each integration scheme has established "free trade among members" as its fundamental objective. Difficulties in moving beyond that point, however, tend to increase at a progressive rate, and some level of political integration is usually necessary to pave the way to higher economic integration goals.

Whatever the level of unity, the economic integration movement is a well-established contemporary phenomenon. Despite its popularity in some regions, this question might be asked: Is it really a useful economic approach? The question is extremely difficult to answer with any degree of certainty because empirical evidence is confused by crosscurrents of social, political, and economic forces that make it difficult to draw definite conclusions. Nevertheless, some kind of analysis is in order. The anticipated advantages of regional economic integration include the following:

1. *Increased trade*—trade among members will normally expand as governmental barriers are reduced or eliminated.
2. *Lower costs*—the cost of production may decrease if free internal movement of labor and capital is encouraged.
3. *Greater specialization*—a freer market will encourage a regional division of labor and a consequent specialization.
4. *Increased investment*—investment may be spurred by the mobility of capital and labor and by the expanded demand of a larger market.
5. *Expanded production*—a freer and larger market with close economic ties among members will tend to stimulate production to fill a larger demand.

6. *Monetary stability*—balance of payments disequilibriums with outside nations may be ameliorated by increased trade within the market. Ultimately, a common currency could resolve most monetary and exchange problems among members.

7. *Greater efficiency*—more highly competitive conditions within the free trade area may result in greater efficiency and higher productivity. Economies of scale from larger production units may result from the expanded market.

8. *Improved terms of trade*—the elimination of artificial barriers to trade within the market area may have the effect of evening out the price exchange ratio among members. In the trade relations of members with nonmembers, domestic competition may result in lower consumer prices for imports and hence improved terms of trade.

9. *A better bargaining position*—members as a bloc may substantially increase their bargaining power in tariff negotiations.

To this list, functionalists might add that regional economic arrangements may serve as a base for building political integration. A regional market's institutional machinery, its harmonization of economic policies, and the spillover effect of its successes may help create an awareness within the region of the advantages of the integrative process.

Some of the highly vocal proponents of a regional approach to economic problems bear some resemblance to the old-time huckster peddling snake oil as a cure for all ills. Although the advantages of the regional approach are real and potentiality great (and it should not be equated with snake oil), it also has some significant drawbacks. Foremost among these is the basic *discriminatory* nature of a free trade area or common market. Each member of the regional group agrees to give preferential trade treatment to its fellow members. Since other trading nations do not share in this *internal* reduction or elimination of trade barriers, they are, ipso facto, the objects of the regional group's discrimination. Trade discrimination, whether direct or indirect and however good its intentions, is inimical to the development of global multilateralism.

Within a free trade area or common market, partially dormant forces of the marketplace are awakened. As governments remove their protective mantles, competition becomes keen. If economic growth falters or the business cycle takes an adverse swing, keen competition can turn to cutthroat competition in a battle for survival. No regional group has yet had to face this kind of challenge. Even during prosperity, free trade is most advantageous for the stronger trading partners. If economic freedom within a regional group permits one or several members to attract a major portion of available investment funds and to dominate the marketplace, economic integration will merely serve to accelerate the process of enriching the rich and impoverishing the poor.

Although a common market may stimulate efficiency and productivity, it may also drive marginal producers out of business, a process that could redound to the disadvantage of market consumers. The natural forces of a free economy encourage the concentration of business into larger units. This concentration and the specialization promoted by common policies increase the possibility that businessmen will reach an understanding with one another, divide up the market, and raise prices. In the EC, for example, leading industrialists in all member countries supported the common market idea partly because of the opportunities for dividing up the continental market that they believed it would provide. A high and growing incidence of mergers and cartel arrangements in EC countries raises the threat of monopoly pricing that may develop once competition with outside firms has been reduced by the cost differential between members and nonmembers. Although cartels could be brought under governmental regulation—and the EC's Treaty of Rome contains provisions that authorize such action—the continental tradition of restrictive marketing practices, augmented by the political power of the giants of industry, militates against it.

A free trade area or common market represents a *substantial* movement toward laissez-faire. Governmental restrictive and promotional systems are dismantled by common agreement to eliminate artificial cost differentials and restraints on trade within the market. The impact of such policies may be a collapse in the delicately engineered internal equilibrium of power among business, labor, and agriculture.

In a regional group composed of Third World developing states, many of these same infirmities may exist. Extremes in levels of development and economic potentials may bestow even greater favors on the more advanced members of the market than in a group composed wholly of developed states. Although the classical economists argued that free trade would tend to equalize incomes in all states, the evidence negates this theory. Within a free market the state that develops most rapidly will attract additional shares of investment capital and skilled labor from neighboring states. Competitive advantages in a free market will tend to increase the rate of industrial development in more advanced states and will frustrate the attempts of weaker states to industrialize.

Finally, the development of common market arrangements, whether in developed or developing states, may have an unhealthy impact on the building of a global multilateral system. The very factors that lend strength to a common market system may also limit world trade. Preferential treatment for members' trade, for example, may encourage retaliation by outsiders. The movement to reduce world trade barriers may be stymied by the realization that freer trade with the rest of the world will weaken the rationale for a regional preferential system. In a common market the "invasion" of external capital to surmount the common external tariff by investing "inside" the market causes balance of payments disequilibriums and reactions within member countries against foreign domination of their economies. Moreover, the discriminatory features of a free trade area or a common market encourage the development of rival trading blocs. If common markets multiply—and evidence of planning for market arrangements in Asia and Africa lends credence to this assumption—a world of regional blocs may restore much of the rivalry that characterized the economic nationalism of the 1930s.

On balance, the development of regional market arrangements has probably been a healthy one. The objective of using a regional market to promote economic development, however, remains largely untested. And as an element related to the problem of political unity, no one has yet been able to unravel the tangled skein of economic factors to produce a definitive explanation of which factors produce closer ties and which invite disunity. Perhaps the main reason why free trade areas and common markets will continue to find favor is the *psychological* satisfactions that major interest groups derive from them. One observer's evaluation of the European Community, for example, concludes that

> it is not surprising that everyone sees something for himself in the Rome Treaty—it is all things to all men. The free trader sees a cutting down of the internal barriers to trade. The protectionist sees the building of a new tariff wall around Western Europe. The right wing sees the strengthening of business interests and the possibility of stiffer resistance to wage demands on the grounds of competitive requirements. The left wing looks to the international unity of workers and sees the approach of the ideal of world brotherhood. The federalists see the creation of new supranational powers and the gradual emergence of a federal government. The confederalists look forward to *l'Europe des patries*—the Europe of nation states. The Europeans see the growth of a new European spirit and self-consciousness. The supporters of an Atlantic Community see the development of much broader loyalties. The one thing that is clear is that not all of these views can be right.[8]

THE PURSUIT OF INTERNATIONAL LIQUIDITY

The removal of barriers to trade through actions by GATT and UNCTAD may spur the exchange of goods, but another factor—the means of payment for goods received—also determines the volume of the goods exchanged. When businessmen in India buy Japanese Toyotas, for example, they must pay for them, not in Indian rupees, but in Japanese yen or in an "international" currency such as the American dollar or the British pound. Foreign currencies needed for carrying on trade are known as foreign exchange. They may be obtained from a free foreign exchange market or, in the case of a state using some form of exchange control, a governmental agency determines whether the projected transaction warrants the use of scarce foreign exchange. In a free exchange market, the rate of exchange between domestic and foreign currency is determined by supply and demand forces similar to those operating in a stock market or a commodity market. In a controlled market, the price of foreign currencies is pegged at an official rate favorable to the exchange control state. This system, often supplemented by a "black market" exchange system, is used in Communist states and in most Third World nations.

One of the main objectives of states in the area of international finance is to accumulate sufficient reserves of foreign currencies to carry them over a lean period. Two types of currencies, distinguished from each other by the role that each plays in relation to international trade and finance, are useful in providing that kind of security. The first type is an international "trading" currency that businessmen use to carry on their day-to-day transactions in foreign markets. Bankers use trading currency to make loans and investments in most countries of the world. The trading currency is the working currency accepted as an international monetary unit in a world of diverse national currencies. For some years the dollar has functioned as the major trading currency, with many billions of dollars currently in the hands of foreign bankers and businessmen. Almost all world oil business, for example, has been transacted in dollars, although the Japanese yen may now be making inroads. The second type is a "reserve" currency that provides governments with the means for protecting the value of their national currencies in foreign exchange markets. When the value of a national currency threatens to drop below its parity or stability level, the government purchases quantities of its own currency in the free market using its international reserves. If a national currency becomes overvalued in the free market, the government reverses the process, accumulating reserves in exchange for its national currency. Countries, therefore, need sizable amounts of reserves to keep the value of their national currency stable. This is especially true of the developed countries of the West, which operate on the basis of a largely free-floating flexible exchange system in which currency values are determined by supply-demand market conditions. The international reserves held by countries are in the form of gold, special drawing rights (SDRs), and foreign exchange. The last of these consists mainly of American dollars and the currencies of Japan, Britain, Germany, France, and other Western states.

After World War II the dollar became the kingpin of the international monetary system for several reasons. For one, the United States was committed to buy gold from foreign monetary authorities or to sell gold to them at the fixed price of $35 an ounce. Because gold was in short supply, American dollars supplemented the gold in national reserves, with the understanding that those dollars could be converted into gold. Consequently, all other currencies were tied to the dollar in terms of their exchange relationship with it and to the extent that they held dollars as a reserve currency. The preeminence of the dollar as a reserve currency was not planned; it occurred because of the willingness of private businessmen, bankers, and public officials in various countries to hold dollars as a safe, universal currency. Since the U.S. government was ready to redeem dollar reserves for gold, there was a general acceptance of dollars in lieu of gold in what might be described as a gold-exchange-standard system. The unrivaled prosperity of the United States and the immersion of its businessmen in business operations around the globe also helped place the dollar in the center of the world monetary stage at that time.

The American dollar also became the world's reserve currency because unprecedented numbers of dollars were available to foreign traders and monetary agencies. This bonanza of dollars resulted from a series of annual deficits in the American balance of payments, which grew in magnitude for forty years. These deficits put hundreds of billions of dollars into foreign hands—much in the form of official reserves. They also provided the liquidity that fostered a high level of world prosperity—especially in the developed nations—over four decades. In addition, billions of dollars were exchanged for gold, thereby reducing American gold reserves substantially. American policies for many years sought to reduce or eliminate the balance of payments deficit and to reduce the outflow of dollars. Had these policies been successful, they would have halted the growth of reserves abroad at the very time when greater international liquidity was needed to support expanding trade and general prosperity. Before the denouement of the gold-dollar crisis and the challenge of the current world debt crisis are examined, a survey of the UN system for creating and safeguarding monetary stability is in order.

The Role of the International Monetary Fund (IMF)

The world's monetary system, weakened during the period of economic nationalism of the 1930s, emerged from World War II in almost complete disarray. In planning for the postwar world, the concern given to creating an orderly international payments system was equal to that given to building a new trading system free of restrictionism and to establishing a lending agency that would aid in the recovery from war and the development of poor societies. One of the three legs of the stool that was to support international economic well-being was the International Monetary Fund. The Articles of Agreement for the Fund and the World Bank were fitted together into the broad framework of a world economic policy at the Bretton Woods Conference of 1944. Although the IMF is a specialized agency of the United Nations, its membership is open to any nation that subscribes to its Articles of Agreement. Its members (151 in 1987) include most of the world's nations. Among them are seven Communist countries, although the Soviet Union and China remain outside the club. In the Soviet view, the World Bank and the IMF are merely crutches to prolong the life of international capitalism. IMF headquarters are in Washington, where a staff of about 1,600, including 750 economists, help the Managing Director and his Board make decisions on loans. In 1985 the IMF had assets of $86 billion, a lending pool of approximately $35 billion, and 31 outstanding loans totaling over $7 billion. It makes loans to rich as well as poor countries. Its main purposes, as set forth in its Articles of Agreement, are

1. To promote *international monetary cooperation*.
2. To facilitate the *expansion of international trade*.
3. To promote *exchange stability*.
4. To assist in the establishment of a *multilateral system of payments*.
5. To give *confidence* to members by making its resources available.
6. To *shorten the duration* and *lessen the degree of disequilibrium* in members' balances of payments.

In summary, IMF operations seek to stabilize the currencies and national economies of members. But how are these objectives to be achieved? The following game plan was envisioned by the architects of the Bretton Woods system:

1. National economic policies should be freely pursued in each member state's efforts to achieve full employment, economic growth, and price stability. Keynesian domestic policies would, it was believed, avoid the general catastrophe of another Great Depression.

2. Exchange rates between currencies should be fixed and tied directly or indirectly to gold. This approach was aimed at avoiding the wildly fluctuating rates that prevailed during the early 1920s and 1930s.

3. Currencies should be freely convertible with one another. The exchange control systems that emerged during the Great Depression and World War II must be avoided during the postwar period.

4. The IMF should play a leading role in lending international funds to cover the balance of payments deficits that were certain to occur as a result of the operations of the first three features.

5. When necessary, countries should alter their exchange rates in order to deal with the reality of a "fundamental disequilibrium." These should be altered, however, only through international agreement.

These system features and IMF objectives together reflected the founders' concern that the world not slip back into the financial anarchy of the 1930s or retain strangling wartime controls. As in the proposals for a world trade system, the Fund's originators foresaw a new, orderly world of international finance based on a common code to guide the actions of member states and governed by an international institution that could determine exchange and payments policies.

The Fund's primary role takes it along this pathway. It is first and foremost an institution through which governments can consult on major monetary questions. Beyond this, it seeks to provide exchange stability by two means: influencing currency values and permitting members to draw foreign exchange from the Fund to tide them over periods of serious financial hardship.

The plan underlying the use of the Fund as a pooling arrangement is fairly simple. All members contribute to a common bank of monetary reserves that they can draw on to overcome short-term disequilibriums in their balances of payments. The contributions are based on a quota system that reflects national income, gold reserves, and other factors related to ability to contribute. The Fund's voting system is weighted according to each member's contribution, and the United States casts about one fifth of all the votes. Initially, each member was required to contribute 25 percent of its quota in gold—the so-called gold tranche—but the remainder could be in its own currency. Each member may annually purchase from the Fund amounts of foreign exchange up to the value of its gold tranche; the maximum ordinarily permitted, however, amounts to 200 percent of its quota. Other lending arrangements supplement the quota system. By 1987 members' subscriptions provided a pool of billions of dollars available for drawing purposes, although as a practical matter the portion of the Fund made up of soft Third World currencies is of little use. When a state withdraws an amount from the Fund for an emergency, it actually purchases the foreign exchange with its own domestic currency; when it repays the amount, it returns foreign exchange to the Fund for its own currency. In this way, the reserve pool as a revolving fund remains fairly constant in the total value of its holdings, but the amounts of different currencies fluctuate, depending on the demand for them. Because of the debt crisis in the Third World, the IMF fund has become increasingly dependent on huge contributions from the industrialized states, especially the United States.

The objective underlying the currency pool is to maintain fairly stable exchange values for members' currencies. When a member suffers a short-term deficit in its balance of payments, purchases of foreign exchange from the Fund are ordinarily expected to carry it through the crisis. Despite the Fund, however, a number of Third World states have been forced to devalue their currencies and undertake protectionist policies to combat their deficits. Major devaluations have resulted from such factors as massive international debt, heavy domestic inflation, and international market forces beyond the state's control.

The Monetary and Debt Crises

Over the years the International Monetary Fund has coped with numerous minor problems but has faced two major crises. One of these, involving mainly the Western industrialized and major trading nations, came to a climax in the early 1970s. The second, involving Third World debtor countries, occurred during the 1980s. An examination of these two crises will provide the reader with a better understanding of the problems of the international monetary system and the role of the IMF in managing them.

The first crisis grew out of the post-World War II international monetary system's dependence on one national currency—the American dollar. As many nations recovered from the economic trauma of the war period, they expanded their export trade and built up huge dollar balances. These balances served as claims against the American gold hoard, which at that time amounted to over two-thirds of the world's available gold. The gold-dollar exchange system, constructed on the assumption that dollars were as good as gold because they could be exchanged at the fixed rate of $35 for one fine ounce of gold, began to waver as dollars were rapidly converted into gold.

By 1970 the drain of American dollars and gold into the global economy had become a virtual gusher. All attempts to stanch the outflow of dollars and stabilize the gold-dollar exchange system were of no avail. A more flexible system was needed to supplement the dollar as an international currency supporting the expansion of world trade and providing ready reserves to protect national currencies. In 1969 the International Monetary Fund began to issue special drawing rights to augment the gold and the dollars and other key currencies that were being used as international reserves, with an initial issue of $3 billion. Since SDRs are a form of fiat money, created as bookkeeping entries in the IMF accounting system, they have been called "paper gold." Their value is related to the value of a weighted basket of the currencies of the five leading export nations. SDRs continue to be used today, and periodically the IMF issues additional amounts. Although SDRs are issued to IMF members on the basis of their contributions to the capitalization of the Fund (and hence their voting power), for many years Third World countries have attempted to obtain a larger share, especially for use as developmental capital. This attempt has been resisted by the West, which regards issuance of SDRs as a means for promoting monetary stability rather than for subsidizing economic development.

By 1971 hundreds of billions of dollars in the world constituted claims against a dwindling supply of American gold and the existing international monetary system was in a state of full crisis. This situation forced the Nixon Administration to abandon the official fixed rate of exchange between gold and the dollar. That same year, in a meeting at the Smithsonian Institution in Washington, the ministers of the Group of Ten (a caucusing group composed of the ten leading contributors to the Fund) promulgated the "Smithsonian Agreement," which resulted in a 10 percent devaluation of the dollar and a realignment of exchange rates. In 1973, after another dollar devaluation, the national currencies of the developed states were permitted to "float" through the workings of a flexible exchange rate system, with occasional individual and collective governmental interventions in the free exchange market to stabilize currency values. The first crisis was thus overcome by permitting the market mechanism to determine national currency exchange values.

The second major IMF crisis began to evolve slowly during the 1960s and early 1970s, as Third World countries desperately sought to borrow the capital they needed to fuel the engine of economic growth. The world oil crisis of the 1970s and the global recession of the early 1980s changed the slow, incremental increase in their debt into a virtual avalanche. Although no one could accurately measure the exact size of the Third World's international debt, by 1987 it was estimated at more than $900 billion, with the accrual of unpaid interest moving it over the $1 trillion mark. As the crisis mounted and the threat of a general default in payments increased, the role of the IMF as the lender "of last resort" emerged. IMF loans were aimed, not at solving the problem, but rather at providing the means by which Third World states could continue to make payments on their huge debts. With each new loan the IMF imposed requirements that the receiving state adopt draconian economic measures to reduce living standards so that debt payments could be made.

In playing the role of rescuer of troubled economies, the IMF has come to be viewed from two different perspectives. Its supporters in both the First and Third Worlds see it as the defender of economic viability, harsh though austerity measures may be. In their view, the IMF is a handy scapegoat for reckless spending by Third World countries. So long as money was available from private and public lending agencies, nations borrowed it with no regard to how repayment would occur. Without the IMF's demand for economic reforms as a condition of new loans, many Third world countries would be financially paralyzed, according to IMF supporters.

On the other hand, many Third World leaders view the IMF as a troublemaker that is intervening in the domestic politics of sovereign states.[9] Austerity measures demanded by the IMF as a condition for granting loans have resulted in reduced government services, heavy unemployment, and, in many countries, an end to economic growth. Leaders of the political left in debtor countries charge the IMF with trying to impose capitalist values on all developing states. Cuba's Fidel Castro, for example, in 1985 hosted a conference of Latin American debtor nations at which he called for the formation of a "debtor's organization" and a refusal of all Third World countries to make full payments on their debts. In some debtor countries, austerity programs have resulted in rioting and the threat of open revolution. In 1984 IMF policies were blamed for causing riots in the Dominican Republic that left more than fifty people dead. Clearly, IMF policies and actions are stirring up anger and defiance in Third World countries, but the IMF appears to be locked into a very difficult situation. Many economists believe that if another world recession develops during the latter part of the 1980s, a general default leading to a global banking crisis could usher in a major depression even more catastrophic than that of the 1930s. Aware of this danger, IMF decision makers are also cognizant that forces beyond their control may be moving the world economy to the brink.[10]

The effort to avoid a general default of Third World debtors has led many observers to propose a working alliance between the IMF and the World Bank. While the IMF provided major support to debtor countries for a decade or more, by 1985 its net loans to all borrowers dwindled to only $560 million from a peak of $12 billion in 1983.[11] The result was that the World Bank, under the new leadership of former Republican congressman A. W. (Tom) Clausen, has been called on to seize the lead role from the IMF in managing the debt crisis.

In 1985, U.S. Treasury Secretary James A. Baker III set forth a new initiative for dealing with the debt problem. At a joint meeting of the IMF and World Bank, Baker offered to substantially increase loans to the fifteen major debtors over a three-year period if the recipient countries would change their state-managed economies and open themselves to major investments from the West. In 1986, World Bank President Clausen offered a counterplan by which there would be a substantial write-off of debt, interest payments would be reduced, and Japan's huge financial resources would provide a new source of funds for debtor countries.

Despite the Baker and Clausen initiatives, the main problem remains. Even with huge loans to the debtor countries, the net transfer of funds is not enough to get the economies of the debtor countries growing at a rate whereby their debts would in time become manageable. The new emphasis on economic growth rather than austerity may prove effective in the long run, but the debt crisis may become critical for the world economy in the short run.

CONCLUSION

Working within the broad framework of the UN system, nearly all states have joined together to build an institutional structure for economic cooperation. Parts of the structure are integrated with central UN decision machinery dominated by the General Assembly; other parts, perhaps the most useful and effective, operate on the periphery of the organization. Despite the decentralized structure, all the operational units of the structure have had the primary goal of avoiding a return to the narrow and bitter economic nationalism of the Great Depression. The battle is never won once and for all, but in moving toward the half-century mark of UN operations, the world can still celebrate the continuing achievement of that goal.

GATT has eliminated some barriers to trade, reduced many others, and learned to live with the rest. GATT has also provided an open forum in which states have developed rules of the trading game and worked out solutions to disputes arising over their application. UNCTAD has supplemented the work of GATT by providing a forum for the creation of new trading policies to encourage the exchange of goods between developing and developed countries. Some UNCTAD recommendations have been implemented through the cooperation of GATT. Although trade cooperation may have suffered from the failure to create the International Trade Organization envisaged by the founding fathers of the UN system, GATT and UNCTAD have done much to fill that vacuum. Many problems remain in the field of trade policy, but none on the horizon is serious enough to produce a major collapse in the world trade mechanism that now exists.

In the related field of monetary policy, the role of the International Monetary Fund has been essential. Problems exist, such as major inflation in many developing countries and the huge debts owed by Third World countries to private and public banks in the West. But the IMF has succeeded in keeping these problems under a measure of control. Its role will become ever more decisive if problems worsen and threaten the stability of the world economy. They are unlikely to be solved, but they must somehow be managed. Although the IMF does not have the power to keep such problems from arising, it becomes the lender of last resort on behalf of the world community in a major effort to avoid international bankruptcy, default, and collapse that would paralyze creditor and debtor nations alike. There is no foreseeable end to this effort; the world seems destined to move from one monetary crisis to another without benefit of a respite.

From this review of post-World War II international economic problems and policies, we can conclude that the Keynesian approach of building institutions of intergovernmental cooperation has produced some handsome achievements. But the test continues. With two thirds of the world's peoples living in poverty, international cooperation obviously has its limits. The future of the world economy may be determined by the efforts of the Third World to achieve development and modernization goals and by the support of those efforts that is elicited from the developed states. Here the role of another major international institutional structure—the World Bank Group—may prove decisive. This is so because the flow of trade and the payment of international debts are intimately related to the level of growth in the developing world. In the next chapter we turn our attention to the subject of economic development and to the role of agencies functioning within the UN system in providing aid for such development.

NOTES

1. Clair Wilcox, *A Charter for World Trade* (New York: Macmillan, 1949), p. 214. This volume is the most thorough analysis available on the Havana Charter.

2. At Geneva, 123 bilateral talks were held over a period of six months in which tariff reductions were considered on fifty thousand items of commerce. The results of these negotiations were incorporated into a single document, the General Agreement on Tariffs and Trade (GATT), and all concessions became applicable to each of the twenty-three participating countries.

3. For a lively discussion of GATT's current operations and future prospects, see John Starrel's, "Trade—To Free or Not to Free, GATT Is the Question," *Europe*, no. 234 (November-December 1982), pp. 4–5.

4. "GATT Chairman Addresses 39th Session," *UN Chronicle* 21, no 1 (January 1984), pp. 96–97.

5. For a more recent assessment of the role of the Group of 77, see "Remember the G77?" *Interdependent* 10, no. 4 (July-August 1984), pp. 1–7.

6. General Assembly Resolution 1995 (XIX), December 30, 1964.

7. For an excellent discussion of the role of the Generalized System of Preferences in North-South trade reform, see William Loehr and John P. Powelson, *Threat to Development—Pitfalls of the NIEO* (Boulder, Colo.: Westview Press, 1983), pp. 37–62.

8. Sidney Dell, *Trade Blocs and Common Markets* (New York: Alfred A. Knopf, 1963), pp. 360–61.

9. See, for example, "World Bank, IMF—Do They Help or Hurt Third World?" *U.S. News & World Report,* April 29, 1985, pp. 43–48.

10. To avoid such a catastrophe, Richard N. Cooper, a leading economist, recommends in "A Monetary System for the Future," *Foreign Affairs* 673, no. 1 (Fall 1984), pp. 166–84, the return to a system of fixed exchange rates and the creation of a World Bank of Issue that would issue a world currency in somewhat the same manner as the Federal Reserve System does in the United States.

11. Hobart Rowen, "Conable's World Bank—It May Hold the Solution to the Debt Crisis," *The Washington Post,* July 14, 1986, pp. 6–7.

SELECTED READINGS

BALASSA, BELA. *Change and Challenge in the World Economy*. New York: St. Martin's Press, 1985.

BROWN, LESTER R., et al. *State of the World, 1986*. New York: W. W. Norton, 1986.

CHILCOTE, RONALD H., ed. *Dependency and Marxism—Toward a Resolution of the Debate*. Boulder, Colo.: Westview Press, 1982.

COOPER, RICHARD N. "A Monetary System for the Future." *Foreign Affairs* 673, no 1 (Fall 1984).

CURTIS, MICHAEL. *Western European Integration*. New York: Harper & Row, 1965.

GARDNER, RICHARD N. "GATT and the United Nations Conference on Trade and Development." *International Organization* 18, no 4 (Autumn 1964), pp. 685–704.

GAUTAM, SEN. *The Military Origins of Industrialization and International Trade Rivalry*. New York: St. Martin's Press, 1984.

JACOBSON, HAROLD K. *Networks of Interdependence: International Organizations and the Global Political System*. 2nd ed. New York: Alfred A. Knopf, 1984.

————, et al. "National Entanglements in International Governmental Organizations." *American Political Science Review* 80, no 1 (March 1986).

KIHL, YOUNG WHAN, and JAMES M. LUTZ. *World Trade Issues: Regime, Structure, and Policy*. New York: Praeger Publishers, 1985.

LOEHR, WILLIAM, and JOHN P. POWELSON. *Threat to Development—Pitfalls of the NIEO*. Boulder, Colo.: Westview Press, 1983.

ROTHSTEIN, ROBERT I. *Global Bargaining: UNCTAD and the Quest for a New International Economic Order*. Princeton: Princeton University Press, 1979.

STERN, ROBERT M. "Policies for Trade and Development." *International Conciliation,* no. 548 (May 1964).

WILCOX, CLAIR. *A Charter for World Trade*. New York: Macmillan, 1949.

11

Promoting Economic Development

Promoting economic development is the decisive test of functional cooperation. An awakening of aspirations for material betterment has fired the imagination of deprived millions throughout the world. Two thirds of mankind are caught up in a revolution of rising expectations that has triggered profound social changes. For more than forty years the leaders of preindustrial societies have looked to the industrialized countries for the keys that will unlock the door to material prosperity.

This revolution of rising expectations has opened a Pandora's box of problems. How can ancient societies be ushered quickly and peacefully into the twentieth century? What basic societal and governmental changes are necessary? What are the keys to economic growth and modernization? From whence will come the help that is so desperately needed? What impact will urbanism and industrialism have on peasant cultures? What role should the United Nations play in the revolution? Obviously, there are no ready answers to these and similar questions, but the challenge is real and it will face the world for a long time to come.

To meet this global challenge, the United Nations, regional international organizations, and individual governments have launched a series of programs aimed at helping the developing or less developed countries (LDCs) to help themselves. In no other field has the United Nations developed institutions, policies, and programs of such variety and scope. These approaches combine technical assistance and capital loans and grants with a broad range of educational, health, welfare, and internal improvement programs to build a base from which each society may try to launch itself into the stage of self-sustaining economic growth.

Despite these efforts, in most developing countries change is slow and seldom measures up to expectations. Societies steeped in tradition and guided by conservative values resist the onslaught of change. Societies in transition grope for new values to replace those that have been rejected. Improved health conditions produce population explosions that cancel out gains in national income. But poverty-stricken societies no longer accept their lot as the will of the gods, and the disparity between expectations and realities has produced a dangerous "frustration gap." Next to the problem of avoiding global war, closing this gap is the major problem that faces the United Nations today and that will face it for the remainder of the twentieth century and perhaps for most of the twenty-first century.

PROBLEMS OF DEVELOPMENT

The less developed world covers vast areas of the planet stretching eastward from Latin America through Africa and the Middle East to South and Southeast Asia and the islands of the Pacific littoral. In meeting the problems of development, states are in some respects like individuals. No two individuals are exactly alike, but individuals living in poverty have many common characteristics and environmental problems that help explain their plight. Ending poverty for individuals depends not only on improving their economic lot but also on changing their thinking, their attitude, their environment—in effect, their whole way of life.

Leaders of the developing countries are generally committed to making the transition to the world reflected in Western material values. What they really want is the kind of production of wealth that the West enjoys, but not necessarily the Western values essential to that goal, such as the work ethic, competitiveness, the elimination of class status, and the freedom that goes along with democracy and capitalism. Yet their centuries-old traditional societies are slowly giving way to modern demands. Whether such changes will solve their problems and enrich their lives is a moot question; they have caught a vision of plenty through the windows of the Western world, and they want to have a share in it.

A Profile of a Less Developed Country (LDC)

Our understanding of the problem of economic development may be promoted if we put together a profile of the features that characterize most developing states. Such a picture of a typical developing state's base or starting point will highlight what needs to be done for economic development and will point up the difficulties of doing it. A note of caution is in order, however, since great differences in size, population, resources, power supplies, native skills, and other natural and human variables exist in developing states as diverse as Brazil and Sierra Leone, Nigeria and Afghanistan. Moreover, the profile does not apply to the oil-rich states of the Third World or to the developing states that have made great progress in recent years, such as South Korea.

First, and most basic, our profile state is *poor.* A comprehensive UN study in 1949, at the start of the modernization campaign, showed that about two thirds of the world's population produced less than one sixth of the world's income. Great disparities also exist in per capita income. Although statistics for the developing states are less accurate than those for advanced states, in some developing states the annual per capita figure has been as low as $100 when the incomes of the few well-to-do have been excluded from the average.

Millions in the Third World today live in conditions that can be described as absolute poverty, as distinguished from general income inequality. Although all Third World states are "less developed" than states in the First World, the poorest states are often referred to as the "least developed" or the Fourth World.[1] Absolute poverty is income below the level that provides the bare essentials of food, clothing, and shelter. World Bank economists have defined the poverty line as the income needed to give each individual in a society a daily supply of 2,250 calories. This required a per capita annual income of $200 in 1975. In that year an estimated 644 million people, or 38 percent of the populations of the LDCs, lived in absolute poverty. World Bank economists have projected that 475 million people will still be living in absolute poverty by the year 2000, although by that time the percentage of such poor people may have fallen to as low as 16 percent. These figures indicate that large numbers of Third World people are desperately striving to improve their conditions of life and that some positive movement is occurring.

Second, the profile state is located to the south of most of the developed countries and has a *tropical* climate. More precisely, the poorest of the developing countries are with few exceptions located south of thirty degrees north latitude, which runs along the southern boundary of the United States and along the northern reaches of the African continent. Tropical jungles, vast mountain ranges, arid deserts, and wild bush country make up great portions of the landmasses of these countries, forcing the people to carry on a daily struggle with nature to eke out a bare existence. High temperatures and humidity and soils leached by tropical rains make the job of wresting a living a precarious one. The profile state lacks the energy sources of coal and oil, although potential hydroelectric power sources exist in the form of great tropical rivers that wind through the mountains and jungles. In some Third World countries, tropical forests are being destroyed because wood is the only available energy supply for cooking and heating. Third World countries also suffer economically because of the high shipping costs that result from the great distances separating most of them from the industrial countries, which increase the prices of both their exports and their imports.

Third, the profile state is experiencing a great *population surge* that in some Third World countries is rapidly assuming the proportions of an "explosion." Birthrates continue high, as they have for centuries, but a new factor—death control—has been added to the equation. The first benefits of modernization to reach many of the developing nations have been drugs and medicines to save lives, chemicals to control mosquitoes and other disease carriers, and water-purifying agents. Technical assistance programs have likewise concentrated on teaching people good health and sanitation habits through public health programs. The result has been a lengthening of the life span in the profile state and a pronounced population imbalance favoring those under eighteen. The second UN World Population Conference, held in Mexico City in 1984, concluded that world population should stabilize at about 10.2 billion by the year 2100. From 1985 to 2100, Africa and Latin America will have the highest growth rates, followed closely by South and East Asia.[2] Actually these projections are based on an anticipated slowing down of population growth that has not yet been achieved.

Fourth, the profile state often lacks the ability to support itself because of the low productivity of *primitive agriculture.* Peasant families painfully tilling their small plots or working on large haciendas or plantations for absentee landlords are living symbols of the plight of agriculture in such countries. Much of the profile state's farming is geared to a subsistence level, with little or no effort or capability to develop a cash crop that could earn foreign exchange. Farming is intensive, with peasants crowded onto the arable land in such numbers that the soil's fertility is low. Crop diseases, insects, wild animals, and rodents and unpredictable natural disasters in the forms of droughts, floods, and hurricanes can ruin the efforts of months of toil. Primitive, handmade plows pulled by plodding buffalos or oxen, and sometimes by human beings, and wooden hoes in some cases provide the only mechanical aids to productivity. Out of this syndrome of inefficiency must come the surpluses to provide "social capital" for community improvements, labor for the hoped-for factories, and the extra food needed to feed those who leave the land. All Third World peoples living under conditions of absolute poverty are undernourished, and millions are seriously malnourished.[3] A substantial increase in agricultural production would be a great boon to their development programs.

Fifth, the profile state has a *colonial background* that has helped determine the direction of modernization and continues to affect the thought and action of its people. In many cases the rudimentary physical framework for development was laid out by the colonial power in the nineteenth century and the first half of the twentieth century. Surpassing the influence of that framework, however, is the lasting imprint that colonialism left on the attitudes and emotions of the people. The humiliation and sense of frustration fostered by foreign rule left scars of anti-Westernism that remain today. In such states internal disunity often still exists as a holdover of a carefully cultivated colonial policy of "divide and rule" or as a result of boundary lines drawn by imperial design that sundered established communities or tribes and mixed traditional enemies within the same political unit. In societies lacking most of the internal impulses and capabilities necessary for modernization, the unity produced by the effort to end foreign rule produced a ferment for change that independence and UN programs have encouraged.

Sixth, the profile state is built on the social fabric of a *traditional society.* Custom and tradition provide the social cement; and religion and conservative values provide the guidelines for human action. Small elite groups dominate the society and often oppose virtually all change because change would mean a loss of their status. Rigid class structures immobilize even the able and ambitious individual. Objective conditions of social stagnation are reinforced by group attitudes, requiring a revolution of perspectives as a prelude to modernity. No society completely abandons its traditional culture; transitional societies in a state of vigorous change reshape the old values, resulting in a social, political, and economic restlessness and rootlessness. Interaction between the old and the new may yield turmoil, revolution, or civil war as rival groups offer the people new ideologies imported from foreign sources, each seeking to capture the modernization process and to direct it toward ideologically determined goals.

Seventh, the profile state is characterized by *mass illiteracy.* Contrasted with the United States and Europe, where illiteracy rates range from 1 to 8 percent, in most Third World countries the proportion of illiterates ranges from 20 to 80 percent. In some countries of the Middle East and tropical Africa, illiteracy reaches 90 percent, and few nations in these areas can claim 50 percent literacy. Latin-American illiteracy rates are high except in Cuba and in countries with predominantly European populations, such as Argentina and Costa Rica.

But educational needs to achieve modernization go beyond basic literacy to include technical, secondary, and university training. A university-trained elite exists in most of the underdeveloped countries, but it is extremely small in number and it consists for the most part of specialists in law, the humanities, and the social sciences. This elite provided the leadership in the march to independence, but a new elite of entrepreneurs, managers, scientists, engineers, and technicians is needed to exploit resources and organize the productive machinery.

Eighth, in its trade relations with the rest of the world, the profile state rests on a *weak economic base.* The export trade of most developing countries is based on the production or extraction of one or a few primary commodities. Living standards beyond the subsistence level provided by local agriculture depend on the export market for these commodities. Foreign exchange earnings desperately needed for buying capital goods from the advanced countries are limited by adverse world market conditions. These include (1) an oversupply of most primary commodities; (2) competition from advanced states with greater productive efficiency; (3) fluctuating prices resulting from speculation among buyers, changes in supply, and other conditions beyond the control of the developing states; (4) the introduction of synthetics and substitutes to replace natural commodities; (5) high shipping costs in getting commodities to distant markets; and (6) deteriorating terms of trade resulting in lower prices for primary commodity exports and higher prices for imports of manufactured consumer and capital goods. A recognition that the world economy, as reflected in the foregoing, is stacked against their interests led the LDCs in the 1970s and 1980s to demand fundamental changes through the creation of a New International Economic Order (NIEO).

Ninth, the profile state suffers from *political instability.* Most developing states are characterized by one-party, authoritarian regimes. Some are ruled by royal autocrats; others, as in many countries of Latin America, are run by a strong man or dictator supported by the landed aristocracy and the military. In many of the new nations, early attempts to establish democratic systems failed when the promised bounty of independence could not be delivered. A strong man, usually exuding charisma and often a military officer, or a group of oligarchs, typically a military clique, then seized power. Opposition groups and parties either do not exist or exist in a highly innocuous form to provide the shadow but not the substance of a democratic system. Political activity is generally confined to the capital city and involves only infighting among the political elite jockeying for positions of strength or attempting a coup. In Third World countries, changes of government through free elections have been rare occurrences. Of all the problems facing the developing states, effective UN support to build political stability is perhaps the most difficult and frustrating.

In summary, a typical underdeveloped state suffers from chronic mass poverty; its location, topography, and climate limit its potentials; its predominantly young population threatens to outstrip economic growth; its inefficient economy rests on an outmoded agricultural base; its customs and traditions thwart change; its colonial background induces contemporary conflicts; its illiteracy rate is high; its competitive position in world trade is poor; its people are largely apolitical; and its government is authoritarian. These human and environmental conditions should give rise to little but despair. They are, however, counterbalanced by an overriding urge to develop and by the help offered by other states, regional groups, and the United Nations. Together, these counterbalancing forces may yet produce dramatic results in economic development.

A BLUEPRINT FOR ECONOMIC DEVELOPMENT

Governmental action to promote economic growth and modernization requires judicious planning so that strategies will match national needs and capabilities. Careful planning is also needed to ensure that resources provided through international agencies are put to productive use. Old prejudices against planning held by the Governing Board of the World Bank and some of the leading capitalist states have largely disappeared, and recipient countries are now required to have developmental blueprints to show how foreign assistance will fit into their master strategies.

Acceptance of government planning for economic development has been accompanied by a recognition that positive governmental action to promote development programs is an essential follow-up. Whether an economy is predicated on free enterprise principles or Soviet-style total planning, or falls somewhere on the vast spectrum between these two extremes, government will in any case play a significant role in budgeting, taxing, spending, regulating, promoting, programming, and determining foreign economic policies. Government planning and programs will vary, of course, according to the indigenous conditions of each country; no two cases will be exactly alike.

Governmental programs cannot, however, provide a shortcut or easy route to modernization. Economic development has always been a slow and painful process. Despite unprecedented amounts of outside help from the United Nations and other sources, the job remains largely one of local initiative and self-help. Today a race is on between rival ideologies and their respective approaches. But within each developing society there is a greater race that involves a desperate attempt to push development ahead of its two most dangerous competitors—hunger and mass frustration.

Preparing the Base

Except for certain natural factors not subject to human alteration, most of the characteristics of our profile state are susceptible to change and improvement. Governmental development plans and UN programs aim at modifying these factors to support a virtual economic and social revolution of modernization. The proximate objective of every developing society is to reach the point from which the society will launch itself into an upward trend of steady, self-sustaining growth.

Sociological and Political Changes. An adequate "takeoff" base requires a modernization of social and political institutions and practices. The following changes are fundamental to that objective.

1. Attitudinal Changes. In many countries a privileged elite will be challenged to adopt new attitudes favoring a modernization that may threaten its traditional status. The choice, however, is not always between self-instituted change and the status quo. The alternative may be a violent revolt that would sweep away all elements of feudal privilege, carried out by those in the society whose attitudes have changed more rapidly than those of the elite. Other critical value changes may involve new orientations toward "worldliness" and "getting ahead," the psychic satisfactions of work, the profit incentive, and other sometimes crass but essential motivations to economic advances.

2. Political Evolution. Tangible societal changes must proceed apace of changing attitudes. First, a political socialization must occur, taking the form of support for a minimally effective national political system. Government, a distant power that extracts taxes and drafts village youth for military service, must take on a new image through directing and servicing functions. Political leadership must be selected on the basis of abilities and policies rather than inherited status or wealth. A corps of administrators recruited and trained in modern governmental techniques must provide a degree of unity for the entire country, reaching even remote villages.

3. Educational Development. Education may be the keystone in building a modern society. Not only do technicians of varying degrees of skills need to be trained, but fundamental learning in the "three R's" must be imparted to a large portion of the population. In many developing countries a majority of the people are dispersed in agricultural pursuits and few have the barest claim to literacy. Schools can serve an integrating function in selecting the best and most compatible traits of the old world to mesh with those of the new world of modernity. As in the advanced states, education must also provide a nationalizing force in developing a single language and in cultivating national myths, traditions, and popular heroes. Beyond the production of a literate, informed citizenry and a trained labor force, elites with secondary and college education must be developed to direct the nation's changeover to a world of business, commerce, industry, and modern administration. The quality of human resources has increasingly come to be recognized in the emerging nations as a critical factor in the modernization process, with education seen as the pathway to opportunity for the nation.

4. Population Control. Population control is widely perceived as crucial to developmental success but may in fact be primarily a problem of education. Demographers speak of the self-limiting nature of the population explosion, noting that rising living standards in the advanced nations had the effect of reducing birthrates drastically. If preindustrialization birthrates had continued in Europe during the nineteenth and twentieth centuries, for example, some European countries would now have populations almost ten times larger. But in the developing world of today, the problem is that the population surge is of such a magnitude that living standards can scarcely be raised to the point where they constitute a self-limiting control on family size. Where will the savings come from if every increment of national income is used to maintain an ever-increasing population? How can rising labor productivity be achieved from an undernourished population whose individual diets are often less than 2,000 calories daily and deficient in proteins? Questions such as these served as the focus for debate at the First (Bucharest in 1974) and Second (Mexico City in 1984) UN World Population Conferences.

One of the major issues confronting the United Nations in its efforts to control population is that of abortion. In the 1980s, for example, the United States declared that it would no longer support UN population control programs in those countries, such as China, where the government administered a proabortion policy. Birth control is a logical answer to the problem of abortion, but the technical potentialities of birth control are widely thwarted by the vast human barriers of religion, morality, economics, apathy, and ignorance. In a major program for population control supported by the United Nations, governmental and private organizations in India have distributed birth control information widely and provided the means of contraception, but with little apparent result. Positive governmental programs may go beyond this approach to encourage smaller families. In the West such programs have included (1) prohibitions against child labor, (2) policies and programs for the emancipation of women, (3) social mobility leading to the economic independence of children from their parents, (4) mechanization of agriculture, and (5) social insurance freeing parents from dependence on children in their old age. When large families become an economic burden rather than an asset, when children can no longer be exploited for economic and dowry purposes, when large families are no longer accepted as a status symbol, populations may be brought under a measure of control. Regardless of the gains made in national income and development, if population growth exceeds or equals them, no improvement in standards of living can result and frustration and revolutionary zeal may intensify.

5. Community Development. Finally, social change in local communities must be stressed. The potentials for modernization rest on a base of village life that has not changed in its social characteristics for many centuries. Villagers must discover that working together can enrich their lives, improve their living conditions, and reduce social barriers. Through increasing self-reliance, awakened by UN-supported programs of community development, villages can implement national programs, thereby reducing the shock impact of urbanism and industrialism on the new society.

Economic Changes.   The central objective of modernization in all developing societies is economic betterment. Social and political changes are aimed mainly at making these societies more receptive to and more efficient at promoting economic development. But the economic problem remains of how to achieve a modern economy, of how to move a largely undeveloped state to the takeoff point from which it can progress through self-sustaining growth.

What are the economic variables in the development equation? How can an underdeveloped state marshal its forces in a collective economic offensive? A UN delegate once observed apropos economic development that "it was easy enough to recognize what had to be done but difficult to decide how to go about it." Though no two states would proceed in exactly the same way, some common approaches can be suggested as "prescriptions for development." Remember, however, that much controversy exists over the best way to achieve development.

1. Increase Agricultural Output.   The objectives of greater farm productivity are a healthier, better-fed, harder-working population; increased foreign exchange earnings through exports; and a savings—extracted from increased output—destined for investment. In the early stages of development, there may be no increase in the peasant's food consumption, but there must be a rise in food production to support a growing urban work force. The most useful means of expanding productivity fall into the category of improved farming technology—modern implements, fertilizers, insect and disease control, good seed stocks, weed control, and scientific farming techniques. In all of these areas, the United Nations has provided leadership, loans, grants, and specific programs. Agrarian reform is another approach that has proved successful in a few societies. Basic to agrarian reform is a land redistribution among the peasants, achieved by splitting up large estates. Although such a redistribution would increase incentives, small holdings are generally uneconomic because they cannot take advantage of economies of scale and because mechanization of such holdings is nearly impossible. Peasant cooperatives to encourage joint production, aided by a reform of inheritance laws that would end fragmentation of plots, may provide an answer to this dilemma. Credit to finance purchases of seeds and fertilizer is a critical element in efforts to boost production. In 1979 the United Nations sought to expand credit for the rural poor through the creation of the International Fund for Agricultural Development (IFAD), which has since dispensed over $2 billion in project loans.[4]

The North-South Institute, which conducts policy-oriented research on Third World issues, concluded in a 1984 report that (1) agricultural development would take longer than experts had predicted in the 1970s; (2) government must play a major role by providing an incentive structure for millions of small farmers; (3)

smaller projects generally yield higher returns than major programs; and (4) concentration on industrialization to the neglect of agriculture had weakened the agricultural base.[5]

2. Develop Simple Industries.   Agricultural production must be supplemented by the development of fishing, mining, and raw material potentials. Most of the new nations have access to the world's oceans and some have sizable inland lakes—both of which are sources for food rich in protein. Expansion in the production of primary commodities may help underdeveloped states to earn critically needed foreign exchange, although lower prices resulting from highly competitive conditions in the world commodity market may negate increased production. Increased productivity, however, will enable such states to take advantage of periods of peak demand and high prices when the advanced countries are engaged in high levels of military spending or enjoy economic boom conditions.

3. Invest in Social Overhead.   A modern economy can be built only on a broad economic base or infrastructure. This means that each underdeveloped country professing modernization as a goal must be prepared to devote human and financial resources to the building of facilities for basic transport, communication, irrigation, and power supplies. The manpower needs to carry out such projects might be available if the labor surplus engaged in inefficient agricultural pursuits could be taken off the land, mobilized into construction units, and utilized in simple "social capital" projects. Added incentives underlying this approach may include reduced unemployment, increased agricultural production as laborsaving techniques are introduced, and an efficient use of foreign exchange to buy machinery from the industrial nations. Psychologically, the personal involvement of thousands of young men in social projects of this kind may help unleash a national pride and a surge of development spirit, thus giving purpose to their lives. Recognizing that the world youth population would increase from 738 million in 1975 to 1.18 billion by 2000, the United Nations proclaimed the International Youth Year in 1985 as a call for governmental action to produce jobs for young people.

4. Acquire Technical Skills.   Modern factories and transportation, communication, and power facilities can be operated only with skilled personnel. An industrializing society faces an enormous task in forging a new labor force of energetic and capable workers from a peasant society. Trainees must be supported out of the savings yielded from a surplus of production over consumption. Exceptions to this rule may be found in apprentice-type training programs and in the technical assistance rendered by advanced states or international institutions. New workers must adjust to the strict discipline of industrial life—regular hours, machine-dictated work speeds, the rhythmic monotony of life on a production line. Managerial and administrative personnel will constitute a new elite, culled out of the indigenous population through ruthless competition for unprecedented rewards.

5. Foster Industrialization.   The capstone of the host of social, political, and economic changes predicated as useful or necessary to modernization can be summed up in the word *industrialization*. Many leaders in developing states equate development and industrialization, and stress the latter as the key to growth and prosperity. However, if industries are created before a proper base has been prepared, they will exist precariously in a modernizing enclave while the rest of the country and most of its people sink deeper into poverty. Sometimes overlooked by developing societies are nonindustrialized states with high productivity and living standards, such as New Zealand and the Netherlands.

For a developing state to industrialize, it must import most of the necessary machinery, tools, and skills. Unlike social capital improvements, which often need sheer muscle power, industrial capital can be built locally only *after* some measure of industrialization has occurred. If modernizing states had the time and patience, they could follow the lead of the West in moving from primitive handicraft to increasingly complex machines over a century or more, but their societies demand rapid action. Quite naturally, most leaders of the new nations prefer to hurdle the successive steps of development and start with modern, sophisticated—even automated—factories. Since the more efficient factory uses less labor, the rise of a large, disgruntled, unemployed urban proletariat seems unavoidable and a dangerous by-product of that kind of industrialization. However, experts from advanced nations who urge leaders to build simple, labor-intensive industries may be suspected of having protectionist motives or, worse still, neocolonialist attitudes.

Industrialization, if it occurs, can produce many salutary results for the underdeveloped society. For one thing, manufactured goods become more readily available and cheaper for the masses. Foreign exchange formerly expended on imports of consumer items can be saved. Savings for investment should increase substantially once industrialization has begun, since national income will be higher. Industrialized plants may also contribute to a local fabrication of capital goods. Despite its pitfalls and the problems it may create, industrialization may be a logical route for many developing countries to take in their attempted "great leap forward" to modernization. The extent, however, to which their people may view it as a singularly facile solution to problems of mass poverty is likely to be more an emotional than a rational reaction.

Acquiring the Means

Capital accumulation is the sine qua non of every development plan. Capital can be defined as the factor of production—along with land and labor, the other factors of production—that takes the form of money or producer goods. Like a catalytic agent in a chemical process, capital, especially in the form of foreign exchange, can produce a desirable reaction between the human and mechanical elements in the economic equation by providing supplies, tools, plant facilities, power, and modern production machines. It can also attract foreign technicians and pay for training local personnel to fill skilled and semiskilled positions. Capital is most useful when it is applied to a carefully prepared social and economic base, when it is invested in sound ventures rather than projects aimed at feeding national egos, and when it is used to produce goods that have a market abroad.

Because Third World leaders believe that capital accumulation will set the pace for industrialization, it has become their main objective. This overriding fascination with capital as the central theme of developmental programs has not always been shared by foreign advisers and planners, or by international institutions and aid-supplying nations. Their restraint is voiced in favor of a "balanced, overall process," but it may also reflect a fear that developing states will be unable to compete effectively in world markets or that, from a narrower viewpoint, industrial development in the Third World may cut into their own foreign markets. Most Western countries, for example, prefer to offer various kinds of development aid, but not capital for industrialization. From their perspective, capital will flow from developed to developing states whenever investment opportunities make such movement profitable, and most capital transfers should therefore be kept in the private sector. Regardless of these caveats, the hunt for capital to supply the voracious appetites of the developing nations accelerates each year. Major sources of capital include (1) local savings, (2) foreign trade, (3) private investment, (4) loans, and (5) foreign aid. Each of these sources has received various kinds of support from the United Nations.

Local Savings.   Leadership elites within developing states must come to grips with two fundamental economic imperatives. First, domestic consumption must be restrained so that production yields a surplus; second, the surplus or savings must be invested creatively to increase production. A surplus can be provided (1) by raising output but not consumption, (2) by reducing consumption but not output, or (3) by raising output faster than consumption. The first two choices are clearly dangerous to the stability of the state since they could provoke a bitter reaction from workers who either work harder for the same pay or receive pay cuts in the interest of development. In none of the three options will domestic consumption be likely to measure up to popular demand, reflecting the harshness of economic development and the resort in some societies to authoritarian methods to force savings through work pressures and through controlled, subsistence-level standards of living.

Local savings can be accrued through taxation, private profit, profit from socialized industries, expropriation, rationing, or inflation. All involve some ingredients of compulsion or exploitation, but the objective is to move as rapidly as possible to a stage of development where progress is reflected in expanded output and in increased consumption that attracts capital investments from abroad. Local savings, however, have a limited applicability to this early forward movement since the germinal core of industrial goods must come from abroad and thus must be paid for in foreign exchange. Local savings are best fitted for "social overhead" projects, which contribute to the building of an infrastructure base that may help attract foreign capital.

Foreign Trade.   Many Third World countries seek to industrialize by replacing imports with locally produced articles of commerce (the import substitution approach) and by expanding exports. An import substitution strategy increases the role of government in managing the economy and is often implemented through a system of tariffs. Foreign markets, particularly those of the advanced countries of the West, are the major source of capital useful to economic development. During the past forty years, foreign trade earnings have accounted for about 80 percent of the foreign exchange funds of the developing countries as a group. Most of their exports have been primary commodities. Many of the advanced countries followed this same route to industrialization and diversification. In the first half of the nineteenth century, for example, the United States depended heavily on cotton exports to feed the engine of economic growth. Foreign earnings financed a growing textile industry, which in turn increased exports and spurred the growth of related industries, such as iron foundries and machine tool and farm implement manufactures.

The leaders of developing countries, whether they accept this approach or not, believe that the cards are stacked against them in the world of trade realities. First, they point out, seesawing demand for primary commodities brought about by war-peace and boom-recession fluctuations in the West has produced chaos in the development of supply sources. Second, specialization in primary products tends to perpetuate existing trade patterns and to condemn Third World states to remain dependent on Western markets for their exports, and on Western suppliers for imports of industrial products. Third, supplies of primary commodities have tended to exceed demand because of productivity increases in Third World states, the increasing development of primary production in advanced states, the substitution of synthetics for natural products, and a change in consumer demand toward more sophisticated products having a smaller raw material content. Protectionist trade policies, price-support programs for marginal domestic producers, and subsidies for exporters have helped Western states accelerate this trend toward securing primary commodities from local producers. Fourth, the terms of trade between the developed and the developing nations have generally tended to favor the former. The terms of trade problem involves the prices that developing states receive for their exports in relationship to the prices that they pay for goods and machinery imported from the advanced states. Over the past seventy years the trend has favored higher prices for industrial goods and lower prices for primary commodities, with the exceptions of the periods encompassing World War I, World War II, and the Korean and Vietnam Wars. This problem can be illustrated by a simple example: In 1956, Morocco had to export 200 tons of phosphate abroad to pay for one imported truck; in 1963, Morocco had to export 318 tons of phosphate to pay for the same truck.[6] That trend has continued, although phosphate prices have fluctuated over the years. Such marketing conditions have undermined development plans, arrested economic growth, and produced widespread despair in the developing world. Under such conditions, increases in the productivity of Third World countries inescapably lead to greater supplies and lower prices.

In the desperate search for capital through trade, the Third World bloc decided to use its growing political decision-making power to hold a world trade conference. In 1964 the UN Conference on Trade and Development (UNCTAD) convened at Geneva to try to remedy some of the problems underlying the Third World's weak position in world trade. The Conference was so successful in offering the developing states a forum to "educate" the developed states on their economic needs that the General Assembly thereafter converted UNCTAD into a permanent trade and development organization, with global meetings held every three or four years.*

To meet the challenge posed by their inferior economic bargaining and trading position, Third World countries began to lobby at meetings of UNCTAD for a more favorable trade position vis-à-vis the industrialized countries. By 1970 UNCTAD had reached agreement on a Generalized System of Preferences (GSP), and the next year the West-oriented General Agreement on Tariffs and Trade (GATT) gave its members authority to offer tariff preferences to LDCs. Today most of the industrialized, market economy countries of the West offer GSP treatment on designated products, in many cases permitting them duty-free entry. In the United States, for example, billions of dollars worth of dutiable imports from developing countries have entered the country duty free each year since the adoption of GSP. Excluded by the United States from GSP treatment are such categories as Communist countries, members of OPEC, countries that have nationalized American-owned properties without compensation, and countries that grant sanctuary to terrorists. Nearly three thousand tariff categories are eligible for duty-free treatment, including many agricultural items, wood and paper products, and a broad range of manufactured articles.

The GSP approach is based on the "infant industry" concept that new industries in the LDCs cannot compete effectively with older, more efficient firms in the industrialized countries. GSP is a means of equalizing the competition and giving the developing states an opportunity to enter the markets of the developed countries. The foreign exchange they earn in this way can be directed into support for economic development programs. Although GSP has been helpful, a shrinking world market for many articles of commerce, growing competition from the developed countries, and the failure to open markets to most Third World goods have kept such gains limited. Increased trade remains the best hope of the developing countries, but only those that produce and export large quantities of oil, gas, and other products high in market demand in the West have thus far been able to successfully translate trade into modernization. The share of developing country exports in the consumption of manufactured goods in the industrial countries doubled over the decade of the 1970s, from 1.7 percent in 1970 to 3.4 percent in 1980, yet the position of these goods in the development equation was not substantially improved.[7] The low prices charged for them to make them competitive combined with the high prices paid for imports from the industrialized countries worked to reduce the amount of net capital available for development projects from trade earnings.

The Third World bloc never believed that GSP alone would solve their trade and development problems. Indeed, it became increasingly clear to the developing states that the existing world economy had to be liquidated and replaced with a new system more favorable to the interests of the LDCs. At the Sixth Special Session of the General Assembly, called in 1974 to deal explicitly with trade and development

---

*The origins and role of UNCTAD are discussed in Chapter 10.

problems, the Third World's caucusing Group of 77 proclaimed the need to establish a New International Economic Order (NIEO). The existing world economic system, according to NIEO proponents, was hopelessly rigged against the interests and needs of the developing countries. This view was supported by a "dependency theory" that has been generally accepted throughout the Third World to explain its failure to make rapid development progress. Dependency theorists argue that the world economy is divided into an exploitive northern tier and a dependent southern tier, which is a carryover from the colonial era. Low prices for raw materials and high prices for industrialized goods, they claim, keep the South in bondage. Hence a new system based on economic realities, fairness, and justice is needed. Later that same year, the General Assembly followed up the Special Session Declaration by approving a Charter of Economic Rights and Duties of States, which sought to convert the general principles of NIEO into a statement of the concrete actions needed to implement the new approach. Since 1974 numerous confrontations have occurred between the First and Third Worlds, with the latter constantly on the offensive and the former typically in a defensive posture.

The demand for NIEO is basically an attempt by the developing states to restructure the international economic system and provide for the redistribution of the world's wealth. In their view, prices for primary commodities have been kept artificially low and those of industrial goods excessively high in world trade as a result of colonialism and neocolonialism. Moreover, in the general workings of the world economy—interest rates, shipping costs, protectionism, insurance rates, and decisions made in GATT, the IMF, and the World Bank Group, for example—the nations of the West dominate the decision processes. Increased trade and other economic actions that support development programs are desperately needed by the LDCs— hence the demand for NIEO.

By the mid-1980s the leaders of the Third World backed away from their persistent demands for NIEO and began to focus on more immediate and pragmatic issues. NIEO, however, is not dead, and efforts to reinvigorate it can be expected. It has taken on the nature of a holy crusade, a sacred mission to convince the rich countries of the world that the existing international system should be modified in the interest of all.

Private Investment. Historically, most funds for the development of emergent economies have come from capital transfers in the form of investments by individuals and corporations from capital-surplus countries. The significance of this source was recognized by President George D. Woods of the International Bank when he stressed that "economic development in many countries will never really get into high gear until they find a way to tap the vast resources of capital and know-how that are available in the private sector of the industrialized nations."[8]

The major obstacle, over which the developing countries have little or no control, is the vast lucrative investment opportunities that are available in the advanced countries themselves. Most private investment capital flows through domestic stock exchanges or is invested directly in business expansions in the United States, Western

Europe, Japan, Australia, and other relatively "safe" countries. Not only are these countries politically stable and economically viable, but investments are safe from governmental expropriation, skilled labor is available, mass consumer markets provide local outlets for manufactured goods, and conversions of profits into dollars or other hard currencies and their transfer to investors are a simple matter. None of these conditions generally obtains in the developing countries of Africa, Asia, and Latin America.

Unlike the flow of governmental funds, which is determined by political and military objectives, private capital transfer is influenced mainly by commercial considerations. Various UN agencies have searched for answers to the problem of making emergent economies more attractive as investment opportunities. Among the proposals that have been made are (1) tax exemptions or reductions and governmental investment guarantees by the developed countries; (2) informational, promotional, and technical assistance centers set up by the developing countries and international institutions; (3) cooperation between private investors and local entrepreneurs aimed at encouraging a "reinvestment of profits"; and (4) studies by the International Bank leading to the establishment of international investment insurance, machinery for arbitrating disputes, and guarantees for the securities of developing states in world capital markets.

Private Loans.   Private borrowing is related to private investment but poses some additional problems. As with young married couples, the attraction of consumer goods from the advanced countries may lead newly independent and underdeveloped countries to live beyond their means. In the competition for overseas markets, many private firms may be far too willing to risk loans to facilitate the peddling of their wares. The result may be a growth in private debts that sacrifices future capital needs, raises false expectations of higher living standards, and causes a disastrous inflation within the underdeveloped country. In addition to consumer loans, Third World nations may make loans to underwrite major development projects, with the expectation that increased foreign exchange earnings will enable them to pay off the loans plus interest over a period of years. If the anticipated expansion in sales in the world market does not occur, both the Third World nations and the lending banks may be in serious trouble. If private loans have been supplemented by loans from national, regional, and UN lending agencies, the recipient governments may find it impossible to come up with the foreign exchange needed for annual payments.

This situation came to pass in the 1980s. During the 1970s and early 1980s, vast surpluses of capital were loaned by private and public banks to Third World states, especially in Latin America. LDC debt grew from about $329 billion in 1977 to about $812 billion in 1984. As a major world economic recession deepened in the early 1980s, while the export income of Third World nations decreased, their payment obligations increased as interest rates tied to market conditions rose precipitously. In 1982 shock waves rocked the world banking community when Mexico announced that it could no longer meet its foreign debt payments. The result was a devaluation of the peso and a rescheduling of Mexico's massive debt by the International Monetary Fund (IMF), the Bank for International Settlements (BIS), and a number of central banks and commercial banks in the United States, Western Europe, and Japan. But Mexico was not alone. By 1983, 34 countries were trying to reschedule their foreign debt payments. Rescheduling an international debt means that missed interest and amortization payments are canceled and then added to the aggregate debt owed by the defaulting state, typically with a lengthening of the overall period for the repayment of the debt. Additional loans were granted by the IMF so that hard-pressed debtor countries would not have to default on their loans or have them rescheduled. Such additional loans were granted only on the condition that each recipient country adopt rigorous austerity measures and adhere to stabilization guidelines laid down by the IMF. Austerity led to economic stagnation, heavy unemployment, and vilification of the IMF by debtor countries. The Group of 77, representing the interests of the developing states, called on the West to restructure debt payments in ways that would revive the momentum of development and increase access to new loans, a position also proclaimed by the UN Conference on Trade and Development at its 1983 meeting in Yugoslavia (UNCTAD VI).

For the foreseeable future, loans are a negative factor. New loans have been made to Third World countries in recent years, but most of these loans have been aimed only at providing the foreign exchange necessary to make installment payments on the principal and interest of debts to commercial banks so as to avoid a massive default and a major international banking crisis. No one can foretell the ultimate impact of this huge international debt, and the crisis deepens with each new loan and each increase in interest rates.

Foreign Aid.   Capital inflows in the form of public grants or loans have been a significant development financing source for four decades. Foreign economic assistance offers the advantage of reducing the harshness of life in an industrializing society, which without this alternative must employ painful methods of economic "forced marches" and compulsorily reduced consumption to achieve a surplus. Regardless of the motivations underlying foreign aid—national self-interest, philanthropy, ideological rivalry, economic dependence, regional growth, or global stability—it has become an established institution of the contemporary state system. For many years the developing states have offered proposals within the UN system for massive transfers of capital. In the early years of the United Nations, such demands were aimed at the creation of a Special UN Fund for Economic Development (the SUNFED proposal), through which huge amounts of capital would be transferred to the LDCs. Under the proposal each developed state would contribute 1 percent of its annual GNP to the capital fund, an amount far in excess of most national aid programs. The United States and other capital-surplus countries rejected the SUNFED idea, holding that existing international institutions such as the World Bank were sufficient to meet the need for capital. Moreover, it was clear that the market economy states of the West offered foreign aid predominantly to prepare the LDCs for an infusion of *private* capital. The West viewed foreign aid as a means for unlocking vast opportunities for profitable investments, thus providing extensive benefits for both donor and recipient states. Foreign aid, in other words, was to "prepare the base" for investment by building infrastructure, improving health, expanding agriculture, conquering illiteracy, and teaching modern skills. These advancements were expected to attract the private capital needed for meaningful economic growth in the developing state. To funnel capital into the LDCs through intergovernmental programs would tend to promote socialism, not capitalism.

The developing states, however, remained steadfast in their search for capital through foreign aid. Their demands for capital aid resulted in 1956 in the creation of the International Finance Corporation (IFC) as an affiliate of the International Bank for Reconstruction and Development (IBRD).* The new lending institution was authorized to make loans to and investments in private companies in developing countries. By the mid-1980s the IFC had provided loans to the LDCs totaling more than $5 billion, which was a small drop in the aid bucket demanded by the developing states. In 1960, in response to criticisms by the LDCs that the repayment terms for IBRD and IFC loans were too harsh, the International Development Association (IDA) was established as an affiliate of the World Bank to grant interest-free "soft loans" with a fifty-year repayment schedule and a slow amortization rate (a ten-year period of grace, then 1 percent of the loan repayable annually for the next ten years and 3 percent repayable annually for the next thirty years). IDA has made a great many loans over the years, but it often suffers from a lack of capital because, unlike IBRD and IFC, it cannot raise loanable funds from private world capital markets. Its funds come mainly from direct contributions by some of its richer members, but this aid is tendered only sporadically.

These efforts to placate the developing bloc through operations of the World Bank Group failed, and pressures continued to mount for the SUNFED proposal. Finally, in 1966, the Third World bloc had sufficient votes in the General Assembly to raise a two-thirds majority in favor of the SUNFED idea. The creation of the UN Capital Development Fund (UNCDF) capped, under a new title, more than a decade of effort to implement the SUNFED proposal. The capital-surplus states of the First World, however, refused to put a single dollar, mark, franc, yen, pound, or other hard currency into the UNCDF, and the Communist countries of the Second World followed their example by likewise refusing to participate.

Other efforts to secure capital through the UN system have also failed. These included a proposal to distribute exclusively to the LDCs the new special drawing rights (SDRs) created by the International Monetary Fund (IMF) to supplement international reserves. The major capital states rejected this proposal and used their majority voting power to distribute newly created SDRs largely to themselves by apportioning them on the basis of each member's subscription to the Fund. A proposal under the new Law of the Sea Treaty was to have the income from the World Ocean and its seabed apportioned among the LDCs for development purposes. Much

---

*The origins and role of the World Bank Group are discussed more extensively in the latter part of this chapter.

of this proposal was emasculated during the ten-year negotiation process, and after the treaty emerged, several of the key parties—including Britain, West Germany, and the United States—rejected it by refusing to sign the treaty. Finally, a breakthrough occurred outside the United Nations. Huge amounts of capital accumulated in the developed states were loaned to the LDCs by commercial banks of the West, with aggregate Third World debt totaling more than $1 trillion. The problems of repayment created by those capital transfers have been discussed above.

PROMOTING INTERNATIONAL ACTION

The major responsibility for economic development quite naturally falls to the lot of the developing states themselves. Indeed, it would be difficult to discover a single "poor" state whose people did not regard economic betterment as the major objective and whose government did not regard it as the most pressing problem. Yet the need for outside help has become an accepted tenet of international economic orthodoxy that few challenge today; and "foreign aid" is widely regarded as a moral and political obligation of developed states. In response to numerous appeals, diverse programs of assistance have been planned and executed over a period of four decades, starting with the Point Four Program of the United States in 1949. These international efforts, although based on converging interests of donors and recipients, have for the most part been shaped and directed by donor countries and have reflected their political, economic, military, moral, or community interests. This relationship between donors and recipients has produced problems of coordinating aid programs so that they will fit constructively with the developmental plans of the recipients. Major issues have arisen, and these issues have occasionally embroiled relations between giver and receiver.

Should Donors Use Bilateral or Multilateral Channels?

One such issue involves the means by which aid is funneled into developing economies. Although most aid of this kind comes from about a dozen capital-surplus countries, each contributor may use a variety of approaches.

Most donor states favor bilateral aid because with such aid they can exercise control over programs by imposing conditions on recipient states. In this way, industries competitive with those of the donor state can be discouraged, economic and social reforms can be encouraged, and counterpart funds can be required. Cold war ideological and political objectives have often been critical determinants of the direction, kinds, and amounts of bilateral aid. Propaganda advantages are also not overlooked by donor governments, since local populations can easily be made aware of the identity of their benefactor. Large amounts of foreign aid may permit the donor state to influence the recipient state's foreign policy, and directed trade patterns together with a need for spare parts may foster its economic dependence.

Most developing countries prefer to receive aid through multilateral channels because this is likely to minimize interference in their domestic and foreign affairs. Exceptions to this preference are found in states that have a close and favorable relationship with major aid-givers and states that for strategic reasons have been able to secure large amounts of aid from competitive East-West assistance programs. The United Nations probably offers the best hope for a fair and impartial aid program worked out through a partnership of donor and recipient countries, and most LDCs have accorded this approach their full support. Donor countries, however, while participating in various UN aid programs, have chosen to administer most of their aid through bilateral channels so as to retain full control over its distribution.

Should Capital Transfers Have Priority?

A well-planned and rationally executed aid program should match up inputs of capital and technical assistance so that balanced growth can occur. This rarely happens even under the very best aid programs. Donor countries, while often generous to a fault in providing technical assistance, are reluctant to provide capital through governmental channels. But the leaders of the developing countries, under great pressure from their peoples to produce tangible results, clamor for capital.

Should Aid Funds Be Granted or Loaned?

To give or to lend is a perennial problem facing aid-giving states and international institutions. In bilateral programs the United States has moved from a predominantly grant basis to a basis of mainly granting low-interest loans, often repayable in local currencies, while the Soviet Union gives its aid in the form of long-term, low-interest loans, often repayable in local commodities. International institutions such as the World Bank generally extend short-term loans at moderate to high interest rates and expect repayment in hard currency.

Those who favor grants over loans argue that grants are more flexible than loans because they can be used to develop educational and other social overhead facilities, whereas loans must ordinarily be used to expand self-liquidating productive facilities so that interest payments can be made and the principal of the loan amortized. Since grants do not have to be repaid, they have a minimally disturbing impact on the recipient country's balance of payments, unlike hard currency loans, which force the aid-receiving country to increase its exports or decrease its imports to obtain foreign exchange for installment payments. Grants, therefore, permit a better allocation of resources within a state and speed up economic growth by permitting a more rational application of aid funds.

The most compelling argument favoring loans over grants is that the need to repay loans with interest may encourage the recipient countries to devote the borrowed funds to productive projects rather than to monuments or imported luxury goods. Furthermore, within donor countries loans are more acceptable politically than grants. American congressmen, for example, have been able to gain the support of their constituents for loan programs of foreign aid—bilateral, regional, and through UN agencies—at times when the American public was reacting negatively to "giveaway" programs.

Like most aid issues, that of loans versus grants poses a somewhat false dichotomy. Both grants and loans are needed in underdeveloped societies—grants to help develop a substantial and suitable infrastructure, loans to provide the capital required for industrial growth and diversification. To increase the capacity of developing states to pay off loans, however, expanding world trade, and open markets in the advanced countries, and higher prices for primary commodities are necessary.[9]

Regional Programs

Most foreign aid to developing countries since 1945 has been administered through bilateral programs, particularly those of the United States and the Soviet Union, and sizable proportions of such aid have been in the forms of military aid and defense support projects. Here we are mainly concerned with international programs taking the form of global multilateralism under UN auspices. Regional groups, however, have also developed aid programs, encouraged and supported by the United Nations. Several of the more prominent regional programs will be examined in this section, and then the diverse approaches and programs of the United Nations will be surveyed and evaluated. But one caveat is in order. Regional aid programs may appear to be multilateral in nature, meaning that decisions concerning foreign aid are apparently developed collectively by the members of the group. This is not necessarily true in fact. Although a regional program is proclaimed to be multilateral, it may in fact be largely bilateral because the donor country retains the ultimate decision powers over which nations receive the aid, what terms and conditions are attached to the aid, and what type of aid is offered. Only UN programs can safely be regarded as truly multilateral in both decision making and administration.

The Colombo Plan. The first regional technical assistance and capital aid program emerged out of a Commonwealth Conference in 1950 at Colombo, Ceylon. The Colombo Plan initially provided for a development program in which the advanced Commonwealth states—the United Kingdom, Canada, Australia, and New Zealand—furnished half of the needed capital, with the other half supplied by recipient Asian governments. The United States has since joined as a contributor of aid, and the recipients today include not only Commonwealth states but other Asian countries as well.

The Colombo Plan represents a balance between a regional and a bilateral approach to development. International machinery has been kept to a minimum. A Consultative Committee representing all the participating states meets annually to review past activities, plan specific programs for the year ahead, and provide a forum in which recipient nations can lobby for more aid and donors can announce new projects. Contributions take the form of both grants and loans, and all aid funds are provided through bilateral arrangements, although multilateral consultation is a factor in coordinating the program. An auxiliary program of technical assistance operates under the Plan through a permanent secretariat at Colombo known as the Council for Technical Cooperation in South and Southeast Asia. Every effort is made to balance inputs of capital with improved absorptive capacities so that balanced growth can occur. Technical cooperation has flourished not only between donor and recipient countries but also among the Asian members themselves. Almost $100 billion in loans and grants has been extended to Asian nations for agricultural and developmental purposes since 1950, with fantastic developmental results in many of the recipient countries.

The European Development Fund.   A program similar to the Colombo Plan is carried on by the European Community (EC) through the European Development Fund, which was created in 1958 to offer aid to members' dependent territories in Africa. The program continued after Belgium and France granted independence to their colonies and the aid goes to the European Community's African associated states, most of which are former members of the French Community. Control over dispensing aid from the Fund is exercised by the European Community's Council of Ministers, whose members cast weighted votes on projects recommended by the EC Commission. The latter body supervises negotiations and submits proposals to the former body for official consideration, then oversees the administration of the approved programs.

The European Development Fund started with an initial $581 million for the first five-year period, and additional funds have been contributed periodically. Most of its credits are granted for improving economic infrastructure, such as railways, ports, roads, telecommunications, and urban development. Modernization of agriculture has had the second highest priority. Since 1964 the Fund has also supplied the recipient countries with technical assistance in the form of advice from experts, technicians, economic surveys, and aid for vocational and professional training. Despite the grave problems confronting many African states today, those aided by the European Development Fund have achieved substantial developmental progress.

The Organization for Economic Cooperation and Development.   The Organization for Economic Cooperation and Development (OECD) is unique as a regional organization fostering technical and developmental assistance because its twenty-four members include only donor nations. The OECD was created in 1961 as an outgrowth of the Organization for European Economic Cooperation (OEEC), which had been established in 1948 to coordinate Marshall Plan aid, and its members are European states plus Australia, New Zealand, Turkey, the United States, and Japan. One of the OECD's initial goals was to expand aid to developing states. This goal could more frankly be explained as an effort by the United States—the main force behind the establishment of the OECD—to encourage European and other member states to carry a larger share of economic development financing.

The OECD pursues its aid-fostering role through a Development Assistance Committee (DAC), which establishes general policies and reviews annually the aid efforts of its members. No aid is offered through the organization's channels, however; in all cases aid is dispensed through bilateral actions or multilateral programs that are part of the UN system. The OECD's role is mainly one of stimulating and harmonizing its members' efforts in providing aid and technical assistance to developing countries, and expanding trade with them. The OECD includes in its membership many of the leading industrial countries of the world, which are also the main aid-givers, along with the Soviet Union.

The Alliance for Progress.   In the western hemisphere the regional approach to economic development has been spurred by the Alliance for Progress program adopted at the Punta del Este Conference of 1961. The Punta del Este Charter provided for an economic alliance between the United States and nineteen governments of Latin America (Cuba's government was excepted) aimed at realizing a steady increase in living standards through joint action. Specifically, the program called for (1) a substantial inflow of capital to Latin America, (2) the implementation of various social and economic reforms within each of the recipient countries, (3) a strengthening of democratic institutions and the role of private enterprise in Latin America, and (4) a stabilization of markets and prices for Latin-American primary commodities.

The large capital inflow was predicated on a sizable investment of private capital from North America, Western Europe, and Japan and on annual transfers of public funds from the United States through low- or no-interest loans. Public funds have been directed to high-priority "social overhead" projects, especially in agriculture, education, communications, and transportation, to build sturdy countrywide bases for private investments in industry.

Has the Alliance for Progress succeeded in achieving its original objectives? There is evidence that can be used to criticize or to praise its operations over the past twenty-five years. On the negative side, much capital has been poured into Latin America, but this has left many Latin-American countries deep in debt and facing financial crises. Moreover, much of the capital that has flowed into Latin America has ended up in the pockets of rich elites that have then invested it in the United States, Europe, or Japan. Internal land and tax reforms have lagged in most countries, and runaway population growth has canceled out much of the gross development gains. Commodity prices have fallen steadily, except during a few unusual years.

On the other hand, some positive elements have emerged from the Alliance for Progress. Over the past twenty-five years, for example, the real economic product of the Latin-American region has increased fourfold in aggregate terms and doubled on a per capita basis. Almost three fourths of Latin America's population is now literate; life expectancy at birth has increased from fifty-six years in 1960 to sixty-five in 1986; and infant mortality rates have fallen by 40 percent. Industry has become equal to agriculture in its contribution to GNP throughout the region, and electric power generating capacity has doubled every six years. It is difficult indeed to determine, on balance, whether the Alliance has been a success or a failure. As with most development programs, there have been elements of both success and failure, and because many of these elements are intangible, it is difficult to measure them in a comparative way.

The Regional Banks.   The regional approach to providing assistance for economic development is rounded out by three international banks—the Inter-American Development Bank, established in 1959; the African Development Bank, established in 1964; and the Asian Development Bank, established in 1966. The initial capital subscriptions for the three banks were: Inter-American, $1 billion; African, $250 million; and Asian, $1 billion. The UN Economic Commissions for Latin America (ECLA), for Africa (ECA), and for Asia and the Far East (ECAFE) laid the groundwork for and fostered the development of these financial institutions. As a rule, each of these banks extends loans repayable over twenty-five to thirty years in hard currencies and give preference to loans that encourage further inflows of public and private capital to its region. Priorities in loans are also given to national, subregional, and regional projects that promote harmonious regional growth and meet the needs of small or less developed countries in the region. The relatively small capitalization of the African Development Bank results from a membership that is limited to the members of the Organization for African Unity, which are at the same time contributors to and beneficiaries of the bank's resources.

The three regional banks have been busily engaged in making loans to support hundreds of development projects in their respective regions. By the mid-1980s loaned funds provided by the Inter-American Development Bank totaled over $20 billion in support of almost two thousand development projects. Much of the bank's funds came from the United States. By that time the Asian Development Bank had committed over $10 billion in support of more than five hundred projects. Generous backing from such members as the United States, twelve European countries, Canada, Australia, New Zealand, and Japan enabled it to perform effectively. Not so with the African Development Bank, which with its strictly African membership has had few hard currency resources available for loan purposes. This weakness led to creation in 1972 of a supporting unit, the African Development Fund, as a means for securing Western financial support while retaining African control over the bank's policies.

In addition to the three regional banks, a number of subregional financial institutions have been established that directly or indirectly relate to the objective of economic development. One of these, the European Investment Bank, an agency of the European Community that was established in 1958 with a capitalization of $1 billion, provides loans for economically distressed areas in Europe as well as associated Third World countries. Two financial institutions—the International Bank for Economic Cooperation (IBEC) and the International Investment Bank—have been created within the framework of COMECON to encourage the trade and development of Socialist members. Other subregional banks include the Central American Bank for Economic Integration (CABEI), which became operational in 1961 as an agency of the Central American Common Market; the East African Development Bank, consisting of Kenya, Tanzania, and Uganda, which was established in 1967; and the Nordic Investment Bank, created in 1967, with five Scandinavian countries as members.

In conclusion, the regional approach to economic development affords a viable compromise between outright bilateralism and a globalism that suffers from a dearth of donor countries and a surfeit of countries desperately in need. Most regional approaches, however, involve only consultation, coordination, and review, leaving the hard decisions on contributions, projects, and priorities to be made bilaterally (and often unilaterally) by the major donor members. The regional banks, with their Councils of Governors determining basic policies and their Boards of Directors making loan decisions, may more closely approximate models of true multilateralism. But even here multilateralism may be modified by a voting system weighted by amounts of capital contributed. Most of the regional and subregional organizations, including two of the three development banks, are also instruments of cold war policy, as their memberships, financial support, and loan clientele clearly indicate. Major contributors regard serving the donor's national interests as a sine qua non of aid given. Recipients desperate in their need for help willingly accept bilateral and regional aid on such terms, but little doubt remains that most of the developing states would prefer more or all assistance to be allotted, administered, and supervised through the truly *international* channels of the United Nations.

UN PROGRAMS

Economic development has become the major focus of debate in the General Assembly, the Economic and Social Council, and various subsidiary organs of the United Nations. Most UN programs have economic development as their basic objective, and most UN personnel administer development programs. Even such crucial questions as disarmament, collective security, and pacific settlement are smothered under an avalanche of words paying homage to the great god of economic development. How can this feverish, almost single-minded, activity be explained?

So great have been LDC pressures on donor countries that the developed states have agreed to participate in a variety of global programs. The Soviet Union, for example, looked askance in 1945 at the creation of an Economic and Social Council and disdainfully regarded economic aid programs as no more than neocapitalistic imperialism. It has since succumbed to the same pressures, however, and contributed sizable amounts to many UN development programs. Soviet contributions have encouraged economic progress in new states whose peoples, without UN help, might be prone to Communist-directed revolutions.

The Soviet Union's early lack of concern for solving problems of economic development was in fact shared by other original members of the United Nations. It was reflected in the UN Charter, which contains only one broad, general provision directly charging the United Nations with fostering economic development. Article 55 provides, among other objectives, that "the United Nations shall promote: (a) higher standards of living, full employment, and conditions of economic and social progress and development." The Charter provides no authority to require any governmental or organizational action in the economic field, and aid programs must rest on a foundation of cooperation and voluntary contributions. The organization has in no way been deterred by the Charter's reticence, however, and a great variety of UN programs, resembling an "alphabet soup" in their shorthand acronymic symbolization, have been established in three broad categories—planning and research, technical assistance, and capital financing.[10]

Building Support for Development

The leaders of most developing countries recognize that the principal responsibility for promoting economic advancement is theirs, that foreign aid and international cooperation are not substitutes for national action. But nations newly launched on programs of modernization lack the experience and sophistication needed to avoid costly mistakes and dead-end objectives. One of the most significant approaches of the United Nations, consequently, has been to create opportunities for a meaningful dialogue between industrialized countries and countries seeking that status, and among the developing countries themselves. The dialogue has been carried on almost endlessly for many years, constituting a novel "school" for imparting desire, knowledge, judgment, and common sense to national purveyors of development schemes. The principal forums for carrying on the dialogue have been the Economic and Social Council (ECOSOC), the General Assembly in regular and special sessions, the Second (Economic and Financial) Committee of the Assembly, the informal forum of UN headquarters, and countless conferences, committees, commissions, and agencies of the UN system.

The UN dialogue has also been a learning experience for the developed countries. From 1946 onward, the chambers of the United Nations have rung with the clamor of many voices setting forth the views of the world's less fortunate on the urgency of economic development, the causes and cures for poverty, and the responsibilities of the more fortunate to alleviate poverty through substantial aid. The main cleavage between the developing states and the developed states has been over the approach to development, with the Western states advocating gradualist policies tested in their centuries-long development struggles and the developing states demanding rapid progress through shortcuts and massive technical and capital assistance programs. The Communist-bloc states have increasingly joined the fray, offering a socialist pattern as the best means for achieving progress.

Out of the debates has emerged not only a communication of existing ideas but also new approaches, increased knowledge, and a better understanding of the problems of development. This interchange has been complemented by special studies, by information gathering and analysis conducted by various secretariats, and by widespread publication of the findings. In fact, so extensive has been the research on problems of development that ECOSOC delegates have complained that they are being drowned in a flood of resolutions, reports, and discussions "beyond the analytical capacity and memory of the human brain." In recent years computers have come into common use to help bring some semblance of order out of this chaos. But the search for shortcuts, for new formulas, for sound plans continues, with the demands of the developing bloc appearing evermore insatiable to the advanced states, placing the latter increasingly on the defensive.

The Regional Commissions.   On urging from the General Assembly, the Economic and Social Council in 1947 established the Economic Commission for Europe (ECE) and the Economic Commission for Asia and the Far East (ECAFE) to give aid to countries devastated by the war. The following year Latin-American demands that economic development be recognized as a problem of equal significance resulted in the creation of the Economic Commission for Latin America (ECLA). In 1958 the Economic Commission for Africa (ECA) was established to help plan and organize economic development drives for the new nations of that continent. Lack of regional harmony caused plans for a Middle East regional commission to be abandoned in the 1960s, but a new Economic Commission for Western Asia (ECWA) was established in 1974, with its headquarters in Beirut. In 1974 the title of ECAFE was changed to the Economic and Social Commission for Asia and the Pacific (ESCAP).

The members of the regional commissions include the countries within their respective areas and certain others having special interests in those areas. The role of these commissions has been one of forging a regional outlook among diverse nations with different economic and social systems and, in some cases, with long histories of mutual hostilities. Nonmembers of the United Nations are eligible for membership on the commissions, but they may choose a consultative or advisory status. Cooperation within each of the regions has been fostered by numerous conferences, regular exchanges of information, the development of personal and official contacts, and an atmosphere of unity created and fostered mainly by the work of each commission's secretariat. Each of the commissions makes annual and special reports to ECOSOC on progress within its area and recommendations to increase the pace of development. Each also makes recommendations to member governments and the specialized agencies on matters falling within their competences.

The main objective of the commissions has been to provide research and planning that can stimulate a spirit of self-help in meeting regional problems. Annual economic surveys of the commissions have served as bases for the development of "country plans," for the distribution of aid by donor countries as well as regional and UN agencies, and for the creation of new regional programs, such as the Inter-American, African, and Asian Development Banks. The commissions have also functioned as catalysts in promoting movements toward regional economic integration, such as the European Community, the Latin American Free Trade Association, and several regional common markets. Annual sessions of the commissions have become major economic planning conferences with broad participation.

The Development Decade.   Three major campaigns to speed Third World development have taken the form of Development Decades for the 1960s, the 1970s, and the 1980s. The first was undertaken in 1961, when the sixteenth General Assembly proclaimed a UN Development Decade to dramatize the organization's efforts, to call attention to the need for long-range planning, and

> to mobilize and to sustain support for the measures required on the part of both developed and developing countries to accelerate progress towards self-sustaining growth of the economy of the individual nations and their social advancement.[11]

The target set by the Assembly in this initial campaign was to raise the annual rate of growth in the developing countries from a 1960 average of about 3.5 percent to a 1970 minimum of 5 percent. All UN member states were urged to pursue policies and adopt measures aimed at achieving this goal. The Assembly's resolution also requested the Secretary-General to consult with UN economic organs and agencies to develop proposals to intensify UN development activity. Secretary-General Dag Hammarskjöld proposed on the basis of his consultations that the Development Decade be devoted to (1) more systematic surveys of conditions and needs, (2) the development and use of physical and human resources, (3) the formulation of "true" development plans free of exaggerated goals, (4) improved administration, (5) better production incentives, (6) the redirection of science and technology to the problems of low-income countries, (7) increased export earnings, and (8) a larger and steadier flow of capital.

The First Development Decade lacked planning and suffered from weak implementation of UN recommendations. The Second and Third Development Decades benefited from improved planning, but major development goals have not been achieved. Nevertheless, the Development Decade approach has succeeded in dramatizing UN development efforts and in stimulating new approaches and new programs. Country economic planning for development has been almost universally accepted and implemented, technical assistance programs have been accelerated, and new research institutes and planning agencies have become operational.

One major problem has been the failure of many developing countries to carry out economic, political, and social reforms. Another has been that the flow of development capital has not measured up to expectations, wreaking havoc with the development goals of most states and leading Secretary-General U Thant to comment during the First Development Decade that financial assistance programs appeared to have "lost the *elan* of a new venture before they had acquired the respectability of old usage."[12] For each decade the goal of a transfer of 1 percent of total GNP from each of the developed states to the developing states was established as the primary objective. In fact, such assistance fell from 0.51 percent of GNP in 1960 to below 0.40 percent in the 1970s and 1980s. In 1982, according to World Bank figures, official development assistance amounted to the following: United States, $8.3 billion; France, $3.9 billion; West Germany, $3 billion; Japan, $3 billion; and OPEC countries, $7.8 billion.[13] Burgeoning population growth has further atrophied program goals by diverting attention within the developing countries to the need for increasing food production to avert mass famine and by emasculating aggregate national gains when measured in terms of per capita standards of living.

In the Third Development Decade the United Nations adopted a New International Development Strategy (NIDS) and also established a Substantial New Program of Action (SNPA) for the Least Developed Countries. The New International Development Strategy is aimed at getting each developed country to transfer 0.7 percent of its GNP each year to Third World development assistance. This figure was lower than the long-heralded 1 percent of GNP demanded in the first two Decades, but it was much higher than the actual development aid. The United States, for example, has varied in the late 1970s and early 1980s from 0.20 percent to 0.27 percent of GNP, a substantial reduction from American figures for the 1960s. Other developed countries have likewise shown evidence of "donor fatigue" in the 1980s, including the Scandinavian countries, which have usually met or exceeded target rates for aid. The global recession of the early 1980s added to the drying up of sources of capital, and inflation has reduced the buying power of aid funds.

SNPA requested that donor countries contribute an additional 0.15 percent of GNP each year during the 1980s for the benefit of the poorest or least developed countries. It also strongly recommended that the industrialized countries convert their public loans to the poorest countries into outright grants. Supporters of SNPA argued that this would be a realistic approach since the alternative would probably be a general default by these countries.

To ensure that the Development Decade campaigns moved the developing states in the "right" direction, the General Assembly in 1967 established the UN Industrial Development Organization (UNIDO). The main objective of UNIDO is "to promote the industrial development . . . and accelerate the industrialization of the developing countries, with particular emphasis on the manufacturing sector." The establishment of UNIDO reflected the emphasis that the developing states place on industrialization, an emphasis that has not always been shared by the developed states. The creation of UNIDO demonstrated once again the determination and the voting power of the Third World bloc of states in the General Assembly. UNIDO has not, however, received heavy financial support from industrialized countries.

UNIDO functioned as an "autonomous" organization within the United Nations until January 1, 1986, when it became a UN specialized agency. Its responsibilities are to strengthen, coordinate, and expedite international efforts to promote industrial development, through such activities as conducting research, making surveys, carrying on training programs, holding seminars, furnishing technical aid, and exchanging information. Its main activity, however, is to apply continual pressures on the industrialized states to provide greater help to the developing states in their modernization drive. This role follows naturally because UNIDO's governing Industrial Development Board is elected by the General Assembly, and African, Asian, and Latin-American states hold a majority of the Assembly seats. Examples of specific projects aided by UNIDO include the production of raw materials from sugarcane waste in Trinidad, the construction of a steel-rolling plant in Jordan, and textile manufacturing in the Sudan. Dr. Abd-El Rahman Khane, Executive Director of UNIDO, has often proclaimed that the organization's goal is to have the Third World account for 25 percent of the world's industrial output by the year 2000. In 1975 it accounted for only 10 percent, and by 1985 it had not yet reached 11 percent. To speed up this process, UNIDO is giving the highest priority to "human resource development," holding that this rather than technology transfers is the key to industrial development. UNIDO has also recognized that Africa is a special problem area where little has been done in getting industrialization started. When the General Assembly in 1980 proclaimed the Industrial Development Decade for Africa, UNIDO threw its full support to building a self-sustaining industrial framework on that continent.

Finally, one of the best approaches to building support for development is communication. The United Nations applies this approach effectively by publishing a vast amount of technical and nontechnical literature. Of special importance is *Development Forum,* ten issues of which are published in English, French, and Spanish each year by the United Nations University and the Division for Economic and Social Information/Department of Public Information. *Development Forum* is a cornucopia of information on development programs, problems, and progress. It is not only an indispensable guide to development for the scholar but also for the planner, the engineer, the government official, and all others who are caught up in the campaign to change and modernize the Third World. All of the UN specialized agencies and various other organizations contribute to its coverage.

Technical Assistance Programs

Technical assistance, which involves the teaching of skills and new technologies, is an indispensable instrument of any development program. Of the three main legs of the development stool—the infrastructure base, technical competence, and development capital—technical cooperation is the least controversial. It has consumed a sizable portion of the energies and funds of the advanced countries and of UN development programs. The transfer of any skill—from the most rudimentary to the most complex, from teaching a farmer how to wield a steel hoe most effectively to training technicians to run an atomic power plant—falls within the scope of technical assistance. The most significant categories are the technological, managerial, administrative, educational, and medical, in all of which there has been a sharing of skills but a growing scarcity of technicians.

Fortunately, some modern skills were transmitted to societies in the developing states during the nineteenth century and the first half of the twentieth century by the colonialists, missionaries, League of Nations programs, or private business and philanthropic organizations. The first government program of technical assistance on a substantial scale began during World War II, when the United States sought to increase the production of primary commodities essential to the war effort through a major program of technical and cultural exchange with Latin-American countries. American experts in agriculture, mining, and education accepted in-service posts in Latin America, while large numbers of Latin Americans received training in the United States as medical doctors and technicians, engineers, agronomists, and public administrators. This program was phased out after the war, but in 1949 President

Harry S Truman urged Americans to adopt "a bold new program for making the benefits of our scientific advances and industrial progress available for the improvement and growth of under-developed areas." Set forth in his inaugural address as the last of four policies aimed at achieving peace and security in the world, Point Four was implemented by Congress in the Act for International Development. The Act provided for two programs: (1) an expanded program of technical assistance carried out through the United Nations and (2) a bilateral program of technical cooperation. With some changes in titles and administrative procedures, both programs continue today as the world's leading multilateral and bilateral technical assistance programs.

UN Development Program. The American decision in 1949 to offer the underdeveloped world a large-scale technical assistance program led the General Assembly in November of that year to adopt an Expanded Program of Technical Assistance (EPTA). It went beyond the existing meager program and was financed through voluntary contributions rather than through the regular budget. Nine years later, in October 1958, the Assembly complemented the EPTA by establishing a Special Fund to lay the groundwork for encouraging capital flows into developing states. In November 1965 the Assembly combined the EPTA and Special Fund into a new UN Development Program (UNDP) to secure a unified approach. Although administratively joined, each of the approaches of the two-phase program needs some individual background treatment to place the UNDP in perspective.

Expanded Program of Technical Assistance (EPTA). The EPTA was hailed in the General Assembly as "the true expression of that spirit of international cooperation which was envisaged by the founders" and as "one of the most constructive acts of international statesmanship ever undertaken under the auspices of the United Nations." The EPTA incorporated three main forms of assistance: (1) providing experts, including some from the underdeveloped countries themselves, to train cadres of technicians; (2) awarding fellowships for technical training in advanced countries; and (3) supplying limited amounts of equipment for training and demonstration purposes. Funds for the EPTA came from voluntary contributions offered at annual pledging conferences, a system continued by the Development Program. Contributions may be made in both local and hard currencies, but donors may not attach any conditions to the use of their contributions.

Five specialized agencies, along with the UN Organization itself, constituted the initial "participating organizations" of the EPTA: (1) the International Labor Organization (ILO), (2) the Food and Agriculture Organization (FAO), (3) the UN Educational, Scientific and Cultural Organization (UNESCO), (4) the International Civil Aviation Organization (ICAO), and (5) the World Health Organization (WHO). Five additional organizations subsequently joined the program: (6) the International Telecommunication Union (ITU) and (7) the World Meteorological Organization (WMO), in 1951; (8) the International Atomic Energy Agency (IAEA), in 1959; (9) the Universal Postal Union (UPU), in 1962; and (10) the Inter-Governmental Maritime Consultative Organization (now the International Maritime Organization (IMO), in

1964. In 1965 the World Bank joined in the new Development Program, bringing the number of participating organizations (including the UN Organization) to twelve. All are represented on the Inter-Agency Consultative Board for the Development Program, which coordinates all UN technical assistance and related programs. The International Monetary Fund, although not participating directly in the program, works closely with the Consultative Board to aid in moderating balance of payments problems affecting development programs.

Resident Representatives in the field assist governments in developing sound programs and advise a Consultative Board on their feasibility in relation to local conditions. Offices around the globe, most of which are organized on a single-country basis, coordinate technical assistance programs, function as "country representatives" for some of the specialized agencies, lend assistance on preinvestment surveys, and serve as a link between the United Nations and the recipient government. The Resident Representative's office has grown in significance as efforts have increased to achieve a greater measure of coordination and unity of purpose in UN assistance programs.

Evaluating the United Nations' contribution of technical assistance to economic development over a forty-year period is a hazardous undertaking, considering the diverse activities and the far-flung programs. The need for skilled persons is so great that the entire program could easily and profitably be absorbed by a single developing country if capital inflow and development projects proceeded apace. No one can accurately calculate the "multiplier effect" by which the skills initially transmitted might spread within countries at a geometric rate. The fact that developing states have not been critical of the pace of the UN technical assistance program may lend some support to their claim that other crucial factors in the development equation—particularly capital transfers—have lagged seriously over the years of UN technical assistance activity. Such a lag would reduce the need for skilled personnel. Leaders recognize that large-scale frustration and political unrest find fertile ground among people who have acquired modern skills but are unable to apply them because of lack of progress in industrialization, land reform, and other aspects of the nation's economy.

The Special Fund.   In an effort to correct this imbalance, a Special Fund was established by the General Assembly in 1958 to provide "systematic and sustained assistance in fields essential to the integrated technical, economic and social development of the less developed countries."[14] The Special Fund reflected a growing recognition by the advanced states that the fruits of technical assistance would be increased if it were supported by inputs of capital. At that, the Special Fund was only a compromise falling far short of the perennial demands of the developing states for a massive development fund to provide capital grants and to be replenished annually at a contributory rate of 1 percent of the GNP of each industrialized state. The developed states, however, prefer that capital flows take the form of private investments, which some developing states regard as a form of economic imperialism.

The Special Fund compromise embodied the concept of paving the way for increased private, national, and international investment by conducting "preinvestment" surveys, by discovering the wealth-producing potentials of unsurveyed natural resources, by establishing training and research institutes, and by preparing "feasibility reports on the practicability, requirements, and usefulness" of development projects. Although the EPTA and the Special Fund were to be coordinated from the start, the Special Fund functioned independently in allocating money and determining priorities. The amalgamation of the two in 1966 in the UN Development Program (UNDP) gave some assurance that both programs would operate thereafter under a single source of direction. The UNDP is the world's largest agency for technical cooperation, currently supporting several thousand development projects.

Miscellaneous Technical Assistance Programs.   The diversity of needs in the developing world has helped spawn a variety of special UN projects, each devoted to an attack on some particular problem of economic development not covered or covered inadequately by the general technical assistance program. To fill a need for top-level administrators in developing societies, a new Operational, Executive, and Administrative (OPEX) personnel service was established in 1958 by the General Assembly. Internationally recruited experts are assigned under OPEX to governments, with the proviso that their duties include training nationals to replace them. Another complementary personnel program emerged in 1963, when the General Assembly established the UN Institute for Training and Research (UNITAR). Fully operational by 1966, UNITAR specializes in conducting training seminars for new members of government delegations and their staffs and for individuals in UN-related civil service positions. Its faculty are recruited through fellowship programs and through the voluntary participation of eminent scholars and statesmen.

A number of programs, peripheral yet significant to economic development, complete the UN effort to provide technical assistance. UN conferences on a host of topics such as population control, desertification, science and technology, world fisheries, and the role of women have been convened over the years to foster development attuned to the needs of particular regions and countries. An Industrial Development Center functions as a clearinghouse in the fields of economics and industrial technology, and an Economic Projections and Programming Center develops long-term projections of world economic and industrial trends to facilitate national planning. Both of these centers are located at UN headquarters, although the latter center also operates through regional subcenters.

A World Food Program was undertaken jointly in 1963 by the United Nations and the FAO to provide food for economic and social development projects and to supply food aid in emergencies. Under this program food aid constituted a partial substitute for cash wages for workers in such fields as mining, industry, community development, and irrigation. In the field of demography, the UN Population Commission conducts extensive research on population problems affecting the ability of states to develop and has sponsored two World Population Conferences. Other programs that contribute indirectly to technical cooperation include the UNICEF program for fostering the development of future leaders and technicians through food and educational programs for children. The United Nations itself trains political leaders in statesmanship, and Secretariat technicians learn modern administrative techniques. Many other types of aid programs include provisions for technical assistance as well. For example, the International Bank has become active in the field of technical assistance through project preparation, development programming, and the training of senior development officials.

The United Nations University, headquartered in Tokyo, carries on a fellowship program that is linked with national and regional development organizations in over sixty countries. Its objective is to supply scholars, scientists, and government officials to help fill some of the knowledge gaps in the areas of poverty, famine, and resource management. In the ten years from 1976 to 1986, the university has dispatched around six hundred fellows to various trouble spots in the developing world. Some of these fellows are experienced specialists, whereas others are graduate students, mainly from Third World countries.

The Future of Technical Assistance. Technical assistance programs enable some nations to help other nations, making all of them better off. The donor countries benefit because the poorer countries make better trading partners as their living conditions improve and because societies moving toward a brighter economic future are less prone to revolutionary violence. There has been little criticism of the principle of technical cooperation, from either the developed or the developing countries. Duplication and overlapping of jurisdictions have abounded in UN programs, however, and between these programs and bilateral and regional programs; and this has sometimes aroused petty jealousies and conflicts. Efforts within the United Nations to coordinate programs have been only partially effective, and future consolidations and partnership arrangements, such as that carried out by the EPTA and the Special Fund through the UN Development Program, are needed in order to employ limited resources and personnel more advantageously. Finally, as already noted, no technical assistance program, no matter how well financed and administered, can achieve major development goals unless capital accumulation, investment, and transfers of technology move forward in tandem with it. We now turn our attention to the UN role of fostering inflows of capital into developing economies to obtain the balance that is so essential for economic development.

UN DEVELOPMENT FINANCING PROGRAMS

Most UN efforts to finance economic development have taken the form of loan programs carried on by the World Bank Group—the International Bank for Reconstruction and Development (IBRD), the International Finance Corporation (IFC), and the International Development Association (IDA)—and, indirectly, by the International Monetary Fund (IMF). Although all of these are specialized agencies that function within the broad framework of the UN system, each is involved in its own fundraising and decision-making operations. Developing states have not given up their attempts to establish an effective capital grants type of UN organization, but they have realistically turned to the World Bank Group and the IMF for capital aid in the form of loans to supplement loans from national, regional, and private sources.

The Role of the World Bank Group

The leading role in the global effort to stimulate development through massive capital transfers has been played by the World Bank and its two affiliates, the International Finance Corporation and the International Development Association.

The International Bank. The International Bank for Reconstruction and Development, with a current membership that includes most nations, was intended from its inception to be the central unit in UN lending operations. The Bank was established under the Articles of Agreement drawn up at the Bretton Woods Monetary and Financial Conference of 1944. Its lending operations began in 1946. Since private international capital had virtually disappeared during the 1930s, the World Bank reflected the prevailing attitude that some form of public international financing was essential as a supplement to private loans. From the Bank's inception to 1949, virtually all of its loans were directed to the urgent task of restoring Europe's war-torn economies, with only seven loans committed to developing countries by the end of 1949. The pace of development loans quickened, however, rising by billions of dollars in each subsequent decade. In its 1985 fiscal year, for example, the Bank made loan commitments valued at $11.4 billion to forty-four countries. In the forty years since it was established, it has approved $113 billion in loans to over one hundred countries, almost all of which has been aimed at promoting economic growth in developing countries. This expansion in the Bank's lending capacities continues today and in all likelihood will continue to the year 2000 and beyond.

Within guidelines laid down by member states, the Bank's lending policies are developed by its Board of Governors, using a weighted voting system based on subscribed capital. The Bank makes "hard loans," repayable in convertible currency, and most of its loans have run for twenty-five to thirty-five years at less than commercial rates of interest. Emphasis has been placed on the financing of power, transport, and communication infrastructure projects, with less than 20 percent of the loans devoted to industry and mining. Loans are made either to member governments or to private firms if such loans are guaranteed by a member government. Loans to private firms have been minimal because firms have found it impossible to obtain their government's guarantee or have preferred not to get involved with governmental red tape. Moreover, the Bank has no facilities for investigating and administering loan applications from small businesses and few locally owned large firms exist in the developing states. To meet this problem, the Bank has increasingly granted loans to private banks and loan and investment agencies so that they can relend those funds to private companies and entrepreneurs.

The World Bank is run by bankers, giving it a conservative image that its Board of Governors regards as a proper one. It operates on sound principles of international finance, and its loan criteria are aimed at protecting its interests and those of its creditors. This image of soundness is necessary since most of the Bank's loan funds are obtained, not from governments, but from borrowing in private capital markets. Loan applicants must use a "project" approach in which the applicant demonstrates that the loan will finance a carefully planned undertaking that will contribute to the productive and earning capacity of the country. For many years the Bank frowned on social project loans (for building hospitals and schools or for slum clearance), general-purpose loans, and loans to meet rising debt or to resolve balance of payments problems, but it has given such loans some support in recent years. In fact, the Bank's lending policies have been substantially modified by its efforts in the latter half of the 1980s to encourage economic growth in major debtor countries of the Third World. For some years the Bank limited its use of funds to "self-liquidating projects"—projects that would provide revenues large enough to service debt payments—but it now measures the repayment capacity of the nation's entire economy in making its loans. On average, World Bank loans have financed only 25 percent of the cost of projects with other investors often joining the Bank to provide the balance.

Over the years the World Bank has undergone a change, both in its self-image and in its operations, from a strictly financial institution to that of a development agency intimately concerned with solving problems of economic development. Instead of remaining aloof and merely passing judgment on loan applications, it now assists states in their development planning, helps prepare project proposals, and provides training for senior development officials. Its economic survey missions check resource and investment potentials in member countries and determine priorities for country and regional projects. The World Bank has also participated increasingly in consortium arrangements for financing major projects, with funds provided jointly by global, regional, and local public and private lending institutions. The World Bank has demonstrated that it can use its funds to secure the cooperation of political enemies on a mutually beneficial development plan, as in the joint development of a common river control system by India and Pakistan. New loan funds and changing attitudes toward economic development have led the Bank to further liberalize its lending criteria by granting loans to countries not fully measuring up to its high standards of fiscal management.

Despite its increased pace of activity, the World Bank has been severely limited in its capacity to meet the vast capital demands of developing states. For one thing, repayment of loans in hard currencies imposes grave difficulties on borrowing states that do not rank high as foreign exchange earners. Many developing states have been overstraining their debt-servicing capacities, and new loans might add to the world debt crisis. Moreover, since economic activity in many developing states is carried on predominantly by private companies, a practical means of making loans to relatively small firms without government guarantees has been considered essential to economic development. These weaknesses of the World Bank have been partly mitigated by the establishment of two additional lending affiliates.

The International Finance Corporation (IFC).   From the start of the World Bank's operations, many observers recognized that some kind of affiliate was needed to help finance private investment. Such an affiliate would permit the stimulation of private companies by injections of international capital secured mainly from private sources. This kind of financing was provided by the establishment of the International Finance Corporation in 1956. The IFC promotes the flow of capital from world money markets, stimulates the formation of investment capital within member countries, and encourages private enterprise and private investment opportunities. It makes loans and direct equity investments in private companies, including companies owned jointly by local and foreign interests. The IFC, for example, has entered into mixed equity loan commitments in such industries as steel, textiles, cement, jute, pulp, food processing, and pharmaceuticals. During the thirty years of its existence, it has channeled $5.6 billion to developing societies in its efforts to mobilize private sector development. In 1985 it committed $937 million in loans and equity capital directly to private businesses in thirty-eight developing countries.

Obviously, the IFC is merely scratching the surface of world needs for public capital to stimulate private investment. Loans to small and medium-sized firms are not included in its scope of operations, although it has encouraged members to establish local development banks to do this job and has offered to help finance them. The IFC itself has been authorized to borrow large sums from the International Bank. The result is effective but circular: The International Bank secures funds from private capital markets, lends some of these finds to the IFC, which in turn lends some to country development banks, from which the funds finally return through direct loans to private businesses. Are these international and national institutional middlemen really necessary? They obviously are, since they were created in response to urgent needs. Most investors refuse to risk their capital in developing states without governmental guarantee programs. The stage of self-sustaining economic growth may finally be reached by a developing country when significant inflows of private funds occur without global, regional, or local institutional stimulation or direct protection.

The International Development Association (IDA).   In response to a growing chorus of demands for a capital grants program and a continuing criticism of the conservative nature of the International Bank's operations, the International Development Association was established in 1960 as a "soft loan" affiliate. The IDA was also a response by the United States (the idea was developed in Congress) to a stepped-up Soviet aid/trade offensive. Although IDA is a separate legal entity and its funds and reserves are separate from those of the International Bank, the management and staff of the two institutions are the same.

The "soft loan" features of IDA pertain to the long period for repayment (fifty years), the slow amortization rate (which begins after a ten-year period of grace, with 1 percent of the loan's principal repayable annually during the second ten years and 3 percent payable annually for the remaining thirty years), and the low cost of the loan (no interest but a three fourths of 1 percent annual service charge). IDA loans are not "soft," however, in one highly significant respect—they must be paid off in "hard" (convertible) foreign exchange. This usually means American dollars or a currency freely convertible into dollars.

Developing states, recognizing the advantages of IDA's terms—especially the provision that no payments on a loan are due for ten years—quickly depleted the initial and subsequent subscriptions. As with International Bank loans, recipients of IDA funds must finance a portion of all loan projects, usually with local currency. IDA's loans go mainly to government agencies in the poorest countries for projects similar to those financed in other developing countries by the International Bank. Whether IDA loans will continue to be paid off when the ten-year grace period ends will depend on a country's progress in economic development and its export trade. It will also depend on general world conditions—war or peace, boom or bust, population control or population explosion, the terms of trade, the development of synthetics, changes in consumer tastes, and numerous other unpredictable factors that may either ease repayments in the 1980s and 1990s or, for all practical purposes, turn current loans into grants. In 1985 IDA loaned more than $3 billion to forty-five countries, bringing its cumulative total for twenty-five years of lending operations to $37 billion. Most of this amount remains outstanding, part of the mammoth Third World debt.

The World Bank Group: An Evaluation

The World Bank Group operates on a professional, nonpolitical level. The activities of the International Bank and its two affiliates have benefited almost every developing state, and indications are that the pace of their lending operations will accelerate over the next decade. Yet the Group's operations have been subject to extensive criticism. The fact that the Group is controlled by Western (former colonial) powers, through a voting system that is weighted on the basis of contributions, has aroused widespread suspicion of its motives and its policies. Some Communist and Socialist states have consistently criticized the Group as exemplars of neo-imperialism and neocolonialism. Critics point out that the International Bank's loan terms are no bargain—that they are usually only slightly easier, and sometimes even harsher, than those of private banks. In many cases states borrow from the Bank despite its high rates because their low credit rating prevents them from securing private loans. The International Finance Corporation, critics charge, has never gained general acceptance in the advanced donor states or, for that matter, in the developing world, as evidenced by its inadequate funding and its modest lending activity. Its objective of furthering private investment by meshing capital from both the public and private sectors is a novel approach but has been implemented at a level that has failed to effectively stimulate growth capitalism within recipient states. The International Development Association has enjoyed a singular success in dispensing funds, probably because it comes closest to the capital grants system unsuccessfully sought by developing states for many years. It is, however, frequently "loaned out," with no loanable funds available until a new pledging conference provides a replenishment.

Despite criticism, the World Bank Group has retained the support of its members, whether developed or developing countries. The Group's loans have helped more than one hundred countries to finance useful development projects, and it has often successfully encouraged internal financial reforms within borrowing countries.

This last role, sometimes referred to as "the art of development diplomacy," may go beyond domestic matters, as in the World Bank's negotiation of the Indus River Agreement between India and Pakistan. Given the fantastic capital needs for economic development in the world today and the failure of the UN Capital Development Fund, one can only conclude that the role of the World Bank Group will continue to grow.

CONCLUSION ON ECONOMIC DEVELOPMENT

Where, on balance, do the developing states stand today? Where will they stand in terms of economic development when the Third Development Decade ends in 1990? What are the prospects for development in the decades beyond 1990? Although more has been done to promote world economic development during the last two decades than in all the past aeons of history, more also has been needed and expected. Progress, if defined as an improvement in mass standards of living, has failed to measure up to optimistic hopes. Agricultural output, while increasing substantially in many developing states, has barely kept pace with population growth, and millions remain undernourished. Famines in Africa during the 1980s may be a harbinger for much of the Third World, with the danger that undernourishment in many countries may turn first to serious malnutrition and then to large-scale famine. In the field of housing, millions of new dwellings must be built each year merely to stay abreast of population growth. Education, despite extensive UN and national programs fostered by UNESCO, remains a major problem at all points on the educational scale—too many illiterates, too few trained technicians, and a great paucity of university-trained professionals. Unemployment and underemployment also pose a serious problem in many countries.

Although some countries and subregions have failed to dent the problem of economic stagnation, others—such as Yugoslavia, South Korea, and Brazil—have been making determined efforts to join the world of developed states. Some societies have received huge infusions of aid but have failed to use that aid effectively to broaden the base of their economies or to integrate new productive enterprises with the demands of the world market. Efforts of the international community through bilateral, regional, and global programs have been scattered and largely uncoordinated, often characterized by wasteful duplication and overlap. Yet a variety of programs encourage experimentation and are likely to extract greater support from capital-surplus states than a single program.

Clearly, most developing states prefer to receive aid through UN programs that leave them unencumbered politically and militarily and avoid damage to national egos. The United Nations offers a partnership arrangement with assisted countries, cooperating in planning, developing, and administering aid programs that are somewhat freer of power rivalries than other aid programs. No other organization can provide such a storehouse of development information and experience or possess so many useful contacts beneficial to developing states. The United Nations also provides a natural focus for coordinating development programs, an "agitation chamber" for debating and stimulating action by member states, a forum for the exchange of information and ideas, and a repository of skills that are available to developing states. But the key objective of the great majority of members—obtaining the full support of the developed states for a large-scale capital grants program—has not been realized. Although the developing states won a voting victory in setting up the UN Capital Development Fund, the refusal of capital-surplus states to volunteer large contributions made it impossible for the Fund to serve its intended purpose. Without it or some similar program, other UN development programs have remained useful and desirable, but not central to development in the eyes of the leaders of developing states.

Leaders in the developed states of the West see the situation differently. For them, the greatest need of the Third World is much greater political and economic freedom. Freer trade, reduced restrictions on investment opportunities, internal reforms, an end to nationalizations and expropriations without full compensation, free exchange of currencies—these and many similar changes would do much to hasten the pace of progress in developing states. For the West, additional capital-dispensing organizations are not necessary and would perhaps do more harm than good because they would tend to spread capital more widely, unfairly, and ineffectively. From the Western perspective, World Bank Group and International Monetary Fund decision making based on weighted voting systems is realistic, whereas financial programs based on voting equality are totally unrealistic.

Future progress in the development and modernization of Third World societies will depend on a reconciliation of the interests and perspectives of the developed and developing states. It would be unrealistic indeed to expect the leading capitalistic states of the world to promote socialism by providing large amounts of capital to support the growth of governmentally owned and operated industries. Conversely, societies that exist on a bare subsistence level cannot be expected to generate the savings needed for private investment on a large scale, or to gladly accept domination of their economies by huge multinational corporations. A major challenge for the United Nations is to try to reduce the levels of disagreement and conflict between the two groups and to somehow get them working together for common objectives advantageous to both. This may mean that, in the process of development within Third World states, a balance must be struck between the building of government-owned and -operated industries and the operations of a laissez-faire free market system. Surely the United Nations will be confronted with developmental challenges for as long as it exists.

NOTES

1. The least developed countries, according to UN classification, are Bangladesh, Benin, Bhutan, Botswana, Burundi, Cape Verde, Central African Republic, Chad, Comoros, Gambia, Guinea, Haiti, Lesotho, Malawi, Maldives, Mali, Nepal, Rwanda, Somalia, Sudan, Tanzania, Uganda, Upper Volta, Western Samoa, and the Yemen Arab Republic. These countries are sometimes referred to as the "Fourth World."

2. "International Conference on Population," *Development Forum*, United Nations University and the Division for Economic and Social Information/Department of Public Information 12, no. 5 (June 1984), p. 13.

3. E. Wayne Nafziger, *The Economics of Developing Countries* (Belmont, Calif.: Wadsworth Publishing, 1984), chap. 5.

4. "Credit for the Poor," *Development Forum*, United Nations University and the Division for Economic and Social Information/Department of Public Information 12, no. 1 (January–February, 1984), p. 6.

5. *World Development Forum*, "The Hunger Project," June 15, 1984, p. 6.

6. UN Document E/CONF.46/C.1/SR.9, May 1, 1964, p. 8.

7. For an excellent analysis of these problems, see the article "Trade and Debt: The Vital Linkage," by U.S. Trade Representative William E. Brock III, in *Foreign Affairs* 62, no. 5 (Summer 1984), pp. 1037–57.

8. George D. Woods, "World Bank and Affiliates Examine Pressing Problems of Economic Development," *United Nations Monthly Chronicle* 1 (November 1964), p. 60. The statement was made in relation to strengthening the International Finance Corporation so that it could encourage greater use of private resources for development purposes.

9. For an analysis of the relationship between loans and trade, see Brock, "Trade and Debt: The Vital Linkage."

10. For a summarized view of the broad range of UN activities in the field of economic development, see Roy Blough, "The Furtherance of Economic Development," *International Organization* 19, no. 3 (Summer 1965), pp. 562–80. Blough's list of UN activities includes "economic and social theories of economic development, and theory and practice of development planning; science and technology; land tenure, taxation, and budgeting; improvement of public administration; economic 'infrastructure' of harbors, airports, transportation, and communication facilities, electric power and other public utilities; industrial development; health, housing, education, 'community development,' and other aspects of social development; population, vocational training of workers, labor organizations, cooperatives, improvements of labor, and social security laws; regional river development; and agriculture, fishing, forestry, mining and manufacturing."

11. General Assembly Resolution 1710 (XVI), December 19, 1961.

12. "The United Nations Development Decade at Mid-Point: An Appraisal by the Secretary-General," UN Doc. E/4071, June 11, 1965, pp. 3–28.

13. *World Bank Development Report, 1983* (New York: Oxford University Press, 1983).

14. General Assembly Resolution 1219 (XII), December 14, 1957.

SELECTED READINGS

Ascher, William. *Scheming for the Poor: The Politics of Redistribution in Latin America*. Cambridge, Mass.: Harvard University Press, 1984.

Bell, David E. "The Quality of Aid." *Foreign Affairs* 44, no. 4 (July 1966), pp. 601–7.

Brock, William E. "Trade and Debt: The Vital Linkage," *Foreign Affairs* 62, no. 5 (Summer 1984), pp. 1037–57.

Drucker, Peter F. "The Changed World Economy," *Foreign Affairs* 64, no. 4 (Spring 1986), pp. 768–91.

Eckhard, Frederic, ed. "Economics and Development," *Issues before the 40th General Assembly of the United Nations, 1985–1986*. New York: UNA/USA, 1985. Pp. 64–84.

KIM, SAMUEL S. *The Quest for a Just World Order*. Boulder, Colo.: Westview Press, 1984.

MIKESELL, RAYMOND F. *Public International Lending for Development*. New York: Random House, 1966.

NAFZIGER, E. WAYNE. *The Economics of Developing Countries*. Belmont, Calif.: Wadsworth Publishing, 1984.

ROSTOW, W. W. *The Process of Economic Growth*. 2nd ed. New York: W. W. Norton, 1962.

TINBERGEN, JAN. "International Economic Planning," *Daedalus* 95, no. 2 (Spring 1966), pp. 530–57.

WARD, BARBARA. *The Rich Nations and the Poor Nations*. New York: W. W. Norton, 1962.

WEISS, THOMAS G., and ANTHONY JENNINGS. *More for the Least? Prospects for Poorest Countries in the Eighties*. Lexington, Mass.: D. C. Heath, 1983.

12

The United Nations Evaluated

A study of the United Nations is necessarily the study of particular institutions, processes, and functions. No subject of such breadth and complexity can be digested unless it is examined piece by piece. At some point, however, the institution as a whole should be evaluated. This chapter will attempt that appraisal.[1]

A PERSPECTIVE

The past two centuries have witnessed technological change at an ever-increasing rate, leaving a mark on every aspect of human behavior. In the twentieth century advancing technology has created close and extensive contact among the peoples of the world that was unimagined in any previous era. This in turn has brought a dramatic increase in opportunities for conflict and cooperation among geographically distant peoples.

The new closeness makes international organization essential, indeed inevitable, as long as humanity survives and resists fusion into a single world state. The roots of the UN system of specialized agencies reach back at least to the creation of the International Telegraphic Union in 1865. Emerging technological capabilities made international organization useful then, and such organizations have persisted and proliferated because they continue to serve important needs. Security agencies of the United Nations had their counterpart in the early nineteenth-century European Concert, and the United Nations is a direct successor to the League of Nations, which was created at the end of World War I to rid the world of war. The League was widely regarded as a failure because it did not restrain aggressors between the two world wars. Yet it was reincarnated in 1945 with a new name and more enthusiastic support than the old League had ever enjoyed. In more than four decades the United Nations has experienced substantial institutional growth.

If broadbrush strokes create an encouraging image of the United Nations, the warts become more visible on a close-up viewing. Public enthusiasm has waned since 1945. The organization has many detractors, and its supporters are often disappointed with its performance.[2] The United Nations leaves a host of problems unresolved, frequently including those it addresses. Hypocrisy abounds. Self-interest, often unenlightened, motivates most UN participants. The common ills of large bureaucracies are all too evident, and politically recruited staff frequently place national above international interests. Using democratic forms, majorities in the General Assembly often run roughshod over minorities, without the restraint induced in democratic societies by shared democratic values, a spirit of fair play, and electoral accountability.

But even close up, the picture is not all bad. If the organization performs poorly at times, effective administration and genuine international cooperation can also be found. If rampant majoritarianism often overrides fair play in the Assembly, other bodies within the UN system are usually constrained by the limited focus of their subject matter, and some by special voting arrangements, to seek more realistic and acceptable outcomes.

A look at national governments can provide a useful perspective on UN shortcomings. Governments also suffer from hypocrisy, unenlightened self-interest, entrenched bureaucracy, and, in many instances, downright despotism. Governments perennially struggle with problems that evade solution. Yet only a few odd anarchists regard government as unnecessary. A better government, not elimination of government, is always the answer. If the United Nations were to collapse through alienation of essential supporters, most of its functions would in all likelihood be assigned to other international organizations, or to a new organization, because multilateral cooperation is a sensible way to deal with the hazards and opportunities presented by a technologically shrunken world.

For over forty years the United Nations has been a "going concern" in international affairs, leaving its imprint, for better or worse, on nearly every major political, economic, social, and humanitarian problem that has arisen. During this period the world has witnessed the breakup of colonial empires and the emergence of more than eighty new nations; a massive nuclear arms race; the economic struggles of nations seeking to develop and modernize; several international wars; numerous uprisings, revolutions, and civil wars; and the growth of international communication on an unprecedented scale. The United Nations has played a role in each of these problem areas. Sometimes the role has been to reduce conflict, encourage agreement, and help nations to act cooperatively. Sometimes the effect has been the opposite as passions and prejudices, or even righteous indignation, have demanded condemnation in place of conciliation. More than forty years ago Albert Einstein stated that nuclear weapons had changed everything except our way of thinking. Too often the behavior of states within the UN framework serves only to illustrate the truth of Einstein's observation.

GLOBAL SECURITY

After more than four decades of the United Nations, the world remains a dangerous place. If nuclear arms have not been unleashed in anger since 1945, conventional arms have found frequent use in major and minor conflicts around the globe and threatened use almost daily. Faced with armed conflict or the threat of it, the organization is often ineffectual and sometimes irrelevant. The Vietnam War dragged on for years with a frustrated United Nations confined to the sidelines. The heralded UN enforcement capability never materialized as a genuine deterrent to aggession, and occasionally UN majorities have themselves given aid and comfort to military action by "liberation movements" carried on against colonial powers.

Amid all of this insecurity, one can scarcely argue that the United Nations has made the world secure. But preceding chapters suggest that the organization has made modest contributions to peace and security. Hostilities anywhere in the world bring a UN response, generally as a moderating and pacifying influence. The Secretary-General almost invariably seeks a mediating role. Often these efforts are vain, but not always. Because of UN influence, the violence accompanying decolonization was probably a good deal less than it would have been otherwise. In the Middle East, where the legacy of colonialism has been almost perpetual strife, the UN presence has helped keep local conflicts from escalating into superpower confrontations. UN forces also helped reduce violence in the Congo during the early years of independence, and the United Nations played an important mediating role in Indonesia's transition to independence as well as in the subsequent disposition of West Irian. Although many international quarrels remain resistant to settlement, any UN contribution is welcome. The same is true of arms control. Arms levels continue to rise, but a number of limited arms control measures owe their adoption, at least in part, to UN encouragement, including the partial nuclear test ban treaty, the banning of nuclear weapons from outer space and the seabed, and the nuclear nonproliferation treaty. The United Nations has also helped to strengthen the nonuse of aggressive force as an international norm. Though inconsistent in its response to international violence, and in its identification of aggression, the organization has nonetheless substantially increased the risk that aggressive use of force will be subject to international censure.

ECONOMIC AND SOCIAL WELL-BEING

A favorable balance sheet for UN functional cooperation is fairly easy to draft. The work of UN agencies in such areas as health, transportation, communication, and weather reporting speaks for itself. In these matters states have important, largely uncontroversial, shared interests that can be served effectively only through multilateral cooperation. Cooperation enables all to reap greater benefits from scientific advances. Trade and monetary institutions are somewhat more controversial in their operations, but on balance they have also performed a service in reducing trade barriers and facilitating international payments.

Through programs in the field, the United Nations has given international protection and material assistance to millions of refugees and has aided children and other groups with special needs. The UN system has also fostered a substantial flow of technical assistance and development capital to poor countries. Although the gap between rich and poor states remains wide, development has been encouraged; and the United Nations has made a significant contribution to the growth of a new international ethic of social responsibility to the poorer states.

The UN role in promoting human rights has been limited largely to rule-making, and abuses by governments abound. UN action is all too often characterized by a double standard that selects certain countries for condemnation and ignores grievous violations by other countries. Nevertheless, through discussions, investigations, reports, declarations, and international covenants sponsored by the United Nations, the organization has promoted a body of norms supporting more humane treatment of people by governments, and these norms appear to be slowly infiltrating national practice.

In all areas of its activity, the United Nations has fostered dialogue on global issues. It sometimes appears to be a "deaf man's dialogue," everyone speaking and no one hearing. Much that is said may not be worth listening to, especially when— as frequently occurs in UN debates—it is untrue, misleading, or insulting. But this is only part of the story. Quiet, less publicized exchanges at the United Nations are an important source of information for most governments. For many small states, the United Nations is a convenient place to conduct some of their international business because they cannot afford to maintain diplomatic missions around the world. The United Nations is a particularly important meeting place for heads of state and foreign ministers. Regional groups use their UN representatives to deal with problems of regional interest. Even the public debates can convey a depth of feeling and a breadth of opinion that would be difficult to assess in multiple bilateral settings. No one can deny that UN discussions have raised global awareness on such matters as the plight of the developing countries, the specter of nuclear war, the dangers of nuclear testing, the problems of children, the role of women, the needs of the handicapped, the fragility of the global environment, and the value of human rights.

THE LIMITS OF UN ACTION

In relation to needs and aspirations, UN accomplishments have been modest. Given the practical limits on effective international action, however, this is understandable. The global environment has not been very friendly to multilateral cooperation, and the divisive effects of differing cultures, ideologies, and levels of development have taken their toll. To some extent, technical and humanitarian activities have found the global environment less hostile. But in the more controversial areas, where national security, power, prestige, and resource allocation are at issue, the United Nations has from the beginning been hampered by serious and persisting cleavages—East-West, North-South, colonial-anticolonial, Arab-Israeli, and many others of lesser dimensions. This is not the setting for easy or expeditious resolution of serious international conflicts, whether by national or international agencies.

Achievement has also been limited by the inability of the United Nations to enforce its decisions on states reluctant to conform. This is particularly true of the superpowers and their friends, but the United Nations has few effective sanctions to impose on any state. The organization depends on the willingness of members to support its decisions and encourage others to comply. Although many states would like to use the United Nations to coerce others in particular cases, few, if any, states are willing to cede the organization general authority to coerce. Each state values its own sovereign independence. The UN system was founded on the bedrock of state sovereignty, and it remains so today. It cannot realistically be otherwise until a global sense of community becomes strong enough to bear the weight of more authoritative institutions.

THE VIEW FROM THE UNITED STATES

The United States, more than any other country, was responsible for the creation of the United Nations. American planning, American initiative, and American support in the postwar negotiations led to its establishment. The final proposal represented the views of many countries, but it owed at least as much to the United States as the League Covenant did to President Woodrow Wilson. For a decade after its creation, the United Nations justified that support by responding readily to American wishes. Moved by U.S. resources and leadership, and perhaps too by U.S. ideals, UN majorities were available to endorse almost any proposal that embodied an important U.S. interest. The organization could not make the Soviet Union yield, but it could and did legitimize American policies. When the Security Council was immobilized by the veto, the United States encouraged the General Assembly to fill the vacuum.

The beginning of the end to U.S. dominance in the United Nations came in 1955, when a long-standing blockade was lifted on admission to membership and sixteen countries were added to the UN roster. Twenty-four more were added in the next five years, and by the middle 1960s, with UN membership exceeding 120, the United States had fallen to a minority position on more than half of UN contested votes. The new members were largely products of the decolonization process, a political movement enthusiastically supported by the United Nations. Typically, each new member brought to the United Nations a sense of injustice suffered under European masters, a fixation on the threat of "neocolonialism" represented by exploitative foreign economic interests, and great economic need. This was translated into suspicion of Western motives and actions, a passion to eradicate all vestiges of colonialism and neocolonialist exploitation, and demands for economic assistance and vast changes in the global economic system. Such demands were often put forth as entitlements, justly deserved reparation for ills suffered for years under the colonial yoke.

Although lacking experience in diplomacy, the new nations were politically sophisticated enough to recognize that their common interests could be best achieved through political unity. The result was the emergence of the Third World as a powerful bloc taking the form of the Non-Aligned Movement in political matters and the

Group of 77 in economic areas. This solidarity produced a transfer of voting dominance from the United States and the West to the Third World, often supported, at least rhetorically, by the Eastern bloc. That situation obtains today. The Third World now dominates UN political processes, and the agenda contains mainly Third World issues.

The changed Western position is reflected in changed American attitudes toward the United Nations. Officially the United States still supports the organization, and financially its share of assessed contributions to the UN system has been about 25 percent—roughly a billion dollars in 1986, nearly as much as the next four contributors combined. But its support has become more grudging and its comment more critical, in both private and governmental circles.[3] Among the general public, support is also lower than it was in previous decades, although a 1985 *New York Times* poll found three out of four respondents still convinced that the world was better off because of the United Nations.[4]

The present American role within the United Nations is not an easy one. Although the United States remains an influential member of the organization, it no longer plays a decisive part in most of the organization's decision processes. American positions usually receive serious consideration, but votes in the Assembly and the Council often find U.S. representatives ineffectually trying to block majority action, or else abstaining as a means of displaying dissatisfaction or lack of interest. This happens time and again, and helps to explain U.S disillusionment with the United Nations.

Many U.S. criticisms of the organization are rooted in substance. One problem is the decision-making process itself. Each member, regardless of its size, population, power position, economic strength, or financial contributions, has one vote. This reflects the "sovereign equality of states," which are equal in no other respect. Prospects for change in voting arrangements are dim, since no change that would improve the relative position of the United States is likely to receive majority approval.

The United States has also objected to "politicization" of UN agencies by the Third World, aided and abetted by the Eastern bloc. Third World majorities have undoubtedly used UN agencies to promote their own political agendas, sometimes to the detriment of the legitimate work of the organization. Harassment of Israel has been one of the more common ploys. This was one of the grounds for U.S. withdrawal from UNESCO in 1984, and the complaint was legitimate. Yet the American objection to politicization is not wholly principled. As one careful UN observer has noted, "Politicization has long figured in US policy toward the United Nations." In past years, when voting alignments were different,

> Washington induced UNESCO and other UN agencies to support its role in the 1950 Korean conflict, and for more than 20 years waged a campaign to deny international recognition to Peking. Even today the United States presses hard within the International Labor Organization for condemnation of Communist Poland's treatment of the labor union Solidarity, while showing little concern over abuses of trade union rights in friendly Chile, for example.[5]

The practical problem of politicization for the United States is its loss of the ability to politicize the organization in a manner compatible with American interests.

The United States has also grown restive about carrying 25 percent of the UN budget. Until 1985 most of the dissatisfaction was verbal, although selective unilateral cuts in American contributions, including assessed obligations, occurred. In 1985, however, the U.S. Congress enacted the so-called Kassebaum Amendment, which limits the U.S. contribution to no more than 20 percent of the assessed budget of the United Nations or any specialized agency unless voting rights on budgetary matters are made proportional to each state's contribution.[6] The restriction was mandated to take effect with the 1987 UN fiscal year and beyond. Additional reductions in the U.S. contribution were made necessary by subsequent congressional action. Legally, refusal to pay a budgetary assessment is a UN Charter violation and could in theory lead to loss of voting rights in the General Assembly. Practically, it imposes serious financial hardship on the United Nations. Adoption of proportional voting on budget matters is unlikely.[7]

U.S. concern with the UN budget process is understandable, because Third World countries, most of which contribute very small amounts, have the ultimate say in determining how UN funds are spent. But there is another side. No other country has an ability to pay approaching that of the United States, and money does to some extent buy influence. The views of the biggest contributor are given a serious hearing, even though in many instances they may not be heeded. As the level of American financial support drops, American influence can be expected to wane further, thus provoking domestic demands for additional cuts. As the cycle continues, the United Nations, its major programs, and U.S. influence will become the big losers.

The process of disillusionment is a two-way street. If U.S. officials and the American public are critical of much that goes on within the UN system, the majority of member nations are frequently critical of U.S. policies and practices within the organization. As in an arms race cycle, each side's critical rhetoric and hostile actions tend to widen the cleavage between them and escalate the level of hostility.

But hostilities can be de-escalated as well. When the United Nations is viewed as a forum for cooperation rather than political conflict (or at best damage limitation), worthwhile things can happen. Cooperation does not mean abandoning principle, or any vital interests. It simply implies a willingness to undertake a genuine search for common ground. Many American criticisms of the organization and the role of competitive blocs are justified; but the ancient axiom that "participation generates influence" should remind American decision makers that opportunity is still there.

The costs of lost opportunity may be great. The United Nations was created to deal with real problems, and the problems have not gone away. They may never be fully resolved, but they must be dealt with. The United Nations is one means we have for dealing with them. Its friends are partly right: it can be used to good purpose. Its critics are also partly right: it needs to be improved. But no country's interest, ultimately, is served by abandoning the effort to promote multilateral cooperation. A recent critique of the United Nations and of U.S. policy toward it captures the essence of the problem:

> Any crisis of multilateralism is a crisis of humankind, for the human agenda is coming to be dominated by more, not fewer, issues of global proportions. International institutions can resolve none of these issues on their own, but neither can national states resolve them without international institutions. For better or worse, then, we are condemned to improve existing international institutions or to invent new ones to take their place.[8]

TOWARD WORLD ORDER

During the present century the world has witnessed the disintegration of colonial empires, two world wars, an almost unbroken series of local conflicts, and a variety of hostile rivalries among nations large and small. Amid these signs of political disintegration, a technological revolution in transportation, communication, and industry has vastly increased the points of social contact across national boundaries and thus the opportunities for both cooperation and hostile collision. At the same time military technology has substantially increased the penalties of resort to organized violence and brought added incentive to avoid at least the most destructive forms of warfare. Faced with the social consequences of technological progress, as they affect international relations, governments have increasingly turned to international organization as a means of eliminating frictions and resolving differences through nonviolent means.

More than a hundred years of experience with functional international organizations, now greatly augmented by the growth of the UN system, has not produced a global political community. It has, however, produced a practical approach to international cooperation. The processes of international organization are geared to a world in which common problems must be attacked by multilateral means, while making full allowance for local particularisms and national freedom of action. As vessels for common action, these processes have proved adaptable and adequate to bear all of the international cooperation that existing bonds of community will generate. Genuine community, with freedom from oppression and want, still lies at the top of distant peaks. That ideal may be unattainable. But international organization points in that direction, even though, as a human institution, it reflects the divisions and the follies of the world we live in.

NOTES

1. For a thoughtful evaluation by a former Secretary-General, see Kurt Waldheim, "The United Nations: The Tarnished Image," *Foreign Affairs* 63, no. 1 (Fall 1984), pp. 93–107.
2. See, e.g., Edward C. Luck, "The U.N. at 40: A Supporter's Lament," *Foreign Policy*, no. 57 (Winter 1984–85), pp. 143–59.
3. In 1985 a respected academic commentator and former UN official, no spokesman for the ultra-conservative fringe groups, seriously suggested that the United States consider withdrawal as a

viable option. Thomas M. Franck, *Nation against Nation: What Happened to the U.N. Dream and What the U.S. Can Do about It* (New York: Oxford University Press, 1985), pp. 271–72. He concluded, however: "For the present, the U.S. national interest is better served by a muscular strategy of staying in." For sober, but generally sympathetic, analyses of U.S. relations with the United Nations, see Donald J. Puchala, "American Interests and the United Nations," *Political Science Quarterly* 97, no. 4 (Winter 1982–83), pp. 571–88; Toby Trister Gati, ed., *The US, the UN, and the Management of Global Change* (New York: New York University Press, 1983); and John Gerard Ruggie, "The United States and the United Nations: Toward a New Realism," *International Organization* 39, no. 2 (Spring 1985), pp. 343–56.

4. *New York Times*, June 26, 1985, sec. 1, p. 8. The poll was conducted for the *New York Times*, CBS News, and the *International Herald Tribune*. Among U.S. respondents, 78 percent answered no to the question "Would the world be better off without the U.N.?" For respondents in West Germany, Britain, France, and Japan the no responses were 56 percent, 69 percent, 45 percent, and 56 percent, respectively. The American Institute of Public Opinion (Gallup Poll) has periodically asked Americans, "In general, do you feel the United Nations is doing a good job or a poor job in trying to solve the problems it has had to face?" Over the years responses have tended to become less favorable, as shown by the following table:

Month and Year	Good Job	Poor Job	Don't Know, No Opinion
July 1954	59%	26%	15%
July 1967	49	35	16
October 1970	44	40	16
January 1975	41	38	21
April–May 1980	31	53	16
February 1985	38	44	18

SOURCE: American Institute of Public Opinion, *The Gallup Poll, 1935–1971*, 3 vols. (New York: Random House, 1972); and American Institute of Public Opinion, *The Gallup Opinion Index*, Report 117 (March 1975), Report 177 (April-May 1980), and Report 237 (June 1985).

The 1985 *New York Times* poll, cited above, elicited a response more favorable to the United Nations. Of 1,509 persons who were asked, "How is the U.N. doing in solving the problems it has had to face?" 5 percent said the United Nations was doing a "very good job" and 46 percent said it was doing a "good job."

5. Leon Gordenker, "Washington's UN Policy Choice: Try to Get Along or Try to Win," *Interdependent* 10, no. 3 (May-June 1984), p. 2.

6. Public Law 99–93, Title I, Sec. 143, August 16, 1985, 99 Stat. 424.

7. In December 1986 the General Assembly moved part way toward the U.S. position by agreeing that spending limits set by its Committee for Program and Coordination during the budget discussion process would not be subsequently overridden by the Assembly. The United States is represented on the CPC and decisions are made by consensus, which, in practical terms, gives the United States (and every other member of the committee) a veto on the size of the UN biennial budget. Whether this will induce Congress to repeal the Kassebaum Amendment is uncertain at this writing.

8. Ruggie, "The United States and the United Nations," p. 356.

SELECTED READINGS

BAEHR, PETER R., and LEON GORDENKER, *The United Nations: Reality and Ideal.* New York: Praeger Publishers, 1984.

FINGER, SEYMOUR MAXWELL, and JOSEPH R. HARBERT, eds. *U.S. Policy in International Institutions*. Rev. ed. Boulder, Colo.: Westview Press, 1982.

FRANCK, THOMAS M. *Nation against Nation: What Happened to the U.N. Dream and What the U.S. Can Do about It*. New York: Oxford University Press, 1985.

GATI, TOBY TRISTER, ed. *The US, the UN, and the Management of Global Change*. New York: New York University Press, 1983.

KAY, DAVID A., ed. *The Changing United Nations: Options for the United States*. New York: Praeger Publishers, 1977.

KIRKPATRICK, JEANE J. *The Reagan Phenomenon—and Other Speeches on Foreign Policy*. Washington, D.C.: American Enterprise Institute for Public Policy Research, 1983.

MOYNIHAN, DANIEL PATRICK. *A Dangerous Place*. New York: Berkley Books, 1980.

PINES, BURTON YALE, ed. *A World without a U.N.: What Would Happen if the U.N. Shut Down*. Washington, D.C.: Heritage Foundation, 1984.

A

The Covenant of the League of Nations[1]

The High Contracting Parties,

In order to promote international cooperation and to achieve international peace and security

by the acceptance of obligations not to resort to war,

by the prescription of open, just and honorable relations between nations,

by the firm establishment of the understandings of international law as the actual rule of conduct among Governments, and

by the maintenance of justice and a scrupulous respect for all treaty obligations in the dealings of organized peoples with one another,

Agree to this Covenant of the League of Nations.

ARTICLE 1. Membership and Withdrawal

1. The original Members of the League of Nations shall be those of the Signatories which are named in the Annex to this Covenant and also such of those other States named in the Annex as shall accede without reservation to this Covenant. Such accessions shall be effected by a declaration deposited with the Secretariat within two months of the coming into force of the Covenant. Notice thereof shall be sent to all other Members of the League.

2. Any fully self-governing State, Dominion or Colony not named in the Annex may become a Member of the League if its admission is agreed to by two-thirds of the Assembly, provided that it shall give effective guaranties of its sincere intention to observe its international obligations, and shall accept such regulations as may be

---

[1]Amendments in italics.

prescribed by the League in regard to its military, naval and air forces and armaments.

3. Any Member of the League may, after two years' notice of its intention so to do, withdraw from the League, provided that all its international obligations and all its obligations under this Covenant shall have been fulfilled at the time of its withdrawal.

ARTICLE 2. Major Organs

The action of the League under this Covenant shall be effected through the instrumentality of an Assembly and of a Council, with a permanent Secretariat.

ARTICLE 3. Assembly

1. The Assembly shall consist of representatives of the Members of the League.

2. The Assembly shall meet at stated intervals and from time to time, as occasion may require, at the Seat of the League or at such other place as may be decided upon.

3. The Assembly may deal at its meetings with any matter within the sphere of action of the League or affecting the peace of the world.

4. At meetings of the Assembly each Member of the League shall have one vote and may have not more than three Representatives.

ARTICLE 4. Council

1. The Council shall consist of representatives of the Principal Allied and Associated Powers, together with Representatives of four other Members of the League. These four Members of the League shall be selected by the Assembly from time to time in its discretion. Until the appointment of the Representatives of the four Members of the League first selected by the Assembly, Representatives of Belgium, Brazil, Greece and Spain shall be Members of the Council.

2. With the approval of the majority of the Assembly, the Council may name additional Members of the League, whose Representatives shall always be Members of the Council; the Council with like approval may increase the number of Members of the League to be selected by the Assembly for representation on the Council.

2. The Assembly shall fix by a two-thirds' majority the rules dealing with the election of the non-permanent Members of the Council, and particularly such regulations as relate to their term of office and the conditions of re-eligibility.

3. The Council shall meet from time to time as occasion may require, and at least once a year, at the Seat of the League, or at such other place as may be decided upon.

4. The Council may deal at its meetings with any matter within the sphere of action of the League or affecting the peace of the world.

5. Any Member of the League not represented on the Council shall be invited to send a Representative to sit as a member at any meeting of the Council during the consideration of matters specially affecting the interests of that Member of the League.

6. At meetings of the Council, each Member of the League represented on the Council shall have one vote, and may have not more than one Representative.

ARTICLE 5. Voting and Meeting Procedures

1. Except where otherwise expressly provided in this Covenant or by the terms of the present Treaty, decisions at any meeting of the Assembly or of the Council shall require the agreement of all the Members of the League represented at the meeting.

2. All matters of procedure at meetings of the Assembly or of the Council, including the appointment of Committees to investigate particular matters, shall be regulated by the Assembly or by the Council and may be decided by a majority of the Members of the League represented at the meeting.

3. The first meeting of the Assembly and the first meeting of the Council shall be summoned by the President of the United States of America.

ARTICLE 6. Secretariat, Secretary-General and Expenses

1. The permanent Secretariat shall be established at the Seat of the League. The Secretariat shall comprise a Secretary-General and such secretaries and staff as may be required.

2. The first Secretary-General shall be the person named in the Annex; thereafter the Secretary-General shall be appointed by the Council with the approval of the majority of the Assembly.

3. The secretaries and the staff of the Secretariat shall be appointed by the Secretary-General with the approval of the Council.

4. The Secretary-General shall act in that capacity at all meetings of the Assembly and of the Council.

5. *The expenses of the League shall be borne by the Members of the League in the proportion decided by the Assembly.*

ARTICLE 7. Seat, Qualifications and Immunities

1. The Seat of the League is established at Geneva.

2. The Council may at any time decide that the Seat of the League shall be established elsewhere.

3. All positions under or in connection with the League, including the Secretariat, shall be open equally to men and women.

4. Representatives of the Members of the League and officials of the League when engaged on the business of the League shall enjoy diplomatic privileges and immunities.

5. The buildings and other property occupied by the League or its officials or by Representatives attending its meetings shall be inviolable.

ARTICLE 8. Reduction of Armaments

1. The Members of the League recognize that the maintenance of peace requires the reduction of national armaments to the lowest point consistent with national safety and the enforcement by common action of international obligations.

2. The Council, taking account of the geographical situation and circumstances of each State, shall formulate plans for such reduction for the consideration and action of the several Governments.

3. Such plans shall be subject to reconsideration and revision at least every ten years.

4. After these plans shall have been adopted by the several Governments, the limits of armaments therein fixed shall not be exceeded without the concurrence of the Council.

5. The Members of the League agree that the manufacture by private enterprise of munitions and implements of war is open to grave objections. The Council shall advise how the evil effects attendant upon such manufacture can be prevented, due regard being had to the necessities of those Members of the League which are not able to manufacture the munitions and implements of war necessary for their safety.

6. The Members of the League undertake to interchange full and frank information as to the scale of their armaments, their military, naval and air programs and the condition of such of their industries as are adaptable to warlike purposes.

ARTICLE 9. Permanent Military, Naval and Air Commission

A permanent Commission shall be constituted to advise the Council on the execution of the provisions of Articles 1 and 8 and on military, naval and air questions generally.

ARTICLE 10. Guaranties Against Aggression

The Members of the League undertake to respect and preserve as against external aggression the territorial integrity and existing political independence of all Members of the League. In case of any such aggression or in case of any threat or danger of such aggression the Council shall advise upon the means by which this obligation shall be fulfilled.

ARTICLE 11. Collective Action

1. Any war or threat of war, whether immediately affecting any of the Members of the League or not, is hereby declared a matter of concern to the whole League, and the League shall take any action that may be deemed wise and effectual to safeguard the peace of nations. In case any such emergency should arise the Secretary-General shall on the request of any Member of the League forthwith summon a meeting of the Council.

2. It is also declared to be the friendly right of each Member of the League to bring to the attention of the Assembly or the Council any circumstance whatever affecting international relations which threatens to disturb international peace or the good understanding between nations upon which peace depends.

ARTICLE 12. Disputes

1. The Members of the League agree that, if there should arise between them any dispute likely to lead to a rupture, they will submit the matter either to arbitra-

tion *or judicial settlement* or to inquiry by the Council, and they agree in no case to resort to war until three months after the award by the arbitrators *or the judicial decision,* or the report by the Council.

2. In any case under this Article the award of the arbitrators *or the judicial decision* shall be made within a reasonable time, and the report of the Council shall be made within six months after the submission of the dispute.

ARTICLE 13. Arbitration or Judicial Settlement

1. The Members of the League agree that, whenever any dispute shall arise between them which they recognize to be suitable for submission to arbitration *or judicial settlement,* and which can not be satisfactorily settled by diplomacy, they will submit the whole subject-matter to arbitration *or judicial settlement.*

2. Disputes as to the interpretation of a treaty, as to any question of international law, as to the existence of any fact which, if established, would constitute a breach of any international obligation, or as to the extent and nature of the reparation to be made for any such breach, are declared to be among those which are generally suitable for submission to arbitration *or judicial settlement.*

3. For the consideration of any such dispute, the court to which the case is referred shall be the Permanent Court of International Justice, established in accordance with Article 14, or any tribunal agreed on by the parties to the dispute or stipulated in any convention existing between them.

4. The Members of the League agree that they will carry out in full good faith any award *or decision* that may be rendered, and that they will not resort to war against a Member of the League which complies therewith. In the event of any failure to carry out such an award *or decision,* the Council shall propose what steps should be taken to give effect thereto.

ARTICLE 14. Permanent Court of International Justice

The Council shall formulate and submit to the Members of the League for adoption plans for the establishment of a Permanent Court of International Justice. The Court shall be competent to hear and determine any dispute of an international character which the parties thereto submit to it. The Court may also give an advisory opinion upon any dispute or question referred to it by the Council or by the Assembly.

ARTICLE 15. Disputes not Submitted to Arbitration or Judicial Settlement

1. If there should arise between Members of the League any dispute likely to lead to a rupture, which is not submitted to arbitration *or judicial settlement* in accordance with Article 13, the Members of the League agree that they will submit the matter to the Council. Any party to the dispute may effect such submission by giving notice of the existence of the dispute to the Secretary-General, who will make all necessary arrangements for a full investigation and consideration thereof.

2. For this purpose, the parties to the dispute will communicate to the Secretary-General, as promptly as possible, statements of their case with all the relevant facts and papers, and the Council may forthwith direct the publication thereof.

3. The Council shall endeavor to effect a settlement of the dispute, and, if such efforts are successful, a statement shall be made public giving such facts and explanations regarding the dispute and the terms of settlement thereof as the Council may deem appropriate.

4. If the dispute is not thus settled, the Council either unanimously or by a majority vote shall make and publish a report containing a statement of the facts of the dispute and the recommendations which are deemed just and proper in regard thereto.

5. Any member of the League represented on the Council may make public a statement of the facts of the dispute and of its conclusions regarding the same.

6. If a report by the Council is unanimously agreed to by the Members thereof other than the Representatives of one or more of the parties to the dispute, the Members of the League agree that they will not go to war with any party to the dispute which complies with the recommendations of the report.

7. If the Council fails to reach a report which is unanimously agreed to by the members thereof, other than the Representatives of one or more of the parties to the dispute, the Members of the League reserve to themselves the right to take such action as they shall consider necessary for the maintenance of right and justice.

8. If the dispute between the parties is claimed by one of them, and is found by the Council, to arise out of a matter which by international law is solely within the domestic jurisdiction of that party, the Council shall so report, and shall make no recommendation as to its settlement.

9. The Council may in any case under this Article refer the dispute to the Assembly. The dispute shall be so referred at the request of either party to the dispute, provided that such request be made within 14 days after the submission of the dispute to the Council.

10. In any case referred to the Assembly, all the provisions of this Article and of Article 12 relating to the action and powers of the Council shall apply to the action and powers of the Assembly, provided that a report made by the Assembly, if concurred in by the Representatives of those Members of the League represented on the Council and of a majority of the other Members of the League, exclusive in each case of the Representatives of the parties to the dispute, shall have the same force as a report by the Council concurred in by all the members thereof other than the Representatives of one or more of the parties to the dispute.

ARTICLE 16. Sanctions and Expulsion

1. Should any Member of the League resort to war in disregard of its covenants under Articles 12, 13, or 15, it shall *ipso facto* be deemed to have committed an act of war against all other Members of the League, which hereby undertake immediately to subject it to the severance of all trade or financial relations, the prohibition of all intercourse between their nationals and the nationals of the covenant-breaking State, and the prevention of all financial, commercial or personal intercourse between the nationals of the covenant-breaking State and the nationals of any other State, whether a Member of the League or not.

2. It shall be the duty of the Council in such case to recommend to the several Governments concerned what effective military, naval or air force the Members of the League shall severally contribute to the armed forces to be used to protect the covenants of the League.

3. The Members of the League agree, further, that they will mutually support one another in the financial and economic measures which are taken under this Article, in order to minimize the loss and inconvenience resulting from the above measures, and that they will mutually support one another in resisting any special measures aimed at one of their number by the covenant-breaking State, and that they will take the necessary steps to afford passage through their territory to the forces of any of the Members of the League which are cooperating to protect the covenants of the League.

4. Any Member of the League which has violated any covenant of the League may be declared to be no longer a Member of the League by a vote of the Council concurred in by the Representatives of all the other Members of the League represented thereon.

ARTICLE 17. Disputes Involving Non-Members

1. In the event of a dispute between a Member of the League and a State which is not a Member of the League, or between States not Members of the League, the State or States not Members of the League shall be invited to accept the obligations of membership in the League for the purposes of such dispute, upon such conditions as the Council may deem just. If such invitation is accepted, the provisions of Articles 12 to 16 inclusive shall be applied with such modifications as may be deemed necessary by the Council.

2. Upon such invitation being given, the Council shall immediately institute an inquiry into the circumstances of the dispute and recommend such action as may seem best and most effectual in the circumstances.

3. If a State so invited shall refuse to accept the obligations of membership in the League for the purposes of such dispute, and shall resort to war against a Member of the League, the provisions of Article 16 shall be applicable as against the State taking such action.

4. If both parties to the dispute when so invited refuse to accept the obligations of membership in the League for the purposes of such dispute, the Council may take such measures and make such recommendations as will prevent hostilities and will result in the settlement of the dispute.

ARTICLE 18. Registration and Publication of Treaties

Every treaty or international engagement entered into hereafter by any Member of the League shall be forthwith registered with the Secretariat and shall as soon as possible be published by it. No such treaty or international engagement shall be binding until so registered.

ARTICLE 19. Review of Treaties

The Assembly may from time to time advise the reconsideration by Members of the League of treaties which have become inapplicable, and the consideration of international conditions whose continuance might endanger the peace of the world.

ARTICLE 20. Abrogation of Inconsistent Obligations

1. The Members of the League severally agree that this Covenant is accepted as abrogating all obligations or understandings *inter se* which are inconsistent with the terms thereof, and solemnly undertake that they will not hereafter enter into any engagements inconsistent with the terms thereof.

2. In case any Member of the League shall, before becoming a Member of the League, have undertaken any obligations inconsistent with the terms of this Covenant, it shall be the duty of such Member to take immediate steps to procure its release from such obligations.

ARTICLE 21. Engagements that Remain Valid

Nothing in this Covenant shall be deemed to affect the validity of international engagements, such as treaties of arbitration or regional understandings like the Monroe doctrine, for securing the maintenance of peace.

ARTICLE 22. Mandates System

1. To those colonies and territories which as a consequence of the late war have ceased to be under the sovereignty of the States which formerly governed them and which are inhabited by peoples not yet able to stand by themselves under the strenuous conditions of the modern world, there should be applied the principle that the well-being and development of such peoples form a sacred trust of civilization and that securities for the performance of this trust should be embodied in this Covenant.

2. The best method of giving practical effect to this principle is that the tutelage of such peoples should be intrusted to advanced nations who by reason of their resources, their experience or their geographical position can best undertake this responsibility, and who are willing to accept it, and that this tutelage should be exercised by them as Mandatories on behalf of the League.

3. The character of the mandate must differ according to the stage of the development of the people, the geographical situation of the territory, its economic conditions and other similar circumstances.

4. Certain communities formerly belonging to the Turkish Empire have reached a stage of development where their existence as independent nations can be provisionally recognized subject to the rendering of administrative advice and assistance by a Mandatory until such time as they are able to stand alone. The wishes of these communities must be a principal consideration in the selection of the Mandatory.

5. Other peoples, especially those of Central Africa, are at such a stage that the Mandatory must be responsible for the administration of the territory under conditions which will guarantee freedom of conscience and religion, subject only to the maintenance of public order and morals, the prohibition of abuses such as the slave trade, the arms traffic and the liquor traffic, and the prevention of the establishment

of fortifications or military and naval bases and of military training of the natives for other than police purposes and the defense of territory, and will also secure equal opportunities for the trade and commerce of other Members of the League.

6. There are territories, such as South West Africa and certain of the South Pacific islands, which, owing to the sparseness of their population, or their small size, or their remoteness from the centers of civilization, or their geographical contiguity to the territory of the Mandatory, and other circumstances, can be best administered under the laws of the Mandatory as integral portions of its territory, subject to the safeguards above mentioned in the interests of the indigenous population.

7. In every case of mandate, the Mandatory shall render to the Council an annual report in reference to the territory committed to its charge.

8. The degree of authority, control or administration to be exercised by the Mandatory shall, if not previously agreed upon by the Members of the League, be explicitly defined in each case by the Council.

9. A permanent Commission shall be constituted to receive and examine the annual reports of the Mandatories and to advise the Council on all matters relating to the observance of the mandates.

ARTICLE 23. Social Responsibilities

Subject to and in accordance with the provisions of international conventions existing or hereafter to be agreed upon, the Members of the League:

(a) will endeavor to secure and maintain fair and humane conditions of labor for men, women and children, both in their own countries and in all countries to which their commercial and industrial relations extend, and for that purpose will establish and maintain the necessary international organizations;

(b) undertake to secure just treatment of the native inhabitants of territories under their control;

(c) will intrust the League with the general supervision over the execution of agreements with regard to the traffic in women and children, and the traffic in opium and other dangerous drugs;

(d) will intrust the League with the general supervision of the trade in arms and ammunition with the countries in which the control of this traffic is necessary in the common interest;

(e) will make provision to secure and maintain freedom of communications and of transit and equitable treatment for the commerce of all Members of the League. In this connection, the special necessities of the regions devastated during the war of 1914–1918 shall be borne in mind;

(f) will endeavor to take steps in matters of international concern for the prevention and control of disease.

ARTICLE 24. International Bureaus

1. There shall be placed under the direction of the League all international bureaus already established by general treaties if the parties to such treaties consent. All such international bureaus and all commissions for the regulation of matters of

international interest hereafter constituted shall be placed under the direction of the League.

2. In all matters of international interest which are regulated by general conventions but which are not placed under the control of international bureaus or commissions, the Secretariat of the League shall, subject to the consent of the Council and if desired by the parties, collect and distribute all relevant information and shall render any other assistance which may be necessary or desirable.

3. The Council may include as part of the expenses of the Secretariat the expenses of any bureau or commission which is placed under the direction of the League.

ARTICLE 25. Promotion of Red Cross

The Members of the League agree to encourage and promote the establishment and cooperation of duly authorized voluntary national Red Cross organizations having as purposes the improvement of health, the prevention of disease and the mitigation of suffering throughout the world.

ARTICLE 26. Amendments

1. Amendments to this Covenant will take effect when ratified by the Members of the League whose Representatives compose the Council and by a majority of the Members of the League whose Representatives compose the Assembly.

2. No such amendment shall bind any Member of the League which signifies its dissent therefrom, but in that case it shall cease to be a Member of the League.

ANNEX I. Original Members of the League of Nations, Signatories of the Treaty of Peace

United States of America*	Guatemala
Belgium	Haiti
Bolivia	Hedjaz*
Brazil	Honduras
British Empire	Italy
Canada	Japan
Australia	Liberia
South Africa	Nicaragua
New Zealand	Panama
India	Peru
China	Poland
Cuba	Portugal
Czechoslovakia	Romania
Ecuador**	Serb-Croat-Slovene State [Yugoslavia]
France	Siam
Greece	Uruguay

*Did not ratify.

**Did not ratify peace treaty but was admitted to membership in 1934.

States Invited to Accede to the Covenant

Argentine Republic	Persia
Chile	Salvador
Colombia	Spain
Denmark	Sweden
Netherlands	Switzerland
Norway	Venezuela
Paraguay	

ANNEX II. First Secretary-General of the League of Nations The Honorable Sir James Eric Drummond, K.C.M.G., C.B.

B

The Charter of the United Nations

We the Peoples of the United Nations Determined

to save succeeding generations from the scourge of war, which twice in our lifetime has brought untold sorrow to mankind, and

to reaffirm faith in fundamental human rights, in the dignity and worth of the human person, in the equal rights of men and women and of nations large and small, and

to establish conditions under which justice and respect for the obligations arising from treaties and other sources of international law can be maintained, and

to promote social progress and better standards of life in larger freedom,

And for These Ends

to practice tolerance and live together in peace with one another as good neighbors, and

to unite our strength to maintain international peace and security, and

to ensure, by the acceptance of principles and the institution of methods, that armed force shall not be used, save in the common interest, and

to employ international machinery for the promotion of the economic and social advancement of all peoples,

Have Resolved to Combine Our Efforts to Accomplish These Aims.

Accordingly, our respective Governments, through representatives assembled in the city of San Francisco, who have exhibited their full powers found to be in good and due form, have agreed to the present Charter of the United Nations and do hereby establish an international organization to be known as the United Nations.

Chapter I
Purposes and Principles

ARTICLE 1. The Purposes of the United Nations are:

1. To maintain international peace and security, and to that end: to take effective collective measures for the prevention and removal of threats to the peace, and for the suppression of acts of aggression and other breaches of the peace, and to bring about by peaceful means, and in conformity with the principles of justice and international law, adjustment or settlement of international disputes or situations which might lead to a breach of the peace;

2. To develop friendly relations among nations based on respect for the principle of equal rights and self-determination of peoples, and to take other appropriate measures to strengthen universal peace;

3. To achieve international cooperation in solving international problems of an economic, social, cultural, or humanitarian character, and in promoting and encouraging respect for human rights and for fundamental freedoms for all without distinction as to race, sex, language, or religion; and

4. To be a center for harmonizing the actions of nations in the attainment of these common ends.

ARTICLE 2. The Organization and its Members, in pursuit of the Purposes stated in Article 1, shall act in accordance with the following Principles.

1. The Organization is based on the principle of the sovereign equality of all its Members.

2. All Members, in order to ensure to all of them the rights and benefits resulting from membership, shall fulfil in good faith the obligations assumed by them in accordance with the present Charter.

3. All Members shall settle their international disputes by peaceful means in such a manner that international peace and security, and justice, are not endangered.

4. All Members shall refrain in their international relations from the threat or use of force against the territorial integrity or political independence of any state, or in any other manner inconsistent with the Purposes of the United Nations.

5. All Members shall give the United Nations every assistance in any action it takes in accordance with the present Charter, and shall refrain from giving assistance to any state against which the United Nations is taking preventive or enforcement action.

6. The Organization shall ensure that states which are not Members of the United Nations act in accordance with these Principles so far as may be necessary for the maintenance of international peace and security.

7. Nothing contained in the present Charter shall authorize the United Nations to intervene in matters which are essentially within the domestic jurisdiction of any

state or shall require the Members to submit such matters to settlement under the present Charter; but this principle shall not prejudice the application of enforcement measures under Chapter VII.

Chapter II
Membership

ARTICLE 3. The original Members of the United Nations shall be the states which, having participated in the United Nations Conference on International Organization at San Francisco, or having previously signed the Declaration by United Nations of January 1, 1942, sign the present Charter and ratify it in accordance with Article 110.

ARTICLE 4. 1. Membership in the United Nations is open to all other peace-loving states which accept the obligations contained in the present Charter and, in the judgment of the Organization, are able and willing to carry out these obligations.

2. The admission of any such state to membership in the United Nations will be effected by a decision of the General Assembly upon the recommendation of the Security Council.

ARTICLE 5. A Member of the United Nations against which preventive or enforcement action has been taken by the Security Council may be suspended from the exercise of the rights and privileges of membership by the General Assembly upon the recommendation of the Security Council. The exercise of these rights and privileges may be restored by the Security Council.

ARTICLE 6. A Member of the United Nations which has persistently violated the Principles contained in the present Charter may be expelled from the Organization by the General Assembly upon the recommendation of the Security Council.

Chapter III
Organs

ARTICLE 7. 1. There are established as the principal organs of the United Nations: a General Assembly, a Security Council, an Economic and Social Council, a Trusteeship Council, an International Court of Justice, and a Secretariat.

2. Such subsidiary organs as may be found necessary may be established in accordance with the present Charter.

ARTICLE 8. The United Nations shall place no restrictions on the eligibility of men and women to participate in any capacity and under conditions of equality in its principal and subsidiary organs.

Chapter IV
The General Assembly

COMPOSITION

ARTICLE 9. 1. The General Assembly shall consist of all the Members of the United Nations.

2. Each Member shall not have more than five representatives in the General Assembly.

FUNCTIONS AND POWERS

ARTICLE 10. The General Assembly may discuss any questions or any matters within the scope of the present Charter or relating to the powers and functions of any organs provided for in the present Charter, and, except as provided in Article 12, may make recommendations to the Members of the United Nations or to the Security Council or to both on any such questions or matters.

ARTICLE 11. 1. The General Assembly may consider the general principles of cooperation in the maintenance of international peace and security, including the principles governing disarmament and the regulation of armaments, and may make recommendations with regard to such principles to the Members or to the Security Council or to both.

2. The General Assembly may discuss any questions relating to the maintenance of international peace and security brought before it by any Member of the United Nations, or by the Security Council, or by a state which is not a Member of the United Nations in accordance with Article 35, paragraph 2, and, except as provided in Article 12, may make recommendations with regard to any such questions to the state or states concerned or to the Security Council or to both. Any such question on which action is necessary shall be referred to the Security Council by the General Assembly either before or after discussion.

3. The General Assembly may call the attention of the Security Council to situations which are likely to endanger international peace and security.

4. The powers of the General Assembly set forth in this Article shall not limit the general scope of Article 10.

ARTICLE 12. 1. While the Security Council is exercising in respect of any dispute or situation the functions assigned to it in the present Charter, the General Assembly shall not make any recommendation with regard to that dispute or situation unless the Security Council so requests.

2. The Secretary-General, with the consent of the Security Council, shall notify the General Assembly at each session of any matters relative to the maintenance of international peace and security which are being dealt with by the Security Council and shall similarly notify the General Assembly, or the Members of the United Nations if the General Assembly is not in session, immediately the Security Council ceases to deal with such matters.

ARTICLE 13. 1. The General Assembly shall initiate studies and make recommendations for the purpose of:

a. promoting international cooperation in the political field and encouraging the progressive development of international law and its codification;

b. promoting international cooperation in the economic, social, cultural, educational, and health fields, and assisting in the realization of human rights and fundamental freedoms for all without distinction as to race, sex, language, or religion.

2. The further responsibilities, functions and powers of the General Assembly with respect to matters mentioned in paragraph 1(b) above are set forth in Chapters IX and X.

ARTICLE 14. Subject to the provisions of Article 12, the General Assembly may recommend measures for the peaceful adjustment of any situation, regardless of origin, which it deems likely to impair the general welfare or friendly relations among nations, including situations resulting from a violation of the provisions of the present Charter setting forth the Purposes and Principles of the United Nations.

ARTICLE 15. 1. The General Assembly shall receive and consider annual and special reports from the Security Council; these reports shall include an account of the measures that the Security Council has decided upon or taken to maintain international peace and security.

2. The General Assembly shall receive and consider reports from the other organs of the United Nations.

ARTICLE 16. The General Assembly shall perform such functions with respect to the international trusteeship system as are assigned to it under Chapters XII and XIII, including the approval of the trusteeship agreements for areas not designated as strategic.

ARTICLE 17. 1. The General Assembly shall consider and approve the budget of the Organization.

2. The expenses of the Organization shall be borne by the Members as apportioned by the General Assembly.

3. The General Assembly shall consider and approve any financial and budgetary arrangements with specialized agencies referred to in Article 57 and shall examine the administrative budgets of such specialized agencies with a view to making recommendations to the agencies concerned.

VOTING

ARTICLE 18. 1. Each member of the General Assembly shall have one vote.

2. Decisions of the General Assembly on important questions shall be made by a two-thirds majority of the members present and voting. These questions shall include: recommendations with respect to the maintenance of international peace and

security, the election of the non-permanent members of the Security Council, the election of the members of the Economic and Social Council, the election of members of the Trusteeship Council in accordance with paragraph 1(c) of Article 86, the admission of new Members to the United Nations, the suspension of the rights and privileges of membership, the expulsion of Members, questions relating to the operation of the trusteeship system, and budgetary questions.

3. Decisions on other questions, including the determination of additional categories of questions to be decided by a two-thirds majority, shall be made by a majority of the members present and voting.

ARTICLE 19. A Member of the United Nations which is in arrears in the payment of its financial contributions to the Organization shall have no vote in the General Assembly if the amount equals or exceeds the amount of the contributions due from it for the preceding two full years. The General Assembly may, nevertheless, permit such a Member to vote if it is satisfied that the failure to pay is due to conditions beyond the control of the Member.

PROCEDURE

ARTICLE 20. The General Assembly shall meet in regular annual sessions and in such special sessions as occasion may require. Special sessions shall be convoked by the Secretary-General at the request of the Security Council or of a majority of the Members of the United Nations.

ARTICLE 21. The General Assembly shall adopt its own rules of procedure. It shall elect its President for each session.

ARTICLE 22. The General Assembly may establish such subsidiary organs as it deems necessary for the performance of its functions.

Chapter V
The Security Council

COMPOSITION

ARTICLE 23. 1. The Security Council shall consist of eleven[1] Members of the United Nations. The Republic of China, France, the Union of Soviet Socialist Republics, the United Kingdom of Great Britain and Northern Ireland, and the United States of America shall be permanent members of the Security Council. The General Assembly shall elect six[2] other Members of the United Nations to be non-permanent members of the Security Council, due regard being specially paid, in the first instance to the contribution of Members of the United Nations to the maintenance of international peace and security and to the other purposes of the Organization, and also to equitable geographical distribution.

---

[1]Expanded to fifteen members by Charter amendment in 1965.

[2]Ten elective members, five chosen each year, provided for by Charter amendment in 1965.

2. The non-permanent members of the Security Council shall be elected for a term of two years. In the first election of non-permanent members, however, three shall be chosen for a term of one year. A retiring member shall not be eligible for immediate re-election.

3. Each member of the Security Council shall have one representative.

FUNCTIONS AND POWERS

ARTICLE 24. 1. In order to ensure prompt and effective action by the United Nations, its Members confer on the Security Council primary responsibility for the maintenance of international peace and security, and agree that in carrying out its duties under this responsibility the Security Council acts on their behalf.

2. In discharging these duties the Security Council shall act in accordance with the Purposes and Principles of the United Nations. The specific powers granted to the Security Council for the discharge of these duties are laid down in Chapters VI, VII, VIII, and XII.

3. The Security Council shall submit annual and, when necessary, special reports to the General Assembly for its consideration.

ARTICLE 25. The Members of the United Nations agree to accept and carry out the decisions of the Security Council in accordance with the present Charter.

ARTICLE 26. In order to promote the establishment and maintenance of international peace and security with the least diversion for armaments of the world's human and economic resources, the Security Council shall be responsible for formulating, with the assistance of the Military Staff Committee referred to in Article 47, plans to be submitted to the Members of the United Nations for the establishment of a system for the regulation of armaments.

VOTING

ARTICLE 27. 1. Each member of the Security Council shall have one vote.

2. Decisions of the Security Council on procedural matters shall be made by an affirmative vote of seven[3] members.

3. Decisions of the Security Council on all other matters shall be made by an affirmative vote of seven[4] members including the concurring votes of the permanent members; provided that, in decisions under Chapter VI, and under paragraph 3 of Article 52, a party to a dispute shall abstain from voting.

PROCEDURE

ARTICLE 28. 1. The Security Council shall be so organized as to be able to function continuously. Each member of the Security Council shall for this purpose be represented at all times at the seat of the Organization.

---

[3]Changed to nine members by Charter amendment in 1965.

[4]Changed to nine members by Charter amendment in 1965.

2. The Security Council shall hold periodic meetings at which each of its members may, if it so desires, be represented by a member of the government or by some other specially designated representative.

3. The Security Council may hold meetings at such places other than the seat of the Organization as in its judgment will best facilitate its work.

ARTICLE 29. The Security Council may establish such subsidiary organs as it deems necessary for the performance of its functions.

ARTICLE 30. The Security Council shall adopt its own rules of procedure, including the method of selecting its President.

ARTICLE 31. Any Member of the United Nations which is not a member of the Security Council may participate, without vote, in the discussion of any question brought before the Security Council whenever the latter considers that the interests of that Member are specially affected.

ARTICLE 32. Any Member of the United Nations which is not a member of the Security Council or any state which is not a Member of the United Nations, if it is a party to a dispute under consideration by the Security Council, shall be invited to participate, without vote, in the discussion relating to the dispute. The Security Council shall lay down such conditions as it deems just for the participation of a state which is not a Member of the United Nations.

Chapter VI
Pacific Settlement of Disputes

ARTICLE 33. 1. The parties to any dispute, the continuance of which is likely to endanger the maintenance of international peace and security, shall, first of all, seek a solution by negotiation, enquiry, mediation, conciliation, arbitration, judicial settlement, resort to regional agencies or arrangements, or other peaceful means of their own choice.

2. The Security Council shall, when it deems necessary, call upon the parties to settle their disputes by such means.

ARTICLE 34. The Security Council may investigate any dispute, or any situation which might lead to international friction or give rise to a dispute, in order to determine whether the continuance of the dispute or situation is likely to endanger the maintenance of international peace and security.

ARTICLE 35. 1. Any Member of the United Nations may bring any dispute, or any situation of the nature referred to in Article 34, to the attention of the Security Council or of the General Assembly.

2. A state which is not a Member of the United Nations may bring to the attention of the Security Council or of the General Assembly any dispute to which it is a party if it accepts in advance, for the purposes of the dispute, the obligations of pacific settlement provided in the present Charter.

3. The proceedings of the General Assembly in respect of matters brought to its attention under this Article will be subject to the provisions of Articles 11 and 12.

ARTICLE 36. 1. The Security Council may, at any stage of a dispute of the nature referred to in Article 33 or of a situation of like nature, recommend appropriate procedures or methods of adjustment.

2. The Security Council should take into consideration any procedures for the settlement of the dispute which have already been adopted by the parties.

3. In making recommendations under this Article the Security Council should also take into consideration that legal disputes should as a general rule be referred by the parties to the International Court of Justice in accordance with the provisions of the Statute of the Court.

ARTICLE 37. 1. Should the parties to a dispute of the nature referred to in Article 33 fail to settle it by the means indicated in that Article, they shall refer it to the Security Council.

2. If the Security Council deems that the continuance of the dispute is in fact likely to endanger the maintenance of international peace and security, it shall decide whether to take action under Article 36 or to recommend such terms of settlement as it may consider appropriate.

ARTICLE 38. Without prejudice to the provisions of Articles 33 to 37, the Security Council may, if all the parties to any dispute so request, make recommendations to the parties with a view to a pacific settlement of the dispute.

Chapter VII
Action with Respect to Threats to the Peace, Breaches of the Peace, and Acts of Aggression

ARTICLE 39. The Security Council shall determine the existence of any threat to the peace, breach of the peace, or act of aggression and shall make recommendations, or decide what measures shall be taken in accordance with Articles 41 and 42, to maintain or restore international peace and security.

ARTICLE 40. In order to prevent an aggravation of the situation, the Security Council may, before making the recommendations or deciding upon the measures provided for in Article 39, call upon the parties concerned to comply with such provisional measures as it deems necessary or desirable. Such provisional measures shall be without prejudice to the rights, claims, or position of the parties concerned.

The Security Council shall duly take account of failure to comply with such provisional measures.

ARTICLE 41. The Security Council may decide what measures not involving the use of armed force are to be employed to give effect to its decisions, and it may call upon the Members of the United Nations to apply such measures. These may include complete or partial interruption of economic relations and of rail, sea, air, postal, telegraphic, radio, and other means of communication, and the severance of diplomatic relations.

ARTICLE 42. Should the Security Council consider that measures provided for in Article 41 would be inadequate or have proved to be inadequate, it may take such action by air, sea, or land forces as may be necessary to maintain or restore international peace and security. Such action may include demonstrations, blockade, and other operations by air, sea, or land forces of Members of the United Nations.

ARTICLE 43. 1. All Members of the United Nations, in order to contribute to the maintenance of international peace and security, undertake to make available to the Security Council, on its call and in accordance with a special agreement or agreements, armed forces, assistance, and facilities, including rights of passage, necessary for the purpose of maintaining international peace and security.
2. Such agreement or agreements shall govern the numbers and types of forces, their degree of readiness and general location, and the nature of the facilities and assistance to be provided.
3. The agreement or agreements shall be negotiated as soon as possible on the initiative of the Security Council. They shall be concluded between the Security Council and Members or between the Security Council and groups of Members and shall be subject to ratification by the signatory states in accordance with their respective constitutional processes.

ARTICLE 44. When the Security Council has decided to use force it shall, before calling upon a Member not represented on it to provide armed forces in fulfilment of the obligations assumed under Article 43, invite that Member, if the Member so desires, to participate in the decisions of the Security Council concerning the employment of contingents of that Member's armed forces.

ARTICLE 45. In order to enable the United Nations to take urgent military measures, Members shall hold immediately available national air-force contingents for combined international enforcement action. The strength and degree of readiness of these contingents and plans for their combined action shall be determined, within the limits laid down in the special agreement or agreements referred to in Article 43, by the Security Council with the assistance of the Military Staff Committee.

ARTICLE 46. Plans for the application of armed force shall be made by the Security Council with the assistance of the Military Staff Committee.

ARTICLE 47. 1. There shall be established a Military Staff Committee to advise and assist the Security Council on all questions relating to the Security Council's military requirements for the maintenance of international peace and security, the employment and command of forces placed at its disposal, the regulation of armaments, and possible disarmament.

2. The Military Staff Committee shall consist of the Chiefs of Staff of the permanent Members of the Security Council or their representatives. Any Member of the United Nations not permanently represented on the Committee shall be invited by the Committee to be associated with it when the efficient discharge of the Committee's responsibilities requires the participation of that Member in its work.

3. The Military Staff Committee shall be responsible under the Security Council for the strategic direction of any armed forces placed at the disposal of the Security Council. Questions relating to the command of such forces shall be worked out subsequently.

4. The Military Staff Committee, with the authorization of the Security Council and after consultation with appropriate regional agencies, may establish regional subcommittees.

ARTICLE 48. 1. The action required to carry out the decisions of the Security Council for the maintenance of international peace and security shall be taken by all the Members of the United Nations or by some of them, as the Security Council may determine.

2. Such decisions shall be carried out by the Members of the United Nations directly and through their action in the appropriate international agencies of which they are members.

ARTICLE 49. The Members of the United Nations shall join in affording mutual assistance in carrying out the measures decided upon by the Security Council.

ARTICLE 50. If preventive or enforcement measures against any state are taken by the Security Council, any other state, whether a Member of the United Nations or not, which finds itself confronted with special economic problems arising from the carrying out of those measures shall have the right to consult the Security Council with regard to a solution of those problems.

ARTICLE 51. Nothing in the present Charter shall impair the inherent right of individual or collective self-defense if an armed attack occurs against a Member of the United Nations, until the Security Council has taken measures necessary to maintain international peace and security. Measures taken by Members in the exercise of this right of self-defense shall be immediately reported to the Security Council and shall not in any way affect the authority and responsibility of the Security

Council under the present Charter to take at any time such action as it deems necessary in order to maintain or restore international peace and security.

Chapter VIII
Regional Arrangements

ARTICLE 52. 1. Nothing in the present Charter precludes the existence of regional arrangements or agencies for dealing with such matters relating to the maintenance of international peace and security as are appropriate for regional action, provided that such arrangements or agencies and their activities are consistent with the Purposes and Principles of the United Nations.

2. The Members of the United Nations entering into such arrangements or constituting such agencies shall make every effort to achieve pacific settlement of local disputes through such regional arrangements or by such regional agencies before referring them to the Security Council.

3. The Security Council shall encourage the development of pacific settlement of local disputes through such regional arrangements or by such regional agencies either on the initiative of the states concerned or by reference from the Security Council.

4. This Article in no way impairs the application of Articles 34 and 35.

ARTICLE 53. 1. The Security Council shall, where appropriate, utilize such regional arrangements or agencies for enforcement action under its authority. But no enforcement action shall be taken under regional arrangements or by regional agencies without the authorization of the Security Council, with the exception of measures against any enemy state, as defined in paragraph 2 of this Article, provided for pursuant to Article 107 or in regional arrangements directed against renewal of aggressive policy on the part of any such state, until such time as the Organization may, on request of the Governments concerned, be charged with the responsibility for preventing further aggression by such a state.

2. The term enemy state as used in paragraph 1 of this Article applies to any state which during the Second World War has been an enemy of any signatory of the present Charter.

ARTICLE 54. The Security Council shall at all times be kept fully informed of activities undertaken or in contemplation under regional arrangements or by regional agencies for the maintenance of international peace and security.

Chapter IX
International Economic and Social Cooperation

ARTICLE 55. With a view to the creation of conditions of stability and well-being which are necessary for peaceful and friendly relations among nations based on respect for the principle of equal rights and self-determination of peoples, the United Nations shall promote:

a. higher standards of living, full employment, and conditions of economic and social progress and development;

b. solutions of international economic, social, health, and related problems; and international cultural and educational cooperation; and

c. universal respect for, and observance of, human rights and fundamental freedoms for all without distinction as to race, sex, language, or religion.

ARTICLE 56. All Members pledge themselves to take joint and separate action in cooperation with the Organization for the achievement of the purposes set forth in Article 55.

ARTICLE 57. 1. The various specialized agencies, established by intergovernmental agreement and having wide international responsibilities, as defined in their basic instruments, in economic, social, cultural, educational, health and related fields, shall be brought into relationship with the United Nations in accordance with the provisions of Article 63.

2. Such agencies thus brought into relationship with the United Nations are hereinafter referred to as specialized agencies.

ARTICLE 58. The Organization shall make recommendations for the coordination of the policies and activities of the specialized agencies.

ARTICLE 59. The Organization shall, where appropriate, initiate negotiations among the states concerned for the creation of any new specialized agencies required for the accomplishment of the purposes set forth in Article 55.

ARTICLE 60. Responsibility for the discharge of the functions of the Organization set forth in this Chapter shall be vested in the General Assembly and, under the authority of the General Assembly, in the Economic and Social Council, which shall have for this purpose the powers set forth in Chapter X.

Chapter X
The Economic and Social Council

COMPOSITION

ARTICLE 61. 1. The Economic and Social Council shall consist of eighteen[5] Members of the United Nations elected by the General Assembly.

2. Subject to the provisions of paragraph 3, six[6] members of the Economic and

---

[5]Expanded to twenty-seven members by Charter amendment in 1965 and to fifty-four members by Charter amendment in 1973.

[6]Changed to provide for the election of nine members each year by Charter amendment in 1965 and eighteen members each year by Charter amendment in 1973.

Social Council shall be elected each year for a term of three years. A retiring member shall be eligible for immediate reelection.

3. At the first election, eighteen members of the Economic and Social Council shall be chosen. The term of office of six members so chosen shall expire at the end of one year, and of six other members at the end of two years, in accordance with arrangements made by the General Assembly.

4. Each member of the Economic and Social Council shall have one representative.

FUNCTIONS AND POWERS

ARTICLE 62. 1. The Economic and Social Council may make or initiate studies and reports with respect to international economic, social, cultural, educational, health, and related matters and may make recommendations with respect to any such matters to the General Assembly, to the Members of the United Nations, and to the specialized agencies concerned.

2. It may make recommendations for the purpose of promoting respect for, and observance of, human rights and fundamental freedoms for all.

3. It may prepare draft conventions for submission to the General Assembly, with respect to matters falling within its competence.

4. It may call, in accordance with the rules prescribed by the United Nations, international conferences on matters falling within its competence.

ARTICLE 63. 1. The Economic and Social Council may enter into agreements with any of the agencies referred to in Article 57, defining the terms on which the agency concerned shall be brought into relationship with the United Nations. Such agreements shall be subject to approval by the General Assembly.

2. It may coordinate the activities of the specialized agencies through consultation with and recommendations to such agencies and through recommendations to the General Assembly and to the Members of the United Nations.

ARTICLE 64. 1. The Economic and Social Council may take appropriate steps to obtain regular reports from the specialized agencies. It may make arrangements with the Members of the United Nations and with the specialized agencies to obtain reports on the steps taken to give effect to its own recommendations and to recommendations on matters falling within its competence made by the General Assembly.

2. It may communicate its observations on these reports to the General Assembly.

ARTICLE 65. The Economic and Social Council may furnish information to the Security Council and shall assist the Security Council upon its request.

ARTICLE 66. 1. The Economic and Social Council shall perform such functions as fall within its competence in connection with the carrying out of the recommendations of the General Assembly.

2. It may, with the approval of the General Assembly, perform services at the request of Members of the United Nations and at the request of specialized agencies.

3. It shall perform such other functions as are specified elsewhere in the present Charter or as may be assigned to it by the General Assembly.

VOTING

ARTICLE 67. 1. Each member of the Economic and Social Council shall have one vote.

2. Decisions of the Economic and Social Council shall be made by a majority of the members present and voting.

PROCEDURE

ARTICLE 68. The Economic and Social Council shall set up commissions in economic and social fields and for the promotion of human rights, and such other commissions as may be required for the performance of its functions.

ARTICLE 69. The Economic and Social Council shall invite any Member of the United Nations to participate, without vote, in its deliberations on any matter of particular concern to that Member.

ARTICLE 70. The Economic and Social Council may make arrangements for representatives of the specialized agencies to participate, without vote, in its deliberations and in those of the commissions established by it, and for its representatives to participate in the deliberations of the specialized agencies.

ARTICLE 71. The Economic and Social Council may make suitable arrangements for consultation with non-governmental organizations which are concerned with matters within its competence. Such arrangements may be made with international organizations and, where appropriate, with national organizations after consultation with the Member of the United Nations concerned.

ARTICLE 72. 1. The Economic and Social Council shall adopt its own rules of procedure, including the method of selecting its President.

2. The Economic and Social Council shall meet as required in accordance with its rules, which shall include provision for the convening of meetings on the request of a majority of its members.

Chapter XI
Declaration Regarding Non-Self-Governing Territories

ARTICLE 73. Members of the United Nations which have or assume responsibilities for the administration of territories whose peoples have not yet attained a full measure of self-government recognize the principle that the interests of the inhabitants of these territories are paramount, and accept as a sacred trust the obligation to promote to the utmost, within the system of international peace and security established by the present Charter, the well-being of the inhabitants of these territories, and, to this end:

a. to ensure, with due respect for the culture of the peoples concerned, their political, economic, social, and educational advancement, their just treatment, and their protection against abuses;

b. to develop self-government, to take due account of the political aspirations of the peoples, and to assist them in the progressive development of their free political institutions, according to the particular circumstances of each territory and its peoples and their varying stages of advancement;

c. to further international peace and security;

d. to promote constructive measures of development, to encourage research, and to cooperate with one another and, when and where appropriate, with specialized international bodies with a view to the practical achievement of the social, economic, and scientific purposes set forth in this Article; and

e. to transmit regularly to the Secretary-General for information purposes, subject to such limitation as security and constitutional considerations may require, statistical and other information of a technical nature relating to economic, social, and educational conditions in the territories for which they are respectively responsible other than those territories to which Chapters XII and XIII apply.

ARTICLE 74. Members of the United Nations also agree that their policy in respect of the territories to which this Chapter applies, no less than in respect of their metropolitan areas, must be based on the general principle of good-neighborliness, due account being taken of the interests and well-being of the rest of the world, in social, economic, and commercial matters.

Chapter XII
International Trusteeship System

ARTICLE 75. The United Nations shall establish under its authority an international trusteeship system for the administration and supervision of such territories as may be placed thereunder by subsequent individual agreements. These territories are hereinafter referred to as trust territories.

ARTICLE 76. The basic objectives of the trusteeship system, in accordance with the Purposes of the United Nations laid down in Article 1 of the present Charter, shall be:

a. to further international peace and security;

b. to promote the political, economic, social, and educational advancement of the inhabitants of the trust territories, and their progressive development towards self-government or independence as may be appropriate to the particular circumstances of each territory and its peoples and the freely expressed wishes of the peoples concerned, and as may be provided by the terms of each trusteeship agreement;

c. to encourage respect for human rights and for fundamental freedoms for all without distinction as to race, sex, language, or religion, and to encourage recognition of the interdependence of the peoples of the world; and

d. to ensure equal treatment in social, economic, and commercial matters for all Members of the United Nations and their nationals, and also equal treatment for the latter in the administration of justice, without prejudice to the attainment of the foregoing objectives and subject to the provisions of Article 80.

ARTICLE 77. 1. The trusteeship system shall apply to such territories in the following categories as may be placed thereunder by means of trusteeship agreements:

a. territories now held under mandate;

b. territories which may be detached from enemy states as a result of the Second World War; and

c. territories voluntarily placed under the system by states responsible for their administration.

2. It will be a matter for subsequent agreement as to which territories in the foregoing categories will be brought under the trusteeship system and upon what terms.

ARTICLE 78. The trusteeship system shall not apply to territories which have become Members of the United Nations, relationship among which shall be based on respect for the principle of sovereign equality.

ARTICLE 79. The terms of trusteeship for each territory to be placed under the trusteeship system, including any alteration or amendment, shall be agreed upon by the states directly concerned, including the mandatory power in the case of territories held under mandate by a Member of the United Nations, and shall be approved as provided for in Articles 83 and 85.

ARTICLE 80. 1. Except as may be agreed upon in individual trusteeship agreements, made under Articles 77, 79, and 81, placing each territory under the trusteeship system, and until such agreements have been concluded, nothing in this Chapter shall be construed in or of itself to alter in any manner the rights whatsoever of any states or any peoples or the terms of existing international instruments to which Members of the United Nations may respectively be parties.

2. Paragraph 1 of this Article shall not be interpreted as giving grounds for delay or postponement of the negotiation and conclusion of agreements for placing mandated and other territories under the trusteeship system as provided for in Article 77.

ARTICLE 81. The trusteeship agreement shall in each case include the terms under which the trust territory will be administered and designate the authority which will exercise the administration of the trust territory. Such authority, hereinafter called the administering authority, may be one or more states or the Organization itself.

ARTICLE 82. There may be designated, in any trusteeship agreement, a strategic area or areas which may include part or all of the trust territory to which the agreement applies, without prejudice to any special agreement or agreements made under Article 43.

ARTICLE 83. 1. All functions of the United Nations relating to strategic areas, including the approval of the terms of the trusteeship agreements and of their alteration or amendment, shall be exercised by the Security Council.

2. The basic objectives set forth in Article 76 shall be applicable to the people of each strategic area.

3. The Security Council shall, subject to the provisions of the trusteeship agreements and without prejudice to security considerations, avail itself of the assistance of the Trusteeship Council to perform those functions of the United Nations under the trusteeship system relating to political, economic, social, and educational matters in the strategic areas.

ARTICLE 84. It shall be the duty of the administering authority to ensure that the trust territory shall play its part in the maintenance of international peace and security. To this end the administering authority may make use of volunteer forces, facilities, and assistance from the trust territory in carrying out the obligations towards the Security Council undertaken in this regard by the administering authority, as well as for local defense and the maintenance of law and order within the trust territory.

ARTICLE 85. 1. The functions of the United Nations with regard to trusteeship agreements for all areas not designated as strategic, including the approval of the terms of the trusteeship agreements and of their alteration or amendment, shall be exercised by the General Assembly.

2. The Trusteeship Council, operating under the authority of the General Assembly, shall assist the General Assembly in carrying out these functions.

Chapter XIII
The Trusteeship Council

COMPOSITION

ARTICLE 86. 1. The Trusteeship Council shall consist of the following Members of the United Nations:

a. those Members administering trust territories;

b. such of those Members mentioned by name in Article 23 as are not administering trust territories; and

c. as many other Members elected for three-year terms by the General Assembly as may be necessary to ensure that the total number of members of the Trusteeship Council is equally divided between those Members of the United Nations which administer trust territories and those which do not.

2. Each member of the Trusteeship Council shall designate one specially qualified person to represent it therein.

FUNCTIONS AND POWERS

ARTICLE 87. The General Assembly and, under its authority, the Trusteeship Council, in carrying out their functions, may:

a. consider reports submitted by the administering authority;

b. accept petitions and examine them in consultation with the administering authority;

c. provide for periodic visits to the respective trust territories at times agreed upon with the administering authority; and

d. take these and other actions in conformity with the terms of the trusteeship agreements.

ARTICLE 88. The Trusteeship Council shall formulate a questionnaire on the political, economic, social, and educational advancement of the inhabitants of each trust territory, and the administering authority for each trust territory within the competence of the General Assembly shall make an annual report to the General Assembly upon the basis of such questionnaire.

VOTING

ARTICLE 89. 1. Each member of the Trusteeship Council shall have one vote.

2. Decisions of the Trusteeship Council shall be made by a majority of the members present and voting.

PROCEDURE

ARTICLE 90. 1. The Trusteeship Council shall adopt its own rules of procedure, including the method of selecting its President.

2. The Trusteeship Council shall meet as required in accordance with its rules, which shall include provision for the convening of meetings on the request of a majority of its members.

ARTICLE 91. The Trusteeship Council shall, when appropriate, avail itself of the assistance of the Economic and Social Council and of the specialized agencies in regard to matters with which they are respectively concerned.

Chapter XIV
The International Court of Justice

ARTICLE 92. The International Court of Justice shall be the principal judicial organ of the United Nations. It shall function in accordance with the annexed Statute, which is based upon the Statute of the Permanent Court of International Justice and forms an integral part of the present Charter.

ARTICLE 93. 1. All Members of the United Nations are *ipso facto* parties to the Statute of the International Court of Justice.

2. A state which is not a Member of the United Nations may become a party to the Statute of the International Court of Justice on conditions to be determined in each case by the General Assembly upon the recommendation of the Security Council.

ARTICLE 94. 1. Each Member of the United Nations undertakes to comply with the decision of the International Court of Justice in any case to which it is a party.

2. If any party to a case fails to perform the obligations incumbent upon it under a judgment rendered by the Court, the other party may have recourse to the Security Council, which may, if it deems necessary, make recommendations or decide upon measures to be taken to give effect to the judgment.

ARTICLE 95. Nothing in the present Charter shall prevent Members of the United Nations from entrusting the solution of their differences to other tribunals by virtue of agreements already in existence or which may be concluded in the future.

ARTICLE 96. 1. The General Assembly or the Security Council may request the International Court of Justice to give an advisory opinion on any legal question.

2. Other organs of the United Nations and specialized agencies, which may at any time be so authorized by the General Assembly, may also request advisory opinions of the Court on legal questions arising within the scope of their activities.

Chapter XV
The Secretariat

ARTICLE 97. The Secretariat shall comprise a Secretary-General and such staff as the Organization may require. The Secretary-General shall be appointed by the General Assembly upon the recommendation of the Security Council. He shall be the chief administrative officer of the Organization.

ARTICLE 98. The Secretary-General shall act in that capacity in all meetings of the General Assembly, of the Security Council, of the Economic and Social Council, and of the Trusteeship Council, and shall perform such other functions as are entrusted to him by these organs. The Secretary-General shall make an annual report to the General Assembly on the work of the Organization.

ARTICLE 99. The Secretary-General may bring to the attention of the Security Council any matter which in his opinion may threaten the maintenance of international peace and security.

ARTICLE 100. 1. In the performance of their duties the Secretary-General and the staff shall not seek or receive instructions from any government or from any other authority external to the Organization. They shall refrain from any action which might reflect on their position as international officials responsible only to the Organization.

2. Each Member of the United Nations undertakes to respect the exclusively international character of the responsibilities of the Secretary-General and the staff and not to seek to influence them in the discharge of their responsibilities.

ARTICLE 101. 1. The staff shall be appointed by the Secretary-General under regulations established by the General Assembly.

2. Appropriate staffs shall be permanently assigned to the Economic and Social Council, the Trusteeship Council, and, as required, to other organs of the United Nations. These staffs shall form a part of the Secretariat.

3. The paramount consideration in the employment of the staff and in the determination of the conditions of service shall be the necessity of securing the highest standards of efficiency, competence, and integrity. Due regard shall be paid to the importance of recruiting the staff on as wide a geographical basis as possible.

Chapter XVI
Miscellaneous Provisions

ARTICLE 102. 1. Every treaty and every international agreement entered into by any Member of the United Nations after the present Charter comes into force shall as soon as possible be registered with the Secretariat and published by it.

2. No party to any such treaty or international agreement which has not been registered in accordance with the provisions of paragraph 1 of this Article may invoke that treaty or agreement before any organ of the United Nations.

ARTICLE 103. In the event of a conflict between the obligations of the Members of the United Nations under the present Charter and their obligations under any other international agreement, their obligations under the present Charter shall prevail.

ARTICLE 104. The Organization shall enjoy in the territory of each of its Members such legal capacity as may be necessary for the exercise of its functions and the fulfilment of its purposes.

ARTICLE 105. 1. The Organization shall enjoy in the territory of each of its Members such privileges and immunities as are necessary for the fulfilment of its purposes.

2. Representatives of the Members of the United Nations and officials of the Organization shall similarly enjoy such privileges and immunities as are necessary for the independent exercise of their functions in connection with the Organization.

3. The General Assembly may make recommendations with a view to determining the details of the application of paragraphs 1 and 2 of this Article or may propose conventions to the Members of the United Nations for this purpose.

Chapter XVII
Transitional Security Arrangements

ARTICLE 106. Pending the coming into force of such special agreements referred to in Article 43 as in the opinion of the Security Council enable it to begin the exercise of its responsibilities under Article 42, the parties to the Four-Nation Declaration, signed at Moscow, October 30, 1943, and France, shall, in accordance with the provisions of paragraph 5 of that Declaration, consult with one another and as occasion requires with other Members of the United Nations with a view to such joint action on behalf of the Organization as may be necessary for the purpose of maintaining international peace and security.

ARTICLE 107. Nothing in the present Charter shall invalidate or preclude action, in relation to any state which during the Second World War has been an enemy of any signatory to the present Charter, taken or authorized as a result of that war by the Governments having responsibility for such action.

Chapter XVIII
Amendments

ARTICLE 108. Amendments to the present Charter shall come into force for all Members of the United Nations when they have been adopted by a vote of two thirds of the members of the General Assembly and ratified in accordance with their respective constitutional processes by two thirds of the Members of the United Nations, including all the permanent members of the Security Council.

ARTICLE 109. 1. A General Conference of the Members of the United Nations for the purpose of reviewing the present Charter may be held at a date and place to be fixed by a two-thirds vote of the members of the General Assembly and by a vote of any seven members of the Security Council. Each Member of the United Nations shall have one vote in the conference.
2. Any alteration of the present Charter recommended by a two-thirds vote of the conference shall take effect when ratified in accordance with their respective constitutional processes by two thirds of the Members of the United Nations including all the permanent members of the Security Council.
3. If such a conference has not been held before the tenth annual session of the General Assembly following the coming into force of the present Charter, the proposal to call such a conference shall be placed on the agenda of that session of the General Assembly, and the conference shall be held if so decided by a majority vote

of the members of the General Assembly and by a vote of any seven members of the Security Council.

Chapter XIX
Ratification and Signature

ARTICLE 110. 1. The present Charter shall be ratified by the signatory states in accordance with their respective constitutional processes.

2. The ratifications shall be deposited with the Government of the United States of America, which shall notify all the signatory states of each deposit as well as the Secretary-General of the Organization when he has been appointed.

3. The present Charter shall come into force upon the deposit of ratifications by the Republic of China, France, the Union of Soviet Socialist Republics, the United Kingdom of Great Britain and Northern Ireland, and the United States of America, and by a majority of the other signatory states. A protocol of the ratifications deposited shall thereupon be drawn up by the Government of the United States of America which shall communicate copies thereof to all the signatory states.

4. The states signatory to the present Charter which ratify it after it has come into force will become original members of the United Nations on the date of the deposit of their respective ratifications.

ARTICLE 111. The present Charter, of which the Chinese, French, Russian, English, and Spanish texts are equally authentic, shall remain deposited in the archives of the Government of the United States of America. Duly certified copies thereof shall be transmitted by that Government to the Governments of the other signatory states.

IN FAITH WHEREOF the representatives of the Governments of the United Nations have signed the present Charter.

DONE at the city of San Francisco the twenty-sixth day of June, one thousand nine hundred and forty-five.

C

Members of the United Nations (August 1987)

Country	Estimated Population, Mid-1984 (000)	UN Budget Assessment, 1986	Date of Admission to United Nations
Afghanistan	17,672	0.01	1946
Albania	2,899	0.01	1955
Algeria	20,841	0.14	1962
Angola	8,339*	0.01	1976
Antigua-Barbuda	78*	0.01	1981
Argentina	30,097	0.62	1945
Australia	15,544	1.66	1945
Austria	7,553	0.74	1955
Bahamas	226	0.01	1973
Bahrain	400	0.02	1971
Bangladesh	97,986	0.02	1974
Barbados	252*	0.01	1966
Belgium	9,856*	1.18	1945
Belize	162	0.01	1981
Benin	3,825	0.01	1960
Bhutan	1,285†	0.01	1971
Bolivia	6,082*	0.01	1945
Botswana	1,047	0.01	1966
Brazil	132,580	1.40	1945
Brunei Darussalam	216	0.04	1984
Bulgaria	8,972	0.16	1955
Burkina Faso	6,470*	0.01	1960
Burma	36,392	0.01	1948
Burundi	4,537	0.01	1962

Country	Estimated Population, Mid-1984 (000)	UN Budget Assessment, 1986	Date of Admission to United Nations
Byelorussian SSR	9,942†	0.34	1945
Canada	25,124	3.06	1945
Cape Verde	296‡	0.01	1975
Central African Republic	2,442§	0.01	1960
Chad	4,944	0.01	1960
Chile	11,878	0.07	1945
China	1,036,040	0.79	1945
Colombia	28,217	0.13	1945
Comoros	421*	0.01	1975
Congo	1,719	0.01	1960
Costa Rica	2,417	0.02	1945
Côte d'Ivore	9,743	0.02	1960
Cuba	10,043	0.09	1945
Cyprus	657	0.02	1960
Czechoslovakia	15,415*	0.70	1945
Democratic Kampuchea	7,200	0.01	1955
Democratic Yemen	2,225	0.01	1967
Denmark	5,112	0.72	1945
Djibouti	405	0.01	1977
Dominica	74‖	0.01	1978
Dominican Republic	6,102	0.03	1945
Ecuador	8,823	0.03	1945
Egypt	45,915*	0.07	1945
El Salvador	4,780	0.01	1945
Equatorial Guinea	300*	0.01	1968
Ethiopia	42,169	0.01	1945
Federal Republic of Germany	61,181	8.26	1973
Fiji	691	0.01	1970
Finland	4,894	0.50	1955
France	54,947	6.37	1945
Gabon	1,127*	0.03	1960
Gambia	696*	0.01	1965
German Democratic Republic	16,699*	1.33	1973
Ghana	12,206	0.01	1957
Greece	9,896	0.44	1945
Grenada	113§	0.01	1974
Guatemala	8,161	0.02	1945
Guinea	5,177*	0.01	1948
Guinea-Bissau	810‖	0.01	1974
Guyana	759‡	0.01	1966
Haiti	5,185	0.01	1945
Honduras	3,717	0.01	1945
Hungary	10,679	0.22	1955

Country	Estimated Population, Mid-1984 (000)	UN Budget Assessment, 1986	Date of Admission to United Nations
Iceland	240	0.03	1946
India	732,256*	0.35	1945
Indonesia	161,632	0.14	1955
Iran	43,414	0.63	1945
Iraq	14,110§	0.12	1945
Ireland	3,535	0.18	1955
Israel	4,106*	0.22	1949
Italy	56,836*	3.79	1955
Jamaica	2,096§	0.02	1962
Japan	120,235	10.84	1956
Jordan	3,247*	0.01	1955
Kenya	19,536	0.01	1963
Kuwait	1,636	0.29	1963
Lao People's Democratic Republic	3,585†	0.01	1955
Lebanon	2,644	0.01	1945
Lesotho	1,481	0.01	1966
Liberia	2,109	0.01	1945
Libyan Arab Jamahiriya	3,624	0.26	1955
Luxembourg	366	0.05	1945
Madagascar	9,400*	0.01	1960
Malawi	6,839	0.01	1964
Malaysia	15,270	0.10	1957
Maldives	180†	0.01	1965
Mali	7,719	0.01	1960
Malta	360§	0.01	1964
Mauritania	1,779*	0.01	1961
Mauritius	1,002*	0.01	1968
Mexico	76,792	0.89	1945
Mongolia	1,820	0.01	1961
Morocco	20,420§	0.05	1956
Mozambique	13,427	0.01	1975
Nepal	16,600	0.01	1955
Netherlands	14,420	1.74	1945
New Zealand	3,266	0.24	1945
Nicaragua	3,058*	0.01	1945
Niger	5,686‖	0.01	1960
Nigeria	92,037	0.19	1960
Norway	4,134	0.54	1945
Oman	1,181	0.02	1971
Pakistan	93,286	0.06	1947
Panama	2,134	0.02	1945
Papua New Guinea	3,239	0.01	1975

Country	Estimated Population, Mid-1984 (000)	UN Budget Assessment, 1986	Date of Admission to United Nations
Paraguay	3,278	0.02	1945
Peru	19,198	0.07	1945
Philippines	53,351	0.10	1945
Poland	37,063	0.64	1945
Portugal	10,089	0.18	1955
Qatar	270	0.04	1971
Romania	22,625	0.19	1955
Rwanda	5,757*	0.01	1962
St. Christopher and Nevis	45§	0.01	1983
St. Lucia	134	0.01	1979
St. Vincent and the Grenadines	128§	0.01	1980
Samoa	159	0.01	1976
São Tomé and Principe	92*	0.01	1975
Saudi Arabia	10,421*	0.97	1945
Senegal	6,316*	0.01	1960
Seychelles	65†	0.01	1976
Sierra Leone	3,518†	0.01	1961
Singapore	2,529	0.10	1965
Solomon Islands	244§	0.01	1978
Somalia	5,269*	0.01	1960
South Africa	30,802*	0.44	1945
Spain	38,997	2.03	1955
Sri Lanka	15,599	0.01	1955
Sudan	20,564*	0.01	1956
Suriname	364§	0.01	1975
Swaziland	605*	0.01	1968
Sweden	8,343	1.25	1946
Syria	9,934	0.04	1945
Thailand	50,588	0.09	1946
Togo	2,747§	0.01	1960
Trinidad and Tobago	1,149*	0.04	1962
Tunisia	6,886*	0.03	1956
Turkey	51,429†	0.34	1945
Uganda	12,630‡	0.01	1962
Ukrainian SSR	50,840†	1.28	1945
Union of Soviet Socialist Republics	276,290†	10.20	1945
United Arab Emirates	1,622†	0.18	1971
United Kingdom and Northern Ireland	56,488	4.86	1945
United Republic of Cameroon	9,165*	0.01	1960
United Republic of Tanzania	21,062	0.01	1961
United States	236,681	25.00	1945

Country	Estimated Population, Mid-1984 (000)	UN Budget Assessment, 1986	Date of Admission to United Nations
Uruguay	2,922†	0.04	1945
Vanuatu	136†	0.01	1981
Venezuela	16,851	0.60	1945
Vietnam	57,020*	0.01	1977
Yemen Arab Republic	6,232*	0.01	1947
Yugoslavia	22,963	0.46	1945
Zaire	29,671	0.01	1960
Zambia	6,242*	0.01	1964
Zimbabwe	7,980	0.02	1980
		100.00	

*Estimate for 1983.
†Estimate for 1985.
‡Estimate for 1980.
§Estimate for 1982.
‖Estimate for 1981.

SOURCE (for population figures): *The Europa Yearbook, 1986: A World Survey,* vol. 1 (London: Europa Publications, 1986).

D

The Universal Declaration of Human Rights

(Adopted December 10, 1948)

Preamble

Whereas recognition of the inherent dignity and of the equal and inalienable rights of all members of the human family is the foundation of freedom, justice and peace in the world,

Whereas disregard and contempt for human rights have resulted in barbarous acts which have outraged the conscience of mankind, and the advent of a world in which human beings shall enjoy freedom of speech and belief and freedom from fear and want has been proclaimed as the highest aspiration of the common people,

Whereas it is essential, if man is not to be compelled to have recourse, as a last resort, to rebellion against tyranny and oppression, that human rights should be protected by the rule of law,

Whereas it is essential to promote the development of friendly relations between nations,

Whereas the peoples of the United Nations have in the Charter reaffirmed their faith in fundamental human rights, in the dignity and worth of the human person and in the equal rights of men and women and have determined to promote social progress and better standards of life in larger freedom,

Whereas Member States have pledged themselves to achieve, in co-operation with the United Nations, the promotion of universal respect for and observance of human rights and fundamental freedoms,

Whereas a common understanding of these rights and freedoms is of the greatest importance for the full realization of this pledge,

Now, therefore,

The General Assembly

Proclaims this Universal Declaration of Human Rights as a common standard of achievement for all peoples and all nations, to the end that every individual and every organ of society, keeping this Declaration constantly in mind, shall strive by teaching and education to promote respect for these rights and freedoms and by progressive measures, national and international, to secure their universal and effective recognition and observance, both among the peoples of Member States themselves and among the peoples of territories under their jurisdiction.

Article 1

All human beings are born free and equal in dignity and rights. They are endowed with reason and conscience and should act towards one another in a spirit of brotherhood.

Article 2

Everyone is entitled to all the rights and freedoms set forth in this Declaration, without distinction of any kind, such as race, colour, sex, language, religion, political or other opinion, national or social origin, property, birth or other status.

Furthermore, no distinction shall be made on the basis of the political, jurisdictional or international status of the country or territory to which a person belongs, whether it be independent, trust, non-self-governing or under any other limitation of sovereignty.

Article 3

Everyone has the right to life, liberty and the security of person.

Article 4

No one shall be held in slavery or servitude; slavery and the slave trade shall be prohibited in all their forms.

Article 5

No one shall be subjected to torture or to cruel, inhuman or degrading treatment or punishment.

Article 6

Everyone has the right to recognition everywhere as a person before the law.

Article 7

All are equal before the law and are entitled without any discrimination to equal protection of the law. All are entitled to equal protection against any discrimination in violation of this Declaration and against any incitement to such discrimination.

Article 8

Everyone has the right to an effective remedy by the competent national tribunals for acts violating the fundamental rights granted him by the constitution or by law.

Article 9

No one shall be subjected to arbitrary arrest, detention or exile.

Article 10

Everyone is entitled in full equality to a fair and public hearing by an independent and impartial tribunal, in the determination of his rights and obligations and of any criminal charge against him.

Article 11

1. Everyone charged with a penal offence has the right to be presumed innocent until proved guilty according to law in a public trial at which he has had all the guarantees necessary for his defence.

2. No one shall be held guilty of any penal offence on account of any act or omission which did not constitute a penal offence, under national or international law, at the time when it was committed. Nor shall a heavier penalty be imposed than the one that was applicable at the time the penal offence was committed.

Article 12

No one shall be subjected to arbitrary interference with his privacy, family, home or correspondence, nor to attacks upon his honour and reputation. Everyone has the right to the protection of the law against such interference or attacks.

Article 13

1. Everyone has the right to freedom of movement and residence within the borders of each State.

2. Everyone has the right to leave any country, including his own, and to return to his country.

Article 14

1. Everyone has the right to seek and to enjoy in other countries asylum from persecution.

2. This right may not be invoked in the case of prosecutions genuinely arising from non-political crimes or from acts contrary to the purposes and principles of the United Nations.

Article 15

1. Everyone has the right to a nationality.
2. No one shall be arbitrarily deprived of his nationality nor denied the right to change his nationality.

Article 16

1. Men and women of full age, without any limitation due to race, nationality or religion, have the right to marry and to found a family. They are entitled to equal rights as to marriage, during marriage and at its dissolution.
2. Marriage shall be entered into only with the free and full consent of the intending spouses.
3. The family is the natural and fundamental group unit of society and is entitled to protection by society and the State.

Article 17

1. Everyone has the right to own property alone as well as in association with others.
2. No one shall be arbitrarily deprived of his property.

Article 18

Everyone has the right to freedom of thought, conscience and religion; this right includes freedom to change his religion or belief, and freedom, either alone or in community with others and in public or private, to manifest his religion or belief in teaching, practice, worship and observance.

Article 19

Everyone has the right to freedom of opinion and expression; this right includes freedom to hold opinions without interference and to seek, receive and impart information and ideas through any media and regardless of frontiers.

Article 20

1. Everyone has the right to freedom of peaceful assembly and association.
2. No one may be compelled to belong to an association.

Article 21

1. Everyone has the right to take part in the government of his country, directly or through freely chosen representatives.

2. Everyone has the right of equal access to public service in his country.

3. The will of the people shall be the basis of the authority of government; this will shall be expressed in periodic and genuine elections which shall be by universal and equal suffrage and shall be held by secret vote or by equivalent free voting procedures.

Article 22

Everyone, as a member of society, has the right to social security and is entitled to realization, through national effort and international co-operation and in accordance with the organization and resources of each State, of the economic, social and cultural rights indispensable for his dignity and the free development of his personality.

Article 23

1. Everyone has the right to work, to free choice of employment, to just and favourable conditions of work and to protection against unemployment.

2. Everyone, without any discrimination, has the right to equal pay for equal work.

3. Everyone who works has the right to just and favourable remuneration ensuring for himself and his family an existence worthy of human dignity, and supplemented, if necessary, by other means of social protection.

4. Everyone has the right to form and to join trade unions for the protection of his interests.

Article 24

Everyone has the right to rest and leisure, including reasonable limitation of working hours and periodic holidays with pay.

Article 25

1. Everyone has the right to a standard of living adequate for the health and well-being of himself and of his family, including food, clothing, housing and medical care and necessary social services, and the right to security in the event of unemployment, sickness, disability, widowhood, old age or other lack of livelihood in circumstances beyond his control.

2. Motherhood and childhood are entitled to special care and assistance. All children, whether born in or out of wedlock, shall enjoy the same social protection.

Article 26

1. Everyone has the right to education. Education shall be free, at least in the elementary and fundamental stages. Elementary education shall be compulsory. Technical and professional education shall be made generally available and higher education shall be equally accessible to all on the basis of merit.

2. Education shall be directed to the full development of the human personality and to the strengthening of respect for human rights and fundamental freedoms. It shall promote understanding, tolerance and friendship among all nations, racial or religious groups, and shall further the activities of the United Nations for the maintenance of peace.

3. Parents have a prior right to choose the kind of education that shall be given to their children.

Article 27

1. Everyone has the right freely to participate in the cultural life of the community, to enjoy the arts and to share in scientific advancement and its benefits.

2. Everyone has the right to the protection of the moral and material interests resulting from any scientific, literary or artistic production of which he is the author.

Article 28

Everyone is entitled to a social and international order in which the rights and freedoms set forth in this Declaration can be fully realized.

Article 29

1. Everyone has duties to the community in which alone the free and full development of his personality is possible.

2. In the exercise of his rights and freedoms, everyone shall be subject only to such limitations as are determined by law solely for the purpose of securing due recognition and respect for the rights and freedoms of others and of meeting the just requirements of morality, public order and the general welfare in a democratic society.

3. These rights and freedom may in no case be exercised contrary to the purposes and principles of the United Nations.

Article 30

Nothing in this Declaration may be interpreted as implying for any State, group or person any right to engage in any activity or to perform any act aimed at the destruction of any of the rights and freedoms set forth herein.

Name Index

Subject Index

ABOUT THE AUTHORS

Robert E. Riggs is Professor of Law and Professor of Political Science at Brigham Young University. He received a B.A. (1949) and an M.A. (1952) from the University of Arizona, a Ph.D. (1955) from the University of Illinois, and an LL.B. (1963) from the University of Arizona. He also studied at Brigham Young University and at Oxford University (St. Catherine's).

Professor Riggs has focused his intellectual interest, his teaching, and his scholarly writing in the field of international organization and law. He has published ten books and monographs and forty articles on this field in scholarly journals and related publications. He has received many awards and scholastic honors, including membership in Phi Beta Kappa and Phi Kappa Phi and receipt of the Phi Kappa Phi Plaque and the Phi Delta Phi University of Arizona Law School Award.

This book, *The United Nations,* is the third book that Professor Riggs and Professor Plano have co-authored. The other two are *Forging World Order* and *The Dictionary of Political Analysis.*

Jack C. Plano is Professor of Political Science and Editor of the New Issues Press of Western Michigan University. His main field of interest is international organization and law. He received an A.B. from Ripon College (1949) and an M.A. (1950) and Ph.D. (1954) from the University of Wisconsin, Madison.

Professor Plano has published several articles and three books and one monograph on this subject: *The United Nations and the India-Pakistan Dispute; Forging World Order,* with Robert E. Riggs; *United Nations Capital Development Fund—Poor and Rich Worlds in Collision,* with Marjon Vashti Kamara; and *International Approaches to Problems of Marine Pollution.* In addition, Professor Plano has co-authored or edited twenty political dictionaries. Professor Plano has received many awards, including a Ford Foundation grant and membership in Phi Beta Kappa and Pi Gamma Mu. He has been an active member of the International Studies Association and the American Political Science Association for many years and has appeared on several programs and panels with these organizations.

A NOTE ON THE TYPE

The text of this book was set in 10/12 Times Roman, a film version of the face designed by Stanley Morison, which was first used by *The Times* (of London) in 1932. Part of Morison's special intent for Times Roman was to create a face that was editorially neutral. It is an especially compact, attractive, and legible typeface, which has come to be seen as the "most important type design of the twentieth century."

Composed by Weimer Typesetting Co., Inc., Indianapolis, Indiana.

Printed and bound by Malloy Lithographing, Inc., Ann Arbor, Michigan.